GEORGE GORDON, LORD BYRON

495

Selected Works

REVISED AND ENLARGED

Manfred on the Jungfrau. Watercolor by John Martin.
Courtesy City of Birmingham Museum and Art Gallery.

GEORGE GORDON, LORD BYRON

Selected Works
REVISED AND ENLARGED

Including Cain
Beppo, Don Juan
Letters and Journals

Edited with an introduction and notes by
EDWARD E. BOSTETTER

HOLT, RINEHART AND WINSTON, INC.
New York   Chicago   San Francisco   Atlanta
Dallas   Montreal   Toronto   London   Sydney

Acknowledgments

The text of the poems is based on that of *The Poetry of Lord Byron*, ed. Ernest Hartley Coleridge, published by John Murray, Ltd.

The selections from letters and journals have been printed by permission of John Murray, controller of Byron copyrights. The text of the letter to Lady Byron, 14 April 1816, first appeared in *Astarte* by Ralph Milbanke, Earl of Lovelace, New Edition ed. Mary, Countess of Lovelace, and published by Christophers, Ltd., 1921. The texts of three letters (to Miss Milbanke, 18 September 1814; to Augusta Leigh, 17 September 1816; and to Douglas Kinnaird, 26 October 1819) have been taken from *Byron: A Self-Portrait*, ed. Peter Quennell and published by John Murray, Ltd. The texts of the other letters and journals have been taken from *Letters and Journals*, ed. R. E. Prothero and published by John Murray, Ltd.

The frontispiece, "Manfred on the Jungfrau," has been reproduced by permission of the Birmingham (England) Museum and Art Gallery, which possesses the original watercolor painted by John Martin in 1837.

Library of Congress Catalog Card Number: 73–165351
ISBN: 0-03-083990-4
Printed in the United States of America
67890 065 98765432

Contents

Selections FROM *Letters, Diary,* AND
Detached Thoughts   *635*

Introduction

On October 15, 1821, Byron jotted down in his *Detached Thoughts* a list of some forty persons or things to which he had seen himself compared "personally or poetically" in English or European journals. The list included Rousseau, Goethe, Shakespeare, Milton, and Pope; Napoleon and Henry VIII; Harlequin, Timon of Athens, and Satan. "The object of so many contradictory comparisons," he decided, "must probably be like something different from them all; but what *that* is, is more than *I* know, or anybody else." And in one of the famous conversations with Lady Blessington in the spring of 1823 when he was speculating complacently on the difficulties of his future biographers, he said, "Now, if I know myself, I should say, that I have no character at all . . . what I think of myself is, that I am so changeable, being everything by turns and nothing long — I am such a strange *mélange* of good and evil, that it would be difficult to describe me."

This fascinated bewilderment of Byron confronted by his own personality has been shared by all who have been swept into his orbit. That he is "something different" is plain enough from the fact that the word "Byronic" has become part of the language and Byron himself a kind of mythical hero like Oedipus or Prometheus. But to say what is different has been as difficult as Byron hoped it would be. The best we can do is to spread the paradoxical elements of his character before us and see if by describing them we can find the clue to understanding the man.

Perhaps the most important and familiar of the paradoxes is the juxtaposition of romantic and neoclassical characteristics in his life and art. On the one hand, Byron was the incarnation of the Romantic Ego. "The wandering outlaw of his own dark mind," cursed by a wild half-mad ancestry, his ancestral home a mouldering Gothic abbey, he was driven to every excess. Haunted by remorse for the "unmentionable" sin, he defied the authority of God, man, and devil, sought to identify with the elemental forces of nature, and died miserably in Greece in one final, frustrated gesture of revolt. John Galt's startling memory of him, sitting in the moonlight "amidst the shrouds and railings" of the boat carrying him to Malta in 1810, is the perfect evocation of the Romantic Byron. "He was," said Galt, "as a mystery in a winding sheet, crowned with a halo."

On the other hand, Byron was the complete Regency gentleman and man of letters. For his romantic contemporaries, with the exception of Shelley and Scott whom he admired as his peers, he had little respect. His critical allegiance was to the neoclassical tradition; indeed, in his admiration for Pope he was almost idolatrous. He pretended to look upon writing as the avocation of a gentleman; his naively arrogant statement of this attitude in the Preface to *Hours of Idleness* led to the attack upon him in the *Edinburgh Review* which in turn provoked his first major poem, the Popean satire, *English Bards and Scotch Reviewers*. In this he accepted the neoclassic theory that one of the chief functions of poetry is to expose and ridicule social cant and hypocrisy, a theory which he defended to the end of his life. In fact, it became the principal motivation of *Don Juan*. It was as social satirist that Byron took most seriously his responsibilities as an artist; and, as we shall see, it was as satirist in *Don Juan* that he finally effected a reconciliation of the romantic and neoclassic elements in his art.

Within this paradox was contained, as within a Chinese puzzle, an infinite number of other paradoxes. As a romantic, Byron was a revolutionary. He ardently espoused the cause of the French Revolution and proclaimed in ringing rhetoric the ultimate triumph of freedom throughout the world. Freedom was the big Byronic word, and by it he ambiguously meant many things. For nations he meant freedom from subjugation to other nations, and for this end he intrigued in Italy and fought in Greece. For the citizens of each nation, he meant freedom from tyranny, particularly the tyranny of monarchy.

His most spectacular eruptions of invective flowed down upon kings and those he considered their tools — the Castlereaghs, Wellingtons, and Southeys. He had genuine sympathy for the poor and oppressed; two of his three speeches in Parliament were on behalf of Catholic emancipation and the Luddites, the weavers of Nottingham who had tried desperately to break the machines they thought were depriving them of livelihoods. For himself and his heroes he meant by freedom complete anarchy and independence from all law and authority outside the individual mind which "is its own origin of ill and end/ And its own place and time."

And yet Byron never forgot that he was an aristocrat whose noble lineage could be traced back to the days of William the Conqueror. Partly because he had inherited the title unexpectedly after a childhood of poverty and neglect, he never felt at ease in his rank and he paraded it with insolent and sometimes ludicrous ostentation. His behavior toward those who failed to show proper deference was childishly rude. Many of his most romantic and anarchistic actions were simply dramatizations of the privileges and customs of the Regency nobleman. Though he admired the United States, he hated democracy, which he called the worst of governments, "an aristocracy of Blackguards." Undoubtedly he would have been greatly tempted by the rumored suggestion that he be the first king of Greece following liberation. We must remember, however, that the paradox of the revolutionary aristocrat is much more apparent today than in Byron's day. Many of the great revolutionaries in England and France were aristocrats. What they sought was a republic in which each would be free within his class, with the benevolent aristocrat as the freely chosen leader. Though he was aware of and amused by his own vanity as a lord of the realm, Byron would have seen no inconsistency in this attitude.

To most people in his own age, Byron was above all notorious for his love affairs. Even today, we are likely to be so hypnotized by the details of his relations with his half-sister Augusta, his marriage and its aftermath, and his numerous other affairs that we are in danger of overlooking or dismissing him as artist. This is not to say that we should try to read and evaluate Byron's poetry without reference to his life. On the contrary, there is, as I hope to show, a vital relationship between them unequaled in literature. But even as lover, Byron was much more than the sum of his affairs. He was rake, Puritan, and romantic idealist. Physically he was extraordinarily beautiful, with a mysterious lameness or deformity that, in marring, enhanced his beauty. He possessed, said Trelawney extravagantly, "the form and features of an Apollo with the feet and legs of a sylvan satyr." In addition, his beauty was precariously held through bouts of excessive dieting and strong purgatives against the pressing threats of obesity. It was the dieting which probably gave to his face the pallor that made it look, according to Scott, "like an alabaster vase lighted up from within." Abnormally sensitive about his lameness and tendency to corpulence, Byron was also shy, and he developed the pose of the "marble heart" both as protection and compensation. He was, in fact, strangely passive in his role as lover, rarely seeking an affair, but rather fatalistically accepting those thrust upon him. "I have been more ravished myself than anybody since the Trojan War," he wrote indignantly in 1819 in denying a rumor that he had carried off a girl from a convent.

Allied to his passivity was a strong Puritan strain. For his own conduct he suffered constant remorse. Peter Quennell, in *Byron: The Years of Fame*, states succinctly that Byron was "a man who sins with a consciousness of wrong-doing and sins again because the sense of guilt demands always fresh fuel." Puritanic sadism helps to account for the ruthless cruelty of his behavior toward Caroline Lamb and Claire Clairmont. His sense of guilt, aggravated by the self-righteous humorless tolerance of his wife, drove him to the hysterical brutality which resulted in their separation. The sense of guilt was also fed by a sexual ambivalence which drew him at various times in his life toward homosexual relations. In this ambivalence Byron was the true narcissistic romantic, dreaming of the mirror image of his own idealized self. The search for the ideal love combined with what Du Bos called the "need of fatality" led to the affair with Augusta in which we can see most clearly the whole nature of Byron as lover.

It is perhaps through an understanding of this "need of fatality" that we can best understand the paradoxes in Byron's religious and philosophical beliefs. To the end of his life, Byron could not shake off the baleful influence of the Calvinistic training with its emphasis upon predestination, sin, and damnation which he received as a child from his mother and nurse. It was fused in his mind with the superstitious awe with which he brooded over the fates of his ancestors, and it underlay his conviction that he had been doomed from birth. He revolted violently against it, both emotionally and intellectually. Emotionally he asserted the independence of his own will against the tyranny of destiny; intellectually he became a free thinker and skeptic, unable to accept the doctrine of Christianity or to put another in its place. He could only insist that the meaning of existence must be found in terms of the human mind. "Matter is eternal," he wrote in his *Detached Thoughts*, "and why not Mind? Why should not the Mind act with and upon the Universe? As portions of it act upon and with the congregated dust called Mankind?" Yet, at the same time, he was fitfully attracted by Catholicism. He insisted that his daughter Allegra be raised a Catholic, and he wrote Moore, "I incline, myself, very much to the Catholic doctrines." Nor did he ever overcome his sense of fatality, which increasingly took the form of morbid superstition. In 1801 a fortuneteller had warned his mother that he should beware of his thirty-seventh year. He set sail for Greece convinced that he would die there. And, as Mr. Nicolson points out, "It was with the reckless fatalism thus engendered that he chose as the defiant date of his embarcation a Sunday and the 13th of the month."

Byron's failure, indeed his refusal, to resolve his intellectual and emotional conflicts should not be shrugged away as evidence of superficiality or irresponsibility. On the contrary, Byron reflected more honestly and expressed more dramatically than most of his contemporaries the basic philosophic conflicts of an age of transition. He faced squarely, particularly in *Don Juan*, the implications of new scientific and social theory, and if he was unable to rationalize his doubts into an optimistic philosophy such as Wordsworth's, this is a sign of his intellectual honesty.

These are perhaps the most fascinating and important of the Byronic paradoxes, but there are many more. Byron was the generous, warmhearted friend, craving affection and lavishing it in return; but he was also the misanthrope, cynical and vindictive, believing the worst of his friends, capable of savage cruelty and petty malice. He was a profligate, recklessly squandering his income, quixotically displaying his rank and wealth, as when he lumbered through Italy with "seven servants, five carriages, nine horses, a monkey, a bull-dog and a mastiff, two cats, three pet fowls and some hens." Yet he was eminently sensible and practical in the conduct of his affairs, as in his handling of the situation in Greece. And in his last years he even took up the "good old gentlemanly vice" of avarice and became a "damned close calculating fellow," to the great disgust of such borrowers as Leigh Hunt. In Byron the antithetical characteristics of human nature existed unrepressed, unresolved, each expressed dramatically and unpredictably with equal power and sincerity. When he said to Lady Blessington, "If I know myself, I have no character at all," he was in a sense right; he had the character of Everyman.

II

But at the same time he had molded the romantic elements of the paradox into a character which set him apart from Everyman and which has ever since borne his name — the character of the Byronic hero. It was an inseparable interweaving of life and art, bearing a startling resemblance to the hero of myth and tragic drama. His life had from the beginning, as Mr. Quennell points out, "something in common with that of Oedipus, a descendant of kings, reared amid humble surroundings . . . Oedipus the lame-footed who returned to his birthright only to involve those who were nearest him in death and disaster. If Oedipus was a predestined being, so was Byron." Or, what is as important, Byron thought that he was and tried to give his life the inevitability of myth. Consequently his development as an artist can best be understood by tracing the relation of the poet to the hero.

The chief characteristics of the Byronic hero were melancholy and ennui; misanthropy, defiant pride, and remorse. These were fashionable characteristics of the age found in varying degrees in the heroes and villains of Gothic romances and in such men of feeling as Goethe's Werther and Chateaubriand's René. They had been widely affected, particularly the melancholy and ennui, by young sentimentalists. That even in adolescence Byron dramatized himself in these terms is evident from the poem "Childish Recollections":

> Weary of love, of life, devour'd with spleen,
> I rest, a perfect Timon, not nineteen:
> World! I renounce thee! All my hope's o'ercast!
> One sigh I give thee, but that sigh's the last.

To his humorless friend Dallas who believed all he was told, Byron wrote grandly at the age of twenty, "The events of my short life have been of so singular a nature that . . . . I have been already held up as the votary of licentiousness, and the disciple of infidelity . . . . My hand is almost as bad as my character." Such words and the deeds that accompanied them — such as the revels of the Merry Monks of Newstead and the drinking from a skull — were pretty much playacting, although there was undoubtedly a hard substratum of belief. It is probable that up to the morning of the publication of *Childe Harold* when he awoke to find himself famous, Byron's conduct differed little from that of his peers: the difference lay in his flair for self-dramatization, a morbid sensitivity of conscience, an "inverted hypocrisy" which led him to brood over, boast about, or even invent misdeeds which his more calloused and hypocritical contemporaries perpetrated without thought.

This difference helps us understand why during the two years of his travels he could have a wonderful time, indeed look back upon them as perhaps the happiest years of his life, and at the same time, interpret them through the gloomy eyes of Childe Harold. Childe Harold was, in part, a dramatic pose, a dream figure, and Byron was probably sincere in disavowing any connection between himself and this "child of the imagination." On the other hand, by the very fact that he was a dream figure, Childe Harold represented the poet's deepest convictions and emotions, his unconscious drives. Perhaps when Byron projected such a dream picture of himself and then lived it out to the last nightmarish detail, he was really acting out "his need of fatality." Ten years afterward, in 1821, Byron gives a brief but fascinating glimpse into his attitude toward the poem: "My passions were developed very early — so early, that few would believe me, if I were to state the period and the facts which accompanied it. Perhaps this was one of the reasons which caused the anticipated melancholy of my thoughts — having anticipated life . . . . The two first Cantos of Ce. Hd. were completed at twenty two, and they are written as if by a man older than I shall probably ever be."

The modern reader may find it difficult to understand the immediate and sensational success of the first two cantos of *Childe Harold*. To him the poem may seem tawdry, trite, and even dull. But for Byron's contemporaries there had been nothing like it. It came at a moment when they were most ready for it and perhaps needed it most. Here was a hero who, unlike the heroes of Scott or the Gothic novels, lived in the contemporary world. His affectation of an archaic name and style nostalgically and quaintly brought the past into the present. He was presented in shockingly memorable phrases and with contagious conviction. To a people isolated and sick of a war which had lasted twenty years, he was the roving columnist, commenting on lands they had known through the war like Portugal and Spain and exotic lands beyond the war like Albania and Greece. His disillusion, his terrible remorse, and his unmentionable guilt were theirs, particularly for those who felt uneasily that they had betrayed the principles of the French Revolution. As the fascinating letters in Quennell's *Byron: The Years of Fame* testify, Childe Harold made an appeal to all classes. To the lives of the jaded, bored aristocracy, he gave meaning and glamor; through him they could see themselves in a new perspective. To the mass of people he was an exciting escape from humdrum existence; for them he was like the sensational movie hero of our day who springs to stardom in one Class B picture. For the Puritans — and there were many — he was a mysterious evil to be vicariously enjoyed and vigorously reformed: an exhilarating challenge. Every reader immediately identified the hero with the author and directly or indirectly with himself. Byron became overnight the expression of the English libido so long repressed by religion, government, and war.

He was quick to exploit his fame. Between 1812 and 1816 he wrote at breakneck speed a series of melodramatic oriental verse narratives in which against the background of dark and violent deeds he filled out in lurid detail the portrait of his hero. The most elaborate attempts to probe the psychology of the hero are found in the *Corsair* and *Lara*; even today there is power in the faded rhetoric of such a passage as the following from *Lara*:

> There was in him a vital scorn of all:
> As if the worst had fall'n which could befall.
> He stood a stranger in this breathing world,
> An erring spirit from another hurl'd;
> A thing of dark imaginings, that shaped
> By choice the perils he by chance escaped:
> But 'scaped in vain, for in their memory yet
> His mind would half exult and half regret.

> • • • • • •

> But haughty still and loth himself to blame,
> He called on Nature's self to share the shame,
> And charged all faults upon the fleshly form
> She gave to clog the soul and feast the worm;
> Till he at last confounded good and ill,
> And half mistook for fate the acts of will.

The last two lines might be taken as Byron's epigram upon his own life during this period. It was easy for him to look and act the part of his hero; he wanted to and society was determined that he should. Soon there was no chance of escape. From acting the role, he turned to living it and what suited a part became the habit of his mind. With the rapidity of one of his own narratives, he was driven to those acts that led to his disgrace and exile. That his life had taken on the characteristics of art was evident to his contemporaries. Goethe is reported as saying of the separation from Lady Byron, "that in its circumstances and the mystery in which it is involved it is so poetical that if Lord Byron had invented it he could hardly have had a more fortunate subject for his genius." His exile, though voluntary, had the inevitability and cathartic effect of drama. Both Byron and society demanded it; it was necessary to complete the pattern of his life. Macaulay points out that Byron had become for the British public a kind of ritual scapegoat or expiatory sacrifice "by whose vicarious agonies all the other transgressors of the same class are, it is supposed, sufficiently chastised," and, he might have added, the superiority of conventional morality is triumphantly reasserted.

The moment of exile is in Byron's life and art the moment, to use Kenneth Burke's phrase, of "symbolic action." It is the moment toward which the first cantos of *Childe Harold* and the Oriental tales have led and from which the later poems take their rise. But it is also the moment which makes possible Byron's emancipation from the hero. For now that the identification is complete, he is set free imaginatively. He is forced into a self-searching analysis which enables him to see himself and his hero in proper perspective and to obtain the aesthetic distance and artistic control without which *Don Juan* could not have been written. In short, it is the moment which makes Byron a great poet.

In the summer of 1816 Byron wrote his first great poems, the *Epistle to Augusta* and the third canto of *Childe Harold*. If in the earlier *Childe Harold* he had anticipated life, he was now reflecting it. He had "outlived himself by many a day," had suffered the experiences which might have filled a century. Where he had posed as the jaded profligate or the Satanic outlaw, he was now defiantly himself, Byron broken by society, frustrated in the "nobler aim" he had once beheld, "one the more/ To baffled millions which have gone before." Standing "as a ruin amidst ruins," he boldly made his experiences symbolize the experiences of an era. By his analyses of the characteristics of Napoleon and Rousseau in terms of his own, he set himself up as the typical man of his age. By his contemplation of Waterloo and the defeat of the hopes of the French Revolution, he identified his failure with the failure of his generation. His mood, however, was not simply one of hopeless defeat. He found a "very life," a "vitality of poison" in despair which sustained and strengthened him and became the source of his artistic power. He discovered the purpose of art: "to create, and in creating live a being more intense" than the life he had "outlived." Through his poetry, through this "soul of his thought" he could triumph in defeat. He could assert that his mind was an indestructible force like the nature of which it was a part; that he had a force within him "which shall tire/ Torture and Time, and breathe when I expire"; that this power which found expression in his poetry was the same as the revolutionary force in society which, though temporarily eclipsed, would ultimately prevail. In this way, he made the Byronic hero not only the symbol of a lost generation but also the prophetic voice of a revolutionary future; and, above all, he made him the expression of the eternally defiant mind of man, unconquerable in its will to freedom.

The one step necessary to give his life truly universal significance Byron took in *Manfred*. This was to detach the hero from himself and from time and place and set him in conflict with cosmic forces. As Manfred, he aspired more or less successfully to the knowledge which would give him control over nature. But he aspired also to an ideal happiness, a union with one like himself which resulted in the destruction of the loved one. It is the unappeasable remorse which followed and Manfred's hysterical efforts to use his knowledge and power to obtain oblivion that Byron made the subject of his drama. But this subject became subordinate to Manfred's refusal to make any pact with or submit in any way to forces external to him, even in the moment of death that is foreordained by these very forces. It is obvious that Byron had translated his relationship with Augusta, his remorse and despair, his isolation and defiance into a dramatic myth of the superman. The superior individual's struggle for self-realization and fulfillment — his desire to be more than man — inevitably entails, he seems to say, a fatal violation of conventional morality. Yet somehow only in this way can the mind of man establish its identity, its independence, the responsibility for its own acts; only in this way may human existence become meaningful.

By finding in *Manfred* the perfect artistic expression for his experiences, Byron achieved an emotional release, a separation from his hero which freed him to develop the larger view of himself and the world in which the hero became increasingly unnecessary, even a little silly. To be sure, Byron used him as protagonist in *Cain* and the classical dramas, but these were simply interludes within the greater drama of *Don Juan*. One noticeable characteristic of the hero had been his lack of humor, his tendency to take himself very seriously indeed. In

Don Juan, Byron at last could laugh at him. Don Juan is a mild, cheerful fellow, a far cry from Manfred or even from the legendary hero whose name he bears. True, he is a wanderer and has numerous affairs, but in both cases he is an unwitting victim of circumstances rather than an aggressive agent. He is very brave, a man of quick and intelligent action, kind and generous, in fact — high-minded. He commits no crime, suffers no remorse, and, far from revolting against society, adjusts quickly and beautifully to every environment whether it be the Turkish harem, the Russian army, or an English house party. In England, he is the polished diplomat, tactful, modest, a good listener, respected by men as much as he is pursued by women. He is the hero as he might be after successful psychoanalytic treatment, and one feels that Byron is really quite fond of him and would like to think that this is what he would or could have been if fate had permitted. Juan becomes the perfect straight man for Byron's own role in the poem which, in a sense, is that of the retired hero who somehow has been denied the oblivion he so defiantly sought and is now anticlimactically living on as the aging lover of the young countess. In relating Juan's life, he looks back with wry amusement on his own, and in a casual conversational way applies the wisdom he has acquired to any subject that comes to hand. He is cynical, mocking, sentimental, realistic by turns in pointing out the incongruities between man's aspirations and his achievements, between his real and pretended motives, between the grandiose picture he draws of himself and the ridiculous figure he really is. In general, he delights in emphasizing the insignificance of man in the universe and showing that life is not worth a potato. He turns upon the society which had hounded him and exposes with pitiless satire its pretensions and hypocrisies. From time to time, he forgets himself and strikes the old pose, but just as rapidly he perceives the absurdity and by the twist of a rhyme turns the pose to burlesque. Over all there is a gusto, an enjoyment of himself and all that he observes that gives him the superiority to his environment he had always sought. Through laughter he has found the freedom he could never obtain through defiance.

The appeal of the Byronic hero is not hard to understand. He exists in one form or another in the dream life of all of us, whether we like it or not, as the embodiment of those impulses cramped or inhibited by society. By the absolute courage of his defiance of moral and social taboos he is, in Herbert Read's phrase, "the unconfessed hero of humanity." He is the expression of our social insecurity, our distrust of our fellows, our dissatisfaction with authority, our disillusionment with social achievement. He is the symbol of our defiant refusal to accept the insignificant role of the individual ego in society or the universe which modern science and technology forces upon us. In short, he represents the ego in conflict with the forces battering to subdue or destroy it — the ego which triumphs even in the moment of defeat.

In the twentieth century the Byronic hero has cast a long shadow. Perhaps it would be more accurate to say that the tensions that created him are stronger than ever before and have resulted in the constant recreation of the hero of which he is the prototype. As we read *Childe Harold, Manfred* and *Don Juan*, we are struck by the similarities with the heroes or anti-heroes produced in our literature and society by the anxieties that have haunted us since the first world war. We think of the Hemingway hero, the product like Childe Harold of a lost generation disillusioned by the results of war, dramatizing the meaninglessness of his existence through self-indulgence and the violation of conventions. Or of the existentialist hero (in Sartre's words "condemned to be free" in an alien universe) and his successors in the literature of the absurd. And there is more than a touch of the Byronic hero in the Beat Generation of the fifties, and its violent and nonviolent descendants in the sixties. His voice can be heard in the protest against the cant of the Establishment; in the cry for the emancipation of the four-letter word and sexual mores; in the rhetoric of revolutionary leaders from Che Guevara to Malcolm X to the student militant. And he can be seen in the dramatic experimentation with dress, appearance, and manner of living; in the defiant rejection of all authority outside the self; in the search for identity through heightened sensation — "the great object of life is sensation — to feel that we exist, even in pain," Byron wrote in a letter quoted below (p. 640). Indeed the descendants today of the Byronic hero are, to use a word that would carry for Byron the proper Satanic overtones, legion.

III

As an artist, Byron has only recently been taken as seriously as he deserves. For one thing, to separate his work from his life and personality is, as we have seen, almost impossible; too often, therefore, the poetry is discussed simply as illustration of the life. For another, it is easier to point out the faults than to analyze the merits; and many critics no doubt have found in this way sweet revenge for the restlessness they have felt in the presence of his personality or the response they could not help making at one time or another to *Childe Harold* or *Manfred*. In one sense, Byron asked for this cavalier condescension toward himself as an artist. Not only did he assert loudly and aggressively at frequent intervals throughout his life that poetry was simply an avocation or diversion, thereby attempting to excuse his faults, but, to add insult to injury, he boasted of the ease and rapidity with which he wrote. He could compose "in the bath, in the study, or on horseback": the *Bride of Abydos*, 732 lines, was written in "four nights to distract my dreams," and another favorite time for composition was at two or three in the morning after a party.

He hated to revise or correct: "I am like the Tiger: if I miss the first spring, I go growling back to my Jungle again, but if I *do hit*, it is crushing." Actually he reworked much more than he liked to confess; in fact, he became quite painstaking and conscientious in the composition of the later poems. It is obvious that he was proud of being a poet, and we have seen that after 1816 poetry became in a very real sense his life. Yet he could never bring himself to admit it without hedging; and is is not surprising that more often than not he has been taken at his word.

Furthermore, from the point of view of the twentieth-century poet, Byron was guilty of the most heinous of artistic crimes: he wrote too much. T. S. Eliot put the criticism bluntly: "The bulk of Byron's poetry is distressing in proportion to its quality." Byron would have readily agreed. "I have had a devilish deal of wear and tear of mind and body in my time, besides having published too often and much already," he wrote Murray in 1817 upon the completion of *Childe Harold* IV, one of the many occasions when he threatened to write no more. Undoubtedly the body of his poetry has suffered a devilish deal of wear and tear during the last century. The present selection indicates fairly, I think, what has held up — in general, what was written after his exile in 1816. This is the poetry upon which an evaluation of Byron as an artist must be based. And immediately we see that bulk remains an essential characteristic of this poetry inseparable from the qualities which make it great. The full appreciation of Byron as an artist comes only through the accumulative impact of reading a lot of him. For it is by repetition and digression, by accumulation and expansion that Byron achieves the intensity a modern poet might achieve through compression. His method is the statement of a theme and the development of variations upon it as in *Childe Harold* or the contrapuntal interweaving of many themes as in *Don Juan*. As the themes are large, so must be the forms through which they realize themselves. The abundance and exuberance of his imagination can find expression in no other way. And in the rush of words to fill the forms there is created for the reader an effect of inexhaustible vitality unsurpassed in poetry. "Exuberance is beauty," cried Blake in one of the Proverbs of Hell, and this could serve as Byron's artistic credo.

But in our intoxication with the rush of words, we are apt to pay little attention to the details of diction and imagery sweeping by. Critics like Eliot would say sourly that it is just as well. They point to an artificiality of diction and a falsity of tone, to an incongruity between language and emotion and a commonplaceness of imagery and idea. Indeed, Eliot made the sweeping charge that "of Byron one can say as of no other English poet of his eminence that he added nothing to the language, that he discovered nothing in the sounds and developed nothing in the meaning of individual words."

It is true that Byron never consciously broke with the neoclassic tradition, or experimented with language as did contemporaries like Wordsworth. His vocabulary was conventionally literary with a high concentration of "poetic diction," except in such poems as *Don Juan*. But into this conventional mold he poured his personality. The tension between language and emotion so created was the artistic manifestation of the fundamental conflict in Byron's character: that of the Regency gentleman who was also the wandering outlaw of his own dark mind. The latter could express himself only in the language of the former. Just as the man struggled for freedom within the social convention, so the poet's imagination struggled for expression within the literary convention. The result was a conventional language highly personalized, charged with meaning drawn from himself, tightened to epigrammatic incisiveness. "If I *do* hit," he said, "it is crushing." He hit crushingly his own character and moods:

> But there is that within me which shall tire
> Torture and Time, and breathe when I expire. . . .

> I have been cunning in mine overthrow,
> The careful pilot of my proper woe. . . .
> Could I embody and unbosom now
> That which is most within me. . . .
>   into *one* word
> And that one word were Lightning, I would speak;
> But as it is, I live and die unheard
> With a most voiceless thought, sheathing it as a sword.

> I have not loved the World, nor the World me:
> I have not flattered its rank breath, nor bowed
> To its idolatries a patient knee. . . .

He caught in a phrase the places he saw, like Venice, "fairy city of the heart,"

> Rising with her tiara of proud towers
> At airy distance, with majestic motion. . . .

or Rome "mother of dead empires," the "Niobe of nations,"

> An empty urn within her withered hands,
> Whose holy dust was scattered long ago. . . .

And in an epigram he epitomized the great men of his age, like Napoleon "Conqueror and Captive of the Earth," or Rousseau "self-torturing sophist,"

. . . . phrensied by disease or war
To that worst pitch of all, which wears a reasoning
    show,

or Gibbon "sapping a solemn creed with solemn sneer." In
this way Byron revitalized the conventional idiom into the
"thoughts that breathe and words that burn."

The content of Byron's poetry, said Hazlitt, "consists mostly
of a tissue of superb commonplaces." The large fundamental
relationships of life, love and death, man, society, and nature
are the subjects of all poetry, but Byron never bothered to
mask them in intricacies of language or symbol and so trans-
form them into vistas new and strange. Nor could he bring
himself to set them within the frame of an elaborately optimistic philosophy like Wordsworth and Shelley and so turn
them from commonplaces into profundities. For these reasons
above all, his poetic stature suffered severely at the hands of
the Victorians, who measured him against his romantic contemporaries, and again under the scrutiny of twentieth-century
new critics who measured him against the metaphysical poets.
But in recent years critics have come to view Byron's artistic
achievement with increasing respect. They have become aware
of a controlling purpose and conscious skill in the use of
familiar images and ideas. They have seen what earlier un-
sympathetic critics did not, that Byron's poems can be read as
a body of poetry in which a complex point of view gives co-
herence and unity to all the works, serious and satiric, from the
earliest to the last. Artistically this point of view expresses itself through recurring thematic and imagistic patterns like fire
and dust, light and darkness, growth and decay, sea and mountain, garden and desert. These are used with great variety and
flexibility to convey Byron's sense of the irreconcilable conflicts
between mind and body, and the unanswerable questions
about the meaning of the universe and man's role in it. Behind
all of Byron's poetry lies the vision of an ideal world, a paradise, which at one moment he laments as something possessed
in his youth and now irretrievably lost, at another as something realizable in the future through revolutionary action,
at still another as something existing only in the mind's eye
momentarily attainable in love, or nature, or even in the crea-

tion of poetry, but lost in the very moment of attainment. Byron's pervasive commonplace is of the fallen man; though often used in its biblical context, it is not a theological but rather a psychological metaphor used by the idealist, continually disillusioned by his own behavior, to express his sense of the unbridgeable gap between the ideal and real in our imperfect universe. Byron achieves much of his effect by the remarkable range of tones in which he expresses himself: from despair to outrage, to defiance, to hope, to stoicism and resignation, and finally to amused contemplation. And there are the bewildering, shifting perspectives in which he builds up "common things with commonplaces." In *Don Juan* he takes a position of complete skepticism and cultivates, as Michael Cooke has said, "the imagery of contradiction."

> For me, I know nought; nothing I deny,
>   Admit — reject — contemn: and what know *you*,
> Except perhaps that you were born to die?
>   And both may after all turn out untrue.

His commonplaces have become the means for expressing his sense of the absurdity of life in a "universe of unpredictability."

Don Juan and its small companion masterpieces *Beppo* and *The Vision of Judgment* represent Byron's apotheosis of the commonplace, the poems in which he truly adds to the language of poetry. Perhaps the best introduction to these poems are his letters, because it is the characteristics of the letters carried over into the poetry that make the poems unique. The letters themselves are among the most wonderful ever written. Freed of the inhibitions and cramping restrictions of literary convention, Byron developed in them an easy flexible style which became a magic mirror reflecting day by day his ever-changing personality. In his casual reading of Pulci and a contemporary English imitation of Pulci by "the brothers Whistlecraft" (pseudonym of John Hookham Frere), he found the equivalent verse style. He discovered delightedly that in the *ottava rima* "without straining hard to versify," he could "rattle on exactly as I talk/With anybody in a ride or walk."

When he began *Don Juan,* Byron seemed to have no purpose except "to giggle and make giggle" through a playful burlesque of the epic manner. But almost haphazardly through the process of writing, a more definite purpose evolved; it was to write an "epic satire" which by carrying the hero through the situations of the heroic epic would reveal "things as they really are," the essentially unheroic motivations and actions of modern man. The loud-mouthed and self-righteous outcry against the immorality of the first five cantos set Byron in a rage, and he settled down in deadly earnest to expose the cant and hypocrisy of society. "Don Juan will be known by and bye, for what it is intended," he wrote Murray in December, 1822, "a *Satire* on *abuses* of the present states of Society, and not an eulogy of vice." The change of purpose is shown in the change of narrative structure of the poem. The first eight cantos contain well-developed episodes "of love, tempest, travel, war. All very accurate . . . and *epic*"; but beginning with Canto 9, plot elements almost disappear and the narrative becomes a thin thread on which to hang satiric comments and character sketches. How the poem would have ended, to how many cantos it would have run, Byron did not know. In February, 1821 he wrote Murray "The 5th. is so far from being the last of D. J., that it is hardly the beginning. I meant to take him the tour of Europe, with a proper mixture of siege, battle, and adventure, and to make him finish as *Anacharsis Cloots*[1] in the French Revolution. To how many cantos this may extend, I know not, nor whether (even if I live) I shall complete it; but this was my notion: I meant to have made him a *Cavalier Servente* in Italy, and a cause for a divorce in England and a Sentimental 'Werther-faced man'[2] in Germany, so as to show the different ridicules of the society in each of those countries, and to have displayed him gradually *gâté* and *blasé* as he grew older, as is natural. But I had not quite fixed whether to make him end in Hell, or in an unhappy marriage, not knowing which would be the severest. The Spanish tradition says Hell: but it is probably only an Allegory of the other state. You are now in possession of my

[1] Anacharsis Cloots was a Prussian Baron who took an active part in the French Revolution, proclaiming himself the Orator of the Human Race. He was executed in March, 1794, by order of Robespierre.

[2] In Goethe's novel *The Sorrows of Young Werther* the hero pines away because of unrequited love and finally commits suicide.

notions on the subject." It really doesn't matter, for *Don Juan* by its very nature could not have a conventional ending; like Byron's letters and conversation, it could end only with the death of its author.

Although the narrative becomes of secondary importance, Byron's narrative skill and versatility have been surpassed in English poetry perhaps only by Chaucer. The Rabelaisian gusto of the first canto and of the night in the harem; the brutal realism of the shipwreck and the Siege of Ismail; the lyric loveliness of the Don Juan–Haidee romance; and the acid satire of the "monstrous" house party — these indicate his extraordinary range and power. But the unique greatness of *Don Juan* lies finally in the omnipresence of the author's comments. "Why, Man," he cried to Murray, "the Soul of such writing is its license; at least the *liberty* of that *license*." He never abused the license: the clarity and sanity of his comic sense prevented that. But he used it to add to the language of poetry the colloquial richness and informality of prose and conversation. He developed as no other poet ever had the language's apparently inexhaustible potentialities for multiple rime. He made the *ottava rima* the most flexible of verse forms by molding it with equal skill for lyric, dramatic, or satiric purposes. In particular, he used his license to develop the device of incongruity, the lightning shift from one state of mind to its opposite. In its simplest form, the device takes on something of the characteristics of the practical joke. Byron leads us to make all the proper psychological responses to a stock situation; then by a phrase or rhyme — his favorite weapon is the end couplet of the stanza — he whips the situation, like a chair, out from under us. As a satiric device, it takes the form of debunking, of stripping the mask from our pretenses, and showing us our true motivations. In its most subtle and complicated form, it becomes romantic irony — the half-sad, half-comic juxtaposition of the illusion and the reality, of the ideal and the actual, of what we should be and what we are. In this form it establishes the dominant mood of the poem.

The most frequent criticism of *Don Juan* has been that it is superficially and cheaply cynical, that its destructive satire is not balanced by any constructive philosophy, that, in De

Selincourt's phrase, it lacks *vision*. Such criticism was more understandable in the days of Victorian illusion than now, but I cannot see that it ever had much validity. In replying to the charge of immorality, Byron said, "No Girl will ever be seduced by reading D. J. — no, no," and we could add that no man will ever put a bullet through his head either. On the contrary, the sustained intellectual shock, by which are forced continually to re-examine the illusions by which we live, is one of the most salutary and exhilarating experiences we can receive in literature. For it shakes us out of apathy and into action as no doctrine of optimism could ever do. There is a brief statement in the *Detached Thoughts* which sums up the final Byronic view of life: "Man is born *passionate* of body, but with an innate though secret tendency to the love of Good in his Mainspring of Mind. But God help us all! It is at present a sad jar of atoms." When we read *Don Juan* we want, like Byron, to do something about it.

Seattle, Wash.   E.E.B.

Chronology

1788	January 22. Born in London.
1790	Taken by mother to Aberdeen, Scotland.
1791	Father, Captain ("Mad Jack") Byron, dies in France.
1792	Attends day school in Aberdeen. Later privately tutored.
1794	Becomes heir to the title of his grand-uncle, the "wicked" Lord Byron.
1798	Inherits title and Newstead Abbey upon death of grand-uncle. Moves to Newstead.
1799	Attends Dr. Glennie's Academy at Dulwich.
1801–1805	Attends Harrow. Falls in love with Mary Chaworth, grand-niece of Lord Chaworth, killed by "wicked" Lord Byron in a duel. She laughs at him and in 1805 marries John Muster (Cf. *The Dream*).
1805	Enters Trinity College, Cambridge.
1806	*Fugitive Pieces,* first volume of poems, privately printed and then destroyed upon the Rev. John Becher's protests against certain of the poems.
1807	*Poems on Various Occasions,* an expurgated edition, again privately printed. In June publicly printed as *Hours of Idleness.*
1808	Attack on *Hours of Idleness* by Henry Brougham in *Edinburgh Review.* Receives M.A. degree at Cambridge, July 4th.
1809	Attains majority; takes seat in House of Lords. *English Bards and Scotch Reviewers* published in March. With Hobhouse sails from England, July 2, for Lisbon. Journeys through Portugal and Spain, sails to Albania by way of Malta, visits the Albanian leader, Ali Pasha,

and reaches Athens by the end of the year. Completes first canto of *Childe Harold*, Dec. 30th.

1810   Travels through Greece and Turkey; swims Hellespont, May 3. Completes second canto of *Childe Harold* in Athens, March 28.

1811   Returns to England in July. Mother dies in August.

1812   Gives three speeches in House of Lords. *Childe Harold* published in March by John Murray who remains Byron's publisher until 1822. Immediate fame. Affair with Lady Caroline Lamb.

1813   In June begins affair with Augusta. First Oriental tales, *The Giaour* and *The Bride of Abydos*, published.

1814   Daughter, Medora, born to Augusta in April. Engaged to Annabella Milbanke in September. *Corsair* and *Lara* published.

1815   Married to Annabella, Jan. 2. Daughter, Augusta Ada, born Dec. 10. *Hebrew Melodies* published.

1816   Lady Byron leaves Byron in January. Formal separation agreed upon and signed in April. Ostracized by society. Byron leaves England for good, April 25. Journeys through Belgium and up the Rhine to Geneva. Spends summer in company of Shelley, Mary Godwin, and Claire Clairmont. Travels to Venice with Hobhouse. *The Siege of Corinth, Parisina* published in February; *Childe Harold* III in November; *The Prisoner of Chillon* in December.

1817   Allegra, daughter of Byron and Claire Clairmont, born Jan. 12. Byron makes Venice his home. Takes trip to Florence and Rome. Sells Newstead Abbey. *Manfred* published in June.

1818   The Shelleys come to Italy in March. Byron and Shelley frequently together until November when Shelleys go to Rome. Byron begins *Don Juan* in July. *Beppo* (first experiment in style of *Don Juan*) published in February; *Childe Harold* IV in April.

1819   Meets Teresa, Countess Guiccioli, in Venice in April. At end of year moves to Ravenna to be with her. *Mazeppa* published in June; *Don Juan* I and II in July.

1820   Becomes involved through the Gambas, Teresa's father

and brothers, in the revolutionary Carbonari movement to free Italy from Austrian rule. Byron lives in the Guiccioli palace with his daughter Allegra.

1821   Carbonari movement defeated; Gambas banished to Pisa where Byron joins them. *Don Juan* III, IV, V, published in August. Byron promises Countess to write no more of *Don Juan*. In the meantime has turned to classical dramas: *Marino Faliero* published in April; *Cain, Two Foscari,* and *Sardanapalus* in December.

1822   Byron meets Trelawney. In April Allegra dies in convent where Byron had placed her. Leigh Hunt moves to Byron's house in June. Byron returns to *Don Juan*. Shelley drowned in July. Byron moves to Genoa. Supports Leigh Hunt in publication of periodical, *The Liberal*. *The Vision of Judgment* published in October.

1823   In July Byron sails for Greece. Arrives in Missolonghi, after many delays and misadventures, on Dec. 30. Cantos VI to XIV of *Don Juan* published.

1824   Is taken ill, April 9, after horseback ride in heavy downpour. Dies April 19. Buried July 16 in Hucknell Torkard Church near Newstead. Cantos XV, XVI of *Don Juan* published in March.

Selected Bibliography

I. EDITIONS

1. *Poetry*

The Works of Lord Byron: Poetry, ed. Ernest Hartley Coleridge. 7 vols. London, 1898–1904.

The Complete Poetical Works of Lord Byron, ed. Paul Elmer Moore. Cambridge, Mass., 1905; reissue, 1952. The best complete one-volume edition.

Byron's Don Juan, ed. Truman Guy Steffan and Willis W. Pratt. 4 vols. Austin, Texas, 1957. A Variorium Edition. Vol. I is a general introduction; vols. II and III, the text with manuscript variants; vol. IV, the notes and critical commentary.

Don Juan, ed. Leslie Marchand. Boston, 1958.

Lord Byron's Cain, ed. Truman Guy Steffan. Austin, Texas, 1968. A Variorum Edition.

2. *Letters and Journals*

The Works of Lord Byron: Letters and Journals, ed. Rowland E. Prothero. 6 vols. London, 1898–1901.

Lord Byron's Correspondence, ed. John Murray. 2 vols. London, 1922. Supplements the Prothero edition.

Byron: A Self-Portrait: Letters and Diaries, 1798 to 1824, ed. Peter Quennell. 2 vols. London, 1950. Includes over fifty new letters.

II. MEMOIRS BY CONTEMPORARIES OF BYRON

Blessington, The Countess of. *Conversations of Lord Byron.* London, 1834. Ed. Ernest J. Lovell, Jr. Princeton, N.J., 1969.

Dallas, R. C. *Recollections of the Life of Lord Byron from the Year 1808 to the End of 1814.* London, 1824.

Galt, John. *The Life of Lord Byron.* London, 1830.

Gamba, Pietro. *A Narrative of Lord Byron's Last Journey to Greece.* London, 1825. Gamba who accompanied Byron, was the brother of the Countess Guiccioli.

Guiccioli, Teresa, Countess. *My Recollections of Lord Byron.* London, 1869.

Hobhouse, John Cam (Lord Broughton). *Recollections of a Long Life.* 4 vols. Ed. Lady Dorchester. London, 1909–1911.

Hunt, Leigh. *Lord Byron and Some of His Contemporaries.* 2 vols. London, 1828.

Lovell, Ernest J., ed. *His Very Self and Voice: The Collected Conversations of Lord Byron.* New York, 1954. Excludes Blessington and Medwin.

Medwin, Thomas. *Journal of the Conversations of Lord Byron. . . . At Pisa.* London, 1824. Ed. Ernest J. Lovell, Jr. Princeton, N.J., 1966.

Moore, Thomas. *Letters and Journals of Lord Byron: with Notices of his Life.* 2 vols. London, 1830. The first "official" biography.

Trelawney, Edward John. *Recollections of the Last Days of Shelley and Byron*. London, 1858. (Revised as *Records of Shelley, Byron, and the Author*. London, 1878).

III. BIOGRAPHY

Borst, William A. *Byron's First Pilgrimage*. New Haven, Conn., 1948. Byron's travels in 1809–1811.

Cline, C. L. *Byron, Shelley and their Pisan Circle*. Austin, Texas, 1952.

Du Bos, Charles. *Byron and the Need of Fatality*. Trans. E. C. Mayne. London, 1932.

Elwin, Malcolm. *Lord Byron's Wife*. London, 1962.

Fox, Sir John C. *The Byron Mystery*. London, 1924. On the separation and the relation with Augusta.

Knight, G. Wilson. *Lord Byron's Marriage: The Evidence of Asterisks*. London, 1957.

Lovelace, Ralph, Earl of. *Astarte*. London, 1905. Revised and enlarged, 1921. First publication of important letters on the separation and the relation with Augusta.

Marchand, Leslie A. *Byron: A Biography*. 3 vols. New York, 1957. The most complete and accurate biography. Revised and condensed as *Byron: A Portrait*. 1 vol. New York, 1970.

Marshall, William H. *Byron, Shelley, Hunt, and The Liberal*. Philadelphia, 1960.

Maurois, André. *Byron*. English translation. London, 1930.

Mayne, Ethel. *Byron*. 2 vols. London, 1912. Revised edition, 1 vol. 1924.

———. *The Life and Letters of Lady Byron*. London, 1929.

Moore, Doris Langley. *The Late Lord Byron*. London, 1961. An account of the burning of Byron's *Memoirs* after his death, with flashbacks into the events and relationships leading to the burning.

Nicholson, Harold. *Byron: the Last Journey: April 1823–April 1824*. London, 1924.

Origo, Iris. *The Last Attachment: the Story of Byron and Teresa Guiccioli*. London, 1949.

Pratt, Willis W. *Byron at Southwell: The Making of a Poet*. Austin, Texas, 1948. Background of Byron's early poems.

Quennell, Peter. *Byron, The Years of Fame*. London, 1935. Byron's life in London, 1811–1816.

————. *Byron in Italy*. London, 1941.

IV. CRITICISM

Arnold, Matthew. "Byron." *Essays in Criticism*. Second Series. London, 1888.

Bloom, Harold. "George Gordon, Lord Byron." *The Visionary Company: A Reading of English Romantic Poetry*. New York, 1961.

Bostetter, Edward E. "Byron." *The Romantic Ventriloquists*. Seattle, Wash., 1963.

————, ed. *Twentieth Century Interpretations of Don Juan: A Collection of Critical Essays*. Englewood Cliffs, N.J., 1969.

Boyd, Elizabeth. *Byron's Don Juan: A Critical Study*. New Brunswick, N.J., 1945.

Calvert, W. J. *Byron: Romantic Paradox*. Chapel Hill, N.C., 1935.

Chew, Samuel C. *Byron in England: His Fame and After Fame*. London, 1924.

Cooke, Michael G. *The Blind Man Traces the Circle: On the Patterns and Philosophy of Byron's Poetry*. Princeton, N.J., 1968.

Eliot, T. S. "Byron." *On Poetry and Poets*. London, 1937.

Elledge, W. Paul. *Byron and the Dynamics of Metaphor*. Nashville, Tenn., 1968.

Fairchild, H. N. "Byron." *Religious Trends in English Poetry*, vol. III. New York, 1949.

Gleckner, Robert F. *Byron and the Ruins of Paradise*. Baltimore, Md., 1967.

Joseph, M. K. *Byron the Poet*. London, 1964.

Knight, G. Wilson. *Lord Byron: Christian Virtues*. London, 1952.

————. *Byron and Shakespeare*. London, 1966.

Lovell, Ernest J., Jr. *Byron: The Record of a Quest: Studies in a Poet's Concept and Treatment of Nature*. Austin, Texas, 1949.

Marchand, Leslie. *Byron's Poetry: A Critical Introduction*. Boston, 1965.

Marjarum, E. W. *Byron as Skeptic and Believer*. Princeton, N.J., 1938.

Marshall, W. H. *The Structure of Byron's Major Poems*. Philadelphia, 1962.

McGann, Jerome J. *Fiery Dust: Byron's Poetic Development*. Chicago, 1968.

Ridenour, George M. *The Style of Don Juan*. New Haven, Conn., 1960.

Russell, Bertrand. "Byron." *History of Western Philosophy*. New York, 1945.

Rutherford, Andrew. *Byron: A Critical Study*. Edinburgh, 1961.

Thorslev, Peter L. Jr. *The Byronic Hero: Types and Prototypes*. Minneapolis, Minn., 1962.

Trueblood, Paul. *The Flowering of Byron's Genius: Studies in Don Juan*. Stanford University, 1945.

West, Paul. *Byron and the Spoiler's Art*. London, 1960.

————, ed. *Byron: A Collection of Critical Essays*. Englewood Cliffs, N.J., 1963.

V. BIBLIOGRAPHICAL GUIDES

The New Cambridge Bibliography of English Literature. Vol. 3: 1800–1900. Cambridge, Eng., 1969.

Chew, Samuel C. "Byron." *The English Romantic Poets: A Review of Research,* revised ed. New York, 1956.

Fogle, Richard Harter. *Romantic Poets and Prose Writers*. Goldentree Bibliographies, New York, 1967.

Jack, Ian. *English Literature, 1815–1832. (Oxford History of English Literature)*. Oxford, 1963.

See also the Annual Bibliographies: "The Romantic Movement: a Selective and Critical Bibliography," *English Language Notes, Supplement,* since 1965. Previously in *English Literary History,* 1937–49; and *Philological Quarterly,* 1950–64. Other annual bibliographies appear in *PMLA* and the *Keats-Shelley Journal*.

Early Lyrics
and
Shorter Poems

Lines Inscribed upon a Cup

Formed from a Skull

When a skull "of giant size and in a perfect state of preservation" was found in the garden of Newstead Abbey, "a strange fancy seized me," Byron told Medwin, "of having it mounted as a drinking cup. I accordingly sent it to town, and it returned with a very high polish and of a mottled colour like tortoise-shell."

1

START NOT — nor deem my spirit fled:
    In me behold the only skull,
From which, unlike a living head,
    Whatever flows is never dull.

2

I liv'd, I lov'd, I quaff'd, like thee:
    I died: let the earth my bones resign;
Fill up — thou canst not injure me;
    The worm hath fouler lips than thine.

3

Better to hold the sparkling grape,
    Than nurse the earth-worm's slimy brood;
And circle in the goblet's shape
    The drink of Gods, than reptiles' food.

4

Where once my wit, perchance, hath shone,
    In aid of others' let me shine;
And when, alas! our brains are gone,
    What nobler substitute than wine?

5

Quaff while thou canst: another race,
    When thou and thine, like me, are sped,

> May rescue thee from Earth's embrace,
>   And rhyme and revel with the dead.

6

> Why not? since through life's little day
>   Our heads such sad effects produce;
> Redeem'd from worms and wasting clay,
>   This chance is theirs, to be of use.

Newstead Abbey, 1808   *1814*

Inscription on the Monument
of a Newfoundland Dog

When Byron's dog Boatswain died he was buried in a vault in the garden at Newstead Abbey and a monument with this verse inscribed was erected. The verse was preceded by a prose inscription which reads in part:

> Near this spot
> Are deposited the remains of one
> Who possessed Beauty without Vanity
> Strength without Insolence
> Courage without Ferocity
> And all the Virtues of Man without his Vices.

WHEN some proud son of man returns to earth,
Unknown to glory, but upheld by birth,
The sculptor's art exhausts the pomp of woe
And storied urns record who rest below:
When all is done, upon the tomb is seen,   5
Not what he was, but what he should have been:
But the poor dog, in life the firmest friend,
The first to welcome, foremost to defend,
Whose honest heart is still his master's own,
Who labours, fights, lives, breathes for him alone,   10
Unhonour'd falls unnotic'd all his worth —

Denied in heaven the soul he held on earth:
While Man, vain insect! hopes to be forgiven,
And claims himself a sole exclusive Heaven.
Oh Man! thou feeble tenant of an hour,   15
Debas'd by slavery, or corrupt by power,
Who knows thee well must quit thee with disgust,
Degraded mass of animated dust!
Thy love is lust, thy friendship all a cheat,
Thy smiles hypocrisy, thy words deceit!   20
By nature vile, ennobled but by name,
Each kindred brute might bid thee blush for shame.
Ye! who perchance behold its simple urn,
Pass on — it honours none you wish to mourn:
To mark a Friend's remains these stones arise;   25
I never knew but one — and here he lies.

Newstead Abbey, October 30, 1808   *1809*

Written after Swimming from

Sestos to Abydos

On May 3, 1810 Byron and a friend Ekenhead swam the
Hellespont from the European to Asian side. The legendary
Leander swam nightly from Abydos to Sestos to see Hero and
had to swim back at daybreak. One stormy night he drowned
and Hero threw herself into the sea. In a letter Byron wrote,
"The immediate distance is not above a mile but the current
renders it hazardous, so much so, that I doubt whether Leander's conjugal powers must not have been exhausted in his
passage to Paradise."

1

IF, in the month of dark December,
   Leander, who was nightly wont
(What maid will not the tale remember?)
   To cross thy stream, broad Hellespont!

2

If, when the wintry tempest roared,
  He sped to Hero, nothing loth,
And thus of old thy current poured,
  Fair Venus! how I pity both!

3

For *me*, degenerate modern wretch,
  Though in the genial month of May
My dripping limbs I faintly stretch,
  And think I've done a feat to-day.

4

But since he crossed the rapid tide,
  According to the doubtful story,
To woo, — and — Lord knows what beside,
  And swam for Love, as I for Glory;

5

'Twere hard to say who fared the best:
  Sad mortals! thus the Gods still plague you!
He lost his labour, I my jest:
  For he was drowned, and I've the ague.

May 9, 1810   *1812*

Maid of Athens Ere We Part

Supposedly addressed to Theresa Macri, daughter of Byron's landlady. The Greek motto means "My life, I love you."

1

MAID of Athens, ere we part,
Give, oh give me back my heart!
Or, since that has left my breast,
Keep it now, and take the rest!
Hear my vow before I go,
Ζωή μου, σᾶς ἀγαπῶ.

2

By those tresses unconfined,
Wooed by each Ægean wind;
By those lids whose jetty fringe
Kiss thy soft cheeks' blooming tinge;
By those wild eyes like the roe,
Ζωή μου, σᾶς ἀγαπῶ.

3

By that lip I long to taste;
By that zone-encircled waist;
By all the token-flowers that tell
What words can never speak so well;
By love's alternate joy and woe,
Ζωή μου, σᾶς ἀγαπῶ.

4

Maid of Athens! I am gone:
Think of me, sweet! when alone.
Though I fly to Istambol,
Athens holds my heart and soul:
Can I cease to love thee? No!
Ζωή μου, σᾶς ἀγαπῶ.

1810   1812

Remember Thee! Remember Thee!

After Byron had broken with Lady Caroline Lamb in the
latter part of 1812, she had visited his apartment during his
absence and written in his copy of *Vathek* the words "Remember me!" According to Medwin, "Byron immediately wrote
under the ominous warning these two stanzas."

Remember thee! remember thee!
  Till Lethe quench Life's burning stream
Remorse and Shame shall cling to thee,
  And haunt thee like a feverish dream!

> Remember thee! Ay, doubt it not.
> Thy husband too shall think of thee!
> By neither shalt thou be forgot,
> Thou *false* to him, thou *fiend* to me!

1813   *1824*

Stanzas for Music

> Probably addressed to Augusta Leigh.

1

I SPEAK not, I trace not, I breathe not thy name,
There is grief in the sound, there is guilt in the fame:
But the tear which now burns on my cheek may impart
The deep thoughts that dwell in that silence of heart.

2

Too brief for our passion, too long for our peace,
Were those hours — can their joy or their bitterness cease?
We repent, we abjure, we will break from our chain, —
We will part, we will fly to — unite it again!

3

Oh! thine be the gladness, and mine be the guilt!
Forgive me, adored one! — forsake, if thou wilt; —
But the heart which is thine shall expire undebased
And *man* shall not break it — whatever *thou* mayst.

4

And stern to the haughty, but humble to thee,
This soul, in its bitterest blackness, shall be:
And our days seem as swift, and our moments more sweet,
With thee by my side, than with worlds at our feet.

5

One sigh of thy sorrow, one look of thy love,
Shall turn me or fix, shall reward or reprove;

And the heartless may wonder at all I resign —
Thy lip shall reply, not to them, but to *mine*.

May 4, 1814   *1830*

She Walks in Beauty

    Written after meeting at a ball his beautiful cousin, Mrs.
Wilmot, who was in mourning and wore a spangled black
dress. On returning home, Byron called for a "tumbler of
Brandy" which he drank at once to her health; he was "in a
sad state all night," and next morning dashed off this lyric.

1

SHE walks in Beauty, like the night
  Of cloudless climes and starry skies;
And all that's best of dark and bright
  Meet in her aspect and her eyes:
Thus mellowed to that tender light
  Which Heaven to gaudy day denies.

2

One shade the more, one ray the less,
  Had half impaired the nameless grace
Which waves in every raven tress,
  Or softly lightens o'er her face;
Where thoughts serenely sweet express,
  How pure, how dear their dwelling-place.

3

And on that cheek, and o'er that brow,
  So soft, so calm, yet eloquent,
The smiles that win, the tints that glow,
  But tell of days in goodness spent,
A mind at peace with all below,
  A heart whose love is innocent!

June 12, 1814   *1815*

The Destruction of Sennacherib

The poem is based on the Biblical account in II *Kings* 19:35. Sennacherib was king of the Assyrians.

1

THE Assyrian came down like the wolf on the fold,
And his cohorts were gleaming in purple and gold;
And the sheen of their spears was like stars on the sea,
When the blue wave rolls nightly on deep Galilee.

2

Like the leaves of the forest when Summer is green,
That host with their banners at sunset were seen:
Like the leaves of the forest when Autumn hath blown,
That host on the morrow lay withered and strown.

3

For the Angel of Death spread his wings on the blast,
And breathed in the face of the foe as he passed;
And the eyes of the sleepers waxed deadly and chill,
And their hearts but once heaved — and for ever grew still!

4

And there lay the steed with his nostril all wide,
But through it there rolled not the breath of his pride;
And the foam of his gasping lay white on the turf,
And cold as the spray of the rock-beating surf.

5

And there lay the rider distorted and pale,
With the dew on his brow, and the rust on his mail:
And the tents were all silent — the banners alone —
The lances unlifted — the trumpet unblown.

6

And the widows of Ashur are loud in their wail,
And the idols are broke in the temple of Baal;

And the might of the Gentile, unsmote by the sword,
Hath melted like snow in the glance of the Lord!

Feb. 17, 1815   *1815*

Stanzas for Music

> Byron sent these lines to Moore on March 2, 1815, with the comment: "I feel merry enough to send you a sad song." Later he said that it was the death of the Duke of Dorset, a school friend, that "set me pondering."

1

THERE'S NOT a joy the world can give like that it takes away,
When the glow of early thought declines in Feeling's dull
  decay;
'Tis not on Youth's smooth cheek the blush alone, which
  fades so fast,
But the tender bloom of heart is gone, ere Youth itself be
  past.

2

Then the few whose spirits float above the wreck of
  happiness
Are driven o'er the shoals of guilt or ocean of excess:
The magnet of their course is gone, or only points in vain
The shore to which their shivered sail shall never stretch
  again.

3

Then the mortal coldness of the soul like Death itself comes
  down;
It cannot feel for others' woes, it dare not dream its own;
That heavy chill has frozen o'er the fountain of our tears,
And though the eye may sparkle still, 'tis where the ice
  appears.

4

Though wit may flash from fluent lips, and mirth distract
    the breast,
Through midnight hours that yield no more their former
    hope of rest;
'Tis but as ivy-leaves around the ruined turret wreath,
All green and wildly fresh without, but worn and grey
    beneath.

5

Oh, could I feel as I have felt, — or be what I have been,
Or weep as I could once have wept, o'er many a vanished
    scene;
As springs, in deserts found, seem sweet, all brackish though
    they be,
So, midst the withered waste of life, those tears would flow
    to me.

March, 1815   *1816*

Stanzas for Music

    Because the poem was published in 1816, the usual assumption has been that it was addressed to Claire Clairmont, to whom Shelley also wrote lyrics in praise of her singing. But Marchand (*Byron,* I, 313) suggests that it may have been addressed to John Edleston, the Cambridge Chorister, whom Byron met in 1805 and upon whose death in 1811 he wrote a number of elegiac poems.

1

THERE BE NONE of Beauty's daughters
    With a magic like thee;
And like music on the waters
    Is thy sweet voice to me:
When, as if its sound were causing
The charméd Ocean's pausing,

The waves lie still and gleaming,
And the lulled winds seem dreaming:

2

And the Midnight Moon is weaving
   Her bright chain o'er the deep;
Whose breast is gently heaving,
   As an infant's asleep:
So the spirit bows before thee,
To listen and adore thee;
With a full but soft emotion,
Like the swell of Summer's ocean.

?   *1816*

When We Two Parted

Enclosed in a letter to John Murray on February 16, 1816, and addressed to Lady Frances Webster with whom Byron had had a passionate but unconsummated romance in 1813 (see below, *Don Juan*, 14, 100:8, note), the poem was apparently written when Byron learned that Lady Frances had become involved with the Duke of Wellington at Brussels after the battle of Waterloo. (See Marchand, II, 580–581). When the poem was published in *Poems*, 1816, the last stanza was omitted. What aroused Byron's indignation was that he had been the "dupe of the few good feelings I could ever boast of" in "sparing" Lady Frances, who then had become involved with one he detested as both soldier and man (and later in *Don Juan* called "Villainton").

1

WHEN we two parted
   In silence and tears,
Half broken-hearted
   To sever for years,
Pale grew thy cheek and cold,
   Colder thy kiss;

Truly that hour foretold
 Sorrow to this.

2

The dew of the morning
 Sunk chill on my brow —
It felt like the warning
 Of what I feel now.
Thy vows are all broken,
 And light is thy fame:
I hear thy name spoken,
 And share in its shame.

3

They name thee before me,
 A knell to mine ear;
A shudder comes o'er me —
 Why wert thou so dear?
They know not I knew thee,
 Who knew thee too well: —
Long, long shall I rue thee,
 Too deeply to tell.

4

In secret we met —
 In silence I grieve,
That thy heart could forget,
 Thy spirit deceive.
If I should meet thee
 After long years,
How should I greet thee? —
 With silence and tears.

5

Then fare thee well, Fanny,
 Now doubly undone,
To prove false unto many
 As faithless to one.

Thou art past all recalling
　　Even would I recall,
For the woman once falling
　　Forever must fall.

1815?　　　　　　　　　　　　　　　　　　　　　*1816*

Fare Thee Well

Addressed to Lady Byron and printed by Byron on April 4, 1816, for private circulation, these lines achieved wide notoriety when published on April 14 in John Scott's *Champion* and on April 21 in Leigh Hunt's *Examiner*.

FARE thee well! and if for ever,
　　Still for ever, fare *thee well*:
Even though unforgiving, never
　　'Gainst thee shall my heart rebel.
Would that breast were bared before thee 　　　　5
　　Where thy head so oft hath lain,
While that placid sleep came o'er thee
　　Which thou ne'er canst know again:
Would that breast, by thee glanced over,
　　Every inmost thought could show! 　　　　　10
Then thou would'st at last discover
　　'Twas not well to spurn it so.
Though the world for this commend thee —
　　Though it smile upon the blow,
Even its praises must offend thee, 　　　　　　15
　　Founded on another's woe:
Though my many faults defaced me,
　　Could no other arm be found,
Than the one which once embraced me,
　　To inflict a cureless wound? 　　　　　　　20
Yet, oh yet, thyself deceive not —
　　Love may sink by slow decay,
But by sudden wrench, believe not
　　Hearts can thus be torn away:

Still thine own its life retaineth —
    Still must mine, though bleeding, beat;
And the undying thought which paineth
    Is — that we no more may meet.
These are words of deeper sorrow
    Than the wail above the dead;
Both shall live — but every morrow
    Wake us from a widowed bed.
And when thou would'st solace gather —
    When our child's first accents flow —
Wilt thou teach her to say "Father!"
    Though his care she must forego?
When her little hands shall press thee —
    When her lip to thine is pressed —
Think of him whose prayer shall bless thee —
    Think of him thy love *had* blessed!
Should her lineaments resemble
    Those thou never more may'st see,
Then thy heart will softly tremble
    With a pulse yet true to me.
All my faults perchance thou knowest —
    All my madness — none can know;
All my hopes — where'er thou goest —
    Wither — yet with *thee* they go.
Every feeling hath been shaken;
    Pride — which not a world could bow —
Bows to thee — by thee forsaken,
    Even my soul forsakes me now.
But 'tis done — all words are idle —
    Words from me are vainer still;
But the thoughts we cannot bridle
    Force their way without the will.
Fare thee well! thus disunited —
    Torn from every nearer tie —
Seared in heart — and lone — and blighted —
    More than this I scarce can die.

March 18, 1816   *1816*

Stanzas to Augusta

Both this and the following poem, *Epistle to Augusta,* were written in July, 1816, and sent to Murray to be published, if Augusta would consent. She reluctantly agreed to the publication of the *Stanzas* but withheld consent for publication of the *Epistle,* which was not printed until 1830.

1

THOUGH the day of my Destiny's over,
   And the star of my Fate hath declined,
Thy soft heart refused to discover
   The faults which so many could find;
Though thy Soul with my grief was acquainted,
   It shrunk not to share it with me,
And the Love which my Spirit hath painted
   It never hath found but in *Thee.*

2

Then when Nature around me is smiling,
   The last smile which answers to mine,
I do not believe it beguiling,
   Because it reminds me of thine;
And when winds are at war with the ocean,
   As the breasts I believed in with me,
If their billows excite an emotion,
   It is that they bear me from *Thee.*

3

Though the rock of my last Hope is shivered,
   And its fragments are sunk in the wave,
Though I feel that my soul is delivered
   To Pain — it shall not be its slave.
There is many a pang to pursue me:
   They may crush, but they shall not contemn;
They may torture, but shall not subdue me;
   'Tis of *Thee* that I think — not of them.

4

Though human, thou didst not deceive me,
    Though woman, thou didst not forsake,
Though loved, thou forborest to grieve me,
    Though slandered, thou never couldst shake;
Though trusted, thou didst not disclaim me,
    Though parted, it was not to fly,
Though watchful, 'twas not to defame me,
    Nor, mute, that the world might belie.

5

Yet I blame not the World, nor despite it,
    Nor the war of the many with one;
If my Soul was not fitted to prize it,
    'Twas folly not sooner to shun:
And if dearly that error hath cost me,
    And more than I once could foresee,
I have found that, whatever it lost me,
    It could not deprive me of *Thee*.

6

From the wreck of the past, which hath perished,
    Thus much I at least may recall,
It hath taught me that what I most cherished
    Deserved to be dearest of all:
In the Desert a fountain is springing,
    In the wide waste there still is a tree,
And a bird in the solitude singing,
    Which speaks to my spirit of *Thee*.

July 24, 1816   *1816*

Epistle to Augusta

1

MY Sister! my sweet Sister! if a name
Dearer and purer were, it should be thine.
Mountains and seas divide us, but I claim
No tears, but tenderness to answer mine:
Go where I will, to me thou art the same —

A loved regret which I would not resign.
There yet are two things in my destiny, —
A world to roam through, and a home with thee.

2

The first were nothing — had I still the last,
It were the haven of my happiness;
But other claims and other ties thou hast,
And mine is not the wish to make them less.
A strange doom is thy father's son's, and past
Recalling, as it lies beyond redress;
Reversed for him our grandsire's fate of yore, —
He had no rest at sea, nor I on shore.

3

If my inheritance of storms hath been
In other elements, and on the rocks
Of perils, overlooked or unforeseen,
I have sustained my share of worldly shocks,
The fault was mine; nor do I seek to screen
My errors with defensive paradox;
I have been cunning in mine overthrow,
The careful pilot of my proper woe.

4

Mine were my faults, and mine be their reward.
My whole life was a contest, since the day
That gave me being, gave me that which marred
The gift, — a fate, or will, that walked astray;
And I at times have found the struggle hard,
And thought of shaking off my bonds of clay:
But now I fain would for a time survive,
If but to see what next can well arrive.

5

Kingdoms and Empires in my little day
I have outlived, and yet I am not old;

2:8. *no rest at sea*: Byron's grandfather, Admiral John Byron, was called "Foul Weather Jack" because of the legend that whenever he put to sea, he met with a storm.

And when I look on this, the petty spray
Of my own years of trouble, which have rolled
Like a wild bay of breakers, melts away:
Something — I know not what — does still uphold
A spirit of slight patience; — not in vain,
Even for its own sake, do we purchase Pain.

6

Perhaps the workings of defiance stir
Within me — or, perhaps, a cold despair
Brought on when ills habitually recur, —
Perhaps a kinder clime, or purer air,
(For even to this may change of soul refer,
And with light armour we may learn to bear,)
Have taught me a strange quiet, which was not
The chief companion of a calmer lot.

7

I feel almost at times as I have felt
In happy childhood; trees, and flowers, and brooks,
Which do remember me of where I dwelt,
Ere my young mind was sacrificed to books,
Come as of yore upon me, and can melt
My heart with recognition of their looks;
And even at moments I could think I see
Some living thing to love — but none like thee.

8

Here are the Alpine landscapes which create
A fund for contemplation; — to admire
Is a brief feeling of a trivial date;
But something worthier do such scenes inspire:
Here to be lonely is not desolate,
For much I view which I could most desire,
And, above all, a Lake I can behold
Lovelier, not dearer, than our own of old.

8:7. *a lake*: Lake Geneva (Leman) contrasted with the Lake at Newstead Abbey.

9

Oh that thou wert but with me! — but I grow
The fool of my own wishes, and forget
The solitude which I have vaunted so
Has lost its praise in this but one regret;
There may be others which I less may show; —
I am not of the plaintive mood, and yet
I feel an ebb in my philosophy,
And the tide rising in my altered eye.

10

I did remind thee of our own dear Lake,
By the old Hall which may be mine no more.
Leman's is fair; but think not I forsake
The sweet remembrance of a dearer shore:
Sad havoc Time must with my memory make,
Ere that or thou can fade these eyes before;
Though, like all things which I have loved, they are
Resigned for ever, or divided far.

11

The world is all before me; I but ask
Of Nature that with which she will comply —
It is but in her Summer's sun to bask,
To mingle with the quiet of her sky,
To see her gentle face without a mask,
And never gaze on it with apathy.
She was my early friend, and now shall be
My sister — till I look again on thee.

12

I can reduce all feelings but this one;
And that I would not; — for at length I see
Such scenes as those wherein my life begun —
The earliest — even the only paths for me —
Had I but sooner learnt the crowd to shun,
I had been better than I now can be;
The Passions which have torn me would have slept;
I had not suffered, and *thou* hadst not wept.

13

With false Ambition what had I to do?
Little with Love, and least of all with Fame;
And yet they came unsought, and with me grew,
And made me all which they can make — a Name.
Yet this was not the end I did pursue;
Surely I once beheld a nobler aim.
But all is over — I am one the more
To baffled millions which have gone before.

14

And for the future, this world's future may
From me demand but little of my care;
I have outlived myself by many a day;
Having survived so many things that were;
My years have been no slumber, but the prey
Of ceaseless vigils; for I had the share
Of life which might have filled a century,
Before its fourth in time had passed me by.

15

And for the remnant which may be to come,
I am content; and for the past I feel
Not thankless, — for within the crowded sum
Of struggles, Happiness at times would steal,
And for the present, I would not benumb
My feelings farther. — Nor shall I conceal
That with all this I still can look around,
And worship Nature with a thought profound.

16

For thee, my own sweet sister, in thy heart
I know myself secure, as thou in mine;
We were and are — I am, even as thou art —
Beings who ne'er each other can resign;
It is the same, together or apart,
From Life's commencement to its slow decline

We are entwined — let Death come slow or fast,
The tie which bound the first endures the last!

July, 1816   *1830*

The Dream

Written in Switzerland in the summer of 1816, *The Dream* is in reality a versified daydream or reverie in which the memory of his youthful infatuation for Mary Chaworth, his distant cousin, leads Byron into a sentimentalized self-history, moving, as Marchand says, "from youthful idealism through disillusionment to sad resignation and melancholy despair." Byron had fallen in love with Mary in 1803, when he was fifteen and she seventeen. Stanzas 2 and 3 probably give an accurate account of his emotional attachment in 1803 and 1804 when he visited her at her home, Annesley Hall, which was near Newstead Abbey. But she rebuffed him and married in 1805 John Musters, a handsome young squire. Her married life was miserable because of her husband's infidelities and in 1814 she separated from him and suffered a temporary mental breakdown. Late in 1813 she renewed her correspondence with Byron and wrote him many letters pleading that he visit her again. But he found excuses for avoiding her, and never saw her before he left England in 1816. The main reason was that from 1804 on she had become for him an important romantic memory and he was afraid of the effect the intrusion of the real woman would have on it. Mary remained a dream ideal to the end of his life. In 1822 he told Medwin ". . . those were the days of romance! She was the beau ideal of all that my youthful fancy could paint of beautiful; and I have taken all my fables about the celestial nature of women from the perfection my imagination created in her — I say created, for I found her, like the rest of the sex, anything but angelic."

1

OUR life is twofold: Sleep hath its own world,
A boundary between the things misnamed
Death and existence: Sleep hath its own world,

And a wide realm of wild reality,
And dreams in their development have breath, 5
And tears, and tortures, and the touch of Joy;
They leave a weight upon our waking thoughts,
They take a weight from off our waking toils,
They do divide our being; they become
A portion of ourselves as of our time, 10
And look like heralds of Eternity;
They pass like spirits of the past, — they speak
Like Sibyls of the future; they have power —
The tyranny of pleasure and of pain;
They make us what we were not — what they will, 15
And shake us with the vision that's gone by,
The dread of vanished shadows — Are they so?
Is not the past all shadow? — What are they?
Creations of the mind? — The mind can make
Substance, and people planets of its own 20
With beings brighter than have been, and give
A breath to forms which can outlive all flesh.
I would recall a vision which I dreamed
Perchance in sleep — for in itself a thought,
A slumbering thought, is capable of years, 25
And curdles a long life into one hour.

2

I saw two beings in the hues of youth
Standing upon a hill, a gentle hill,
Green and of mild declivity, the last
As 'twere the cape of a long ridge of such, 30
Save that there was no sea to lave its base,
But a most living landscape, and the wave
Of woods and cornfields, and the abodes of men
Scattered at intervals, and wreathing smoke
Arising from such rustic roofs; — the hill 35
Was crowned with a peculiar diadem
Of trees, in circular array, so fixed,

27. The scene of stanzas 2 and 3 is Annesley Hall.

Not by the sport of nature, but of man:
These two, a maiden and a youth, were there
Gazing — the one on all that was beneath   *40*
Fair as herself — but the Boy gazed on her;
And both were young, and one was beautiful:
And both were young — yet not alike in youth.
As the sweet moon on the horizon's verge,
The Maid was on the eve of Womanhood;   *45*
The Boy had fewer summers, but his heart
Had far outgrown his years, and to his eye
There was but one belovéd face on earth,
And that was shining on him: he had looked
Upon it till it could not pass away;   *50*
He had no breath, no being, but in hers;
She was his voice; he did not speak to her,
But trembled on her words; she was his sight,
For his eye followed hers, and saw with hers,
Which coloured all his objects: — he had ceased   *55*
To live within himself; she was his life,
The ocean to the river of his thoughts,
Which terminated all: upon a tone,
A touch of hers, his blood would ebb and flow,
And his cheek change tempestuously — his heart   *60*
Unknowing of its cause of agony.
But she in these fond feelings had no share:
Her sighs were not for him; to her he was
Even as a brother — but no more; 'twas much,
For brotherless she was, save in the name   *65*
Her infant friendship had bestowed on him;
Herself the solitary scion left
Of a time-honoured race. — It was a name
Which pleased him, and yet pleased him not — and why?
Time taught him a deep answer — when she loved   *70*
Another: even *now* she loved another,
And on the summit of that hill she stood
Looking afar if yet her lover's steed
Kept pace with her expectancy, and flew.

3

A change came o'er the spirit of my dream.   75
There was an ancient mansion, and before
Its walls there was a steed caparisoned:
Within an antique Oratory stood
The Boy of whom I spake; — he was alone,
And pale, and pacing to and fro: anon   80
He sate him down, and seized a pen, and traced
Words which I could not guess of; then he leaned
His bowed head on his hands, and shook as 'twere
With a convulsion — then arose again,
And with his teeth and quivering hands did tear   85
What he had written, but he shed no tears.
And he did calm himself, and fix his brow
Into a kind of quiet: as he paused,
The Lady of his love re-entered there;
She was serene and smiling then, and yet   90
She knew she was by him beloved — she knew,
For quickly comes such knowledge, that his heart
Was darkened with her shadow, and she saw
That he was wretched, but she saw not all.
He rose, and with a cold and gentle grasp   95
He took her hand; a moment o'er his face
A tablet of unutterable thoughts
Was traced, and then it faded, as it came;
He dropped the hand he held, and with slow steps
Retired, but not as bidding her adieu,   100
For they did part with mutual smiles; he passed
From out the massy gate of that old Hall,
And mounting on his steed he went his way;
And ne'er repassed that hoary threshold more.

4

A change came o'er the spirit of my dream.   105
The Boy was sprung to manhood: in the wilds

105–125. The recollection of episodes in his travels in the Near East
in 1810.

Of fiery climes he made himself a home,
And his Soul drank their sunbeams: he was girt
With strange and dusky aspects; he was not
Himself like what he had been; on the sea   *110*
And on the shore he was a wanderer;
There was a mass of many images
Crowded like waves upon me, but he was
A part of all; and in the last he lay
Reposing from the noontide sultriness,   *115*
Couched among fallen columns, in the shade
Of ruined walls that had survived the names
Of those who reared them; by his sleeping side
Stood camels grazing, and some goodly steeds
Were fastened near a fountain; and a man   *120*
Clad in a flowing garb did watch the while,
While many of his tribe slumbered around:
And they were canopied by the blue sky,
So cloudless, clear, and purely beautiful,
That God alone was to be seen in Heaven.   *125*

5

A change came o'er the spirit of my dream.
The Lady of his love was wed with One
Who did not love her better: — in her home,
A thousand leagues from his, — her native home,
She dwelt, begirt with growing Infancy,   *130*
Daughters and sons of Beauty, — but behold!
Upon her face there was the tint of grief,
The settled shadow of an inward strife,
And an unquiet drooping of the eye,
As if its lid were charged with unshed tears.   *135*
What could her grief be? — she had all she loved,
And he who had so loved her was not there
To trouble with bad hopes, or evil wish,
Or ill-repressed affliction, her pure thoughts.
What could her grief be? — she had loved him not,   *140*
Nor given him cause to deem himself beloved,

Nor could he be a part of that which preyed
Upon her mind — a spectre of the past.

6

A change came o'er the spirit of my dream.
The Wanderer was returned. — I saw him stand   *145*
Before an Altar — with a gentle bride;
Her face was fair, but was not that which made
The Starlight of his Boyhood; — as he stood
Even at the altar, o'er his brow there came
The self-same aspect, and the quivering shock   *150*
That in the antique Oratory shook
His bosom in its solitude; and then —
As in that hour — a moment o'er his face
The tablet of unutterable thoughts
Was traced, — and then it faded as it came,   *155*
And he stood calm and quiet, and he spoke
The fitting vows, but heard not his own words,
And all things reeled around him; he could see
Not that which was, nor that which should have been —
But the old mansion, and the accustomed hall,   *160*
And the remembered chambers, and the place,
The day, the hour, the sunshine, and the shade,
All things pertaining to that place and hour
And her who was his destiny, came back
And thrust themselves between him and the light: *165*
What business had they there at such a time?

7

A change came o'er the spirit of my dream.
The Lady of his love; — Oh! she was changed
As by the sickness of the soul; her mind

144–166. This episode must be read with the context in which it was
written in mind — the self-pitying bitterness of Byron in the months following the separation from his wife. By publishing *The Dream*, he was
humiliating her as cruelly as she had humiliated him. The erratic behavior which he ascribes to himself is similar to the behavior Hobhouse,
his best man, noticed in him before and during the wedding.

Had wandered from its dwelling, and her eyes   170
They had not their own lustre, but the look
Which is not of the earth; she was become
The Queen of a fantastic realm; her thoughts
Were combinations of disjointed things;
And forms, impalpable and unperceived   175
Of others' sight, familiar were to hers.
And this the world calls frenzy; but the wise
Have a far deeper madness — and the glance
Of melancholy is a fearful gift;
What is it but the telescope of truth?   180
Which strips the distance of its fantasies,
And brings life near in utter nakedness,
Making the cold reality too real!

8

A change came o'er the spirit of my dream.
The Wanderer was alone as heretofore,   185
The beings which surrounded him were gone,
Or were at war with him; he was a mark
For blight and desolation, compassed round
With Hatred and Contention; Pain was mixed
In all which was served up to him, until,   190
Like to the Pontic monarch of old days,
He fed on poisons, and they had no power,
But were a kind of nutriment; he lived
Through that which had been death to many men,
And made him friends of mountains: with the stars   195
And the quick Spirit of the Universe
He held his dialogues; and they did teach
To him the magic of their mysteries;
To him the book of Night was opened wide,
And voices from the deep abyss revealed   200
A marvel and a secret — Be it so.

191. *Pontic Monarch*: Mithridates, King of Pontius (120–163 B.C.), is
said to have protected himself against poisoning so effectively through the
use of antidotes that when as an old man he tried to poison himself he
could not do so.

9

My dream was past; it had no further change.
It was of a strange order, that the doom
Of these two creatures should be thus traced out
Almost like a reality — the one   205
To end in madness — both in misery.

July, 1816   *1816*

Darkness

> Written in the summer of 1816, *Darkness* reflects the re-
> current mood of bleak desolation that haunted Byron in the
> months following the separation. The theme of the last man
> and the end of the world was a popular one in Romantic
> literature. Byron may have remembered some details from an
> anonymous novel entitled *The Last Man, or . . . A Romance
> in Futurity* (2 vols., 1806). Later Thomas Campbell wrote
> a sentimental poem (1823) and Mary Shelley a novel (1826)
> both entitled *The Last Man*. But Byron's poem is unique in
> its harsh realism and ruthless accumulation of detail.

I HAD a dream, which was not all a dream.
The bright sun was extinguished, and the stars
Did wander darkling in the eternal space,
Rayless, and pathless, and the icy Earth
Swung blind and blackening in the moonless air;   5
Morn came and went — and came, and brought no day,
And men forgot their passions in the dread
Of this their desolation; and all hearts
Were chilled into a selfish prayer for light:
And they did live by watchfires — and the thrones,   10
The palaces of crownéd kings — the huts,
The habitations of all things which dwell,
Were burnt for beacons; cities were consumed,
And men were gathered round their blazing homes
To look once more into each other's face;   15
Happy were those who dwelt within the eye
Of the volcanos, and their mountain-torch:

A fearful hope was all the World contained;
Forests were set on fire — but hour by hour
They fell and faded — and the crackling trunks   20
Extinguished with a crash — and all was black.
The brows of men by the despairing light
Wore an unearthly aspect, as by fits
The flashes fell upon them; some lay down
And hid their eyes and wept; and some did rest   25
Their chins upon their clenchéd hands, and smiled;
And others hurried to and fro, and fed
Their funeral piles with fuel, and looked up
With mad disquietude on the dull sky,
The pall of a past World; and then again   30
With curses cast them down upon the dust,
And gnashed their teeth and howled: the wild birds shrieked,
And, terrified, did flutter on the ground,
And flap their useless wings; the wildest brutes
Came tame and tremulous; and vipers crawled   35
And twined themselves among the multitude,
Hissing, but stingless — they were slain for food:
And War, which for a moment was no more,
Did glut himself again: — a meal was bought
With blood, and each sate sullenly apart   40
Gorging himself in gloom: no Love was left;
All earth was but one thought — and that was Death,
Immediate and inglorious; and the pang
Of famine fed upon all entrails — men
Died, and their bones were tombless as their flesh;   45
The meagre by the meagre were devoured,
Even dogs assailed their masters, all save one,
And he was faithful to a corse, and kept
The birds and beasts and famished men at bay,
Till hunger clung them, or the dropping dead   50
Lured their lank jaws; himself sought out no food,
But with a piteous and perpetual moan,
And a quick desolate cry, licking the hand
Which answered not with a caress — he died.

50. *clung*: Shriveled.

The crowd was famished by degrees; but two   55
Of an enormous city did survive,
And they were enemies: they met beside
The dying embers of an altar-place
Where had been heaped a mass of holy things
For an unholy usage; they raked up,   60
And shivering scraped with their cold skeleton hands
The feeble ashes, and their feeble breath
Blew for a little life, and made a flame
Which was a mockery; then they lifted up
Their eyes as it grew lighter, and beheld   65
Each other's aspects — saw, and shrieked, and died —
Even of their mutual hideousness they died,
Unknowing who he was upon whose brow
Famine had written Fiend. The World was void,
The populous and the powerful was a lump,   70
Seasonless, herbless, treeless, manless, lifeless —
A lump of death — a chaos of hard clay.
The rivers, lakes, and ocean all stood still,
And nothing stirred within their silent depths;
Ships sailorless lay rotting on the sea,   75
And their masts fell down piecemeal: as they dropped
They slept on the abyss without a surge —
The waves were dead; the tides were in their grave,
The Moon, their mistress, had expired before;
The winds were withered in the stagnant air,   80
And the clouds perished; Darkness had no need
Of aid from them — She was the Universe.

July, 1816   *1816*

Prometheus

Also written in the summer of 1816 and presenting the counter-mood to *Darkness*. From his boyhood, Byron had admired Prometheus as a symbol of the defiant and unconquerable mind of man. His first English exercise at Harrow had been a paraphrase of a chorus from the *Prometheus*

Bound of Aeschylus. His portrait of Prometheus in this poem, particularly in the last stanza, should be compared with the final speeches of *Manfred*. Referring to *Manfred,* he wrote that the *Prometheus* of Aeschylus "if not exactly in my plan, has always been so much in my head, that I can easily conceive its influence over all or anything I have written." For other allusions in Byron to Prometheus, see Peter Thorslev, *The Byronic Hero* (1962).

1

TITAN! to whose immortal eyes
  The sufferings of mortality,
  Seen in their sad reality,
Were not as things that gods despise;
What was thy pity's recompense?   5
A silent suffering, and intense;
The rock, the vulture, and the chain,
All that the proud can feel of pain,
The agony they do not show,
The suffocating sense of woe,   10
  Which speaks but in its loneliness,
And then is jealous lest the sky
Should have a listener, nor will sigh
  Until its voice is echoless.

2

Titan! to thee the strife was given   15
  Between the suffering and the will,
  Which torture where they cannot kill;
And the inexorable Heaven,
And the deaf tyranny of Fate,
The ruling principle of Hate,   20
Which for its pleasure doth create
The things it may annihilate,
Refused thee even the boon to die:
The wretched gift Eternity
Was thine — and thou hast borne it well. 25
All that the Thunderer wrung from thee

26. *Thunderer*: Zeus.

Was but the menace which flung back
On him the torments of thy rack;
The fate thou didst so well foresee,
But would not to appease him tell; 30
And in thy Silence was his Sentence,
And in his Soul a vain repentance,
And evil dread so ill dissembled,
That in his hand the lightnings trembled.

3

Thy Godlike crime was to be kind, 35
  To render with thy precepts less
  The sum of human wretchedness,
And strengthen Man with his own mind;
But baffled as thou wert from high,
Still in thy patient energy, 40
In the endurance, and repulse
  Of thine impenetrable Spirit,
Which Earth and Heaven could not convulse,
  A mighty lesson we inherit:
Thou art a symbol and a sign 45
  To Mortals of their fate and force;
Like thee, Man is in part divine,
  A troubled stream from a pure source;
And Man in portions can foresee
His own funereal destiny; 50
His wretchedness, and his resistance,
And his sad unallied existence:
To which his Spirit may oppose
Itself — an equal to all woes —
  And a firm will, and a deep sense, 55
Which even in torture can descry
  Its own concentered recompense,
Triumphant where it dares defy,
And making Death a Victory.

July, 1816   *1816*

29. *The fate . . . foresee*: Prometheus foresaw but would not reveal the
circumstances that could cause the overthrow of Zeus.

Sonnet on Chillon

In late June, 1816, Byron and Shelley visited the Castle of Chillon at the head of Lake Geneva, and there Byron heard the story of François Bonivard (1496–1570), who had been imprisoned by Duke Charles III of Savoy in a dungeon "lower than the lake" for four years (1532–1536). There is no record of any brothers being imprisoned with him, and though he was a political opponent of the Duke he was probably not as idealistic an exponent of liberty as Byron believed him to be. He also lived a very full life after his release, achieving considerable reputation as a scholar and author. But the historical details are not necessary to an appreciation of Byron's poems, which are his own imaginative creations and owe much of their power to the conflicting moods of his own "dark mind." Between the sonnet (which was written last) and the tale there is an interesting difference of tone. The sonnet is in the spirit of *Prometheus* and *Manfred*, but the narrative of the Prisoner is closer to the spirit of *Darkness*. It is a dramatic monologue of alienation under the impact of imprisonment and isolation — of gradual despair, apathy, and finally resignation so that the Prisoner learns "to love despair" and regains "his freedom with a sigh." For further interpretations see W. H. Marshall, *The Structure of Byron's Major Poems* (1962) and Andrew Rutherford, *Byron: A Critical Study* (1961). For the tale, see p. 111 below.

ETERNAL Spirit of the chainless Mind!
   Brightest in dungeons, Liberty! thou art:
   For there thy habitation is the heart —
The heart which love of thee alone can bind;
And when thy sons to fetters are consigned —   5
   To fetters, and the damp vault's dayless gloom,
   Their country conquers with their martyrdom,
And Freedom's fame finds wings on every wind.
Chillon! thy prison is a holy place,
   And thy sad floor an altar — for 'twas trod,   10
Until his very steps have left a trace
   Worn, as if thy cold pavement were a sod,

By Bonnivard! — May none those marks efface!
For they appeal from tyranny to God.

1816   *1816*

Stanzas Written on the Road

Between Florence and Pisa

1

OH, talk not to me of a name great in story —
The days of our Youth are the days of our glory;
And the myrtle and ivy of sweet two-and-twenty
Are worth all your laurels, though ever so plenty.

2

What are garlands and crowns to the brow that is wrinkled?
'Tis but as a dead flower with May-dew besprinkled:
Then away with all such from the head that is hoary,
What care I for the wreaths that can *only* give glory?

3

Oh FAME! — if I e'er took delight in thy praises,
'Twas less for the sake of thy high-sounding phrases,
Than to see the bright eyes of the dear One discover,
She thought that I was not unworthy to love her.

4

There chiefly I sought thee, *there* only I found thee;
Her Glance was the best of the rays that surround thee,
When it sparkled o'er aught that was bright in my story,
I knew it was Love, and I felt it was Glory.

1821   *1830*

On This Day I Complete

My Thirty-sixth Year

Probably addressed to Loukas Chalandritsanos, Byron's page, who had accompanied him from Cephalonia to Missolonghi.

1

'T is time this heart should be unmoved,
　　Since others it hath ceased to move:
Yet, though I cannot be beloved,
　　　　Still let me love!

2

My days are in the yellow leaf;
　　The flowers and fruits of Love are gone;
The worm, the canker, and the grief
　　　　Are mine alone!

3

The fire that on my bosom preys
　　Is lone as some Volcanic isle;
No torch is kindled at its blaze —
　　　　A funeral pile.

4

The hope, the fear, the jealous care,
　　The exalted portion of the pain
And power of love, I cannot share,
　　　　But wear the chain.

5

But 't is not *thus* — and 't is not *here* —
　　Such thoughts should shake my soul, nor *now*
Where Glory decks the hero's bier,
　　　　Or binds his brow.

6

The Sword, the Banner, and the Field,
   Glory and Greece, around me see!
The Spartan, borne upon his shield,
      Was not more free.

7

Awake! (not Greece — she *is* awake!)
   Awake, my spirit! Think through *whom*
Thy life-blood tracks its parent lake,
      And then strike home!

8

Tread those reviving passions down,
   Unworthy manhood! — unto thee
Indifferent should the smile or frown
      Of Beauty be.

9

If thou regret'st thy youth, *why live?*
   The land of honourable death
Is here: — up to the Field, and give
      Away thy breath!

10

Seek out — less often sought than found —
   A soldier's grave, for thee the best;
Then look around, and choose thy ground,
      And take thy Rest.

Jan. 22, 1824   *Oct. 1824*

Selections *from* Childe Harold's Pilgrimge

Childe Harold's Pilgrimage

In the first two cantos of *Childe Harold,* written in 1808–1810 during his travels in the Mediterranean countries, Byron had maintained a careful distinction between himself and his fictitious hero. He had also exploited the currently fashionable literary antiquarianism by his use of the Spenserian stanza, labored archaic diction, and the terminology of chivalry ("Childe" was a chivalric term for a "youth of noble birth").

But in the third canto, completed on the shores of Lake Geneva in the summer of 1816, he soon abandoned the attempt to maintain the distinction between himself and his hero, and the poem became openly the record of his own experiences and reflections. He also gave up the archaisms with a resulting directness and intensity of expression. Like the earlier cantos, this canto is a meditative travel poem, organized around his experiences in crossing the English channel, touring the battlefield of Waterloo, journeying down the Rhine river into Switzerland, contemplating Lake Geneva and the Alps, and anticipating the crossing into Italy. But a dramatic unity lacking in the earlier cantos is provided by the opening and closing apostrophes to his infant daughter and by the tension created by juxtaposing imagistic and thematic patterns involving the relation of man and society, and man and nature. In particular, the first section of the poem pivots around the reflections about man and society provoked by viewing the battlefield of Waterloo, and the latter section revolves around the reflections about man and nature inspired by Lake Geneva and the Alps, with the journey down the Rhine rimmed by the ruined castles of robber barons providing the connecting link. The influence of his companionship with Shelley (who "dosed him with Wordsworth") is evident in the nature stanzas. For Byron's own comment on Canto III see his letter of January 28, 1817, to Thomas Moore.

Canto IV was written at Venice between June, 1817, and January, 1818, and grew out of his travels in 1817 from Venice to Rome. His intent, as he says in stanza 25, was "to meditate amongst decay and stand / A ruin amidst ruins . . .". The following excerpts in which he contemplates the decaying grandeur of Venice and the ruined monuments of ancient Rome show off the dazzling virtuosity Byron had achieved in his use of the Spenserian stanza for the purposes of dramatic description and self-analysis. In the famous apostrophe to the Ocean with which the canto ends, the perishable works of man are set against the background of the inexorable indifferent power of nature, a more fundamentally "Byronic" view of the relation of man to nature than in the third canto. For further critical comment, see general introduction above pp. xvii–xix.

CANTO THE THIRD

"Afin que cette application vous forçât de penser à autre chose; il n'y a en vérîté de remède que celui-là et le temps.
        Lettre du Roi de Prusse à D'Alembert, Sept. 7, 1776.

1

Is thy face like thy mother's, my fair child!
    ADA! sole daughter of my house and heart?
When last I saw thy young blue eyes they smiled,
And then we parted, — not as now we part,
But with a hope. —
                    Awaking with a start,
The waters heave around me; and on high
The winds lift up their voices: I depart,
Whither I know not; but the hour's gone by,
When Albion's lessening shores could grieve or glad mine eye.

Epigraph: "In order that this application might force you to think of something else; there is in truth no remedy but that and time." The letter is from Frederick the Great to D'Alembert, the French Philosopher, urging him to apply himself to a difficult problem in order to overcome his grief at a deep personal loss. For Byron the "application" for loss of wife, daughter and homeland is of course the writing of this canto.

1:4. *parted*: Ada was only five weeks old when Lady Byron left Byron in January 1816. He never saw his daughter again.

1:9. *Albion's*: England's. Byron sailed from Dover on April 25, 1816.

2

Once more upon the waters! yet once more!
 And the waves bound beneath me as a steed
 That knows his rider. Welcome to their roar!
 Swift be their guidance, wheresoe'er it lead!
 Though the strained mast should quiver as a reed,
 And the rent canvass fluttering strew the gale,
 Still must I on; for I am as a weed,
 Flung from the rock, on Ocean's foam, to sail
Where'er the surge may sweep, the tempest's breath prevail.

3

In my youth's summer I did sing of One,
 The wandering outlaw of his own dark mind;
 Again I seize the theme, then but begun,
 And bear it with me, as the rushing wind
 Bears the cloud onwards: in that Tale I find
 The furrows of long thought, and dried-up tears,
 Which, ebbing, leave a sterile track behind,
 O'er which all heavily the journeying years
Plod the last sands of life, — where not a flower appears.

4

Since my young days of passion — joy, or pain —
 Perchance my heart and harp have lost a string —
 And both may jar: it may be, that in vain
 I would essay as I have sung to sing:
 Yet, though a dreary strain, to this I cling;
 So that it wean me from the weary dream
 Of selfish grief or gladness — so it fling
 Forgetfulness around me — it shall seem
To me, though to none else, a not ungrateful theme.

5

He, who grown agèd in this world of woe,
 In deeds, not years, piercing the depths of life,

3:1. *my youth's summer*: Byron began *Childe Harold* in 1809 when he was twenty-one years old.

So that no wonder waits him — nor below
  Can Love or Sorrow, Fame, Ambition, Strife,
  Cut to his heart again with the keen knife
  Of silent, sharp endurance — he can tell
  Why Thought seeks refuge in lone caves, yet rife
  With airy images, and shapes which dwell
Still unimpaired, though old, in the Soul's haunted cell.

6

'Tis to create, and in creating live
  A being more intense that we endow
  With form our fancy, gaining as we give
  The life we image, even as I do now —
  What am I? Nothing: but not so art thou,
  Soul of my thought! with whom I traverse earth,
  Invisible but gazing, as I glow
  Mixed with thy spirit, blended with thy birth,
And feeling still with thee in my crushed feelings' dearth.

7

Yet must I think less wildly: — I *have* thought
  Too long and darkly, till my brain became,
  In its own eddy boiling and o'erwrought,
  A whirling gulf of phantasy and flame:
  And thus, untaught in youth my heart to tame,
  My springs of life were poisoned. 'Tis too late:
  Yet am I changed; though still enough the same
  In strength to bear what Time can not abate,
And feed on bitter fruits without accusing Fate.

8

Something too much of this: — but now 'tis past,
  And the spell closes with its silent seal —
  Long absent HAROLD re-appears at last;
  He of the breast which fain no more would feel,
  Wrung with the wounds which kill not, but ne'er heal;
  Yet Time, who changes all, had altered him
  In soul and aspect as in age: years steal

Fire from the mind as vigour from the limb;
And Life's enchanted cup but sparkles near the brim.

9

His had been quaffed too quickly, and he found
   The dregs were wormwood; but he filled again,
   And from a purer fount, on holier ground,
   And deemed its spring perpetual — but in vain!
   Still round him clung invisibly a chain
   Which galled for ever, fettering though unseen,
   And heavy though it clanked not; worn with pain,
   Which pined although it spoke not, and grew keen,
Entering with every step he took through many a scene.

10

Secure in guarded coldness, he had mixed
   Again in fancied safety with his kind,
   And deemed his spirit now so firmly fixed
   And sheathed with an invulnerable mind,
   That, if no joy, no sorrow lurked behind;
   And he, as one, might 'midst the many stand
   Unheeded, searching through the crowd to find
   Fit speculation — such as in strange land
He found in wonder-works of God and Nature's hand.

11

But who can view the ripened rose, nor seek
   To wear it? who can curiously behold
   The smoothness and the sheen of Beauty's cheek,
   Nor feel the heart can never all grow old?
   Who can contemplate Fame through clouds unfold
   The star which rises o'er her steep, nor climb?
   Harold, once more within the vortex, rolled
   On with the giddy circle, chasing Time,
Yet with a nobler aim than in his Youth's fond prime.

9:3. *holier ground*: Greece. The reference is to the experiences described in Canto II.
11:9. *fond*: Foolish.

12

But soon he knew himself the most unfit
  Of men to herd with Man, with whom he held
  Little in common; untaught to submit
  His thoughts to others, though his soul was quelled
  In youth by his own thoughts; still uncompelled,
  He would not yield dominion of his mind
  To Spirits against whom his own rebelled,
  Proud though in desolation — which could find
A life within itself, to breathe without mankind.

13

Where rose the mountains, there to him were friends;
  Where rolled the ocean, thereon was his home;
  Where a blue sky, and glowing clime, extends,
  He had the passion and the power to roam;
  The desert, forest, cavern, breaker's foam,
  Were unto him companionship; they spake
  A mutual language, clearer than the tome
  Of his land's tongue, which he would oft forsake
For Nature's pages glassed by sunbeams on the lake.

14

Like the Chaldean, he could watch the stars,
  Till he had peopled them with beings bright
  As their own beams; and earth, and earth-born jars,
  And human frailties, were forgotten quite:
  Could he have kept his spirit to that flight
  He had been happy; but this clay will sink
  Its spark immortal, envying it the light
  To which it mounts, as if to break the link
That keeps us from yon heaven which woos us to its brink.

15

But in Man's dwellings he became a thing
  Restless and worn, and stern and wearisome,

14:1. *Chaldean*: The Babylonians, who were noted for their knowledge
of astronomy.

Drooped as a wild-born falcon with clipt wing,
To whom the boundless air alone were home:
Then came his fit again, which to o'ercome,
As eagerly the barred-up bird will beat
His breast and beak against his wiry dome
Till the blood tinge his plumage — so the heat
Of his impeded Soul would through his bosom eat.

16

Self-exiled Harold wanders forth again,
With nought of Hope left — but with less of gloom;
The very knowledge that he lived in vain,
That all was over on this side the tomb,
Had made Despair a smilingness assume,
Which, though 'twere wild, — as on the plundered wreck
When mariners would madly meet their doom
With draughts intemperate on the sinking deck, —
Did yet inspire a cheer, which he forbore to check.

17

Stop! — for thy tread is on an Empire's dust!
An Earthquake's spoil is sepulchred below!
Is the spot marked with no colossal bust?
Nor column trophied for triumphal show?
None; but *the moral's truth* tells simpler so. —
As the ground was before, thus let it be; —
How that red rain hath made the harvest grow!
And is this all the world has gained by thee,
Thou first and last of Fields! king-making Victory?

18

And Harold stands upon this place of skulls,
The grave of France, the deadly Waterloo!
How in an hour the Power which gave annuls
Its gifts, transferring fame as fleeting too! —

17:1. *Empire's dust*: The battlefield of Waterloo. Napoleon had been
defeated on June 18, 1815.

In "pride of place" here last the Eagle flew,
Then tore with bloody talon the rent plain,
Pierced by the shaft of banded nations through;
Ambition's life and labours all were vain —
He wears the shattered links of the World's broken chain.

19

Fit retribution! Gaul may champ the bit
And foam in fetters; — but is Earth more free?
Did nations combat to make *One* submit?
Or league to teach all Kings true Sovereignty?
What! shall reviving Thraldom again be
The patched-up Idol of enlightened days?
Shall we, who struck the Lion down, shall we
Pay the Wolf homage? proffering lowly gaze
And servile knees to Thrones? No! *prove* before ye praise!

20

If not, o'er one fallen Despot boast no more!
In vain fair cheeks were furrowed with hot tears
For Europe's flowers long rooted up before
The trampler of her vineyards; in vain, years
Of death, depopulation, bondage, fears,
Have all been borne, and broken by the accord
Of roused-up millions: all that most endears
Glory, is when the myrtle wreathes a Sword,
Such as Harmodius drew on Athens' tyrant Lord.

18:5. *Eagle flew*: "Pride of Place" is a falconry term meaning the
highest point of flight. The eagle was Napoleon.

19:5. *reviving Thraldom*: One result of Waterloo had been to restore
the conditions that had led to the French Revolution. A Bourbon king had
been restored to the French throne, and the forces of reaction were
strengthened throughout Europe. Napoleon is the "Lion" (1. 7) and the
victorious monarchs, "the Wolf" (1. 8).

20:9. *Harmodius*: In 514 B.C. Harmodius and his friend, Aristogiton,
hiding daggers in myrtle, attempted to assassinate Hippias, Tyrant of
Athens, and his brother, Hipparchus. Harmodius, cut down by the guards
after killing Hipparchus, became a symbol of the martyr-patriot.

21

There was a sound of revelry by night,
  And Belgium's Capital had gathered then
  Her Beauty and her Chivalry — and bright
  The lamps shone o'er fair women and brave men;
  A thousand hearts beat happily; and when
  Music arose with its voluptuous swell,
  Soft eyes looked love to eyes which spake again,
  And all went merry as a marriage bell;
But hush! hark! a deep sound strikes like a rising knell!

22

Did ye not hear it? — No — 'twas but the Wind,
  Or the car rattling o'er the stony street;
  On with the dance! let joy be unconfined;
  No sleep till morn, when Youth and Pleasure meet
  To chase the glowing Hours with flying feet —
  But hark! — that heavy sound breaks in once more,
  As if the clouds its echo would repeat;
  And nearer — clearer — deadlier than before!
Arm! Arm! it is — it is — the cannon's opening roar!

23

Within a windowed niche of that high hall
  Sate Brunswick's fated Chieftain; he did hear
  That sound the first amidst the festival,
  And caught its tone with Death's prophetic ear;
  And when they smiled because he deemed it near,
  His heart more truly knew that peal too well
  Which stretched his father on a bloody bier,
  And roused the vengeance blood alone could quell;
He rushed into the field, and, foremost fighting, fell.

21:1. *sound of revelry*: The Duchess of Richmond's famous ball, given on the eve of the battle of Quatre-Bras, three days before Waterloo.
23:2. *Brunswick's fated chieftan*: The Duke of Brunswick was killed at Quatre-Bras. His father had been killed in battle in 1806.

24

Ah! then and there was hurrying to and fro —
   And gathering tears, and tremblings of distress,
   And cheeks all pale, which but an hour ago
   Blushed at the praise of their own loveliness —
   And there were sudden partings, such as press
   The life from out young hearts, and choking sighs
   Which ne'er might be repeated; who could guess
   If ever more should meet those mutual eyes,
Since upon night so sweet such awful morn could rise!

25

And there was mounting in hot haste — the steed,
   The mustering squadron, and the clattering car,
   Went pouring forward with impetuous speed,
   And swiftly forming in the ranks of war —
   And the deep thunder peal on peal afar;
   And near, the beat of the alarming drum
   Roused up the soldier ere the Morning Star;
   While thronged the citizens with terror dumb,
Or whispering, with white lips — "The foe! They come! they
   come!"

26

And wild and high the "Cameron's Gathering" rose!
   The war-note of Lochiel, which Albyn's hills
   Have heard, and heard, too, have her Saxon foes: —
   How in the noon of night that pibroch thrills,
   Savage and shrill! But with the breath which fills
   Their mountain-pipe, so fill the mountaineers
   With the fierce native daring which instils
   The stirring memory of a thousand years,
And Evan's — Donald's fame rings in each clansman's ears!

26:1. *Cameron's gathering*: War song of the Cameron clan, whose chief
was called "Lochiel" after his estate.
26:2. *Albyn's*: Scotland's.
26:4. *pibroch*: Martial bagpipe music.
26:9. *Evan's, Donald's*: Sir Evan Cameron (1629–1719) had fought

27

And Ardennes waves above them her green leaves,
  Dewy with Nature's tear-drops, as they pass —
  Grieving, if aught inanimate e'er grieves,
  Over the unreturning brave, — alas!
  Ere evening to be trodden like the grass
  Which now beneath them, but above shall grow
  In its next verdure, when this fiery mass
  Of living Valour, rolling on the foe
And burning with high Hope, shall moulder cold and low.

28

Last noon beheld them full of lusty life; —
  Last eve in Beauty's circle proudly gay;
  The Midnight brought the signal-sound of strife,
  The Morn the marshalling in arms, — the Day
  Battle's magnificently-stern array!
  The thunder-clouds close o'er it, which when rent
  The earth is covered thick with other clay
  Which her own clay shall cover, heaped and pent,
Rider and horse, — friend, — foe, — in one red burial blent!

29

Their praise is hymned by loftier harps than mine;
  Yet one I would select from that proud throng,
  Partly because they blend me with his line,
  And partly that I did his Sire some wrong,
  And partly that bright names will hallow song;
  And his was of the bravest, and when showered
  The death-bolts deadliest the thinned files along,
  Even where the thickest of War's tempest lowered,
They reached no nobler breast than thine, young, gallant
  Howard!

against Cromwell. His grandson, Donald Cameron (1695–1748), had fought
on behalf of the Young Pretender at the battle of Culloden in 1746.
  27:1. *Ardennes*: The forest in Belgium and northern France which became a battlefield in both World Wars.
  29:2. *one I would select*: Frederick Howard, son of the Earl of Carlisle,
whom Byron had viciously satirized in *English Bards and Scotch Reviewers*.

30

There have been tears and breaking hearts for thee,
   And mine were nothing, had I such to give;
   But when I stood beneath the fresh green tree,
   Which living waves where thou didst cease to live,
   And saw around me the wide field revive
   With fruits and fertile promise, and the Spring
   Come forth her work of gladness to contrive,
   With all her reckless birds upon the wing,
I turned from all she brought to those she could not bring.

31

I turned to thee, to thousands, of whom each
   And one as all a ghastly gap did make
   In his own kind and kindred, whom to teach
   Forgetfulness were mercy for their sake;
   The Archangel's trump, not Glory's, must awake
   Those whom they thirst for; though the sound of Fame
   May for a moment soothe, it cannot slake
   The fever of vain longing, and the name
So honoured but assumes a stronger, bitter claim.

32

They mourn, but smile at length — and, smiling, mourn:
   The tree will wither long before it fall;
   The hull drives on, though mast and sail be torn;
   The roof-tree sinks, but moulders on the hall
   In massy hoariness; the ruined wall
   Stands when its wind-worn battlements are gone;
   The bars survive the captive they enthral;
   The day drags through though storms keep out the sun;
And thus the heart will break, yet brokenly live on:

33

Even as a broken Mirror, which the glass
   In every fragment multiplies — and makes
   A thousand images of one that was,
   The same — and still the more, the more it breaks;

And thus the heart will do which not forsakes,
   Living in shattered guise; and still, and cold,
   And bloodless, with its sleepless sorrow aches,
   Yet withers on till all without is old,
Showing no visible sign, for such things are untold.

34

There is a very life in our despair,
   Vitality of poison, — a quick root
   Which feeds these deadly branches; for it were
   As nothing did we die; but Life will suit
   Itself to Sorrow's most detested fruit,
   Like to the apples on the Dead Sea's shore,
   All ashes to the taste: Did man compute
   Existence by enjoyment, and count o'er
Such hours 'gainst years of life, — say, would he name three-
   score?

35

The Psalmist numbered out the years of man:
   They are enough; and if thy tale be *true,*
   Thou, who didst grudge him even that fleeting span,
   More than enough, thou fatal Waterloo!
   Millions of tongues record thee, and anew
   Their children's lips shall echo them, and say —
   "Here, where the sword united nations drew,
   Our countrymen were warring on that day!"
And this is much — and all — which will not pass away.

36

There sunk the greatest, nor the worst of men,
   Whose Spirit, antithetically mixed,
   One moment of the mightiest, and again
   On little objects with like firmness fixed;
   Extreme in all things! hadst thou been betwixt,
   Thy throne had still been thine, or never been;

36:1. *greatest*: Napoleon.

For Daring made thy rise as fall: thou seek'st
Even now to re-assume the imperial mien,
And shake again the world, the Thunderer of the scene!

37

Conqueror and Captive of the Earth art thou!
She trembles at thee still, and thy wild name
Was ne'er more bruited in men's minds than now
That thou art nothing, save the jest of Fame,
Who wooed thee once, thy Vassal, and became
The flatterer of thy fierceness — till thou wert
A God unto thyself; nor less the same
To the astounded kingdoms all inert,
Who deemed thee for a time whate'er thou didst assert.

38

Oh, more or less than man — in high or low —
Battling with nations, flying from the field;
Now making monarchs' necks thy footstool, now
More than thy meanest soldier taught to yield;
An Empire thou couldst crush, command, rebuild,
But govern not thy pettiest passion, nor,
However deeply in men's spirits skilled,
Look through thine own, nor curb the lust of War,
Nor learn that tempted Fate will leave the loftiest Star.

39

Yet well thy soul hath brooked the turning tide
With that untaught innate philosophy,
Which, be it Wisdom, Coldness, or deep Pride,
Is gall and wormwood to an enemy.
When the whole host of hatred stood hard by,
To watch and mock thee shrinking, thou hast smiled
With a sedate and all-enduring eye; —
When Fortune fled her spoiled and favourite child,
He stood unbowed beneath the ills upon him piled.

40

Sager than in thy fortunes; for in them
   Ambition steeled thee on too far to show
   That just habitual scorn, which could contemn
   Men and their thoughts; 'twas wise to feel, not so
   To wear it ever on thy lip and brow,
   And spurn the instruments thou wert to use
   Till they were turned unto thine overthrow:
   'Tis but a worthless world to win or lose;
So hath it proved to thee, and all such lot who choose.

41

If, like a tower upon a headlong rock,
   Thou hadst been made to stand or fall alone,
   Such scorn of man had helped to brave the shock;
   But men's thoughts were the steps which paved thy throne,
   Their admiration thy best weapon shone;
   The part of Philip's son was thine, not then
   (Unless aside thy Purple had been thrown)
   Like stern Diogenes to mock at men —
For sceptered Cynics Earth were far too wide a den.

42

But Quiet to quick bosoms is a Hell,
   And *there* hath been thy bane; there is a fire
   And motion of the Soul which will not dwell
   In its own narrow being, but aspire
   Beyond the fitting medium of desire;
   And, but once kindled, quenchless evermore,
   Preys upon high adventure, nor can tire
   Of aught but rest; a fever at the core,
Fatal to him who bears, to all who ever bore.

43

This makes the madmen who have made men mad

41:6. *Philip's Son*: Alexander the Great.
41:8. *Diogenes*: The Greek cynic philosopher who sought in vain for
an honest man.

By their contagion; Conquerors and Kings,
  Founders of sects and systems, to whom add
  Sophists, Bards, Statesmen, all unquiet things
  Which stir too strongly the soul's secret springs,
  And are themselves the fools to those they fool;
  Envied, yet how unenviable! what stings
  Are theirs! One breast laid open were a school
Which would unteach Mankind the lust to shine or rule:

44

Their breath is agitation, and their life
  A storm whereon they ride, to sink at last,
  And yet so nursed and bigoted to strife,
  That should their days, surviving perils past,
  Melt to calm twilight, they feel overcast
  With sorrow and supineness, and so die;
  Even as a flame unfed, which runs to waste
  With its own flickering, or a sword laid by,
Which eats into itself, and rusts ingloriously.

45

He who ascends to mountain-tops, shall find
  The loftiest peaks most wrapt in clouds and snow;
  He who surpasses or subdues mankind,
  Must look down on the hate of those below.
  Though high *above* the Sun of Glory glow,
  And far *beneath* the Earth and Ocean spread,
  Round him are icy rocks, and loudly blow
  Contending tempests on his naked head,
And thus reward the toils which to those summits led.

46

Away with these! true Wisdom's world will be
  Within its own creation, or in thine,
  Maternal Nature! for who teems like thee,
  Thus on the banks of thy majestic Rhine?
  There Harold gazes on a work divine,
  A blending of all beauties; streams and dells,

Fruit, foliage, crag, wood, cornfield, mountain, vine,
  And chiefless castles breathing stern farewells
From gray but leafy walls, where Ruin greenly dwells,

47

And there they stand, as stands a lofty mind,
  Worn, but unstooping to the baser crowd,
  All tenantless, save to the crannying Wind,
  Or holding dark communion with the Cloud
  There was a day when they were young and proud;
  Banners on high, and battles passed below;
  But they who fought are in a bloody shroud,
  And those which waved are shredless dust ere now,
And the bleak battlements shall bear no future blow.

48

Beneath these battlements, within those walls,
  Power dwelt amidst her passions; in proud state
  Each robber chief upheld his arméd halls,
  Doing his evil will, nor less elate
  Than mightier heroes of a longer date.
  What want these outlaws conquerors should have
  But History's purchased page to call them great?
  A wider space — an ornamented grave?
Their hopes were not less warm, their souls were full as brave.

49

In their baronial feuds and single fields,
  What deeds of prowess unrecorded died!
  And Love, which lent a blazon to their shields,
  With emblems well devised by amorous pride,
  Through all the mail of iron hearts would glide;
  But still their flame was fierceness, and drew on
  Keen contest and destruction near allied,
  And many a tower for some fair mischief won,
Saw the discoloured Rhine beneath its ruin run.

49:3. *Love, which lent a blazon*: The usual device on the shields was
a bleeding heart.

50

But Thou, exulting and abounding river!
  Making thy waves a blessing as they flow
  Through banks whose beauty would endure for ever
  Could man but leave thy bright creation so,
  Nor its fair promise from the surface mow
  With the sharp scythe of conflict, — then to see
  Thy valley of sweet waters, were to know
  Earth paved like Heaven — and to seem such to me,
Even now what wants thy stream? — that it should Lethe be.

51

A thousand battles have assailed thy banks,
  But these and half their fame have passed away,
  And Slaughter heaped on high his weltering ranks:
  Their very graves are gone, and what are they?
  Thy tide washed down the blood of yesterday,
  And all was stainless, and on thy clear stream
  Glassed, with its dancing light, the sunny ray;
  But o'er the blacken'd memory's blighting dream
Thy waves would vainly roll, all sweeping as they seem.

52

Thus Harold inly said, and passed along,
  Yet not insensible to all which here
  Awoke the jocund birds to early song
  In glens which might have made even exile dear:
  Though on his brow were graven lines austere,
  And tranquil sternness, which had ta'en the place
  Of feelings fierier far but less severe —
  Joy was not always absent from his face,
But o'er it in such scenes would steal with transient trace.

53

Nor was all Love shut from him, though his days
  Of Passion had consumed themselves to dust.

50:9. *Lethe*: River of oblivion.

It is in vain that we would coldly gaze
On such as smile upon us; the heart must
Leap kindly back to kindness, though Disgust
Hath weaned it from all worldlings: thus he felt,
For there was soft Remembrance, and sweet Trust
In one fond breast, to which his own would melt,
And in its tenderer hour on that his bosom dwelt.

54

And he learned to love, — I know not why,
   For this in such as him seems strange of mood, —
   The helpless looks of blooming Infancy,
   Even in its earliest nurture; what subdued,
   To change like this, a mind so far imbued
   With scorn of man, it little boots to know;
   But thus it was; and though in solitude
   Small power the nipped affections have to grow,
In him this glowed when all beside had ceased to glow.

55

And there was one soft breast, as hath been said,
   Which unto his was bound by stronger ties
   Than the church links withal; and — though unwed,
   That love was pure — and, far above disguise,
   Had stood the test of mortal enmities
   Still undivided, and cemented more
   By peril, dreaded most in female eyes;
   But this was firm, and from a foreign shore
Well to that heart might his these absent greetings pour!

I

The castled Crag of Drachenfels
Frowns o'er the wide and winding Rhine,
Whose breast of waters broadly swells

53:8. *one fond breast*: His half sister Augusta to whom the following
lyric is addressed.
   Song: 1. 1. *Drachenfels* (Dragon's rock): The ruins of a castle on the right
bank of the Rhine near Bonn.

Between the banks which bear the vine,
And hills all rich with blossomed trees,
And fields which promise corn and wine,
And scattered cities crowning these,
Whose far white walls along them shine,
Have strewed a scene, which I should see
With double joy wert *thou* with me.

II

And peasant girls, with deep blue eyes,
And hands which offer early flowers,
Walk smiling o'er this Paradise;
Above, the frequent feudal towers
Through green leaves lift their walls of gray;
And many a rock which steeply lowers,
And noble arch in proud decay,
Look o'er this vale of vintage-bowers;
But one thing want these banks of Rhine, —
Thy gentle hand to clasp in mine!

III

I send the lilies given to me —
Though long before thy hand they touch,
I know that they must withered be,
But yet reject them not as such;
For I have cherished them as dear,
Because they yet may meet thine eye,
And guide thy soul to mine even here,
When thou behold'st them drooping nigh,
And know'st them gathered by the Rhine,
And offered from my heart to thine!

IV

The river nobly foams and flows —
The charm of this enchanted ground,
And all its thousand turns disclose
Some fresher beauty varying round:
The haughtiest breast its wish might bound

Through life to dwell delighted here;
Nor could on earth a spot be found
To Nature and to me so dear —
Could thy dear eyes in following mine
Still sweeten more these banks of Rhine!

56

By Coblentz, on a rise of gentle ground,
  There is a small and simple Pyramid,
Crowning the summit of the verdant mound;
  Beneath its base are Heroes' ashes hid —
  Our enemy's — but let not that forbid
Honour to Marceau! o'er whose early tomb
  Tears, big tears, gushed from the rough soldier's lid,
Lamenting and yet envying such a doom,
Falling for France, whose rights he battled to resume.

57

Brief, brave, and glorious was his young career, —
  His mourners were two hosts, his friends and foes;
And fitly may the stranger lingering here
  Pray for his gallant Spirit's bright repose; —
  For he was Freedom's Champion, one of those,
The few in number, who had not o'erstept
  The charter to chastise which she bestows
On such as wield her weapons; he had kept
The whiteness of his soul — and thus men o'er him wept.

58

Here Ehrenbreitstein, with her shattered wall
  Black with the miner's blast, upon her height
Yet shows of what she was, when shell and ball
  Rebounding idly on her strength did light: —

56:6. *Marceau*: François Marceau (1769–1796), a French revolutionary general, noted for his devotion to republican ideals, killed in battle on the Rhine.
58:1. *Ehrenbreitstein*: Fortress on the Rhine, captured by the French after a prolonged siege in 1799, and dismantled and blown up upon the French evacuation in 1801.

A Tower of Victory! from whence the flight
Of baffled foes was watched along the plain:
But Peace destroyed what War could never blight,
And laid those proud roofs bare to Summer's rain —
On which the iron shower for years had poured in vain.

59

Adieu to thee, fair Rhine! How long delighted
  The stranger fain would linger on his way!
  Thine is a scene alike where souls united
  Or lonely Contemplation thus might stray;
  And could the ceaseless vultures cease to prey
  On self-condemning bosoms, it were here,
  Where Nature, nor too sombre nor too gay,
  Wild but not rude, awful yet not austere,
Is it to the mellow Earth as Autumn to the year.

60

Adieu to thee again! a vain adieu!
  There can be no farewell to scene like thine;
  The mind is coloured by thy every hue;
  And if reluctantly the eyes resign
  Their cherished gaze upon thee, lovely Rhine!
  'Tis with the thankful glance of parting praise;
  More mighty spots may rise — more glaring shine,
  But none unite in one attaching maze
The brilliant, fair, and soft, — the glories of old days,

61

The negligently grand, the fruitful bloom
  Of coming ripeness, the white city's sheen,
  The rolling stream, the precipice's gloom,
  The forest's growth, and Gothic walls between, —
  The wild rocks shaped, as they had turrets been,
  In mockery of man's art; and these withal
  A race of faces happy as the scene,
  Whose fertile bounties here extend to all,
Still springing o'er thy banks, though Empires near them fall.

62

But these recede. Above me are the Alps,
  The Palaces of Nature, whose vast walls
  Have pinnacled in clouds their snowy scalps,
  And throned Eternity in icy halls
  Of cold Sublimity, where forms and falls
  The Avalanche — the thunderbolt of snow!
  All that expands the spirit, yet appals,
  Gather around these summits, as to show
How Earth may pierce to Heaven, yet leave vain man below.

63

But ere these matchless heights I dare to scan,
  There is a spot should not be passed in vain, —
  Morat! the proud, the patriot field! where man
  May gaze on ghastly trophies of the slain,
  Nor blush for those who conquered on that plain;
  Here Burgundy bequeathed his tombless host,
  A bony heap, through ages to remain,
  Themselves their monument; — the Stygian coast
Unsepulchred they roamed, and shrieked each wandering ghost.

64

While Waterloo with Cannæ's carnage vies,
  Morat and Marathon twin names shall stand;
  They were true Glory's stainless victories,
  Won by the unambitious heart and hand
  Of a proud, brotherly, and civic band,
  All unbought champions in no princely cause
  Of vice-entailed Corruption; they no land
  Doomed to bewail the blasphemy of laws
Making Kings' rights divine, by some Draconic clause.

63:3. *Morat*: In 1476 the Swiss defeated an invading Burgundian army. An estimated 20,000 Burgundians were killed and left unburied. A small pyramid of bones still remained in 1816 and Byron carried off as souvenir "as much as may have made a quarter of a hero."

64:1. *Cannae*: Bloody battle in which Hannibal defeated the Romans in 216 B.C. At Marathon (1. 2) the Greeks, like the Swiss fighting for their freedom, defeated the invading Persians in 490 B.C.

65

By a lone wall a lonelier column rears
  A gray and grief-worn aspect of old days;
  'Tis the last remnant of the wreck of years,
  And looks as with the wild-bewildered gaze
  Of one to stone converted by amaze,
  Yet still with consciousness; and there it stands
  Making a marvel that it not decays,
  When the coeval pride of human hands,
Levelled Aventicum, hath strewed her subject lands.

66

And there — oh! sweet and sacred be the name! —
  Julia — the daughter — the devoted — gave
  Her youth to Heaven; her heart, beneath a claim
  Nearest to Heaven's, broke o'er a father's grave.
  Justice is sworn 'gainst tears, and hers would crave
  The life she lived in — but the Judge was just —
  And then she died on him she could not save.
  Their tomb was simple, and without a bust,
And held within their urn one mind — one heart — one dust.

67

But these are deeds which should not pass away,
  And names that must not wither, though the Earth
  Forgets her empires with a just decay,
  The enslavers and the enslaved — their death and birth;
  The high, the mountain-majesty of Worth
  Should be — and shall, survivor of its woe,
  And from its immortality, look forth
  In the sun's face, like yonder Alpine snow,
Imperishably pure beyond all things below.

65:9. *Adventicum*: The Roman capital of Switzerland, long since destroyed.

66:2. *Julia*: An inscription, afterward proved to be forged, led Byron to believe that Julia Alpinula had died here after a vain effort to save her father, executed in A.D. 69 for leading a rebellion against Roman rule.

68

Lake Leman woos me with its crystal face,
  The mirror where the stars and mountains view
  The stillness of their aspect in each trace
  Its clear depth yields of their far height and hue:
  There is too much of Man here, to look through
  With a fit mind the might which I behold;
  But soon in me shall Loneliness renew
  Thoughts hid, but not less cherished than of old,
Ere mingling with the herd had penned me in their fold.

69

To fly from, need not be to hate, mankind:
  All are not fit with them to stir and toil,
  Nor is it discontent to keep the mind
  Deep in its fountain, lest it overboil
  In the hot throng, where we become the spoil
  Of our infection, till too late and long
  We may deplore and struggle with the coil,
  In wretched interchange of wrong for wrong
Midst a contentious world, striving where none are strong.

70

There, in a moment, we may plunge our years
  In fatal penitence, and in the blight
  Of our own Soul turn all our blood to tears,
  And colour things to come with hues of Night;
  The race of life becomes a hopeless flight
  To those that walk in darkness: on the sea
  The boldest steer but where their ports invite —
  But there are wanderers o'er Eternity
Whose bark drives on and on, and anchored ne'er shall be.

71

Is it not better, then, to be alone,
  And love Earth only for its earthly sake?

68:1. *Lake Leman*: Lake Geneva.

By the blue rushing of the arrowy Rhone,
Or the pure bosom of its nursing Lake,
Which feeds it as a mother who doth make
A fair but froward infant her own care,
Kissing its cries away as these awake; —
Is it not better thus our lives to wear,
Than join the crushing crowd, doomed to inflict or bear?

72

I live not in myself, but I become
Portion of that around me; and to me
High mountains are a feeling, but the hum
Of human cities torture: I can see
Nothing to loathe in Nature, save to be
A link reluctant in a fleshly chain,
Classed among creatures, when the soul can flee,
And with the sky — the peak — the heaving plain
Of Ocean, or the stars, mingle — and not in vain.

73

And thus I am absorbed, and this is life: —
I look upon the peopled desert past,
As on a place of agony and strife,
Where, for some sin, to Sorrow I was cast,
To act and suffer, but remount at last
With a fresh pinion; which I feel to spring,
Though young, yet waxing vigorous as the Blast
Which it would cope with, on delighted wing,
Spurning the clay-cold bonds which round our being cling.

74

And when, at length, the mind shall be all free
From what it hates in this degraded form,
Reft of its carnal life, save what shall be
Existent happier in the fly and worm, —
When Elements to Elements conform,
And dust is as it should be, shall I not
Feel all I see less dazzling but more warm?

The bodiless thought? the Spirit of each spot?
Of which, even now, I share at times the immortal lot?

75

Are not the mountains, waves, and skies, a part
  Of me and of my Soul, as I of them?
  Is not the love of these deep in my heart
  With a pure passion? should I not contemn
  All objects, if compared with these? and stem
  A tide of suffering, rather than forego
  Such feelings for the hard and worldly phlegm
  Of those whose eyes are only turned below,
Gazing upon the ground, with thoughts which dare not glow?

76

But this is not my theme; and I return
  To that which is immediate, and require
  Those who find contemplation in the urn,
  To look on One, whose dust was once all fire, —
  A native of the land where I respire
  The clear air for a while — a passing guest,
  Where he became a being, — whose desire
  Was to be glorious; 'twas a foolish quest,
The which to gain and keep, he sacrificed all rest.

77

Here the self-torturing sophist, wild Rousseau,
  The apostle of Affliction, he who threw
  Enchantment over Passion, and from Woe
  Wrung overwhelming eloquence, first drew
  The breath which made him wretched; yet he knew
  How to make Madness beautiful, and cast
  O'er erring deeds and thoughts, a heavenly hue
  Of words, like sunbeams, dazzling as they past
The eyes, which o'er them shed tears feelingly and fast.

76:4. *One*: Jean Jacques Rousseau (1712–1778), who was born in Geneva.

78

His love was Passion's essence — as a tree
  On fire by lightning; with ethereal flame
  Kindled he was, and blasted; for to be
  Thus, and enamoured, were in him the same.
  But his was not the love of living dame,
  Nor of the dead who rise upon our dreams,
  But of ideal Beauty, which became
  In him existence, and o'erflowing teems
Along his burning page, distempered though it seems.

79

This breathed itself to life in Julie, *this*
  Invested her with all that's wild and sweet;
  This hallowed, too, the memorable kiss
  Which every morn his fevered lip would greet,
  From hers, who but with friendship his would meet;
  But to that gentle touch, through brain and breast
  Flashed the thrilled Spirit's love-devouring heat;
  In that absorbing sigh perchance more blest
Than vulgar minds may be with all they seek possest.

80

His life was one long war with self-sought foes,
  Or friends by him self-banished; for his mind
  Had grown Suspicion's sanctuary, and chose,
  For its own cruel sacrifice, the kind,
  'Gainst whom he raged with fury strange and blind.
  But he was phrensied, — wherefore, who may know?
  Since cause might be which Skill could never find;
  But he was phrensied by disease or woe,
To that worst pitch of all, which wears a reasoning show.

79:1. *Julie*: Heroine of Rousseau's novel, *La Nouvelle Héloïse*.
79:3. *memorable kiss*: In his *Confessions*, Book 9, Rousseau tells of his "pure" passion for the Comtesse d'Houdetot, and his long walk every morning for the single kiss which was the common salutation of French acquaintances.

81

For then he was inspired, and from him came,
  As from the Pythian's mystic cave of yore,
  Those oracles which set the world in flame,
  Nor ceased to burn till kingdoms were no more:
  Did he not this for France? which lay before
  Bowed to the inborn tyranny of years?
  Broken and trembling to the yoke she bore,
  Till by the voice of him and his compeers,
Roused up to too much wrath which follows o'ergrown fears?

82

They made themselves a fearful monument!
  The wreck of old opinions — things which grew,
  Breathed from the birth of Time: the veil they rent,
  And what behind it lay, all earth shall view.
  But good with ill they also overthrew,
  Leaving but ruins, wherewith to rebuild
  Upon the same foundation, and renew
  Dungeons and thrones, which the same hour refilled,
As heretofore, because Ambition was self-willed.

83

But this will not endure, nor be endured!
  Mankind have felt their strength, and made it felt.
  They might have used it better, but, allured
  By their new vigour, sternly have they dealt
  On one another; Pity ceased to melt
  With her once natural charities. But they,
  Who in Oppression's darkness caved had dwelt,
  They were not eagles, nourished with the day;
What marvel then, at times, if they mistook their prey?

84

What deep wounds ever closed without a scar?
  The heart's bleed longest, and but heal to wear

81:2. *Pythian's mystic cave*: Apollo's oracle at Delphi.

That which disfigures it; and they who war
With their own hopes, and have been vanquished, bear
Silence, but not submission: in his lair
Fixed Passion holds his breath, until the hour
Which shall atone for years; none need despair:
It came — it cometh — and will come, — the power
To punish or forgive — in *one* we shall be slower.

85

Clear, placid Leman! thy contrasted lake,
With the wild world I dwelt in, is a thing
Which warns me, with its stillness, to forsake
Earth's troubled waters for a purer spring.
This quiet sail is as a noiseless wing
To waft me from distraction; once I loved
Torn Ocean's roar, but thy soft murmuring
Sounds sweet as if a Sister's voice reproved,
That I with stern delights should e'er have been so moved.

86

It is the hush of night, and all between
Thy margin and the mountains, dusk, yet clear,
Mellowed and mingling, yet distinctly seen,
Save darkened Jura, whose capt heights appear
Precipitously steep; and drawing near,
There breathes a living fragrance from the shore,
Of flowers yet fresh with childhood; on the ear
Drops the light drip of the suspended oar,
Or chirps the grasshopper one good-night carol more.

87

He is an evening reveller, who makes
His life an infancy, and sings his fill;
At intervals, some bird from out the brakes
Starts into voice a moment, then is still.
There seems a floating whisper on the hill,
But that is fancy — for the Starlight dews
All silently their tears of Love instil,

Weeping themselves away, till they infuse
Deep into Nature's breast the spirit of her hues.

88

Ye Stars! which are the poetry of Heaven!
  If in your bright leaves we would read the fate
  Of men and empires, — 'tis to be forgiven,
  That in our aspirations to be great,
  Our destinies o'erleap their mortal state,
  And claim a kindred with you; for ye are
  A Beauty and a Mystery, and create
  In us such love and reverence from afar,
That Fortune, — Fame, — Power, — Life, have named themselves a Star.

89

All Heaven and Earth are still — though not in sleep,
  But breathless, as we grow when feeling most;
  And silent, as we stand in thoughts too deep: —
  All Heaven and Earth are still: From the high host
  Of stars, to the lulled lake and mountain-coast,
  All is concentered in a life intense.
  Where not a beam, nor air, nor leaf is lost,
  But hath a part of Being, and a sense
Of that which is of all Creator and Defence.

90

Then stirs the feeling infinite, so felt
  In solitude, where we are *least* alone;
  A truth, which through our being then doth melt,
  And purifies from self: it is a tone,
  The soul and source of Music, which makes known
  Eternal harmony, and sheds a charm
  Like to the fabled Cytherea's zone,
  Binding all things with beauty; — 'twould disarm
The spectre Death, had he substantial power to harm.

90:7. *Cytherea's zone*: The Girdle of Venus which endowed the wearer
with the power to inspire love.

91

Not vainly did the early Persian make
  His altar the high places, and the peak
  Of earth-o'ergazing mountains, and thus take
  A fit and unwalled temple, there to seek
  The Spirit, in whose honour shrines are weak
  Upreared of human hands. Come, and compare
  Columns and idol-dwellings — Goth or Greek —
  With Nature's realms of worship, earth and air —
Nor fix on fond abodes to circumscribe thy prayer!

92

The sky is changed! — and such a change! Oh Night,
  And Storm, and Darkness, ye are wondrous strong,
  Yet lovely in your strength, as is the light
  Of a dark eye in Woman! Far along,
  From peak to peak, the rattling crags among
  Leaps the live thunder! Not from one lone cloud,
  But every mountain now hath found a tongue,
  And Jura answers, through her misty shroud,
Back to the joyous Alps, who call to her aloud!

93

And this is in the Night: — Most glorious Night!
  Thou wert not sent for slumber! let me be
  A sharer in thy fierce and far delight, —
  A portion of the tempest and of thee!
  How the lit lake shines, a phosphoric sea,
  And the big rain comes dancing to the earth!
  And now again 'tis black, — and now, the glee
  Of the loud hills shakes with its mountain-mirth,
As if they did rejoice o'er a young Earthquake's birth.

94

Now, where the swift Rhone cleaves his way between
  Heights which appear as lovers who have parted
  In hate, whose mining depths so intervene,
  That they can meet no more, though broken-hearted:

Though in their souls, which thus each other thwarted,
Love was the very root of the fond rage
Which blighted their life's bloom, and then departed: —
Itself expired, but leaving them an age
Of years all winters, — war within themselves to wage:

95

Now, where the quick Rhone thus hath cleft his way,
The mightiest of the storms hath ta'en his stand:
For here, not one, but many, make their play,
And fling their thunder-bolts from hand to hand,
Flashing and cast around: of all the band,
The brightest through these parted hills hath forked
His lightnings, — as if he did understand,
That in such gaps as Desolation worked,
There the hot shaft should blast whatever therein lurked.

96

Sky — Mountains — River — Winds — Lake — Lightnings!
   ye!
With night, and clouds, and thunder — and a Soul
To make these felt and feeling, well may be
Things that have made me watchful; the far roll
Of your departing voices, is the knoll
Of what in me is sleepless, — if I rest.
But where of ye, O Tempests! is the goal?
Are ye like those within the human breast?
Or do ye find, at length, like eagles, some high nest?

97

Could I embody and unbosom now
That which is most within me, — could I wreak
My thoughts upon expression, and thus throw
Soul — heart — mind — passions — feelings — strong or
   weak —
All that I would have sought, and all I seek,

96:5. *Knoll*: Knell.

Bear, know, feel — and yet breathe — into *one* word,
And that one word were Lightning, I would speak;
But as it is, I live and die unheard,
With a most voiceless thought, sheathing it as a sword.

98

The Morn is up again, the dewy Morn,
With breath all incense, and with cheek all bloom —
Laughing the clouds away with playful scorn,
And living as if earth contained no tomb, —
And glowing into day: we may resume
The march of our existence: and thus I,
Still on thy shores, fair Leman! may find room
And food for meditation, nor pass by
Much, that may give us pause, if pondered fittingly.

99

Clarens! sweet Clarens birthplace of deep Love!
Thine air is the young breath of passionate Thought;
Thy trees take root in Love; the snows above,
The very Glaciers have his colours caught,
And Sun-set into rose-hues sees them wrought
By rays which sleep there lovingly: the rocks,
The permanent crags, tell here of Love, who sought
In them a refuge from the worldly shocks,
Which stir and sting the Soul with Hope that woos, then mocks.

100

Clarens! by heavenly feet thy paths are trod, —
Undying Love's, who here ascends a throne
To which the steps are mountains; where the God
Is a pervading Life and Light, — so shown
Not on those summits solely, nor alone
In the still cave and forest; o'er the flower
His eye is sparkling, and his breath hath blown,
His soft and summer breath, whose tender power
Passes the strength of storms in their most desolate hour.

99:1. *Clarens*: A village on Lake Geneva, scene of *La Nouvelle Héloïse*.

101

All things are here of *Him;* from the black pines,
  Which are his shade on high, and the loud roar
  Of torrents, where he listeneth, to the vines
  Which slope his green path downward to the shore,
  Where the bowed Waters meet him, and adore,
  Kissing his feet with murmurs; and the Wood,
  The covert of old trees, with trunks all hoar,
  But light leaves, young as joy, stands where it stood,
Offering to him, and his, a populous solitude.

102

A populous solitude of bees and birds,
  And fairy-formed and many-coloured things,
  Who worship him with notes more sweet than words,
  And innocently open their glad wings,
  Fearless and full of life: the gush of springs,
  And fall of lofty fountains, and the bend
  Of stirring branches, and the bud which brings
  The swiftest thought of Beauty, here extend
Mingling — and made by Love — unto one mighty end.

103

He who hath loved not, here would learn that lore,
  And make his heart a spirit; he who knows
  That tender mystery, will love the more;
  For this is Love's recess, where vain men's woes,
  And the world's waste, have driven him far from those,
  For 'tis his nature to advance or die;
  He stands not still, but or decays, or grows
  Into a boundless blessing, which may vie
With the immortal lights, in its eternity!

104

'Twas not for fiction chose Rousseau this spot,
  Peopling it with affections; but he found
  It was the scene which Passion must allot
  To the Mind's purified beings; 'twas the ground

Where early Love his Psyche's zone unbound,
And hallowed it with loveliness: 'tis lone,
And wonderful, and deep, and hath a sound,
And sense, and sight of sweetness; here the Rhone
Hath spread himself a couch, the Alps have reared a throne.

105

Lausanne! and Ferney! ye have been the abodes
Of Names which unto you bequeathed a name;
Mortals, who sought and found, by dangerous roads,
A path to perpetuity of Fame:
They were gigantic minds, and their steep aim
Was, Titan-like, on daring doubts to pile
Thoughts which should call down thunder, and the flame
Of Heaven again assailed — if Heaven, the while,
On man and man's research could deign do more than smile.

106

The one was fire and fickleness, a child
Most mutable in wishes, but in mind
A wit as various, — gay, grave, sage, or wild, —
Historian, bard, philosopher, combined;
He multiplied himself among mankind,
The Proteus of their talents: But his own
Breathed most in ridicule, — which, as the wind,
Blew where it listed, laying all things prone, —
Now to o'erthrow a fool, and now to shake a throne.

107

The other, deep and slow, exhausting thought,
And hiving wisdom with each studious year,
In meditation dwelt — with learning wrought,
And shaped his weapon with an edge severe,

105:1. *Lausanne and Ferney*: Edward Gibbon (1737–1794), described in
stanza 107, finished *Decline and Fall of the Roman Empire* at Lausanne
in 1788; Voltaire (1694–1778), described in stanza 106, had lived at
Ferney near Geneva many years before his death. Both Gibbon and Voltaire were hostile to Christianity, the "solemn creed" (107:5), and were
critical of the social and political evils of their age.

Sapping a solemn creed with solemn sneer;
The lord of irony, — that master-spell,
Which stung his foes to wrath, which grew from fear
And doomed him to the zealot's ready Hell,
Which answers to all doubts so eloquently well.

108

Yet, peace be with their ashes, — for by them,
  If merited, the penalty is paid;
  It is not ours to judge, — far less condemn;
  The hour must come when such things shall be made
  Known unto all, — or hope and dread allayed
  By slumber, on one pillow, in the dust,
  Which, thus much we are sure, must lie decayed;
  And when it shall revive, as is our trust,
'Twill be to be forgiven — or suffer what is just.

109

But let me quit Man's works, again to read
  His Maker's, spread around me, and suspend
  This page, which from my reveries I feed,
  Until it seems prolonging without end.
  The clouds above me to the white Alps tend,
  And I must pierce them, and survey whate'er
  May be permitted, as my steps I bend
  To their most great and growing region, where
The earth to her embrace compels the powers of air.

110

Italia too! Italia! looking on thee,
  Full flashes on the Soul the light of ages,
  Since the fierce Carthaginian almost won thee,
  To the last halo of the Chiefs and Sages
  Who glorify thy consecrated pages;
  Thou wert the throne and grave of empires; still,
  The fount at which the panting Mind assuages

110:3. *Carthaginian*: Hannibal.

Her thirst of knowledge, quaffing there her fill,
Flows from the eternal source of Rome's imperial hill.

111

Thus far have I proceeded in a theme
    Renewed with no kind auspices: — to feel
    We are not what we have been, and to deem
    We are not what we should be, — and to steel
    The heart against itself; and to conceal,
    With a proud caution, love, or hate, or aught, —
    Passion or feeling, purpose, grief, or zeal, —
    Which is the tyrant Spirit of our thought,
Is a stern task of soul: — No matter, — it is taught.

112

And for these words, thus woven into song,
    It may be that they are a harmless wile, —
    The colouring of the scenes which fleet along,
    Which I would seize, in passing, to beguile
    My breast, or that of others, for a while.
    Fame is the thirst of youth, — but I am not
    So young as to regard men's frown or smile,
    As loss or guerdon of a glorious lot; —
I stood and stand alone, — remembered or forgot.

113

I have not loved the World, nor the World me;
    I have not flattered its rank breath, nor bowed
    To its idolatries a patient knee,
    Nor coined my cheek to smiles, — nor cried aloud
    In worship of an echo: in the crowd
    They could not deem me one of such — I stood
    Among them, but not of them — in a shroud
    Of thoughts which were not their thoughts, and still could,
Had I not filed my mind, which thus itself subdue.

113:9. *filed*: defiled.

114

I have not loved the World, nor the World me, —
  But let us part fair foes; I do believe,
  Though I have found them not, that there may be
  Words which are things, — hopes which will not deceive,
  And Virtues which are merciful, nor weave
  Snares for the failing; I would also deem
  O'er others' griefs that some sincerely grieve —
  That two, or one, are almost what they seem, —
That Goodness is no name — and Happiness no dream.

115

My daughter! with thy name this song begun!
  My daughter! with thy name thus much shall end! —
  I see thee not — I hear thee not — but none
  Can be so wrapt in thee; Thou art the Friend
  To whom the shadows of far years extend:
  Albeit my brow thou never should'st behold,
  My voice shall with thy future visions blend,
  And reach into thy heart, — when mine is cold, —
A token and a tone, even from thy father's mould.

116

To aid thy mind's development, — to watch
  Thy dawn of little joys, — to sit and see
  Almost thy very growth, — to view thee catch
  Knowledge of objects, — wonders yet to thee!
  To hold thee lightly on a gentle knee,
  And print on thy soft cheek a parent's kiss, —
  This, it should seem, was not reserved for me —
  Yet this was in my nature: — as it is,
I know not what is there, yet something like to this.

117

Yet, though dull Hate as duty should be taught,
  I know that thou wilt love me: though my name
  Should be shut from thee, as a spell still fraught

With desolation, and a broken claim:
Though the grave closed between us, — 'twere the same,
I know that thou wilt love me — though to drain
My blood from out thy being were an aim,
And an attainment, — all would be in vain, —
Still thou would'st love me, still that more than life retain.

118

The child of Love! though born in bitterness,
    And nurtured in Convulsion! Of thy sire
    These were the elements, — and thine no less.
    As yet such are around thee, — but thy fire
    Shall be more tempered, and thy hope far higher!
    Sweet be thy cradled slumbers! O'er the sea
    And from the mountains where I now respire,
    Fain would I waft such blessing upon thee,
As — with a sigh — I deem thou might'st have been to me!

1816   *1816*

CANTO THE FOURTH

1

I STOOD in Venice, on the "Bridge of Sighs;"
    A Palace and a prison on each hand:
    I saw from out the wave her structures rise
    As from the stroke of the Enchanter's wand:
    A thousand Years their cloudy wings expand
    Around me, and a dying Glory smiles
    O'er the far times, when many a subject land
    Looked to the wingéd Lion's marble piles,
Where Venice sate in state, throned on her hundred isles!

1:1. *Bridge of Sighs*: A covered bridge between the Doge's palace and
the prison of San Marco.
1:7. *winged Lion*: Emblem of St. Mark, patron saint of Venice.

2

She looks a sea Cybele, fresh from Ocean,
 Rising with her tiara of proud towers
 At airy distance, with majestic motion,
 A Ruler of the waters and their powers:
 And such she was; — her daughters had their dowers
 From spoils of nations, and the exhaustless East
 Poured in her lap all gems in sparkling showers.
 In purple was she robed, and of her feast
Monarchs partook, and deemed their dignity increased.

3

In Venice Tasso's echoes are no more,
 And silent rows the songless Gondolier;
 Her palaces are crumbing to the shore,
 And Music meets not always now the ear:
 Those days are gone — but Beauty still is here.
 States fall — Arts fade — but Nature doth not die,
 Nor yet forget how Venice once was dear,
 The pleasant place of all festivity,
The Revel of the earth — the Masque of Italy!

4

But unto us she hath a spell beyond
 Her name in story, and her long array
 Of mighty shadows, whose dim forms despond
 Above the Dogeless city's vanished sway;
 Ours is a trophy which will not decay
 With the Rialto; Shylock and the Moor,

2:1. *Cybele*: Mother of the Gods in Greek mythology who was generally represented in art as wearing a crown of towers.

3:1. *Tasso's echoes*: Until the latter part of the eighteenth century
gondoliers were accustomed to sing to each other alternate stanzas of
Tasso's *Jerusalem Delivered*.

4:4. *dogeless city*: The last doge (duke) of Venice was deposed by
Napoleon in 1797. In 1817 Venice was an Austrian possession.

4:6. *Rialto*: The site of the original city and once the financial and

And Pierre, can not be swept or worn away —
The keystones of the Arch! though all were o'er,
For us repeopled were the solitary shore.

5

The Beings of the Mind are not of clay:
Essentially immortal, they create
And multiply in us a brighter ray
And more beloved existence: that which Fate
Prohibits to dull life in this our state
Of mortal bondage, by these Spirits supplied,
First exiles, then replaces what we hate;
Watering the heart whose early flowers have died,
And with a fresher growth replenishing the void.

6

Such is the refuge of our youth and age —
The first from Hope, the last from Vacancy;
And this wan feeling peoples many a page —
And, may be, that which grows beneath mine eye:
Yet there are things whose strong reality
Outshines our fairy-land; in shape and hues
More beautiful than our fantastic sky,
And the strange constellations which the Muse
O'er her wild universe is skilful to diffuse:

7

I saw or dreamed of such, — but let them go, —
They came like Truth — and disappeared like dreams;
And whatsoe'er they were — are now but so:
I could replace them if I would; still teems
My mind with many a form which aptly seems
Such as I sought for, and at moments found;

commercial center. Byron uses the word symbolically for the former greatness of Venice as the center of Mediterranean trade.
    Shylock and the Moor: In Shakespeare's *Merchant of Venice* and *Othello*.
    4:7. *Pierre*: A tragic character in Thomas Otway's *Venice Preserved*
(1682).

Let these too go — for waking Reason deems
Such over-weening phantasies unsound,
And their voices speak, and other sights surround.

8

I've taught me other tongues — and in strange eyes
Have made me not a stranger; to the mind
Which is itself, no changes bring surprise;
Nor is it harsh to make, nor hard to find
A country with — aye, or without mankind;
Yet was I born where men are proud to be, —
Not without cause; and should I leave behind
The inviolate Island of the sage and free,
And seek me out a home by a remoter sea,

9

Perhaps I loved it well; and should I lay
My ashes in a soil which is not mine,
My Spirit shall resume it — if we may
Unbodied choose a sanctuary. I twine
My hopes of being remembered in my line
With my land's language: if too fond and far
These aspirations in their scope incline, —
If my Fame should be, as my fortunes are,
Of hasty growth and blight, and dull Oblivion bar

10

My name from out the temple where the dead
Are honoured by the Nations — let it be —
And light the Laurels on a loftier head!
And be the Spartan's epitaph on me —
"Sparta hath many a worthier son than he."
Meantime I seek no sympathies, nor need —
The thorns which I have reaped are of the tree

10:4. *Spartan's epitaph*: Answer of the mother of Brasidas, Spartan
general, killed in battle in 422 B.C., when he was praised by strangers as
a hero.

I planted, — they have torn me, — and I bleed:
I should have known what fruit would spring from such a seed.

* * * * * * *

18

I loved her from my boyhood — she to me
  Was as a fairy city of the heart,
  Rising like water-columns from the sea —
  Of Joy the sojourn, and of Wealth the mart;
  And Otway, Radcliffe, Schiller, Shakespeare's art,
  Had stamped her image in me, and even so,
  Although I found her thus, we did not part;
  Perchance even dearer in her day of woe,
Than when she was a boast, a marvel, and a show.

19

I can repeople with the past — and of
  The present there is still for eye and thought,
  And meditation chastened down, enough;
  And more, it may be, than I hoped or sought;
  And of the happiest moments which were wrought
  Within the web of my existence, some
  From thee, fair Venice! have their colours caught:
  There are some feelings Time can not benumb,
Nor Torture shake, or mine would now be cold and dumb.

20

But from their nature will the Tannen grow
  Loftiest on loftiest and least sheltered rocks,
  Rooted in barrenness, where nought below
  Of soil supports them 'gainst the Alpine shocks
  Of eddying storms; yet springs the trunk, and mocks
  The howling tempest, till its height and frame
  Are worthy of the mountains from whose blocks

18:5. *Radcliffe, Schiller*: Mrs. Ann Radcliffe wrote the *Mysteries of Udolpho* (1794); J. C. F. von Schiller, *The Ghost Seer* (1789).
20:1. *Tannen*: Firs.

Of bleak, gray granite into life it came,
And grew a giant tree; — the Mind may grow the same.

21

Existence may be borne, and the deep root
    Of life and sufferance make its firm abode
    In bare and desolated bosoms: mute
    The camel labours with the heaviest load,
    And the wolf dies in silence — not bestowed
    In vain should such example be; if they,
    Things of ignoble or of savage mood,
    Endure and shrink not, we of nobler clay
May temper it to bear, — it is but for a day.

22

All suffering doth destroy, or is destroyed,
    Even by the sufferer — and, in each event,
    Ends: — Some, with hope replenished and rebuoyed,
    Return to whence they came — with like intent,
    And weave their web again; some, bowed and bent,
    Wax gray and ghastly, withering ere their time,
    And perish with the reed on which they leant;
    Some seek devotion — toil — war — good or crime,
According as their souls were formed to sink or climb.

23

But ever and anon of griefs subdued
    There comes a token like a Scorpion's sting,
    Scarce seen, but with fresh bitterness imbued;
    And slight withal may be the things which bring
    Back on the heart the weight which it would fling
    Aside for ever: it may be a sound —
    A tone of music — summer's eve — or spring —
    A flower — the wind — the Ocean — which shall wound,
Striking the electric chain wherewith we are darkly bound;

24

And how and why we know not, nor can trace
    Home to its cloud this lightning of the mind,

But feel the shock renewed, nor can efface
The blight and blackening which it leaves behind,
Which out of things familiar, undesigned,
When least we deem of such, calls up to view
The Spectres whom no exorcism can bind, —
The cold — the changed — perchance the dead, anew —
The mourned — the loved — the lost — too many! yet how few!

25

But my Soul wanders; I demand it back
To meditate amongst decay, and stand
A ruin amidst ruins; there to track
Fall'n states and buried greatness, o'er a land
Which *was* the mightiest in its old command,
And *is* the loveliest, and must ever be
The master-mould of Nature's heavenly hand;
Wherein were cast the heroic and the free, —
The beautiful — the brave — the Lords of earth and sea,

26

The Commonwealth of Kings — the Men of Rome!
And even since, and now, fair Italy!
Thou art the Garden of the World, the Home
Of all Art yields, and Nature can decree;
Even in thy desert, what is like to thee?
Thy very weeds are beautiful — thy waste
More rich than other climes' fertility;
Thy wreck a glory — and thy ruin graced
With an immaculate charm which cannot be defaced.

27

The Moon is up, and yet it is not night —
Sunset divides the sky with her — a sea
Of glory streams along the Alpine height
Of blue Friuli's mountains; Heaven is free
From clouds, but of all colours seems to be, —
Melted to one vast Iris of the West, —
Where the Day joins the past Eternity;

While, on the other hand, meek Dian's crest
Floats through the azure air — an island of the blest!

28

A single star is at her side, and reigns
  With her o'er half the lovely heaven; but still
  Yon sunny Sea heaves brightly, and remains
  Rolled o'er the peak of the far Rhætian hill,
  As Day and Night contending were, until
  Nature reclaimed her order: — gently flows
  The deep-dyed Brenta, where their hues instil
  The odorous purple of a new-born rose,
Which streams upon her stream, and glassed within it glows,

29

Filled with the face of heaven, which, from afar,
  Comes down upon the waters! all its hues,
  From the rich sunset to the rising star,
  Their magical variety diffuse:
  And now they change — a paler Shadow strews
  Its mantle o'er the mountains; parting Day
  Dies like the Dolphin, whom each pang imbues
  With a new colour as it gasps away —
The last still loveliest, till — 'tis gone — and all is gray.

• • • • • • •

78

Oh, Rome! my Country! City of the Soul!
  The orphans of the heart must turn to thee,
  Lone Mother of dead Empires! and control
  In their shut breasts their petty misery.
  What are our woes and sufferance? Come and see
  The cypress — hear the owl — and plod your way
  O'er steps of broken thrones and temples — Ye!
  Whose agonies are evils of a day —
A world is at our feet as fragile as our clay.

79

The Niobe of nations! there she stands,
  Childless and crownless, in her voiceless woe;
  An empty urn within her withered hands,
  Whose holy dust was scattered long ago;
  The Scipios' tomb contains no ashes now;
  The very sepulchres lie tenantless
  Of their heroic dwellers: dost thou flow,
  Old Tiber! through a marble wilderness?
Rise, with thy yellow waves, and mantle her distress.

80

The Goth, the Christian — Time — War — Flood, and Fire,
  Have dealt upon the seven-hilled City's pride;
  She saw her glories star by star expire,
  And up the steep barbarian Monarchs ride,
  Where the car climbed the Capitol; far and wide
  Temple and tower went down, nor left a site:
  Chaos of ruins! who shall trace the void,
  O'er the dim fragments cast a lunar light,
And say, "here was, or is," where all is doubly night?

81

The double night of ages, and of her,
  Night's daughter, Ignorance, hath wrapt and wrap
  All around us; we but feel our way to err:
  The Ocean hath his chart, the Stars their map,
  And Knowledge spreads them on her ample lap;
  But Rome is as the desert — where we steer
  Stumbling o'er recollections; now we clap
  Our hands, and cry "Eureka!" "it is clear" —
When but some false Mirage of ruin rises near.

79:1. *Niobe*: In Greek mythology the queen whose twelve children were killed before her eyes and who became the symbol of eternal sorrow.
  79:5. *Scipios' tomb*: Discovered and rifled in 1780.
  80:5. *car*: The chariot during celebrations of the Roman Triumphs.

82

Alas! the lofty city! and alas!
  The trebly hundred triumphs! and the day
  When Brutus made the dagger's edge surpass
  The Conqueror's sword in bearing fame away!
  Alas, for Tully's voice and Virgil's lay,
  And Livy's pictured page! — but these shall be
  Her resurrection; all beside — decay.
  Alas, for Earth, for never shall we see
That brightness in her eye she bore when Rome was free!

•   •   •   •   •   •   •

93

What from this barren being do we reap?
  Our senses narrow, and our reason frail,
  Life short, and truth a gem which loves the deep,
  And all things weighed in Custom's falsest scale;
  Opinion an Omnipotence, — whose veil
  Mantles the earth with darkness, until right
  And wrong are accidents, and Men grow pale
  Lest their own judgments should become too bright,
And their free thoughts be crimes, and Earth have too much
  light.

94

And thus they plod in sluggish misery,
  Rotting from sire to son, and age to age,
  Proud of their trampled nature, and so die,
  Bequeathing their hereditary rage
  To the new race of inborn slaves, who wage
  War for their chains, and rather than be free,
  Bleed gladiator-like, and still engage

82:2. *trebly hundred triumphs*: The 320 triumphs, honoring successful
generals, which were supposed to have taken place from the founding
of Rome to its decline.
82:5. *Tully's voice*: Cicero's.

Within the same Arena where they see
Their fellows fall before, like leaves of the same tree.

95

I speak not of men's creeds — they rest between
   Man and his Maker — but of things allowed,
   Averred, and known, and daily, hourly seen —
   The yoke that is upon us doubly bowed,
   And the intent of Tyranny avowed,
   The edict of Earth's rulers, who are grown
   The apes of him who humbled once the proud,
   And shook them from their slumbers on the throne;
Too glorious, were this all his mighty arm had done.

96

Can tyrants but by tyrants conquered be,
   And Freedom find no Champion and no Child
   Such as Columbia saw arise when she
   Sprung forth a Pallas, armed and undefiled?
   Or must such minds be nourished in the wild,
   Deep in the unpruned forest, 'midst the roar
   Of cataracts, where nursing Nature smiled
   On infant Washington? Has Earth no more
Such seeds within her breast, or Europe no such shore?

97

But France got drunk with blood to vomit crime;
   And fatal have her Saturnalia been
   To Freedom's cause, in every age and clime;
   Because the deadly days which we have seen,
   And vile Ambition, that built up between
   Man and his hopes an adamantine wall,
   And the base pageant last upon the scene,
   Are grown the pretext for the eternal thrall

96:4. *Pallas*: Pallas Athena, Goddess of Wisdom. According to legend, she sprang full grown and armed from the head of her father, Zeus.

97:7. *base pageant*: The Congress of Vienna (1815) and the Holy Alliance. See Canto III, stanza 19.

Which nips Life's tree, and dooms Man's worst — his second
    fall.

98

Yet, Freedom! yet thy banner, torn, but flying,
    Streams like the thunder-storm *against* the wind;
    Thy trumpet voice, though broken now and dying,
    The loudest still the Tempest leaves behind;
    Thy tree hath lost its blossoms, and the rind,
    Chopped by the axe, looks rough and little worth,
    But the sap lasts, — and still the seed we find
    Sown deep, even in the bosom of the North;
So shall a better spring less bitter fruit bring forth.

• • • • • • •

107

Cypress and ivy, weed and wallflower grown
    Matted and massed together — hillocks heaped
    On what were chambers — arch crushed, column strown
    In fragments — chocked up vaults, and frescos steeped
    In subterranean damps, where the owl peeped,
    Deeming it midnight: — Temples — Baths — or Halls?
    Pronounce who can: for all that Learning reaped
    From her research hath been, that these are walls —
Behold the Imperial Mount! 'tis thus the Mighty falls.

108

There is the moral of all human tales;
    'Tis but the same rehearsal of the past,
    First Freedom, and then Glory — when that fails,
    Wealth — Vice — Corruption, — Barbarism at last.
    And History, with all her volumes vast,
    Hath but *one* page, — 'tis better written here,
    Where gorgeous Tyranny hath thus amassed
    All treasures, all delights, that Eye or Ear,

107:9. *Imperial Mount*: The Palatine hill, most important of the seven
hills of Rome, where the Caesars built their palaces.

Heart, Soul could seek — Tongue ask — Away with words!
  draw near,

109

Admire — exult — despise — laugh — weep, — for here
  There is such matter for all feeling: — Man!
  Thou pendulum betwixt a smile and tear,
  Ages and Realms are crowded in this span,
  This mountain, whose obliterated plan
  The pyramid of Empires pinnacled,
  Of Glory's gewgaws shining in the van
  Till the Sun's rays with added flame were filled!
Where are its golden roofs? where those who dared to build?

• • • • • • •

120

Alas! our young affections run to waste,
  Or water but the desert! whence arise
  But weeds of dark luxuriance, tares of haste,
  Rank at the core, though tempting to the eyes
  Flowers whose wild odours breathe but agonies,
  And trees whose gums are poison; such the plants
  Which spring beneath her steps as Passion flies
  O'er the World's wilderness, and vainly pants
For some celestial fruit forbidden to our wants.

121

Oh, Love! no habitant of earth thou art —
  An unseen Seraph, we believe in thee, —
  A faith whose martyrs are the broken heart, —
  But never yet hath seen, nor e'er shall see
  The naked eye, thy form, as it should be;
  The mind hath made thee, as it peopled Heaven,
  Even with its own desiring phantasy,
  And to a thought such shape and image given,

  109:9. *golden roofs*: Nero's *Domus Aurea* (Golden House), the most
spectacular of the palaces.

As haunts the unquenched soul — parched — wearied —
wrung — and riven.

122

Of its own beauty is the mind diseased,
   And fevers into false creation: — where,
   Where are the forms the sculptor's soul hath seized?
   In him alone. Can Nature show so fair?
   Where are the charms and virtues which we dare
   Conceive in boyhood and pursue as men,
   The unreached Paradise of our despair,
   Which o'er-informs the pencil and the pen,
And overpowers the page where it would bloom again?

123

Who loves, raves — 'tis youth's frenzy — but the cure
   Is bitterer still, as charm by charm unwinds
   Which robed our idols, and we see too sure
   Nor Worth nor Beauty dwells from out the mind's
   Ideal shape of such; yet still it binds
   The fatal spell, and still it draws us on,
   Reaping the whirlwind from the oft-sown winds;
   The stubborn heart, its alchemy begun,
Seems ever near the prize — wealthiest when most undone.

124

We wither from our youth, we gasp away —
   Sick — sick; unfound the boon — unslaked the thirst,
   Though to the last, in verge of our decay,
   Some phantom lures, such as we sought at first —
   But all too late, — so are we doubly curst.
   Love, Fame, Ambition, Avarice — 'tis the same,
   Each idle — and all ill — and none the worst —
   For all are meteors with a different name,
And Death the sable smoke where vanishes the flame.

125

Few — none — find what they love or could have loved,
   Though accident, blind contact, and the strong

Necessity of loving, have removed
Antipathies — but to recur, ere long,
Envenomed with irrevocable wrong;
And Circumstance, that unspiritual God
And Miscreator, makes and helps along
Our coming evils with a crutch-like rod,
Whose touch turns Hope to dust, — the dust we all have trod.

126

Our life is a false nature — 'tis not in
The harmony of things, — this hard decree,
This uneradicable taint of Sin,
This boundless Upas, this all-blasting tree,
Whose root is Earth — whose leaves and branches be
The skies which rain their plagues on men like dew —
Disease, death, bondage — all the woes we see,
And worse, the woes we see not — which throb through
The immedicable soul, with heart-aches ever new.

127

Yet let us ponder boldly — 'tis a base
Abandonment of reason to resign
Our right of thought — our last and only place
Of refuge; this, at least, shall still be mine:
Though from our birth the Faculty divine
Is chained and tortured — cabined, cribbed, confined,
And bred in darkness, lest the Truth should shine
Too brightly in the unpreparéd mind,
The beam pours in — for Time and Skill will couch the blind.

128

Arches on arches! as it were that Rome,
Collecting the chief trophies of her line,
Would build up all her triumphs in one dome,
Her Coliseum stands; the moonbeams shine

126:4. *upas*: A Javanese tree that yields an intensely poisonous milky juice used as an arrow poison. There was a widespread legend in the late eighteenth century that the tree destroyed all animal life within a radius of 15 miles.

As 'twere its natural torches — for divine
  Should be the light which streams here, — to illume
  This long-explored but still exhaustless mine
  Of Contemplation; and the azure gloom
Of an Italian night, where the deep skies assume

129

Hues which have words, and speak to ye of Heaven,
  Floats o'er this vast and wondrous monument,
  And shadows forth its glory. There is given
  Unto the things of earth, which Time hath bent,
  A Spirit's feeling, and where he hath leant
  His hand, but broke his scythe, there is a power
  And magic in the ruined battlement,
  For which the Palace of the present hour
Must yield its pomp, and wait till Ages are its dower.

130

Oh, Time! the Beautifier of the dead,
  Adorner of the ruin — Comforter
  And only Healer when the heart hath bled;
  Time! the Corrector where our judgments err,
  The test of Truth, Love — sole philosopher,
  For all beside are sophists — from thy thrift,
  Which never loses though it doth defer —
  Time, the Avenger! unto thee I lift
My hands, and eyes, and heart, and crave of thee a gift:

131

Amidst this wreck, where thou hast made a shrine
  And temple more divinely desolate —
  Among thy mightier offerings here are mine,
  Ruins of years — though few, yet full of fate: —
  If thou hast ever seen me too elate,
  Hear me not; but if calmly I have borne
  Good, and reserved my pride against the hate
  Which shall not whelm me, let me not have worn
This iron in my soul in vain — shall *they* not mourn?

132

And Thou, who never yet of human wrong
  Left the unbalanced scale, great Nemesis!
  Here, where the ancient paid thee homage long —
  Thou, who didst call the Furies from the abyss,
  And round Orestes bade them howl and hiss
  For that unnatural retribution — just,
  Had it but been from hands less near — in this
  Thy former realm, I call thee from the dust!
Dost thou not hear my heart? — Awake! thou shalt, and must.

133

It is not that I may not have incurred,
  For my ancestral faults or mine, the wound
  I bleed withal; and, had it been conferred
  With a just weapon, it had flowed unbound;
  But now my blood shall not sink in the ground —
  To thee I do devote it — *Thou* shalt take
  The vengeance, which shall yet be sought and found —
  Which if *I* have not taken for the sake ——
But let that pass — I sleep — but Thou shalt yet awake.

134

And if my voice break forth, 'tis not that now
  I shrink from what is suffered: let him speak
  Who hath beheld decline upon my brow,
  Or seen my mind's convulsion leave it weak;
  But in this page a record will I seek.
  Not in the air shall these my words disperse,
  Though I be ashes; a far hour shall wreak
  The deep prophetic fulness of this verse,
And pile on human heads the mountain of my curse!

132:2. *Nemesis*: Greek goddess representing fortune and specifically the avenger of crimes. Orestes had killed his mother, Clytemnestra, to avenge his father, Agamemnon, and in punishment had been hounded by the Furies. Byron's meaning is that, unlike Orestes, he will not take vengeance for his disgrace upon himself but will leave the retribution to Nemesis.

135

That curse shall be Forgiveness. — Have I not —
  Hear me, my mother Earth! behold it, Heaven! —
  Have I not had to wrestle with my lot?
  Have I not suffered things to be forgiven?
  Have I not had my brain seared, my heart riven,
  Hopes sapped, name blighted. Life's life lied away?
  And only not to desperation driven,
  Because not altogether of such clay
As rots into the souls of those whom I survey.

136

From mighty wrongs to petty perfidy
  Have I not seen what human things could do?
  From the loud roar of foaming calumny
  To the small whisper of the as paltry few —
  And subtler venom of the reptile crew,
  The Janus glance of whose significant eye,
  Learning to lie with silence, would *seem* true —
  And without utterance, save the shrug or sigh,
Deal round to happy fools its speechless obloquy.

137

But I have lived, and have not lived in vain:
  My mind may lose its force, my blood its fire,
  And my frame perish even in conquering pain;
  But there is that within me which shall tire
  Torture and Time, and breathe when I expire;
  Something unearthly, which they deem not of,
  Like the remembered tone of a mute lyre,
  Shall on their softened spirits sink, and move
In hearts all rocky now the late remorse of Love.

138

The seal is set. — Now welcome, thou dread Power!
  Nameless, yet thus omnipotent, which here

136:6. *Janus glance*: A Roman god with two faces, one seeing the past, the other the future. Byron uses the word here in the sense of "two-faced." He is accusing his wife and her supporters of duplicity.

Walk'st in the shadow of the midnight hour
With a deep awe, yet all distinct from fear;
Thy haunts are ever where the dead walls rear
Their ivy mantles, and the solemn scene
Derives from thee a sense so deep and clear
That we become a part of what has been,
And grow upon the spot — all-seeing but unseen.

139

And here the buzz of eager nations ran,
  In murmured pity, or loud-roared applause,
  As man was slaughtered by his fellow man.
  And wherefore slaughtered? wherefore, but because
  Such were the bloody Circus' genial laws,
  And the imperial pleasure. — Wherefore not?
  What matters where we fall to fill the maws
  Of worms — on battle-plains or listed spot?
Both are but theatres — where the chief actors rot.

140

I see before me the Gladiator lie:
  He leans upon his hand — his manly brow
  Consents to death, but conquers agony,
  And his drooped head sinks gradually low —
  And through his side the last drops, ebbing slow
  From the red gash, fall heavy, one by one,
  Like the first of a thunder-shower; and now
  The arena swims around him — he is gone,
Ere ceased the inhuman shout which hailed the wretch who won.

141

He heard it, but he heeded not — his eyes
  Were with his heart — and that was far away;
  He recked not of the life he lost nor prize,

139:8. *listed spot*: The field of the list of tournament, such as the arena
of the Coliseum.
140:1. *Gladiator*: Byron's description is suggested by the famous statue,
usually called the *Dying Gaul*.

But where his rude hut by the Danube lay —
There were his young barbarians all at play,
There was their Dacian mother — he, their sire,
Butchered to make a Roman holiday —
All this rushed with his blood — Shall he expire
And unavenged? — Arise! ye Goths, and glut your ire!

142

But here, where Murder breathed her bloody steam; —
And here, where buzzing nations choked the ways,
And roared or murmured like a mountain stream
Dashing or winding as it torrent strays;
Here, where the Roman million's blame or praise
Was Death or Life — the playthings of a crowd —
My voice sounds much — and fall the stars' faint rays
On the arena void — seats crushed — walls bowed —
And galleries, where my steps seem echoes strangely loud.

143

A Ruin — yet what Ruin! from its mass
Walls — palaces — half-cities, have been reared;
Yet oft the enormous skeleton ye pass,
And marvel where the spoil could have appeared.
Hath it indeed been plundered, or but cleared?
Alas! developed, opens the decay,
When the colossal fabric's form is neared:
It will not bear the brightness of the day,
Which streams too much on all — years — man — have reft
away.

144

But when the rising moon begins to climb
Its topmost arch, and gently pauses there —

141:6. *Dacian*: The Roman Emperor Trajan conquered Dacia (modern Rumania) in A.D. 101 and brought 10,000 Dacians back to Rome as gladiators.
141:9. *Arise! ye Goths*: The Goths under Alaric sacked Rome in A.D. 410.
142:6. *playthings of a crowd*: According to its whim, a crowd spared or condemned to death a wounded gladiator, by turning thumbs up or down.

When the stars twinkle through the loops of Time,
And the low night-breeze waves along the air
The garland-forest, which the gray walls wear,
Like laurels on the bald first Cæsar's head —
When the light shines serene but doth not glare —
Then in this magic circle raise the dead; —
Heroes have trod this spot — 'tis on their dust ye tread.

145

"While stands the Coliseum, Rome shall stand:
"When falls the Coliseum, Rome shall fall;
"And when Rome falls — the World." From our own land
Thus spake the pilgrims o'er this mighty wall
In Saxon times, which we are wont to call
Ancient; and these three mortal things are still
On their foundations, and unaltered all —
Rome and her Ruin past Redemption's skill —
The World — the same wide den — of thieves, or what ye will.

• • • • • • •

153

But lo! the Dome — the vast and wondrous Dome,
To which Diana's marvel was a cell —
Christ's mighty shrine above His martyr's tomb!
I have beheld the Ephesian's miracle —
Its columns strew the wilderness, and dwell
The hyæna and the jackal in their shade;

144:6. *bald first Caesar's head*: "Suetonius," says Byron, "informs us
that Julius Caesar was particularly gratified by that decree of the senate
which enabled him to wear a wreath of laurel on all occasions. He was
anxious not to show that he was conqueror of the world, but to hide that
he was bald."

145:1-3. *"While stands the Coliseum. . . ."* Quoted by Gibbon in *Decline and Fall of the Roman Empire* from the Venerable Bede and
ascribed to Anglo-Saxon pilgrims of the eighth century.

153:1. *the dome*: Church of St. Peter's.

153:2. *Diana's marvel*: the second temple of Artemis (Diana) at Ephesus.
The ruins (l. 4) that Byron saw in 1810 were not, however, those of the
temple, which was not uncovered until 1870, but probably of the gym-
nasium.

I have beheld Sophia's bright roofs swell
    Their glittering mass i' the Sun, and have surveyed
Its sanctuary the while the usurping Moslem prayed;

154

But thou, of temples old, or altars new,
    Standest alone — with nothing like to thee —
    Worthiest of God, the Holy and the True!
    Since Zion's desolation, when that He
    Forsook his former city, what could be,
    Of earthly structures, in His honour piled,
    Of a sublimer aspect? Majesty —
    Power — Glory — Strength — and Beauty all are aisled
In this eternal Ark of worship undefiled.

155

Enter: its grandeur overwhelms thee not;
    And why? it is not lessened — but thy mind,
    Expanded by the Genius of the spot,
    Has grown colossal, and can only find
    A fit abode wherein appear enshrined
    Thy hopes of Immortality — and thou
    Shalt one day, if found worthy, so defined
    See thy God face to face, as thou dost now
His Holy of Holies — nor be blasted by his brow.

156

Thou movest — but increasing with the advance,
    Like climbing some great Alp, which still doth rise,
    Deceived by its gigantic elegance —
    Vastness which grows, but grows to harmonize —
    All musical in its immensities;
    Rich marbles, richer painting — shrines where flame
    The lamps of gold — and haughty dome which vies
    In air with Earth's chief structures, though their frame
Sits on the firm-set ground — and this the clouds must claim.

153:7. *Sophia's bright roofs*: Church of St. Sophia in Constantinople.

157

Thou seest not all — but piecemeal thou must break,
  To separate contemplation, the great whole;
  And as the Ocean many bays will make
  That ask the eye — so here condense thy soul
  To more immediate objects, and control
  Thy thoughts until thy mind hath got by heart
  Its eloquent proportions, and unroll
  In mighty graduations, part by part,
The Glory which at once upon thee did not dart,

158

Not by its fault — but thine: Our outward sense
  Is but of gradual grasp — and as it is
  That what we have of feeling most intense
  Outstrips our faint expression; even so this
  Outshining and o'erwhelming edifice
  Fools our fond gaze, and greatest of the great
  Defies at first our Nature's littleness,
  Till, growing with its growth, we thus dilate
Our Spirits to the size of that they contemplate.

159

Then pause, and be enlightened; there is more
  In such a survey than the sating gaze
  Of wonder pleased, or awe which would adore
  The worship of the place, or the mere praise
  Of Art and its great Masters, who could raise
  What former time, nor skill, nor thought could plan:
  The fountain of Sublimity displays
  Its depth, and thence may draw the mind of Man
Its golden sands, and learn what great Conceptions can.

160

Or, turning to the Vatican, go see
  Laocoön's torture dignifying pain —

160:2. *Laocoön's torture*: A sculptured group in the Vatican museum
shows Laocoon and his two sons being squeezed to death by sea-serpents.

A Father's love and Mortal's agony
With an Immortal's patience blending: — Vain
The struggle — vain, against the coiling strain
And gripe, and deepening of the dragon's grasp,
The Old Man's clench; the long envenomed chain
Rivets the living links, — the enormous Asp
Enforces pang on pang, and stifles gasp on gasp.

161

Or view the Lord of the unerring bow,
The God of Life, and Poesy, and Light —
The Sun in human limbs arrayed, and brow
All radiant from his triumph in the fight;
The shaft hath just been shot — the arrow bright
With an Immortal's vengeance — in his eye
And nostril beautiful Disdain, and Might
And Majesty, flash their full lightnings by,
Developing in that one glance the Deity.

162

But in his delicate form — a dream of Love,
Shaped by some solitary Nymph, whose breast
Longed for a deathless lover from above,
And maddened in that vision — are exprest
All that ideal Beauty ever blessed
The mind with in its most unearthly mood,
When each Conception was a heavenly Guest —
A ray of Immortality — and stood,
Starlike, around, until they gathered to a God!

163

And if it be Prometheus stole from Heaven
The fire which we endure — it was repaid
By him to whom the energy was given
Which this poetic marble hath arrayed
With an eternal Glory — which, if made

161:1. *Lord of the unerring bow*: The Apollo Belvedere.

By human hands, is not of human thought —
And Time himself hath hallowed it, nor laid
One ringlet in the dust — nor hath it caught
A tinge of years, but breathes the flame with which 'twas
wrought.

• • • • • • •

175

But I forget. — My Pilgrim's shrine is won,
And he and I must part, — so let it be, —
His task and mine alike are nearly done;
Yet once more let us look upon the Sea;
The Midland Ocean breaks on him and me,
And from the Alban Mount we now behold
Our friend of youth, that Ocean, which when we
Beheld it last by Calpe's rock unfold
Those waves, we followed on till the dark Euxine rolled

176

Upon the blue Symplegades: long years —
Long, though not very many — since have done
Their work on both; some suffering and some tears
Have left us nearly where we had begun:
Yet not in vain our mortal race hath run —
We have had our reward — and it is here, —
That we can yet feel gladdened by the Sun,
And reap from Earth — Sea — joy almost as dear
As if there were no Man to trouble what is clear.

175:1. *But I forget*: Byron's reflections on Rome have led him into
numerous digressions.
175:5. *Midland Ocean*: The Mediterranean.
175:6. *Alban Mount*: The Alban hills near Rome.
175:8. *Calpe's rock*: Gibraltar. Byron is recalling his voyage through
the Mediterranean in 1809.
175:9. *Euxine*: Black Sea.
176:1. *Symplegades*: Two islands in the passage between the Black Sea
and the Bosporus.

177

Oh! that the Desert were my dwelling-place,
   With one fair Spirit for my minister,
   That I might all forget the human race,
   And, hating no one, love but only her!
   Ye elements! — in whose ennobling stir
   I feel myself exalted — Can ye not
   Accord me such a Being? Do I err
   In deeming such inhabit many a spot?
Though with them to converse can rarely be our lot.

178

There is a pleasure in the pathless woods,
   There is a rapture on the lonely shore,
   There is society, where none intrudes,
   By the deep Sea, and Music in its roar:
   I love not Man the less, but Nature more,
   From these our interviews, in which I steal
   From all I may be, or have been before,
   To mingle with the Universe, and feel
What I can ne'er express — yet can not all conceal.

179

Roll on, thou deep and dark blue Ocean — roll!
   Ten thousand fleets sweep over thee in vain;
   Man marks the earth with ruin — his control
   Stops with the shore; — upon the watery plain
   The wrecks are all thy deed, nor doth remain
   A shadow of man's ravage, save his own,
   When, for a moment, like a drop of rain,
   He sinks into thy depths with bubbling groan —
Without a grave — unknelled, uncoffined, and unknown.

177:2. Byron is probably thinking of Augusta.
178:8. See Canto III, stanza 72 ff. But note the difference between the views of nature presented there and in the following apostrophe to the ocean.

180

His steps are not upon thy paths, — thy fields
  Are not a spoil for him, — thou dost arise
  And shake him from thee; the vile strength he wields
  For Earth's destruction thou dost all despise,
  Spurning him from thy bosom to the skies —
  And send'st him, shivering in thy playful spray
  And howling, to his Gods, where haply lies
  His petty hope in some near port or bay,
And dashest him again to Earth: — there let him lay.

181

The armaments which thunderstrike the walls
  Of rock-built cities, bidding nations quake,
  And Monarchs tremble in their Capitals,
  The oak Leviathans, whose huge ribs make
  Their clay creator the vain title take
  Of Lord of thee, and Arbiter of War —
  These are thy toys, and, as the snowy flake,
  They melt into thy yeast of waves, which mar
Alike the Armada's pride or spoils of Trafalgar.

182

Thy shores are empires, changed in all save thee —
  Assyria — Greece — Rome — Carthage — what are they?
  Thy waters washed them power while they were free,
  And many a tyrant since; their shores obey
  The stranger, slave, or savage; their decay
  Has dried up realms to deserts: — not so thou,
  Unchangeable save to thy wild waves' play,
  Time writes no wrinkle on thine azure brow —
Such as Creation's dawn beheld, thou rollest now.

180:9. *lay*: A common substitution for "lie" in Byron's day.
181:9. *Armada's pride or spoils of Trafalgar*: Over half of the Spanish fleet invading England in 1588 was destroyed by storms; another storm destroyed most of the French ships captured by Nelson at Trafalgar in 1805.

183

Thou glorious mirror, where the Almighty's form
   Glasses itself in tempests; in all time,
   Calm or convulsed — in breeze, or gale, or storm —
   Icing the Pole, or in the torrid clime
   Dark-heaving — boundless, endless, and sublime —
   The image of Eternity — the throne
   Of the Invisible; even from out thy slime
   The monsters of the deep are made — each Zone
Obeys thee — thou goest forth, dread, fathomless, alone.

184

And I have loved thee, Ocean! and my joy
   Of youthful sports was on thy breast to be
   Borne, like thy bubbles, onward: from a boy
   I wantoned with thy breakers — they to me
   Were a delight; and if the freshening sea
   Made them a terror — 'twas a pleasing fear,
   For I was as it were a Child of thee,
   And trusted to thy billows far and near,
And laid my hand upon thy mane — as I do here.

185

My task is done — my song hath ceased — my theme
   Has died into an echo; it is fit
   The spell should break of this protracted dream.
   The torch shall be extinguished which hath lit
   My midnight lamp — and what is writ, is writ, —
   Would it were worthier! but I am not now
   That which I have been — and my visions flit
   Less palpably before me — and the glow
Which in my Spirit dwelt is fluttering, faint, and low.

186

Farewell! a word that must be, and hath been —
   A sound which makes us linger; — yet — farewell!
   Ye! who have traced the Pilgrim to the scene

Which is his last — if in your memories dwell
A thought which once was his — if on ye swell
A single recollection — not in vain
He wore his sandal-shoon, and scallop-shell;
Farewell! with *him* alone may rest the pain,
If such there were — with *you*, the Moral of his Strain.

1817   *1818*

186:7. Sandals indicated travel by land and a scallop shell, worn in the hat, travel by sea.

Tales

The Prisoner of Chillon

See headnote to *Sonnet on Chillon,* p. 35, above.

1

My hair is grey, but not with years,
   Nor grew it white
   In a single night,
As men's have grown from sudden fears:
My limbs are bowed, though not with toil,   5
   But rusted with a vile repose,
For they have been a dungeon's spoil,
   And mine has been the fate of those
To whom the goodly earth and air
Are banned, and barred — forbidden fare;   10
But this was for my father's faith
I suffered chains and courted death;
That father perished at the stake
For tenets he would not forsake;
And for the same his lineal race   15
In darkness found a dwelling place;
We were seven — who now are one,
   Six in youth, and one in age,
Finished as they had begun,
   Proud of Persecution's rage;   20
One in fire, and two in field,
Their belief with blood have sealed,
Dying as their father died,
For the God their foes denied; —
Three were in a dungeon cast,   25
Of whom this wreck is left the last.

2

There are seven pillars of Gothic mould,
In Chillon's dungeons deep and old,
There are seven columns, massy and grey,
Dim with a dull imprisoned ray,   30
A sunbeam which hath lost its way,
And through the crevice and the cleft
Of the thick wall is fallen and left;
Creeping o'er the floor so damp,
Like a marsh's meteor lamp: 35
And in each pillar there is a ring,
  And in each ring there is a chain;
That iron is a cankering thing,
  For in these limbs its teeth remain,
With marks that will not wear away,   40
Till I have done with this new day,
Which now is painful to these eyes,
Which have not seen the sun so rise
For years — I cannot count them o'er,
I lost their long and heavy score   45
When my last brother drooped and died,
And I lay living by his side.

3

They chained us each to a column stone,
And we were three — yet, each alone;
We could not move a single pace,   50
We could not see each other's face,
But with that pale and livid light
That made us strangers in our sight:
And thus together — yet apart,
Fettered in hand, but joined in heart,   55
'Twas still some solace in the dearth
Of the pure elements of earth,
To hearken to each other's speech,
And each turn comforter to each
With some new hope, or legend old,   60
Or song heroically bold;

But even these at length grew cold.
Our voices took a dreary tone,
An echo of the dungeon stone,
    A grating sound, not full and free,   65
    As they of yore were wont to be:
    It might be fancy — but to me
They never sounded like our own.

4

I was the eldest of the three,
    And to uphold and cheer the rest   70
    I ought to do — and did my best —
And each did well in his degree.
    The youngest, whom my father loved,
Because our mother's brow was given
To him, with eyes as blue as heaven —   75
    For him my soul was sorely moved:
And truly might it be distressed
To see such bird in such a nest;
For he was beautiful as day —
    (When day was beautiful to me   80
    As to young eagles, being free) —
    A polar day, which will not see
A sunset till its summer's gone,
    Its sleepless summer of long light,
The snow-clad offspring of the sun: 85
    And thus he was as pure and bright,
And in his natural spirit gay,
With tears for nought but others' ills,
And then they flowed like mountain rills,
Unless he could assuage the woe   90
Which he abhorred to view below.

5

The other was as pure of mind,
But formed to combat with his kind;
Strong in his frame, and of a mood
Which 'gainst the world in war had stood,   95

And perished in the foremost rank
   With joy: — but not in chains to pine:
His spirit withered with their clank,
   I saw it silently decline —
   And so perchance in sooth did mine: *100*
But yet I forced it on to cheer
Those relics of a home so dear.
He was a hunter of the hills,
   Had followed there the deer and wolf;
   To him this dungeon was a gulf,   *105*
And fettered feet the worst of ills.

6

   Lake Leman lies by Chillon's walls:
A thousand feet in depth below
Its massy waters meet and flow;
Thus much the fathom-line was sent   *110*
From Chillon's snow-white battlement,
   Which round about the wave inthralls:
A double dungeon wall and wave
Have made — and like a living grave.
Below the surface of the lake   *115*
The dark vault lies wherein we lay:
We heard it ripple night and day;
   Sounding o'er our heads it knocked;
And I have felt the winter's spray
Wash through the bars when winds were high   *120*
And wanton in the happy sky;
   And then the very rock hath rocked,
   And I have felt it shake, unshocked,
Because I could have smiled to see
The death that would have set me free.   *125*

7

I said my nearer brother pined,
I said his mighty heart declined,
He loathed and put away his food;
It was not that 'twas coarse and rude,

For we were used to hunter's fare, 130
And for the like had little care:
The milk drawn from the mountain goat
Was changed for water from the moat,
Our bread was such as captives' tears
Have moistened many a thousand years, 135
Since man first pent his fellow men
Like brutes within an iron den;
But what were these to us or him?
These wasted not his heart or limb;
My brother's soul was of that mould 140
Which in a palace had grown cold,
Had his free breathing been denied
The range of the steep mountain's side;
But why delay the truth? — he died.
I saw, and could not hold his head, 145
Nor reach his dying hand — nor dead, —
Though hard I strove, but strove in vain,
To rend and gnash my bonds in twain.
He died — and they unlocked his chain,
And scooped for him a shallow grave 150
Even from the cold earth of our cave.
I begged them, as a boon, to lay
His corse in dust whereon the day
Might shine — it was a foolish thought,
But then within my brain it wrought, 155
That even in death his freeborn breast
In such a dungeon could not rest.
I might have spared my idle prayer —
They coldly laughed — and laid him there:
The flat and turfless earth above 160
The being we so much did love;
His empty chain above it leant,
Such Murder's fitting monument!

8

But he, the favourite and the flower,
Most cherished since his natal hour, 165

His mother's image in fair face,
The infant love of all his race,
His martyred father's dearest thought,
My latest care, for whom I sought
To hoard my life, that his might be   170
Less wretched now, and one day free;
He, too, who yet had held untired
A spirit natural or inspired —
He, too, was struck, and day by day
Was withered on the stalk away.   175
Oh, God! it is a fearful thing
To see the human soul take wing
In any shape, in any mood:
I've seen it rushing forth in blood,
I've seen it on the breaking ocean   180
Strive with a swoln convulsive motion,
I've seen the sick and ghastly bed
Of Sin delirious with its dread:
But these were horrors — this was woe
Unmixed with such — but sure and slow: 185
He faded, and so calm and meek,
So softly worn, so sweetly weak,
So tearless, yet so tender — kind,
And grieved for those he left behind;
With all the while a cheek whose bloom   190
Was as a mockery of the tomb,
Whose tints as gently sunk away
As a departing rainbow's ray;
An eye of most transparent light,
That almost made the dungeon bright;   195
And not a word of murmur — not
A groan o'er his untimely lot, —
A little talk of better days,
A little hope my own to raise,
For I was sunk in silence — lost   200
In this last loss, of all the most;
And then the sighs he would suppress
Of fainting Nature's feebleness,

More slowly drawn, grew less and less:
I listened, but I could not hear;   205
I called, for I was wild with fear;
I knew 'twas hopeless, but my dread
Would not be thus admonishéd;
I called, and thought I heard a sound —
I burst my chain with one strong bound,   210
And rushed to him: — I found him not,
I only stirred in this black spot,
I only lived, *I* only drew
The accursed breath of dungeon-dew;
The last, the sole, the dearest link   215
Between me and the eternal brink,
Which bound me to my failing race,
Was broken in this fatal place.
One on the earth, and one beneath —
My brothers — both had ceased to breathe: 220
I took that hand which lay so still,
Alas! my own was full as chill;
I had not strength to stir, or strive,
But felt that I was still alive —
A frantic feeling, when we know   225
That what we love shall ne'er be so.
   I know not why
   I could not die,
I had no earthly hope — but faith,
And that forbade a selfish death.   230

      9

What next befell me then and there
   I know not well — I never knew —
First came the loss of light, and air,
   And then of darkness too:
I had no thought, no feeling — none —   235
Among the stones I stood a stone,
And was, scarce conscious what I wist,
As shrubless crags within the mist;
For all was blank, and bleak, and grey;

It was not night — it was not day;   240
It was not even the dungeon-light,
So hateful to my heavy sight,
But vacancy absorbing space,
And fixedness — without a place;
There were no stars — no earth — no time —   245
No check — no change — no good — no crime —
But silence, and a stirless breath
Which neither was of life nor death;
A sea of stagnant idleness,
Blind, boundless, mute, and motionless!   250

10

A light broke in upon my brain, —
   It was the carol of a bird;
It ceased, and then it came again,
   The sweetest song ear ever heard,
And mine was thankful till my eyes   255
Ran over with the glad surprise,
And they that moment could not see
I was the mate of misery;
But then by dull degrees came back
My senses to their wonted track;   260
I saw the dungeon walls and floor
Close slowly round me as before,
I saw the glimmer of the sun
Creeping as it before had done,
But through the crevice where it came   265
That bird was perched, as fond and tame,
   And tamer than upon the tree;
A lovely bird, with azure wings,
And song that said a thousand things,
   And seemed to say them all for me!   270
I never saw its like before,
I ne'er shall see its likeness more:
It seemed like me to want a mate,
But was not half so desolate,
And it was come to love me when   275

None lived to love me so again,
And cheering from my dungeon's brink,
Had brought me back to feel and think.
I know not if it late were free,
   Or broke its cage to perch on mine,   *280*
But knowing well captivity,
   Sweet bird! I could not wish for thine!
Or if it were, in wingéd guise,
A visitant from Paradise;
For — Heaven forgive that thought! the while   *285*
Which made me both to weep and smile —
I sometimes deemed that it might be
My brother's soul come down to me;
But then at last away it flew,
And then 'twas mortal well I knew,   *290*
For he would never thus have flown —
And left me twice so doubly lone, —
Lone — as the corse within its shroud,
Lone — as a solitary cloud,
   A single cloud on a sunny day,   *295*
While all the rest of heaven is clear,
A frown upon the atmosphere,
That hath no business to appear
   When skies are blue, and earth is gay.

11

A kind of change came in my fate,   *300*
My keepers grew compassionate;
I know not what had made them so,
They were inured to sights of woe,
But so it was: — my broken chain
With links unfastened did remain,   *305*
And it was liberty to stride
Along my cell from side to side,
And up and down, and then athwart,
And tread it over every part;
And round the pillars one by one,   *310*
Returning where my walk begun,

Avoiding only, as I trod,
My brothers' graves without a sod;
For if I thought with heedless tread
My step profaned their lowly bed,   315
My breath came gaspingly and thick,
And my crushed heart felt blind and sick.

12

I made a footing in the wall,
    It was not therefrom to escape,
For I had buried one and all,   320
    Who loved me in a human shape;
And the whole earth would henceforth be
A wider prison unto me:
No child — no sire — no kin had I,
No partner in my misery;   325
I thought of this, and I was glad,
For thought of them had made me mad;
But I was curious to ascend
To my barred windows, and to bend
Once more, upon the mountains high,   330
The quiet of a loving eye.

13

I saw them — and they were the same,
They were not changed like me in frame;
I saw their thousand years of snow
On high — their wide long lake below,   335
And the blue Rhone in fullest flow;
I heard the torrents leap and gush
O'er channelled rock and broken bush;
I saw the white-walled distant town,
And whiter sails go skimming down;   340
And then there was a little isle,
Which in my very face did smile,
    The only one in view;
A small green isle, it seemed no more,
Scarce broader than my dungeon floor,   345

But in it there were three tall trees,
And o'er it blew the mountain breeze,
And by it there were waters flowing,
And on it there were young flowers growing,
   Of gentle breath and hue. 350
The fish swam by the castle wall,
And they seemed joyous each and all;
The eagle rode the rising blast,
Methought he never flew so fast
As then to me he seemed to fly; 355
And then new tears came in my eye,
And I felt troubled — and would fain
I had not left my recent chain;
And when I did descend again,
The darkness of my dim abode 360
Fell on me as a heavy load;
It was as is a new-dug grave,
Closing o'er one we sought to save, —
And yet my glance, too much opprest,
Had almost need of such a rest. 365

14

It might be months, or years, or days —
   I kept no count, I took no note —
I had no hope my eyes to raise,
   And clear them of their dreary mote;
At last men came to set me free; 370
   I asked not why, and recked not where;
It was at length the same to me,
Fettered or fetterless to be,
I'd learned to love despair.
And thus when they appeared at last, 375
And all my bonds aside were cast,
These heavy walls to me had grown
A hermitage — and all my own!
And half I felt as they were come
To tear me from a second home: 380
With spiders I had friendship made,

And watched them in their sullen trade,
Had seen the mice by moonlight play,
And why should I feel less than they?
We were all inmates of one place,   385
And I, the monarch of each race,
Had power to kill — yet, strange to tell!
In quiet we had learned to dwell;
My very chains and I grew friends,
So much a long communion tends   390
To make us what we are: — even I
Regained my freedom with a sigh.

1816   1816

Mazeppa

Byron found the bare bones of his narrative — the intrigue, the discovery, the wild ride, the rescue — in Voltaire's *Histoire de Charles XII,* in a passage which he quoted in an "Advertisement" or head note to the first edition of the poem. The use of the frame tale and the details of the ride are his own invention. The historical Mazeppa (1645?–1710) was for twenty years a hetman or chief of the Cossacks, who turned against Peter the Great and became an ally of Charles II.

1

'Twas after dread Pultowa's day,
   When Fortune left the royal Swede —
Around a slaughtered army lay,
   No more to combat and to bleed.
The power and glory of the war,   5
   Faithless as their vain votaries, men,
Had passed to the triumphant Czar,
   And Moscow's walls were safe again —
Until a day more dark and drear,
And a more memorable year,   10
Should give to slaughter and to shame
A mightier host and haughtier name;

1. *Pultowa's day*: On July 8, 1709, the Russian army under Peter the Great defeated the Swedes under Charles XII at Pultowa in the northern Ukraine.
9. *day more dark and drear*: The burning of Moscow by Napoleon's army on October 15, 1812.

A greater wreck, a deeper fall,
A shock to one — a thunderbolt to all.

2

Such was the hazard of the die;   15
The wounded Charles was taught to fly
By day and night through field and flood,
Stained with his own and subjects' blood;
For thousands fell that flight to aid:
And not a voice was heard to upbraid   20
Ambition in his humbled hour,
When Truth had nought to dread from Power.
His horse was slain, and Gieta gave
His own — and died the Russians' slave.
This, too, sinks after many a league   25
Of well-sustained, but vain fatigue;
And in the depth of forests darkling,
The watch-fires in the distance sparkling —
    The beacons of surrounding foes —
A King must lay his limbs at length.   30
    Are these the laurels and repose
For which the nations strain their strength?
They laid him by a savage tree,
In outworn Nature's agony;
His wounds were stiff, his limbs were stark;   35
The heavy hour was chill and dark;
The fever in his blood forbade
A transient slumber's fitful aid:
And thus it was; but yet through all,
Kinglike the monarch bore his fall,   40
And made, in this extreme of ill,
His pangs the vassals of his will:
All silent and subdued were they,
As once the nations round him lay.

---

16. *the wounded Charles*: The king had been wounded in the foot.
23. *Gieta*: A colonel in the Swedish army who, according to Voltaire, though himself wounded, gave the king his horse and thus gave up his own chance to avoid capture.

3

A band of chiefs! — alas! how few,   45
    Since but the fleeting of a day
Had thinned it; but this wreck was true
    And chivalrous: upon the clay
Each sate him down, all sad and mute,
    Beside his monarch and his steed;   50
For danger levels man and brute,
    And all are fellows in their need.
Among the rest, Mazeppa made
His pillow in an old oak's shade —
Himself as rough, and scarce less old,   55
The Ukraine's Hetman, calm and bold;
But first, outspent with this long course,
The Cossack prince rubbed down his horse,
And made for him a leafy bed,
    And smoothed his fetlocks and his mane,   60
    And slacked his girth, and stripped his rein,
And joyed to see how well he fed;
For until now he had the dread
His wearied courser might refuse
To browse beneath the midnight dews: 65
But he was hardy as his lord,
And little cared for bed and board;
But spirited and docile too,
Whate'er was to be done, would do.
Shaggy and swift, and strong of limb,   70
All Tartar-like he carried him;
Obeyed his voice, and came to call,
And knew him in the midst of all:
Though thousands were around, — and Night,
Without a star, pursued her flight, —   75
That steed from sunset until dawn
His chief would follow like a fawn.

56. *Hetman*: Chieftain, military leader.

4

This done, Mazeppa spread his cloak,
And laid his lance beneath his oak,
Felt if his arms in order good   80
The long day's march had well withstood —
If still the powder filled the pan,
   And flints unloosened kept their lock —
His sabre's hilt and scabbard felt,
And whether they had chafed his belt;   85
And next the venerable man,
From out his havresack and can,
   Prepared and spread his slender stock;
And to the Monarch and his men
The whole or portion offered then   90
With far less of inquietude
Than courtiers at a banquet would.
And Charles of this his slender share
With smiles partook a moment there,
To force of cheer a greater show,   95
And seem above both wounds and woe; —
And then he said — "Of all our band,
Though firm of heart and strong of hand,
In skirmish, march, or forage, none
Can less have said or more have done   100
Than thee, Mazeppa! On the earth
So fit a pair had never birth,
Since Alexander's days till now,
As thy Bucephalus and thou:
All Scythia's fame to thine should yield   105
For pricking on o'er flood and field."
Mazeppa answered — "Ill betide
The school wherein I learned to ride!"
Quoth Charles — "Old Hetman, wherefore so,

104. *Bucephalus*: The name of Alexander the Great's horse, and thus
by extension any war horse.
105. *Scythia*: Ancient region of south Europe and Asia, traditionally
associated with South Russia and the Black Sea. The Scythians flourished
from the ninth to the fourth centuries, B.C.

Since thou hast learned the art so well?"   *110*
Mazeppa said — " 'Twere long to tell;
And we have many a league to go,
With every now and then a blow,
And ten to one at least the foe,
Before our steeds may graze at ease,   *115*
Beyond the swift Borysthenes:
And, Sire, your limbs have need of rest,
And I will be the sentinel
Of this your troop." — "But I request,"
Said Sweden's monarch, "thou wilt tell   *120*
This tale of thine, and I may reap,
Perchance, from this the boon of sleep;
For at this moment from my eyes
The hope of present slumber flies."

"Well, Sire, with such a hope, I'll track   *125*
My seventy years of memory back:
I think 'twas in my twentieth spring, —
Aye 'twas, — when Casimir was king —
John Casimir, — I was his page
Six summers, in my earlier age: *130*
A learnéd monarch, faith! was he,
And most unlike your Majesty;
He made no wars, and did not gain
New realms to lose them back again;
And (save debates in Warsaw's diet)   *135*
He reigned in most unseemly quiet;
Not that he had no cares to vex;
He loved the Muses and the Sex;
And sometimes these so froward are,
They made him wish himself at war;   *140*
But soon his wrath being o'er, he took
Another mistress — or new book:

116. *Borysthenes*: The Dnieper River.
129. *John Casimer*: King of Poland from 1648 to 1668. He had previously been a Jesuit and Cardinal which points up the irony of lines 138 ff.
135. *Warsaw's diet*: Parliament.

And then he gave prodigious fêtes —
All Warsaw gathered round his gates
To gaze upon his splendid court,   145
And dames, and chiefs, of princely port.
He was the Polish Solomon.
So sung his poets, all but one,
Who, being unpensioned, made a satire,
And boasted that he could not flatter.   150
It was a court of jousts and mimes,
Where every courtier tried at rhymes;
Even I for once produced some verses,
And signed my odes 'Despairing Thyrsis.'
There was a certain Palatine,   155
    A Count of far and high descent,
Rich as a salt or silver mine;
And he was proud, ye may divine,
    As if from Heaven he had been sent;
He had such wealth in blood and ore   160
    As few could match beneath the throne;
And he would gaze upon his store,
And o'er his pedigree would pore,
Until by some confusion led,
Which almost looked like want of head,   165
    He thought their merits were his own.
His wife was not of this opinion;
    His junior she by thirty years,
Grew daily tired of his dominion;
    And, after wishes, hopes, and fears,   170
    To virtue a few farewell tears,
A restless dream or two — some glances
At Warsaw's youth — some songs, and dances,
Awaited but the usual chances,
Those happy accidents which render   175
The coldest dames so very tender,

155. *Palatine*: Nobleman possessing royal prerogatives. His name was
Lord Falbowski.
157. *Salt or silver mine*: Salt mines were major sources of income in
Poland.

To deck her Count with titles given,
'Tis said, as passports into Heaven;
But, strange to say, they rarely boast
Of these, who have deserved them most.   *180*

5

"I was a goodly stripling then;
   At seventy years I so may say,
That there were few, or boys or men,
   Who, in my dawning time of day,
Of vassal or of knight's degree,   *185*
Could vie in vanities with me;
For I had strength — youth — gaiety,
A port, not like to this ye see,
But smooth, as all is rugged now;
   For Time, and Care, and War, have ploughed   *190*
My very soul from out my brow;
   And thus I should be disavowed
By all my kind and kin, could they
Compare my day and yesterday;
This change was wrought, too, long ere age   *195*
Had ta'en my features for his page:
With years, ye know, have not declined
My strength — my courage — or my mind,
Or at this hour I should not be
Telling old tales beneath a tree,   *200*
With starless skies my canopy.
   But let me on: Theresa's form —
Methinks it glides before me now,
Between me and yon chestnut's bough,
   The memory is so quick and warm;   *205*
And yet I find no words to tell
The shape of her I loved so well:
She had the Asiatic eye,
   Such as our Turkish neighbourhood
   Hath mingled with our Polish blood,   *210*
Dark as above us is the sky;
But through it stole a tender light,

Like the first moonrise of midnight;
Large, dark, and swimming in the stream,
Which seemed to melt to its own beam;   215
All love, half languor, and half fire,
Like saints that at the stake expire,
And lift their raptured looks on high,
As though it were a joy to die.
A brow like a midsummer lake,   220
   Transparent with the sun therein,
When waves no murmur dare to make,
   And heaven beholds her face within.
A cheek and lip — but why proceed?
   I loved her then, I love her still;   225
And such as I am, love indeed
   In fierce extremes — in good and ill.
But still we love even in our rage,
And haunted to our very age
With the vain shadow of the past, —   230
As is Mazeppa to the last.

6

"We met — we gazed — I saw, and sighed;
She did not speak, and yet replied;
There are ten thousand tones and signs
We hear and see, but none defines —   235
Involuntary sparks of thought,
Which strike from out the heart o'erwrought,
And form a strange intelligence,
Alike mysterious and intense,
Which link the burning chain that binds,   240
Without their will, young hearts and minds;
Conveying, as the electric wire,
We know not how, the absorbing fire.
I saw, and sighed — in silence wept,
And still reluctant distance kept,   245
Until I was made known to her,
And we might then and there confer
Without suspicion — then, even then,
   I longed, and was resolved to speak;

But on my lips they died again,   250
  The accents tremulous and weak,
Until one hour. — There is a game,
  A frivolous and foolish play,
  Wherewith we while away the day;
It is — I have forgot the name —   255
And we to this, it seems, were set,
By some strange chance, which I forget:
I recked not if I won or lost,
  It was enough for me to be
  So near to hear, and oh! to see   260
The being whom I loved the most.
I watched her as a sentinel,
(May ours this dark night watch as well!)
  Until I saw, and thus it was,
That she was pensive, nor perceived   265
Her occupation, nor was grieved
Nor glad to lose or gain; but still
Played on for hours, as if her will
Yet bound her to the place, though not
That hers might be the winning lot.   270
  Then through my brain the thought did pass,
Even as a flash of lightning there,
That there was something in her air
Which would not doom me to despair;
And on the thought my words broke forth,   275
  All incoherent as they were;
Their eloquence was little worth,
But yet she listened — 'tis enough —
  Who listens once will listen twice;
  Her heart, be sure, is not of ice —   280
And one refusal no rebuff.

7

"I loved, and was beloved again —
  They tell me, Sire, you never knew
  Those gentle frailties; if 'tis true,
I shorten all my joy or pain;   285
To you 'twould seem absurd as vain;

But all men are not born to reign,
Or o'er their passions, or as you
Thus o'er themselves and nations too.
I am — or rather *was* — a Prince,   *290*
    A chief of thousands, and could lead
        Them on where each would foremost bleed;
But could not o'er myself evince
The like control — But to resume:
    I loved, and was beloved again;   *295*
In sooth, it is a happy doom,
    But yet where happiest ends in pain. —
We met in secret, and the hour
Which led me to that lady's bower
Was fiery Expectation's dower.   *300*
My days and nights were nothing — all
Except that hour which doth recall,
In the long lapse from youth to age,
    No other like itself: I'd give
        The Ukraine back again to live   *305*
It o'er once more, and be a page,
The happy page, who was the lord
Of one soft heart, and his own sword,
And had no other gem nor wealth,
Save Nature's gift of Youth and Health.   *310*
We met in secret — doubly sweet,
Some say, they find it so to meet;
I know not that — I would have given
    My life but to have called her mine
In the full view of Earth and Heaven;   *315*
    For I did oft and long repine
That we could only meet by stealth.

8

"For lovers there are many eyes,
    And such there were on us; the Devil
    On such occasions should be civil —   *320*
The Devil! — I'm loth to do him wrong,
    It might be some untoward saint,
Who would not be at rest too long,

But to his pious bile gave vent —
But one fair night, some lurking spies   325
Surprised and seized us both.
The Count was something more than wroth —
I was unarmed; but if in steel,
All cap-à-pie from head to heel,
What 'gainst their numbers could I do?   330
'Twas near his castle, far away
   From city or from succour near,
And almost on the break of day;
I did not think to see another,
   My moments seemed reduced to few;   335
And with one prayer to Mary Mother,
   And, it may be, a saint or two,
As I resigned me to my fate,
They led me to the castle gate:
   Theresa's doom I never knew,   340
Our lot was henceforth separate.
An angry man, ye may opine,
Was he, the proud Count Palatine;
And he had reason good to be,
   But he was most enraged lest such   345
   An accident should chance to touch
Upon his future pedigree;
Nor less amazed, that such a blot
His noble 'scutcheon should have got,
While he was highest of his line;   350
   Because unto himself he seemed
   The first of men, nor less he deemed
In others' eyes, and most in mine.
'Sdeath! with a *page* — perchance a king
Had reconciled him to the thing;   355
But with a stripling of a page —
I felt — but cannot paint his rage.

           9
" 'Bring forth the horse!' — the horse was brought!
In truth, he was a noble steed,
   A Tartar of the Ukraine breed,   360

Who looked as though the speed of thought
Were in his limbs; but he was wild,
  Wild as the wild deer, and untaught,
With spur and bridle undefiled —
  'Twas but a day he had been caught;   *365*
And snorting, with erected mane,
And struggling fiercely, but in vain,
In the full foam of wrath and dread
To me the desert-born was led:
They bound me on, that menial throng,   *370*
Upon his back with many a thong;
They loosed him with a sudden lash —
Away! — away! — and on we dash! —
Torrents less rapid and less rash.

10

"Away! — away! — My breath was gone,   *375*
I saw not where he hurried on:
'Twas scarcely yet the break of day,
And on he foamed — away! — away!
The last of human sounds which rose,
As I was darted from my foes,   *380*
With the wild shout of savage laughter,
Which on the wind came roaring after
A moment from that rabble rout:
With sudden wrath I wrenched my head,
  And snapped the cord, which to the mane   *385*
  Had bound my neck in lieu of rein,
And, writhing half my form about,
Howled back my curse; but 'midst the tread,
The thunder of my courser's speed,
Perchance they did not hear nor heed: *390*
It vexes me — for I would fain
Have paid their insult back again.
I paid it well in after days:
There is not of that castle gate,
Its drawbridge and portcullis' weight,   *395*
Stone — bar — moat — bridge — or barrier left;

Nor of its fields a blade of grass,
  Save what grows on a ridge of wall,
  Where stood the hearth-stone of the hall;
And many a time ye there might pass, 400
Nor dream that e'er the fortress was.
I saw its turrets in a blaze,
Their crackling battlements all cleft,
  And the hot lead pour down like rain
From off the scorched and blackening roof, 405
Whose thickness was not vengeance-proof.
  They little thought that day of pain,
When launched, as on the lightning's flash,
They bade me to destruction dash,
  That one day I should come again, 410
With twice five thousand horse, to thank
  The Count for his uncourteous ride.
They played me then a bitter prank,
  When, with the wild horse for my guide,
They bound me to his foaming flank: 415
At length I played them one as frank —
For Time at last sets all things even —
  And if we do but watch the hour,
  There never yet was human power
Which could evade, if unforgiven, 420
The patient search and vigil long
Of him who treasures up a wrong.

11
"Away! — away! — my steed and I,
  Upon the pinions of the wind!
  All human dwellings left behind, 425
We sped like meteors through the sky,
When with its crackling sound the night
Is chequered with the Northern light.
Town — village — none were on our track,
  But a wild plain of far extent, 430
And bounded by a forest black;
  And, save the scarce seen battlement

On distant heights of some strong hold,
Against the Tartars built of old,
No trace of man. The year before   *435*
A Turkish army had marched o'er;
And where the Spahi's hoof hath trod,
The verdure flies the bloody sod:
The sky was dull, and dim, and gray,
    And a low breeze crept moaning by —   *440*
    I could have answered with a sigh —
But fast we fled, — away! — away! —
And I could neither sigh nor pray;
And my cold sweat-drops fell like rain
Upon the courser's bristling mane;   *445*
But, snorting still with rage and fear,
He flew upon his far career:
At times I almost thought, indeed,
He must have slackened in his speed;
But no — my bound and slender frame   *450*
    Was nothing to his angry might,
And merely like a spur became:
Each motion which I made to free
My swoln limbs from their agony
    Increased his fury and affright: *455*
I tried my voice, — 'twas faint and low —
But yet he swerved as from a blow;
And, starting to each accent, sprang
As from a sudden trumpet's clang:
Meantime my cords were wet with gore,   *460*
Which, oozing through my limbs, ran o'er;
And in my tongue the thirst became
A something fierier far than flame.

                        12
"We neared the wild wood — 'twas so wide,
I saw no bounds on either side: *465*
'Twas studded with old sturdy trees,

437. *Spahi's hoof*: An elite cavalry corps under the Turkish empire
(disbanded 1826).

That bent not to the roughest breeze
Which howls down from Siberia's waste,
And strips the forest in its haste, —
But these were few and far between,   *470*
Set thick with shrubs more young and green,
Luxuriant with their annual leaves,
Ere strown by those autumnal eves
That nip the forest's foliage dead,
Dicoloured with a lifeless red,   *475*
Which stands thereon like stiffened gore
Upon the slain when battle's o'er;
And some long winter's night hath shed
Its frost o'er every tombless head —
So cold and stark — the raven's beak   *480*
May peck unpierced each frozen cheek:
'Twas a wild waste of underwood,
And here and there a chestnut stood,
The strong oak, and the hardy pine;
  But far apart — and well it were,   *485*
Or else a different lot were mine —
  The boughs gave way, and did not tear
My limbs; and I found strength to bear
My wounds, already scarred with cold;
My bonds forbade to loose my hold.   *490*
We rustled through the leaves like wind, —
Left shrubs, and trees, and wolves behind;
By night I heard them on the track,
Their troop came hard upon our back,
With their long gallop, which can tire   *495*
The hound's deep hate, and hunter's fire:
Where'er we flew they followed on,
Nor left us with the morning sun;
Behind I saw them, scarce a rood,
At day-break winding through the wood,   *500*
And through the night had heard their feet
Their stealing, rustling step repeat.
Oh! how I wished for spear or sword,
At least to die amidst the horde,

And perish — if it must be so — 505
At bay, destroying many a foe!
When first my courser's race begun,
I wished the goal already won;
But now I doubted strength and speed:
Vain doubt! his swift and savage breed 510
Had nerved him like the mountain-roe —
Nor faster falls the blinding snow
Which whelms the peasant near the door
Whose threshold he shall cross no more,
Bewildered with the dazzling blast, 515
Than through the forest-paths he passed —
Untired, untamed, and worse than wild —
All furious as a favoured child
Balked of its wish; or — fiercer still —
A woman piqued — who has her will! 520

13

"The wood was passed; 'twas more than noon,
But chill the air, although in June;
Or it might be my veins ran cold —
Prolonged endurance tames the bold;
And I was then not what I seem, 525
But headlong as a wintry stream,
And wore my feelings out before
I well could count their causes o'er:
And what with fury, fear, and wrath,
The tortures which beset my path — 530
Cold — hunger — sorrow — shame — distress —
Thus bound in Nature's nakedness;
Sprung from a race whose rising blood
When stirred beyond its calmer mood,
And trodden hard upon, is like 535
The rattle-snake's, in act to strike —
What marvel if this worn-out trunk
Beneath its woes a moment sunk?
The earth gave way, the skies rolled round,
I seemed to sink upon the ground; 540

But erred — for I was fastly bound.
My heart turned sick, my brain grew sore,
And throbbed awhile, then beat no more:
The skies spun like a mighty wheel;
I saw the trees like drunkards reel,   545
And a slight flash sprang o'er my eyes,
Which saw no farther. He who dies
Can die no more than then I died,
O'ertortured by that ghastly ride.
I felt the blackness come and go,   550
    And strove to wake; but could not make
My senses climb up from below:
I felt as on a plank at sea,
When all the waves that dash o'er thee,
At the same time upheave and whelm,   555
And hurl thee towards a desert realm.
My undulating life was as
The fancied lights that flitting pass
Our shut eyes in deep midnight, when
Fever begins upon the brain;   560
But soon it passed, with little pain,
    But a confusion worse than such:
    I own that I should deem it much,
Dying, to feel the same again;
And yet I do suppose we must   565
Feel far more ere we turn to dust!
No matter! I have bared my brow
Full in Death's face — before — and now.

                    14
"My thoughts came back. Where was I? Cold,
    And numb, and giddy: pulse by pulse   570
Life reassumed its lingering hold,
And throb by throb, — till grown a pang
    Which for a moment would convulse,
    My blood reflowed, though thick and chill;
My ear with uncouth noises rang,   575
    My heart began once more to thrill;

My sight returned, though dim; alas!
And thickened, as it were, with glass.
Methought the dash of waves was nigh;
There was a gleam too of the sky,   *580*
Studded with stars; — it is no dream;
The wild horse swims the wilder stream!
The bright broad river's gushing tide
Sweeps, winding onward, far and wide,
And we are half-way, struggling o'er   *585*
To yon unknown and silent shore.
The waters broke my hollow trance,
And with a temporary strength
   My stiffened limbs were rebaptized.
My courser's broad breast proudly braves,   *590*
And dashes off the ascending waves,
And onward we advance!
We reach the slippery shore at length,
   A haven I but little prized,
For all behind was dark and drear,   *595*
And all before was night and fear.
How many hours of night or day
In those suspended pangs I lay,
I could not tell; I scarcely knew
If this were human breath I drew.   *600*

15

"With glossy skin, and dripping mane,
   And reeling limbs, and reeking flank,
The wild steed's sinewy nerves still strain
   Up the repelling bank.
We gain the top: a boundless plain   *605*
Spreads through the shadow of the night,
   And onward, onward, onward — seems,
   Like precipices in our dreams,
To stretch beyond the sight;
And here and there a speck of white,   *610*
   Or scattered spot of dusky green,
In masses broke into the light,

And rose the moon upon my right:
   But nought distinctly seen
In the dim waste would indicate   *615*
The omen of a cottage gate;
No twinkling taper from afar
Stood like a hospitable star;
Not even an ignis-fatuus rose
To make him merry with my woes: *620*
   That very cheat had cheered me then!
Although detected, welcome still,
Reminding me, through every ill,
   Of the abodes of men.

16

"Onward we went — but slack and slow;   *625*
   His savage force at length o'erspent,
The drooping courser, faint and low,
   All feebly foaming went:
A sickly infant had had power
To guide him forward in that hour!   *630*
   But, useless all to me,
His new-born tameness nought availed —
My limbs were bound; my force had failed,
   Perchance, had they been free.
With feeble effort still I tried   *635*
To rend the bonds so starkly tied,
   But still it was in vain;
My limbs were only wrung the more,
And soon the idle strife gave o'er,
   Which but prolonged their pain.   *640*
The dizzy race seemed almost done,
Although no goal was nearly won:
Some streaks announced the coming sun —
   How slow, alas! he came!
Methought that mist of dawning gray   *645*
Would never dapple into day,
How heavily it rolled away!
   Before the eastern flame

Rose crimson, and deposed the stars,
And called the radiance from their cars,   650
And filled the earth, from his deep throne,
With lonely lustre, all his own.

17

"Uprose the sun; the mists were curled
Back from the solitary world
Which lay around — behind — before.   655
What booted it to traverse o'er
Plain — forest — river? Man nor brute,
Nor dint of hoof, nor print of foot,
Lay in the wild luxuriant soil —
No sign of travel, none of toil —   660
The very air was mute:
And not an insect's shrill small horn,
Nor matin bird's new voice was borne
From herb nor thicket. Many a *werst,*
Panting as if his heart would burst,   665
The weary brute still staggered on;
And still we were — or seemed — alone:
At length, while reeling on our way,
Methought I heard a courser neigh,
From out yon tuft of blackening firs.   670
Is it the wind those branches stirs?
No, no! from out the forest prance
    A trampling troop; I see them come!
In one vast squadron they advance!
    I strove to cry — my lips were dumb!   675
The steeds rush on in plunging pride;
But where are they the reins to guide?
A thousand horse, and none to ride!
With flowing tail, and flying mane,
Wide nostrils never stretched by pain,   680
Mouths bloodless to the bit or rein,
And feet that iron never shod,

---

664. *werst*: A Russian measure equivalent to 3510 feet.

And flanks unscarred by spur or rod,
A thousand horse, the wild, the free,
Like waves that follow o'er the sea,   685
   Came thickly thundering on,
As if our faint approach to meet!
The sight re-nerved my courser's feet,
A moment staggering, feebly fleet,
A moment, with a faint low neigh,   690
   He answered, and then fell!
With gasps and glazing eyes he lay,
   And reeking limbs immoveable,
     His first and last career is done!
On came the troop — they saw him stoop,   695
   They saw me strangely bound along
   His back with many a bloody thong.
They stop — they start — they snuff the air,
Gallop a moment here and there,
Approach, retire, wheel round and round,   700
Then plunging back with sudden bound,
Headed by one black mighty steed,
Who seemed the Patriarch of his breed,
   Without a single speck or hair
Of white upon his shaggy hide;   705
They snort — they foam — neigh — swerve aside,
And backward to the forest fly,
By instinct, from a human eye.
   They left me there to my despair,
Linked to the dead and stiffening wretch,   710
Whose lifeless limbs beneath me stretch,
Relieved from that unwonted weight,
From whence I could not extricate
Nor him nor me — and there we lay,
   The dying on the dead!   715
I little deemed another day
   Would see my houseless, helpless head.

"And there from morn to twilight bound,
I felt the heavy hours toil round,

With just enough of life to see 720
My last of suns go down on me,
In hopeless certainty of mind,
That makes us feel at length resigned
To that which our foreboding years
Present the worst and last of fears: 725
Inevitable — even a boon,
Nor more unkind for coming soon,
Yet shunned and dreaded with such care,
As if it only were a snare
   That Prudence might escape: 730
At times both wished for and implored,
At times sought with self-pointed sword,
Yet still a dark and hideous close
To even intolerable woes,
   And welcome in no shape. 735
And, strange to say, the sons of pleasure,
They who have revelled beyond measure
In beauty, wassail, wine, and treasure,
Die calm, or calmer, oft than he
Whose heritage was Misery. 740
For he who hath in turn run through
All that was beautiful and new,
   Hath nought to hope, and nought to leave;
And, save the future, (which is viewed
Not quite as men are base or good, 745
But as their nerves may be endued,)
   With nought perhaps to grieve:
The wretch still hopes his woes must end,
And Death, whom he should deem his friend,
Appears, to his distempered eyes, 750
Arrived to rob him of his prize,
The tree of his new Paradise.
To-morrow would have given him all,
Repaid his pangs, repaired his fall;
To-morrow would have been the first 755
Of days no more deplored or curst,
But bright, and long, and beckoning years,

Seen dazzling through the mist of tears,
Guerdon of many a painful hour;
To-morrow would have given him power   *760*
To rule — to shine — to smite — to save —
And must it dawn upon his grave?

18

"The sun was sinking — still I lay
   Chained to the chill and stiffening steed!
I thought to mingle there our clay;   *765*
   And my dim eyes of death had need,
   No hope arose of being freed.
I cast my last looks up the sky,
   And there between me and the sun
I saw the expecting raven fly,   *770*
Who scarce would wait till both should die,
   Ere his repast begun;
He flew, and perched, then flew once more,
And each time nearer than before;
I saw his wing through twilight flit,   *775*
And once so near me he alit
   I could have smote, but lacked the strength;
But the slight motion of my hand,
And feeble scratching of the sand,
The exerted throat's faint struggling noise,   *780*
Which scarcely could be called a voice,
   Together scared him off at length.
I knew no more — my last dream
   Is something of a lovely star
   Which fixed my dull eyes from afar,   *785*
And went and came with wandering beam,
And of the cold — dull — swimming — dense
Sensation of recurring sense,
And then subsiding back to death,
And then again a little breath,   *790*
A little thrill — a short suspense,
   An icy sickness curdling o'er
My heart, and sparks that crossed my brain —

A gasp — a throb — a start of pain,
　A sigh — and nothing more.　　　　　　　　795

19

"I woke — where was I? — Do I see
A human face look down on me?
And doth a roof above me close?
Do these limbs on a couch repose?
Is this a chamber where I lie?　　　　　　　800
And is it mortal yon bright eye,
That watches me with gentle glance?
　I closed my own again once more,
As doubtful that my former trance
　Could not as yet be o'er.　　　　　　　805
A slender girl, long-haired, and tall,
Sate watching by the cottage wall.
The sparkle of her eye I caught,
Even with my first return of thought;
For ever and anon she threw　　　　　　　810
　A prying, pitying glance on me
　With her black eyes so wild and free:
I gazed, and gazed, until I knew
　No vision it could be, —
But that I lived, and was released　　　　815
From adding to the vulture's feast:
And when the Cossack maid beheld
My heavy eyes at length unsealed,
She smiled — and I essayed to speak,
　But failed — and she approached, and made　820
　With lip and finger signs that said,
I must not strive as yet to break
The silence, till my strength should be
Enough to leave my accents free;
And then her hand on mine she laid,　　　825
And smoothed the pillow for my head,
And stole along on tiptoe tread,
　And gently oped the door, and spake
In whispers — ne'er was voice so sweet!

Even music followed her light feet.   *830*
   But those she called were not awake,
And she went forth; but, ere she passed,
Another look on me she cast,
   Another sign she made, to say,
That I had nought to fear, that all   *835*
Were near, at my command or call,
   And she would not delay
Her due return: — while she was gone,
Methought I felt too much alone.

20

"She came with mother and with sire —   *840*
What need of more? — I will not tire
With long recital of the rest,
Since I became the Cossack's guest.
They found me senseless on the plain,
   They bore me to the nearest hut,   *845*
They brought me into life again —
Me — one day o'er their realm to reign!
   Thus the vain fool who strove to glut
His rage, refining on my pain,
   Sent me forth to the wilderness,   *850*
Bound — naked — bleeding — and alone,
To pass the desert to a throne, —
   What mortal his own doom may guess?
   Let none despond, let none despair!
To-morrow the Borysthenes   *855*
May see our coursers graze at ease
Upon his Turkish bank, — and never
Had I such welcome for a river
   As I shall yield when safely there.
Comrades, good night!" — The Hetman threw   *860*
   His length beneath the oak-tree shade,
   With leafy couch already made —

---

859. The king and Mazeppa barely escaped the pursuing Russian
cavalry, but they at last safely reached Turkey, where Mazeppa died soon
after.

A bed nor comfortless nor new
To him, who took his rest whene'er
The hour arrived, no matter where: 865
　　His eyes the hastening slumbers steep.
And if ye marvel Charles forgot
To thank his tale, *he* wondered not, —
　　The King had been an hour asleep!

1818   *1819*

Beppo

A VENETIAN STORY

Byron wrote Beppo in September and October 1817. The poem was his first experiment in the *ottava rima* stanza and the mock heroic style he was to develop so effectively in *Don Juan* and *The Vision of Judgment*. In a letter to John Murray, October 12, 1817, Byron said that he wrote the poem "in or after the excellent manner of Mr. Whistlecraft (whom I take to be Frere) on a Venetian anecdote which amused me." The poem by John Hookham Frere was titled *Prospectus and Specimen of an Intended National Work,* by William and Robert Whistlecraft (more familiarly known as *The Monks and The Giants*), and was in turn modeled upon the manner of Italian mock-epic poets like Luigi Pulci (1432–1484). But of these Byron then apparently knew nothing. The anecdote which amused Byron was concerned with a Turk arriving at an Inn and revealing himself to the hostess, now living with her "amoroso," as her husband long since presumed lost at sea. He had made a fortune in Turkey, and, according to Byron's friend Hobshouse who recorded the story, he made three offers to his wife "either to quit your amoroso and come with me or to stay with your amoroso or to accept a pension and live alone. The lady has not yet given an answer." The anecdote was told to Byron appropriately enough by the husband of Marianna Segati, who was at the time Byron's mistress and living in his house. See Letters to Thomas Moore, November 17, 1816, and January 28, 1817, below, pp. 652–656.

Rosalind. *Farewell, Monsieur Traveller; Look, you lisp, and wear strange suits: disable all the benefits of your own country; be out of love with your Nativity, and almost chide*

149

*God for making you that countenance you are; or I will scarce
think you have swam in a Gondola.*

> *As You Like It, Act IV, Scene i.*

ANNOTATION OF THE COMMENTATORS

*That is, been at Venice, which was much visited by the
young English gentlemen of those times, and was then what
Paris is now — the seat of all dissoluteness. — S.A.*

1

'Tis known, at least it should be, that throughout
   All countries of the Catholic persuasion,
Some weeks before Shrove Tuesday comes about,
   The People take their fill of recreation,
And buy repentance, ere they grow devout,
   However high their rank, or low their station,
With fiddling, feasting, dancing, drinking, masquing,
And other things which may be had for asking.

2

The moment night with dusky mantle covers
   The skies (and the more duskily the better),
The Time less liked by husbands than by lovers
   Begins, and Prudery flings aside her fetter;
And Gaiety on restless tiptoe hovers,
   Giggling with all the gallants who beset her;
And there are songs and quavers, roaring, humming,
Guitars, and every other sort of strumming.

3

And there are dresses splendid, but fantastical,
   Masks of all times and nations, Turks and Jews,
And harlequins and clowns, with feats gymnastical,
   Greeks, Romans, Yankee-doodles, and Hindoos;
All kinds of dress, except the ecclesiastical,
   All people, as their fancies hit, may choose,

Epigraph: The "annotation" is from Samuel Ayscough, *The Dramatic
Works of William Shakespeare with Explanatory Notes* (1807), I, 242.

But no one in these parts may quiz the Clergy, —
Therefore take heed, ye Freethinkers! I charge ye.

4

You'd better walk about begirt with briars,
   Instead of coat and smallclothes, than put on
A single stitch reflecting upon friars,
   Although you swore it only was in fun;
They'd haul you o'er the coals, and stir the fires
   Of Phlegethon with every mother's son,
Nor say one mass to cool the cauldron's bubble
That boiled your bones, unless you paid them double.

5

But saving this, you may put on whate'er
   You like by way of doublet, cape, or cloak,
Such as in Monmouth-street, or in Rag Fair,
   Would rig you out in seriousness or joke;
And even in Italy such places are,
   With prettier name in softer accents spoke,
For, bating Covent Garden, I can hit on
No place that's called "Piazza" in Great Britain.

6

This feast is named the Carnival, which being
   Interpreted, implies "farewell to flesh:"
So called, because the name and thing agreeing,
   Through Lent they live on fish both salt and fresh.
But why they usher Lent with so much glee in,
   Is more than I can tell, although I guess
'Tis as we take a glass with friends at parting,
In the Stage-Coach or Packet, just at starting.

4:6. *Phlegethon*: The river of fire in Hades, the underworld of Greek myth.
   5:3. *Monmouth-street, or . . . Rag Fair*: Known in the eighteenth century as centers for the sale of second hand clothes.
   5:8. *Piazza*: The arcades in Covent Garden Market were called piazzas. In Venice the piazzas or squares were frequently market places.
   6:2. *"farewell to flesh"*: "Carnevale" in Italian.

7

And thus they bid farewell to carnal dishes,
  And solid meats, and highly spiced ragouts,
To live for forty days on ill-dressed fishes,
  Because they have no sauces to their stews;
A thing which causes many "poohs" and "pishes,"
  And several oaths (which would not suit the Muse),
From travellers accustomed from a boy
To eat their salmon, at the least, with soy;

8

And therefore humbly I would recommend
  "The curious in fish-sauce," before they cross
The sea, to bid their cook, or wife, or friend,
  Walk or ride to the Strand, and buy in gross
(Or if set out beforehand, these may send
  By any means least liable to loss),
Ketchup, Soy, Chili-vinegar, and Harvey,
Or, by the Lord! a Lent will well nigh starve ye;

9

That is to say, if your religion's Roman,
  And you at Rome would do as Romans do,
According to the proverb, — although no man,
  If foreign, is obliged to fast; and you,
If Protestant, or sickly, or a woman,
  Would rather dine in sin on a ragout —
Dine and be d — d! I don't mean to be coarse,
But that's the penalty, to say no worse.

10

Of all the places where the Carnival
  Was most facetious in the days of yore,
For dance, and song, and serenade, and ball,
  And Masque, and Mime, and Mystery, and more
Than I have time to tell now, or at all,
  Venice the bell from every city bore, —
And at the moment when I fix my story,
That sea-born city was in all her glory.

11

They've pretty faces yet, those same Venetians,
    Black eyes, arched brows, and sweet expressions still;
Such as of old were copied from the Grecians,
    In ancient arts by moderns mimicked ill;
And like so many Venuses of Titian's
    (The best's at Florence — see it, if ye will,)
They look when leaning over the balcony,
Or stepped from out a picture by Giorgione,

12

Whose tints are Truth and Beauty at their best;
    And when you to Manfrini's palace go,
That picture (howsoever fine the rest)
    Is loveliest to my mind of all the show;
It may perhaps be also to *your* zest,
    And that's the cause I rhyme upon it so:
'Tis but a portrait of his Son, and Wife,
And self; but *such* a Woman! Love in life!

13

Love in full life and length, not love ideal,
    No, nor ideal beauty, that fine name,
But something better still, so very real,
    That the sweet Model must have been the same;
A thing that you would purchase, beg, or steal,
    Wer't not impossible, besides a shame:
The face recalls some face, as 'twere with pain,
You once have seen, but ne'er will see again;

14

One of those forms which flit by us, when we
    Are young, and fix our eyes on every face;
And, oh! the Loveliness at times we see
    In momentary gliding, the soft grace,

12:8. *Love in life!*: The picture by Giorgione (1478–1511) that Byron
admired represents "an almost nude woman, probably a gypsy, seated with
a child in her lap, and a standing warrior gazing upon her, a storm
breaking over the landscape." Byron was wrong on one point: Giorgione
was never married.

The Youth, the Bloom, the Beauty which agree,
   In many a nameless being we retrace,
Whose course and home we knew not, nor shall know,
Like the lost Pleiad seen no more below.

15

I said that like a picture by Giorgione
   Venetian women were, and so they *are*,
Particularly seen from a balcony,
   (For beauty's sometimes best set off afar)
And there, just like a heroine of Goldoni,
   They peep from out the blind, or o'er the bar;
And truth to say, they're mostly very pretty,
And rather like to show it, more's the pity!

16

For glances beget ogles, ogles sighs,
   Sighs wishes, wishes words, and words a letter,
Which flies on wings of light-heeled Mercuries,
   Who do such things because they know no better;
And then, God knows what mischief may arise,
   When Love links two young people in one fetter,
Vile assignations, and adulterous beds,
Elopements, broken vows, and hearts, and heads.

17

Shakespeare described the sex in Desdemona
   As very fair, but yet suspect in fame,
And to this day from Venice to Verona
   Such matters may be probably the same,
Except that since those times was never known
   Husband whom mere suspicion could inflame
To suffocate a wife no more than twenty,
Because she had a "Cavalier Servente."

14:8. *lost Pleiad*: The Pleiads, according to Greek myth, were the seven daughters of Atlas changed into stars.

15:5. *Goldoni*: Italian comic playwright (1707–1793).

17:8. *"Cavalier Servente"*: Among the Italian aristocracy, the official

18

Their jealousy (if they are ever jealous)
  Is of a fair complexion altogether,
Not like that sooty devil of Othello's,
  Which smothers women in a bed of feather,
But worthier of these much more jolly fellows,
  When weary of the matrimonial tether
His head for such a wife no mortal bothers,
But takes at once another, or *another's*.

19

Didst ever see a Gondola? For fear
  You should not, I'll describe it you exactly:
'Tis a long covered boat that's common here,
  Carved at the prow, built lightly, but compactly,
Rowed by two rowers, each call'd "Gondolier,"
  It glides along the water looking blackly,
Just like a coffin clapt in a canoe,
Where none can make out what you say or do.

20

And up and down the long canals they go,
  And under the Rialto shoot along,
By night and day, all paces, swift or slow,
  And round the theatres, a sable throng,
They wait in their dusk livery of woe, —
  But not to them do woeful things belong,
For sometimes they contain a deal of fun,
Like mourning coaches when the funeral's done.

21

But to my story. — 'Twas some years ago,
  It may be thirty, forty, more or less,
The Carnival was at its height, and so
  Were all kinds of buffoonery and dress;

lover of a married woman who accompanied her everywhere and was
openly accepted in society. See below stanzas 36ff.
   20:2. *Rialto*: The bridge leading to the island, which is properly the
Rialto. See note to *Childe Harold*, IV, 4:6.

A certain lady went to see the show,
   Her real name I know not, nor can guess,
And so we'll call her Laura, if you please,
Because it slips into my verse with ease.

22

She was not old, nor young, nor at the years
   Which certain people call a *"certain age,"*
Which yet the most uncertain age appears,
   Because I never heard, nor could engage
A person yet by prayers, or bribes, or tears,
   To name, define by speech, or write on page,
The period meant precisely by that word, —
Which surely is exceedingly absurd.

23

Laura was blooming still, had made the best
   Of Time, and Time returned the compliment,
And treated her genteelly, so that, dressed,
   She looked extremely well where'er she went;
A pretty woman is a welcome guest,
   And Laura's brow a frown had rarely bent;
Indeed, she shone all smiles, and seemed to flatter
Mankind with her black eyes for looking at her.

24

She was a married woman; 'tis convenient,
   Because in Christian countries 'tis a rule
To view their little slips with eyes more lenient;
   Whereas if single ladies play the fool,
(Unless within the period intervenient
   A well-timed wedding makes the scandal cool)
I don't know how they ever can get over it,
Except they manage never to discover it.

25

Her husband sailed upon the Adriatic,
   And made some voyages, too, in other seas,

And when he lay in Quarantine for pratique
   (A forty days' precaution 'gainst disease),
His wife would mount, at times, her highest attic,
   For thence she could discern the ship with ease:
He was a merchant trading to Aleppo,
His name Giuseppe, called more briefly, Beppo.

26

He was a man as dusky as a Spaniard,
   Sunburnt with travel, yet a portly figure;
Though coloured, as it were, within a tanyard,
   He was a person both of sense and vigour —
A better seaman never yet did man yard;
   And she, although her manners showed no rigour,
Was deemed a woman of the strictest principle,
So much as to be thought almost invincible.

27

But several years elapsed since they had met;
   Some people thought the ship was lost, and some
That he had somehow blundered into debt,
   And did not like the thought of steering home;
And there were several offered any bet,
   Or that he would, or that he would not come;
For most men (till by losing rendered sager)
Will back their own opinions with a wager.

28

'Tis said that their last parting was pathetic,
   As partings often are, or ought to be,
And their presentiment was quite prophetic,
   That they should never more each other see,
(A sort of morbid feeling, half poetic,
   Which I have known occur in two or three,)

25:3. *Pratique*: A clean bill of health.
25:7. *Aleppo*: A city in north west Syria.
25:8. *Beppo*: "Joe," the nickname for Giuseppe (Joseph).

When kneeling on the shore upon her sad knee
He left this Adriatic Ariadne.

29

And Laura waited long, and wept a little,
   And thought of wearing weeds, as well she might;
She almost lost all appetite for victual,
   And could not sleep with ease alone at night;
She deemed the window-frames and shutters brittle
   Against a daring housebreaker or sprite,
And so she thought it prudent to connect her
With a vice-husband, *chiefly* to *protect her.*

30

She chose, (and what is there they will not choose,
   If only you will but oppose their choice?)
Till Beppo should return from his long cruise,
   And bid once more her faithful heart rejoice,
A man some women like, and yet abuse —
   A Coxcomb was he by the public voice;
A Count of wealth, they said, as well as quality,
And in his pleasures of great liberality.

31

And then he was a Count, and then he knew
   Music, and dancing, fiddling, French and Tuscan;
The last not easy, be it known to you,
   For few Italians speak the right Etruscan.
He was a critic upon operas, too,
   And knew all niceties of sock and buskin;
And no Venetian audience could endure a
Song, scene, or air, when he cried "seccatura!"

28:8. *Ariadne*: In Greek myth, the Cretan princess who gave Theseus the clue that enabled him to kill the Minotaur and who was later abandoned by him at Naxos.

31:6. *sock and buskin*: Comedy and tragedy.

31:8. *"seccatura"*: Nuisance, bore.

32

His "bravo" was decisive, for that sound
　　Hushed "Academie" sighed in silent awe;
The fiddlers trembled as he looked around,
　　For fear of some false note's detected flaw;
The "Prima Donna's" tuneful heart would bound,
　　Dreading the deep damnation of his "Bah!"
Soprano, Basso, even the Contra-Alto,
Wished him five fathom under the Rialto.

33

He patronised the Improvisatori,
　　Nay, could himself extemporise some stanzas,
Wrote rhymes, sang songs, could also tell a story,
　　Sold pictures, and was skilful in the dance as
Italians can be, though in this their glory
　　Must surely yield the palm to that which France has;
In short, he was a perfect Cavaliero,
And to his very valet seemed a hero.

34

Then he was faithful too, as well as amorous;
　　So that no sort of female could complain,
Although they're now and then a little clamorous,
　　He never put the pretty souls in pain;
His heart was one of those which most enamour us,
　　Wax to receive, and marble to retain:
He was a lover of the good old school,
Who still become more constant as they cool.

35

No wonder such accomplishments should turn
　　A female head, however sage and steady —
With scarce a hope that Beppo could return,
　　In law he was almost as good as dead, he
Nor sent, nor wrote, nor showed the least concern,
　　And she had waited several years already:

And really if a man won't let us know
That he's alive, he's *dead* — or should be so.

36

Besides, within the Alps, to every woman,
   (Although, God knows, it is a grievous sin,)
'Tis, I may say, permitted to have *two* men;
   I can't tell who first brought the custom in,
But "Cavalier Serventes" are quite common,
   And no one notices or cares a pin;
And we may call this (not to say the worst)
A *second* marriage which corrupts the *first*.

37

The word was formerly a "Ciscisbeo,"
   But *that* is now grown vulgar and indecent;
The Spaniards call the person a *"Cortejo,"*
   For the same mode subsists in Spain, though recent;
In short it reaches from the Po to Teio,
   And may perhaps at last be o'er the sea sent:
But Heaven preserve Old England from such courses!
Or what becomes of damage and divorces?

38

However, I still think, with all due deference
   To the fair *single* part of the creation,
That married ladies should preserve the preference
   In *tête à tête* or general conversation —
And this I say without peculiar reference
   To England, France, or any other nation —
Because they know the world, and are at ease,
And being natural, naturally please.

39

'Tis true, your budding Miss is very charming,
   But shy and awkward at first coming out,

37:5. *Po to Teio*: Po, a river in northern Italy flowing into the Adriatic, and Teio (Tagus), a river in Spain and Portugal flowing into the Atlantic.

So much alarmed, that she is quite alarming,
 All Giggle, Blush; half Pertness, and half Pout;
And glancing at *Mamma,* for fear there's harm in
 What you, she, it, or they, may be about:
The Nursery still lisps out in all they utter —
Besides, they always smell of bread and butter.

40

But "Cavalier Servente" is the phrase
 Used in politest circles to express
This supernumerary slave, who stays
 Close to the lady as a part of dress,
Her word the only law which he obeys.
 His is no sinecure, as you may guess;
Coach, servants, gondola, he goes to call,
And carries fan and tippet, gloves and shawl.

41

With all its sinful doings, I must say,
 That Italy's a pleasant place to me,
Who love to see the Sun shine every day,
 And vines (not nailed to walls) from tree to tree
Festooned, much like the back scene of a play,
 Or melodrame, which people flock to see,
When the first act is ended by a dance
In vineyards copied from the South of France.

42

I like on Autumn evenings to ride out,
 Without being forced to bid my groom be sure
My cloak is round his middle strapped about,
 Because the skies are not the most secure;
I know too that, if stopped upon my route,
 Where the green alleys windingly allure,
Reeling with *grapes* red wagons choke the way, —
In England 'twould be dung, dust, or a dray.

43

I also like to dine on becaficas,
   To see the Sun set, sure he'll rise to-morrow,
Not through a misty morning twinkling weak as
   A drunken man's dead eye in maudlin sorrow,
But with all Heaven t'himself; the day will break as
   Beauteous as cloudless, nor be forced to borrow
That sort of farthing candlelight which glimmers
Where reeking London's smoky cauldron simmers.

44

I love the language, that soft bastard Latin,
   Which melts like kisses from a female mouth,
And sounds as if it should be writ on satin,
   With syllables which breathe of the sweet South,
And gentle liquids gliding all so pat in,
   That not a single accent seems uncouth,
Like our harsh northern whistling, grunting gutteral,
Which we're obliged to hiss, and spit, and sputter all.

45

I like the women too (forgive my folly!),
   From the rich peasant cheek of ruddy bronze,
And large black eyes that flash on you a volley
   Of rays that say a thousand things at once,
To the high Dama's brow, more melancholy,
   But clear, and with a wild and liquid glance,
Heart on her lips, and soul within her eyes,
Soft as her clime, and sunny as her skies.

46

Eve of the land which still is Paradise!
   Italian Beauty didst thou not inspire
Raphael, who died in thy embrace, and vies
   With all we know of Heaven, or can desire,

43:1. *becaficas*: Songbirds, delicacies particularly in an autumn after they have fattened on fruits.
46:3. *Raphael* (1483–1520) died of a fever after, according to Vasari, "an unusually wild debauch."

In what he hath bequeathed us? — in what guise,
   Though flashing from the fervour of the Lyre,
Would *words* describe thy past and present glow,
While yet Canova can create below ?

47

"England! with all thy faults I love thee still,"
   I said at Calais, and have not forgot it;
I like to speak and lucubrate my fill;
   I like the government (but that is not it);
I like the freedom of the press and quill;
   I like the Habeas Corpus (when we've got it);
I like a Parliamentary debate,
Particularly when 'tis not too late;

48

I like the taxes, when they're not too many;
   I like a seacoal fire, when not too dear;
I like a beef-steak, too, as well as any;
   Have no objection to a pot of beer;
I like the weather, — when it is not rainy,
   That is, I like two months of every year.
And so God save the Regent, Church, and King!
Which means that I like all and every thing.

49

Our standing army, and disbanded seamen,
   Poor's rate, Reform, my own, the nation's debt,
Our little riots just to show we're free men,
   Our trifling bankruptcies in the Gazette,
Our cloudy climate, and our chilly women,
   All these I can forgive, and those forget,
And greatly venerate our recent glories,
And wish they were not owing to the Tories.

46:8. *Canova* (1757–1822), Italian sculptor.
47:1. William Cowper, *The Task*, II, 206.

50

But to my tale of Laura, — for I find
   Digression is a sin, that by degrees
Becomes exceeding tedious to my mind,
   And, therefore, may the reader too displease —
The gentle reader, who may wax unkind,
   And caring little for the Author's ease,
Insist on knowing what he means — a hard
And hapless situation for a Bard.

51

Oh! that I had the art of easy writing
   What should be easy reading! could I scale
Parnassus, where the Muses sit inditing
   Those pretty poems never known to fail,
How quickly would I print (the word delighting)
   A Grecian, Syrian, or Assyrian tale;
And sell you, mixed with western Sentimentalism,
Some samples of the *finest Orientalism.*

52

But I am but a nameless sort of person,
   (A broken Dandy lately on my travels)
And take for rhyme, to hook my rambling verse on,
   The first that Walker's Lexicon unravels,
And when I can't find that, I put a worse on,
   Not caring as I ought for critics' cavils;
I've half a mind to tumble down to prose,
But verse is more in fashion — so here goes!

53

The Count and Laura made their new arrangement,
   Which lasted, as arrangements sometimes do,

51:8. Byron is poking fun at the vogue for Oriental verse tales, and
in the last lines is probably laughing at his own enormously popular
"Tales."

52:4. *Walker's Lexicon*: *A Rhyming Dictionary* (1775) by James Walker
(1732–1807).

For half a dozen years without estrangement;
   They had their little differences, too;
Those jealous whiffs, which never any change meant;
   In such affairs there probably are few
Who have not had this pouting sort of squabble,
From sinners of high station to the rabble.

54

But, on the whole, they were a happy pair,
   As happy as unlawful love could make them;
The gentleman was fond, the lady fair,
   Their chains so slight, 'twas not worth while to break them:
The World beheld them with indulgent air;
   The pious only wished "the Devil take them!"
He took them not; he very often waits,
And leaves old sinners to be young ones' baits.

55

But they were young: Oh! what without our Youth
   Would Love be! What would Youth be without Love!
Youth lends its joy, and sweetness, vigour, truth,
   Heart, soul, and all that seems as from above;
But, languishing with years, it grows uncouth —
   One of few things Experience don't improve;
Which is, perhaps, the reason why old fellows
Are always so preposterously jealous.

56

It was the Carnival, as I have said
   Some six and thirty stanzas back, and so
Laura the usual preparations made,
   Which you do when your mind's made up to go
To-night to Mrs. Boehm's masquerade,
   Spectator, or Partaker in the show;

56:5. *Mrs. Boehm's masquerade*: On June 17, 1817, the *London Morning Chronicle* reported "On Monday evening this distinguished lady of the *haut ton* gave a splendid masquerade at her residence in St. James Square." It was the kind of party Byron had often attended before he left England.

The only difference known between the cases
Is — *here*, we have six weeks of "varnished faces."

57

Laura, when dressed, was (as I sang before)
   A pretty woman as was ever seen,
Fresh as the Angel o'er a new inn door,
   Or frontispiece of a new Magazine,
With all the fashions which the last month wore,
   Coloured, and silver paper leaved between
That and the title-page, for fear the Press
Should soil with parts of speech the parts of dress.

58

They went to the Ridotto; 'tis a hall
   Where People dance, and sup, and dance again;
Its proper name, perhaps, were a masqued ball,
   But that's of no importance to my strain;
'Tis (on a smaller scale) like our Vauxhall,
   Excepting that it can't be spoit by rain;
The company is "mixed" (the phrase I quote is
As much as saying, they're below your notice);

59

For a "mixed company" implies that, save
   Yourself and friends, and half a hundred more,
Whom you may bow to without looking grave,
   The rest are but a vulgar set, the Bore
Of public places, where they basely brave
   The fashionable stare of twenty score
Of well-bred persons, called *"The World;"* but I,
Although I know them, really don't know why.

60

This is the case in England; at least was
   During the dynasty of Dandies, now

58:1. *Ridotto*: Public entertainment; synonym for masquerade.
58:5. *Vauxhall*: Public entertainment gardens in London which closed in 1859.

Perchance succeeded by some other class
    Of imitated Imitators: — how
Irreparably soon decline, alas!
    The Demagogues of fashion: all below
Is frail; how easily the world is lost
By Love, or War, and, now and then, — by Frost!

61

Crushed was Napoleon by the northern Thor,
    Who knocked his army down with icy hammer,
Stopped by the *Elements* — like a Whaler — or
    A blundering novice in his new French grammar;
Good cause had he to doubt the chance of war,
    And as for Fortune — but I dare not d—n her,
Because, were I to ponder to Infinity,
The more I should believe in her Divinity.

62

She rules the present, past, and all to be yet,
    She gives us luck in lotteries, love, and marriage;
I cannot say that she's done much for me yet;
    Not that I mean her bounties to disparage,
We've not yet closed accounts, and we shall see yet
    How much she'll make amends for past miscarriage;
Meantime the Goddess I'll no more importune,
Unless to thank her when she's made my fortune.

63

To turn, — and to return; — the Devil take it!
    This story slips for ever through my fingers,
Because, just as the stanza likes to make it,
    It needs must be — and so it rather lingers;
This form of verse began, I can't well break it,
    But must keep time and tune like public singers;
But if I once get through my present measure,
I'll take another when I'm next at leisure.

61:1. *Crushed was Napoleon*: Napoleon's retreat from Russia in the winter of 1812 was turned into a rout by the severe weather.

64

They went to the Ridotto ('tis a place
   To which I mean to go myself to-morrow,
Just to divert my thoughts a little space
   Because I'm rather hippish, and may borrow
Some spirits, guessing at what kind of face
   May lurk beneath each mask; and as my sorrow
Slackens its pace sometimes, I'll make, or find,
Something shall leave it half an hour behind.)

65

Now Laura moves along the joyous crowd,
   Smiles in her eyes, and simpers on her lips;
To some she whispers, others speaks aloud;
   To some she curtsies, and to some she dips,
Complains of warmth, and this complaint avowed,
   Her lover brings the lemonade, she sips;
She then surveys, condemns, but pities still
Her dearest friends for being dressed so ill.

66

One has false curls, another too much paint,
   A third — where did she buy that frightful turban?
A fourth's so pale she fears she's going to faint,
   A fifth's look's vulgar, dowdyish, and suburban,
A sixth's white silk has got a yellow taint,
   A seventh's thin muslin surely will be her bane,
And lo! an eighth appears, — "I'll see no more!"
For fear, like Banquo's kings, they reach a score.

67

Meantime, while she was thus at others gazing,
   Others were levelling their looks at her;
She heard the men's half-whispered mode of praising
   And, till 'twas done, determined not to stir;
The women only thought it quite amazing
   That, at her time of life, so many were

66:7–8. See *Macbeth* IV. i. 112–118.

Admirers still, — but "Men are so debased,
Those brazen Creatures always suit their taste."

68

For my part, now, I ne'er could understand
   Why naughty women — but I won't discuss
A thing which is a scandal to the land,
   I only don't see why it should be thus;
And if I were but in a gown and band,
   Just to entitle me to make a fuss,
I'd preach on this till Wilberforce and Romilly
Should quote in their next speeches from my homily.

69

While Laura thus was seen, and seeing, smiling,
   Talking, she knew not why, and cared not what,
So that her female friends, with envy broiling,
   Beheld her airs, and triumph, and all that;
And well-dressed males still kept before her filing,
   And passing bowed and mingled with her chat;
More than the rest one person seemed to stare
With pertinacity that's rather rare.

70

He was a Turk, the colour of mahogany;
   And Laura saw him, and at first was glad,
Because the Turks so much admire philogyny,
   Although their usage of their wives is sad;
'Tis said they use no better than a dog any
   Poor woman, whom they purchase like a pad:
They have a number, though they ne'er exhibit 'em,
Four wives by law, and concubines "ad libitum."

71

They lock them up, and veil, and guard them daily,
   They scarcely can behold their male relations,

68:7. William *Wilberforce* (1759–1833) who fought successfully for the abolition of the slave trade, and Sir Samuel *Romilly* (1757–1818). See *Don Juan*, I, 15:4, note.

So that their moments do not pass so gaily
   As is supposed the case with northern nations;
Confinement, too, must make them look quite palely;
   And as the Turks abhor long conversations,
Their days are either passed in doing nothing,
Or bathing, nursing, making love, and clothing.

72

They cannot read, and so don't lisp in criticism;
   Nor write, and so they don't affect the Muse;
Were never caught in epigram or witticism,
   Have no romances, sermons, plays, reviews, —
In Harams learning soon would make a pretty schism,
   But luckily these Beauties are no "Blues;"
No bustling *Botherby* have they to show 'em
"That charming passage in the last new poem:"

73

No solemn, antique gentleman of rhyme,
   Who having angled all his life for Fame,
And getting but a nibble at a time,
   Still fussily keeps fishing on, the same
Small "Triton of the minnows," the sublime
   Of Mediocrity, the furious tame,
The Echo's echo, usher of the school
Of female wits, boy bards — in short, a fool!

74

A stalking oracle of awful phrase,
   The approving *"Good!"* (by no means GOOD in law)
Humming like flies around the newest blaze,
   The bluest of bluebottles you e'er saw,
Teasing with blame, excruciating with praise,
   Gorging the little fame he gets all raw,

72:6. *"Blues"*: Bluestockings, nick-name for lady intellectuals.
72:7. *Botherby*: William Sotheby (1757–1833), poet, translator and patron of the arts. Like Southey, he had incurred Byron's wrath for a presumed insulting remark, and is pilloried here as Poet-Fool.

Translating tongues he knows not even by letter,
And sweating plays so middling, bad were better.

75

One hates an author that's *all author* — fellows
   In foolscap uniforms turned up with ink,
So very anxious, clever, fine, and jealous,
   One don't know what to say to them, or think,
Unless to puff them with a pair of bellows;
   Of Coxcombry's worst coxcombs e'en the pink
Are preferable to these shreds of paper,
These unquenched snuffings of the midnight taper.

76

Of these same we see several, and of others,
   Men of the world, who know the World like Men,
Scott, Rogers, Moore, and all the better brothers,
   Who think of something else besides the pen;
But for the children of the "Mighty Mother's,"
   The would-be wits, and can't-be gentlemen,
I leave them to their daily "tea is ready,"
Smug coterie, and literary lady.

77

The poor dear Mussul*women* whom I mention
   Have none of these instructive pleasant people,
And *one* would seem to them a new invention,
   Unknown as bells within a Turkish steeple;
I think 'twould almost be worth while to pension
   (Though best-sown projects very often reap ill)
A missionary author — just to preach
Our Christian usage of the parts of speech.

76:3. Sir Walter Scott (1771–1832), Samuel Rogers (1763–1855), and Thomas Moore (1779–1852) were contemporary writers Byron held up as models. See below *Don Juan*, I, 205.

76:8. Probably a reference to "Wordsworth and Co." Byron in a letter referred to the "tea-drinking neutrality of morals" of the Lake school of poets.

78

No Chemistry for them unfolds her gases,
  No Metaphysics are let loose in lectures,
No Circulating Library amasses
  Religious novels, moral tales, and strictures
Upon the living manners, as they pass us;
  No Exhibition glares with annual pictures;
They stare not on the stars from out their attics,
Nor deal (thank God for that!) in Mathematics.

79

Why I thank God for that is not great matter,
  I have my reasons, you no doubt suppose,
And as, perhaps, they would not highly flatter,
  I'll keep them for my life (to come) in prose;
I fear I have a little turn for Satire,
  And yet methinks the older that one grows
Inclines us more to laugh than scold, though Laughter
Leaves us so doubly serious shortly after.

80

Oh, Mirth and Innocence! Oh, Milk and Water!
  Ye happy mixtures of more happy days!
In these sad centuries of sin and slaughter,
  Abominable Man no more allays
His thirst with such pure beverage. No matter,
  I love you both, and both shall have my praise:
Oh, for old Saturn's reign of sugar-candy! —
Meantime I drink to your return in brandy.

81

Our Laura's Turk still kept his eyes upon her,
  Less in the Mussulman than Christian way,
Which seems to say, "Madam, I do you honour,
  And while I please to stare, you'll please to stay."
Could staring win a woman, this had won her,
  But Laura could not thus be led astray;

78:8. Probably a stab at Lady Byron. See *Don Juan*, I, 12:1.

She had stood fire too long and well, to boggle
Even at this Stranger's most outlandish ogle.

82

The morning now was on the point of breaking,
   A turn of time at which I would advise
Ladies who have been dancing, or partaking
   In any other kind of exercise,
To make their preparations for forsaking
   The ball-room ere the Sun begins to rise,
Because when once the lamps and candles fail,
His blushes make them look a little pale.

83

I've seen some balls and revels in my time,
   And stayed them over for some silly reason,
And then I looked (I hope it was no crime)
   To see what lady best stood out the season;
And though I've seen some thousands in their prime
   Lovely and pleasing, and who still may please on,
I never saw but one (the stars withdrawn)
Whose bloom could after dancing dare the Dawn.

84

The name of this Aurora I'll not mention,
   Although I might, for she was nought to me
More than that patent work of God's invention,
   A charming woman, whom we like to see;
But writing names would merit reprehension,
   Yet if you like to find out this fair *She*,
At the next London or Parisian ball
You still may mark her cheek, out-blooming all.

85

Laura, who knew it would not do at all
   To meet the daylight after seven hours' sitting
Among three thousand people at a ball,
   To make her curtsey thought it right and fitting;

The Count was at her elbow with her shawl,
    And they the room were on the point of quitting,
When lo! those curséd Gondoliers had got
Just in the very place where they *should not*.

86

In this they're like our coachmen, and the cause
    Is much the same — the crowd, and pulling, hauling,
With blasphemies enough to break their jaws,
    They make a never intermitted bawling.
At home, our Bow-street gem'men keep the laws,
    And here a sentry stands within your calling;
But for all that, there is a deal of swearing,
And nauseous words past mentioning or bearing.

87

The Count and Laura found their boat at last,
    And homeward floated o'er the silent tide,
Discussing all the dances gone and past;
    The dancers and their dresses, too, beside;
Some little scandals eke; but all aghast
    (As to their palace-stairs the rowers glide)
Sate Laura by the side of her adorer,
When lo! the Mussulman was there before her!

88

"Sir," said the Count, with brow exceeding grave,
    "Your unexpected presence here will make
It necessary for myself to crave
    Its import? But perhaps 'tis a mistake;
I hope it is so; and, at once to waive
    All compliment, I hope so for *your* sake;
You understand my meaning, or you *shall*."
"Sir," (quoth the Turk) " 'tis no mistake at all:

86:5. *Bow-street gem'men*: The Bow Street Runners, appointed in 1805 and attached to Bow Street Court, were the precursors of Scotland Yard.

89

"That Lady is *my wife!*" Much wonder paints
   The lady's changing cheek, as well it might;
But where an Englishwoman sometimes faints,
   Italian females don't do so outright;
They only call a little on their Saints,
   And then come to themselves, almost, or quite;
Which saves much hartshorn, salts, and sprinkling faces,
And cutting stays, as usual in such cases.

90

She said, — what could she say? Why, not a word;
   But the Count courteously invited in
The Stranger, much appeased by what he heard:
   "Such things, perhaps, we'd best discuss within,"
Said he; "don't let us make ourselves absurd
   In public, by a scene, nor raise a din,
For then the chief and only satisfaction
Will be much quizzing on the whole transaction."

91

They entered, and for Coffee called — it came,
   A beverage for Turks and Christians both,
Although the way they make it's not the same.
   Now Laura, much recovered, or less loth
To speak, cries "Beppo! what's your pagan name?
   Bless me! your beard is of amazing growth!
And how came you to keep away so long?
Are you not sensible 'twas very wrong?

92

"And are you *really, truly,* now a Turk?
   With any other women did you wive?
Is't true they use their fingers for a fork?
   Well, that's the prettiest Shawl — as I'm alive!

89:7. *Hartshorn*: Volatile preparation of ammonia, used as smelling-salts.

You'll give it me? They say you eat no pork.
 And how so many years did you contrive
To — Bless me! did I ever? No, I never
Saw a man grown so yellow! How's your liver?

93

"Beppo! that beard of yours becomes you not;
 It shall be shaved before you're a day older:
Why do you wear it? Oh! I had forgot —
 Pray don't you think the weather here is colder?
How do I look? You shan't stir from this spot
 In that queer dress, for fear that some beholder
Should find you out, and make the story known.
How short your hair is! Lord! how grey it's grown!"

94

What answer Beppo made to these demands
 Is more than I know. He was cast away
About where Troy stood once, and nothing stands;
 Became a slave of course, and for his pay
Had bread and bastinadoes, till some bands
 Of pirates landing in a neighbouring bay,
He joined the rogues and prospered, and became
A renegado of indifferent fame.

95

But he grew rich, and with his riches grew so
 Keen the desire to see his home again,
He thought himself in duty bound to do so,
 And not be always thieving on the main;
Lonely he felt, at times, as Robin Crusoe,
 And so he hired a vessel come from Spain,
Bound for Corfu: she was a fine polacca,
Manned with twelve hands, and laden with tobacco.

95:7. *Palacca*: A three-masted merchant vessel.

96

Himself, and much (heaven knows how gotten!) cash,
  He then embarked, with risk of life and limb,
And got clear off, although the attempt was rash;
  He said that *Providence* protected him —
For my part, I say nothing — lest we clash
  In our opinions: — well — the ship was trim,
Set sail, and kept her reckoning fairly on,
Except three days of calm when off Cape Bonn.

97

They reached the Island, he transferred his lading,
  And self and live stock to another bottom,
And passed for a true Turkey-merchant, trading
  With goods of various names — but I've forgot 'em.
However, he got off by this evading,
  Or else the people would perhaps have shot him;
And thus at Venice landed to reclaim
His wife, religion, house, and Christian name.

98

His wife received, the Patriarch re-baptised him,
  (He made the Church a present, by the way;)
He then threw off the garments which disguised him,
  And borrowed the Count's smallclothes for a day:
His friends the more for his long absence prized him,
  Finding he'd wherewithal to make them gay,
With dinners, where he oft became the laugh of them,
For stories — but *I* don't believe the half of them.

99

Whate'er his youth had suffered, his old age
  With wealth and talking made him some amends;
Though Laura sometimes put him in a rage,
  I've heard the Count and he were always friends.

96:8. *Cape Bonn*: Northernmost point of Tunis.

My pen is at the bottom of a page,
    Which being finished, here the story ends:
'Tis to be wished it had been sooner done,
But stories somehow lengthen when begun.

1817   1818

Plays

Manfred
A DRAMATIC POEM

On February 15, 1817, Byron wrote to John Murray: ". . . . I forgot to mention to you that a kind of Poem in dialogue (in blank verse) or drama, begun last summer in Switzerland, is finished; it is in three acts; but of a very wild, metaphysical, and inexplicable kind. Almost all the persons — but two or three — are spirits of the earth and air, or the waters; the scene is in the Alps; the hero a kind of magician, who is tormented by a species of remorse, the cause of which is left half unexplained. He wanders about invoking these spirits, which appear to him, and are of no use; he at last goes to the very abode of the Evil principle in *propria persona,* to evocate a ghost, which appears, and gives him an ambiguous and disagreeable answer; and in the 3d act he is found by his attendants dying in a tower where he studied his art. You may perceive by this outline that I have no great opinion of this piece of phantasy; but I have at least rendered it *quite impossible* for the stage, for which my intercourse with D[rury] Lane has given me the greatest contempt.

I have not even copied it off, and feel too lazy at present to attempt the whole; but when I have, I will send it you, and you may either throw it into the fire or not."

In spite of the assumed nonchalance of the letter, Byron thought highly enough of "this piece of phantasy" to rewrite carefully the third act, when the original version (in which the Abbot is carried off by a devil in a slapstick scene and Manfred is found dying by his servants in a brief final scene) was severely criticized by William Gifford, whose opinion Byron greatly respected.

Byron also vigorously defended his play against the charges in various reviews that he had borrowed from Goethe's *Faust* and Marlowe's *Faustus.* To Murray on October 23, 1817 he

181

snapped, "The devil may take both the Faustuses, German and English, — I have taken neither." He insisted that he never read or saw Marlowe's *Faustus* and that "Goethe's Faust I never read, for I don't know German; but Matthew Monk Lewis in 1816, at Coligny, translated most of it to me viva voce, and I was naturally much struck with it; but it was the *Staubach* (sic) and the *Jungfrau,* and something else, much more than *Faustus,* that made me write *Manfred.* The first scene, however, and that of Faustus are very similar." (Letter to Murray, June 7, 1820.) The Staubback is a waterfall; the Jungfrau a mountain in the Swiss Alps; the "something else" is an oblique reference to Augusta. In an earlier letter, he had said, "As to the germs of *Manfred,* they may be found in the Journal which I sent to Mrs. Leigh." (See below, pp. 647–651.)

Byron is justified in defending himself. Manfred is almost the opposite of Faust. Where Faust makes a contract with Mephistopheles, Manfred refuses to make any pact with the spirits he evokes. Where Faust seeks youth, power, and knowledge, and so is led to sin, Manfred seeks forgetfulness, self-oblivion, for sins already committed. Ironically through the series of confrontations that make up the action of the drama, Manfred is condemned to increased self-awareness, and in the end accepts full responsibility for his actions. He dies independent and alone, without excuse or fear. The relation to modern existentialist drama is evident. (For further critical comment, see Introduction, p. xix above.)

*"There are more things in heaven and earth, Horatio,
Than are dreamt of in your philosophy."*

DRAMATIS PERSONAE

MANFRED	WITCH OF THE ALPS
CHAMOIS HUNTER	ARIMANES
ABBOT OF ST. MAURICE	NEMESIS
MANUEL	THE DESTINIES
HERMAN	SPIRITS, ETC.

Epigraph: "There are more things . . . ." *Hamlet* I. v. 166–67.

The Scene of the Drama is amongst the Higher Alps — partly in the Castle of Manfred, and partly in the Mountains.

ACT I

SCENE I. — MANFRED *alone. — Scene, a Gothic Gallery. — Time, Midnight.*

Manfred. The lamp must be replenished, but even then
It will not burn so long as I must watch:
My slumbers — if I slumber — are not sleep,
But a continuance of enduring thought,
Which then I can resist not: in my heart   5
There is a vigil, and these eyes but close
To look within; and yet I live, and bear
The aspect and the form of breathing men.
But Grief should be the Instructor of the wise;
Sorrow is Knowledge: they who know the most   10
Must mourn the deepest o'er the fatal truth,
The Tree of Knowledge is not that of Life.
Philosophy and science, and the springs
Of Wonder, and the wisdom of the World,
I have essayed, and in my mind there is   15
A power to make these subject to itself —
But they avail not: I have done men good,
And I have met with good even among men —
But this availed not: I have had my foes,
And none have baffled, many fallen before me —   20
But this availed not: — Good — or evil — life —
Powers, passions — all I see in other beings,
Have been to me as rain unto the sands,
Since that all-nameless hour. I have no dread,
And feel the curse to have no natural fear,   25
Nor fluttering throb, that beats with hopes or wishes,
Or lurking love of something on the earth.
Now to my task. —
                    Mysterious Agency!
Ye Spirits of the unbounded Universe!
Whom I have sought in darkness and in light —   30
Ye, who do compass earth about, and dwell

In subtler essence — ye, to whom the tops
Of mountains inaccessible are haunts,
And Earth's and Ocean's caves familiar things —
I call upon ye by the written charm   35
Which gives me power upon you — Rise! Appear!

                                                        [*A pause.*]

They come not yet. — Now by the voice of him
Who is the first among you — by this sign,
Which makes you tremble — by the claims of him
Who is undying, — Rise! Appear! —— Appear!   40

                                                        [*A pause.*]

If it be so. — Spirits of Earth and Air,
Ye shall not so elude me! By a power,
Deeper than all yet urged, a tyrant-spell,
Which had its birthplace in a star condemned,
The burning wreck of a demolished world,   45
A wandering hell in the eternal Space;
By the strong curse which is upon my Soul,
The thought which is within me and around me,
I do compel ye to my will. — Appear!

[*A star is seen at the darker end of the gallery: it is
stationary; and a voice is heard singing.*]

FIRST SPIRIT

Mortal! to thy bidding bowed,   50
From my mansion in the cloud,
Which the breath of Twilight builds,
And the Summer's sunset gilds
With the azure and vermilion,
Which is mixed for my pavilion;   55
Though thy quest may be forbidden,
On a star-beam I have ridden,
To thine adjuration bowed:
Mortal — be thy wish avowed!

Voice of the SECOND SPIRIT.

Mont Blanc is the Monarch of mountains;   60
  They crowned him long ago

On a throne of rocks, in a robe of clouds,
  With a Diadem of snow.
Around his waist are forests braced,
  The Avalanche in his hand; 65
But ere it fall, that thundering ball
  Must pause for my command.
The Glacier's cold and restless mass
  Moves onward day by day;
But I am he who bids it pass, 70
  Or with its ice delay.
I am the Spirit of the place,
  Could make the mountain bow
And quiver to his caverned base —
  And what with me would'st *Thou?* 75

Voice of the THIRD SPIRIT.

In the blue depth of the waters,
  Where the wave hath no strife,
Where the Wind is a stranger,
  And the Sea-snake hath life,
Where the Mermaid is decking 80
  Her green hair with shells,
Like the storm on the surface
  Came the sound of thy spells;
O'er my calm Hall of Coral
  The deep Echo rolled — 85
To the Spirit of Ocean
  Thy wishes unfold!

FOURTH SPIRIT.

Where the slumbering Earthquake
  Lies pillowed on fire,
And the lakes of bitumen 90
  Rise boilingly higher;
Where the roots of the Andes
  Strike deep in the earth,
As their summits to heaven

Shoot soaringly forth;   95
I have quitted my birthplace,
   Thy bidding to bide —
Thy spell hath subdued me,
   Thy will be my guide!

FIFTH SPIRIT.

I am the Rider of the wind,   100
   The Stirrer of the storm;
The hurricane I left behind
   Is yet with lightning warm;
To speed to thee, o'er shore and sea
   I swept upon the blast: 105
The fleet I met sailed well — and yet
   'Twill sink ere night be past.

SIXTH SPIRIT.

My dwelling is the shadow of the Night,
Why doth thy magic torture me with light?

SEVENTH SPIRIT.

The Star which rules thy destiny   110
Was ruled, ere earth began, by me:
It was a World as fresh and fair
As e'er revolved round Sun in air;
Its course was free and regular,
Space bosomed not a lovelier star.   115
The Hour arrived — and it became
A wandering mass of shapeless flame,
A pathless Comet, and a curse,
The menace of the Universe;
Still rolling on with innate force,   120
Without a sphere, without a course,
A bright deformity on high,
The monster of the upper sky!
And Thou! beneath its influence born —
Thou worm! whom I obey and scorn —   125

Forced by a Power (which is not thine,
And let thee but to make thee mine)
For this brief moment to descend,
Where these weak Spirits round thee bend
And parley with a thing like thee —   130
What would'st thou, Child of Clay! with me?

The SEVEN SPIRITS.

Earth — ocean — air — night — mountains — winds — thy
    Star,
    Are at thy beck and bidding, Child of Clay!
Before thee at thy quest their Spirits are —
    What would'st thou with us, Son of mortals — say?   135
    Manfred. Forgetfulness ——
    First Spirit.   Of what — of whom — and why?
    Manfred. Of that which is within me; read it there —
Ye know it — and I cannot utter it.
    Spirit. We can but give thee that which we possess:
Ask of us subjects, sovereignty, the power   140
O'er earth — the whole, or portion — or a sign
Which shall control the elements, whereof
We are the dominators, — each and all,
These shall be thine.
    Manfred.   Oblivion — self-oblivion!
Can ye not wring from out the hidden realms   145
Ye offer so profusely — what I ask?
    Spirit. It is not in our essence, in our skill;
But — thou may'st die.
    Manfred.   Will Death bestow it on me?
    Spirit. We are immortal, and do not forget;
We are eternal; and to us the past   150
Is, as the future, present. Art thou answered?
    Manfred. Ye mock me — but the Power which brought ye
        here
Hath made you mine. Slaves, scoff not at my will!
The Mind — the Spirit — the Promethean spark,
The lightning of my being, is as bright,   155
Pervading, and far darting as your own,

And shall not yield to yours, though cooped in clay!
Answer, or I will teach you what I am.
    Spirit. We answer — as we answered; our reply
Is even in thine own words.
    Manfred.   Why say ye so?   *160*
    Spirit. If, as thou say'st, thine essence be as ours,
We have replied in telling thee, the thing
Mortals call death hath nought to do with us.
    Manfred. I then have called ye from your realms in vain;
Ye cannot, or ye will not, aid me.
    Spirit.   Say —   *165*
What we possess we offer; it is thine:
Bethink ere thou dismiss us; ask again;
Kingdom, and sway, and strength, and length of days —
    Manfred. Accurséd! what have I to do with days?
They are too long already. — Hence — begone!   *170*
    Spirit. Yet pause: being here, our will would do thee service;
Bethink thee, is there then no other gift
Which we can make not worthless in thine eyes?
    Manfred. No, none: yet stay — one moment, ere we part,
I would behold ye face to face. I hear   *175*
Your voices, sweet and melancholy sounds,
As Music on the waters; and I see
The steady aspect of a clear large Star;
But nothing more. Approach me as ye are,
Or one — or all — in your accustomed forms.   *180*
    Spirit. We have no forms, beyond the elements
Of which we are the mind and principle:
But choose a form — in that we will appear.
    Manfred. I have no choice; there is no form on earth
Hideous or beautiful to me. Let him,   *185*
Who is most powerful of ye, take such aspect
As unto him may seem most fitting — Come!

    Seventh Spirit [*appearing in the shape of a beautiful female
      figure*].

I. i. 187. . . . *beautiful female figure*: The seventh spirit evidently
takes the form of Astarte. See below II. iv. 83 ff.

Behold!
Manfred. Oh God! if it be thus, and *thou*
Art not a madness and a mockery,
I yet might be most happy. I will clasp thee,   190
And we again will be ——

[*The figure vanishes.*]

My heart is crushed!

[MANFRED *falls senseless.*]

[*A voice is heard in the Incantation which follows.*]

When the Moon is on the wave,   4 ems
   And the glow-worm in the grass,
And the meteor on the grave,
   And the wisp on the morass;   195
When the falling stars are shooting,
And the answered owls are hooting,
And the silent leaves are still
In the shadow of the hill,
Shall my soul be upon thine,   200
With a power and with a sign.

Though thy slumber may be deep,
Yet thy Spirit shall not sleep;
There are shades which will not vanish,
There are thoughts thou canst not banish;   205
By a Power to thee unknown,
Thou canst never be alone;
Thou art wrapt as with a shroud,
Thou art gathered in a cloud;
And for ever shalt thou dwell   210
In the spirit of this spell.

Though thou seest me not pass by,
Thou shalt feel me with thine eye

As a thing that, though unseen,
Must be near thee, and hath been;   215
And when in that secret dread
Thou hast turned around thy head,
Thou shalt marvel I am not
As thy shadow on the spot,
And the power which thou dost feel   220
Shall be what thou must conceal.

And a magic voice and verse
Hath baptized thee with a curse;
And a Spirit of the air
Hath begirt thee with a snare;   225
In the wind there is a voice
Shall forbid thee to rejoice;
And to thee shall Night deny
All the quiet of her sky;
And the day shall have a sun,   230
Which shall make thee wish it done.

From thy false tears I did distil
An essence which hath strength to kill;
From thy own heart I then did wring
The black blood in its blackest spring;   235
From thy own smile I snatched the snake,
For there it coiled as in a brake;
From thy own lip I drew the charm
Which gave all these their chiefest harm;
In proving every poison known,   240
I found the strongest was thine own.

By the cold breast and serpent smile,
By thy unfathomed gulfs of guile,
By that most seeming virtuous eye,
By thy shut soul's hypocrisy;   245
By the perfection of thine art

I. i. 237. *brake*: Thicket.

Which passed for human thine own heart;
By thy delight in others' pain,
And in thy brotherhood of Cain,
I call upon thee! and compel   250
Thyself to be thy proper Hell!

And on thy head I pour the vial
Which doth devote thee to this trial;
Nor to slumber, nor to die,
Shall be in thy destiny;   255
Though thy death shall still seem near
To thy wish, but as a fear;
Lo! the spell now works around thee,
And the clankless chain hath bound thee;
O'er thy heart and brain together   260
Hath the word been passed — now wither!

SCENE II. — *The Mountain of the Jungfrau. — Time,
Morning.* — MANFRED *alone upon the cliffs.*

Manfred. The spirits I have raised abandon me,
The spells which I have studied baffle me,
The remedy I recked of tortured me;
I lean no more on superhuman aid;
It hath no power upon the past, and for   5
The future, till the past be gulfed in darkness,
It is not of my search. — My Mother Earth!
And thou fresh-breaking Day, and you, ye Mountains,
Why are ye beautiful? I cannot love ye.
And thou, the bright Eye of the Universe,   10
That openest over all, and unto all
Art a delight — thou shin'st not on my heart.
And you, ye crags, upon whose extreme edge
I stand, and on the torrent's brink beneath
Behold the tall pines dwindled as to shrubs   15

I. i. 251. *Thyself . . . hell*: Cf. Satan in *Paradise Lost*, I. 254–255: "The
mind is its own place, and in itself/Can make a Heaven of Hell, a Hell of
Heaven."

In dizziness of distance; when a leap,
A stir, a motion, even a breath, would bring
My breast upon its rocky bosom's bed
To rest for ever — wherefore do I pause?
I feel the impulse — yet I do not plunge;   20
I see the peril — yet do not recede;
And my brain reels — and yet my foot is firm:
There is a power upon me which withholds,
And makes it my fatality to live, —
If it be life to wear within myself   25
This barrenness of Spirit, and to be
My own Soul's sepulchre, for I have ceased
To justify my deeds unto myself —
The last infirmity of evil. Aye,
Thou winged and cloud-cleaving minister,   30

                             [An Eagle passes.]

Whose happy flight is highest into heaven,
Well may'st thou swoop so near me — I should be
Thy prey, and gorge thine eaglets; thou art gone
Where the eye cannot follow thee; but thine
Yet pierces downward, onward, or above,   35
With a pervading vision. — Beautiful!
How beautiful is all this visible world!
How glorious in its action and itself!
But we, who name ourselves its sovereigns, we,
Half dust, half deity, alike unfit   40
To sink or soar, with our mixed essence make
A conflict of its elements, and breathe
The breath of degradation and of pride,
Contending with low wants and lofty will,
Till our Mortality predominates,   45
And men are — what they name not to themselves,
And trust not to each other. Hark! the note,

       [The Shepherd's pipe in the distance is heard.]

I. ii. 37 ff. *How beautiful* . . . : See Hamlet's "quintessence of dust"
speech, *Hamlet* II. ii. 304 ff.

The natural music of the mountain reed —
For here the patriarchal days are not
A pastoral fable — pipes in the liberal air,   50
Mixed with the sweet bells of the sauntering herd;
My soul would drink those echoes. Oh, that I were
The viewless spirit of a lovely sound,
A living voice, a breathing harmony,
A bodiless enjoyment — born and dying   55
With the blest tone which made me!

> *Enter from below a* CHAMOIS HUNTER.

Chamois Hunter.   Even so
This way the Chamois leapt: her nimble feet
Have baffled me; my gains to-day will scarce
Repay my break-neck travail. — What is here?
Who seems not of my trade, and yet hath reached   60
A height which none even of our mountaineers,
Save our best hunters, may attain: his garb
Is goodly, his mien manly, and his air
Proud as a free-born peasant's, at this distance:
I will approach him nearer.

Manfred. [*not perceiving the other*]. To be thus —   65
Grey-haired with anguish, like these blasted pines,
Wrecks of a single winter, barkless, branchless,
A blighted trunk upon a curséd root,
Which but supplies a feeling to Decay —
And to be thus, eternally but thus,   70
Having been otherwise! Now furrowed o'er
With wrinkles, ploughed by moments, not by years
And hours, all tortured into ages — hours
Which I outlive! — Ye toppling crags of ice!
Ye Avalanches, whom a breath draws down   75
In mountainous o'erwhelming, come and crush me!
I hear ye momently above, beneath,
Crash with a frequent conflict; but ye pass,
And only fall on things that still would live;

I. ii. 57. *Chamois*: Wild mountain antelope.

On the young flourishing forest, or the hut   80
And hamlet of the harmless villager.

    Chamois Hunter. The mists begin to rise from up the valley;
I'll warn him to descend, or he may chance
To lose at once his way and life together.

    Manfred. The mists boil up around the glaciers; clouds   85
Rise curling fast beneath me, white and sulphury,
Like foam from the roused ocean of deep Hell,
Whose every wave breaks on a living shore,
Heaped with the damned like pebbles. — I am giddy.

    Chamois Hunter. I must approach him cautiously; if near, 90
A sudden step will startle him, and he
Seems tottering already.

    Manfred.   Mountains have fallen,
Leaving a gap in the clouds, and with the shock
Rocking their Alpine brethren; filling up
The ripe green valleys with Destruction's splinters;   95
Damming the rivers with a sudden dash,
Which crushed the waters into mist, and made
Their fountains find another channel — thus,
Thus, in its old age, did Mount Rosenberg —
Why stood I not beneath it?

    Chamois Hunter.   Friend! have a care,   100
Your next step may be fatal! — for the love
Of Him who made you, stand not on that brink!

    Manfred. (not hearing him). Such would have been for me
    a fitting tomb;
My bones had then been quiet in their depth;
They had not then been strewn upon the rocks   105
For the wind's pastime — as thus — thus they shall be —
In this one plunge. — Farewell, ye opening Heavens!
Look not upon me thus reproachfully —
You were not meant for me — Earth! take these atoms!

    [*As* MANFRED *is in act to spring from the cliff, the*
    CHAMOIS HUNTER *seizes and retains him with a sudden*
                   grasp.]

    I. ii. 99. *Mount Rosenberg:* Mt. Rossberg in Switzerland from which
a landslide in 1806 destroyed several villages and killed over 450 people.

Chamois Hunter. Hold, madman! — though aweary of thy
    life,   *110*
Stain not our pure vales with thy guilty blood:
Away with me —— I will not quit my hold.
    Manfred. I am most sick at heart — nay, grasp me not —
I am all feebleness — the mountains whirl
Spinning round me —— I grow blind —— What art thou? *115*
    Chamois Hunter. I'll answer that anon. — Away with
    me ——
The clouds grow thicker —— there — now lean on me —
Place your foot here — here, take this staff, and cling
A moment to that shrub — now give me your hand,
And hold fast by my girdle — softly — well —   *120*
The Chalet will be gained within an hour:
Come on, we'll quickly find a surer footing,
And something like a pathway, which the torrent
Hath washed since winter. — Come, 'tis bravely done —
You should have been a hunter. — Follow me.   *125*

    [*As they descend the rocks with difficulty, the scene
        closes.*]

ACT II

SCENE I. — *A Cottage among the Bernese Alps.* —
MANFRED *and the* CHAMOIS HUNTER.

    Chamois Hunter. No — no — yet pause — thou must not
    yet go forth:
Thy mind and body are alike unfit
To trust each other, for some hours, at least;
When thou art better, I will be thy guide —
But whither?
    Manfred. It imports not: I do know   *5*
My route full well, and need no further guidance.
    Chamois Hunter. Thy garb and gait bespeak thee of high
    lineage —
One of the many chiefs, whose castled crags
Look o'er the lower valleys — which of these
May call thee lord? I only know their portals;   *10*

My way of life leads me but rarely down
To bask by the huge hearths of those old halls,
Carousing with the vassals; but the paths,
Which step from out our mountains to their doors,
I know from childhood — which of these is thine?   15
   Manfred.   No matter.
   Chamois Hunter.   Well, Sir, pardon me the question,
And be of better cheer. Come, taste my wine;
'Tis of an ancient vintage; many a day
'T has thawed my veins among our glaciers, now
Let it do thus for thine — Come, pledge me fairly!   20
   Manfred. Away, away! there's blood upon the brim!
Will it then never — never sink in the earth?
   Chamois Hunter. What dost thou mean? thy senses wander
     from thee.
   Manfred. I say 'tis blood — my blood! the pure warm
     stream
Which ran in the veins of my fathers, and in ours   25
When we were in our youth, and had one heart,
And loved each other as we should not love,
And this was shed: but still it rises up,
Colouring the clouds, that shut me out from Heaven,
Where thou art not — and I shall never be.   30
   Chamois Hunter. Man of strange words, and some half-
     maddening sin,
Which makes thee people vacancy, whate'er
Thy dread and sufferance be, there's comfort yet —
The aid of holy men, and heavenly patience ——
   Manfred. Patience — and patience! Hence that word was
     made   35
For brutes of burthen, not for birds of prey!
Preach it to mortals of a dust like thine, —
I am not of thine order.
   Chamois Hunter. Thanks to Heaven!
I would not be of thine for the free fame
Of William Tell; but whatsoe'er thine ill,   40
It must be borne, and these wild starts are useless.
   Manfred. Do I not bear it? — Look on me — I live.

Chamois Hunter. This is convulsion, and no healthful life.

Manfred. I tell thee, man! I have lived many years,
Many long years, but they are nothing now   45
To those which I must number: ages — ages —
Space and eternity — and consciousness,
With the fierce thirst of death — and still unslaked!

Chamois Hunter. Why on thy brow the seal of middle age
Hath scarce been set; I am thine elder far.   50

Manfred. Think'st thou existence doth depend on time?
It doth; but actions are our epochs: mine
Have made my days and nights imperishable,
Endless, and all alike, as sands on the shore,
  Innumerable atoms; and one desert,   55
Barren and cold, on which the wild waves break,
But nothing rests, save carcasses and wrecks,
Rocks, and the salt-surf weeds of bitterness.

Chamois Hunter. Alas! he's mad — but yet I must not leave
    him.

Manfred. I would I were — for then the things I see   60
Would be but a distempered dream.

Chamois Hunter.   What is it
That thou dost see, or think thou look'st upon?

Manfred. Myself, and thee — a peasant of the Alps —
Thy humble virtues, hospitable home,
And spirit patient, pious, proud, and free;   65
Thy self-respect, grafted on innocent thoughts;
Thy days of health, and nights of sleep; thy toils,
By danger dignified, yet guiltless; hopes
Of cheerful old age and a quiet grave,
With cross and garland over its green turf,   70
And thy grandchildren's love for epitaph!
This do I see — and then I look within —
It matters not — my Soul was scorched already!

Chamois Hunter. And would'st thou then exchange thy lot
    for mine?

Manfred. No, friend! I would not wrong thee,
    nor exchange   75
My lot with living being: I can bear —

However wretchedly, 'tis still to bear —
In life what others could not brook to dream,
But perish in their slumber.
  Chamois Hunter. And with this —
This cautious feeling for another's pain   *80*
Canst thou be black with evil? — say not so.
Can one of gentle thoughts have wreaked revenge
Upon his enemies?
  Manfred. Oh! no, no, no!
My injuries came down on those who loved me —
On those whom I best loved: I never quelled   *85*
An enemy, save in my just defence —
But my embrace was fatal.
  Chamois Hunter. Heaven give thee rest!
And Penitence restore thee to thyself;
My prayers shall be for thee.
  Manfred.   I need them not,
But can endure thy pity. I depart —   *90*
'Tis time — farewell! — Here's gold, and thanks for thee —
No words — it is thy due. — Follow me not —
I know my path the mountain peril's past:
And once again I charge thee, follow not!

             [*Exit* MANFRED.]

   SCENE II. — *A lower Valley in the Alps.* — *A Cataract.*

      [*Enter* MANFRED.]

It is not noon — the Sunbow's rays still arch
The torrent with the many hues of heaven,
And roll the sheeted silver's waving column
O'er the crag's headlong perpendicular,
And fling its lines of foaming light along,   *5*
And to and fro, like the pale courser's tail,
The Giant steed, to be bestrode by Death,
As told in the Apocalypse. No eyes
But mine now drink this sight of loveliness;

 II. ii. 8. *told in the Apocalypse*: See *Revelations* 6:8.

I should be sole in this sweet solitude, 10
And with the Spirit of the place divide
The homage of these waters. — I will call her.

[MANFRED *takes some of the water into the palm of his
hand and flings it into the air, muttering the adjuration.
After a pause, the* WITCH OF THE ALPS *rises beneath the
arch of the sunbow of the torrent.*]

Beautiful Spirit! with thy hair of light,
And dazzling eyes of glory, in whose form
The charms of Earth's least mortal daughters grow 15
To an unearthly stature, in an essence
Of purer elements; while the hues of youth, —
Carnationed like a sleeping Infant's cheek,
Rocked by the beating of her mother's heart,
Or the rose tints, which Summer's twilight leaves 20
Upon the lofty Glacier's virgin snow,
The blush of earth embracing with her Heaven, —
Tinge thy celestial aspect, and make tame
The beauties of the Sunbow which bends o'er thee.
Beautiful Spirit! in thy calm clear brow, 25
Wherein is glassed serenity of Soul,
Which of itself shows immortality,
I read that thou wilt pardon to a Son
Of Earth, whom the abstruser powers permit
At times to commune with them — if that he 30
Avail him of his spells — to call thee thus,
And gaze on thee a moment.
  Witch.   Son of Earth!
I know thee, and the Powers which give thee power!
I know thee for a man of many thoughts,
And deeds of good and ill, extreme in both, 35
Fatal and fated in thy sufferings.
I have expected this — what would'st thou with me?
  Manfred. To look upon thy beauty — nothing further.
The face of the earth hath maddened me, and I
Take refuge in her mysteries, and pierce 40
To the abodes of those who govern her —

But they can nothing aid me. I have sought
From them what they could not bestow, and now
I search no further.
    Witch.   What could be the quest
Which is not in the power of the most powerful,   *45*
The rulers of the invisible?
    Manfred   A boon; —
But why should I repeat it? 'twere in vain.
    Witch. I know not that; let thy lips utter it.
    Manfred. Well, though it torture me, 'tis but the same;
My pang shall find a voice. From my youth upwards   *50*
My Spirit walked not with the souls of men,
Nor looked upon the earth with human eyes;
The thirst of their ambition was not mine,
The aim of their existence was not mine;
My joys — my griefs — my passions — and my powers,   *55*
Made me a stranger; though I wore the form,
I had no sympathy with breathing flesh,
Nor midst the Creatures of Clay that girded me
Was there but One who — but of her anon.
I said with men, and with the thoughts of men,   *60*
I held but slight communion; but instead,
My joy was in the wilderness, — to breathe
The difficult air of the iced mountain's top,
Where the birds dare not build — nor insect's wing
Flit o'er the herbless granite; or to plunge   *65*
Into the torrent, and to roll along
On the swift whirl of the new-breaking wave
Of river-stream, or Ocean, in their flow.
In these my early strength exulted; or
To follow through the night the moving moon,   *70*
The stars and their development; or catch
The dazzling lightnings till my eyes grew dim;
Or to look, list'ning, on the scattered leaves,
While Autumn winds were at their evening song.
These were my pastimes, and to be alone;   *75*
For if the beings, of whom I was one, —
Hating to be so, — crossed me in my path,

I felt myself degraded back to them,
And was all clay again. And then I dived,
In my lone wanderings, to the caves of Death,   80
Searching its cause in its effect; and drew
From withered bones, and skulls, and heaped up dust,
Conclusions most forbidden. Then I passed
The nights of years in sciences untaught,
Save in the old-time; and with time and toil,   85
And terrible ordeal, and such penance
As in itself hath power upon the air,
And spirits that do compass air and earth,
Space, and the peopled Infinite, I made
Mine eyes familiar with Eternity,   90
Such as, before me, did the Magi, and
He who from out their fountain-dwellings raised
Eros and Anteros, at Gadara,
As I do thee; — and with my knowledge grew
The thirst of knowledge, and the power and joy   95
Of this most bright intelligence, until ——
    Witch. Proceed.
    Manfred.   Oh! I but thus prolonged my words,
Boasting these idle attributes, because
As I approach the core of my heart's grief —
But — to my task. I have not named to thee   100
Father or mother, mistress, friend, or being,
With whom I wore the chain of human ties;
If I had such, they seemed not such to me —
Yet there was One ——
    Witch.   Spare not thyself — proceed.
    Manfred. She was like me in lineaments — her eyes —   105
Her hair — her features — all, to the very tone
Even of her voice, they said were like to mine;
But softened all, and tempered into beauty:

II. ii. 91. *Magi*: Philosopher-priests of ancient Persia.
II. ii. 92–93. *He . . . Gadara*: Iamblichus, a neoplatonic philosopher of
the fourth century, was reported to have called up Eros, the god of love,
and his brother Anteros, the god who avenged unrequited love, from the
springs in Gadara, Syria, which bore their names.

She had the same lone thoughts and wanderings,
The quest of hidden knowledge, and a mind   *110*
To comprehend the Universe: nor these
Alone, but with them gentler powers than mine,
Pity, and smiles, and tears — which I had not;
And tenderness — but that I had for her;
Humility — and that I never had.   *115*
Her faults were mine — her virtues were her own —
I loved her, and destroyed her!
    Witch.   With thy hand?
    Manfred. Not with my hand, but heart, which broke her
    heart;
It gazed on mine, and withered. I have shed
Blood, but not hers — and yet her blood was shed; *120*
I saw — and could not stanch it.
    Witch.   And for this —
A being of the race thou dost despise —
The order, which thine own would rise above,
Mingling with us and ours, — thou dost forego
The gifts of our great knowledge, and shrink'st back *125*
To recreant mortality —— Away!
    Manfred. Daughter of Air! I tell thee, since that hour —
But words are breath — look on me in my sleep,
Or watch my watchings — Come and sit by me!
My solitude is solitude no more,   *130*
But peopled with the Furies; — I have gnashed
My teeth in darkness till returning morn,
Then cursed myself till sunset; — I have prayed
For madness as a blessing — 'tis denied me.
I have affronted Death — but in the war   *135*
Of elements the waters shrunk from me,
And fatal things passed harmless; the cold hand
Of an all-pitiless Demon held me back,
Back by a single hair, which would not break.
In Fantasy, Imagination, all   *140*
The affluence of my soul — which one day was
A Crœsus in creation — I plunged deep,
But, like an ebbing wave, it dashed me back

Into the gulf of unfathomed thought.
I plunged amidst Mankind — Forgetfulness   *145*
I sought in all, save where 'tis to be found —
And that I have to learn — my Sciences,
My long pursued and superhuman art,
Is mortal here: I dwell in my despair —
And live — and live for ever.
   Witch.   It may be   *150*
That I can aid thee.
   Manfred.   To do this thy power
Must wake the dead, or lay me low with them.
Do so — in any shape — in any hour —
With any torture — so it be the last.
   Witch. That is not in my province; but if thou   *155*
Wilt swear obedience to my will, and do
My bidding, it may help thee to thy wishes.
   Manfred. I will not swear — Obey! and whom? the Spirits
Whose presence I command, and be the slave
Of those who served me — Never!
   Witch.   Is this all?   *160*
Hast thou no gentler answer? — Yet bethink thee,
And pause ere thou rejectest.
   Manfred.   I have said it.
   Witch. Enough! I may retire then — say!
   Manfred.   Retire!

                      [*The* WITCH *disappears.*]

   Manfred. [*alone*]. We are the fools of Time and Terror:
Steal on us, and steal from us; yet we live,   *165*
Loathing our life, and dreading still to die.
In all the days of this detested yoke —
This vital weight upon the struggling heart,
Which sinks with sorrow, or beats quick with pain,
Or joy that ends in agony or faintness —   *170*
In all the days of past and future — for
In life there is no present — we can number
How few — how less than few — wherein the soul
Forbears to pant for death, and yet draws back

As from a stream in winter, though the chill   175
Be but a moment's. I have one resource
Still in my science — I can call the dead,
And ask them what it is we dread to be:
The sternest answer can but be the Grave,
And that is nothing: if they answered not ——   180
The buried Prophet answered to the Hag
Of Endor; and the Spartan Monarch drew
From the Byzantine maid's unsleeping spirit
An answer and his destiny — he slew
That which he loved, unknowing what he slew,   185
And died unpardoned — though he called in aid
The Phyxian Jove, and in Phigalia roused
The Arcadian Evocators to compel
The indignant shadow to depose her wrath,
Or fix her term of vengeance — she replied   190
In words of dubious import, but fulfilled.
If I had never lived, that which I love
Had still been living; had I never loved,
That which I love would still be beautiful,
Happy and giving hapiness. What is she?   195
What is she now? — a sufferer for my sins —
A thing I dare not think upon — or nothing.
Within few hours I shall not call in vain —
Yet in this hour I dread the thing I dare:
Until this hour I never shrunk to gaze   200
On spirit, good or evil — now I tremble,
And feel a strange cold thaw upon my heart.

II. ii. 181–182. *buried prophet . . . Endor*: The spirit of Samuel, raised by the witch of Endor, prophesied to King Saul that he would be killed in battle. See *I Samuel*, 28.

II. ii. 182–191. *Spartan . . . destiny*: Pausanius (d. 470 B.C.) had demanded Cleonice for his mistress, but when she entered his room in the dark, he had mistaken her for an assassin and killed her. Overcome by remorse he asked the priests of Phigalia (in Arcadia in the Peloponnesus) to summon up her spirit so that he could ask her pardon. She replied that he would soon be delivered from his troubles, a prophecy shortly fulfilled by his death.

II. ii. 187. *Phyxian Jove*: Protector of fugitives.

But I can act even what I most abhor,
And champion human fears. — The night approaches.

[*Exit.*]

SCENE III. — *The summit of the Jungfrau Mountain.*

[*Enter* FIRST DESTINY.]

The Moon is rising broad, and round, and bright;
And here on snows, where never human foot
Of common mortal trod, we nightly tread,
And leave no traces: o'er the savage sea,
The glassy ocean of the mountain ice,   5
We skim its rugged breakers, which put on
The aspect of a tumbling tempest's foam,
Frozen in a moment — a dead Whirlpool's image:
And this most steep fantastic pinnacle,
The fretwork of some earthquake — where the clouds   10
Pause to repose themselves in passing by —
Is sacred to our revels, or our vigils;
Here do I wait my sisters, on our way
To the Hall of Arimanes — for to-night
Is our great festival — 'tis strange they come not.   15

A VOICE *without, singing.*

The Captive Usurper,
  Hurled down from the throne,
Lay buried in torpor,
  Forgotten and lone;
I broke through his slumbers,   20
  I shivered his chain,
I leagued him with numbers —
  He's Tyrant again!

With the blood of a million he'll answer my care,
With a Nation's destruction — his flight and despair!   25

SECOND VOICE, *without.*

The Ship sailed on, the Ship sailed fast,
But I left not a sail, and I left not a mast;
There is not a plank of the hull or the deck,
And there is not a wretch to lament o'er his wreck;
Save one, whom I held, as he swam, by the hair,   30
And he was a subject well worthy my care;
A traitor on land, and a pirate at sea —
But I saved him to wreak further havoc for me!

FIRST DESTINY, *answering.*

The City lies sleeping;
    The morn, to deplore it,   35
May dawn on it weeping:
    Sullenly, slowly,
The black plague flew o'er it —
    Thousands lie lowly;
Tens of thousands shall perish;   40
    The living shall fly from
The sick they should cherish;
    But nothing can vanquish
The touch that they die from.
    Sorrow and anguish,   45
And evil and dread,
    Envelope a nation;
The blest are the dead,
    Who see not the sight
    Of their own desolation;   50
This work of a night —

This wreck of a realm — this deed of my doing —
For ages I've done, and shall still be renewing!

Enter the SECOND *and* THIRD DESTINIES.

THE THREE.

Our hands contain the hearts of men,
    Our footsteps are their graves;   55

We only give to take again
The Spirits of our slaves!

First Destiny. Welcome! — Where's Nemesis?
Second Destiny. At some great work;
But what I know not, for my hands were full.
Third Destiny. Behold she cometh.

Enter NEMESIS.

First Destiny. Say, where hast thou been? 60
My Sisters and thyself are slow to-night.
Nemesis. I was detained repairing shattered thrones —
Marrying fools, restoring dynasties —
Avenging men upon their enemies,
And making them repent their own revenge; 65
Goading the wise to madness; from the dull
Shaping out oracles to rule the world
Afresh — for they were waxing out of date,
And mortals dared to ponder for themselves,
To weigh kings in the balance — and to speak 70
Of Freedom, the forbidden fruit. — Away!
We have outstayed the hour — mount we our clouds!

[*Exeunt.*]

SCENE IV. — *The Hall of Arimanes. — Arimanes on his
Throne, a Globe of Fire, surrounded by the Spirits.*

Hymn of the SPIRITS.

Hail to our Master! — Prince of Earth and Air!
Who walks the clouds and waters — in his hand
The sceptre of the Elements, which tear
Themselves to chaos at his high command!
He breatheth — and a tempest shakes the sea; 5
He speaketh — and the clouds reply in thunder;
He gazeth — from his glance the sunbeams flee;
He moveth — Earthquakes rend the world asunder.

II. iii. 58. *Nemesis*: See *Childe Harold* IV. 132.2 and note. Here Nemesis is presented as the chief assistant to Arimanes.

Beneath his footsteps the Volcanoes rise;
   His shadow is the Pestilence: his path   *10*
The comets herald through the crackling skies;
   And Planets turn to ashes at his wrath.
To him War offers daily sacrifice;
   To him Death pays his tribute; Life is his,
With all its Infinite of agonies —   *15*
   And his the Spirit of whatever is!

[*Enter the* DESTINIES *and* NEMESIS.]

First Destiny. Glory to Arimanes! on the earth
His power increaseth — both my sisters did
His bidding, nor did I neglect my duty!
   Second Destiny. Glory to Arimanes! we who bow   *20*
The necks of men, bow down before his throne!
   Third Destiny. Glory to Arimanes! we await
His nod!
   Nemesis. Sovereign of Sovereigns! we are thine,
And all that liveth, more or less, is ours,
And most things wholly so; still to increase   *25*
Our power, increasing thine, demands our care,
And we are vigilant. Thy late commands
Have been fulfilled to the utmost.

[*Enter* MANFRED]

A Spirit.   What is here?
A mortal! — Thou most rash and fatal wretch,
Bow down and worship!
   Second Spirit.   I do know the man —   *30*
A Magian of great power, and fearful skill!

II. iv. 17. *Arimanes*: Ahriman, the name of the principle of evil in
the Persian religion of Zoroaster (c. 628–551 B.C.). Like Blake's "God of
this World" Arimanes controls the physical universe and inflicts evil
upon man by way of natural catastrophies and institutional tyrannies.
As "Prince of Earth and Air," he is obviously ruler of the spirits Manfred
evokes in the first act. Note that he and Nemesis can raise the spirit of
Astarte, but they cannot make her speak: she "belongs to the other
powers" (II. iv. 115).

Third Spirit. Bow down and worship, slave! — What, know'st thou not
Thine and our Sovereign? — Tremble, and obey!
 All the Spirits. Prostrate thyself, and thy condemnéd clay,
Child of the Earth! or dread the worst.
 Manfred.   I know it;   *35*
And yet ye see I kneel not.
 Fourth Spirit.   'Twill be taught thee.
 Manfred. 'Tis taught already; — many a night of the earth,
On the bare ground, have I bowed down my face,
And strewed my head with ashes; I have known
The fulness of humiliation — for   *40*
I sunk before my vain despair, and knelt
To my own desolation.
 Fifth Spirit.   Dost thou dare
Refuse to Arimanes on his throne
What the whole earth accords, beholding not
The terror of his Glory? — Crouch! I say.   *45*
 Manfred. Bid *him* bow down to that which is above him,
The overruling Infinite — the Maker
Who made him not for worship — let him kneel,
And we will kneel together.
 The Spirits.   Crush the worm!
Tear him in pieces! —
 First Destiny. Hence! Avaunt! — he's mine. *50*
Prince of the Powers invisible! This man
Is of no common order, as his port
And presence here denote: his sufferings
Have been of an immortal nature — like
Our own; his knowledge, and his powers and will, *55*
As far as is compatible with clay,
Which clogs the ethereal essence, have been such
As clay hath seldom borne; his aspirations
Have been beyond the dwellers of the earth,
And they have only taught him what we know — *60*
That knowledge is not happiness, and science
But an exchange of ignorance for that
Which is another kind of ignorance.

This is not all — the passions, attributes
Of Earth and Heaven, from which no power, nor being,   65
Nor breath from the worm upwards is exempt,
Have pierced his heart; and in their consequence
Made him a thing — I who pity not,
Yet pardon those who pity. He is mine —
And thine it may be; be it so, or not —   70
No other Spirit in this region hath
A soul like his — or power upon his soul.
   Nemesis. What doth he here then?
   First Destiny.   Let *him* answer that.
   Manfred. Ye know what I have known; and without power
I could not be amongst ye: but there are   75
Powers deeper still beyond — I come in quest
Of such, to answer unto what I seek.
   Nemesis. What would'st thou?
   Manfred.   *Thou* canst not reply to me.
Call up the dead — my question is for them.
   Nemesis. Great Arimanes, doth thy will avouch   80
The wishes of this mortal?
   Arimanes.   Yea.
   Nemesis.   Whom wouldst thou
Uncharnel?
   Manfred. One without a tomb — call up
Astarte.

NEMESIS

Shadow! or Spirit!
  Whatever thou art,   85
Which still doth inherit
  The whole or a part
Of the form of thy birth,
  Of the mould of thy clay,
Which returned to the earth,   90
  Re-appear to the day!

II. iv. 83. *Astarte*: the name is that of the ancient Phoenician goddess
of love, equivalent to the Greek Aphrodite.

Bear what thou borest,
   The heart and the form,
And the aspect thou worest
   Redeem from the worm.   *95*
Appear! — Appear! — Appear!
Who sent thee there requires thee here!

[*The Phantom of* ASTARTE *rises and stands in the midst.*]

Manfred. Can this be death? there's bloom upon her cheek;
But now I see it is no living hue,
But a strange hectic — like the unnatural red   *100*
Which Autumn plants upon the perished leaf.
It is the same! Oh, God! that I should dread
To look upon the same — Astarte! — No,
I cannot speak to her — but bid her speak —
Forgive me or condemn me.   *105*

NEMESIS.

By the Power which hath broken
   The grave which enthralled thee,
Speak to him who hath spoken,
   Or those who have called thee!
Manfred.   She is silent,
And in that silence I am more than answered.   *110*
  Nemesis. My power extends no further. Prince of Air!
It rests with thee alone — command her voice.
  Arimanes. Spirit — obey this sceptre!
  Nemesis.   Silent still!
She is not of our order, but belongs
To the other powers. Mortal! thy quest is vain,   *115*
And we are baffled also.
    Manfred.   Hear me, hear me —
Astarte! my belovéd! speak to me:
I have so much endured — so much endure —
Look on me! the grave hath not changed thee more
Than I am changed for thee. Thou lovedst me   *120*
Too much, as I loved thee: we were not made

To torture thus each other — though it were
The deadliest sin to love as we have loved.
Say that thou loath'st me not — that I do bear
This punishment for both — that thou wilt be   125
One of the blesséd — and that I shall die;
For hitherto all hateful things conspire
To bind me in existence — in a life
Which makes me shrink from Immortality —
A future like the past. I cannot rest.   130
I know not what I ask, nor what I seek:
I feel but what thou art, and what I am;
And I would hear yet once before I perish
The voice which was my music — Speak to me!
For I have called on thee in the still night,   135
Startled the slumbering birds from the hushed boughs,
And woke the mountain wolves, and made the caves
Acquainted with thy vainly echoed name,
Which answered me — many things answered me —
Spirits and men — but thou wert silent all.   140
Yet speak to me! I have outwatched the stars,
And gazed o'er heaven in vain in search of thee.
Speak to me! I have wandered o'er the earth,
And never found thy likeness — Speak to me!
Look on the fiends around — they feel for me: 145
I fear them not, and feel for thee alone.
Speak to me! though it be in wrath; — but say —
I reck not what — but let me hear thee once —
This once — once more!

  Phantom of Astarte. Manfred!
  Manfred.   Say on, say on —
I live but in the sound — it is thy voice!   150
  Phantom. Manfred! To-morrow ends thine earthly ills.
   Farewell!
  Manfred. Yet one word more — am I forgiven?
  Phantom. Farewell!
  Manfred.   Say, shall we meet again?
  Phantom.   Farewell!

Manfred. One word for mercy! Say thou lovest me.
Phantom. Manfred!

[*The Spirit of* ASTARTE *disappears.*]

Nemesis. She's gone, and will not be recalled: [155]
Her words will be fulfilled. Return to the earth.
A Spirit. He is convulsed — This is to be a mortal,
And seek the things beyond mortality.
Another Spirit. Yet, see, he mastereth himself, and makes
His torture tributary to his will. [160]
Had he been one of us, he would have made
An awful Spirit.
Nemesis. Hast thou further question
Of our great Sovereign, or his worshippers?
Manfred. None.
Nemesis. Then for a time farewell.
Manfred. We meet then! Where? On the earth? — [165]
Even as thou wilt: and for the grace accorded
I now depart a debtor. Fare ye well!

[*Exit* MANFRED.]

[*Scene closes.*]

ACT III

SCENE I. — *A Hall in the Castle of Manfred.*

MANFRED AND HERMAN

Manfred. What is the hour?
Herman. It wants but one till sunset,
And promises a lovely twilight.
Manfred. Say,
Are all things so disposed of in the tower
As I directed?
Herman. All, my Lord, are ready:

Here is the key and casket.
  Manfred.   It is well: 5
Thou mayst retire.   [*Exit* HERMAN.]

  Manfred. (alone). There is a calm upon me —
Inexplicable stillness! which till now
Did not belong to what I knew of life.
If that I did not know Philosophy
To be of all our vanities the motliest,   10
The merest word that ever fooled the ear
From out the schoolman's jargon, I should deem
The golden secret, the sought "Kalon," found,
And seated in my soul. It will not last,
But it is well to have known it, though but once: 15
It hath enlarged my thoughts with a new sense,
And I within my tablets would note down
That there is such a feeling. Who is there?
                          [*Re-enter* HERMAN.]
  Herman. My Lord, the Abbot of St. Maurice craves
To greet your presence.

          [*Enter the* ABBOT OF ST. MAURICE.]

  Abbot.   Peace be with Count Manfred!   20
  Manfred. Thanks, holy father! welcome to these walls;
Thy presence honours them, and blesseth those
Who dwell within them.
  Abbot.   Would it were so, Count! —
But I would fain confer with thee alone.
  Manfred. Herman, retire. — What would my reverend
      guest?   25
  Abbot. Thus, without prelude: — Age and zeal — my office —
And good intent must plead my privilege;
Our near, though not acquainted neighbourhood,
May also be my herald. Rumours strange,
And of unholy nature, are abroad,   30
And busy with thy name — a noble name

III. i. 13. *"Kalon"*: The beautiful, the highest good of human existence.

For centuries: may he who bears it now
Transmit it unimpaired!

    Manfred.   Proceed, — I listen.

    Abbot. 'Tis said thou holdest converse with the things
Which are forbidden to the search of man;   *35*
That with the dwellers of the dark abodes,
The many evil and unheavenly spirits
Which walk the valley of the Shade of Death,
Thou communest. I know that with mankind,
Thy fellows in creation, thou dost rarely   *40*
Exchange thy thoughts, and that thy solitude
Is as an Anchorite's — were it but holy.

    Manfred. And what are they who do avouch these things?

    Abbot. My pious brethren — the scaréd peasantry —
Even thy own vassals — who do look on thee   *45*
With most unquiet eyes. Thy life's in peril!

    Manfred. Take it.

    Abbot.   I come to save, and not destroy:
I would not pry into thy secret soul;
But if these things be sooth, there still is time
For penitence and pity: reconcile thee   *50*
With the true church, and through the church to Heaven.

    Manfred. I hear thee. This is my reply — whate'er
I may have been, or am, doth rest between
Heaven and myself — I shall not choose a mortal
To be my mediator — Have I sinned   *55*
Against your ordinances? prove and punish!

    Abbot. My son! I did not speak of punishment,
But penitence and pardon; — with thyself
The choice of such remains — and for the last,
Our institutions and our strong belief   *60*
Have given me power to smooth the path from sin
To higher hope and better thoughts; the first
I leave to Heaven, — "Vengeance is mine alone!"
So saith the Lord, and with all humbleness
His servant echoes back the awful word.   *65*

    Manfred. Old man! there is no power in holy men,
Nor charm in prayer, nor purifying form

Of penitence, nor outward look, nor fast,
Nor agony — nor, greater than all these,
The innate tortures of that deep Despair,   70
Which is Remorse without the fear of Hell,
But all in all sufficient to itself
Would make a hell of Heaven — can exorcise
From out the unbounded spirit the quick sense
Of its own sins — wrongs — sufferance — and revenge   75
Upon itself; there is no future pang
Can deal that justice on the self-condemned
He deals on his own soul.

    Abbot.   All this is well;
For this will pass away, and be succeeded
By an auspicious hope, which shall look up   80
With calm assurance to that blessed place,
Which all who seek may win, whatever be
Their earthly errors, so they be atoned:
And the commencement of atonement is
The sense of its necessity. Say on —   85
And all our church can teach thee shall be taught;
And all we can absolve thee shall be pardoned.

    Manfred. When Rome's sixth Emperor was near his last,
The victim of a self-inflicted wound,
To shun the torments of a public death   90
From senates once his slaves, a certain soldier,
With show of loyal pity, would have stanched
The gushing throat with his officious robe;
The dying Roman thrust him back, and said —
Some empire still in his expiring glance —   95
"It is too late — is this fidelity?"

    Abbot. And what of this?

    Manfred.   I answer with the Roman —
"It is too late!"

    Abbot.   It never can be so,
To reconcile thyself with thy own soul,
And thy own soul with Heaven. Hast thou no hope?   100

III. i. 73. *Hell of Heaven*: See I. i. 252 n. above.
III. i. 88. *Rome's sixth emperor*: Nero.

'Tis strange — even those who do despair above,
Yet shape themselves some fantasy on earth,
To which frail twig they cling, like drowning men.
   Manfred. Aye — father! I have had those early visions,
And noble aspirations in my youth,   *105*
To make my own the mind of other men,
The enlightener of nations; and to rise
I knew not wither — it might be to fall;
But fall, even as the mountain-cataract,
Which having leapt from its more dazzling height,   *110*
Even in the foaming strength of its abyss,
(Which casts up misty columns that become
Clouds raining from the re-ascended skies,)
Lies low but mighty still. — But this is past,
My thoughts mistook themselves.
   Abbot.   And wherefore so?   *115*
   Manfred. I could not tame my nature down; for he
Must serve who fain would sway; and soothe, and sue,
And watch all time, and pry into all place,
And be a living Lie, who would become
A mighty thing amongst the mean — and such   *120*
The mass are; I disdained to mingle with
A herd, though to be leader — and of wolves.
The lion is alone, and so am I.
   Abbot. And why not live and act with other men?
   Manfred. Because my nature was averse from life;   *125*
And yet not cruel; for I would not make,
But find a desolation. Like the Wind,
The red-hot breath of the most lone Simoom,
Which dwells but in the desert, and sweeps o'er
The barren sands which bear no shrubs to blast,   *130*
And revels o'er their wild and arid waves,
And seeketh not, so that is is not sought,
But being met is deadly, — such hath been
The course of my existence; but there came
Things in my path which are no more.
   Abbot.   Alas!   *135*
I 'gin to fear that thou art past all aid

From me and from my calling; yet so young,
I still would ——
    Manfred.   Look on me! there is an order
Of mortals on the earth, who do become
Old in their youth, and die ere middle age,   *140*
Without the violence of warlike death;
Some perishing of pleasure — some of study —
Some worn with toil, some of mere weariness, —
Some of disease — and some insanity —
And some of withered, or of broken hearts;   *145*
For this last is a malady which slays
More than are numbered in the lists of Fate,
Taking all shapes, and bearing many names.
Look upon me! for even of all these things
Have I partaken; and of all these things,   *150*
One were enough; then wonder not that I
Am what I am, but that I ever was,
Or having been, that I am still on earth.
    Abbot. Yet, hear me still ——
    Manfred.   Old man! I do respect
Thine order, and revere thine years; I deem   *155*
Thy purpose pious, but it is in vain:
Think me not churlish; I would spare thyself,
Far more than me, in shunning at this time
All further colloquy — and so — farewell.

                       [*Exit* MANFRED.]

    Abbot. This should have been a noble creature: he   *160*
Hath all the energy which would have made
A goodly frame of glorious elements,
Had they been wisely mingled; as it is,
It is an awful chaos — Light and Darkness —
And mind and dust — and passions and pure thoughts   *165*
Mixed, and contending without end or order, —
All dormant or destructive. He will perish —
And yet he must not — I will try once more,
For such are worth redemption; and my duty

Is to dare all things for a righteous end.   170
I'll follow him — but cautiously, though surely.

[*Exit* ABBOT.]

SCENE II. — *Another Chamber.*

MANFRED *and* HERMAN

Herman. My Lord, you bade me wait on you at sunset:
He sinks behind the mountain.
   Manfred.   Doth he so?
I will look on him.

[MANFRED *advances to the Window of the Hall.*]

        Glorious Orb! the idol
Of early nature, and the vigorous race
Of undiseased mankind, the giant sons   5
Of the embrace of Angels, with a sex
More beautiful than they, which did draw down
The erring Spirits who can ne'er return. —
Most glorious Orb! that wert a worship, ere
The mystery of thy making was revealed!   10
Thou earliest minister of the Almighty,
Which gladdened, on their mountain tops, the hearts
Of the Chaldean shepherds, till they poured
Themselves in orisons! Thou material God!
And representative of the Unknown —   15
Who chose thee for his shadow! Thou chief Star!
Centre of many stars! which mak'st our earth
Endurable, and temperest the hues
And hearts of all who walk within thy rays!
Sire of the seasons! Monarch of the climes,   20
And those who dwell in them! for near or far,
Our inborn spirits have a tint of thee
Even as our outward aspects; —thou dost rise,

III. ii. 6. *embrace of angels*: See *Genesis* 6:2–4.

And shine, and set in glory. Fare thee well!
I ne'er shall see thee more. As my first glance   25
Of love and wonder was for thee, then take
My latest look: thou wilt not beam on one
To whom the gifts of life and warmth have been
Of a more fatal nature. He is gone —

                                    [*Exit* MANFRED.]

SCENE III. — *The Mountains* — *The Castle of Manfred
at some distance* — *A Terrace before a Tower.* — *Time,
Twilight.*

HERMAN, MANUEL, *and other dependants of* MANFRED.

Herman. 'Tis strange enough! night after night, for years,
He hath pursued long vigils in this tower,
Without a witness. I have been within it, —
So have we all been oft-times; but from it,
Or its contents, it were impossible   5
To draw conclusions absolute, of aught
His studies tend to. To be sure, there is
One chamber where none enter: I would give
The fee of what I have to come these three years,
To pore upon its mysteries.
Manuel.   'Twere dangerous;   10
Content thyself with what thou know'st already.
Herman. Ah! Manuel! thou art elderly and wise,
And couldst say much; thou hast dwelt within the castle —
How many years is't?
Manuel.   Ere Count Manfred's birth,
I served his father, whom he nought resembles.   15
Herman. There be more sons in like predicament!
But wherein do they differ?
Manuel.   I speak not
Of features or of form, but mind and habits;
Count Sigismund was proud, but gay and free, —
A warrior and a reveller; he dwelt not   20
With books and solitude, nor made the night

A gloomy vigil, but a festal time,
Merrier than day; he did not walk the rocks
And forests like a wolf, nor turn aside
From men and their delights.

    Herman.   Beshrew the hour,   25
But those were jocund times! I would that such
Would visit the old walls again; they look
As if they had forgotten them.

    Manuel.   These walls
Must change their chieftain first. Oh! I have seen
Some strange things in them, Herman.

    Herman.   Come, be friendly;   30
Relate me some to while away our watch:
I've heard thee darkly speak of an event
Which happened hereabouts, by this same tower.

    Manuel. That was a night indeed! I do remember
'Twas twilight, as it may be now, and such   35
Another evening: — yon red cloud, which rests
On Eigher's pinnacle, so rested then, —
So like that it might be the same; the wind
Was faint and gusty, and the mountain snows
Began to glitter with the climbing moon;   40
Count Manfred was, as now, within his tower, —
How occupied, we know not, but with him
The sole companion of his wanderings
And watchings — her, whom of all earthly things
That lived, the only thing he seemed to love, —   45
As he, indeed, by blood was bound to do,
The Lady Astarte, his ——

                 Hush! who comes here?

            [*Enter the* ABBOT.]

    Abbot. Where is your master?
    Herman.   Yonder in the tower.
    Abbot. I must speak with him.
    Manuel.   'Tis impossible;

III. iii. 37. *Eigher's pinnacle*: A mountain east of the Jungfrau.

He is most private, and must not be thus   50
Intruded on.
   Abbot.   Upon myself I take
The forfeit of my fault, if fault there be —
But I must see him.
   Herman.   Thou hast seen him once
This eve already.
   Abbot.   Herman! I command thee,
Knock, and apprize the Count of my approach.   55
   Herman. We dare not.
   Abbot.   Then it seems I must be herald
Of my own purpose.
   Manuel.   Reverend father, stop —
I pray you pause.
   Abbot.   Why so?
   Manuel.   But step this way,
And I will tell you further.   *[Exeunt.]*

SCENE IV. — *Interior of the Tower.*

MANFRED *alone.*

The stars are forth, the moon above the tops
Of the snow-shining mountains. — Beautiful!
I linger yet with Nature, for the Night
Hath been to me a more familiar face
Than that of man; and in her starry shade   5
Of dim and solitary loveliness,
I learned the language of another world.
I do remember me, that in my youth,
When I was wandering, — upon such a night
I stood within the Coliseum's wall,   10
'Midst the chief relics of almighty Rome;
The trees which grew along the broken arches
Waved dark in the blue midnight, and the stars
Shone through the rents of ruin; from afar
The watch-dog bayed beyond the Tiber; and   15

III. iv. 10. *Coliseum's wall*: Compare *Childe Harold*, IV, 128–131.

More near from out the Cæsars' palace came
The owl's long cry, and, interruptedly,
Of distant sentinels the fitful song
Begun and died upon the gentle wind.
Some cypresses beyond the time-worn breach   20
Appeared to skirt the horizon, yet they stood
Within a bowshot. Where the Cæsars dwelt,
And dwell the tuneless birds of night, amidst
A grove which springs through levelled battlements,
And twines its roots with the imperial hearths,   25
Ivy usurps the laurel's place of growth;
But the gladiators' bloody Circus stands,
A noble wreck in ruinous perfection,
While Cæsar's chambers, and the Augustan halls,
Grovel on earth in indistinct decay. —   30
And thou didst shine, thou rolling Moon, upon
All this, and cast a wide and tender light,
Which softened down the hoar austerity
Of rugged desolation, and filled up,
As 'twere anew, the gaps of centuries;   35
Leaving that beautiful which still was so,
And making that which was not — till the place
Became religion, and the heart ran o'er
With silent worship of the Great of old, —
The dead, but sceptred, Sovereigns, who still rule   40
Our spirits from their urns.
                          'Twas such a night!
'Tis strange that I recall it at this time;
But I have found our thoughts take wildest flight
Even at the moment when they should array
Themselves in pensive order.

[*Enter the* ABBOT.]

Abbot.   My good Lord!   45
I crave a second grace for this approach;
But yet let not my humble zeal offend
By its abruptness — all it hath of ill
Recoils on me; its good in the effect

May light upon your head — could I say *heart* —   50
Could I touch *that,* with words or prayers, I should
Recall a noble spirit which hath wandered,
But is not yet all lost.
   Manfred.   Thou know'st me not;
My days are numbered, and my deeds recorded:
Retire, or 'twill be dangerous — Away!   55
   Abbot. Thou dost not mean to menace me?
   Manfred.   Not I!
I simply tell thee peril is at hand,
And would preserve thee.
   Abbot.   What dost thou mean?
   Manfred.   Look there!
What dost thou see?
   Abbot.   Nothing.
   Manfred.   Look there, I say,
And steadfastly; — now tell me what thou seest?   60
   Abbot. That which should shake me, — but I fear it not:
I see a dusk and awful figure rise,
Like an infernal god, from out the earth;
His face wrapt in a mantle, and his form
Robed as with angry clouds: he stands between   65
Thyself and me — but I do fear him not.
   Manfred. Thou hast no cause — he shall not harm thee —
    but
His sight may shock thine old limbs into palsy.
I say to thee — Retire!
   Abbot.   And I reply —
Never — till I have battled with this fiend: —   70
What doth he here?
   Manfred.   Why — aye — what doth he here?
I did not send for him, — he is unbidden.
   Abbot. Alas! lost Mortal! what with guests like these
Hast thou to do? I tremble for thy sake:
Why doth he gaze on thee, and thou on him?   75
Ah! he unveils his aspect: on his brow
The thunder-scars are graven; from his eye
Glares forth the immortality of Hell —

Avaunt! —

   Manfred. Pronounce — what is thy mission?

   Spirit.   Come!

   Abbot. What are thou, unknown being? answer! — speak! [80]

   Spirit. The genius of this mortal. — Come! 'tis time.

   Manfred. I am prepared for all things, but deny

The Power which summons me. Who sent thee here?

   Spirit. Thou'lt know anon — Come! come!

   Manfred.   I have commanded

Things of an essence greater far than thine,   85

And striven with thy masters. Get thee hence!

   Spirit. Mortal! thine hour is come — Away! I say.

   Manfred. I knew, and know my hour is come, but not

To render up my soul to such as thee:

Away! I'll die as I have lived — alone.   90

   Spirit. Then I must summon up my brethren. — Rise!

                        [*Other Spirits rise up.*]

   Abbot. Avaunt! ye evil ones! — Avaunt! I say, —

Ye have no power where Piety hath power,

And I do charge ye in the name —

   Spirit.   Old man!

We know ourselves, our mission, and thine order;   95

Waste not thy holy words on idle uses,

It were in vain: this man is forfeited.

Once more — I summon him — Away! Away!

   Manfred. I do defy ye, — though I feel my soul

Is ebbing from me, yet I do defy ye;   100

Nor will I hence, while I have earthly breath

To breathe my scorn upon ye — earthly strength

To wrestle, though with spirits; what ye take

Shall be ta'en limb by limb.

   Spirit.   Reluctant mortal!

Is this the Magian who would so pervade   105

III. iv. 81. *The genius of this mortal*: See Act I. i. 110. It is evident that the spirits evoked in Act I, the destinies and spirits in the Hall of Arimanes in Act II, and the spirits that come for Manfred are all inter-related.

The world invisible, and make himself
Almost our equal? Can it be that thou
Art thus in love with life? the very life
Which made thee wretched?
    Manfred.   Thou false fiend, thou liest!
My life is in its last hour, — *that* I know,   *110*
Nor would redeem a moment of that hour;
I do not combat against Death, but thee
And thy surrounding angels; my past power
Was purchased by no compact with thy crew,
But by superior science — penance, daring,   *115*
And length of watching, strength of mind, and skill
In knowledge of our Fathers — when the earth
Saw men and spirits walking side by side,
And gave ye no supremacy: I stand
Upon my strength — I do defy — deny —   *120*
Spurn back, and scorn ye! —
    Spirit.   But thy many crimes
Have made thee ——
    Manfred.   What are they to such as thee?
Must crimes be punished but by other crimes,
And greater criminals? — Back to thy hell!
Thou hast no power upon me, *that* I feel;   *125*
Thou never shalt possess me, *that* I know:
What I have done is done; I bear within
A torture which could nothing gain from thine:
The Mind which is immortal makes itself
Requital for its good or evil thoughts, —   *130*
Is its own origin of ill and end —
And its own place and time: its innate sense,
When stripped of this mortality, derives
No colour from the fleeting things without,
But is absorbed in sufferance or in joy,   *135*
Born from the knowledge of its own desert.
Thou didst not tempt me, and thou couldst not tempt me;
I have not been thy dupe, nor am thy prey —

III. iv. 129–132. *mind . . . time*: See I. i. 252 n. above.

But was my own destroyer, and will be
My own hereafter. — Back, ye baffled fiends!   140
The hand of Death is on me — but not yours!

> [*The Demons disappear.*]

   Abbot. Alas! how pale thou art — thy lips are white —
And thy breast heaves — and in thy gasping throat
The accents rattle: Give thy prayers to Heaven —
Pray — albeit but in thought, — but die not thus.   145
   Manfred. 'Tis over — my dull eyes can fix thee not;
But all things swim around me, and the earth
Heaves as it were beneath me. Fare thee well —
Give me thy hand.
   Abbot.   Cold — cold — even to the heart —
But yet one prayer — Alas! how fares it with thee?   150
   Manfred. Old man! 'tis not so difficult to die.

> [MANFRED *expires.*]

   Abbot. He's gone — his soul hath ta'en its earthless flight;
Whither? I dread to think — but he is gone.

1816–17   *1817*

III. iv. 151. *Old man . . . to die*: This line was left out in the first edition at Gifford's suggestion and Byron wrote furiously to Murray (August 12, 1817) "You have destroyed the whole effect and moral of the poem by omitting the last line of Manfred's speaking, and why this was done, I know not."

Cain

A MYSTERY

Byron wrote *Cain* in the summer of 1821 in the interval between beginning and completing *The Vision of Judgment*. The play was published with two others, *The Two Foscari* and *Sardanapalus,* in December, 1821. *Cain* and *The Vision* are interesting viewed side by side, representing as they do the opposite styles of Byron in their most effective forms. *The Vision* is in the mock-heroic "low" colloquial style of *Don Juan,* and *Cain* is in "the gay metaphysical style," as Byron wrote Murray, of *Manfred.* Yet they have much in common. Through both runs the same questioning of divine justice and human rule based upon it. *The Vision* is preoccupied with the politics of eighteenth- and nineteenth-century England and *Cain* with the "politics of Paradise" which underlay and sanctioned the former. Through the questionings of Cain and Lucifer in particular Byron is attacking not dead dogma of the past but theological doctrines very much alive and powerful in his own day.

Byron is essentially correct when he disclaims in his Preface utilizing any sources except the Bible. The situations and characterization of the first two acts are his own imaginative reconstruction of the events leading to the climactic episode of the third chapter of Genesis. From Milton's *Paradise Lost* he obviously took the general suggestion of metaphysical debate in a paradisiacal setting, and some hints for Adam and Eve; and Gessner's *Death of Abel* (see Byron's Preface) provided precedence for the development of the relation of Cain and his sister-wife, the character of Abel, and a few minor details of plot like the whirlwind which destroyed Cain's altar. Lucifer has something of the defiant pride and immortal sorrow of Milton's Satan, and the mocking cynicism of

Mephistopheles in Goethe's *Faust,* but he is finally a very different character from either. Through him Byron raises the question of the origin and nature of evil in its most complex and ambiguous terms. Particularly in the second act, when he carries Cain through space and Hades, Lucifer is truly the devil's advocate indicting God as the father and creator of evil. Byron is engaged in something of the same ironic reversal of the traditional connotations of good and evil as Blake in his use of devils and angels in *The Marriage of Heaven and Hell.* And, although there is no necessity to press an identification of Byron with Lucifer, undoubtedly Lucifer becomes the spokesman for Byron's deepest doubts and questions about the role of man in the cosmos.

Cain stirred up a terrific storm of invective and protest upon its publication, and it has been the object of controversy and debate ever since. For the critical history, as well as details of interpretation, the student should consult the variorum edition of *Cain* by T. G. Steffan (1969).

"Now the Serpent was more subtil than any beast of the field which the Lord God had made."

Genesis iii.1.

DRAMATIS PERSONÆ

Men	Spirits	Women
ADAM	ANGEL OF THE LORD	EVE
CAIN	LUCIFER	ADAH
ABEL		ZILLAH

PREFACE

THE following scenes are entitled "A Mystery," in conformity with the ancient title annexed to dramas upon similar subjects, which were styled "Mysteries, or Moralities."[1] The author has

---

[1] *"Mysteries or Moralities"*: Byron of course here confuses two different types of medieval plays. "Mystery" meant for him simply "a tragedy on a sacred subject," a dramatization of a biblical episode. Byron's direct knowledge of medieval drama was probably slight.

by no means taken the same liberties with his subject which were common formerly, as may be seen by any reader curious enough to refer to those very profane productions, whether in English, French, Italian, or Spanish. The author has endeavoured to preserve the language adapted to his characters; and where it is (and this is but rarely) taken from actual *Scripture*, he has made as little alteration, even of words, as the rhythm would permit. The reader will recollect that the book of Genesis does not state that Eve was tempted by a demon, but by "the Serpent;" and that only because he was "the most subtil of all the beasts of the field."[2] Whatever interpretation the Rabbins and the Fathers may have put upon this, I take the words as I find them, and reply, with Bishop Watson upon similar occasions, when the Fathers were quoted to him as Moderator in the schools of Cambridge, "Behold the Book!" — holding up the Scripture.[3] It is to be recollected, that my present subject has nothing to do with the *New Testament*, to which no reference can be here made without anachronism.[4] With the poems upon similar topics I have not been recently familiar. Since I was twenty I have never read Milton; but I had read him so frequently before, that this may make little difference. Gesner's "Death of Abel"[5] I have never read since I was eight years of age, at Aberdeen. The general impression of my recollection is delight; but of the contents I remember only that Cain's wife was called Mahala, and Abel's Thirza; in the following pages I have called them "Adah" and "Zillah," the earliest female names which occur in Genesis. They were those of Lamech's wives[6]: those of Cain and Abel are not

---

[2] "... *beasts of the field*": See *Genesis*, 3:1.

[3] ... *holding up the scripture*: Richard Watson (1737–1816), Bishop of Llandaff and Professor of Divinity at Cambridge, acknowledged no theological authority except the New Testament and during doctrinal disputes would hold it in his hands and say, "Here is the fountain of truth."

[4] ... *anachronism*. Byron nevertheless permits Lucifer a number of veiled allusions to Christ, justified perhaps on the same grounds that justify Michael's revelations to Adam in *Paradise Lost* (see Act I, ll. 163–166, 541–542 and Act II, sc. 1, ll. 16–20); and he also permits a speculation by Adah and Cain about a future atonement, Act III, ll. 85–92.

[5] *Gesner's Death of Abel*: A sentimental poem (1758) by a Swiss writer, Solomon Gessner (1730–1788).

[6] *Lamech's wives*: See *Genesis*, 4:19. Lamech is a descendant of Cain.

called by their names. Whether, then, a coincidence of subject may have caused the same in expression, I know nothing, and care as little. [I[7] am prepared to be accused of Manicheism,[8] or some other hard name ending in *ism*, which makes a formidable figure and awful sound in the eyes and ears of those who would be as much puzzled to explain the terms so bandied about, as the liberal and pious indulgers in such epithets. Against such I can defend myself, or, if necessary, I can attack in turn. "Claw for claw, as Conan said to Satan, and the deevil take the shortest nails" (Waverley).[9]]

The reader will please to bear in mind (what few choose to recollect), that there is no allusion to a future state in any of the books of Moses, nor indeed in the Old Testament. For a reason for this extraordinary omission he may consult Warburton's "Divine Legation;"[10] whether satisfactory or not, no better has yet been assigned. I have therefore supposed it new to Cain, without, I hope, any perversion of Holy Writ.

With regard to the language of Lucifer, it was difficult for me to make him talk like a clergyman upon the same subjects; but I have done what I could to restrain him within the bounds of spiritual politeness. If he disclaims having tempted Eve in the shape of the Serpent, it is only because the book of Genesis has not the most distant allusion to anything of the kind, but merely to the Serpent in his serpentine capacity.

---

7 [*I am prepared* . . . .]: The bracketed sentences were omitted from the first edition of the play, probably through Murray's timidity.

8 *Manicheism*: The Manichean heresy (derived from Mani, third century A.D. Persian prophet) held that a cosmic conflict existed between coeternal principles of good and evil, the good being the Power of Light and Spirit, the evil being the Power of Darkness and Matter, the ruler of the material world and the body. Man is a warring mixture of soul and body. Byron gives Lucifer several allusions to this eternal dualism (see Act I, 11. 102, 546; Act II, Sc. 2, 1. 404). Since Lucifer (lightbearer), as his name suggests, presents himself as the Power of Light and Reason opposed to the Tyrannical Creator of the Material World, a reversal of the traditional roles of good and evil, Byron could well expect the kind of outraged protest from the orthodox "unco guid" that the play indeed provoked.

9 *Waverley*: In a note to *Waverley*, Scott identifies Conan as a Jester in Irish ballads, who on one occasion in descending to the infernal regions received a cuff from the devil which he instantly returned.

10 *Warburton's Divine Legation*: William Warburton (1698–1779), English Bishop, is best known today for his defence of Pope's *Essay on Man*. *The Divine Legation of Moses* (1737–1741) is an anti-deist polemic.

Note. — The reader will perceive that the author has partly adopted in this poem the notion of Cuvier,[11] that the world had been destroyed several times before the creation of man. This speculation, derived from the different strata and the bones of enormous and unknown animals found in them, is not contrary to the Mosaic account, but rather confirms it; as no human bones have yet been discovered in those strata, although those of many known animals are found near the remains of the unknown. The assertion of Lucifer, that the pre-Adamite world was also peopled by rational beings much more intelligent than man, and proportionably powerful to the mammoth, etc., etc., is, of course, a poetical fiction to help him to make out his case.

I ought to add, that there is a "tramelogedia" of Alfieri, called "Abele."[12] I have never read that, nor any other of the posthumous works of the writer, except his Life.

Ravenna, Sept. 20, 1821

ACT I

SCENE I. — *The Land without Paradise.* — *Time, Sunrise.*

ADAM, EVE, CAIN, ABEL, ADAH, ZILLAH, *offering a Sacrifice.*

Adam. GOD, the Eternal! Infinite! All-wise! —
Who out of darkness on the deep didst make
Light on the waters with a word — All Hail!
Jehovah! with returning light — All Hail!
Eve. God! who didst name the day, and separate   5
Morning from night, till then divided never —

11 *the notion of Cuvier*: Baron Cuvier (1769–1832), French naturalist, in his *Discours sur les révolutions de la surface du Globe* (1812; translated 1813) wrote "judging from the different orders of animals of which we discover the remains in a fossil state, they had probably experienced two or three irruptions of the sea."

12 *"Abele"*: Vittorio Alfieri (1749–1803), Italian dramatist, interpolated the word "melo" in the middle of the word "tragedy" to classify a play which he said was "neither a tragedy, a comedy, a drama, a tragicomedy, nor a Greek tragedy." *Abele* was posthumously published in 1804.

Who didst divide the wave from wave, and call
Part of thy work the firmament — All Hail!

    Abel. God! who didst call the elements into
Earth, ocean, air and fire — and with the day   10
And night, and worlds which these illuminate,
Or shadow, madest beings to enjoy them,
And love both them and thee — All Hail! All Hail!

    Adah. God! the Eternal parent of all things!
Who didst create these best and beauteous beings,   15
To be belovéd, more than all, save thee —
Let me love thee and them: — All Hail! All Hail!

    Zillah. Oh, God! who loving, making, blessing all,
Yet didst permit the Serpent to creep in,
And drive my father forth from Paradise,   20
Keep us from further evil: — Hail! All Hail!

    Adam. Son Cain! my first-born — wherefore art thou silent?

    Cain. Why should I speak?

    Adam.   To pray.

    Cain.   Have ye not prayed?

    Adam. We have, most fervently.

    Cain.   And loudly: I
Have heard you.

    Adam.   So will God, I trust.

    Abel.   Amen!   25

    Adam. But thou my eldest born? art silent still?

    Cain. 'Tis better I should be so.

    Adam.   Wherefore so?

    Cain. I have nought to ask.

    Adam.   Nor aught to thank for?

    Cain.   No.

    Adam. Dost thou not *live?*

    Cain.   Must I not die?

    Eve.   Alas!
The fruit of our forbidden tree begins   30
To fall.

    Adam. And we must gather it again.
Oh God! why didst thou plant the tree of knowledge?

    Cain. And wherefore plucked ye not the tree of life?

Ye might have then defied him.

Adam.   Oh! my son,
Blaspheme not: these are Serpent's words.

Cain.   Why not?   35
The snake spoke *truth;* it *was* the Tree of Knowledge;
It *was* the Tree of Life: knowledge is good,
And Life is good; and how can both be evil?

Eve. My boy! thou speakest as I spoke in sin,
Before thy birth: let me not see renewed   40
My misery in thine. I have repented.
Let me not see my offspring fall into
The snares beyond the walls of Paradise,
Which even in Paradise destroyed his parents.
Content thee with what *is.* Had we been so,   45
Thou now hadst been contented. — Oh, my son!

Adam. Our orisons completed, let us hence,
Each to his task of toil — not heavy, though
Needful: the earth is young, and yields us kindly
Her fruits with little labour.

Eve.   Cain — my son —   50
Behold thy father cheerful and resigned —
And do as he doth.   [*Exeunt* ADAM *and* EVE.]

Zillah.   Wilt thou not, my brother?

Abel. Why wilt thou wear this gloom upon thy brow,
Which can avail thee nothing, save to rouse
The Eternal anger?

Adah.   My belovéd Cain   55
Wilt thou frown even on me?

Cain.   No, Adah! no;
I fain would be alone a little while.
Abel, I'm sick at heart; but it will pass;
Precede me, brother — I will follow shortly.
And you, too, sisters, tarry not behind;   60
Your gentleness must not be harshly met:
I'll follow you anon.

Adah.   If not, I will

Return to seek you here.

   Abel.   The peace of God
Be on your spirit, brother!

                [*Exeunt* ABEL, ZILLAH, *and* ADAH.]

   Cain [*solus*].   And this is
Life? — Toil! and wherefore should I toil? — because   65
My father could not keep his place in Eden?
What had *I* done in this? — I was unborn:
I sought not to be born; nor love the state
To which that birth has brought me. Why did he
Yield to the Serpent and the woman? or   70
Yielding — why suffer? What was there in this?
The tree was planted, and why not for him?
If not, why place him near it, where it grew
The fairest in the centre? They have but
One answer to all questions, " 'Twas *his* will,   75
And *he* is good." How know I that? Because
He is all-powerful, must all-good, too, follow?
I judge but by the fruits — and they are bitter —
Which I must feed on for a fault not mine.
Whom have we here? — A shape like to the angels   80
Yet of a sterner and a sadder aspect
Of spiritual essence: why do I quake?
Why should I fear him more than other spirits,
Whom I see daily wave their fiery swords
Before the gates round which I linger oft,   85
In Twilight's hour, to catch a glimpse of those
Gardens which are my just inheritance,
Ere the night closes o'er the inhibited walls
And the immortal trees which overtop
The Cherubim-defended battlements?   90
If I shrink not from these, the fire-armed angels,
Why should I quail from him who now approaches?
Yet — he seems mightier far than them, nor less
Beauteous, and yet not all as beautiful
As he hath been, and might be: sorrow seems   95

Half of his immortality. And it is
So? and can aught grieve save Humanity?
He cometh.

[*Enter* LUCIFER.]

   Lucifer. Mortal!
    Cain.   Spirit, who art thou?
   Lucifer. Master of spirits.
    Cain.   And being so, canst thou
Leave them, and walk with dust?
   Lucifer.   I know the thoughts   *100*
Of dust, and feel for it, and with you.
    Cain.   How!
You know my thoughts?
   Lucifer.   They are the thoughts of all
Worthy of thought; — 'tis your immortal part
Which speaks within you.
    Cain.   What immortal part?
This has not been revealed: the Tree of Life   *105*
Was withheld from us by my father's folly,
While that of Knowledge, by my mother's haste,
Was plucked too soon; and all the fruit is Death!
   Lucifer. They have deceived thee; thou shalt live.
    Cain.   I live,
But live to die; and, living, see no thing   *110*
To make death hateful, save an innate clinging,
A loathsome, and yet all invincible
Instinct of life, which I abhor, as I
Despise myself, yet cannot overcome —
And so I live. Would I had never lived!   *115*
   Lucifer. Thou livest — and must live for ever. Think not
The Earth, which is thine outward cov'ring, is
Existence — it will cease — and thou wilt be —
No less than thou art now.

   I. 102. See note on Manicheism, above, p. 231. According to the Manicheans, the immortal soul in man is imprisoned in an evil and decaying
body.

Cain.   No *less!* and why
No more?

Lucifer. It may be thou shalt be as we.   *120*

Cain. And ye?

Lucifer.   Are everlasting.

Cain.   Are ye happy?

Lucifer. We are mighty.

Cain.   Are ye happy?

Lucifer.   No: art thou?

Cain. How should I be so? Look on me!

Lucifer.   Poor clay!
And thou pretendest to be wretched! Thou!

Cain. I am: — and thou, with all thy might, what art
      thou?   *125*

Lucifer. One who aspired to be what made thee, and
Would not have made thee what thou art.

Cain.   '   Ah!
Thou look'st almost a god; and ——

Lucifer.   I am none:
And having failed to be one, would be nought
Save what I am. He conquered; let him reign!   *130*

Cain. Who?

Lucifer.   Thy Sire's maker — and the Earth's.

Cain.   And Heaven's,
And all that in them is. So I have heard
His Seraphs sing; and so my father saith.

Lucifer. They say — what they must sing and say, on pain
Of being that which I am, — and thou art —   *135*
Of spirits and of men.

Cain.   And what is that?

Lucifer. Souls who dare use their immortality —
Souls who dare look the Omnipotent tyrant in
His everlasting face, and tell him that
His evil is not good! If he has made,   *140*
As he saith — which I know not, nor believe —
But, if he made us — he cannot unmake:
We are immortal! — nay, he'd *have* us so,
That he may torture: — let him! He is great —

But, in his greatness, is no happier than   145
We in our conflict! Goodness would not make
Evil; and what else hath he made? But let him
Sit on his vast and solitary throne —
Creating worlds, to make eternity
Less burdensome to his immense existence   150
And unparticipated solitude;
Let him crowd orb on orb: he is alone
Indefinite, Indissoluble Tyrant;
Could he but crush himself, 'twere the best boon
He ever granted: but let him reign on!   155
And multiply himself in misery!
Spirits and Men, at least we sympathise —
And, suffering in concert, make our pangs
Innumerable, more endurable,
By the unbounded sympathy of all   160
With all! But *He!* so wretched in his height,
So restless in his wretchedness, must still
Create, and re-create — perhaps he'll make
One day a Son unto himself — as he
Gave you a father — and if he so doth,   165
Mark me! that Son will be a sacrifice!
    Cain. Thou speak'st to me of things which long have swum
In visions through my thought: I never could
Reconcile what I saw with what I heard.
My father and my mother talk to me   170
Of serpents, and of fruits and trees: I see
The gates of what they call their Paradise
Guarded by fiery-sworded Cherubim,
Which shut them out — and me: I feel the weight

   I. 147 ff. Lucifer is here turning the doctrine of Plenitude, widely
accepted in the eighteenth century as an argument for God's Infinite
Goodness, against itself. The orthodox argument was that God might have
refrained from creating and continued alone, self-sufficient and perfect to
all eternity, but his Goodness and Magnanimity obliged him to create
external things, even though they would be necessarily imperfect. For a
detailed discussion of the doctrine, see Arthur Lovejoy, *The Great Chain
of Being*, 1936.
   I. 163. For the allusion to Christ, see Preface n.4, above, p. 230.

Of daily toil, and constant thought: I look 175
Around a world where I seem nothing, with
Thoughts which arise within me, as if they
Could master all things — but I thought alone
This misery was *mine*. My father is
Tamed down; my mother has forgot the mind 180
Which made her thirst for knowledge at the risk
Of an eternal curse; my brother is
A watching shepherd boy, who offers up
The firstlings of the flock to him who bids
The earth yield nothing to us without sweat; 185
My sister Zillah sings an earlier hymn
Than the birds' matins; and my Adah — my
Own and belovéd — she, too, understands not
The mind which overwhelms me: never till
Now met I aught to sympathise with me. 190
'Tis well — I rather would consort with spirits.
    Lucifer. And hadst thou not been fit by thine own soul
For such companionship, I would not now
Have stood before thee as I am: a serpent
Had been enough to charm ye, as before. 195
    Cain. Ah! didst *thou* tempt my mother?
    Lucifer.   I tempt none,
Save with the truth: was not the Tree, the Tree
Of Knowledge? and was not the Tree of Life
Still fruitful? Did *I* bid her pluck them not?
Did I plant things prohibited within 200
The reach of beings innocent, and curious
By their own innocence? I would have made ye
Gods; and even He who thrust ye forth, so thrust ye
Because "ye should not eat the fruits of life,
"And become gods as we." Were those his words? 205
    Cain. They were, as I have heard from those who heard
      them,
In thunder.
    Lucifer. Then who was the Demon? He
Who would not let ye live, or he who would
Have made ye live for ever, in the joy

And power of Knowledge?

   Cain.   Would they had snatched both   *210*
The fruits, or neither!

   Lucifer.   One is yours already,
The other may be still.

   Cain.   How so?

   Lucifer.   By being
Yourselves, in your resistance. Nothing can
Quench the mind, if the mind will be itself
And centre of surrounding things — 'tis made   *215*
To sway.

   Cain. But didst thou tempt my parents?

   Lucifer.   I?
Poor clay — what should I tempt them for, or how?

   Cain. They say the Serpent was a spirit.

   Lucifer.   Who
Saith that? It is not written so on high:
The proud One will not so far falsify,   *220*
Though man's vast fears and little vanity
Would make him cast upon the spiritual nature
His own low failing. The snake *was* the snake —
No more; and yet not less than those he tempted,
In nature being earth also — *more* in *wisdom,*   *225*
Since he could overcome them, and foreknew
The knowledge fatal to their narrow joys.
Think'st thou I'd take the shape of things that die?

   Cain. But the thing had a demon?

   Lucifer.   He but woke one
In those he spake to with his forky tongue.   *230*
I tell thee that the Serpent was no more
Than a mere serpent: ask the Cherubim
Who guard the tempting tree. When thousand ages
Have rolled o'er your dead ashes, and your seed's,
The seed of the then world may thus array   *235*
Their earliest fault in fable, and attribute
To me a shape I scorn, as I scorn all

   I. 223. See Byron's remarks on the serpent in the Preface, above, p. 230.

That bows to him, who made things but to bend
Before his sullen, sole eternity;
But we, who see the truth, must speak it. Thy   *240*
Fond parents listened to a creeping thing,
And fell. For what should spirits tempt them? What
Was there to envy in the narrow bounds
Of Paradise, that spirits who pervade
Space — but I speak to thee of what thou know'st not,   *245*
With all thy Tree of Knowledge.
    Cain.   But thou canst not
Speak aught of Knowledge which I would not know,
And do not thirst to know, and bear a mind
To know.
    Lucifer. And heart to look on?
    Cain.   Be it proved.
    Lucifer. Darest thou look on Death?
    Cain.   He has not yet   *250*
Been seen.
    Lucifer. But must be undergone.
    Cain.   My father
Says he is something dreadful, and my mother
Weeps when he's named; and Abel lifts his eyes
To Heaven, and Zillah casts hers to the earth,
And sighs a prayer; and Adah looks on me,   *255*
And speaks not.
    Lucifer.   And thou?
    Cain.   Thoughts unspeakable
Crowd in my breast to burning, when I hear
Of this almighty Death, who is, it seems,
Inevitable. Could I wrestle with him?
I wrestled with the lion, when a boy,   *260*
In play, till he ran roaring from my gripe.
    Lucifer. It has no shape; but will absorb all things
That bear the form of earth-born being.
    Cain.   Ah!
I thought it was a being: who could do
Such evil things to beings save a being?   *265*
    Lucifer. Ask the Destroyer

Cain.   Who?

Lucifer.   The Maker — Call him
Which name thou wilt: he makes but to destroy.

   Cain. I knew not that, yet thought it, since I heard
Of Death: although I know not what it is —
Yet it seems horrible. I have looked out   270
In the vast desolate night in search of him;
And when I saw gigantic shadows in
The umbrage of the walls of Eden, chequered
By the far-flashing of the Cherub's swords,
I watched for what I thought his coming; for   275
With fear rose longing in my heart to know
What 'twas which shook us all — but nothing came.
And then I turned my weary eyes from off
Our native and forbidden Paradise,
Up to the lights above us, in the azure,   280
Which are so beautiful: shall they, too, die?

   Lucifer. Perhaps — but long outlive both thine and thee.

   Cain. I'm glad of that: I would not have them die —
They are so lovely. What is Death? I fear,
I feel, it is a dreadful thing; but what,   285
I cannot compass: 'tis denounced against us,
Both them who sinned and sinned not, as an ill —
What ill?

   Lucifer. To be resolved into the earth.

   Cain. But shall I know it?

   Lucifer.   As I know not death,
I cannot answer.

   Cain.   Were I quiet earth,   290
That were no evil: would I ne'er had been
Aught else but dust!

   Lucifer.   That is a *grovelling* wish,
Less than thy father's — for he wished to know!

   Cain. But not to live — or wherefore plucked he not
The Life-tree?

   Lucifer.   He was hindered.

   Cain.   Deadly error!   295
Not to snatch first that fruit: — but ere he plucked

The knowledge, he was ignorant of Death.
Alas! I scarcely now know what it is,
And yet I fear it — fear I know not what!
  Lucifer. And I, who know all things, fear nothing; see   *300*
What is true knowledge.
  Cain.   Wilt thou teach me all?
  Lucifer. Aye, upon one condition.
  Cain.   Name it.
  Lucifer.   That
Thou dost fall down and worship me — thy Lord.
  Cain. Thou art not the Lord my father worships.
  Lucifer.   No.
  Cain. His equal?
  Lucifer.   No; — I have nought in common with
  him!   *305*
Nor would: I would be aught above — beneath —
Aught save a sharer or a servant of
His power. I dwell apart; but I am great: —
Many there are who worship me, and more
Who shall — be thou amongst the first.
  Cain.   I never   *310*
As yet have bowed unto my father's God.
Although my brother Abel oft implores
That I would join with him in sacrifice: —
Why should I bow to thee?
  Lucifer.   Hast thou ne'er bowed
To him?
  Cain. Have I not said it? — need I say it?   *315*
Could not thy mighty knowledge teach thee that?
  Lucifer. He who bows not to him has bowed to me.
  Cain. But I will bend to neither.
  Lucifer.   Ne'er the less,
Thou art my worshipper; not worshipping
Him makes thee mine the same.
  Cain.   And what is that?   *320*
  Lucifer. Thou'lt know here — and hereafter.
  Cain.   Let me but
Be taught the mystery of my being.

Lucifer.   Follow
Where I will lead thee.
    Cain.   But I must retire
To till the earth — for I had promised ——
    Lucifer.   What?
    Cain. To cull some first-fruits.
    Lucifer.   Why?
    Cain.   To offer up   *325*
With Abel on an altar.
    Lucifer.   Said'st thou not
Thou ne'er hadst bent to him who made thee?
    Cain.   Yes —
But Abel's earnest prayer has wrought upon me;
The offering is more his than mine — and Adah ——
    Lucifer. Why dost thou hesitate?
    Cain.   She is my sister,   *330*
Born on the same day, of the same womb; and
She wrung from me, with tears, this promise; and
Rather than see her weep, I would, methinks,
Bear all — and worship aught.
    Lucifer.   Then follow me!
    Cain. I will.

[*Enter* ADAH.]

    Adah.   My brother, I have come for thee;   *335*
It is our hour of rest and joy — and we
Have less without thee. Thou hast laboured not
This morn; but I have done thy task: the fruits
Are ripe, and glowing as the light which ripens:
Come away.
    Cain.   Seest thou not?
    Adah.   I see an angel;   *340*
We have seen many: will he share our hour
Of rest? — he is welcome.
    Cain.   But he is not like
The angels we have seen.
    Adah.   Are there, then, others?

But he is welcome, as they were: they deigned
To be our guests — will he?
    Cain (to Lucifer).   Wilt thou?
    Lucifer.   I ask   *345*
Thee to be mine.
    Cain.   I must away with him.
    Adah. And leave us?
    Cain.   Aye.
    Adah.   And *me?*
    Cain.   Belovéd Adah!
    Adah. Let me go with thee.
    Lucifer.   No, she must not.
    Adah.   Who
Art thou that steppest between heart and heart?
    Cain. He is a God.
    Adah.   How know'st thou?
    Cain.   He speaks like   *350*
A God.
    Adah. So did the Serpent, and it lied.
    Lucifer. Thou errest, Adah! — was not the Tree that
Of Knowledge?
    Adah.   Aye — to our eternal sorrow.
    Lucifer. And yet that grief is knowledge — so he lied not:
And if he did betray you, 'twas with Truth;   *355*
And Truth in its own essence cannot be
But good.
    Adah. But all we know of it has gathered
Evil on ill; expulsion from our home,
And dread, and toil, and sweat, and heaviness;
Remorse of that which was — and hope of that   *360*
Which cometh not. Cain! walk not with this Spirit.
Bear with what we have borne, and love me — I
Love thee.
    Lucifer. More than thy mother, and thy sire?
    Adah. I do. Is that a sin, too?
    Lucifer.   No, not yet;
It one day will be in your children.
    Adah.   What!   *365*

Must not my daughter love her brother Enoch?

    Lucifer. Not as thou lovest Cain.

    Adah.   Oh, my God!

Shall they not love and bring forth things that love

Out of their love? have they not drawn their milk

Out of this bosom? was not he, their father,   *370*

Born of the same sole womb, in the same hour

With me? did we not love each other? and

In multiplying our being multiply

Things which will love each other as we love

Them? — And as I love thee, my Cain! go not   *375*

Forth with this spirit; he is not of ours.

    Lucifer. The sin I speak of is not of my making,

And cannot be a sin in you — whate'er

It seem in those who will replace ye in

Mortality.

    Adah. What is the sin which is not   *380*

Sin in itself? Can circumstance make sin

Or virtue? — if it doth, we are the slaves

Of ——

    Lucifer. Higher things than ye are slaves: and higher

Than them or ye would be so, did they not

Prefer an independency of torture   *385*

To the smooth agonies of adulation,

In hymns and harpings, and self-seeking prayers,

To that which is omnipotent, because

It is omnipotent, and not from love,

But terror and self-hope.

    Adah.   Omnipotence   *390*

Must all be goodness

    Lucifer.   Was it so in Eden?

    Adah. Fiend! tempt me not with beauty; thou **art** fairer

Than was the Serpent, and as false.

    Lucifer.   As true.

Ask Eve, your mother: bears she not the knowledge

Of good and evil?

    Adah.   Oh, my mother! thou   *395*

Hast plucked a fruit more fatal to thine offspring

Than to thyself; thou at the least hast passed
Thy youth in Paradise, in innocent
And happy intercourse with happy spirits:
But we, thy children, ignorant of Eden,   *400*
Are girt about by demons, who assume
The words of God, and tempt us with our own
Dissatisfied and curious thoughts — as thou
Wert worked on by the snake, in thy most flushed
And heedless, harmless wantonness of bliss.   *405*
I cannot answer this immortal thing
Which stands before me; I cannot abhor him;
I look upon him with a pleasing fear,
And yet I fly not from him: in his eye
There is a fastening attraction which   *410*
Fixes my fluttering eyes on his; my heart
Beats quick; he awes me, and yet draws me near,
Nearer and nearer: — Cain — Cain — save me from him!
    Cain. What dreads my Adah? This is no ill spirit.
    Adah. He is not God — nor God's: I have beheld   *415*
The Cherubs and the Seraphs; he looks not
Like them.
    Cain.   But there are spirits loftier still —
The archangels.
    Lucifer.   And still loftier than the archangels.
    Adah. Aye — but not blesséd.
    Lucifer.   If the blessedness
Consists in slavery — no.
    Adah.   I have heard it said,   *420*
The Seraphs *love most* — Cherubim *know most* —
And this should be a Cherub — since he loves not.
    Lucifer. And if the higher knowledge quenches love,
What must *he be* you cannot love when known?
Since the all-knowing Cherubim love least,   *425*
The Seraphs' love can be but ignorance:
That they are not compatible, the doom

I. 416. *The Cherubs and the Seraphs*: In the celestial hierarchy, Seraphim, symbolizing divine love and beauty, are of a higher order than Cherubim, symbolizing divine wisdom and justice.

Of thy fond parents, for their daring, proves.
Choose betwixt Love and Knowledge — since there is
No other choice: your sire hath chosen already: *430*
His worship is but fear.
    Adah.   Oh, Cain! choose Love.
    Cain. For thee, my Adah, I choose not — It was
Born with me — but I love nought else.
    Adah.   Our parents?
    Cain. Did they love us when they snatched from the Tree
That which hath driven us all from Paradise?   *435*
    Adah. We were not born then — and if we had been,
Should we not love them — and our children, Cain?
    Cain. My little Enoch! and his lisping sister!
Could I but deem them happy, I would half
Forget —— but it can never be forgotten   *440*
Through thrice a thousand generations! never
Shall men love the remembrance of the man
Who sowed the seed of evil and mankind
In the same hour! They plucked the tree of science
And sin — and, not content with their own sorrow,   *445*
Begot *me* — *thee* — and all the few that are,
And all the unnumbered and innumerable
Multitudes, millions, myriads, which may be,
To inherit agonies accumulated
By ages! — and *I* must be sire of such things!   *450*
Thy beauty and thy love — my love and joy,
The rapturous moment and the placid hour,
All we love in our children and each other,
But lead them and ourselves through many years
Of sin and pain — or few, but still of sorrow,   *455*
Interchecked with an instant of brief pleasure,
To Death — the unknown! Methinks the Tree of Knowledge
Hath not fulfilled its promise: — if they sinned,
At least they ought to have known all things that are
Of knowledge — and the mystery of Death.   *460*
What do they know? — that they are miserable.
What need of snakes and fruits to teach us that?
    Adah. I am not wretched, Cain, and if thou

Wert happy ——
   Cain.   Be thou happy, then, alone —
I will have nought to do with happiness,   *465*
Which humbles me and mine.
   Adah.   Alone I could not,
Nor *would* be happy; but with those around us
I think I could be so, despite of Death,
Which, as I know it not, I dread not, though
It seems an awful shadow — if I may   *470*
Judge from what I have heard.
   Lucifer.   And thou couldst not
Alone, thou say'st, be happy?
   Adah.   Alone! Oh, my God!
Who could be happy and alone, or good?
To me my solitude seems sin; unless
When I think how soon I shall see my brother,   *475*
His brother, and our children, and our parents.
   Lucifer. Yet thy God is alone; and is he happy?
Lonely, and good?
   Adah.   He is not so; he hath
The angels and the mortals to make happy,
And thus becomes so in diffusing joy.   *480*
What else can joy be, but the spreading joy?
   Lucifer. Ask of your sire, the exile fresh from Eden;
Or of his first-born son: ask your own heart;
It is not tranquil.
   Adah.   Alas! no! and you —
Are you of Heaven?
   Lucifer.   If I am not, enquire   *485*
The cause of this all-spreading happiness
(Which you proclaim) of the all-great and good
Maker of life and living things; it is
His secret, and he keeps it. *We* must bear,
And some of us resist — and both in vain,   *490*
His Seraphs say: but it is worth the trial,
Since better may not be without: there is
A wisdom in the spirit, which directs
To right, as in the dim blue air the eye

Of you, young mortals, lights at once upon   *495*
The star which watches, welcoming the morn.
   Adah. It is a beautiful star; I love it for
Its beauty.
   Lucifer. And why not adore?
   Adah.   Our father
Adores the Invisible only.
   Lucifer.   But the symbols
Of the Invisible are the loveliest   *500*
Of what is visible; and yon bright star
Is leader of the host of Heaven.
   Adah.   Our father
Saith that he has beheld the God himself
Who made him and our mother.
   Lucifer.   Hast *thou* seen him?
   Adah. Yes — in his works.
   Lucifer.   But in his being?
   Adah.   No —   *505*
Save in my father, who is God's own image;
Or in his angels, who are like to thee —
And brighter, yet less beautiful and powerful
In seeming: as the silent sunny noon,
All light, they look upon us; but thou seem'st   *510*
Like an ethereal night, where long white clouds
Streak the deep purple, and unnumbered stars
Spangle the wonderful mysterious vault
With things that look as if they would be suns;
So beautiful, unnumbered, and endearing,   *515*
Not dazzling, and yet drawing us to them,
They fill my eyes with tears, and so dost thou.
Thou seem'st unhappy: do not make us so,
And I will weep for thee.
   Lucifer.   Alas! those tears!
Couldst thou but know what oceans will be shed ——   *520*
   Adah. By me?
   Lucifer.   By all.
   Adah.   What all?
   Lucifer.   The million millions —

The myriad myriads — the all-peopled earth —
The unpeopled earth — and the o'er-peopled Hell,
Of which thy bosom is the germ.

   Adah.   O Cain!
This spirit curseth us.

   Cain.   Let him say on;   525
Him will I follow.

   Adah.   Whither?

   Lucifer.   To a place
Whence he shall come back to thee in an hour;
But in that hour see things of many days.

   Adah. How can that be?

   Lucifer.   Did not your Maker make
Out of old worlds this new one in few days?   530
And cannot I, who aided in this work,
Show in an hour what he hath made in many,
Or hath destroyed in few?

   Cain.   Lead on.

   Adah.   Will he,
In sooth, return within an hour?

   Lucifer.   He shall.
With us acts are exempt from time, and we   535
Can crowd eternity into an hour,
Or stretch an hour into eternity:
We breathe not by a mortal measurement —
But that's a mystery. Cain, come on with me.

   Adah. Will he return?

   Lucifer.   Aye, woman! he alone   540
Of mortals from that place (the first and last
Who shall return, save ONE), shall come back to thee,
To make that silent and expectant world
As populous as this: at present there
Are few inhabitants.

   Adah.   Where dwellest thou?   545

   Lucifer. Throughout all space. Where should I dwell?
   Where are

I. 542. For the allusion to Christ, see note on Preface, above, p. 230.
I. 546. See note on Manicheism, above, p. 231.

Thy God or Gods — there am I: all things are
Divided with me: Life and Death — and Time —
Eternity — and heaven and earth — and that
Which is not heaven nor earth, but peopled with   *550*
Those who once peopled or shall people both —
These are my realms! so that I do divide
His, and possess a kingdom which is not
His. If I were not that which I have said,
Could I stand here? His angels are within   *555*
Your vision.

   Adah. So they were when the fair Serpent
Spoke with our mother first.

   Lucifer.   Cain! thou hast heard.
If thou dost long for knowledge, I can satiate
That thirst; nor ask thee to partake of fruits
Which shall deprive thee of a single good   *560*
The Conqueror has left thee. Follow me.

   Cain. Spirit, I have said it.

                     [*Exeunt* LUCIFER *and* CAIN.]

   Adah [*follows exclaiming*]. Cain! my brother! Cain!

ACT II

SCENE I. — *The Abyss of Space.*

   Cain. I tread on air, and sink not — yet I fear
To sink.

   Lucifer. Have faith in me, and thou shalt be
Borne on the air, of which I am the Prince.

   Cain. Can I do so without impiety?

   Lucifer. Believe — and sink not! doubt — and
      perish! thus   *5*
Would run the edict of the other God,
Who names me Demon to his angels; they
Echo the sound to miserable things,

II. i. 3. Lucifer is quoting scripture to his own purpose. See *Ephesians*, 2:2: "Wherein in the past ye walked according to the course of this world, according to the prince of the power of the air, the spirit that now worketh in the children of disobedience. . . ."

Which, knowing nought beyond their shallow senses,
Worship the *word* which strikes their ear, and deem   *10*
Evil or good what is proclaimed to them
In their abasement. I will have none such:
Worship or worship not, thou shalt behold
The worlds beyond thy little world, nor be
Amerced for doubts beyond thy little life,   *15*
With torture of *my* dooming. There will come
An hour, when, tosssed upon some water-drops,
A man shall say to a man, "Believe in me,
And walk the waters;" and the man shall walk
The billows and be safe. *I* will not say,   *20*
Believe in *me,* as a conditional creed
To save thee; but fly with me o'er the gulf
Of space an equal flight, and I will show
What thou dar'st not deny, — the history
Of past — and present, and of future worlds.   *25*
    Cain. Oh God! or Demon! or whate'er thou art,
Is yon our earth?
    Lucifer.   Dost thou not recognise
The dust which formed your father?
    Cain.   Can it be?
Yon small blue circle, swinging in far ether,
With an inferior circlet purpler still,   *30*
Which looks like that which lit our earthly night?
Is this our Paradise? Where are its walls,
And they who guard them?
    Lucifer.   Point me out the site
Of Paradise.
    Cain.   How should I? As we move
Like sunbeams onward, it grows small and smaller,   *35*
And as it waxes little, and then less,
Gathers a halo round it, like the light
Which shone the roundest of the stars, when I
Beheld them from the skirts of Paradise:
Methinks they both, as we recede from them,   *40*

II. i. 16–20. For the allusion to Christ, see note on Preface, above
p. 230. The reference is to *Matthew*, 14:25–31.

Appear to join the innumerable stars
Which are around us; and, as we move on,
Increase their myriads.
  Lucifer.   And if there should be
Worlds greater than thine own — inhabited
By greater things — and they themselves far more   *45*
In number than the dust of thy dull earth,
Though multiplied to animated atoms,
All living — and all doomed to death — and wretched,
What wouldst thou think?
  Cain.   I should be proud of thought
Which knew such things.
  Lucifer.   But if that high thought were *50*
Linked to a servile mass of matter — and,
Knowing such things, aspiring to such things,
And science still beyond them, were chained down
To the most gross and petty paltry wants,
All foul and fulsome — and the very best   *55*
Of thine enjoyments a sweet degradation,
A most enervating and filthy cheat
To lure thee on to the renewal of
Fresh souls and bodies, all foredoomed to be
As frail, and few so happy ——
  Cain.   Spirit! I   *60*
Know nought of Death, save as a dreadful thing
Of which I have heard my parents speak, as of
A hideous heritage I owe to them
No less than life — a heritage not happy,
If I may judge, till now. But, Spirit! if   *65*
It be as thou hast said (and I within
Feel the prophetic torture of its truth),
Here let me die: for to give birth to those
Who can but suffer many years, and die —
Methinks is merely propagating Death,   *70*
And multiplying murder.
  Lucifer.   Thou canst not
All die — there is what must survive.
  Cain.   The Other

Spake not of this unto my father, when
He shut him forth from Paradise, with death
Written upon his forehead. But at least   *75*
Let what is mortal of me perish, that
I may be in the rest as angels are.
    Lucifer. I am angelic: wouldst thou be as I am?
    Cain. I know not what thou art: I see thy power,
And see thou show'st me things beyond my power,   *80*
Beyond all power of my born faculties,
Although inferior still to my desires
And my conceptions.
    Lucifer.   What are they which dwell
So humbly in their pride, as to sojourn
With worms in clay?
    Cain.   And what art thou who dwellest   *85*
So haughtily in spirit, and canst range
Nature and immortality — and yet
Seem'st sorrowful?
    Lucifer.   I seem that which I am;
And therefore do I ask of thee, if thou
Wouldst be immortal?
    Cain.   Thou hast said, I must be   *90*
Immortal in despite of me. I knew not
This until lately — but since it must be,
Let me, or happy or unhappy, learn
To anticipate my immortality.
    Lucifer. Thou didst before I came upon thee.
    Cain.   How?   *95*
    Lucifer. By suffering.
    Cain.   And must torture be immortal?
    Lucifer. We and thy sons will try. But now, behold!
Is it not glorious?
    Cain.   Oh thou beautiful
And unimaginable ether! and
Ye multiplying masses of increased   *100*
And still-increasing lights! what are ye? what

II. i. 83. For Byron's comment on the effect of Cain's sense of inadequacy, see letter to Murray, 3 November 1821, below, p. 687.

Is this blue wilderness of interminable
Air, where ye roll along, as I have seen
The leaves along the limpid streams of Eden?
Is your course measured for ye? Or do ye   105
Sweep on in your unbounded revelry
Through an aërial universe of endless
Expansion — at which my soul aches to think —
Intoxicated with eternity?
Oh God! Oh Gods! or whatsoe'er ye are!   110
How beautiful ye are! how beautiful
Your works, or accidents, or whatsoe'er
They may be! Let me die, as atoms die,
(If that they die), or know ye in your might
And knowledge! My thoughts are not in this hour   115
Unworthy what I see, though my dust is;
Spirit! let me expire, or see them nearer.
  Lucifer. Art thou not nearer? look back to thine earth!
  Cain. Where is it? I see nothing save a mass
Of most innumerable lights.
  Lucifer.   Look there!   120
  Cain. I cannot see it.
  Lucifer.   Yet it sparkles still.
  Cain. That! — yonder!
  Lucifer.   Yea.
  Cain.   And wilt thou tell me so?
Why, I have seen the fire-flies and fire-worms
Sprinkle the dusky groves and the green banks
In the dim twilight, brighter than yon world   125
Which bears them.
  Lucifer.   Thou hast seen both worms and worlds,
Each bright and sparkling — what dost think of them?
  Cain. That they are beautiful in their own sphere,
And that the night, which makes both beautiful,
The little shining fire-fly in its flight,   130
And the immortal star in its great course,
Must both be guided.
  Lucifer.   But by whom or what?
  Cain. Show me.

Lucifer.   Dar'st thou behold?

Cain.   How know I what
I *dare* behold? As yet, thou hast shown nought
I dare not gaze on further.

Lucifer.   On, then, with me.   *135*
Wouldst thou behold things mortal or immortal?

Cain. Why, what are things?

Lucifer.   *Both* partly: but what doth
Sit next thy heart?

Cain.   The things I see.

Lucifer.   But what
Sate nearest it?

Cain.   The things I have not seen,
Nor ever shall — the mysteries of Death.   *140*

Lucifer. What, if I show to thee things which have died,
As I have shown thee much which cannot die?

Cain. Do so.

Lucifer.   Away, then! on our mighty wings!

Cain. Oh! how we cleave the blue! The stars fade from us!
The earth! where is my earth? Let me look on it,   *145*
For I was made of it.

Lucifer.   'Tis now beyond thee,
Less, in the universe, than thou in it;
Yet deem not that thou canst escape it; thou
Shalt soon return to earth, and all its dust:
'Tis part of thy eternity, and mine.   *150*

Cain. Where dost thou lead me?

Lucifer.   To what was before thee!
The phantasm of the world; of which thy world
Is but the wreck.

Cain.   What! is it not then new?

Lucifer. No more than life is; and that was ere thou
Or *I* were, or the things which seem to us   *155*
Greater than either: many things will have
No end; and some, which would pretend to have
Had no beginning, have had one as mean
As thou; and mightier things have been extinct
To make way for much meaner than we can   *160*

Surmise; for *moments* only and the *space*
Have been and must be all *unchangeable.*
But changes make not death, except to clay;
But thou art clay — and canst but comprehend
That which was clay, and such thou shalt behold.   *165*
   Cain. Clay — Spirit — what thou wilt — I can survey.
   Lucifer. Away, then!
   Cain.   But the lights fade from me fast,
And some till now grew larger as we approached,
And wore the look of worlds.
   Lucifer.   And such they are.
   Cain. And Edens in them?
   Lucifer.   It may be.
   Cain.   And men?   *170*
   Lucifer. Yea, or things higher.
   Cain.   Aye! and serpents too?
   Lucifer. Wouldst thou have men without them? must
   no reptiles
Breathe, save the erect ones?
   Cain.   How the lights recede!
Where fly we?
   Lucifer   To the world of phantoms, which
Are beings past, and shadows still to come.   *175*
   Cain. But it grows dark, and dark — the stars are gone!
   Lucifer. And yet thou seest.
   Cain.   'Tis a fearful light!
No sun — no moon — no lights innumerable —
The very blue of the empurpled night
Fades to a dreary twilight — yet I see   *180*
Huge dusky masses; but unlike the worlds
We were approaching, which, begirt with light,
Seemed full of life even when their atmosphere
Of light gave way, and showed them taking shapes
Unequal, of deep valleys and vast mountains;   *185*
And some emitting sparks, and some displaying
Enormous liquid plains, and some begirt
With luminous belts, and floating moons, which took,
Like them, the features of fair earth: — instead,

All here seems dark and dreadful.

Lucifer.   But distinct.   *190*
Thou seekest to behold Death, and dead things?

Cain. I seek it not; but as I know there are
Such, and that my sire's sin makes him and me,
And all that we inherit, liable
To such, I would behold, at once, what I   *195*
Must one day see perforce.

Lucifer.   Behold!

Cain.   'Tis darkness!

Lucifer. And so it shall be ever — but we will
Unfold its gates!

Cain.   Enormous vapours roll
Apart — what's this?

Lucifer.   Enter!

Cain.   Can I return?

Lucifer. Return! be sure: how else should Death be
    peopled?   *200*
Its present realm is thin to what it will be,
Through thee and thine.

Cain.   The clouds still open wide
And wider, and make widening circles round us!

Lucifer. Advance!

Cain.   And thou!

Lucifer.   Fear not — without me thou
Couldst not have gone beyond thy world. On! on!   *205*

                    [*They disappear through the clouds.*]

Scene II. — *Hades*

Enter Lucifer *and* Cain.

Cain. How silent and how vast are these dim worlds!
For they seem more than one, and yet more peopled
Than the huge brilliant luminous orbs which swung
So thickly in the upper air, that I
Had deemed them rather the bright populace   *5*
Of some all unimaginable Heaven,

Than things to be inhabited themselves,
But that on drawing near them I beheld
Their swelling into palpable immensity
Of matter, which seemed made for life to dwell on,   *10*
Rather than life itself. But here, all is
So shadowy, and so full of twilight, that
It speaks of a day past.
    Lucifer.   It is the realm
Of Death. — Wouldst have it present?
    Cain.   Till I know
That which it really is, I cannot answer.   *15*
But if it be as I have heard my father
Deal out in his long homilies, 'tis a thing —
Oh God! I dare not think on't! Curséd be
He who invented Life that leads to Death!
Or the dull mass of life, that, being life,   *20*
Could not retain, but needs must forfeit it —
Even for the innocent!
    Lucifer.   Dost thou curse thy father?
    Cain. Cursed he not me in giving me my birth?
Cursed he not me before my birth, in daring
To pluck the fruit forbidden?
    Lucifer.   Thou say'st well: *25*
The curse is mutual 'twixt thy sire and thee —
But for thy sons and brother?
    Cain.   Let them share it
With me, their sire and brother! What else is
Bequeathed to me? I leave them my inheritance!
Oh, ye interminable gloomy realms   *30*
Of swimming shadows and enormous shapes,
Some fully shown, some indistinct, and all
Mighty and melancholy — what are ye?
Live ye, or have ye lived?
    Lucifer.   Somewhat of both.
    Cain. Then what is Death?
    Lucifer.   What? Hath not he who
      made ye   *35*
Said 'tis another life?

Cain.   Till now he hath
Said nothing, save that all shall die.
 Lucifer.   Perhaps
He one day will unfold that further secret.
 Cain. Happy the day!
 Lucifer.   Yes; happy! when unfolded,
Through agonies unspeakable, and clogged   40
With agonies eternal, to innumerable
Yet unborn myriads of unconscious atoms,
All to be animated for this only!
 Cain. What are these mighty phantoms which I see
Floating around me? — They wear not the form   45
Of the Intelligences I have seen
Round our regretted and unentered Eden;
Nor wear the form of man as I have viewed it
In Adam's and in Abel's, and in mine,
Nor in my sister-bride's, nor in my children's: 50
And yet they have an aspect, which, though not
Of men nor angels, looks like something, which,
If not the last, rose higher than the first,
Haughty, and high, and beautiful, and full
Of seeming strength, but of inexplicable   55
Shape; for I never saw such. They bear not
The wing of Seraph, nor the face of man,
Nor form of mightiest brute, nor aught that is
Now breathing; mighty yet and beautiful
As the most beautiful and mighty which   60
Live, and yet so unlike them, that I scarce
Can call them living.
 Lucifer.   Yet they lived.
 Cain.   Where?
 Lucifer.   Where
Thou livest.

II. ii. 44–62. Cain is being shown "the *rational* Pre-Adamites, beings
endowed with a higher intelligence than man, but totally unlike him in
form, and with much greater strength of mind and person. You may suppose the small talk which takes place between him and Lucifer upon these
matters is not quite canonical" (Letter to Thomas Moore, 19 September
1821). See also Byron's preface, above, p. 232.

Cain.   When?

Lucifer.   On what thou callest earth
They did inhabit.

Cain.   Adam is the first.

Lucifer. Of thine, I grant thee — but too mean to be   65
The last of these.

Cain.   And what are they?

Lucifer.   That which
Thou shalt be.

Cain.   But what *were* they?

Lucifer.   Living, high,
Intelligent, good, great, and glorious things.
As much superior unto all thy sire
Adam could e'er have been in Eden, as   70
The sixty-thousandth generation shall be,
In its dull damp degeneracy, to
Thee and thy son; — and how weak they are, judge
By thy own flesh.

Cain.   Ah me! and did *they* perish?

Lucifer. Yes, from their earth, as thou wilt fade from
    thine.   75

Cain. But was *mine* theirs?

Lucifer.   It was.

Cain.   But not as now.
It is too little and too lowly to
Sustain such creatures.

Lucifer.   True, it was more glorious.

Cain. And wherefore did it fall?

Lucifer.   Ask him who fells.

Cain. But how?

Lucifer.   By a most crushing and inexorable   80
Destruction and disorder of the elements,
Which struck a world to chaos, as a chaos
Subsiding has struck out a world: such things,
Though rare in time, are frequent in eternity. —
Pass on, and gaze upon the past.

Cain.   'Tis awful!   85

Lucifer. And true. Behold these phantoms! they were once

Material as thou art.

Cain.   And must I be
Like them?

Lucifer. Let He who made thee answer that.
I show thee what thy predecessors are,
And what they *were* thou feelest, in degree   *90*
Inferior as thy petty feelings and
Thy pettier portion of the immortal part
Of high intelligence and earthly strength.
What ye in common have with what they had
Is Life, and what ye *shall* have — Death: the rest   *95*
Of your poor attributes is such as suits
Reptiles engendered out of the subsiding
Slime of a mighty universe, crushed into
A scarcely-yet shaped planet, peopled with
Things whose enjoyment was to be in blindness —   *100*
A Paradise of Ignorance, from which
Knowledge was barred as poison. But behold
What these superior beings are or were;
Or, if it irk thee, turn thee back and till
The earth, thy task — I'll waft thee there in safety.   *105*

Cain. No: I'll stay here.

Lucifer.   How long?

Cain.   For ever! Since
I must one day return here from the earth,
I rather would remain; I am sick of all
That dust has shown me — let me dwell in shadows.

Lucifer. It cannot be: thou now beholdest as   *110*
A vision that which is reality.
To make thyself fit for this dwelling, thou
Must pass through what the things thou seest have passed —
The gates of Death.

Cain.   By what gate have we entered
Even now?

Lucifer. By mine! But, plighted to return,   *115*
My spirit buoys thee up to breathe in regions

II. ii. 88. *Let he*: Byron's own careless grammar.

Where all is breathless save thyself. Gaze on;
But do not think to dwell here till thine hour
Is come!
    Cain. And these, too — can they ne'er repass
To earth again?
    Lucifer.   *Their* earth is gone for ever —   *120*
So changed by its convulsion, they would not
Be conscious to a single present spot
Of its new scarcely hardened surface — 'twas —
Oh, what a beautiful world it *was!*
    Cain.   And is!
It is not with the earth, though I must till it,   *125*
I feel at war — but that I may not profit
By what it bears of beautiful, untoiling,
Nor gratify my thousand swelling thoughts
With knowledge, nor allay my thousand fears
Of Death and Life.
    Lucifer.   What thy world is, thou see'st,   *130*
But canst not comprehend the shadow of
That which it was.
    Cain.   And those enormous creatures,
Phantoms inferior in intelligence
(At least so seeming) to the things we have passed,
Resembling somewhat the wild habitants   *135*
Of the deep woods of earth, the hugest which
Roar nightly in the forest, but ten-fold
In magnitude and terror; taller than
The cherub-guarded walls of Eden — with
Eyes flashing like the fiery swords which fence them —   *140*
And tusks projecting like the trees stripped of
Their bark and branches — what were they?
    Lucifer.   That which
The Mammoth is in thy world; — but these lie
By myriads underneath its surface.
    Cain.   But
None on it?

    II. ii. 132–144. This is Byron's adoption of the "notion of Cuvier" as
mentioned in the Preface above, p. 232.

Lucifer. No: for they frail race to war   145
With them would render the curse on it useless —
'Twould be destroyed so early.
    Cain.   But why *war?*
    Lucifer. You have forgotten the denunciation
Which drove your race from Eden — war with all things,
And death to all things, and disease to most things,   150
And pangs, and bitterness; these were the fruits
Of the forbidden tree.
    Cain.   But animals —
Did they, too, eat of it, that they must die?
    Lucifer. Your Maker told ye, *they* were made for you,
As you for him. — You would not have their doom   155
Superior to your own? Had Adam not
Fallen, all had stood.
    Cain.   Alas! the hopeless wretches!
They too must share my sire's fate, like his sons;
Like them, too, without having shared the apple;
Like them, too, without the so dear-bought *knowledge!*   160
It was a lying tree — for we *know* nothing.
At least it *promised knowledge* at the *price*
Of death — but *knowledge* still: but what *knows* man?
    Lucifer. It may be death leads to the *highest* knowledge;
And being of all things the sole thing certain,   165
At least leads to the *surest* science: therefore
The Tree was true, though deadly.
    Cain.   These dim realms!
I see them, but I know them not.
    Lucifer.   Because
Thy hour is yet afar, and matter cannot
Comprehend spirit wholly — but 'tis something   170
To know there are such realms.
    Cain.   We knew already
That there was Death.
    Lucifer.   But not what was beyond it.
    Cain. Nor know I now.
    Lucifer.   Thou knowest that there is
A state, and many states beyond thine own —

And this thou knewest not this morn.

    Cain.   But all   *175*
Seems dim and shadowy.

    Lucifer.   Be content; it will
Seem clearer to thine immortality.

    Cain. And yon immeasurable liquid space
Of glorious azure which floats on beyond us,
Which looks like water, and which I should deem   *180*
The river which flows out of Paradise
Past my own dwelling, but that it is bankless
And boundless, and of an ethereal hue —
What is it?

    Lucifer. There is still some such on earth,
Although inferior, and thy children shall   *185*
Dwell near it — 'tis the phantasm of an Ocean.

    Cain. 'Tis like another world; a liquid sun —
And those inordinate creatures sporting o'er
Its shining surface?

    Lucifer.   Are its inhabitants,
The past Leviathans.

    Cain.   And yon immense   *190*
Serpent, which rears his dripping mane and vasty
Head, ten times higher than the haughtiest cedar,
Forth from the abyss, looking as he could coil
Himself around the orbs we lately looked on —
Is he not of the kind which basked beneath   *195*
The Tree in Eden?

    Lucifer.   Eve, thy mother, best
Can tell what shape of serpent tempted her.

    Cain. This seems too terrible. No doubt the other
Had more of beauty.

    Lucifer.   Hast thou ne'er beheld him?

    Cain. Many of the same kind (at least so called)   *200*
But never that precisely, which persuaded
The fatal fruit, nor even of the same aspect.

    Lucifer. Your father saw him not?

    Cain.   No: 'twas my mother
Who tempted him — she tempted by the serpent.

Lucifer. Good man! whene'er thy wife, or thy sons' wives,[205]
Tempt thee or them to aught that's new or strange,
Be sure thou seest first who hath tempted *them!*

   Cain. Thy precept comes too late: there is no more
For serpents to tempt woman to.

   Lucifer.   But there
Are some things still which woman may tempt man to,   210
And man tempt woman: — let thy sons look to it!
My counsel is a kind one; for 'tis even
Given chiefly at my own expense; 'tis true,
'Twill not be followed, so there's little lost.

   Cain. I understand not this.

   Lucifer.   The happier thou! —   215
Thy world and thou are still too young! Thou thinkest
Thyself most wicked and unhappy — is it
Not so?

   Cain. For crime, I know not; but for pain,
I have felt much.

   Lucifer.   First-born of the first man!
Thy present state of sin — and thou art evil,   220
Of sorrow — and thou sufferest, are both Eden
In all its innocence compared to what
Thou shortly may'st be; and that state again,
In its redoubled wretchedness, a Paradise
To what thy sons' sons' sons, accumulating   225
In generations like to dust (which they
In fact but add to), shall endure and do. —
Now let us back to earth!

   Cain.   And wherefore didst thou
Lead me here only to inform me this?

   Lucifer. Was not thy quest for knowledge?

   Cain.   Yes — as being 230
The road to happiness!

   Lucifer.   If truth be so,
Thou hast it.

   Cain.   Then my father's God did well
When he prohibited the fatal Tree.

   Lucifer. But had done better in not planting it.

But ignorance of evil doth not save   235
From evil; it must still roll on the same,
A part of all things.
  Cain.   Not of all things. No —
I'll not believe it — for I thirst for good.
  Lucifer. And who and what doth not? *Who* covets evil
For its own bitter sake? — *None* — nothing! 'tis   240
The leaven of all life, and lifelessness.
  Cain. Within those glorious orbs which we behold,
Distant, and dazzling, and innumerable,
Ere we came down into this phantom realm,
Ill cannot come: they are too beautiful.   245
  Lucifer. Thou hast seen them from afar.
  Cain.   And what of that?
Distance can but diminish glory — they,
When nearer, must be more ineffable.
  Lucifer. Approach the things of earth most beautiful,
And judge their beauty near.
  Cain.   I have done this —   250
The loveliest thing I know is loveliest nearest.
  Lucifer. Then there must be delusion. — What is that
Which being nearest to thine eyes is still
More beautiful than beauteous things remote?
  Cain. My sister Adah. — All the stars of heaven,   255
The deep blue noon of night, lit by an orb
Which looks a spirit, or a spirit's world —
The hues of twilight — the Sun's gorgeous coming —
His setting indescribable, which fills
My eyes with pleasant tears as I behold   260
Him sink, and feel my heart float softly with him
Along that western paradise of clouds —
The forest shade, the green bough, the bird's voice —
The vesper bird's, which seems to sing of love,
And mingles with the song of Cherubim,   265
As the day closes over Eden's walls; —
All these are nothing, to my eyes and heart,
Like Adah's face: I turn from earth and heaven
To gaze on it.

Lucifer.   'Tis fair as frail mortality,
In the first dawn and bloom of young creation,   270
And earliest embraces of earth's parents,
Can make its offspring; still it is delusion.
  Cain. You think so, being not her brother.
  Lucifer.   Mortal!
My brotherhood's with those who have no children.
  Cain. Then thou canst have no fellowship with us.   275
  Lucifer. It may be that thine own shall be for me.
But if thou dost possess a beautiful
Being beyond all beauty in thine eyes,
Why art thou wretched?
  Cain.   Why do I exist?
Why art *thou* wretched? why are all things so?   280
Ev'n he who made us must be, as the maker
Of things unhappy! To produce destruction
Can surely never be the task of joy,
And yet my sire says he's omnipotent:
Then why is Evil — he being Good? I asked   285
This question of my father; and he said,
Because this Evil only was the path
To Good. Strange Good, that must arise from out
Its deadly opposite. I lately saw
A lamb stung by a reptile: the poor suckling   290
Lay foaming on the earth, beneath the vain
And piteous bleating of its restless dam;
My father plucked some herbs, and laid them to
The wound; and by degrees the helpless wretch
Resumed its careless life, and rose to drain   295
The mother's milk, who o'er it tremulous
Stood licking its reviving limbs with joy.
Behold, my son! said Adam, how from Evil
Springs Good!
  Lucifer.   What didst thou answer?
  Cain.   Nothing; for

II. ii. 287–288. Adam is here giving one of the arguments offered by
theologians in support of the doctrines of *felix culpa* (happy sin) or the
"fortunate fall." The fall of man makes possible the redemption.

He is my father: but I thought, that 'twere   *300*
A better portion for the animal
Never to have been *stung at all*, than to
Purchase renewal of its little life
With agonies unutterable, though
Dispelled by antidotes.

    Lucifer.   But as thou saidst   *305*
Of all belovéd things thou lovest her
Who shared thy mother's milk, and giveth hers
Unto thy children —

    Cain.   Most assuredly:
What should I be without her?

    Lucifer.   What am I?

    Cain. Dost thou love nothing?

    Lucifer.   What does thy God love? *310*

    Cain. All things, my father says; but I confess
I see it not in their allotment here.

    Lucifer. And, therefore, thou canst not see if *I* love
Or no — except some vast and general purpose,
To which particular things must melt like snows.   *315*

    Cain. Snows! what are they?

    Lucifer.   Be happier in not knowing
What thy remoter offspring must encounter;
But bask beneath the clime which knows no winter.

    Cain. But dost thou not love something like thyself?

    Lucifer. And dost thou love *thyself?*

    Cain.   Yes, but love more   *320*
What makes my feelings more endurable,
And is more than myself, because I love it!

    Lucifer. Thou lovest it, because 'tis beautiful,
As was the apple in thy mother's eye;
And when it ceases to be so, thy love   *325*
Will cease, like any other appetite.

    Cain. Cease to be beautiful! how can that be?

    Lucifer. With time.

    Cain.   But time has passed, and hitherto
Even Adam and my mother both are fair:
Not fair like Adah and the Seraphim —   *330*

But very fair.

Lucifer.   All that must pass away
In them and her.

Cain.   I'm sorry for it; but
Cannot conceive my love for her the less:
And when her beauty disappears, methinks
He who creates all beauty will lose more   *335*
Than me in seeing perish such a work.

Lucifer. I pity thee who lovest what must perish.

Cain. And I thee who lov'st nothing.

Lucifer.   And thy brother —
Sits he not near thy heart?

Cain.   Why should he not?

Lucifer. Thy father loves him well — so does thy God. *340*

Cain. And so do I.

Lucifer.   'Tis well and meekly done.

Cain. Meekly!

Lucifer.   He is the second born of flesh,
And is his mother's favourite.

Cain.   Let him keep
Her favour, since the Serpent was the first
To win it.

Lucifer. And his father's?

Cain.   What is that   *345*
To me? should I not love that which all love?

Lucifer. And the Jehovah — the indulgent Lord,
And bounteous planter of barred Paradise —
He, too, looks smilingly on Abel.

Cain.   I
Ne'er saw him, and I know not if he smiles.   *350*

Lucifer. But you have seen his angels.

Cain.   Rarely.

Lucifer.   But
Sufficiently to see they love your brother:
His sacrifices are acceptable.

Cain. So be they! wherefore speak to me of this?

Lucifer. Because thou hast thought of this ere now.

Cain.   And if *355*

I *have* thought, why recall a thought that —— (*he pauses as
    agitated*) — Spirit!
Here we are in *thy* world; speak not of *mine*.
Thou hast shown me wonders: thou hast shown me those
Mighty Pre-Adamites who walked the earth
Of which ours is the wreck; thou hast pointed out   360
Myriads of starry worlds, of which our own
Is the dim and remote companion, in
Infinity of life: thou hast shown me shadows
Of that existence with the dreaded name
Which my sire brought us — Death; thou hast shown me
    much   365
But not all: show me where Jehovah dwells,
In his especial Paradise — or *thine:*
Where is it?
    Lucifer.   *Here,* and o'er all space.
    Cain.   But ye
Have some allotted dwelling — as all things;
Clay has its earth, and other worlds their tenants;   370
All temporary breathing creatures their
Peculiar element; and things which have
Long ceased to breathe *our* breath, have theirs, thou say'st;
And the Jehovah and thyself have thine —
Ye do not dwell together?
    Lucifer.   No, we reign   375
Together; but our dwellings are asunder.
    Cain. Would there were only one of ye! perchance
An unity of purpose might make union
In elements which seem now jarred in storms.
How came ye, being Spirits wise and infinite,   380
To separate? Are ye not as brethren in
Your essence — and your nature, and your glory?
    Lucifer. Art not thou Abel's brother?
    Cain.   We are brethren,
And so we shall remain; but were it not so,
Is spirit like to flesh? can it fall out —   385
Infinity with Immortality?
Jarring and turning space to misery —

For what?

    Lucifer. To reign.

    Cain.   Did ye not tell me that
Ye are both eternal?

    Lucifer.   Yea!

    Cain.   And what I have seen —
Yon blue immensity, is boundless?

    Lucifer.   Aye.   *390*

    Cain. And cannot ye both *reign*, then? — is there not
Enough? — why should ye differ?

    Lucifer.   We *both* reign.

    Cain. But one of you makes evil.

    Lucifer.   Which?

    Cain.   Thou! for
If thou canst do man good, why dost thou not?

    Lucifer. And why not he who made? *I* made ye not;   *395*
Ye are *his* creatures, and not mine.

    Cain.   Then leave us
His creatures, as thou say'st we are, or show me
Thy dwelling, or *his* dwelling.

    Lucifer.   I could show thee
Both; but the time will come thou shalt see one
Of them for evermore.

    Cain.   And why not now?   *400*

    Lucifer. Thy human mind hath scarcely grasp to gather
The little I have shown thee into calm
And clear thought: and *thou* wouldst go on aspiring
To the great double Mysteries! the *two Principles!*
And gaze upon them on their secret thrones!   *405*
Dust! limit thy ambition; for to see
Either of these would be for thee to perish!

    Cain. And let me perish, so I see them!

    Lucifer.   There
The son of her who snatched the apple spake!
But thou wouldst only perish, and not see them;   *410*
That sight is for the other state.

II. ii. 404. See note on Manicheism, above, p. 231.

Cain.   Of Death?

Lucifer. That is the prelude.

Cain.   Then I dread it less,
Now that I know it leads to something definite.

Lucifer. And now I will convey thee to thy world,
Where thou shalt multiply the race of Adam,   *415*
Eat, drink, toil, tremble, laugh, weep, sleep — and die!

Cain. And to what end have I beheld these things
Which thou hast shown me?

Lucifer.   Didst thou not require
Knowledge? And have I not, in what I showed,
Taught thee to know thyself?

Cain.   Alas! I seem   *420*
Nothing.

Lucifer. And this should be the human sum
Of knowledge, to know mortal nature's nothingness;
Bequeath that science to thy children, and
'Twill spare them many tortures.

Cain.   Haughty spirit!
Thou speak'st it proudly; but thyself, though proud,   *425*
Hast a superior.

Lucifer.   No! By heaven, which he
Holds, and the abyss, and the immensity
Of worlds and life, which I hold with him — No!
I have a Victor — true; but no superior.
Homage he has from all — but none from me: *430*
I battle it against him, as I battled
In highest Heaven — through all Eternity,
And the unfathomable gulfs of Hades,
And the interminable realms of space,
And the infinity of endless ages,   *435*
All, all, will I dispute! And world by world,
And star by star, and universe by universe,
Shall tremble in the balance, till the great
Conflict shall cease, if ever it shall cease,
Which it ne'er shall, till he or I be quenched!   *440*

II. ii. 420–421. See letter to Murray, November 3, 1821, below, p. 687.

And what can quench our immortality,
Or mutual and irrevocable hate?
He as a conqueror will call the conquered
Evil; but what will be the *Good* he gives?
Were I the victor, *his* works would be deemed   *445*
The only evil ones. And you, ye new
And scarce-born mortals, what have been his gifts
To you already, in your little world?
    Cain. But few; and some of those but bitter.
    Lucifer.   Back
With me, then, to thine earth, and try the rest   *450*
Of his celestial boons to you and yours.
Evil and Good are things in their own essence,
And not made good or evil by the Giver;
But if he gives you good — so call him; if
Evil springs from *him*, do not name it *mine*,   *455*
Till ye know better its true fount; and judge
Not by words, though of Spirits, but the fruits
Of your existence, such as it must be.
One good gift has the fatal apple given, —
Your *reason:* — let it not be overswayed   *460*
By tyrannous threats to force you into faith
'Gainst all external sense and inward feeling:
Think and endure, — and form an inner world
In your own bosom — where the outward fails;
So shall you nearer be the spiritual   *465*
Nature, and war triumphant with your own.
                               [They disappear.]

ACT III

SCENE I. — *The Earth, near Eden, as in Act I.*

Enter CAIN *and* ADAH.

  Adah. Hush! tread softly, Cain!
  Cain.   I will — but wherefore?

II. ii. 452 ff. For the emphasis on reason and the mind's independence
compare Manfred's dying speeches to the spirits that came for him,
III. iii. 110 ff. and *Childe Harold*, Canto 4, stanza 127.

Adah. Our little Enoch sleeps upon yon bed
Of leaves, beneath the cypress.
    Cain. Cypress! 'tis
A gloomy tree, which looks as if it mourned
O'er what it shadows; wherefore didst thou choose it   5
For our child's canopy?
    Adah. Because its branches
Shut out the sun like night, and therefore seemed
Fitting to shadow slumber.
    Cain. Aye, the last —
And longest; but no matter — lead me to him.

                       [They go up to the child.]
How lovely he appears! his little cheeks,   10
In their pure incarnation, vying with
The rose leaves strewn beneath them.
    Adah. And his lips, too,
How beautifully parted! No; you shall not
Kiss him, at least not now: he will awake soon —
His hour of mid-day rest is nearly over;   15
But it were pity to disturb him till
'Tis closed.
    Cain. You have said well; I will contain
My heart till then. He smiles, and sleeps! — sleep on,
And smile, thou little, young inheritor
Of a world scarce less young: sleep on, and smile!   20
Thine are the hours and days when both are cheering
And innocent! *thou* hast not plucked the fruit —
Thou know'st not thou art naked! Must the time
Come thou shalt be amerced for sins unknown,
Which were not thine nor mine? But now sleep on!   25
His cheeks are reddening into deeper smiles,
And shining lids are trembling o'er his long
Lashes, dark as the cypress which waves o'er them;
Half open, from beneath them the clear blue
Laughs out, although in slumber. He must dream —   30
Of what? Of Paradise! — Aye! dream of it,
My disinherited boy! 'Tis but a dream;
For never more thyself, thy sons, nor fathers,

Shall walk in that forbidden place of joy!

    Adah. Dear Cain! Nay, do not whisper o'er our son   *35*
Such melancholy yearnings o'er the past:
Why wilt thou always mourn for Paradise?
Can we not make another?

    Cain.   Where?

    Adah.   Here, or
Where'er thou wilt: where'er thou art, I feel not
The want of this so much regretted Eden.   *40*
Have I not thee — our boy — our sire, and brother,
And Zillah — our sweet sister, and our Eve,
To whom we owe so much besides our birth?

    Cain. Yes — Death, too, is amongst the debts we owe her.

    Adah. Cain! that proud Spirit, who withdrew thee hence,   *45*
Hath saddened thine still deeper. I had hoped
The promised wonders which thou hast beheld,
Visions, thou say'st, of past and present worlds,
Would have composed thy mind into the calm
Of a contented knowledge; but I see   *50*
Thy guide hath done thee evil: still I thank him,
And can forgive him all, that he so soon
Hath given thee back to us.

    Cain.   So soon?

    Adah.   'Tis scarcely
Two hours since ye departed: two *long* hours
To *me,* but only *hours* upon the sun.   *55*

    Cain. And yet I have approached that sun, and seen
Worlds which he once shone on, and never more
Shall light; and worlds he never lit: methought
Years had rolled o'er my absence.

    Adah.   Hardly hours.

    Cain. The mind then hath capacity of time,   *60*
And measures it by that which it beholds,
Pleasing or painful; little or almighty.
I had beheld the immemorial works
Of endless beings; skirred extinguished worlds;
And, gazing on eternity, methought   *65*
I had borrowed more by a few drops of ages

From its immensity: but now I feel
My littleness again. Well said the Spirit,
That I was nothing!
   Adah.   Wherefore said he so?
Jehovah said not that.
   Cain.   No: *he* contents him   70
With making us the *nothing* which we are;
And after flattering dust with glimpses of
Eden and Immortality, resolves
It back to dust again — for what?
   Adah.   Thou know'st —
Even for our parents' error.
   Cain.   What is that   75
To us? they sinned, then *let them* die!
   Adah. Thou hast not spoken well, nor is that thought
Thy own, but of the Spirit who was with thee.
Would *I* could die for them, so *they* might live!
   Cain. Why, so say I — provided that one victim   80
Might satiate the Insatiable of life,
And that our little rosy sleeper there
Might never taste of death nor human sorrow,
Nor hand it down to those who spring from him.
   Adah. How know we that some such atonement one day 85
May not redeem our race?
   Cain.   By sacrificing
The harmless for the guilty? what atonement
Were there? why, *we* are innocent: what have we
Done, that we must be victims for a deed
Before our birth, or need have victims to   90
Atone for this mysterious, nameless sin —

III. 85–91. Cain is echoing Byron's criticism of the doctrine of the atonement expressed in a letter to his clerical friend Hodgson on September 13, 1811: ". . . the basis of your religion is *injustice*; the *Son* of *God*, the *pure*, the *immaculate*, the *innocent*, is sacrificed for the *Guilty* . . . You degrade the Creator, in the first place, by making him a begetter of children; and in the next you convert him into a Tyrant over an immaculate and injured Being, who is sent into existence to suffer death for the benefit of some millions of Scoundrels who, after all, seem as likely to be damned as ever."

If it be such a sin to seek for knowledge?

   Adah. Alas! thou sinnest now, my Cain: thy words
Sound impious in mine ears.

   Cain.   Then leave me!

   Adah.   Never,
Though thy God left thee.

   Cain.   Say, what have we here?   *95*

   Adah. Two altars, which our brother Abel made
During thine absence, whereupon to offer
A sacrifice to God on thy return.

   Cain. And how knew *he*, that *I* would be so ready
With the burnt offerings, which he daily brings   *100*
With a meek brow, whose base humility
Shows more of fear than worship — as a bribe
To the Creator?

   Adah.   Surely, 'tis well done.

   Cain. One altar may suffice; *I* have no offering.

   Adah. The fruits of the earth, the early, beautiful,   *105*
Blossom and bud — and bloom of flowers and fruits —
These are a goodly offering to the Lord,
Given with a gentle and a contrite spirit.

   Cain. I have toiled, and tilled, and sweaten in the sun,
According to the curse: — must I do more?   *110*
For what should I be gentle? for a war
With all the elements ere they will yield
The bread we eat? For what must I be grateful?
For being dust, and grovelling in the dust,
Till I return to dust? If I am nothing —   *115*
For nothing shall I be an hypocrite,
And seem well-pleased with pain? For what should I
Be contrite? for my father's sin, already
Expiate with what we all have undergone,
And to be more than expiated by   *120*
The ages prophesied, upon our seed.
Little deems our young blooming sleeper, there,
The germs of an eternal misery
To myriads is within him! better 'twere
I snatched him in his sleep, and dashed him 'gainst   *125*

The rocks, than let him live to ——
    Adah.   Oh, my God!
Touch not the child — my child! *thy* child! Oh, Cain!
    Cain. Fear not! for all the stars, and all the power
Which sways them, I would not accost yon infant
With ruder greeting than a father's kiss.   *130*
    Adah. Then, why so awful in thy speech?
    Cain.   I said,
'Twere better that he ceased to live, than give
Life to so much of sorrow as he must
Endure, and, harder still, bequeath; but since
That saying jars you, let us only say —   *135*
'Twere better that he never had been born.
    Adah. Oh, do not say so! Where were then the joys,
The mother's joys of watching, nourishing,
And loving him? Soft! he awakes. Sweet Enoch!

                          [*She goes to the child.*]

Oh, Cain! look on him; see how full of life,   *140*
Of strength, of bloom, of beauty, and of joy —
How like to me — how like to thee, when gentle —
For *then* we are *all* alike; is't not so, Cain?
Mother, and sire, and son, our features are
Reflected in each other; as they are   *145*
In the clear waters, when *they* are *gentle,* and
When *thou* art *gentle.* Love us, then, my Cain!
And love thyself for our sakes, for we love thee.
Look! how he laughs and stretches out his arms,
And opens wide his blue eyes upon thine,   *150*
To hail his father; while his little form
Flutters as winged with joy. Talk not of pain!
The childless cherubs well might envy thee
The pleasures of a parent! Bless him, Cain!
As yet he hath no words to thank thee, but   *155*
His heart will, and thine own too.
    Cain.   Bless thee, boy!
If that a mortal blessing may avail thee,
To save thee from the Serpent's curse!

Adah.   It shall.
Surely a father's blessing may avert
A reptile's subtlety.
   Cain.   Of that I doubt;   *160*
But bless him ne'er the less.
   Adah.   Our brother comes.
   Cain. Thy brother Abel.

[*Enter* ABEL.]

   Abel.   Welcome, Cain! My brother,
The peace of God be on thee!
   Cain.   Abel, hail!
   Abel. Our sister tells me that thou hast been wandering,
In high communion with a Spirit, far   *165*
Beyond our wonted range. Was he of those
We have seen and spoken with, like to our father?
   Cain. No.
   Abel.   Why then commune with him? he may be
A foe to the Most High.
   Cain.   And friend to man.
Has the Most High been so — if so you term him?   *170*
   Abel. Term him! your words are strange to-day, my brother.
My sister Adah, leave us for awhile —
We mean to sacrifice.
   Adah.   Farewell, my Cain;
But first embrace thy son. May his soft spirit,
And Abel's pious ministry, recall thee   *175*
To peace and holiness!
                    [*Exit* ADAH, *with her child.*]
   Abel.   Where hast thou been?
   Cain. I know not.
   Abel.   Nor what thou hast seen?
   Cain.   The dead —
The Immortal — the Unbounded — the Omnipotent —
The overpowering mysteries of space —
The innumerable words that were and are —   *180*
A whirlwind of such overwhelming things,

Suns, moons, and earths, upon their loud-voiced spheres
Singing in thunder round me, as have made me
Unfit for mortal converse: leave me, Abel.

  Abel. Thine eyes are flashing with unnatural light —   *185*
Thy cheek is flushed with an unnatural hue —
Thy words are fraught with an unnatural sound —
What may this mean?

  Cain.   It means — I pray thee, leave me.

  Abel. Not till we have prayed and sacrificed together.

  Cain. Abel, I pray thee, sacrifice alone —   *190*
Jehovah loves thee well.

  Abel.   *Both* well, I hope.

  Cain. But thee the better: I care not for that;
Thou art fitter for his worship than I am;
Revere him, then — but let it be alone —
At least, without me.

  Abel.   Brother, I should ill   *195*
Deserve the name of our great father's son,
If, as my elder, I revered thee not,
And in the worship of our God, called not
On thee to join me, and precede me in
Our priesthood — 'tis thy place.

  Cain.   But I have ne'er   *200*
Asserted it.

  Abel. The more my grief; I pray thee
To do so now: thy soul seems labouring in
Some strong delusion; it will calm thee.

  Cain.   No;
Nothing can calm me more. *Calm!* say I? Never
Knew I what calm was in the soul, although   *205*
I have seen the elements stilled. My Abel, leave me!
Or let me leave thee to thy pious purpose.

  Abel. Neither; we must perform our task together.
Spurn me not.

  Cain. If it must be so —— well, then,
What shall I do?

  Abel.   Choose one of those two altars.   *210*

  Cain. Choose for me: they to me are so much turf

And stone.

  Abel. Choose thou!

  Cain.   I have chosen.

  Abel.   'Tis the highest,

And suits thee, as the elder. Now prepare

Thine offerings.

  Cain.   Where are thine?

  Abel.   Behold them here —

The firstlings of the flock, and fat thereof —

A shepherd's humble offering.

  Cain.   I have no flocks;   215

I am a tiller of the ground, and must

Yield what it yieldeth to my toil — its fruit:

           [*He gathers fruits.*]

Behold them in their various bloom and ripeness.

   [*They dress their altars, and kindle a flame upon them.*]

  Abel. My brother, as the elder, offer first   220

Thy prayer and thanksgiving with sacrifice.

  Cain. No — I am new to this; lead thou the way,

And I will follow — as I may.

  Abel (kneeling).   Oh, God!

Who made us, and who breathed the breath of life

Within our nostrils, who hath blessed us,   225

And spared, despite our father's sin, to make

His children all lost, as they might have been,

Had not thy justice been so tempered with

The mercy which is thy delight, as to

Accord a pardon like a Paradise,   230

Compared with our great crimes: — Sole Lord of light!

Of good, and glory, and eternity!

Without whom all were evil, and with whom

Nothing can err, except to some good end

Of thine omnipotent benevolence!   235

Inscrutable, but still to be fulfilled!

Accept from out thy humble first of shepherds'

III. 213. See *Genesis* 4:2–8.

First of the first-born flocks — an offering,
In itself nothing — as what offering can be
Aught unto thee? — but yet accept it for   240
The thanksgiving of him who spreads it in
The face of thy high heaven — bowing his own
Even to the dust, of which he is — in honour
Of thee, and of thy name, for evermore!
   Cain [*standing erect during this speech*]. Spirit whate'er
     or whosoe'er thou art,   245
Omnipotent, it may be — and, if good,
Shown in the exemption of thy deeds from evil;
Jehovah upon earth! and God in heaven!
And it may be with other names, because
Thine attributes seem many, as thy works: —   250
If thou must be propitiated with prayers,
Take them! If thou must be induced with altars,
And softened with a sacrifice, receive them;
Two beings here erect them unto thee.
If thou lov'st blood, the shepherd's shrine, which smokes   255
On my right hand, hath shed it for thy service
In the first of his flock, whose limbs now reek
In sanguinary incense to thy skies;
Or, if the sweet and blooming fruits of earth,
And milder seasons, which the unstained turf   260
I spread them on now offers in the face
Of the broad sun which ripened them, may seem
Good to thee — inasmuch as they have not
Suffered in limb or life — and rather form
A sample of thy works, than supplication   265
To look on ours! If a shrine without victim,
And altar without gore, may win thy favour,
Look on it! and for him who dresseth it,
He is — such as thou mad'st him; and seeks nothing
Which must be won by kneeling: if he's evil,   270
Strike him! thou art omnipotent, and may'st —
For what can he oppose? If he be good,
Strike him, or spare him, as thou wilt! since all
Rests upon thee; and Good and Evil seem

To have no power themselves, save in thy will —   *275*
And whether that be good or ill I know not,
Not being omnipotent, nor fit to judge
Omnipotence — but merely to endure
Its mandate; which thus far I have endured.

> [*The fire upon the altar of* ABEL *kindles into a column*
> *of the brightest flame, and ascends to heaven; while a*
> *whirlwind throws down the altar of* CAIN, *and scatters*
> *the fruits abroad upon the earth.*]

Abel [*kneeling*]. Oh, brother, pray! Jehovah's wroth with
   thee.   *280*
Cain. Why so?
Abel.   Thy fruits are scattered on the earth.
Cain. From earth they came, to earth let them return;
Their seed will bear fresh fruit there ere the summer:
Thy burnt flesh-offering prospers better; see
How Heaven licks up the flames, when thick with blood!   *285*
Abel. Think not upon my offering's acceptance,
But make another of thine own — before
It is too late.
Cain.   I will build no more altars,
Nor suffer any ——
Abel [*rising*]. Cain! what meanest thou?
Cain. To cast down yon vile flatterer of the clouds,   *290*
The smoky harbinger of thy dull prayers —
Thine altar, with its blood of lambs and kids,
Which fed on milk, to be destroyed in blood.
Abel [*opposing him*]. Thou shalt not: — add not impious
   works to impious
Words! let that altar stand — 'tis hallowed now   *295*

III. 288–316. For Byron's own comment on Cain's motivation in killing
Abel, see the letter to Murray, below, p. 687. Also in the letter to Moore,
19 September 1821, quoted above, Byron writes, "The consequence [of the
journey with Lucifer] is, that Cain comes back and kills Abel in a fit of
dissatisfaction, partly with the politics of Paradise, which has driven them
all out of it, and partly because (as it is written in Genesis) Abel's sacrifice
was the most acceptable to the Deity." For a summary of recent critical
interpretations, see Steffan, *Byron's Cain*, pp. 289 ff.

By the immortal pleasure of Jehovah,
In his acceptance of the victims.

    Cain.   *His!*
His pleasure! what was his high pleasure in
The fumes of scorching flesh and smoking blood,
To the pain of the bleating mothers, which   300
Still yearn for their dead offspring? or the pangs
Of the sad ignorant victims underneath
Thy pious knife? Give way! this bloody record
Shall not stand in the sun, to shame creation!

    Abel. Brother, give back! thou shalt not touch my altar 305
With violence: if that thou wilt adopt it,
To try another sacrifice, 'tis thine.

    Cain. Another sacrifice! Give way, or else
That sacrifice may be ——

    Abel.   What mean'st thou?

    Cain.   Give —
Give way! — thy God loves blood! — then look to it: — 310
Give way, ere he hath *more!*

    Abel.   In *his* great name,
I stand between thee and the shrine which hath
Had his acceptance.

    Cain.   If thou lov'st thyself,
Stand back till I have strewed this turf along
Its native soil: — else ——

    Abel [*opposing him*]. I love God far more 315
Than life.

    Cain [*striking him with a brand, on the temples, which he
       snatches from the altar*]. Then take thy life unto thy God,
Since he loves lives.

    Abel [*falls*].   What hast thou done — my brother?

    Cain. Brother!

    Abel.   Oh, God! receive thy servant! and
Forgive his slayer, for he knew not what
He did — Cain, give me — give me thy hand; and tell 320
Poor Zillah —

   III. 318–320. Abel's words anticipate Jesus' words on the cross, *Luke*
23:34.

Cain [*after a moment's stupefaction*]. My hand! 'tis all red,
and with ——
What?   [*A long pause. — Looking slowly round.*]
         Where am I? alone! Where's Abel? where
Cain? Can it be that I am he? My brother,
Awake! — why liest thou so long on the green earth?
'Tis not the hour of slumber: — why so pale?   325
What hast thou! — thou wert full of life this morn!
Abel! I pray thee, mock me not! I smote
Too fiercely, but not fatally. Ah, why
Wouldst thou oppose me? This is mockery;
And only done to daunt me: — 'twas a blow —   330
And but a blow. Stir — stir — nay, only stir!
Why, so — that's well! — thou breathest! breathe upon me!
Oh God! Oh God!
    Abel [*very faintly*]. What's he who speaks of God?
    Cain. Thy murderer.
    Abel.   Then may God forgive him! Cain,
Comfort poor Zillah: — she has but one brother
Now.   [ABEL *dies.*]

    Cain. And I none! — Who makes me brotherless?   336
His eyes are open! then he is not dead!
Death is like sleep; and sleep shuts down our lids.
His lips, too, are apart; why then he breathes;
And yet I feel it not. — His heart! — his heart! —   340
Let me see, doth it beat? methinks —— No! — no!
This is a vision, else I am become
The native of another and worse world.
The earth swims round me: — what is this? — 'tis wet;
                [*Puts his hand to his brow, and then looks at it.*]

And yet there are no dews! 'Tis blood — my blood —   345
My brother's and my own! and shed by me!
Then what have I further to do with life,
Since I have taken life from my own flesh?
But he can not be dead! — Is silence death?
No; he will wake; then let me watch by him.   350
Life cannot be so slight, as to be quenched

Thus quickly! — he hath spoken to me since —
What shall I say to him? — My brother! — No:
He will not answer to that name; for brethren
Smite not each other. Yet — yet — speak to me.   355
Oh! for a word more of that gentle voice,
That I may bear to hear my own again!

[*Enter* ZILLAH.]

Zillah. I heard a heavy sound; what can it be?
'Tis Cain; and watching by my husband. What
Dost thou there, brother? Doth he sleep? Oh, Heaven!   360
What means this paleness, and yon stream? — No, no!
It is not blood; for who would shed his blood?
Abel! what's this? — who hath done this? He moves not;
He breathes not: and his hands drop down from mine
With stony lifelessness! Ah! cruel Cain!   365
Why camest thou not in time to save him from
This violence? Whatever hath assailed him,
Thou wert the stronger, and shouldst have stepped in
Between him and aggression! Father! — Eve! —
Adah! — come hither! Death is in the world!   370
                    [*Exit* ZILLAH, *calling on her Parents, etc.*]

Cain [*solus*]. And who hath brought him there? — I — who
            abhor
The name of Death so deeply, that the thought
Empoisoned all my life, before I knew
His aspect — I have led him here, and given
My brother to his cold and still embrace,   375
As if he would not have asserted his
Inexorable claim without my aid.
I am awake at last — a dreary dream
Had maddened me; — but *he* shall ne'er awake!

[*Enter* ADAM, EVE, ADAH, *and* ZILLAH.]

Adam. A voice of woe from Zillah brings me here —   380
What do I see? — 'Tis true! — My son! — my son!
Woman, behold the Serpent's work, and thine!   [*To* EVE.]

Eve. Oh! speak not of it now: the Serpent's fangs
Are in my heart! My best beloved, Abel!
Jehovah! this is punishment beyond   *385*
A mother's sin, to take *him* from me!
    Adam.   Who,
Or what hath done this deed? — speak, Cain, since thou
Wert present; was it some more hostile angel,
Who walks not with Jehovah? or some wild
Brute of the forest?
    Eve.   Ah! a livid light   *390*
Breaks through, as from a thunder-cloud! yon brand
Massy and bloody! snatched from off the altar,
And black with smoke, and red with ——
    Adam.   Speak, my son!
Speak, and assure us, wretched as we are,
That we are not more miserable still.   *395*
    Adah. Speak, Cain! and say it was not *thou!*
    Eve.   It was!
I see it now — he hangs his guilty head,
And covers his ferocious eye with hands
Incarnadine!
    Adah.   Mother, thou dost him wrong —
Cain! clear thee from this horrible accusal,   *400*
Which grief wrings from our parent.
    Eve.   Hear, Jehovah!
May the eternal Serpent's curse be on him!
For he was fitter for his seed than ours.
May all his days be desolate! May ——
    Adah.   Hold!
Curse him not, mother, for he is thy son —   *405*
Curse him not, mother, for he is my brother,
And my betrothed.
    Eve.   He hath left thee no brother —
Zillah no husband — me *no son!* for thus
I curse him from my sight for evermore!
All bonds I break between us, as he broke   *410*
That of his nature, *in yon* — Oh Death! Death!
Why didst thou not take *me,* who first incurred thee?

Why dost thou not so now?
   Adam.   Eve! let not this,
Thy natural grief, lead to impiety!
A heavy doom was long forespoken to us;   *415*
And now that it begins, let it be borne
In such sort as may show our God, that we
Are faithful servants to his holy will.
   Eve [*pointing to Cain*]. *His will!* the will of yon Incarnate
     Spirit
Of Death, whom I have brought upon the earth   *420*
To strew it with the dead. May all the curses
Of life be on him! and his agonies
Drive him forth o'er the wilderness, like us
From Eden, till his children do by him
As he did by his brother! May the swords   *425*
And wings of fiery Cherubim pursue him
By day and night — snakes spring up in his path —
Earth's fruits be ashes in his mouth — the leaves
On which he lays his head to sleep be strewed
With scorpions! May his dreams be of his victim!   *430*
His waking a continual dread of Death!
May the clear rivers turn to blood as he
Stoops down to stain them with his raging lip!
May every element shun or change to him!
May he live in the pangs which others die with!   *435*
And Death itself wax something worse than Death
To him who first acquainted him with man!
Hence, fratricide! henceforth that word is *Cain*,
Through all the coming myriads of mankind,
Who shall abhor thee, though thou wert their sire!   *440*
May the grass wither from thy feet! the woods
Deny thee shelter! earth a home! the dust
A grave! the sun his light! and heaven her God!
                              [*Exit* Eve.]

   III. 441–443. Byron added these lines after sending off the manuscript.
In a letter of September 12, 1821, asking Murray to add the lines, he wrote,
"There's as pretty a piece of Imprecation for you, when joined to the lines
already sent, as you may wish to meet with in the course of your business."

Adam. Cain! get thee forth: we dwell no more together.
Depart! and leave the dead to me — I am   445
Henceforth alone — we never must meet more.

 Adah. Oh, part not with him thus, my father: do not
Add thy deep curse to Eve's upon his head!

 Adam. I curse him not: his spirit be his curse.
Come, Zillah!

 Zillah.   I must watch my husband's corse.   450

 Adam. We will return again, when he is gone
Who hath provided for us this dread office.
Come, Zillah!

 Zillah.   Yet one kiss on yon pale clay,
And those lips once so warm — my heart! my heart!

       [*Exeunt* ADAM *and* ZILLAH *weeping.*]

 Adah. Cain! thou hast heard, we must go forth. I am
   ready,   455
So shall our children be. I will bear Enoch,
And you his sister. Ere the sun declines
Let us depart, nor walk the wilderness
Under the cloud of night. — Nay, speak to me.
To *me — thine own.*

 Cain.   Leave me!

 Adah.   Why, all have left thee.   460

 Cain. And wherefore lingerest thou? Dost thou not fear
To dwell with one who hath done this?

 Adah.   I fear
Nothing except to leave thee, much as I
Shrink from the deed which leaves thee brotherless.
I must not speak of this — it is between thee   465
And the great God.

 A Voice from within exclaims. Cain! Cain!

 Adah.   Hear'st thou that voice?

 The Voice within. Cain! Cain!

 Adah.   It soundeth like an angel's tone.

 III. 467. In *Genesis,* 4:9–15 the Lord himself imposes sentence and places the mark on Cain.

[*Enter the* ANGEL *of the Lord.*]

Angel. Where is thy brother Abel?
Cain.   Am I then
My brother's keeper?
     Angel.   Cain! what hast thou done?
The voice of thy slain brother's blood cries out,   490
Even from the ground, unto the Lord! — Now art thou
Cursed from the earth, which opened late her mouth
To drink thy brother's blood from thy rash hand.
Henceforth, when thou shalt till the ground, it shall not
Yield thee her strength; a fugitive shalt thou   475
Be from this day, and vagabond on earth!
     Adah. This punishment is more than he can bear.
Behold thou drivest him from the face of earth,
And from the face of God shall he be hid.
A fugitive and vagabond on earth,   480
'Twill come to pass, that whoso findeth him
Shall slay him.
     Cain.   Would they could! but who are they
Shall slay me? Where are these on the lone earth
As yet unpeopled?
     Angel.   Thou hast slain thy brother,
And who shall warrant thee against thy son?   485
     Adah. Angel of Light! be merciful, nor say
That this poor aching breast now nourishes
A murderer in my boy, and of his father.
     Angel. Then he would but be what his father is.
Did not the milk of Eve give nutriment   490
To him thou now seest so besmeared with blood?
The fratricide might well engender parricides. —
But it shall not be so — the Lord thy God
And mine commandeth me to set his seal
On Cain, so that he may go forth in safety.   495
Who slayeth Cain, a sevenfold vengeance shall
Be taken on his head. Come hither!
     Cain.   What
Wouldst thou with me?

Angel.   To mark upon thy brow
Exemption from such deeds as thou hast done.
   Cain. No, let me die!
   Angel.   It must not be.
      [*The* ANGEL *sets the mark on* CAIN's *brow*.]

   Cain.   It burns   *500*
My brow, but nought to that which is within it!
Is there more? let me meet it as I may.
   Angel. Stern hast thou been and stubborn from the womb,
As the ground thou must henceforth till; but he
Thou slew'st was gentle as the flocks he tended.   *505*
   Cain. After the fall too soon was I begotten;
Ere yet my mother's mind subsided from
The Serpent, and my sire still mourned for Eden.
That which I am, I am; I did not seek
For life, nor did I make myself; but could I   *510*
With my own death redeem him from the dust —
And why not so? let him return to day,
And I lie ghastly! so shall be restored
By God the life to him he loved; and taken
From me a being I ne'er loved to bear.   *515*
   Angel. Who shall heal murder? what is done, is done;
Go forth! fulfil thy days! and be thy deeds
Unlike the last!   [*The* ANGEL *disappears*.]

   Adah.   He's gone, let us go forth;
I hear our little Enoch cry within
Our bower.
   Cain.   Ah! little knows he what he weeps for!   *520*
And I who have shed blood cannot shed tears!
But the four rivers would not cleanse my soul.
Think'st thou my boy will bear to look on me?
   Adah. If I thought that he would not, I would ——
   Cain [*interrupting her*].   No,
No more of threats: we have had too many of them: *525*

   III. 522. *the four rivers*: into which the river flowing out of Eden
divided (*Genesis*, 2:10).

Go to our children — I will follow thee.

    Adah. I will not leave thee lonely with the dead —
Let us depart together.

    Cain.   Oh! thou dead
And everlasting witness! whose unsinking
Blood darkens earth and heaven! what thou *now* art   530
I know not! but if *thou* seest what *I* am,
I think thou wilt forgive him, whom his God
Can ne'er forgive, nor his own soul. — Farewell!
I must not, dare not touch what I have made thee.
I, who sprung from the same womb with thee, drained   535
The same breast, clasped thee often to my own,
In fondness brotherly and boyish, I
Can never meet thee more, nor even dare
To do that for thee, which thou shouldst have done
For me — compose thy limbs into their grave —   540
The first grave yet dug for mortality.
But who hath dug that grave? Oh, earth! Oh, earth!
For all the fruits thou hast rendered to me, I
Give thee back this. — Now for the wilderness!

            [ADAH *stoops down and kisses the body of* ABEL.]

    Adah. A dreary, and an early doom, my brother,   545
Has been thy lot! Of all who mourn for thee,
I alone must not weep. My office is
Henceforth to dry up tears, and not to shed them;
But yet of all who mourn, none mourn like me,
Not only for thyself, but him who slew thee.   550
Now, Cain! I will divide thy burden with thee.

    Cain. Eastward from Eden will we take our way;
'Tis the most desolate, and suits my steps.

    Adah. Lead! thou shalt be my guide, and may our God
Be thine! Now let us carry forth our children.   555

    Cain. And *he* who lieth there was childless! I
Have dried the fountain of a gentle race,
Which might have graced his recent marriage couch,
And might have tempered this stern blood of mine,

III. 552. *Eastward from Eden*: *Genesis,* 4:16.

Uniting with our children Abel's offspring!   *560*
O Abel!
   Adah. Peace be with him!
   Cain.   But with *me!* ——

                                                        [*Exeunt.*]
1821   *1821*

Satires

From English Bards and Scotch Reviewers

Byron had begun a satire in the manner of Pope called "British Bards" as early as October, 1807. After the scathing review of *Hours of Idleness* in the *Edinburgh Review* of January, 1808, he carefully revised and enlarged the satire and published it anonymously under the present title in March, 1809. It was immediately popular, and Byron prepared a second and further expanded edition which was published under his name in October, 1809, after he had left on his travels. Two more editions were published in 1810, but after his return in 1812, Byron suppressed a fifth edition, having become friends with many like Francis Jeffrey and Thomas Moore whom he had attacked.

The excerpt given here opened the first edition of the poem. Byron later came to admire Sir Walter Scott both as man and poet, but he never fundamentally changed his mind about the "Lakers," Southey, Wordsworth and Coleridge, even though in an annotated copy of the fourth edition he makes the marginal comment "unjust" opposite the lines on Wordsworth and Coleridge. For his later feud with Southey see *Vision of Judgment* and the Dedication to *Don Juan* and notes; and for comments on Wordsworth and Coleridge, see the Dedication to *Don Juan,* stanzas 2–6; Canto 1, stanzas 90, 205; and Canto 3, stanzas 93–100.

• • •

Time was, ere yet in these degenerate days
Ignoble themes obtained mistaken praise,
When Sense and Wit with Poesy allied,   *105*

No fabled Graces, flourished side by side,
From the same fount their inspiration drew,
And, reared by Taste, bloomed fairer as they grew.
Then, in this happy Isle, a POPE's pure strain
Sought the rapt soul to charm, nor sought in vain;   *110*
A polished nation's praise aspired to claim,
And raised the people's, as the poet's fame.
Like him great DRYDEN poured the tide of song,
In stream less smooth, indeed, yet doubly strong.
Then CONGREVE's scenes could cheer, or OTWAY's melt;   *115*
For Nature then an English audience felt —
But why these names, or greater still, retrace,
When all to feebler Bards resign their place?
Yet to such times our lingering looks are cast,
When taste and reason with those times are past.   *120*
Now look around, and turn each trifling page,
Survey the precious works that please the age;
This truth at least let Satire's self allow,
No dearth of Bards can be complained of now.
The loaded Press beneath her labour groans,   *125*
And Printers' devils shake their weary bones;
While SOUTHEY's Epics cram the creaking shelves,
And LITTLE's Lyrics shine in hot-pressed twelves.
Thus saith the *Preacher:* "Nought beneath the sun
Is new," yet still from change to change we run.   *130*
What varied wonders tempt us as they pass!
The Cow-pox, Tractors, Galvanism, and Gas,

---

115. William Congreve (1670–1729), most brilliant of the Restoration comic dramatists, and Thomas Otway (1652–1685), whose tragedies (particularly *Venice Preserved*) were often ranked next to Shakespeare's by neoclassic critics.

128. *Little's lyrics*: Little was the name under which Thomas Moore published his early poems.

hot-press'd twelves: Printed sheets were passed between hot rollers to give them smoothness. "Twelves" (duodecimo) refers to the size of the volume.

129. *the Preacher*: *Ecclesiastes* 1:9.

132. *Cow-pox*: Vaccination for small pox.

Tractors: Metal rods for curing "Red Noses, Gouty Toes, Windy Bowels, Broken Legs, Hump backs."

Galvanism: Experiments on corpses with electric currents by Galvani (1737–1798) and his followers.

In turns appear, to make the vulgar stare,
Till the swoln bubble bursts — and all is air!
Nor less new schools of Poetry arise,   135
Where dull pretenders grapple for the prize:
O'er Taste awhile these Pseudo-bards prevail;
Each country Book-club bows the knee to Baal,
And, hurling lawful Genius from the throne,
Erects a shrine and idol of its own;   140
Some leaden calf — but whom it matters not,
From soaring SOUTHEY, down to groveling STOTT.

    Behold! in various throngs the scribbling crew,
For notice eager, pass in long review:
Each spurs his jaded Pegasus apace,   145
And Rhyme and Blank maintain an equal race;
Sonnets on sonnets crowd, and ode on ode;
And Tales of Terror jostle on the road;
Immeasurable measures move along;
For simpering Folly loves a varied song,   150
To strange, mysterious Dulness still the friend,
Admires the strain she cannot comprehend.
Thus Lays of Minstrels — may they be the last! —
On half-strung harps whine mournful to the blast.
While mountain spirits prate to river sprites,   155
That dames may listen to the sound at nights;
And goblin brats, of Gilpin Horner's brood
Decoy young Border-nobles through the wood,
And skip at every step, Lord knows how high,
And frighten foolish babes, the Lord knows why;   160
While high-born ladies in their magic cell,
Forbidding Knights to read who cannot spell,

    Gas: Laughing gas. Byron looks upon all of these as fake "wonders" of
the age and signs of degeneration, like the poetry.
    142. *Stott*: A newspaper poet who wrote under the pseudonym "Hafiz."
"This personage is at present the most profound explorer of the bathos,"
says Byron's note.
    153. *Lays of Minstrels*: Scott's *Lay of the Last Minstrel* (1805) grew
out of a suggestion that he write a ballad on the border legend of Gilpin
Horner (157).

Despatch a courier to a wizard's grave,
And fight with honest men to shield a knave.

Next view in state, proud prancing on his roan,   165
The golden-crested haughty Marmion,
Now forging scrolls, now foremost in the fight,
Not quite a Felon, yet but half a Knight,
The gibbet or the field prepared to grace;
A mighty mixture of the great and base.   170
And think'st thou, SCOTT! by vain conceit perchance,
On public taste to foist thy stale romance,
Though MURRAY with his MILLER may combine
To yield thy muse just half-a-crown per line?
No! when the sons of song descend to trade,   175
Their bays are sear, their former laurels fade,
Let such forego the poet's sacred name,
Who rack their brains for lucre, not for fame:
Still for stern Mammon may they toil in vain!
And sadly gaze on Gold they cannot gain!   180
Such be their meed, such still the just reward
Of prostituted Muse and hireling bard!
For this we spurn Apollo's venal son,
And bid a long "good night to Marmion."

These are the themes that claim our plaudits now;   185
These are the Bards to whom the Muse must bow;
While MILTON, DRYDEN, POPE, alike forgot,
Resign their hallowed Bays to WALTER SCOTT.

The time has been, when yet the Muse was young,
When HOMER swept the lyre, and MARO sung,   190
An Epic scarce ten centuries could claim,
While awe-struck nations hailed the magic name:

173. *Murray with his Miller*: Scott's publisher, Constable, paid him
£1000 for *Marmion*. One half of the copyright was divided between two
London publishers, William Miller and John Murray. Murray later became Byron's publisher.
184. *"Good night to Marmion"*: Spoken by Henry Blount upon the
death of Marmion (*Marmion*, Canto VI, 869).
190. *Maro*: Virgil.

The work of each immortal Bard appears
The single wonder of a thousand years.
Empires have mouldered from the face of earth, 195
Tongues have expired with those who gave them birth,
Without the glory such a strain can give,
As even in ruin bids the language live.
Not so with us, though minor Bards, content,
On one great work a life of labour spent: 200
With eagle pinion soaring to the skies,
Behold the Ballad-monger SOUTHEY rise!
To him let CAMOËNS, MILTON, TASSO yield,
Whose annual strains, like armies, take the field.
First in the ranks see Joan of Arc advance, 205
The scourge of England and the boast of France!
Though burnt by wicked BEDFORD for a witch,
Behold her statue placed in Glory's niche;
Her fetters burst, and just released from prison,
A virgin Phœnix from her ashes risen. 210
Next see tremendous Thalaba come on,
Arabia's monstrous, wild, and wond'rous son;
Domdaniel's dread destroyer, who o'erthrew
More mad magicians than the world e'er knew.
Immortal Hero! all thy foes o'ercome, 215
For ever reign — the rival of Tom Thumb!
Since startled Metre fled before thy face,
Well wert thou doomed the last of all thy race!
Well might triumphant Genii bear thee hence,
Illustrious conqueror of common sense! 220
Now, last and greatest, Madoc spreads his sails,

---

203. *Camoens*: Portuguese poet (1524–1580), author of the epic, *The
Lusiads*.

Tasso: Italian poet (1544–1595), author of the epic, *Jerusalem Delivered*.

205. Southey's *Joan of Arc* was published in 1796; *Thalaba the Destroyer* (211) in 1801; *Madoc* (221) in 1805.

213. *Domdaniel's . . . . destroyer*: Domdaniel was an underwater palace
inhabited by evil magicians, destroyed by Thalaba at the cost of his own
life.

216. *Tom Thumb*: The hero of Henry Fielding's farce, *The Tragedy of
Tragedies*; or *The Life and Death of Tom Thumb the Great* (1730).

Cacique in Mexico, and Prince in Wales;
Tells us strange tales, as other travellers do,
More old than Mandeville's, and not so true.
Oh, SOUTHEY! SOUTHEY! cease thy varied song!   225
A bard may chaunt too often and too long:
As thou art strong in verse, in mercy, spare!
A fourth, alas! were more than we could bear.
But if, in spite of all the world can say,
Thou still wilt verseward plod thy weary way;   230
If still in Berkeley-Ballads most uncivil,
Thou wilt devote old women to the devil,
The babe unborn thy dread intent may rue:
"God help thee," SOUTHEY, and thy readers too.

    Next comes the dull disciple of thy school,   235
That mild apostate from poetic rule,
The simple WORDSWORTH, framer of a lay
As soft as evening in his favourite May,
Who warns his friend "to shake off toil and trouble,
And quit his books, for fear of growing double;"   240
Who, both by precept and example, shows
That prose is verse, and verse is merely prose;
Convincing all, by demonstration plain,
Poetic souls delight in prose insane;
And Christmas stories tortured into rhyme   245
Contain the essence of the true sublime.

222. *Cacique*: Chief. The setting of *Madoc* is first Wales and then Mexico, where Madoc founded a colony.

224. *Mandeville's*: Sir John Mandeville's *Travels*, a book of marvelous adventures written in the fourteenth century (c. 1357).

231. *Berkeley-ballads*: Southey wrote a ballad called *The Old Woman of Berkeley* "wherein an aged gentlewoman is carried away by Beelzebub, on a high trotting horse." (Byron's note.)

234. *"God help thee"*: Byron's note records that the last line "is an evident plagiarism from the *Anti-Jacobin* to Mr. Southey, on his Dactylics: 'God help thee, silly one.'"

239. See Wordsworth's *The Tables Turned*, stanza 1.

242. In the *Preface to the Lyrical Ballads*, Wordsworth had argued that there "neither is, nor can be, any essential difference between the language of prose and metrical composition."

Thus, when he tells the tale of Betty Foy,
The idiot mother of "an idiot Boy;"
A moon-struck, silly lad, who lost his way,
And, like his bard, confounded night with day;   250
So close on each pathetic part he dwells,
And each adventure so sublimely tells,
That all who view the "idiot in his glory"
Conceive the Bard the hero of the story.

   Shall gentle COLERIDGE pass unnoticed here,   255
To turgid ode and tumid stanza dear?
Though themes of innocence amuse him best,
Yet still Obscurity's a welcome guest.
If Inspiration should her aid refuse
To him who takes a Pixy for a muse,   260
Yet none in lofty numbers can surpass
The bard who soars to elegize an ass:
So well the subject suits his noble mind,
He brays, the Laureate of the long-eared kind.

1807–8   *1809*

247. See Wordsworth's poem, *The Idiot Boy*.
259. Byron refers to two of Coleridge's poems: *Songs of the Pixies* and *To a Young Ass*.

The Vision of Judgment

QUEVEDO REDIVIVUS

SUGGESTED BY THE COMPOSITION SO ENTITLED
BY THE AUTHOR OF "WAT TYLER"

When George III died in 1820, Robert Southey, as Poet
Laureate, wrote an almost incredibly pompous eulogy in
labored hexameters entitled *A Vision of Judgment*. The poem
describes the poet's vision of George's arrival before the gates
of Heaven where Satan's accusers, John Wilkes and Junius,
are struck dumb as they confront the saintly old man. George
Washington among the blessed souls absolves him of blame,
and the "Ineffable Presence" itself welcomes him into Heaven. In the preface to the poem, Southey made a gratuitous
attack on the "Satanic school" of poetry, and Byron, already
furious with Southey (see headnote to Dedication to *Don
Juan*), was triggered into writing this magnificent burlesque.
But from the beginning he was caught up in his own exu-
berant vision of judgment, and the reader need know nothing
of Southey's *Vision* to be carried along in the satiric sport
and delighted by the "diabolical" cleverness with which
Southey is introduced into the poem and made the means of
getting George into heaven.

Byron began the *Vision,* according to his own note, "on
May 7, but left off the same day — resumed about the 20th of
September" and concluded on October 4. In the interim he

Title: *Quevedo Redivivus*: "Quevedo Resurrected." Francisco Gomez de
Quevedo y Villegas (1580–1635) had written a series of satiric visions (1635).
The Author of "Wat Tyler": Southey's radical drama, written in 1794,
had been published in 1817 without his permission and had caused the
now Arch-Tory Poet Laureate great embarrassment.

had written *Cain,* to which the *Vision* is a kind of comic counterpart (see headnote to *Cain*). Byron sent the poem to John Murray who, afraid of prosecution, withheld it from publication. In the summer of 1822, Byron ordered Murray to turn the manuscript over to John Hunt, the brother of Leigh Hunt and publisher of the new journal, *The Liberal,* that Byron and Hunt were editing. The poem appeared in the first number on October 15, 1822. In December, John Hunt was indicted for libel against the memory of George III. Byron offered to provide counsel and to come to England to stand trial in his stead, but the case did not come to trial until January, 1824, after Byron had gone to Greece. Hunt was convicted, but the fine was relatively light, indicating in effect a victory for himself and Byron. The full history can be found in William Marshall's *Byron, Shelley, Hunt and The Liberal.*

"A Daniel come to judgment! yea, a Daniel!
I thank thee, Jew, for teaching me that word."

1

SAINT PETER sat by the celestial gate:
  His keys were rusty, and the lock was dull,
So little trouble had been given of late;
  Not that the place by any means was full,
But since the Gallic era "eighty-eight"
  The Devils had ta'en a longer, stronger pull,
And "a pull altogether," as they say
At sea — which drew most souls another way.

2

The Angels all were singing out of tune,
  And hoarse with having little else to do,
Excepting to wind up the sun and moon,
  Or curb a runaway young star or two,

Epigraph. *The Merchant of Venice* IV. i. 223, 341. Shylock speaks the first line; Gratiano the second.

1:5. *"eighty-eight"*: In July, 1788, King Louis XVI was forced to order a meeting of the Estates General for the following year; and thus set the stage for the French Revolution.

Or wild colt of a comet, which too soon
   Broke out of bounds o'er the ethereal blue,
Splitting some planet with its playful tail,
As boats are sometimes by a wanton whale.

3

The Guardian Seraphs had retired on high,
   Finding their charges past all care below;
Terrestrial business filled nought in the sky
   Save the Recording Angel's black bureau;
Who found, indeed, the facts to multiply
   With such rapidity of vice and woe,
That he had stripped off both his wings in quills,
And yet was in arrear of human ills.

4

His business so augmented of late years,
   That he was forced, against his will, no doubt,
(Just like those cherubs, earthly ministers,)
   For some resource to turn himself about,
And claim the help of his celestial peers,
   To aid him ere he should be quite worn out
By the increased demand for his remarks:
Six Angels and twelve Saints were named his clerks.

5

This was a handsome board — at least for Heaven;
   And yet they had even then enough to do,
So many Conquerors' cars were daily driven,
   So many kingdoms fitted up anew;
Each day, too, slew its thousands six or seven,
   Till at the crowning carnage, Waterloo,
They threw their pens down in divine disgust —
The page was so besmeared with blood and dust.

6

This by the way; 'tis not mine to record
   What Angels shrink from: even the very Devil

On this occasion his own work abhorred,
    So surfeited with the infernal revel:
Though he himself had sharpened every sword,
    It almost quenched his innate thirst of evil.
(Here Satan's sole good work deserves insertion —
'Tis, that he has both Generals in reversion.)

7

Let's skip a few short years of hollow peace,
    Which peopled earth no better, Hell as wont,
And Heaven none — they form the tyrant's lease,
    With nothing but new names subscribed upon 't;
'Twill one day finish: meantime they increase,
    "With seven heads and ten horns," and all in front,
Like Saint John's foretold beast; but ours are born
Less formidable in the head than horn.

8

In the first year of Freedom's second dawn
    Died George the Third; although no tyrant, one
Who shielded tyrants, till each sense withdrawn
    Left him nor mental nor external sun:
A better farmer ne'er brushed dew from lawn,
    A worse king never left a realm undone!
He died — but left his subjects still behind,
One half as mad — and t'other no less blind.

9

He died! his death made no great stir on earth:
    His burial made some pomp; there was profusion
Of velvet — gilding — brass — and no great dearth

    6:8. *in reversion*: Satan has a future claim to both Napoleon and Wellington.

    7:7. *foretold beast*: See *Revelations* 13.

    8:1. *Freedom's second dawn*: Revolutionary activity in Italy in which Byron was involved.

    8:4. *nor mental nor external sun*: During the last years of his life, George was mentally incompetent and blind. His son had ruled as Regent since 1811.

Of aught but tears — save those shed by collusion:
For these things may be bought at their true worth;
Of elegy there was the due infusion —
Bought also; and the torches, cloaks and banners,
Heralds, and relics of old Gothic manners,

10

Formed a sepulchral melodrame. Of all
The fools who flocked to swell or see the show,
Who cared about the corpse? The funeral
Made the attraction, and the black the woe,
There throbbed not there a thought which pierced the pall;
And when the gorgeous coffin was laid low,
It seemed the mockery of hell to fold
The rottenness of eighty years in gold.

11

So mix his body with the dust! It might
Return to what it *must* far sooner, were
The natural compound left alone to fight
Its way back into earth, and fire, and air;
But the unnatural balsams merely blight
What Nature made him at his birth, as bare
As the mere million's base unmummied clay —
Yet all his spices but prolong decay.

12

He's dead — and upper earth with him has done;
He's buried; save the undertaker's bill,
Or lapidary scrawl, the world is gone
For him, unless he left a German will:
But where's the proctor who will ask his son?
In whom his qualities are reigning still,
Except that household virtue, most uncommon,
Of constancy to a bad, ugly woman.

12:3. *lapidary scrawl*: Tombstone inscriptions.
12:5. *son*: The rumor was that George IV had hidden his father's will just as George II had hidden George I's "German" will. A proctor was an official of the court of probate.

13

"God save the king!" It is a large economy
    In God to save the like; but if he will
Be saving, all the better; for not one am I
    Of those who think damnation better still:
I hardly know too if not quite alone am I
    In this small hope of bettering future ill
By circumscribing, with some slight restriction,
The eternity of Hell's hot jurisdiction.

14

I know this is unpopular; I know
    'Tis blasphemous; I know one may be damned
For hoping no one else may e'er be so;
    I know my catechism; I know we're crammed
With the best doctrines till we quite o'erflow;
    I know that all save England's Church have shammed,
And that the other twice two hundred churches
And synagogues have made a *damned* bad purchase.

15

God help us all! God help me too! I am,
    God knows, as helpless as the Devil can wish,
And not a whit more difficult to damn,
    Than is to bring to land a late-hooked fish,
Or to the butcher to purvey the lamb;
    Not that I'm fit for such a noble dish,
As one day will be that immortal fry
Of almost every body born to die.

16

Saint Peter sat by the celestial gate,
    And nodded o'er his keys: when, lo! there came
A wondrous noise he had not heard of late —
    A rushing sound of wind, and stream, and flame;
In short, a roar of things extremely great,
    Which would have made aught save a Saint exclaim;
But he, with first a start and then a wink,
Said, "There's another star gone out, I think!"

17

But ere he could return to his repose,
    A Cherub flapped his right wing o'er his eyes —
At which Saint Peter yawned, and rubbed his nose:
    "Saint porter," said the angel, "prithee rise!"
Waving a goodly wing, which glowed, as glows
    An earthy peacock's tail, with heavenly dyes:
To which the saint replied, "Well, what's the matter?
"Is Lucifer come back with all this clatter?"

18

"No," quoth the Cherub: "George the Third is dead."
    "And who *is* George the Third?" replied the apostle:
"What George? what Third?" "The King of England," said
    The angel. "Well! he won't find kings to jostle
Him on his way; but does he wear his head?
    Because the last we saw here had a tustle,
And ne'er would have got into Heaven's good graces,
Had he not flung his head in all our faces.

19

"He was — if I remember — King of France;
    That head of his, which could not keep a crown
On earth, yet ventured in my face to advance
    A claim to those of martyrs — like my own:
If I had my sword, as I had once
    When I cut ears off, I had cut him down;
But having but my *keys*, and not my brand,
I only knocked his head from out his hand.

20

"And then he set up such a headless howl,
    That all the Saints came out and took him in;
And there he sits by Saint Paul, cheek by jowl;

18:6. *last . . . here*: Louis XVI, beheaded in 1793.
19:4. *my own*: St. Peter was crucified in Rome in A.D. 67, according
to tradition. For cutting off the ear of the high priest's servant when
Judas betrays Jesus, see *John*, 18:10.

That fellow Paul — the parvenu! The skin
Of Saint Bartholomew, which makes his cowl
   In heaven, and upon earth redeemed his sin,
So as to make a martyr, never sped
Better than did this weak and wooden head.

21

"But had it come up here upon its shoulders,
   There would have been a different tale to tell:
The fellow-feeling in the Saint's beholders
   Seems to have acted on them like a spell;
And so this very foolish head Heaven solders
   Back on its trunk: it may be very well,
And seems the customs here to overthrow
Whatever has been wisely done below."

22

The Angel answered, "Peter! do not pout:
   The King who comes has head and all entire,
And never knew much what it was about —
   He did as doth the puppet — by its wire,
And will be judged like all the rest, no doubt:
   My business and your own is not to inquire
Into such matters, but to mind our cue —
Which is to act as we are bid to do."

23

While thus they spake, the angelic caravan,
   Arriving like a rush of mighty wind,
Cleaving the fields of space, as doth the swan
   Some silver stream (say Ganges, Nile, or Inde,
Or Thames, or Tweed), and midst them an old man
   With an old soul, and both extremely blind,
Halted before the gate, and, in his shroud,
Seated their fellow-traveller on a cloud.

20:4. *parvenu*: Upstart. Paul was not one of the original apostles and yet his epistles became the basis of Church dogma.
20:5. *Bartholomew*: One of the twelve apostles, who was flayed alive according to tradition.

24

But bringing up the rear of this bright host
   A Spirit of a different aspect waved
His wings, like thunder-clouds above some coast
   Whose barren beach with frequent wrecks is paved;
His brow was like the deep when tempest-tossed;
   Fierce and unfathomable thoughts engraved
Eternal wrath on his immortal face,
And *where* he gazed a gloom pervaded space.

25

As he drew near, he gazed upon the gate
   Ne'er to be entered more by him or Sin,
With such a glance of supernatural hate,
   As made Saint Peter wish himself within;
He pottered with his keys at a great rate,
   And sweated through his Apostolic skin:
Of course his perspiration was but ichor,
Or some such other spiritual liquor.

26

The very Cherubs huddled all together,
   Like birds when soars the falcon; and they felt
A tingling to the tip of every feather,
   And formed a circle like Orion's belt
Around their poor old charge; who scarce knew whither
   His guards had led him, though they gently dealt
With royal Manes (for by many stories,
And true, we learn the Angels all are Tories).

27

As things were in this posture, the gate flew
   Asunder, and the flashing of its hinges
Flung over space an universal hue
   Of many-coloured flame, until its tinges
Reached even our speck of earth, and made a new
   Aurora borealis spread its fringes

O'er the North Pole; the same seen, when ice-bound,
By Captain Parry's crew, in "Melville's Sound."

28

And from the gate thrown open issued beaming
   A beautiful and mighty Thing of Light,
Radiant with glory, like a banner streaming
   Victorious from some world-o'erthrowing fight:
My poor comparisons must needs be teeming
   With earthly likenesses, for here the night
Of clay obscures our best conceptions, saving
Johanna Southcote, or Bob Southey raving.

29

'Twas the Archangel Michael: all men know
   The make of Angels and Archangels, since
There's scarce a scribbler has not one to show,
   From the fiends' leader to the Angels' Prince.
There also are some altar-pieces, though
   I really can't say that they much evince
One's inner notions of immortal spirits;
But let the connoisseurs explain *their* merits.

30

Michael flew forth in glory and in good;
   A goodly work of him from whom all Glory
And Good arise; the portal past — he stood;
   Before him the young Cherubs and Saints hoary —
(I say *young*, begging to be understood
   By looks, not years; and should be very sorry
To state, they were not older than St. Peter,
But merely that they seemed a little sweeter).

27:8. *Captain Parry's crew*: In 1819 while searching for a northwest passage, Parry and his crew wintered in Melville sound, an inlet of northwest Greenland.

28:8. *Johanna Southcote*: Religious fanatic (1750–1814) who prophesied that she would give birth to a new messiah in October, 1814. Her pregnancy turned out to be dropsy, of which she died.

31

The Cherubs and the Saints bowed down before
    That arch-angelic Hierarch, the first
Of Essences angelical who wore
    The aspect of a god; but this ne'er nursed
Pride in his heavenly bosom, in whose core
    No thought, save for his Maker's service, durst
Intrude, however glorified and high;
He knew him but the Viceroy of the sky.

32

He and the sombre, silent Spirit met —
    They knew each other both for good and ill;
Such was their power, that neither could forget
    His former friend and future foe; but still
There was a high, immortal, proud regret
    In either's eye, as if 'twere less their will
Than destiny to make the eternal years
Their date of war, and their "Champ Clos" the spheres.

33

But here they were in neutral space: we know
    From Job, that Satan hath the power to pay
A heavenly visit thrice a-year or so;
    And that the "Sons of God," like those of clay,
Must keep him company; and we might show
    From the same book, in how polite a way
The dialogue is held between the Powers
Of Good and Evil — but 'twould take up hours.

34

And this is not a theologic tract,
    To prove with Hebrew and with Arabic,

32:8. *"Champ Clos"*: Enclosed field for a tournament.
33. Byron refers to the first two chapters of *Job*.
34:1. *theologic tract*: In his introduction to his translation of the
Book of Job (1812) John Mason Good argued for the historical authenticity
of *Job* with learned citations from both Hebrew and Arabic versions.

If Job be allegory or a fact,
    But a true narrative; and thus I pick
From out the whole but such and such an act
    As sets aside the slightest thought of trick.
'Tis every tittle true, beyond suspicion,
And accurate as any other vision.

35

The spirits were in neutral space, before
    The gate of Heaven; like eastern thresholds is
The place where Death's grand cause is argued o'er,
    And souls despatched to that world or to this;
And therefore Michael and the other wore
    A civil aspect: though they did not kiss,
Yet still between his Darkness and his Brightness
There passed a mutual glance of great politeness.

36

The Archangel bowed, not like a modern beau,
    But with a graceful oriental bend,
Pressing one radiant arm just where below
    The heart in good men is supposed to tend;
He turned as to an equal, not too low,
    But kindly; Satan met his ancient friend
With more hauteur, as might an old Castilian
Poor Noble meet a mushroom rich civilian.

37

He merely bent his diabolic brow
    An instant; and then raising it, he stood
In act to assert his right or wrong, and show
    Cause why King George by no means could or should
Make out a case to be exempt from woe
    Eternal, more than other kings, endued
With better sense and hearts, whom History mentions,
Who long have "paved Hell with their good intentions."

35:2. *eastern thresholds*: The city gates of Eastern cities were traditionally used for the administration of justice.

38

Michael began: "What wouldst thou with this man,
   Now dead, and brought before the Lord? What ill
Hath he wrought since his mortal race began,
   That thou canst claim him? Speak! and do thy will,
If it be just: if in this earthly span
   He hath been greatly failing to fulfil
His duties as a king and mortal, say,
And he is thine; if not — let him have way."

39

"Michael!" replied the Prince of Air, "even here
   Before the gate of Him thou servest, must
I claim my subject: and will make appear
   That as he was my worshipper in dust,
So shall he be in spirit, although dear
   To thee and thine, because nor wine nor lust
Were of his weaknesses; yet on the throne
He reigned o'er millions to serve me alone.

40

"Look to *our* earth, or rather *mine; it* was,
   Once, more thy master's: but I triumph not
In this poor planet's conquest; nor alas!
   Need he thou servest envy me my lot:
With all the myriads of bright worlds which pass
   In worship round him, he may have forgot
Yon weak creation of such paltry things:
I think few worth damnation save their kings,

41

"And these but as a kind of quit-rent, to
   Assert my right as Lord: and even had
I such an inclination, 'twere (as you
   Well know) superfluous; they are grown so bad,
That Hell has nothing better left to do
   Than leave them to themselves: so much more mad
And evil by their own internal curse,
Heaven cannot make them better, nor I worse.

42

"Look to the earth, I said, and say again:
  When this old, blind, mad, helpless, weak, poor worm
Began in youth's first bloom and flush to reign,
  The world and he both wore a different form,
And much of earth and all the watery plain
  Of Ocean called him king: through many a storm
His isles had floated on the abyss of Time;
For the rough virtues chose them for their clime.

43

"He came to his sceptre young; he leaves it old:
  Look to the state in which he found his realm,
And left it; and his annals too behold,
  How to a minion first he gave the helm;
How grew upon his heart a thirst for gold,
  The beggar's vice, which can but overwhelm
The meanest hearts; and for the rest, but glance
Thine eye along America and France.

44

" 'Tis true, he was a tool from first to last
  (I have the workmen safe); but as a tool
So let him be consumed. From out the past
  Of ages, since mankind have known the rule
Of monarchs — from the bloody rolls amassed
  Of Sin and Slaughter — from the Cæsars' school,
Take the worst pupil; and produce a reign
More drenched with gore, more cumbered with the slain.

45

"He ever warred with freedom and the free:
  Nations as men, home subjects, foreign foes,
So that they uttered the word 'Liberty!'
  Found George the Third their first opponent. Whose
History was ever stained as his will be

42:3. *youth's first bloom*: George III was twenty-two years old when he
came to the throne in 1760.
43:4. *minion*: John Stuart, Earl of Bute, Prime Minister in 1762–1763.

With national and individual woes?
I grant his household abstinence; I grant
His neutral virtues, which most monarchs want;

46

"I know he was a constant consort; own
    He was a decent sire, and middling lord.
All this is much, and most upon a throne;
    As temperance, if at Apicius' board,
Is more than at an anchorite's supper shown.
    I grant him all the kindest can accord;
And this was well for him, but not for those
Millions who found him what Oppression chose.

47

"The New World shook him off; the Old yet groans
    Beneath what he and his prepared, if not
Completed: he leaves heirs on many thrones
    To all his vices, without what begot
Compassion for him — his tame virtues; drones
    Who sleep, or despots who have now forgot
A lesson which shall be re-taught them, wake
Upon the thrones of earth; but let them quake!

48

"Five millions of the primitive, who hold
    The faith which makes ye great on earth, implored
A *part* of that vast *all* they held of old, —
    Freedom to worship — not alone your Lord,
Michael, but you, and you, Saint Peter! Cold
    Must be your souls, if you have not abhorred
The foe to Catholic participation
In all the license of a Christian nation.

46:4. *Apicius' board*: Apicius was a famous epicure of the time of
Tiberius (first century A.D.).
48:7. *foe . . . . participation*: George III opposed giving political rights
to Roman Catholics.

49

"True! he allowed them to pray God; but as
    A consequence of prayer, refused the law
Which would have placed them upon the same base
    With those who did not hold the Saints in awe."
But here Saint Peter started from his place
    And cried, "You may the prisoner withdraw:
Ere Heaven shall ope her portals to this Guelph,
While I am guard, may I be damned myself!

50

"Sooner will I with Cerberus exchange
    My office (and *his* is no sinecure)
Than see this royal Bedlam-bigot range
    The azure fields of Heaven, of that be sure!"
"Saint!" replied Satan, "you do well to avenge
    The wrongs he made your satellites endure;
And if to this exchange you should be given,
I'll try to coax *our* Cerberus up to Heaven!"

51

Here Michael interposed: "Good Saint! and Devil!
    Pray, not so fast; you both outrun discretion.
Saint Peter! you were wont to be more civil:
    Satan! excuse this warmth of his expression,
And condescension to the vulgar's level:
    Even Saints sometimes forget themselves in session.
Have you got more to say?" — "No." — "If you please,
I'll trouble you to call your witnesses."

52

Then Satan turned and waved his swarthy hand,
    Which stirred with its electric qualities
Clouds farther off than we can understand,

49:7. *Guelph*: The family name of the House of Hanover, to which
George III belonged.
50:1. *Cerberus*: The three-headed dog guarding the gate of hell in
Greek mythology.

Although we find him sometimes in our skies;
Infernal thunder shook both sea and land
   In all the planets — and Hell's batteries
Let off the artillery, which Milton mentions
As one of Satan's most sublime inventions.

53

This was a signal unto such damned souls
   As have the privilege of their damnation
Extended far beyond the mere controls
   Of worlds past, present, or to come; no station
Is theirs particularly in the rolls
   Of Hell assigned; but where their inclination
Or business carries them in search of game,
They may range freely — being damned the same.

54

They are proud of this — as very well they may,
   It being a sort of knighthood, or gilt key
Stuck in their loins; or like to an "entré"
   Up the back stairs, or such free-masonry.
I borrow my comparisons from clay,
   Being clay myself. Let not those spirits be
Offended with such base low likenesses;
We know their posts are nobler far than these.

55

When the great signal ran from Heaven to Hell —
   About ten million times the distance reckoned
From our sun to its earth, as we can tell
   How much time it takes up, even to a second,
For every ray that travels to dispel
   The fogs of London, through which, dimly beaconed,
The weathercocks are gilt some thrice a year,
If that the *summer* is not too severe:

52:7–8. *Milton mentions*: In *Paradise Lost* VI, 469–536.
54:2. *gilt key*: A gold key was the insignia of the office of Lord Chamberlain.

56

I say that I can tell — 'twas half a minute;
   I know the solar beams take up more time
Ere, packed up for their journey, they begin it;
   But then their Telegraph is less sublime,
And if they ran a race, they would not win it
   'Gainst Satan's couriers bound for their own clime.
The sun takes up some years for every ray
To reach its goal — the Devil not half a day.

57

Upon the verge of space, about the size
   Of half-a-crown, a little speck appeared
(I've seen a something like it in the skies
   In the Ægean, ere a squall); it neared,
And, growing bigger, took another guise;
   Like an aërial ship it tacked, and steered,
Or *was* steered (I am doubtful of the grammar
Of the last phrase, which makes the stanza stammer;

58

But take your choice): and then it grew a cloud;
   And so it was — a cloud of witnesses.
But such a cloud! No land ere saw a crowd
   Of locusts numerous as the heavens saw these;
They shadowed with their myriads Space; their loud
   And varied cries were like those of wild geese,
(If nations may be likened to a goose),
And realised the phrase of "Hell broke loose."

59

Here crashed a sturdy oath of stout John Bull,
   Who damned away his eyes as heretofore:
There Paddy brogued "By Jasus!" — "What's your wull?"
   The temperate Scot exclaimed: the French ghost swore
In certain terms I shan't translate in full,
   As the first coachman will; and 'midst the war,
The voice of Jonathan was heard to express,
"*Our* President is going to war, I guess."

60

Besides there were the Spaniard, Dutch, and Dane;
   In short, an universal shoal of shades
From Otaheite's isle to Salisbury Plain,
   Of all climes and professions, years and trades,
Ready to swear against the good king's reign,
   Bitter as clubs in cards are against spades:
All summoned by this grand "subpœna," to
Try if kings mayn't be damned like me or you.

61

When Michael saw this host, he first grew pale,
   As Angels can; next, like Italian twilight,
He turned all colours — as a peacock's tail,
   Or sunset streaming through a Gothic skylight
In some old abbey, or a trout not stale,
   Or distant lightning on the horizon *by* night,
Or a fresh rainbow, or a grand review
Of thirty regiments in red, green, and blue.

62

Then he addressed himself to Satan: "Why —
   My good old friend, for such I deem you, though
Our different parties make us fight so shy,
   I ne'er mistake you for a *personal* foe;
Our difference is *political,* and I
   Trust that, whatever may occur below,
You know my great respect for you: and this
Makes me regret whate'er you do amiss —

63

"Why, my dear Lucifer, would you abuse
   My call for witnesses? I did not mean
That you should half of Earth and Hell produce;
   'Tis even suprfluous, since two honest, clean,

60:3. *Otaheite's isle*: Tahiti.
60:6. *clubs . . . spades*: In the game of ombre, the ace of spades ranks
above the ace of clubs.

True testimonies are enough: we lose
  Our Time, nay, our Eternity, between
The accusation and defence: if we
Hear both, 'twill stretch our immortality."

64

Satan replied, "To me the matter is
  Indifferent, in a personal point of view:
I can have fifty better souls than this
  With far less trouble than we have gone through
Already; and I merely argued his
  Late Majesty of Britain's case with you
Upon a point of form: you may dispose
Of him; I've kings enough below, God knows!"

65

Thus spoke the Demon (late called "multifaced"
  By multo-scribbling Southey). "Then we'll call
One or two persons of the myriads placed
  Around our congress, and dispense with all
The rest," quoth Michael: "Who may be so graced
  As to speak first? there's choice enough — who shall
It be?" Then Satan answered, "There are many;
But you may choose Jack Wilkes as well as any."

66

A merry, cock-eyed, curious-looking Sprite
  Upon the instant started from the throng,
Dressed in a fashion now forgotten quite;
  For all the fashions of the flesh stick long
By people in the next world; where unite
  All the costumes since Adam's, right or wrong,

65:1. *"multi-faced"*: In Southey's *Vision*, V, 70.

65:8. *Jack Wilkes*: John Wilkes (1727–1797) had been one of the most successful of George III's opponents. Elected on three successive occasions to Parliament from Middlesex (London), and twice expelled, he at last triumphed over the opposition and had the expulsion orders stricken from the record. He became Lord Mayor of London in 1774 and turned "half a courtier." In his old age he voted against the Whigs.

From Eve's fig-leaf down to the petticoat,
Almost as scanty, of days less remote.

67

The Spirit looked around upon the crowds
  Assembled, and exclaimed, "My friends of all
The spheres, we shall catch cold amongst these clouds;
  So let's to business: why this general call?
If those are freeholders I see in shrouds,
  And 'tis for an election that they bawl,
Behold a candidate with unturned coat!
Saint Peter, may I count upon your vote?"

68

"Sir," replied Michael, "you mistake; these things
  Are of a former life, and what we do
Above is more august; to judge of kings
  Is the tribunal met: so now you know."
"Then I presume those gentlemen with wings,"
  Said Wilkes, "are Cherubs; and that soul below
Looks much like George the Third, but to my mind
A good deal older — bless me! is he blind?"

69

"He is what you behold him, and his doom
  Depends upon his deeds," the Angel said;
"If you have aught to arraign in him, the tomb
  Gives license to the humblest beggar's head
To lift itself against the loftiest." — "Some,"
  Said Wilkes, "don't wait to see them laid in lead,
For such a liberty — and I, for one,
Have told them what I thought beneath the sun."

70

"*Above* the sun repeat, then, what thou hast
  To urge against him," said the Archangel. "Why,"
Replied the spirit, "since old scores are past,
  Must I turn evidence? In faith, not I.

Besides, I beat him hollow at the last,
  With all his Lords and Commons: in the sky
I don't like ripping up old stories, since
His conduct was but natural in a prince.

71

"Foolish, no doubt, and wicked, to oppress
  A poor unlucky devil without a shilling;
But then I blame the man himself much less
  Than Bute and Grafton, and shall be unwilling
To see him punished here for their excess,
  Since they were both damned long ago, and still in
Their place below: for me, I have forgiven,
And vote his *habeas corpus* into Heaven."

72

"Wilkes," said the Devil, "I understand all this;
  You turned to half a courtier ere you died,
And seem to think it would not be amiss
  To grow a whole one on the other side
Of Charon's ferry; you forget that *his*
  Reign is concluded; whatsoe'er betide,
He won't be sovereign more: you've lost your labour,
For at the best he will but be your neighbour.

73

"However, I knew what to think of it,
  When I beheld you in your jesting way,
Flitting and whispering round about the spit
  Where Belial, upon duty for the day,
With Fox's lard was basting William Pitt,
  His pupil; I knew what to think, I say:

71:4. *Bute and Grafton*: Ministers of George III. Grafton was Prime Minister in 1768–1770.

72:5. *Charon's ferry*: See *Don Juan*, 2, 101:3 n.

73:5. *Fox's lard*: Charles James Fox (1749–1806), famous Whig statesman, was very fat. William Pitt (1759–1806) as Prime Minister had in 1795 pushed through Parliament bills to restrict freedom of press and speech, known as "gagging" bills.

That fellow even in Hell breeds farther ills;
I'll have him *gagged* — 'twas one of his own Bills.

74

"Call Junius!" From the crowd a shadow stalked,
  And at the name there was a general squeeze,
So that the very ghosts no longer walked
  In comfort, at their own aërial ease,
But were all rammed, and jammed (but to be balked,
  As we shall see), and jostled hands and knees,
Like wind compressed and pent within a bladder,
Or like a human colic, which is sadder.

75

The shadow came — a tall, thin, grey-haired figure,
  That looked as it had been a shade on earth;
Quick in its motions, with an air of vigour,
  But nought to mark its breeding or its birth;
Now it waxed little, then again grew bigger,
  With now an air of gloom, or savage mirth;
But as you gazed upon its features, they
Changed every instant — to *what,* none could say.

76

The more intently the ghosts gazed, the less
  Could they distinguish whose the features were;
The Devil himself seemed puzzled even to guess;
  Thy varied like a dream — now here, now there;
And several people swore from out the press,
  They knew him perfectly; and one could swear
He was his father; upon which another
Was sure he was his mother's cousin's brother:

77

Another, that he was a duke, or knight,
  An orator, a lawyer, or a priest,

74:1. *Junius*: Pseudonym of the author of a series of public letters (1769–1771) attacking George III and his ministers. His identity remains uncertain, but Sir Philip Francis (1740–1818), an official in the War Office, is still the most probable choice (79:8).

A nabob, a man-midwife; but the wight
   Mysterious changed his countenance at least
As oft as they their minds: though in full sight
   He stood, the puzzle only was increased;
The man was a phantasmagoria in
Himself — he was so volatile and thin.

78

The moment that you had pronounced him *one,*
   Presto! his face changed, and he was another;
And when that change was hardly well put on,
   It varied, till I don't think his own mother
(If that he had a mother) would her son
   Have known, he shifted so from one to t'other;
Till guessing from a pleasure grew a task,
At this epistolary "Iron Mask."

79

For sometimes he like Cerberus would seem —
   "Three gentlemen at once" (as sagely says
Good Mrs. Malaprop); then you might deem
   That he was not even *one;* now many rays
Were flashing round him; and now a thick steam
   Hid him from sight — like fogs on London days:
Now Burke, now Tooke, he grew to people's fancies
And certes often like Sir Philip Francis.

80

I've an hypothesis — 'tis quite my own;
   I never let it out till now, for fear
Of doing people harm about the throne,
   And injuring some minister or peer,
On whom the stigma might perhaps be blown;
   It is — my gentle public, lend thine ear!

78:8. *"Iron Mask":* The "Man in the Iron Mask" was confined in the Bastille during the reign of Louis XIV. His identity, like that of Junius, remains uncertain.

79:3. *Mrs. Malaprop:* A character in Sheridan's comedy, *The Rivals.* See Act 4, Sc. 2.

79:7. *Tooke:* See below, 84:6 n.

'Tis, that what Junius we are wont to call,
Was *really — truly —* nobody at all.

81

I don't see wherefore letters should not be
 Written without hands, since we daily view
Them written without heads; and books, we see,
 Are filled as well without the latter too:
And really till we fix on somebody
 For certain sure to claim them as his due,
Their author, like the Niger's mouth, will bother
The world to say if *there* be mouth or author.

82

"And who and what art thou?" the Archangel said.
 "For *that* you may consult my title-page,"
Replied this mighty shadow of a shade:
 "If I have kept my secret half an age,
I scarce shall tell it now." — "Canst thou upbraid,"
 Continued Michael, "George Rex, or allege
Aught further?" Junius answered, "You had better
First ask him for *his* answer to my letter:

83

"My charges upon record will outlast
 The brass of both his epitaph and tomb."
"Repent'st thou not," said Michael, "of some past
 Exaggeration? something which may doom
Thyself if false, as him if true? Thou wast
 Too bitter — is it not so? — in thy gloom
Of passion?" — "Passion!" cried the phantom dim,
"I loved my country, and I hated him.

84

"What I have written, I have written: let
 The rest be on his head or mine!" So spoke
Old *"Nominis Umbra;"* and while speaking yet,

84:3. *"Nominis Umbra"*: "Shadow of a name," part of the motto on the
title page of the letters.

Away he melted in celestial smoke.
Then Satan said to Michael, "Don't forget
  To call George Washington, and John Horne Tooke,
And Franklin;" — but at this time there was heard
A cry for room, though not a phantom stirred.

85

At length with jostling, elbowing, and the aid
  Of Cherubim appointed to that post,
The devil Asmodeus to the circle made
  His way, and looked as if his journey cost
Some trouble. When his burden down he laid,
  "What's this" cried Michael; "why, 'tis not a ghost?"
"I know it," quoth the Incubus; "but he
Shall be one, if you leave the affair to me.

86

"Confound the renegado! I have sprained
  My left wing, he's so heavy; one would think
Some of his works about his neck were chained.
  But to the point; while hovering o'er the brink
Of Skiddaw (where as usual it still rained),
  I saw a taper, far below me, wink,
And stooping, caught this fellow at a libel —
No less on History — than the Holy Bible.

87

"The former is the Devil's scripture, and
  The latter yours, good Michael: so the affair
Belongs to all of us, you understand.
  I snatched him up just as you see him there,
And brought him off for sentence out of hand:
  I've scarcely been ten minutes in the air —
At least a quarter it can hardly be:
I dare say that his wife is still at tea."

84:6. *John Horne Tooke*: An English radical leader (1736–1812) who
supported the American and French revolutions.
86:5. *Skiddaw*: A mountain near Southey's home in the Lake country.
86:8. *history . . . Bible*: That is, writing *A Vision of Judgment*.

88

Here Satan said, "I know this man of old,
    And have expected him for some time here;
A sillier fellow you will scarce behold,
    Or more conceited in his petty sphere:
But surely it was not worth while to fold
    Such trash below your wing, Asmodeus dear:
We had the poor wretch safe (without being bored
With carriage) coming of his own accord.

89

"But since he's here, let's see what he has done."
    "Done!" cried Asmodeus, "he anticipates
The very business you are now upon,
    And scribbles as if head clerk to the Fates.
Who knows to what his ribaldry may run,
    When such an ass as this, like Balaam's, prates?"
"Let's hear," quoth Michael, "what he has to say:
You know we're bound to that in every way."

90

Now the bard, glad to get an audience, which
    By no means often was his case below,
Began to cough, and hawk, and hem, and pitch
    His voice into that awful note of woe
To all unhappy hearers within reach
    Of poets when the tide of rhyme's in flow;
But stuck fast with his first hexameter,
Not one of all whose gouty feet would stir.

91

But ere the spavined dactyls could be spurred
    Into recitative, in great dismay
Both Cherubim and Seraphim were heard
    To murmur loudly through their long array;
And Michael rose ere he could get a word

89:6. *Balaam's*: See *Numbers* 22:28.

Of all his foundered verses under way,
And cried, "For God's sake stop, my friend! 'twere best —
'*Non Di, non homines*' — you know the rest."

92

A general bustle spread throughout the throng,
    Which seemed to hold all verse in detestation;
The Angels had of course enough of song
    When upon service; and the generation
Of ghosts had heard too much in life, not long
    Before, to profit by a new occasion:
The Monarch, mute till then, exclaimed, "What! what!
Pye come again? No more — no more of that!"

93

The tumult grew; an universal cough
    Convulsed the skies, as during a debate,
When Castlereagh has been up long enough
    (Before he was first minister of state,
I mean — the *slaves hear now*); some cried "Off, off!"
    As at a farce; till, grown quite desperate,
The Bard Saint Peter prayed to interpose
(Himself an author) only for his prose.

94

The varlet was not an ill-favoured knave;
    A good deal like a vulture in the face,
With a hook nose and a hawk's eye, which gave
    A smart and sharper-looking sort of grace
To his whole aspect, which, though rather grave,
    Was by no means so ugly as his case;
But that, indeed, was hopeless as can be,
Quite a poetic felony "*de se.*"

91:8. *Non Di, non homines*: The reference is to Horace's *Ars Poetica*, 372: "Not men, not Gods, not booksellers will tolerate mediocre poets."
92:8. *Pye*: Henry James Pye (1745–1813) notoriously bad poet, Southey's predecessor as poet laureate.
93:3. *Castlereagh*: See *Don Juan*, Dedication, 11:8, note.
94:8. *felony "de se"*: Suicide.

95

Then Michael blew his trump, and stilled the noise
    With one still greater, as is yet the mode
On earth besides; except some grumbling voice,
    Which now and then will make a slight inroad
Upon decorous silence, few will twice
    Lift up their lungs when fairly overcrowed;
And now the Bard could plead his own bad cause,
With all the attitudes of self-applause.

96

He said — (I only give the heads) — he said,
    He meant no harm in scribbling; 'twas his way
Upon all topics; 'twas, besides, his bread,
    Of which he buttered both sides; 'twould delay
Too long the assembly (he was pleased to dread),
    And take up rather more time than a day,
To name his works — he would but cite a few —
"Wat Tyler" — "Rhymes on Blenheim" — "Waterloo."

97

He had written praises of a Regicide;
    He had written praises of all kings whatever;
He had written for republics far and wide,
    And then against them bitterer than ever;
For pantisocracy he once had cried
    Aloud, a scheme less moral than 'twas clever;
Then grew a hearty anti-jacobin —
Had turned his coat — and would have turned his skin.

98

He had sung against all battles, and again
    In their high praise and glory; he had called

96:8. *Waterloo*: In *Wat Tyler* (1794) and *The Battle of Blenheim* (1798)
Southey had shown himself a radical republican. In *The Poet's Pilgrimage to Waterloo* (1816) he had celebrated the defeat of republicanism.
    97:5. *pantisocracy*: The ideal community that Southey and Coleridge
planned to establish in Pennsylvania in 1794.
    97:7. *anti-jacobin*: Anti-revolutionary; anti-republican.

Reviewing "the ungentle craft," and then
   Became as base a critic as e'er crawled —
Fed, paid, and pampered by the very men
   By whom his muse and morals had been mauled:
He had written much blank verse, and blanker prose,
And more of both than any body knows.

99

He had written Wesley's life: — here turning round
   To Satan, "Sir, I'm ready to write yours,
In two octavo volumes, nicely bound,
   With notes and preface, all that most allures
The pious purchaser; and there's no ground
   For fear, for I can choose my own reviewers:
So let me have the proper documents,
That I may add you to my other saints."

100

Satan bowed, and was silent. "Well, if you,
   With amiable modesty, decline
My offer, what says Michael? There are few
   Whose memoirs could be rendered more divine.
Mine is a pen of all work; not so new
   As it was once, but I would make you shine
Like your own trumpet. By the way, my own
Has more of brass in it, and is as well blown.

101

"But talking about trumpets, here's my 'Vision!'
   Now you shall judge, all people — yes — you shall
Judge with my judgment! and by my decision
   Be guided who shall enter heaven or fall.
I settle all these things by intuition,
   Times present, past, to come — Heaven — Hell — and all,
Like King Alfonso. When I thus see double,
I save the Deity some worlds of trouble."

101:7. *King Alphonso*: King of Castile (c. 1226–1284) whom Byron
quotes in a note as saying in regard to the Ptolomean system that "had
he been consulted at the creation of the world, he would have spared the
Maker some absurdities."

102

He ceased, and drew forth an MS.; and no
   Persuasion on the part of Devils, Saints,
Or Angels, now could stop the torrent; so
   He read the first three lines of the contents;
But at the fourth, the whole spiritual show
   Had vanished, with variety of scents,
Ambrosial and sulphureous, as they sprang,
Like lightning, off from his "melodious twang."

103

Those grand heroics acted as a spell;
   The Angels stopped their ears and plied their pinions;
The Devils ran howling, deafened, down to Hell;
   The ghosts fled, gibbering, for their own dominions —
(For 'tis not yet decided where they dwell,
   And I leave every man to his opinions);
Michael took refuge in his trump — but, lo!
His teeth were set on edge, he could not blow!

104

Saint Peter, who has hitherto been known
   For an impetuous saint, upraised his keys,
And at the fifth line knocked the poet down;
   Who fell like Phaeton, but more at ease,
Into his lake, for there he did not drown;
   A different web being by the Destinies
Woven for the Laureate's final wreath, whene'er
Reform shall happen either here or there.

105

He first sank to the bottom — like his works,
   But soon rose to the surface — like himself;
For all corrupted things are buoyed like corks,
   By their own rottenness, light as an elf,

104:4. *Phaeton*: Son of Apollo who attempting to drive the chariot of
the sun across the sky was killed by Zeus and hurled into the river.

Or wisp that flits o'er a morass: he lurks,
  It may be, still, like dull books on a shelf,
In his own den, to scrawl some "Life" or "Vision,"
  As Welborn says — "the Devil turned precisian."

106

As for the rest, to come to the conclusion
  Of this true dream, the telescope is gone
Which kept my optics free from all delusion,
  And showed me what I in my turn have shown;
All I saw farther, in the last confusion,
  Was, that King George slipped into Heaven for one;
And when the tumult dwindled to a calm,
I left him practising the hundredth psalm.

1821   *1822*

105:8. *precisian*: Puritan. Wellborn is a character in Massinger's play,
A New Way to Pay Old Debts (1633).

Selections *from* Don Juan

Don Juan

Byron began *Don Juan* in July 1818, probably with no more serious purpose than to write a "playful satire" like *Beppo,* centering on a ribald experience related to him by a Venetian friend. As with *Beppo,* he was quickly caught up in the writing and by mid-September had essentially finished the first canto and dedication. On September 19, he wrote Moore, "It is called *Don Juan,* and is meant to be a little quietly facetious upon everything." The use of the name Don Juan, the legendary libertine, for the innocent boy seduced by Donna Julia was part of the fun. Byron's Juan was naive, amiable, possessed of all the natural virtues, and in sexual matters more sinned against than sinning. Thus he became the perfect foil for the sophisticated narrator's facetious commentary on men and morals and "everything."

The idea of an extended mock-epic, as sketched in at the end of Canto 1 (Stanzas 200–203) obviously tempted Byron and he was soon embarked on Canto 2 (the shipwreck and the meeting with Haidee), and by April 3, 1819 had sent it off to John Murray who published the first two cantos anonymously in July, 1819. Cantos 3 and 4 were written between September, 1819 and January, 1820; and Canto 5, which takes place in a Turkish harem, in the autumn of 1820. But the brouhaha among the reviewers over indecency and irreverence stirred up by the first two cantos frightened Murray and he waited until August 1821 to publish the next three. In the meantime, Byron let the poem lie fallow for over a year, though the letter of February 16, 1821 to Murray (see introduction, p.xxvii) indicates that he had great long-range plans for Juan. The ostensible reason he gave was that he had promised the Countess Guiccioli, who had been shocked

341

by the immorality of the poem as she read it in a French translation, that he would write no more, but actually he was using her to justify his immediate preoccupation with other matters. He had become intensely involved in the Carbonari movement for the independence of Northern Italy, and he had also turned to the writing of essentially political plays, *Marino Faliero, The Two Foscari,* and *Sardanapalus.* In the summer and autumn of 1821 he wrote *The Vision of Judgment* and *Cain,* in which the rebellion against tyranny was given cosmic proportions (see headnotes to each).

The failure of the Carbonari movement, the outcry against *Cain* (published in December, 1821) added to the continuing attack on *Don Juan,* strengthened Byron in taking a much more serious view of the purpose and function of his "epic satire." Between April and May 1823, he wrote in a remarkably sustained burst of creative energy Cantos 6 to 16 and a few stanzas of Canto 17. The sixth Canto (which picked Juan up in the Turkish harem where he had been abandoned the year before) was a last gay fling in the old manner, appropriately the most bawdy of the cantos, but beginning with Canto 7 the deepening purpose was made evident in the treatment of the siege of Ismail, the experiences of Juan at the Court of Catherine the Great, and the acid portrait of English society (Cantos 10–16). At that point Byron broke off to begin his preparations for going to Greece, and as far as we know, wrote no more before his death. During this period Cantos 6 to 16 were printed by John Hunt, the radical publisher and brother of Leigh Hunt, to whom Byron gave the rights after quarrelling with Murray, who was increasingly reluctant to publish: Cantos 6–8 in July, 1823; 9–11 in August; 12–14 in December; 15–16 on March 26, 1824, less than a month before Byron's death.

In the present selections an attempt has been made to indicate the range and variety of Don Juan by printing entire the first three cantos and the portion of the fourth as far as the death of Haidee; followed by extensive selections from Cantos 8 and 9 (the war cantos), and from Cantos 10 through 16 (the English cantos). In Cantos 13 through 15 passages have been chosen which best show Byron's delineation of the principal characters of English society with whom Juan becomes acquainted: Lord Henry and Lady Adeline Ammundeville, the Duchess of Fitz-Fulke, and Aurora Raby, so that the wonderful complexities of the encounter with the Ghost in Canto 16 can be fully enjoyed by the reader.

For further critical comment on the poem see the Introduction pp. xix–xx; xxvi–xxix. For remarks on *Don Juan* by Byron himself, see the letters on pp. 660, 668, 671, 680, and 692. The student should consult *The Variorum Don Juan*, ed. Steffan and Pratt, 4 vols., 1957, for full commentary and notes. A survey of modern critical comment on the poem is given in *Twentieth Century Interpretations of Don Juan*, ed. Edward E. Bostetter.

'*Difficile est propriè communia dicere.*'[1]

Horace.

'*Dost thou think, because thou art virtuous, there shall be no more cakes and ale? Yes, by Saint Anne, and ginger shall be hot i' the mouth, too!*'[2]

Shakespeare, Twelfth Night, or What You Will.

FRAGMENT[3]
ON THE BACK OF THE MS. OF CANTO I

I WOULD to Heaven that I were so much clay,
    As I am blood, bone, marrow, passion, feeling —
Because at least the past were passed away,
    And for the future — (but I write this reeling,
Having got drunk exceedingly to-day,
    So that I seem to stand upon the ceiling)

1 *Difficile . . . . dicere*: "Tis no slight task to write on common things" (Byron's translation). This line from Horace, *Ars Poetica*, ii, 3, 128, was used as the motto for Cantos 1–4.

2 "*Dost thou think . . . .*"; This passage from *Twelfth Night* II. iii. 105–108, was used as the motto for Cantos 6–8. The first sentence is spoken by Sir Toby and the second by the Clown to Malvolio.

3 Fragment: This cancelled stanza was first used as a headpiece to the poem by Moore in his 1833 edition. There is no indication that Byron intended it to be so used.

I say — the future is a serious matter —
And so — for God's sake — hock[4] and soda-water!

DEDICATION

On September 19, 1818, Byron wrote to Murray that *Don Juan* "is dedicated to Southey in good, simple, savage verse upon the Laureat's politics, and the way he got them." However, the impetus for the Dedication was not politics but a report relayed to Byron from England that Southey had been spreading the story that he and Shelley had in Switzerland in 1816 "formed a League of Incest, and practiced our principles" with Claire Claremont and Mary Godwin. "He is a burning liar," Byron wrote Murray November 24, 1818, "for the women to whom he alludes are not sisters — one being Godwin's daughter, by Mary Wollstonecraft, and the other daughter of the *present* (second) Mrs. G[n], by a former husband; and in the next place . . . there was no *promiscuous intercourse* whatever."

When it was decided to bring out the first two cantos anonymously, Byron wrote Murray to omit the Dedication: "I won't attack the dog in the dark. Such things are for scoundrels and renegades like himself." Consequently the Dedication was not published until after Byron's death. For Byron's further quarrel with Southey, see headnote to *The Vision of Judgment.*

1

BOB SOUTHEY! You're a poet — Poet-laureate,
    And representative of all the race;
Although 't is true that you turned out a Tory at
    Last, — yours has lately been a common case;
And now, my Epic Renegade! what are ye at?
    With all the Lakers, in and out of place?
A nest of tuneful persons, to my eye
Like "four and twenty Blackbirds in a pye;

---

4 *hock*: A German dry white wine.
1:6. *Lakers*: Southey, Wordsworth and Coleridge. The first two still lived in the Lake District in Northwest England, but Coleridge had left in 1811.

2

"Which pye being opened they began to sing,"
  (This old song and new simile holds good),
"A dainty dish to set before the King,"
  Or Regent, who admires such kind of food; —
And Coleridge, too, has lately taken wing,
  But like a hawk encumbered with his hood, —
Explaining Metaphysics to the nation —
I wish he would explain his Explanation.

3

You, Bob! are rather insolent, you know,
  At being disappointed in your wish
To supersede all warblers here below,
  And be the only Blackbird in the dish;
And then you overstrain yourself, or so,
  And tumble downward like the flying fish
Gasping on deck, because you soar too high, Bob,
And fall, for lack of moisture, quite a-dry, Bob!

4

And Wordsworth, in a rather long "Excursion,"
  (I think the quarto holds five hundred pages),
Has given a sample from the vasty version
  Of this new system to perplex the sages;
'T is poetry — at least by his assertion,
  And may appear so when the dog-star rages —
And he who understands it would be able
To add a story to the Tower of Babel.

5

You — Gentlemen! by dint of long seclusion
  From better company, have kept your own

2:8. *Explanation*: A reference to Coleridge's philosophical discussions in *Biographia Literaria* (1817). Byron was angry with Coleridge because as he wrote Murray "I understand [he] went about repeating Southey's lie with pleasure."

3:8. *quite-a-dry, Bob*: A bawdy pun. In Regency slang a "dry bob" meant coition without emission (Partridge, *Dictionary of Slang*).

4:1. *"Excursion"*: Wordsworth's long philosophical poem was published in 1814. See Canto 3, 94:5–8.

At Keswick, and, through still continued fusion
  Of one another's minds, at last have grown
To deem as a most logical conclusion,
  That Poesy has wreaths for you alone:
There is a narrowness in such a notion,
Which makes me wish you'd change your lakes for Ocean.

6

I would not imitate the petty thought,
  Nor coin my self-love to so base a vice,
For all the glory your conversion brought,
  Since gold alone should not have been its price.
You have your salary; was 't for that you wrought?
  And Wordsworth has his place in the Excise.
You're shabby fellows — true — but poets still,
And duly seated on the Immortal Hill.

7

Your bays may hide the baldness of your brows —
  Perhaps some virtuous blushes; — let them go —
To you I envy neither fruit nor boughs —
  And for the fame you would engross below,
The field is universal, and allows
  Scope to all such as feel the inherent glow:
Scott, Rogers, Campbell, Moore, and Crabbe, will try
'Gainst you the question with posterity.

8

For me, who, wandering with pedestrian Muses,
  Contend not with you on the wingéd steed,
I wish your fate may yield ye, when she chooses,
  The fame you envy, and the skill you need;
And, recollect, a poet nothing loses

6:6. *Excise*: For his aid to the Tory Party, Wordsworth had been appointed Distributor of Stamps for Westmoreland County in 1813. See also Canto 3, 93:3–4.

7:7. These were the contemporary poets for whom Byron held a continuing high regard. See Canto 1, 205; *Beppo*, 76:3.

   In giving to his brethren their full need
Of merit — and complaint of present days
Is not the certain path to future praise.

9

He that reserves his laurels for posterity
   (Who does not often claim the bright reversion)
Has generally no great crop to spare it, he
   Being only injured by his own assertion;
And although here and there some glorious rarity
   Arise like Titan from the sea's immersion,
The major part of such appellants go
To — God knows where — for no one else can know.

10

If, fallen in evil days on evil tongues,
   Milton appealed to the Avenger, Time,
If Time, the Avenger, execrates his wrongs,
   And makes the word "Miltonic" mean *"Sublime,"*
He deigned not to belie his soul in songs,
   Nor turn his very talent to a crime;
He did not loathe the Sire to laud the Son,
But closed the tyrant-hater he begun.

11

Think'st thou, could he — the blind Old Man — arise
   Like Samuel from the grave, to freeze once more
The blood of monarchs with his prophecies,
   Or be alive again — again all hoar
With time and trials, and those helpless eyes,
   And heartless daughters — worn — and pale — and poor;

   10:1–2. *evil tongues*: See *Paradise Lost*, VII, 25–26.
   10:7. *loathe the Sire to laud the Son*: Milton hated both Charles I and Charles II. He did not, in other words, change his politics like Southey and Wordsworth.
   11:2. *Samuel from the grave*: *I Samuel* 28:13–14.
   11:6. *heartless daughters*: "Milton's two elder daughters are said to have robbed him of his books, besides cheating and plaguing him in the economy of his house etc., etc." Byron's note.

Would *he* adore a sultan? *he* obey
The intellectual eunuch Castlereagh?

12

Cold-blooded, smooth-faced, placid miscreant!
  Dabbling its sleek young hands in Erin's gore,
And thus for wider carnage taught to pant,
  Transferred to gorge upon a sister shore,
The vulgarest tool that Tyranny could want,
  With just enough of talent, and no more,
To lengthen fetters by another fixed,
And offer poison long already mixed.

13

An orator of such set trash of phrase
  Ineffably — legitimately vile,
That even its grossest flatterers dare not praise,
  Nor foes — all nations — condescend to smile, —
Nor even a sprightly blunder's spark can blaze
  From that Ixion grindstone's ceaseless toil,
That turns and turns to give the world a notion
Of endless torments and perpetual motion.

14

A bungler even in its disgusting trade,
  And botching, patching, leaving still behind
Something of which its masters are afraid —
  States to be curbed, and thoughts to be confined,

11:8. *Castlereagh*: Robert Stewart, Viscount Castlereagh (1769–1822), chief Tory statesman between 1812 and 1822. As Foreign Secretary he was responsible for the coalition that brought about Napoleon's defeat and settled the peace terms at the Congress of Vienna (stanza 14). In his youth he was responsible for suppressing the Irish Rebellion of 1798 (stanza 12). He was identified with all the repressive legislation following the Napoleonic Wars.

13:1. *set trash of phrase*: Castlereagh was notorious for his inept and confused use of English language.

13:6. *Ixion*: In Greek myth, Ixion was bound in hell to an ever-turning wheel.

Conspiracy or Congress to be made —
   Cobbling at manacles for all mankind —
A tinkering slave-maker, who mends old chains,
With God and Man's abhorrence for its gains.

15

If we may judge of matter by the mind,
   Emasculated to the marrow *It*
Hath but two objects, how to serve, and bind,
   Deeming the chain it wears even men may fit,
Eutropius of its many masters, — blind
   To worth as freedom, wisdom as to wit,
Fearless — because *no* feeling dwells in ice,
Its very courage stagnates to a vice.

16

Where shall I turn not to *view* its bonds,
   For I will never *feel* them? — Italy!
Thy late reviving Roman soul desponds
   Beneath the lie this State-thing breathed o'er thee —
Thy clanking chain, and Erin's yet green wounds,
   Have voices — tongues to cry aloud for me.
Europe has slaves — allies — kings — armies still —
And Southey lives to sing them very ill.

17

Meantime, Sir Laureate, I proceed to dedicate,
   In honest simple verse, this song to you,
And, if in flattering strains I do not predicate,
   'T is that I still retain my "buff and blue;"
My politics as yet are all to educate:
   Apostasy 's so fashionable, too,

15:5. *Entropius*: A eunuch who was minister of the Roman emperor Arcadius (378–408).
16:4. At the Congress of Vienna, Castlereagh insisted that the Italian states were not ready for independence.
17:4. *"buff and blue"*: Colors of the Whig party.

To keep *one* creed's a task grown quite Herculean;
Is it not so, my Tory, ultra-Julian?

Venice, Sept. 16, 1818   *1833*

CANTO THE FIRST

1

I WANT a hero: an uncommon want,
　　When every year and month sends forth a new one,
Till, after cloying the gazettes with cant,
　　The age discovers he is not the true one;
Of such as these I should not care to vaunt,
　　I'll therefore take our ancient friend Don Juan —
We all have seen him, in the pantomime,
Sent to the Devil somewhat ere his time.

2

Vernon, the butcher Cumberland, Wolfe, Hawke,
　　Prince Ferdinand, Granby, Burgoyne, Keppel, Howe,
Evil and good, have had their tithe of talk,
　　And filled their sign-posts then, like Wellesley now;
Each in their turn like Banquo's monarchs stalk,
　　Followers of fame, "nine farrow" of that sow:
France, too, had Buonaparté and Dumourier
Recorded in the Moniteur and Courier.

17:8. *ultra-Julian*: Roman emperor, Julian (331–363), called the Apostate because he renounced the Christian religion in which he had been reared and attempted to restore pagan polytheism as the state religion. Southey had renounced his youthful republican principles and turned Tory.
　1:7. *pantomine*: A favorite pantomine in England during Byron's youth was *Don Juan*, or *The Libertine Destroyed*, by Charles Delpini with music by Gluck.
　2:1–2. *Vernon . . . Howe*: Generals and admirals of the eighteenth century, famous or notorious for particular battles.
　2:4. *Wellesley*: Duke of Wellington. Many squares and streets were named for Wellington, the hero of Waterloo.
　2:5. *Banquo's monarchs*: See *Macbeth* IV. i. 112 ff.
　2:6. *"nine farrow"*: See the witch's chant in Macbeth IV. i. 65.
　2:7. *Dumourier*: French revolutionary general.
　2:8. *Moniteur and Courier*: Well-known French newspapers.

3

Barnave, Brissot, Condorcet, Mirabeau,
  Petion, Clootz, Danton, Marat, La Fayette
Were French, and famous people, as we know;
  And there were others, scarce forgotten yet,
Joubert, Hoche, Marceau, Lannes, Desaix, Moreau,
  With many of the military set,
Exceedingly remarkable at times,
But not at all adapted to my rhymes.

4

Nelson was once Britannia's god of War,
  And still should be so, but the tide is turned;
There 's no more to be said of Trafalgar,
  'T is with our hero quietly inurned;
Because the army 's grown more popular,
  At which the naval people are concerned;
Besides, the Prince is all for the land-service,
Forgetting Duncan, Nelson, Howe, and Jervis.

5

Brave men were living long before Agamemnon
  And since, exceeding valorous and sage,
A good deal like him too, though quite the same none;
  But then they shone not on the poet's page,
And so have been forgotten: — I condemn none,
  But can't find any in the present age
Fit for my poem (that is, for my new one);
So, as I said, I'll take my friend Don Juan.

3:1–2. *Barnave . . . La Fayette*: Famous French philosophers and politicians most of them active in the French Revolution. Several (Barnave, Brissot, Condorcet, Clootz, Danton) were executed in the Reign of Terror.
3:5. *Joubert . . . Moreau*: French generals during the revolutionary and Napoleonic wars.
4:3. *Trafalgar*: Nelson was killed at the battle of Trafalgar, October 21, 1805.
4:7. The Prince Regent urged large allowances for the army at the expense of the navy.
4:8. *Duncan . . . Jervis*: English admirals during the French wars.
5:1. *Agamemnon*: Commanded the Greeks in the Trojan War.

6

Most epic poets plunge *"in medias res"*
　　(Horace makes this the heroic turnpike road),
And then your hero tells, whene'er you please,
　　What went before — by way of episode,
While seated after dinner at his ease,
　　Beside his mistress in some soft abode,
Palace, or garden, paradise, or cavern,
Which serves the happy couple for a tavern.

7

That is the usual method, but not mine —
　　My way is to begin with the beginning;
The regularity of my design
　　Forbids all wandering as the worst of sinning,
And therefore I shall open with a line
　　(Although it cost me half an hour in spinning),
Narrating somewhat of Don Juan's father,
And also of his mother, if you'd rather.

8

In Seville was he born, a pleasant city,
　　Famous for oranges and women, — he
Who has not seen it will be much to pity,
　　So says the proverb — and I quite agree;
Of all the Spanish towns is none more pretty,
　　Cadiz perhaps — but that you soon may see; —
Don Juan's parents lived beside the river,
A noble stream, and called the Guadalquivir.

9

His father's name was Jóse — *Don,* of course —
　　A true Hidalgo, free from every stain

6:1. *"in medias res"*: Into the middle of things. Horace based his critical precept on Homer.
9:1. *Jose*: Byron anglicizes Jose (emphasizing the first syllable) just as he does Juan, partly for humor and partly for meter.
9:2. *Hidalgo*: Title of Spanish nobleman of lesser rank.

Of Moor or Hebrew blood, he traced his source
   Through the most Gothic gentlemen of Spain;
A better cavalier ne'er mounted horse,
   Or, being mounted, e'er got down again,
Than Jóse, who begot our hero, who
Begot — but that's to come — Well, to renew:

10

His mother was a learnéd lady, famed
   For every branch of every science known —
In every Christian language ever named,
   With virtues equalled by her wit alone:
She made the cleverest people quite ashamed,
   And even the good with inward envy groan,
Finding themselves so very much exceeded,
In their own way, by all the things that she did.

11

Her memory was a mine: she knew by heart
   All Calderon and greater part of Lopé,
So, that if any actor missed his part,
   She could have served him for the prompter's copy;
For her Feinagle's were a useless art,
   And he himself obliged to shut up shop — he
Could never make a memory so fine as
That which adorned the brain of Donna Inez.

12

Her favourite science was the mathematical,
   Her noblest virtue was her magnanimity,
Her wit (she sometimes tried at wit) was Attic all,

    10:1. *mother*: The following portrait is, at least in part, a satire on
Byron's wife.
    11:2. *Calderon* (1600–1681) and *Lopé de Vega* (1562–1635): Spanish
dramatists.
    11:5. *Feinagle*: Gregor von Feinagle (1765–1819), inventor of a system
for training the memory.
    12:3. *attic*: Athenian. The ancient Athenians were famous for their
refined wit.

Her serious sayings darkened to sublimity;
In short, in all things she was fairly what I call
   A prodigy — her morning dress was dimity,
Her evening silk, or, in the summer, muslin,
And other stuffs, with which I won't stay puzzling.

13

She knew the Latin — that is, "the Lord's prayer,"
   And Greek — the alphabet — I'm nearly sure;
She read some French romances here and there,
   Although her mode of speaking was not pure;
For native Spanish she had no great care,
   At least her conversation was obscure;
Her thoughts were theorems, her words a problem,
As if she deemed that mystery would ennoble 'em.

14

She liked the English and the Hebrew tongue,
   And said there was analogy between 'em;
She proved it somehow out of sacred song,
   But I must leave the proofs to those who 've seen 'em;
But this I heard her say, and can't be wrong,
   And all may think which way their judgments lean 'em,
" 'T is strange — the Hebrew noun which means 'I am,'
The English always used to govern d—n."

15

Some women use their tongues — she *looked* a lecture,
   Each eye a sermon, and her brow a homily,
An all-in-all sufficient self-director,
   Like the lamented late Sir Samuel Romilly
The Law's expounder, and the State's corrector
   Whose suicide was almost an anomaly —

15:4. *Romilly*: A lawyer (1757–1818) who as solicitor-general and member of Parliament supported many reform measures. Retained by Byron to represent him in the separation proceedings, he became an adviser instead to Lady Byron, and Byron never forgave him. He committed suicide upon the death of his wife. See Byron's comment in the letter to John Murray, below, pp. 666–667.

One sad example more, that "All is vanity," —
(The jury brought their verdict in "Insanity!")

16

In short, she was a walking calculation,
  Miss Edgeworth's novels stepping from their covers,
Or Mrs. Trimmer's books on education,
  Or "Cœlebs' Wife" set out in quest of lovers,
Morality's prim personification,
  In which not Envy's self a flaw discovers;
To others' share let "female errors fall,"
For she had not even one — the worst of all.

17

Oh! she was perfect past all parallel —
  Of any modern female saint's comparison;
So far above the cunning powers of Hell,
  Her Guardian Angel had given up his garrison;
Even her minutest motions went as well
  As those of the best time-piece made by Harrison:
In virtues nothing earthly could surpass her
Save thine "incomparable oil," Macassar!

18

Perfect she was, but as perfection is
  Insipid in this naughty world of ours,
Where our first parents never learned to kiss
  Till they were exiled from their earlier bowers,
Where all was peace, and innocence, and bliss,

16:2. *Edgeworth*: Maria Edgeworth (1767–1849), author of *Castle Rackrent*.

16:3. *Trimmer*: Sarah Trimmer (1741–1810) wrote edifying stories for children and pamphlets on the necessity of moral education.

16:4. *"Coelebs' Wife"*: Hannah More (1745–1833) was the author of many books of moral instruction, including *Coelebs in Search of a Wife*.

16:7. *"let female errors fall"*: Pope, *Rape of the Lock*, II, 17.

17:6. *Harrison*: John "Longitude" Harrison (1693–1776), famous for perfecting a chronometer that determined longitude within half a degree.

17:8. *Macassar*: A popular hair-oil from the island of Macassar, advertised according to Byron's note as "incomparable."

(I wonder how they got through the twelve hours),
Don Jóse, like a lineal son of Eve,
Went plucking various fruit without her leave.

19

He was a mortal of the careless kind,
  With no great love for learning, or the learned,
Who chose to go where'er he had a mind,
  And never dreamed his lady was concerned;
The world, as usual, wickedly inclined
  To see a kingdom or a house o'erturned,
Whispered he had a mistress, some said *two*.
But for domestic quarrels *one* will do.

20

Now Donna Inez had, with all her merit,
  A great opinion of her own good qualities;
Neglect, indeed, requires a saint to bear it,
  And such, indeed, she was in her moralities;
But then she had a devil of a spirit,
  And sometimes mixed up fancies with realities,
And let few opportunities escape
Of getting her liege lord into a scrape.

21

This was an easy matter with a man
  Oft in the wrong, and never on his guard;
And even the wisest, do the best they can,
  Have moments, hours, and days, so unprepared,
That you might "brain them with their lady's fan";
  And sometimes ladies hit exceeding hard,
And fans turn into falchions in fair hands,
And why and wherefore no one understands.

22

'T is pity learnéd virgins ever wed
  With persons of no sort of education,

21:5. *"brain them with their lady's fan"*: See *1 Henry IV* II. iii. 20–21.

Or gentlemen, who, though well born and bred,
   Grow tired of scientific conversation:
I don't choose to say much upon this head,
   I'm a plain man, and in a single station,
But — Oh! ye lords of ladies intellectual,
Inform us truly, have they not hen-pecked you all?

23

Don Jóse and his lady quarrelled — *why,*
   Not any of the many could divine,
Though several thousand people chose to try,
   'T was surely no concern of theirs nor mine;
I loathe that low vice — curiosity;
   But if there's anything in which I shine,
'T is in arranging all my friends' affairs,
Not having, of my own, domestic cares.

24

And so I interfered, and with the best
   Intentions, but their treatment was not kind;
I think the foolish people were possessed,
   For neither of them could I ever find,
Although their porter afterwards confessed —
   But that 's no matter, and the worst 's behind,
For little Juan o'er me threw, down stairs,
A pail of housemaid's water unawares.

25

A little curly-headed, good-for-nothing,
   And mischief-making monkey from his birth;
His parents ne'er agreed except in doting
   Upon the most unquiet imp on earth;
Instead of quarrelling, had they been but both in
   Their senses, they'd have sent young master forth
To school, or had him soundly whipped at home,
To teach him manners for the time to come.

26

Don Jóse and the Donna Inez led
   For some time an unhappy sort of life,

Wishing each other, not divorced, but dead;
   They lived respectably as man and wife,
Their conduct was exceedingly well-bred,
   And gave no outward signs of inward strife,
Until at length the smothered fire broke out,
And put the business past all kind of doubt.

27

For Inez called some druggists and physicians,
   And tried to prove her loving lord was *mad,*
But as he had some lucid intermissions,
   She next decided he was only *bad;*
Yet when they asked her for her depositions,
   No sort of explanation could be had,
Save that her duty both to man and God
Required this conduct — which seemed very odd.

28

She kept a journal, where his faults were noted,
   And opened certain trunks of books and letters,
All which might, if occasion served, be quoted;
   And then she had all Seville for abettors,
Besides her good old grandmother (who doted);
   The hearers of her case became repeaters,
Then advocates, inquisitors, and judges,
Some for amusement, others for old grudges.

29

And then this best and meekest woman bore
   With such serenity her husband's woes,
Just as the Spartan ladies did of yore,
   Who saw their spouses killed, and nobly chose
Never to say a word about them more —
   Calmly she heard each calumny that rose,
And saw *his* agonies with such sublimity,
That all the world exclaimed, "What magnanimity!"

27:2. Byron believed that Lady Byron before their separation had sent
a physician to him to determine his sanity.

30

No doubt this patience, when the world is damning us,
  Is philosophic in our former friends;
'T is also pleasant to be deemed magnanimous,
  The more so in obtaining our own ends;
And what the lawyers call a *"malus animus"*
  Conduct like this by no means comprehends:
Revenge in person 's certainly no virtue,
But then 't is not *my* fault, if *others* hurt you.

31

And if our quarrels should rip up old stories,
  And help them with a lie or two additional,
I'm not to blame, as you well know — no more is
  Any one else — they were become traditional;
Besides, their resurrection aids our glories
  By contrast, which is what we just were wishing all:
And Science profits by this resurrection —
Dead scandals form good subjects for dissection.

32

Their friends had tried at reconciliation,
  Then their relations, who made matters worse.
('T were hard to tell upon a like occasion
  To whom it may be best to have recourse —
I can't say much for friend or yet relation):
  The lawyers did their utmost for divorce,
But scarce a fee was paid on either side
Before, unluckily, Don Jóse died.

33

He died: and most unluckily, because,
  According to all hints I could collect
From Counsel learnéd in those kinds of laws,
  (Although their talk 's obscure and circumspect)
His death contrived to spoil a charming cause;

30:5. *"malus animus"*: Inclination to evil.

A thousand pities also with respect
To public feeling, which on this occasion
Was manifested in a great sensation.

34

But ah! he died; and buried with him lay
   The public feeling and the lawyer's fees:
His house was sold, his servants sent away,
   A Jew took one of his two mistresses,
A priest the other — at least so they say:
   I asked the doctors after his disease —
He died of the slow fever called the tertian,
And left his widow to her own aversion.

35

Yet Jóse was an honourable man,
   That I must say, who knew him very well;
Therefore his frailties I'll no further scan,
   Indeed there were not many more to tell:
And if his passions now and then outran
   Discretion, and were not so peaceable
As Numa's (who was also named Pompilius),
He had been ill brought up, and was born bilious.

36

Whate'er might be his worthlessness or worth,
   Poor fellow! he had many things to wound him.
Let's own — since it can do no good on earth —
   It was a trying moment that which found him
Standing alone beside his desolate hearth,
   Where all his household gods lay shivered round him:
No choice was left his feelings or his pride,
Save Death or Doctors' Commons — so he died.

35:7. *Numa*: Legendary second king of Rome, noted for his wisdom and piety and for his long, peaceable reign.
36:8. *Doctors' Commons*: Divorce court.

37

Dying intestate, Juan was sole heir
    To a chancery suit, and messuages, and lands,
Which, with a long minority and care,
    Promised to turn out well in proper hands:
Inez became sole guardian, which was fair,
    And answered but to Nature's just demands;
An only son left with an only mother
Is brought up much more wisely than another.

38

Sagest of women, even of widows, she
    Resolved that Juan should be quite a paragon,
And worthy of the noblest pedigree,
    (His Sire was of Castile, his Dam from Aragon):
Then, for accomplishments of chivalry,
    In case our Lord the King should go to war again,
He learned the arts of riding, fencing, gunnery,
And how to scale a fortress — or a nunnery.

39

But that which Donna Inez most desired,
    And saw into herself each day before all
The learnéd tutors whom for him she hired,
    Was, that this breeding should be strictly moral:
Much into all his studies she inquired,
    And so they were submitted first to her, all,
Arts, sciences — no branch was made a mystery
To Juan's eyes, excepting natural history.

40

The languages, especially the dead,
    The sciences, and most of all the abstruse,
The arts, at least all such as could be said
    To be the most remote from common use,

37:2. *messuages*: Dwelling houses with adjacent buildings and lands.

In all these he was much and deeply read:
  But not a page of anything that 's loose,
Or hints continuation of the species,
Was ever suffered, lest he should grow vicious.

41

His classic studies made a little puzzle,
  Because of filthy loves of gods and goddesses,
Who in the earlier ages raised a bustle,
  But never put on pantaloons or bodices;
His reverend tutors had at times a tussle,
  And for their Æneids, Iliads, and Odysseys,
Were forced to make an odd sort of apology,
For Donna Inez dreaded the Mythology.

42

Ovid's a rake, as half his verses show him,
  Anacreon's morals are a still worse sample,
Catullus scarcely has a decent poem,
  I don't think Sappho's Ode a good example,
Although Longinus tells us there is no hymn
  Where the Sublime soars forth on wings more ample;
But Virgil's songs are pure, except that horrid one
Beginning with *"Formosum Pastor Corydon."*

43

Lucretius' irreligion is too strong
  For early stomachs, to prove wholesome food;
I can't help thinking Juvenal was wrong,
  Although no doubt his real intent was good,

  42:1–3. *Ovid* (43 B.C.–18 A.D.) wrote the *Art of Love*; *Anacreon* (c. 521 B.C.) and *Catullus* (84?–54 B.C.) were famous for their frank love poetry.
  42:4. *Sappho's Ode*: *Ode to Aphrodite* (sixth century B.C.).
  42:8. *"Formosum Pastor Corydon"*: Virgil's second Eclogue is concerned with the love of the shepherd Corydon for the "beautiful boy" Alexis.
  43:1. *Lucretius' irreligion*: In *De Rerum Natura* (Concerning the Nature of Things) Lucretius (96?–55 B.C.) seeks to show that the universe can be explained without recourse to divine agency.
  43:3. *Juvenal*: The satires on first century A.D. Roman society describe its vices in vivid detail.

For speaking out so plainly in his song,
  So much indeed as to be downright rude;
And then what proper person can be partial
To all those nauseous epigrams of Martial?

44

Juan was taught from out the best edition,
  Expurgated by learnéd men, who place,
Judiciously, from out the schoolboy's vision,
  The grosser parts; but, fearful to deface
Too much their modest bard by this omission,
  And pitying sore his mutilated case,
They only add them in an appendix,
Which saves, in fact, the trouble of an index;

45

For there we have them all "at one fell swoop,"
  Instead of being scattered through the pages;
They stand forth marshalled in a handsome troop,
  To meet the ingenuous youth of future ages,
Till some less rigid editor shall stoop
  To call them back into their separate cages,
Instead of standing staring all together,
Like garden gods — and not so decent either.

46

The Missal too (it was the family Missal)
  Was ornamented in a sort of way
Which ancient mass-books often are, and this all
  Kinds of grotesques illumined; and how they,
Who saw those figures on the margin kiss all,
  Could turn their optics to the text and pray,
Is more than I know — But Don Juan's mother
Kept this herself, and gave her son another.

44:7. *appendix*: "Fact, there is, or was, such an edition with all the obnoxious epigrams of Martial placed by themselves at the end" (Byron's note). This was the Amsterdam edition of 1701. Martial was a Roman poet, first century A.D.

47

Sermons he read, and lectures he endured,
  And homilies, and lives of all the saints;
To Jerome and to Chrysostom inured,
  He did not take such studies for restraints;
But how Faith is acquired, and then insured,
  So well not one of the aforesaid paints
As Saint Augustine in his fine Confessions,
Which make the reader envy his transgressions.

48

This too, was a sealed book to little Juan —
  I can't but say that his mamma was right,
If such an education was the true one.
  She scarcely trusted him from out her sight;
Her maids were old, and if she took a new one,
  You might be sure she was a perfect fright;
She did this during even her husband's life —
I recommend as much to every wife.

49

Young Juan waxed in goodliness and grace;
  At six a charming child, and at eleven
With all the promise of as fine a face
  As e'er to Man's maturer growth was given:
He studied steadily, and grew apace,
  And seemed, at least, in the right road to Heaven,
For half his days were passed at church, the other
Between his tutors, confessor, and mother.

50

At six, I said, he was a charming child,
  At twelve he was a fine, but quiet boy;
Although in infancy a little wild,

47:3. *Jerome and . . . Chrysostom*: Two church fathers of the fourth
century. Jerome's translations became the basis of the Latin version of
the Bible known as the Vulgate.

They tamed him down amongst them: to destroy
His natural spirit not in vain they toiled,
　　At least it seemed so; and his mother's joy
Was to declare how sage, and still, and steady,
Her young philosopher was grown already.

51

I had my doubts, perhaps I have them still,
　　But what I say is neither here nor there:
I knew his father well, and have some skill
　　In character — but it would not be fair
From sire to son to augur good or ill:
　　He and his wife were an ill-sorted pair —
But scandal 's my aversion — I protest
Against all evil speaking, even in jest.

52

For my part I say nothing — nothing — but
　　This I will say — my reasons are my own —
That if I had an only son to put
　　To school (as God be praised that I have none),
'T is not with Donna Inez I would shut
　　Him up to learn his catechism alone,
No — no — I 'd send him out betimes to college,
For there it was I picked up my own knowledge.

53

For there one learns — 't is not for me to boast,
　　Though I acquired — but I pass over *that,*
As well as all the Greek I since have lost: —
　　I say that there 's the place — but *"Verbum sat,"*
I think I picked up too, as well as most,
　　Knowledge of matters — but no matter *what* —
I never married — but, I think, I know
That sons should not be educated so.

53:4. *Verbum sat*: A word to the wise is sufficient.

54

Young Juan now was sixteen years of age,
    Tall, handsome, slender, but well knit: he seemed
Active, though not so sprightly, as a page;
    And everybody but his mother deemed
Him almost man; but she flew in a rage
    And bit her lips (for else she might have screamed)
If any said so — for to be precocious
Was in her eyes a thing the most atrocious.

55

Amongst her numerous acquaintance, all
    Selected for discretion and devotion,
There was the Donna Julia, whom to call
    Pretty were but to give a feeble notion
Of many charms in her as natural
    As sweetness to the flower, or salt to Ocean,
Her zone to Venus, or his bow to Cupid,
(But this last simile is trite and stupid.)

56

The darkness of her Oriental eye
    Accorded with her Moorish origin;
(Her blood was not all Spanish; by the by,
    In Spain, you know, this is a sort of sin;)
When proud Granada fell, and, forced to fly,
    Boabdil wept: of Donna Julia's kin
Some went to Africa, some stayed in Spain —
Her great great grandmamma chose to remain.

57

She married (I forget the pedigree)
    With an Hidalgo, who transmitted down
His blood less noble than such blood should be;
    At such alliances his sires would frown,

56:6. *Boabdil*: Moorish leader who wept as he took a last view of the
city which he had been forced to surrender to the Spaniards in 1492.

In that point so precise in each degree
    That they bred *in and in,* as might be shown,
Marrying their cousins — nay, their aunts, and nieces,
Which always spoils the breed, if it increases.

58

This heathenish cross restored the breed again,
    Ruined its blood, but much improved its flesh;
For from a root the ugliest in Old Spain
    Sprung up a branch as beautiful as fresh;
The sons no more were short, the daughters plain;
    But there 's a rumour which I fain would hush,
'T is said that Donna Julia's grandmamma
Produced her Don more heirs at love than law.

59

However this might be, the race went on
    Improving still through every generation,
Until it centred in an only son,
    Who left an only daughter; my narration
May have suggested that this single one
    Could be but Julia (whom on this occasion
I shall have much to speak about), and she
Was married, charming, chaste, and twenty-three.

60

Her eye (I'm very fond of handsome eyes)
    Was large and dark, suppressing half its fire
Until she spoke, then through its soft disguise
    Flashed an expression more of pride than ire,
And love than either; and there would arise
    A something in them which was not desire,
But would have been, perhaps, but for the soul
Which struggled through and chastened down the whole.

61

Her glossy hair was clustered o'er a brow
    Bright with intelligence, and fair, and smooth;

Her eyebrow's shape was like the aërial bow,
   Her cheek all purple with the beam of youth,
Mounting, at times, to a transparent glow,
   As if her veins ran lightning; she, in sooth,
Possessed an air and grace by no means common:
Her stature tall — I hate a dumpy woman.

62

Wedded she was some years, and to a man
   Of fifty, and such husbands are in plenty;
And yet, I think, instead of such a ONE
   'T were better to have TWO of five-and-twenty,
Especially in countries near the sun:
   And now I think on 't, *"mi vien in mente,"*
Ladies even of the most uneasy virtue
Prefer a spouse whose age is short of thirty.

63

'T is a sad thing, I cannot choose but say,
   And all the fault of that indecent sun,
Who cannot leave alone our helpless clay,
   But will keep baking, broiling, burning on,
That howsoever people fast and pray,
   The flesh is frail, and so the soul undone:
What men call gallantry, and gods adultery,
Is much more common where the climate's sultry.

64

Happy the nations of the moral North!
   Where all is virtue, and the winter season
Sends sin, without a rag on, shivering forth
   ('T was snow that brought St. Anthony to reason):
Where juries cast up what a wife is worth,
   By laying whate'er sum, in mulct, they please on

62:6. *"mi vien in mente"*: It comes to my mind.
64:4. *St. Anthony*: It was St. Francis of Assisi, as Byron remembered in a note, who used snow "as a recipe for hot blood in cold weather."
64:6. *mulct*: Fine or penalty.

The lover, who must pay a handsome price,
Because it is a marketable vice.

65

Alfonso was the name of Julia's lord,
  A man well looking for his years, and who
Was neither much beloved nor yet abhorred:
  They lived together as most people do,
Suffering each other's foibles by accord,
  And not exactly either *one* or *two*;
Yet he was jealous, though he did not show it,
For Jealousy dislikes the world to know it.

66

Julia was — yet I never could see why —
  With Donna Inez quite a favourite friend;
Between their tastes there was small sympathy,
  For not a line had Julia ever penned:
Some people whisper (but, no doubt, they lie,
  For Malice still imputes some private end)
That Inez had, ere Don Alfonso's marriage,
Forgot with him her very prudent carriage;

67

And that still keeping up the old connection,
  Which Time had lately rendered much more chaste,
She took his lady also in affection,
  And certainly this course was much the best:
She flattered Julia with her sage protection,
  And complimented Don Alfonso's taste;
And if she could not (who can?) silence scandal,
At least she left it a more slender handle.

68

I can't tell whether Julia saw the affair
  With other people's eyes, or if her own
Discoveries made, but none could be aware
  Of this, at least no symptom e'er was shown;

Perhaps she did not know, or did not care,
    Indifferent from the first, or callous grown:
I'm really puzzled what to think or say,
She kept her counsel in so close a way.

69

Juan she saw, and, as a pretty child,
    Caressed him often — such a thing might be
Quite innocently done, and harmless styled,
    When she had twenty years, and thirteen he;
But I am not so sure I should have smiled
    When he was sixteen, Julia twenty-three;
These few short years make wondrous alterations,
Particularly amongst sun-burnt nations.

70

Whate'er the cause might be, they had become
    Changed; for the dame grew distant, the youth shy,
Their looks cast down, their greetings almost dumb.
    And much embarrassment in either eye;
There surely will be little doubt with some
    That Donna Julia knew the reason why,
But as for Juan, he had no more notion
Than he who never saw the sea of Ocean.

71

Yet Julia's very coldness still was kind,
    And tremulously gentle her small hand
Withdrew itself from his, but left behind
    A little pressure, thrilling, and so bland
And slight, so very slight, that to the mind
    'T was but a doubt; but ne'er magician's wand
Wrought change with all Armida's fairy art
Like what this light touch left on Juan's heart.

71:7. *Armida's fairy art*: Armida, a sorceress in Tasso's *Jerusalem Delivered*, led Rinaldo to forget his vows as a crusader.

72

And if she met him, though she smiled no more,
 She looked a sadness sweeter than her smile,
As if her heart had deeper thoughts in store
 She must not own, but cherished more the while
For that compression in its burning core;
 Even Innocence itself has many a wile,
And will not dare to trust itself with truth,
And Love is taught hypocrisy from youth.

73

But Passion most dissembles, yet betrays
 Even by its darkness; as the blackest sky
Foretells the heaviest tempest, it displays
 Its workings through the vainly guarded eye,
And in whatever aspect it arrays
 Itself, 't is still the same hypocrisy;
Coldness or Anger, even Disdain or Hate,
Are masks it often wears, and still too late.

74

Then there were sighs, the deeper for suppression,
 And stolen glances, sweeter for the theft,
And burning blushes, though for no transgression,
 Tremblings when met, and restlessness when left;
All these are little preludes to possession,
 Of which young Passion cannot be bereft,
And merely tend to show how greatly Love is
Embarrassed at first starting with a novice.

75

Poor Julia's heart was in an awkward state;
 She felt it going, and resolved to make
The noblest efforts for herself and mate,
 For Honour's, Pride's, Religion's, Virtue's sake:
Her resolutions were most truly great,

And almost might have made a Tarquin quake:
She prayed the Virgin Mary for her grace,
As being the best judge of a lady's case.

76

She vowed she never would see Juan more,
   And next day paid a visit to his mother,
And looked extremely at the opening door,
   Which, by the Virgin's grace, let in another;
Grateful she was, and yet a little sore —
   Again it opens, it can be no other,
'T is surely Juan now — No! I'm afraid
That night the Virgin was no further prayed.

77

She now determined that a virtuous woman
   Should rather face and overcome temptation,
That flight was base and dastardly, and no man
   Should ever give her heart the least sensation,
That is to say, a thought beyond the common
   Preference, that we must feel, upon occasion,
For people who are pleasanter than others,
But then they only seem so many brothers.

78

And even if by chance — and who can tell?
   The Devil's so very sly — she should discover
That all within was not so very well,
   And, if still free, that such or such a lover
Might please perhaps, a virtuous wife can quell
   Such thoughts, and be the better when they're over;
And if the man should ask, 't is but denial:
I recommend young ladies to make trial.

75:6. *Tarquin*: Legendary Roman kings noted for tyranny and cruelty.
One of them is the ravisher in Shakespeare's *Rape of Lucrece*.

79

And, then, there are such things as Love divine,
  Bright and immaculate, unmixed and pure,
Such as the angels think so very fine,
  And matrons, who would be no less secure,
Platonic, perfect, "just such love as mine;"
  Thus Julia said — and thought so, to be sure;
And so I'd have her think, were *I* the man
On whom her reveries celestial ran.

80

Such love is innocent, and may exist
  Between young persons without any danger.
A hand may first, and then a lip be kissed;
  For my part, to such doings I'm a stranger,
But *hear* these freedoms form the utmost list
  Of all o'er which such love may be a ranger:
If people go beyond, 't is quite a crime,
But not my fault — I tell them all in time.

81

. Love, then, but Love within its proper limits,
  Was Julia's innocent determination
In young Don Juan's favour, and to him its
  Exertion might be useful on occasion;
And, lighted at too pure a shrine to dim its
  Ethereal lustre, with what sweet persuasion
He might be taught, by Love and her together —
I really don't know what, nor Julia either.

82

Fraught with this fine intention, and well fenced
  In mail of proof — her purity of soul —
She, for the future, of her strength convinced,
  And that her honour was a rock, or mole,
Exceeding sagely from that hour dispensed
  With any kind of troublesome control;

But whether Julia to the task was equal
Is that which must be mentioned in the sequel.

83

Her plan she deemed both innocent and feasible,
    And, surely, with a stripling of sixteen
Not Scandal's fangs could fix on much that 's seizable,
    Of if they did so, satisfied to mean
Nothing but what was good, her breast was peaceable —
    A quiet conscience makes one so serene!
Christians have burnt each other, quite persuaded
That all the Apostles would have done as they did.

84

And if in the mean time her husband died,
    But Heaven forbid that such a thought should cross
Her brain, though in a dream! (and then she sighed)
    Never could she survive that common loss;
But just suppose that moment should betide,
    I only say suppose it — *inter nos*:
(This should be *entre nous,* for Julia thought
In French, but then the rhyme would go for nought.)

85

I only say, suppose this supposition:
    Juan being then grown up to man's estate
Would fully suit a widow of condition,
    Even seven years hence it would not be too late;
And in the interim (to pursue this vision)
    The mischief, after all, could not be great,
For he would learn the rudiments of Love,
I mean the *seraph* way of those above.

86

So much for Julia! Now we'll turn to Juan.
    Poor little fellow! he had no idea
Of his own case, and never hit the true one;

In feelings quick as Ovid's Miss Medea,
He puzzled over what he found a new one,
But not as yet imagined it could be a
Thing quite in course, and not at all alarming,
Which, with a little patience, might grow charming.

87

Silent and pensive, idle, restless, slow,
His home deserted for the lonely wood,
Tormented with a wound he could not know,
His, like all deep grief, plunged in solitude:
I'm fond myself of solitude or so,
But then, I beg it may be understood,
By solitude I mean a Sultan's (not
A Hermit's), with a haram for a grot.

88

"Oh Love! in such a wilderness as this,
Where Transport and Security entwine,
Here is the Empire of thy perfect bliss,
And here thou art a God indeed divine."
The bard I quote from does not sing amiss,
With the exception of the second line,
For that same twining "Transport and Security"
Are twisted to a phrase of some obscurity.

89

The Poet meant, no doubt, and thus appeals
To the good sense and senses of mankind,
The very thing which everybody feels,
As all have found on trial, or may find,
That no one likes to be disturbed at meals
Or love. — I won't say more about "entwined"

86:4. *Ovid's Miss Medea*: In the *Metamorphoses* (VII, 10–12) Ovid describes Medea's sudden involuntary infatuation for Jason.
88:5. *the Bard*: Thomas Campbell in *Gertrude of Wyoming*, III, 1:1–4.

Or "Transport," as we knew all that before,
But beg "Security" will bolt the door.

90

Young Juan wandered by the glassy brooks,
  Thinking unutterable things; he threw
Himself at length within the leafy nooks
  Where the wild branch of the cork forest grew;
There poets find materials for their books,
  And every now and then we read them through,
So that their plan and prosody are eligible,
Unless, like Wordsworth, they prove unintelligible.

91

He, Juan (and not Wordsworth), so pursued
  His self-communion with his own high soul,
Until his mighty heart, in its great mood,
  Had mitigated part, though not the whole
Of its disease; he did the best he could
  With things not very subject to control,
And turned, without perceiving his condition,
Like Coleridge, into a metaphysician.

92

He thought about himself, and the whole earth,
  Of man the wonderful, and of the stars,
And how the deuce they ever could have birth;
  And then he thought of earthquakes, and of wars,
How many miles the moon might have in girth,
  Of air-balloons, and of the many bars
To perfect knowledge of the boundless skies; —
And then he thought of Donna Julia's eyes.

93

In thoughts like these true Wisdom may discern
  Longings sublime, and aspirations high,
Which some are born with, but the most part learn

To plague themselves withal, they know not why:
'T was strange that one so young should thus concern
   His brain about the action of the sky;
If *you* think 't was Philosophy that this did,
I can't help thinking puberty assisted.

94

He pored upon the leaves, and on the flowers,
   And heard a voice in all the winds; and then
He thought of wood-nymphs and immortal bowers,
   And how the goddesses came down to men:
He missed the pathway, he forgot the hours,
   And when he looked upon his watch again,
He found how much old Time had been a winner —
He also found that he had lost his dinner.

95

Sometimes he turned to gaze upon his book,
   Boscan, or Garcilasso; — by the wind
Even as the page is rustled while we look,
   So by the poesy of his own mind
Over the mystic leaf his soul was shook,
   As if 't were one whereon magicians bind
Their spells, and give them to the passing gale,
According to some good old woman's tale.

96

Thus would he while his lonely hours away
   Dissatisfied, not knowing what he wanted;
Nor glowing reverie, nor poet's lay,
   Could yield his spirit that for which it panted,
A bosom whereon he his head might lay,
   And hear the heart beat with the love it granted,
With — several other things, which I forget,
Or which, at least, I need not mention yet.

95:2. *Boscan* (1500–1544) and *Garcilasso* (1503–1536), Spanish poets
known for their sonnets in the Italian manner.

97

Those lonely walks, and lengthening reveries,
    Could not escape the gentle Julia's eyes;
She saw that Juan was not at his ease;
    But that which chiefly may, and must surprise,
Is, that the Donna Inez did not tease
    Her only son with question or surmise;
Whether it was she did not see, or would not,
Or, like all very clever people, could not.

98

This may seem strange, but yet 't is very common;
    For instance — gentlemen, whose ladies take
Leave to o'erstep the written rights of Woman,
    And break the — Which commandment is't they break?
(I have forgot the number, and think no man
    Should rashly quote, for fear of a mistake;)
I say, when these same gentlemen are jealous,
They make some blunder, which their ladies tell us.

99

A real husband always is suspicious,
    But still no less suspects in the wrong place,
Jealous of some one who had no such wishes,
    Or pandering blindly to his own disgrace,
By harbouring some dear friend extremely vicious;
    The last indeed 's infallibly the case:
And when the spouse and friend are gone off wholly,
He wonders at their vice, and not his folly.

100

Thus parents also are at times short-sighted:
    Though watchful as the lynx, they ne'er discover,
The while the wicked world beholds delighted,
    Young Hopeful's mistress, or Miss Fanny's lover,
Till some confounded escapade has blighted
    The plan of twenty years, and all is over;

And then the mother cries, the father swears
And wonders why the devil he got heirs.

101

But Inez was so anxious, and so clear
   Of sight, that I must think, on this occasion,
She had some other motive much more near
   For leaving Juan to this new temptation,
But what that motive was, I shan't say here;
   Perhaps to finish Juan's education,
Perhaps to open Don Alfonso's eyes,
In case he thought his wife too great a prize.

102

It was upon a day, a summer's day; —
   Summer's indeed a very dangerous season,
And so is spring about the end of May;
   The sun, no doubt, is the prevailing reason;
But whatsoe'er the cause is, one may say,
   And stand convicted of more truth than treason,
That there are months which nature grows more merry in, —
March has its hares, and May must have its heroine.

103

'T was on a summer's day — the sixth of June:
   I like to be particular in dates,
Not only of the age, and year, but moon;
   They are a sort of post-house, where the Fates
Change horses, making History change its tune,
   Then spur away o'er empires and o'er states,
Leaving at last not much besides chronology,
Excepting the post-obits of theology.

103:8. *post-obits*: Literally, bonds that take effect after death. Here figuratively, perhaps, the theological promises of life after death. For the more common use of the term see stanza 125, l.8 below.

104

'T was on the sixth of June, about the hour
　　Of half-past six — perhaps still nearer seven —
When Julia sate within as pretty a bower
　　As e'er held houri in that heathenish heaven
Described by Mahomet, and Anacreon Moore,
　　To whom the lyre and laurels have been given,
With all the trophies of triumphant song —
He won them well, and may he wear them long!

105

She sate, but not alone; I know not well
　　How this same interview had taken place,
And even if I knew, I shall not tell —
　　People should hold their tongues in any case;
No matter how or why the thing befell,
　　But there were she and Juan, face to face —
When two such faces are so, 't would be wise,
But very difficult, to shut their eyes.

106

How beautiful she looked! her conscious heart
　　Glowed in her cheek, and yet she felt no wrong:
Oh Love! how perfect is thy mystic art,
　　Strengthening the weak, and trampling on the strong!
How self-deceitful is the sagest part
　　Of mortals whom thy lure hath led along! —
The precipice she stood on was immense,
So was her creed in her own innocence.

107

She thought of her own strength, and Juan's youth,
　　And of the folly of all prudish fears,
Victorious Virtue, and domestic Truth,
　　And then of Don Alfonso's fifty years:

104:5. *Anacreon Moore*: Thomas Moore had begun his career by publishing a translation of Anacreon's odes. Here the reference is probably
to a tale in *Lalla Rookh* (1817).

I wish these last had not occurred, in sooth,
   Because that number rarely much endears,
And through all climes, the snowy and the sunny,
Sounds ill in love, whate'er it may in money.

108

When people say, "I've told you *fifty* times,"
   They mean to scold, and very often do;
When poets say, "I've written *fifty* rhymes,"
   They make you dread that they'll recite them too;
In gangs of *fifty*, thieves commit their crimes;
   At *fifty* love for love is rare, 't is true,
But then, no doubt, it equally as true is,
A good deal may be bought for *fifty* Louis.

109

Julia had honour, virtue, truth, and love
   For Don Alfonso; and she inly swore,
By all the vows below to Powers above,
   She never would disgrace the ring she wore,
Nor leave a wish which wisdom might reprove;
   And while she pondered this, besides much more,
One hand on Juan's carelessly was thrown,
Quite by mistake — she thought it was her own;

110

Unconsciously she leaned upon the other,
   Which played within the tangles of her hair;
And to contend with thoughts she could not smother
   She seemed by the distraction of her air.
'T was surely very wrong in Juan's mother
   To leave together this imprudent pair,
She who for many years had watched her son so —
I'm very certain *mine* would not have done so.

111

The hand which still held Juan's, by degrees
   Gently, but palpably confirmed its grasp,

As if it said, "Detain me, if you please;"
　　Yet there's no doubt she only meant to clasp
His fingers with a pure Platonic squeeze;
　　She would have shrunk as from a toad, or asp,
Had she imagined such a thing could rouse
A feeling dangerous to a prudent spouse.

112

I cannot know what Juan thought of this,
　　But what he did, is much what you would do;
His young lip thanked it with a grateful kiss,
　　And then, abashed at its own joy, withdrew
In deep despair, lest he had done amiss, —
　　Love is so very timid when 't is new:
She blushed, and frowned not, but she strove to speak,
And held her tongue, her voice was grown so weak.

113

The sun set, and up rose the yellow moon:
　　The Devil 's in the moon for mischief; they
Who called her CHASTE, methinks, began too soon
　　Their nomenclature; there is not a day,
The longest, not the twenty-first of June,
　　Sees half the business in a wicked way,
On which three single hours of moonshine smile —
And then she looks so modest all the while!

114

There is a dangerous silence in that hour,
　　A stillness, which leaves room for the full soul
To open all itself, without the power
　　Of calling wholly back its self-control;
The silver light which, hallowing tree and tower,
　　Sheds beauty and deep softness o'er the whole,
Breathes also to the heart, and o'er it throws
A loving languor, which is not repose.

115

And Julia sate with Juan, half embraced
　　And half retiring from the glowing arm,

Which trembled like the bosom where 't was placed;
　Yet still she must have thought there was no harm,
Or else 't were easy to withdraw her waist;
　But then the situation had its charm,
And then — God knows what next — I can't go on;
I'm almost sorry that I e'er begun.

116

Oh Plato! Plato! you have paved the way,
　With your confounded fantasies, to more
Immoral conduct by the fancied sway
　Your system feigns o'er the controlless core
Of human hearts, than all the long array
　Of poets and romancers: — You 're a bore,
A charlatan, a coxcomb — and have been,
At best, no better than a go-between.

117

And Julia's voice was lost, except in sighs,
　Until too late for useful conversation;
The tears were gushing from her gentle eyes,
　I wish, indeed, they had not had occasion;
But who, alas! can love, and then be wise?
　Not that Remorse did not oppose Temptation;
A little still she strove, and much repented,
And whispering "I will ne'er consent" — consented.

118

'T is said that Xerxes offered a reward
　To those who could invent him a new pleasure:
Methinks the requisition 's rather hard,
　And must have cost his Majesty a treasure:
For my part, I'm a moderate-minded bard,
　Fond of a little love (which I call leisure);
I care not for new pleasures, as the old
Are quite enough for me, so they but hold.

119

Oh Pleasure! you 're indeed a pleasant thing,
　Although one must be damned for you, no doubt:

I make a resolution every spring
   Of reformation, ere the year run out,
But somehow, this my vestal vow takes wing,
   Yet still, I trust, it may be kept throughout:
I 'm very sorry, very much ashamed,
And mean, next winter, to be quite reclaimed.

120

Here my chaste Muse a liberty must take —
   Start not! still chaster reader — she 'll be nice hence-
Forward, and there is no great cause to quake;
   This liberty is a poetic licence,
Which some irregularity may make
   In the design, and as I have a high sense
Of Aristotle and the Rules, 't is fit
To beg his pardon when I err a bit.

121

This licence is to hope the reader will
   Suppose from June the sixth (the fatal day,
Without whose epoch my poetic skill
   For want of facts would all be thrown away),
But keeping Julia and Don Juan still
   In sight, that several months have passed; we 'll say
'T was in November, but I'm not so sure
About the day — the era 's more obscure.

122

We 'll talk of that anon. — 'T is sweet to hear
   At midnight on the blue and moonlit deep
The song and oar of Adria's gondolier,
   By distance mellowed, o'er the waters sweep;
'T is sweet to see the evening star appear;
   'T is sweet to listen as the night-winds creep
From leaf to leaf; 't is sweet to view on high
The rainbow, based on ocean, span the sky.

122:3. *Adria's*: The Adriatic Sea. Here, Venice.

123

'T is sweet to hear the watch-dog's honest bark
  Bay deep-mouthed welcome as we draw near home;
'T is sweet to know there is an eye will mark
  Our coming, and look brighter when we come;
'T is sweet to be awakened by the lark,
  Or lulled by falling waters; sweet the hum
Of bees, the voice of girls, the song of birds,
The lisp of children, and their earliest words.

124

Sweet is the vintage, when the showering grapes
  In Bacchanal profusion reel to earth,
Purple and gushing: sweet are our escapes
  From civic revelry to rural mirth;
Sweet to the miser are his glittering heaps,
  Sweet to the father is his first-born's birth,
Sweet is revenge — especially to women —
Pillage to soldiers, prize-money to seamen.

125

Sweet is a legacy, and passing sweet
  The unexpected death of some old lady,
Or gentleman of seventy years complete,
  Who 've made "us youth" wait too — too long already,
For an estate, or cash, or country seat,
  Still breaking, but with stamina so steady,
That all the Israelites are fit to mob its
Next owner for their double-damned post-obits.

126

'T is sweet to win, no matter how, one's laurels,
  By blood or ink, 't is sweet to put an end
To strife; 't is sometimes sweet to have our quarrels,
  Particularly with a tiresome friend:

125:4. *"us youth"*: See *I Henry IV* II. ii. 93.
125:8. *post-obits*: Loans to an heir, usually at exorbitant interest, which fall due when he receives his inheritance.

Sweet is old wine in bottles, ale in barrels;
  Dear is the helpless creature we defend
Against the world; and dear the schoolboy spot
We ne'er forget, though there we are forgot.

127

But sweeter still than this, than these, than all,
  Is first and passionate Love — it stands alone,
Like Adam's recollection of his fall;
  The Tree of Knowledge has been plucked — all 's known —
And Life yields nothing further to recall
  Worthy of this ambrosial sin, so shown,
No doubt in fable, as the unforgiven
Fire which Prometheus filched for us from Heaven.

128

Man 's a strange animal, and makes strange use
  Of his own nature, and the various arts,
And likes particularly to produce
  Some new experiment to show his parts;
This is the age of oddities let loose,
  Where different talents find their different marts;
You 'd best begin with truth, and when you 've lost your
Labour, there 's a sure market for imposture.

129

What opposite discoveries we have seen!
  (Signs of true genius, and of empty pockets.)
One makes new noses, one a guillotine,
  One breaks your bones, one sets them in their sockets;
But Vaccination certainly has been
  A kind antithesis to Congreve's rockets,
With which the Doctor paid off an old pox,
By borrowing a new one from an ox.

129:3. *new noses*: An American quack, Benjamin Perkins, had advertised metallic tractors guaranteed tð cure among other things "red noses."

129:5. *Congreve's rockets*: Sir William Congreve (1772–1828) had invented a rocket (1808) used at the battle of Leipzig (1813).

129:7. *Doctor*: Edward Jenner (1749–1823) made the first vaccine against smallpox in 1796.

130

Bread has been made (indifferent) from potatoes:
    And Galvanism has set some corpses grinning,
But has not answered like the apparatus
    Of the Humane Society's beginning,
By which men are unsuffocated gratis:
    What wondrous new machines have late been spinning!
I said the small-pox has gone out of late;
Perhaps it may be followed by the great.

131

'T is said the great came from America;
    Perhaps it may set out on its return, —
The population there so spreads, they say
    'T is grown high time to thin it in its turn,
With war, or plague, or famine — any way,
    So that civilisation they may learn;
And which in ravage the more loathsome evil is —
Their real *lues,* or our pseudo-syphillis?

132

This is the patent age of new inventions
    For killing bodies, and for saving souls,
All propagated with the best intentions;
    Sir Humphry Davy's lantern, by which coals
Are safely mined for in the mode he mentions,
    Tombuctoo travels, voyages to the Poles

130:2. *Galvanism*: Experiments had been conducted in 1803 in sending electric currents through the body of a corpse.

130:3–4. *Humane Society's beginning*: The Royal Humane Society was founded in 1774 to resuscitate drowning persons.

130:8. *great*: Syphilis.

131:8. *lues*: *lues venerea* (syphilis). The reference to thinning the population is probably suggested by Malthus' *Essay on the Principle of Population* (1798).

132:4. *lantern*: Sir Humphrey Davy invented the miners' safety lamp in 1815.

132:6. In 1809 James Jackson had published "an account of Tombuctoo, the great Emporium of Central Africa"; Sir John Ross and Sir William Parry (see *Vision of Judgment*, 27:8 n.) were exploring arctic regions at this time.

Are ways to benefit mankind, as true,
Perhaps, as shooting them at Waterloo.

133

Man 's a phenomenon, one knows not what,
    And wonderful beyond all wondrous measure;
'T is pity though, in this sublime world, that
    Pleasure 's a sin, and sometimes Sin 's a pleasure;
Few mortals know what end they would be at,
    But whether Glory, Power, or Love, or Treasure,
The path is through perplexing ways, and when
The goal is gained, we die, you know — and then —

134

What then? — I do not know, no more do you —
    And so good night. — Return we to our story:
'T was in November, when fine days are few,
    And the far mountains wax a little hoary,
And clap a white cape on their mantles blue;
    And the sea dashes round the promontory,
And the loud breaker boils against the rock,
And sober suns must set at five o'clock.

135

'T was, as the watchmen say, a cloudy night;
    No moon, no stars, the wind was low or loud
By gusts, and many a sparkling hearth was bright
    With the piled wood, round which the family crowd;
There 's something cheerful in that sort of light,
    Even as a summer sky's without a cloud:
I 'm fond of fire, and crickets, and all that,
A lobster salad, and champagne, and chat.

136

'T was midnight — Donna Julia was in bed,
    Sleeping, most probably, — when at her door
Arose a clatter might awake the dead,
    If they had never been awoke before,

And that they have been so we all have read,
    And are to be so, at the least, once more; —
The door was fastened, but with voice and fist
First knocks were heard, then "Madam — Madam — hist!

137

"For God's sake, Madam — Madam — here's my master,
    With more than half the city at his back —
Was ever heard of such a curst disaster!
    'T is not my fault — I kept good watch — Alack!
Do pray undo the bolt a little faster —
    They 're on the stair just now, and in a crack
Will all be here; perhaps he yet may fly —
Surely the window 's not so *very* high!"

138

By this time Don Alfonso was arrived,
    With torches, friends, and servants in great number;
The major part of them had long been wived,
    And therefore paused not to disturb the slumber
Of any wicked woman, who contrived
    By stealth her husband's temples to encumber:
Examples of this kind are so contagious,
Were *one* not punished, *all* would be outrageous.

139

I can't tell how, or why, or what suspicion
    Could enter into Don Alfonso's head;
But for a cavalier of his condition
    It surely was exceedingly ill-bred,
Without a word of previous admonition,
    To hold a levee round his lady's bed,
And summon lackeys, armed with fire and sword,
To prove himself the thing he most abhorred.

140

Poor Donna Julia! starting as from sleep,
    (Mind — that I do not say — she had not slept),

Began at once to scream, and yawn, and weep;
  Her maid, Antonia, who was an adept,
Contrived to fling the bed-clothes in a heap,
  As if she had just now from out them crept:
I can't tell why she should take all this trouble
To prove her mistress had been sleeping double.

141

But Julia mistress, and Antonia maid,
  Appeared like two poor harmless women who
Of goblins, but still more of men afraid,
  Had thought one man might be deterred by two,
And therefore side by side were gently laid,
  Until the hours of absence should run through,
And truant husband should return, and say,
"My dear, — I was the first who came away."

142

Now Julia found at length a voice, and cried,
  "In Heaven's name, Don Alfonso, what d' ye mean?
Has madness seized you? would that I had died
  Ere such a monster's victim I had been!
What may this midnight violence betide,
  A sudden fit of drunkenness or spleen?
Dare you suspect me, whom the thought would kill?
Search, then, the room!" — Alfonso said, "I will."

143

He searched, *they* searched, and rummaged everywhere,
  Closet and clothes' press, chest and window-seat,
And found much linen, lace, and several pair
  Of stockings, slippers, brushes, combs, complete
With other articles of ladies fair,
  To keep them beautiful, or leave them neat:
Arras they pricked and curtains with their swords,
And wounded several shutters, and some boards.

144

Under the bed they searched, and there they found —
  No matter what — it was not that they sought;
They opened windows, gazing if the ground
  Had signs of footmarks, but the earth said nought;
And then they stared each others' faces round:
  'T is odd, not one of all these seekers thought,
And seems to me almost a sort of blunder,
Of looking *in* the bed as well as under.

145

During this inquisition Julia's tongue
  Was not asleep — "Yes, search and search," she cried,
"Insult on insult heap, and wrong on wrong!
  It was for this that I became a bride!
For this in silence I have suffered long
  A husband like Alfonso at my side;
But now I 'll bear no more, nor here remain,
If there be law or lawyers in all Spain.

146

"Yes, Don Alfonso! husband now no more,
  If ever you indeed deserved the name,
Is 't worthy of your years? — you have threescore —
  Fifty, or sixty, it is all the same —
Is 't wise or fitting, causeless to explore
  For facts against a virtuous woman's fame?
Ungrateful, perjured, barbarous Don Alfonso,
How dare you think your lady would go on so?

147

"Is it for this I have disdained to hold
  The common privileges of my sex?
That I have chosen a confessor so old
  And deaf, that any other it would vex,
And never once he has had cause to scold,
  But found my very innocence perplex

So much, he always doubted I was married —
How sorry you will be when I 've miscarried!

148

"Was it for this that no Cortejo e'er
  I yet have chosen from out the youth of Seville?
Is it for this I scarce went anywhere,
  Except to bull-fights, mass, play, rout, and revel?
Is it for this, whate'er my suitors were,
  I favoured none — nay, was almost uncivil?
Is it for this that General Count O'Reilly,
Who took Algiers, declares I used him vilely?

149

"Did not the Italian *Musico* Cazzani
  Sing at my heart six months at least in vain?
Did not his countryman, Count Corniani,
  Call me the only virtuous wife in Spain?
Were there not also Russians, English, many?
  The Count Strongstroganoff I put in pain,
And Lord Mount Coffeehouse, the Irish peer,
Who killed himself for love (with wine) last year.

150

"Have I not had two bishops at my feet?
  The Duke of Ichar, and Don Fernan Nunez;
And is it thus a faithful wife you treat?

148:1. *Cortejo*: "The Spanish 'Cortejo' is much the same as the Italian 'Cavalier Servente'" (Byron's note). See *Beppo*, 37.

148:7–8. *O'Reilly*: "Donna Julia here made a mistake. Count O'Reilly did not take Algiers but Algiers very nearly took him; he and his army retreated with great loss, and not much credit, from before that city in the year 1775" (Byron's note). Alexander O'Reilly (1722–1794) was a Spanish general of Irish extraction.

149:1–2. *Cazzani*: Probably Byron's own coinage, but with bawdy echo of *Cazzo* — penis, used figuratively to mean a scamp, rogue (Patridge's *Dictionary of Slang*).

149:3. *Corniani*: Perhaps a play on the word *cornuto* — "horned," meaning a cuckold.

150:2. These are names belonging to well-known noble families of Spain.

I wonder in what quarter now the moon is:
I praise your vast forbearance not to beat
    Me also, since the time so opportune is —
Oh, valiant man! with sword drawn and cocked trigger,
Now, tell me, don't you cut a pretty figure?

151

"Was it for this you took your sudden journey,
    Under pretence of business indispensable
With that sublime of rascals your attorney,
    Whom I see standing there, and looking sensible
Of having played the fool? though both I spurn, he
    Deserves the worst, his conduct 's less defensible,
Because, no doubt, 't was for his dirty fee,
And not from any love to you nor me.

152

"If he comes here to take a deposition,
    By all means let the gentleman proceed;
You 've made the apartment in a fit condition; —
    There's pen and ink for you, sir, when you need —
Let everything be noted with precision,
    I would not you for nothing should be fee'd —
But, as my maid 's undressed, pray turn your spies out."
"Oh!" sobbed Antonia, "I could tear their eyes out."

153

"There is the closet, there the toilet, there
    The antechamber — search them under, over;
There is the sofa, there the great arm-chair,
    The chimney — which would really hold a lover.
I wish to sleep, and beg you will take care
    And make no further noise, till you discover
The secret cavern of this lurking treasure —
And when 't is found, let me, too, have that pleasure.

154

"And now, Hidalgo! now that you have thrown
    Doubt upon me, confusion over all,

Pray have the courtesy to make it known
   Who is the man you search for? how d' ye call
Him? what 's his lineage? let him but be shown —
   I hope he 's young and handsome — is he tall?
Tell me — and be assured, that since you stain
My honour thus, it shall not be in vain.

155

"At least, perhaps, he has not sixty years,
   At that age he would be too old for slaughter,
Or for so young a husband's jealous fears —
   (Antonia! let me have a glass of water.)
I am ashamed of having shed these tears,
   They are unworthy of my father's daughter;
My mother dreamed not in my natal hour,
That I should fall into a monster's power.

156

"Perhaps 't is of Antonia you are jealous,
   You saw that she was sleeping by my side,
When you broke in upon us with your fellows:
   Look where you please — we 've nothing, sir, to hide;
Only another time, I trust you 'll tell us,
   Or for the sake of decency abide
A moment at the door, that we may be
Dressed to receive so much good company.

157

"And now, sir, I have done, and say no more;
   The little I have said may serve to show
The guileless heart in silence may grieve o'er
   The wrongs to whose exposure it is slow: —
I leave you to your conscience as before,
   'T will one day ask you *why* you used me so?
God grant you feel not then the bitterest grief! —
Antonia! where's my pocket-handkerchief?"

158

She ceased and turned upon her pillow; pale
　　She lay, her dark eyes flashing through their tears,
Like skies that rain and lighten; as a veil,
　　Waved and o'ershading her wan cheek, appears
Her streaming hair; the black curls strive, but fail
　　To hide the glossy shoulder, which uprears
Its snow through all; — her soft lips lie apart,
And louder than her breathing beats her heart.

159

The Senhor Don Alfonso stood confused;
　　Antonia bustled round the ransacked room,
And, turning up her nose, with looks abused
　　Her master, and his myrmidons, of whom
Not one, except the attorney, was amused;
　　He, like Achates, faithful to the tomb,
So there were quarrels, cared not for the cause,
Knowing they must be settled by the laws.

160

With prying snub-nose, and small eyes, he stood,
　　Following Antonia's motions here and there,
With much suspicion in his attitude;
　　For reputations he had little care;
So that a suit or action were made good,
　　Small pity had he for the young and fair,
And ne'er believed in negatives, till these
Were proved by competent false witnesses.

161

But Don Alfonso stood with downcast looks,
　　And, truth to say, he made a foolish figure;
When, after searching in five hundred nooks,
　　And treating a young wife with so much rigour,
He gained no point, except some self-rebukes,
　　Added to those his lady with such vigour

159:6. *Achates*: The faithful friend of Aeneas in Virgil's *Aeneid*.

Had poured upon him for the last half-hour,
Quick, thick, and heavy — as a thunder-shower.

162

At first he tried to hammer an excuse,
  To which the sole reply was tears, and sobs,
And indications of hysterics, whose
  Prologue is always certain throes, and throbs,
Gasps, and whatever else the owners choose;
  Alfonso saw his wife, and thought of Job's;
He saw too, in perspective, her relations,
And then he tried to muster all his patience.

163

He stood in act to speak, or rather stammer,
  But sage Antonia cut him short before
The anvil of his speech received the hammer,
  With "Pray, sir, leave the room, and say no more,
Or madam dies." — Alfonso muttered, "D—n her,"
  But nothing else, the time of words was o'er;
He cast a rueful look or two, and did,
He knew not wherefore, that which he was bid.

164

With him retired his *"posse comitatus,"*
  The attorney last, who lingered near the door
Reluctantly, still tarrying there as late as
  Antonia let him — not a little sore
At this most strange and unexplained *"hiatus"*
  In Don Alfonso's facts, which just now wore
An awkward look; as he revolved the case,
The door was fastened in his legal face.

165

No sooner was it bolted, than — Oh Shame!
  Oh Sin! Oh Sorrow! and Oh Womankind!

164:1. his *"posse comitatus"*: His "posse," literally a body of citizens
in a county summoned to keep order.

How can you do such things and keep your fame,
  Unless this world, and t' other too, be blind?
Nothing so dear as an unfilched good name!
  But to proceed — for there is more behind:
With much heartfelt reluctance be it said,
Young Juan slipped, half-smothered, from the bed.

166

He had been hid — I don't pretend to say
  How, nor can I indeed describe the where —
Young, slender, and packed easily, he lay,
  No doubt, in little compass, round or square;
But pity him I neither must nor may
  His suffocation by that pretty pair;
'T were better, sure, to die so, than be shut
With maudlin Clarence in his Malmsey butt.

167

And, secondly, I pity not, because
  He had no businesss to commit a sin,
Forbid by heavenly, fined by human laws; —
  At least 't was rather early to begin,
But at sixteen the conscience rarely gnaws
  So much as when we call our old debts in
At sixty years, and draw the accompts of evil,
And find a deuced balance with the Devil.

168

Of his position I can give no notion:
  'T is written in the Hebrew Chronicle,
How the physicians, leaving pill and potion,
  Prescribed, by way of blister, a young belle,
When old King David's blood grew dull in motion,

166:8. *Clarence*: See *Richard III* I. iv. 276. The Duke of Clarence was thrown into a Spanish sweet wine cask to drown.
168:2. *Hebrew Chronicle*: See *I Kings*, 1:1–3.

And that the medicine answered very well;
Perhaps 't was in a different way applied,
For David lived, but Juan nearly died.

169

What 's to be done? Alfonso will be back
   The moment he has sent his fools away.
Antonia's skill was put upon the rack,
   But no device could be brought into play —
And how to parry the renewed attack?
   Besides, it wanted but few hours of day:
Antonia puzzled; Julia did not speak,
But pressed her bloodless lips to Juan's cheek.

170

He turned his lip to hers, and with his hand
   Called back the tangles of her wandering hair;
Even then their love they could not all command,
   And half forgot their danger and despair:
Antonia's patience now was at a stand —
   "Come, come, 't is no time for fooling there,"
She whispered, in great wrath — "I must deposit
This pretty gentleman within the closet:

171

"Pray, keep your nonsense for some luckier night —
   Who can have put my master in this mood?
What will become on 't — I'm in such a fright,
   The Devil 's in the urchin, and no good —
Is this a time for giggling? this a plight?
   Why don't you know that it may end in blood?
You'll lose your life, and I shall lose my place,
My mistress all, for that half-girlish face.

172

"Had it but been for a stout cavalier
   Of twenty-five or thirty — (come, make haste)
But for a child, what piece of work is here!

I really, madam, wonder at your taste —
 (Come, sir, get in) — my master must be near:
  There, for the present, at the least, he's fast,
And if we can but till the morning keep
Our counsel — (Juan, mind, you must not sleep.)"

173

Now, Don Alfonso entering, but alone,
 Closed the oration of the trusty maid:
She loitered, and he told her to be gone,
 An order somewhat sullenly obeyed;
However, present remedy was none,
 And no great good seemed answered if she staid:
Regarding both with slow and sidelong view,
She snuffed the candle, curtsied, and withdrew.

174

Alfonso paused a minute — then begun
 Some strange excuse for his late proceeding;
He would not justify what he had done,
 To say the best, it was extremely ill-breeding;
But there were ample reasons for it, none
 Of which he specified in this his pleading:
His speech was a fine sample, on the whole,
Of rhetoric, which the learned call *"rigmarole."*

175

Julia said nought; though all the while there rose
 A ready answer, which at once enables
A matron, who her husband's foible knows,
 By a few timely words to turn the tables,
Which, if it does not silence, still must pose, —
 Even if it should comprise a pack of fables;
'T is to retort with firmness, and when he
Suspects with *one,* do you reproach with *three.*

176

Julia, in fact, had tolerable grounds, —
 Alfonso's loves with Inez were well known;

But whether 't was that one's own guilt confounds —
   But that can't be, as has been often shown,
A lady with apologies abounds; —
   It might be that her silence sprang alone
From delicacy to Don Juan's ear,
To whom she knew his mother's fame was dear.

177

There might be one more motive, which makes two;
   Alfonso ne'er to Juan had alluded, —
Mentioned his jealousy, but never who
   Had been the happy lover, he concluded,
Concealed amongst his premises; 't is true,
   His mind the more o'er this its mystery brooded;
To speak of Inez now were, one may say,
Like throwing Juan in Alfonso's way.

178

A hint, in tender cases, is enough;
   Silence is best: besides, there is a *tact* —
(That modern phrase appears to me sad stuff,
   But it will serve to keep my verse compact) —
Which keeps, when pushed by questions rather rough,
   A lady always distant from the fact:
The charming creatures lie with such a grace,
There's nothing so becoming to the face.

179

They blush, and we believe them; at least I
   Have always done so: 't is of no great use,
In any case, attempting a reply,
   For then their eloquence grows quite profuse;
And when at length they 're out of breath, they sigh,
   And cast their languid eyes down, and let loose
A tear or two, and then we make it up;
And then — and then — and then — sit down and sup.

180

Alfonso closed his speech, and begged her pardon,
    Which Julia half withheld, and then half granted,
And laid conditions he thought very hard on,
    Denying several little things he wanted:
He stood like Adam lingering near his garden,
    With useless penitence perplexed and haunted;
Beseeching she no further would refuse,
When, lo! he stumbled o'er a pair of shoes.

181

A pair of shoes! — what then? not much, if they
    Are such as fit with ladies' feet, but these
(No one can tell how much I grieve to say)
    Were masculine; to see them, and to seize,
Was but a moment's act. — Ah! well-a-day!
    My teeth begin to chatter, my veins freeze!
Alfonso first examined well their fashion,
And then flew out into another passion.

182

He left the room for his relinquished sword,
    And Julia instant to the closet flew.
"Fly, Juan, fly! for Heaven's sake — not a word —
    The door is open — you may yet slip through
The passage you so often have explored —
    Here is the garden-key — Fly — fly — Adieu!
Haste — haste! I hear Alfonso's hurrying feet —
Day has not broke — there 's no one in the street."

183

None can say that this was not good advice,
    The only mischief was, it came too late;
Of all experience 't is the usual price,
    A sort of income-tax laid on by fate:
Juan had reached the room-door in a trice,
    And might have done so by the garden-gate,

But met Alfonso in his dressing-gown,
Who threatened death — so Juan knocked him down.

184

Dire was the scuffle, and out went the light;
   Antonia cried out "Rape!" and Julia "Fire!"
But not a servant stirred to aid the fight.
   Alfonso, pommelled to his heart's desire,
Swore lustily he 'd be revenged this night;
   And Juan, too, blasphemed an octave higher;
His blood was up: though young, he was a Tartar.
And not at all disposed to prove a martyr.

185

Alfonso's sword had dropped ere he could draw it,
   And they continued battling hand in hand,
For Juan very luckily ne'er saw it;
   His temper not being under great command,
If at that moment he had chanced to claw it,
   Alfonso's days had not been in the land
Much longer. — Think of husbands', lovers' lives!
And how ye may be doubly widows — wives!

186

Alfonso grappled to detain the foe,
   And Juan throttled him to get away,
And blood ('t was from the nose) began to flow;
   At last, as they more faintly wrestling lay,
Juan contrived to give an awkward blow,
   And then his only garment quite gave way;
He fled, like Joseph, leaving it; but there,
I doubt, all likeness ends between the pair.

187

Lights came at length, and men, and maids, who found
   An awkward spectacle their eyes before;

186:7. *Joseph*: For the story of Joseph and Potiphar's wife, see *Genesis* 39:7–18.

Antonia in hysterics, Julia swooned,
  Alfonso leaning, breathless by the door;
Some half-torn drapery scattered on the ground,
  Some blood, and several footsteps, but no more:
Juan the gate gained, turned the key about,
And liking not the inside, locked the out.

188

Here ends this canto. — Need I sing, or say,
  How Juan, naked, favoured by the night,
Who favours what she should not, found his way,
  And reached his home in an unseemly plight?
The pleasant scandal which arose next day,
  The nine days' wonder which was brought to light,
And how Alfonso sued for a divorce,
Were in the English newspapers, of course.

189

If you would like to see the whole proceedings,
  The depositions, and the Cause at full,
The names of all the witnesses, the pleadings
  Of Counsel to nonsuit, or to annul,
There's more than one edition, and the readings
  Are various, but they none of them are dull:
The best is that in short-hand ta'en by Gurney,
Who to Madrid on purpose made a journey.

190

But Donna Inez, to divert the train
  Of one of the most circulating scandals
That had for centuries been known in Spain,
  At least since the retirement of the Vandals,
First vowed (and never had she vowed in vain)
  To Virgin Mary several pounds of candles;

189:7. *Gurney*: William Gurney (1777–1855), famous shorthand specialist, had reported proceedings of many celebrated English trials in the early nineteenth century.

And then, by the advice of some old ladies,
She sent her son to be shipped off from Cadiz.

191

She had resolved that he should travel through
   All European climes, by land and sea,
To mend his former morals, and get new,
   Especially in France and Italy —
(At least this is the thing most people do.)
   Julia was sent into a convent — she
Grieved — but, perhaps, her feelings may be better
Shown in the following copy of her Letter:

192

"They tell me 't is decided you depart:
   'T is wise — 't is well, but not the less a pain;
I have no further claim on your young heart,
   Mine is the victim, and would be again:
To love too much has been the only art
   I used; — I write in haste, and if a stain
Be on this sheet, 't is not what it appears;
My eyeballs burn and throb, but have no tears.

193

"I loved, I love you, for this love have lost
   State, station, Heaven, Mankind's my own esteem,
And yet can not regret what it hath cost,
   So dear is still the memory of that dream;
Yet, if I name my guilt, 't is not to boast,
   None can deem harshlier of me than I deem:
I trace this scrawl because I cannot rest —
I've nothing to reproach, or to request.

194

"Man's love is of man's life a thing apart,
   'T is a Woman's whole existence; Man may range
The Court, Camp, Church, the Vessel, and the Mart;
   Sword, Gown, Gain, Glory offer, in exchange

Pride, Fame, Ambition, to fill up his heart,
    And few there are whom these can not estrange;
Men have all these resources, We but one —
To love again, and be again undone.

195

"You will proceed in pleasure, and in pride,
    Beloved and loving many; all is o'er
For me on earth, except some years to hide
    My shame and sorrow deep in my heart's core:
These I could bear, but cannot cast aside
    The passion which still rages as before, —
And so farewell — forgive me, love me — No,
That word is idle now — but let it go.

196

"My breast has been all weakness, is so yet;
    But still I think I can collect my mind;
My blood still rushes where my spirit 's set,
    As roll the waves before the settled wind;
My heart is feminine, nor can forget —
    To all, except one image, madly blind;
So shakes the needle, and so stands the pole,
As vibrates my fond heart to my fixed soul.

197

"I have no more to say, but linger still,
    And dare not set my seal upon this sheet,
And yet I may as well the task fulfil,
    My misery can scarce be more complete;
I had not lived till now, could sorrow kill;
    Death shuns the wretch who fain the blow would meet,
And I must even survive this last adieu,
And bear with life, to love and pray for you!"

198

This note was written upon gilt-edged paper
    With a neat little crow-quill, slight and new;

Her small white hand could hardly reach the taper,
　　It trembled as magnetic needles do,
And yet she did not let one tear escape her;
　　The seal a sun-flower; *"Elle vous suit partout,"*
The motto cut upon a white cornelian;
The wax was superfine, its hue vermilion.

199

This was Don Juan's earliest scrape; but whether
　　I shall proceed with his adventures is
Dependent on the public altogether;
　　We 'll see, however, what they say to this:
Their favour in an author's caps 's a feather,
　　And no great mischief 's done by their caprice;
And if their approbation we experience,
Perhaps they'll have some more about a year hence.

200

My poem 's epic, and is meant to be
　　Divided in twelve books; each book containing,
With Love, and War, a heavy gale at sea,
　　A list of ships, and captains, and kings reigning,
New characters; the episodes are three:
　　A panoramic view of Hell 's in training,
After the style of Virgil and of Homer,
So that my name of Epic 's no misnomer.

201

All these things will be specified in time,
　　With strict regard to Aristotle's rules,
The *Vade Mecum* of the true sublime,
　　Which makes so many poets, and some fools:
Prose poets like blank-verse, I 'm fond of rhyme,
　　Good workmen never quarrel with their tools;

198:6. *Elle vous suit partout*: "She follows you everywhere." Byron
had a seal bearing this motto.
198:7. *cornelian*: Stone of translucent quartz.
201:3. *Vade Mecum*: A guide or handbook (lit. "Go with me").

I 've got new mythological machinery,
And very handsome supernatural scenery.

202

There 's only one slight difference between
  Me and my epic brethren gone before,
And here the advantage is my own, I ween,
  (Not that I have not several merits more,
But this will more peculiarly be seen);
  They so embellish, that 't is quite a bore
Their labyrinth of fables to thread through,
Whereas this story 's actually true.

203

If any person doubt it, I appeal
  To History, Tradition, and to Facts,
To newspapers, whose truth all know and feel,
  To plays in five, and operas in three acts;
All these confirm my statement a good deal,
  But that which more completely faith exacts
Is, that myself, and several now in Seville,
Saw Juan's last elopement with the Devil.

204

If ever I should condescend to prose,
  I 'll write poetical commandments, which
Shall supersede beyond all doubt all those
  That went before; in these I shall enrich
My text with many things that no one knows,
  And carry precept to the highest pitch:
I 'll call the work "Longinus o'er a Bottle,
Or, Every Poet his *own* Aristotle."

205

Thou shalt believe in Milton, Dryden, Pope;
  Thou shalt not set up Wordsworth, Coleridge, Southey;
Because the first is crazed beyond all hope,
  The second drunk, the third so quaint and mouthy:

With Crabbe it may be difficult to cope,
   And Campbell's Hippocrene is somewhat drouthy:
Thou shalt not steal from Samuel Rogers, nor
Commit — flirtation with the muse of Moore.

206

Thou shalt not covet Mr. Sotheby's Muse,
   His Pegasus, nor anything that 's his;
Thou shalt not bear false witness like "the Blues" —
   (There 's *one*, at least, is very fond of this);
Thou shalt not write, in short, but what I choose:
   This is true criticism, and you may kiss —
Exactly as you please, or not, — the rod;
But if you don't, I'll lay it on, by G—d!

207

If any person should presume to assert
   This story is not moral, first, I pray,
That they will not cry out before they 're hurt,
   Then that they 'll read it o'er again, and say
(But, doubtless, nobody will be so pert),
   That this is not a moral tale, though gay:
Besides, in Canto Twelfth, I mean to show
The very place where wicked people go.

208

If, after all, there should be some so blind
   To their own good this warning to despise,
Led by some tortuosity of mind,
   Not to believe my verse and their own eyes,
And cry that they "the moral cannot find,"
   I tell him, if a cleryman, he lies;

205:5–8. *Crabbe . . . Moore*: See Dedication 7:7–8.
205:6. *Campbell's Hippocrene* (fountain of the muses in Greek myth) may have been "drouthy" because he had lately turned to prose.
206:1. *Sotheby's Muse*: For Sotheby see *Beppo*, 72:7 n.
206:3. *"the Blues"*: Bluestockings, so called from the color of their hose; women who cultivated an interest in literature and politics. Byron may be referring to his wife.

Should captains the remark, or critics, make,
They also lie too — under a mistake.

209

The public approbation I expect,
    And beg they'll take my word about the moral,
Which I with their amusement will connect
    (So children cutting teeth receive a coral);
Meantime they 'll doubtless please to recollect
    My epical pretensions to the laurel:
For fear some prudish readers should grow skittish,
I've bribed my Grandmother's Review — the British.

210

I sent it in a letter to the Editor,
    Who thanked me duly by return of post —
I 'm for a handsome article his creditor;
    Yet, if my gentle Muse he please to roast,
And break a promise after having made it her,
    Denying the receipt of what it cost,
And smear his page with gall instead of honey,
All I can say is — that he had the money.

211

I think that with this holy *new* alliance
    I may ensure the public, and defy
All other magazines of art or science,
    Daily, or monthly, or three monthly; I
Have not essayed to multiply their clients,
    Because they tell me 't were in vain to try,
And that the Edinburgh Review and Quarterly
Treat a dissenting author very martyrly.

209:8. *my grandmother's review*: The British Review had attacked —
and continued to attack — Byron on moral grounds, and this was Byron's
revenge. The editor of the *Review* took Byron's joke seriously and wrote
a solemn denial in his magazine. Byron carried on the joke in "Letter
to the Editor of My Grandmother's Review" which was published in the
Liberal in 1822.

212

"*Non ego hoc ferrem calidus juventâ*
        Consule Planco," Horace said, and so
Say I; by which quotation there is meant a
        Hint that some six or seven good years ago
(Long ere I dreamt of dating from the Brenta)
        I was most ready to return a blow,
And would not brook at all this sort of thing
In my hot youth — when George the Third was King.

213

But now at thirty years my hair is grey —
        (I wonder what it will be like at forty?
I thought of a peruke the other day —)
        My heart is not much greener; and, in short, I
Have squandered my whole summer while 't was May,
        And feel no more the spirit to retort; I
Have spent my whole life, both interest and principal,
And deem not, what I deemed — my soul invincible.

214

No more — no more — Oh! never more on me
        The freshness of the heart can fall like dew,
Which out of all the lovely things we see
        Extracts emotions beautiful and new,
Hived in our bosoms like the bag o' the bee.
        Think'st thou the honey with those objects grew?
Alas! 't was not in them, but in thy power
To double even the sweetness of a flower.

215

No more — no more — Oh! never more, my heart,
        Canst thou be my sole world, my universe!
Once all in all, but now a thing apart,
        Thou canst not be my blessing or my curse:

212:1-2. "*non ego hoc . . . Planco*": "I should not have endured this in
the heat of youth when Plancus was consul." Horace, *Odes*, III, 14:27–28.
    212:5. *Brenta*: A river near Venice.

The illusion 's gone for ever, and thou art
  Insensible, I trust, but none the worse,
And in thy stead I 've got a deal of judgment,
Though Heaven knows how it ever found a lodgment.

216

My days of love are over; me no more
  The charms of maid, wife, and still less of widow,
Can make the fool of which they made before, —
  In short, I must not lead the life I did do;
The credulous hope of mutual minds is o'er,
  The copious use of claret is forbid too,
So for a good old-gentlemanly vice,
I think I must take up with avarice.

217

Ambition was my idol, which was broken
  Before the shrines of Sorrow, and of Pleasure;
And the two last have left me many a token
  O'er which reflection may be made at leisure:
Now, like Friar Bacon's Brazen Head, I've spoken,
  "Time is, Time was, Time 's past:" — a chymic treasure
Is glittering Youth, which I have spent betimes —
My heart in passion, and my head on rhymes.

218

What is the end of fame? 't is but to fill
  A certain portion of uncertain paper:
Some liken it to climbing up a hill,
  Whose summit, like all hills, is lost in vapour;
For this men write, speak, preach, and heroes kill,
  And bards burn what they call their "midnight taper,"
To have, when the original is dust,
A name, a wretched picture and worse bust.

217:6. *"Time is . . . Time's past"*: In Robert Greene's *Friar Bacon* and *Friar Bungay*, scene xi, 59 ff., the Brazen Head speaks these words to Friar Bacon. "Chymic" means counterfeit.

219

What are the hopes of man? Old Egypt's King
   Cheops erected the first Pyramid
And largest, thinking it was just the thing
   To keep his memory whole, and mummy hid;
But somebody or other rummaging,
   Burglariously broke his coffin's lid:
Let not a monument give you or me hopes,
Since not a pinch of dust remains of Cheops.

220

But I, being fond of true philosophy,
   Say very often to myself, "Alas!
All things that have been born were born to die,
   And flesh (which Death mows down to hay) is grass;
You've passed your youth not so unpleasantly,
   And if you had it o'er again — 't would pass —
So thank your stars that matters are no worse,
And read your Bible, Sir, and mind your purse."

221

But for the present, gentle reader! and
   Still gentler purchaser! the Bard — that's I —
Must with permission, shake you by the hand,
   And so — "your humble servant, and Good-bye!"
We meet again, if we should understand
   Each other; and if not, I shall not try
Your patience further than by this short sample —
'T were well if others followed my example.

222

"Go, little Book, from this my solitude!
   I cast thee on the waters — go thy ways!

219:8. *Cheops*: The Quarterly Review in April, 1818, reported that
when the tomb was opened, it was discovered that "not a bone was left
of Cheops."

222:1–4. Byron quotes from Southey's *Epilogue to the Lay of the
Laureate*.

And if — as I believe, thy vein be good,
   The World will find thee after many days."
When Southey's read, and Wordsworth understood,
   I can't help putting in my claim to praise —
The four first rhymes are Southey's every line:
For God's sake, reader! take them not for mine.

Nov. 1, 1818   *1819*

CANTO THE SECOND

1

OH ye! who teach the ingenuous youth of nations,
   Holland, France, England, Germany, or Spain,
I pray ye flog them upon all occasions —
   It mends their morals, never mind the pain:
The best of mothers and of educations
   In Juan's case were but employed in vain.
Since, in a way that's rather of the oddest, he
Became divested of his native modesty.

2

Had he but been placed at a public school,
   In the third form, or even in the fourth,
His daily task had kept his fancy cool,
   At least, had he been nurtured in the North;
Spain may prove an exception to the rule,
   But then exceptions always prove its worth —
A lad of sixteen causing a divorce
Puzzled his tutors very much, of course.

3

I can't say that it puzzles me at all,
   If all things be considered: first, there was
His lady-mother, mathematical,
   A — never mind; — his tutor, an old ass;
A pretty woman — (that's quite natural,
   Or else the thing had hardly come to pass)

A husband rather old, not much in unity
With his young wife — a time, and opportunity.

4

Well — well; the World must turn upon its axis,
   And all Mankind turn with it, heads or tails,
And live and die, make love and pay our taxes,
   And as the veering wind shifts, shift our sails;
The King commands us, and the Doctor quacks us,
   The Priest instructs, and so our life exhales,
A little breath, love, wine, ambition, fame,
Fighting, devotion, dust, — perhaps a name.

5

I said that Juan had been sent to Cadiz —
   A pretty town, I recollect it well —
'T is there the mart of the colonial trade is,
   (Or was, before Peru learned to rebel),
And such sweet girls! — I mean, such graceful ladies,
   Their very walk would make your bosom swell;
I can't describe it, though so much it strike,
Nor liken it — I never saw the like:

6

An Arab horse, a stately stag, a barb
   New broke, a camelopard, a gazelle,
No — none of these will do; — and then their grab,
   Their veil and petticoat — Alas! to dwell
Upon such things would very near absorb
   A canto — then their feet and ankles, — well,
Thank Heaven I've got no metaphor quite ready,
(And so, my sober Muse — come, let's be steady —

7

Chaste Muse! — well, — if you must, you must) — the veil
   Thrown back a moment with the glancing hand,

5:4. *Peru learn'd to rebel*: Peru and other Latin American countries began their war for independence in 1810.

While the o'erpowering eye, that turns you pale,
    Flashes into the heart: — All sunny land
Of Love! when I forget you, may I fail
    To say my prayers — but never was there planned
A dress through which the eyes give such a volley,
Excepting the Venetian Fazzioli.

8

But to our tale: the Donna Inez sent
    Her son to Cadiz only to embark;
To stay there had not answered her intent,
    But why? — we leave the reader in the dark —
'T was for a voyage the young man was meant,
    As if a Spanish ship were Noah's ark,
To wean him from the wickedness of earth,
And send him like a Dove of Promise forth.

9

Don Juan bade his valet pack his things
    According to directions, then received
A lecture and some money: for four springs
    He was to travel; and though Inez grieved
(As every kind of parting has its stings),
    She hoped he would improve — perhaps believed:
A letter, too, she gave (he never read it)
Of good advice — and two or three of credit.

10

In the mean time, to pass her hours away,
    Brave Inez now set up a Sunday school
For naughty children, who would rather play
    (Like truant rogues) the devil, or the fool;
Infants of three years old were taught that day,
    Dunces were whipped, or set upon a stool:

7:8. *Fazzioli*: "I fazzioli, or kerchiefs (a white kind of veil) which the lower orders wear upon their heads" (letter of Byron to Rogers, March 3, 1818).

The great success of Juan's education
Spurred her to teach another generation.

11

Juan embarked — the ship got under way,
   The wind was fair, the water passing rough;
A devil of a sea rolls in that bay,
   As I, who 've crossed it oft, know well enough;
And, standing on the deck, the dashing spray
   Flies in one's face, and makes it weather-tough:
And there he stood to take, and take again,
His first — perhaps his last — farewell of Spain.

12

I can't but say it is an awkward sight
   To see one's native land receding through
The growing waters; it unmans one quite,
   Especially when life is rather new:
I recollect Great Britain's coast looks white,
   But almost every other country 's blue,
When gazing on them, mystified by distance,
We enter on our nautical existence.

13

So Juan stood, bewildered on the deck:
   The wind sung, cordage strained, and sailors swore,
And the ship creaked, the town became a speck,
   From which away so fair and fast they bore.
The best of remedies is a beef-steak
   Against sea-sickness; try it, Sir, before
You sneer, and I assure you this is true,
For I have found it answer — so may you.

14

Don Juan stood, and, gazing from the stern,
   Beheld his native Spain receding far:
First partings form a lesson hard to learn,
   Even nations feel this when they go to war;

There is a sort of unexpressed concern,
　　A kind of shock that sets one's heart ajar,
At leaving even the most unpleasant people
And places — one keeps looking at the steeple.

15

But Juan had got many things to leave,
　　His mother, and a mistress, and no wife,
So that he had much better cause to grieve
　　Than many persons more advanced in life:
And if we now and then a sigh must heave
　　At quitting even those we quit in strife,
No doubt we weep for those the heart endears —
That is, till deeper griefs congeal our tears.

16

So Juan wept, as wept the captive Jews
　　By Babel's waters, still remembering Sion:
I 'd weep, — but mine is not a weeping Muse,
　　And such light griefs are not a thing to die on:
Young men should travel, if but to amuse
　　Themselves; and the next time their servants tie on
Behind their carriages their new portmanteau,
Perhaps it may be lined with this my canto.

17

And Juan wept, and much he sighed and thought,
　　While his salt tears dropped into the salt sea,
"Sweets to the sweet;" (I like so much to quote;
　　You must excuse this extract, — 't is where she,
The Queen of Denmark, for Ophelia brought
　　Flowers to the grave;) and, sobbing often, he
Reflected on his present situation,
And seriously resolved on reformation.

16:8. Trunk makers often lined their trunks with leaves from books
that failed to sell.
17:3. *"Sweets to the sweet"*: Hamlet V. i. 265.

18

"Farewell, my Spain! a long farewell!" he cried,
 "Perhaps I may revisit thee no more,
But die, as many an exiled heart hath died,
 Of its own thirst to see again thy shore:
Farewell, where Guadalquivir's waters glide!
 Farewell, my mother! and, since all is o'er
Farewell, too, dearest Julia! — (here he drew
Her letter out again, and read it through.)

19

"And oh! if e'er I should forget, I swear —
 But that 's impossible, and cannot be —
Sooner shall this blue Ocean melt to air,
 Sooner shall Earth resolve itself to sea,
Than I resign thine image, oh, my fair!
 Or think of anything, excepting thee;
A mind diseased no remedy can physic —
(Here the ship gave a lurch, and he grew sea-sick.)

20

"Sooner shall Heaven kiss earth — (here he fell sicker)
 Oh Julia! what is every other woe? —
(For God's sake let me have a glass of liquor;
 Pedro, Battista, help me down below.)
Julia, my love! — (you rascal, Pedro, quicker) —
 Oh, Julia! — (this curst vessel pitches so) —
Belovéd Julia, hear me still beseeching!"
(Here he grew inarticulate with retching.)

21

He felt that chilling heaviness of heart,
 Or rather stomach, which, alas! attends,
Beyond the best apothecary's art,
 The loss of Love, the treachery of friends,
Or death of those we dote on, when a part
 Of us dies with them as each fond hope ends:
No doubt he would have been much more pathetic,
But the sea acted as a strong emetic.

22

Love 's a capricious power: I 've known it hold
   Out through a fever caused by its own heat,
But be much puzzled by a cough and cold,
   And find a quinsy very hard to treat;
Against all noble maladies he 's bold,
   But vulgar illnesses don't like to meet,
Nor that a sneeze should interrupt his sigh,
Nor inflammation redden his blind eye.

23

But worst of all is nausea, or a pain
   About the lower region of the bowels;
Love, who heroically breathes a vein,
   Shrinks from the application of hot towels,
And purgatives are dangerous to his reign,
   Sea-sickness death: his love was perfect, how else
Could Juan's passion, while the billows roar,
Resist his stomach, ne'er at sea before?

24

The ship, called the most holy "Trinidada,"
   Was steering duly for the port Leghorn;
For there the Spanish family Moncada
   Were settled long ere Juan's sire was born:
They were relations, and for them he had a
   Letter of introduction, which the morn
Of his departure had been sent him by
His Spanish friends for those in Italy.

25

His suite consisted of three servants and
   A tutor, the licentiate Pedrillo,
Who several languages did understand,
   But now lay sick and speechless on his pillow,
And, rocking in his hammock, longed for land,

23:3. *breathes a vein*: Draws or lets blood.
24:3. *Mancada*: Byron used the name of a neighbor at La Mira in 1818.
25:2. *licentiate*: University graduate, licensed to tutor.

His headache being increased by every billow;
And the waves oozing through the port-hole made
His berth a little damp, and him afraid.

26

'T was not without some reason, for the wind
　　Increased at night, until it blew a gale;
And though 't was not much to a naval mind,
　　Some landsmen would have looked a little pale,
For sailors are, in fact, a different kind:
　　At sunset they began to take in sail,
For the sky showed it would come on to blow,
And carry away, perhaps, a mast or so.

27

At one o'clock the wind with sudden shift
　　Threw the ship right into the trough of the sea,
Which struck her aft, and made an awkward rift,
　　Started the stern-post, also shattered the
Whole of her stern-frame, and, ere she could lift
　　Herself from out her present jeopardy,
The rudder tore away: 't was time to sound
The pumps, and there were four feet water found.

28

One gang of people instantly was put
　　Upon the pumps, and the remainder set
To get up part of the cargo, and what not;
　　But they could not come at the leak as yet;
At last they did get at it really, but
　　Still their salvation was an even bet:
The water rushed through in a way quite puzzling,
While they thrust sheets, shirts, jackets, bales of muslin,

29

Into the opening; but all such ingredients
　　Would have been vain, and they must have gone down,

26:1. Many of the details of the shipwreck were taken from Dalzell's
Shipwrecks and Disasters at Sea (1812). Byron wrote Murray, "There was
not a *single circumstance* of it *not* taken from *fact*."

Despite of all their efforts and expedients,
   But for the pumps: I 'm glad to make them known
To all the brother tars who may have need hence,
   For fifty tons of water were upthrown
By them per hour, and they had all been undone,
But for the maker, Mr. Mann, of London.

30

As day advanced the weather seemed to abate,
   And then the leak they reckoned to reduce,
And keep the ship afloat, though three feet yet
   Kept two hand — and one chain-pump still in use.
The wind blew fresh again: as it grew late
   A squall came on, and while some guns broke loose,
A gust — which all descriptive power transcends —
Laid with one blast the ship on her beam ends.

31

There she lay, motionless, and seemed upset;
   The water left the hold, and washed the decks,
And made a scene men do not soon forget;
   For they remember battles, fires, and wrecks,
Or any other thing that brings regret,
   Or breaks their hopes, or hearts, or heads, or necks:
Thus drownings are much talked of by the divers,
And swimmers, who may chance to be survivors.

32

Immediately the masts were cut away,
   Both main and mizen; first the mizen went,
The main-mast followed: but the ship still lay
   Like a mere log, and baffled our intent.
Foremast and bowsprit were cut down, and they
   Eased her at last (although we never meant
To part with all till every hope was blighted),
And then with violence the old ship righted.

33

It may be easily supposed, while this
   Was going on, some people were unquiet,

That passengers would find it much amiss
  To lose their lives, as well as spoil their diet;
That even the able seaman, deeming his
  Days nearly o'er, might be disposed to riot,
As upon such occasions tars will ask
For grog, and sometimes drink rum from the cask.

34

There 's nought, no doubt; so much the spirit calms
  As rum and true religion: thus it was,
Some plundered, some drank spirits, some sung psalms,
  The high wind made the treble, and as bass
The hoarse harsh waves kept time; fright cured the qualms
  Of all the luckless landsmen's sea-sick maws:
Strange sounds of wailing, blasphemy, devotion,
Clamoured in chorus to the roaring Ocean.

35

Perhaps more mischief had been done, but for
  Our Juan, who, with sense beyond his years,
Got to the spirit-room, and stood before
  It with a pair of pistols; and their fears,
As if Death were more dreadful by his door
  Of fire than water, spite of oaths and tears,
Kept still aloof the crew, who, ere they sunk;
Thought it would be becoming to die drunk.

36

"Give us more grog," they cried, "for it will be
  All one an hour hence." Juan answered, "No!
'T is true that Death awaits both you and me,
  But let us die like men, not sink below
Like brutes:" — and thus his dangerous post kept he,
  And none liked to anticipate the blow;
And even Pedrillo, his most reverend tutor,
Was for some rum a disappointed suitor.

37

The good old gentleman was quite aghast,
   And made a loud and pious lamentation;
Repented all his sins, and made a last
   Irrevocable vow of reformation;
Nothing should tempt him more (this peril past)
   To quit his academic occupation,
In cloisters of the classic Salamanca,
To follow Juan's wake, like Sancho Panca.

38

But now there came a flash of hope once more;
   Day broke, and the wind lulled: the masts were gone,
The leak increased; shoals round her, but no shore,
   The vessel swam, yet still she held her own.
They tried the pumps again, and though, before,
   Their desperate efforts seemed all useless grown,
A glimpse of sunshine set some hands to bale —
The stronger pumped, the weaker thrummed a sail.

39

Under the vessel's keel the sail was passed,
   And for the moment it had some effect;
But with a leak, and not a stick of mast,
   Nor rag of canvas, what could they expect?
But still 't is best to struggle to the last,
   'T is never too late to be wholly wrecked:
And though 't is true that man can only die once,
'T is not so pleasant in the Gulf of Lyons.

40

There winds and waves had hurled them, and from thence,
   Without their will, they carried them away;
For they were forced with steering to dispense,
   And never had as yet a quiet day
On which they might repose, or even commence
   A jurymast or rudder, or could say

The ship would swim an hour, which, by good luck,
Still swam — though not exactly like a duck.

41

The wind, in fact, perhaps, was rather less,
   But the ship laboured so, they scarce could hope
To weather out much longer; the distress
   Was also great with which they had to cope
For want of water, and their solid mess
   Was scant enough: in vain the telescope
Was used — nor sail nor shore appeared in sight,
Nought but the heavy sea, and coming night.

42

Again the weather threatened, — again blew
   A gale, and in the fore and after-hold
Water appeared; yet though the people knew
   All this, the most were patient, and some bold,
Until the chains and leathers were worn through
   Of all our pumps: — a wreck complete she rolled,
At mercy of the waves, whose mercies are
Like human beings during civil war.

43

Then came the carpenter, at last, with tears
   In his rough eyes, and told the captain, he
Could do no more: he was a man in years,
   And long had voyaged through many a stormy sea,
And if he wept at length they were not fears
   That made his eyelids as a woman's be,
But he, poor fellow, had a wife and children, —
Two things for dying people quite bewildering.

44

The ship was evidently settling now
   Fast by the head; and, all distinction gone,
Some went to prayers again, and made a vow
   Of candles to their saints — but there were none

To pay them with; and some looked o'er the bow;
  Some hoisted out the boats; and there was one
That begged Pedrillo for an absolution,
Who told him to be dammed — in his confusion,

45

Some lashed them in their hammocks; some put on
  Their best clothes, as if going to a fair;
Some cursed the day on which they saw the Sun,
  And gnashed their teeth, and, howling, tore their hair;
And others went on as they had begun,
  Getting the boats out, being well aware
That a tight boat will live in a rough sea,
Unless with breakers close beneath her lee.

46

The worst of all was, that in their condition,
  Having been several days in great distress,
'T was difficult to get out such provision
  As now might render their long suffering less:
Men, even when dying, dislike inanition;
  Their stock was damaged by the weather's stress:
Two casks of biscuit, and a keg of butter,
Were all that could be thrown into the cutter.

47

But in the long-boat they contrived to stow
  Some pounds of bread, though injured by the wet;
Water, a twenty-gallon cask or so;
  Six flasks of wine; and they contrived to get
A portion of their beef up from below,
  And with a piece of pork, moreover, met,
But scarce enough to serve them for a luncheon —
Then there was rum, eight gallons in a puncheon.

48

The other boats, the yawl and pinnace, had
  Been stove in the beginning of the gale;

And the long-boat's condition was but bad,
　　As there were but two blankets for a sail,
And one oar for a mast, which a young lad
　　Threw in by good luck over the ship's rail;
And two boats could not hold, far less be stored,
To save one half the people then on board.

49

'T was twilight, and the sunless day went down
　　Over the waste of waters; like a veil,
Which, if withdrawn, would but disclose the frown
　　Of one whose hate is masked but to assail.
Thus to their hopeless eyes the night was shown,
　　And grimly darkled o'er the faces pale,
And the dim desolate deep: twelve days had Fear
Been their familiar, and now Death was here.

50

Some trial had been making at a raft,
　　With little hope in such a rolling sea,
A sort of thing at which one would have laughed,
　　If any laughter at such times could be,
Unless with people who too much have quaffed,
　　And have a kind of wild and horrid glee,
Half epileptical, and half hysterical: —
Their preservation would have been a miracle.

51

At half-past eight o'clock, booms, hencoops, spars,
　　And all things, for a chance, had been cast loose,
That still could keep afloat the struggling tars,
　　For yet they strove, although of no great use:
There was no light in heaven but a few stars,
　　The boats put off o'ercrowded with their crews;
She gave a heel, and then a lurch to port,
And, going down head foremost — sunk, in short.

52

Then rose from sea to sky the wild farewell —
　　Then shrieked the timid, and stood still the brave, —

Then some leaped overboard with dreadful yell,
   As eager to anticipate their grave;
And the sea yawned around her like a hell,
   And down she sucked with her the whirling wave,
Like one who grapples with his enemy,
And strives to strangle him before he die.

53

And first one universal shriek there rushed,
   Louder than the loud Ocean, like a crash
Of echoing thunder; and then all was hushed,
   Save the wild wind and the remorseless dash
Of billows; but at intervals there gushed,
   Accompanied by a convulsive splash,
A solitary shriek, the bubbling cry
Of some strong swimmer in his agony.

54

The boats, as stated, had got off before,
   And in them crowded several of the crew;
And yet their present hope was hardly more
   Than what it had been, for so strong it blew
There was slight chance of reaching any shore;
   And then they were too many, though so few —
Nine in the cutter, thirty in the boat,
Were counted in them when they got afloat.

55

All the rest perished; near two hundred souls
   Had left their bodies; and what 's worse, alas!
When over Catholics the Ocean rolls,
   They must wait several weeks before a mass
Takes off one peak of purgatorial coals,
   Because, till people know what 's come to pass,
They won't lay out their money on the dead —
It costs three francs for every mass that 's said.

56

Juan got into the long-boat, and there
   Contrived to help Pedrillo to a place;

It seemed as if they had exchanged their care,
    For Juan wore the magisterial face
Which courage gives, while poor Pedrillo's pair
    Of eyes were crying for their owner's case:
Battista, though, (a name called shortly Tita),
Was lost by getting at some aqua-vita.

57

Pedro, his valet, too, he tried to save,
    But the same cause, conductive to his loss,
Left him so drunk, he jumped into the wave,
    As o'er the cutter's edge he tried to cross,
And so he found a wine-and-watery grave;
    They could not rescue him although so close,
Because the sea ran higher every minute,
And for the boat — the crew kept crowding in it.

58

A small old spaniel, — which had been Don Jóse's,
    His father's, whom he loved, as ye may think,
For on such things the memory reposes
    With tenderness — stood howling on the brink,
Knowing, (dogs have such intellectual noses!)
    No doubt, the vessel was about to sink;
And Juan caught him up, and ere he stepped
Off threw him in, then after him he leaped.

59

He also stuffed his money where he could
    About his person, and Pedrillo's too,
Who let him do, in fact, whate'er he would,
    Not knowing what himself to say, or do,
As every rising wave his dread renewed;
    But Juan, trusting they might still get through,
And deeming there were remedies for any ill,
Thus re-embarked his tutor and his spaniel.

60

'T was a rough night, and blew so stiffly yet,
    That the sail was becalmed between the seas,

Though on the wave's high top too much to set,
　　They dared not take it in for all the breeze:
Each sea curled o'er the stern, and kept them wet,
　　And made them bale without a moment's ease,
So that themselves as well as hopes were damped,
And the poor little cutter quickly swamped.

61

Nine souls more went in her: the long-boat still
　　Kept above water, with an oar for mast,
Two blankets stitched together, answering ill
　　Instead of sail, were to the oar made fast;
Though every wave rolled menacing to fill,
　　And present peril all before surpassed,
They grieved for those who perished with the cutter,
And also for the biscuit-casks and butter.

62

The sun rose red and fiery, a sure sign
　　Of the continuance of the gale: to run
Before the sea until it should grow fine,
　　Was all that for the present could be done:
A few tea-spoonfuls of their rum and wine
　　Were served out to the people, who begun
To faint, and damaged bread wet through the bags,
And most of them had little clothes but rags.

63

They counted thirty, crowded in a space
　　Which left scarce room for motion or exertion;
They did their best to modify their case,
　　One half sate up, though numbed with the immersion,
While t' other half were laid down in their place,
　　At watch and watch; thus, shivering like the tertian
Ague in its cold fit, they filled their boat,
With nothing but the sky for a great coat.

64

'T is very certain the desire of life
　　Prolongs it: this is obvious to physicians,

When patients, neither plagued with friends nor wife,
   Survive through very desperate conditions,
Because they still can hope, nor shines the knife
   Nor shears of Atropos before their visions:
Despair of all recovery spoils longevity,
And makes men's misery of alarming brevity.

65

'T is said that persons living on annuities
   Are longer lived than others, — God knows why,
Unless to plague the grantors, — yet so true it is,
   That some, I really think, *do* never die:
Of any creditors the worst a Jew it is,
   And *that* 's their mode of furnishing supply:
In my young days they lent me cash that way,
Which I found very troublesome to pay.

66

'T is thus with people in an open boat,
   They live upon the love of Life, and bear
More than can be believed, or even thought,
   And stand like rocks the tempest's wear and tear;
And hardship still has been the sailor's lot,
   Since Noah's ark went cruising here and there;
She had a curious crew as well as cargo,
Like the first old Greek privateer, the Argo.

67

But man is a carnivorous production,
   And must have meals, at least one meal a day;
He cannot live, like woodcocks, upon suction,
   But, like the shark and tiger, must have prey;
Although his anatomical construction

64:6. *Atropos*: In Greek myth, the one among the three fates who cut the thread of life.
65:7–8. Before leaving England in 1816, Byron had contracted debts of about 30,000 pounds.
66:8. *Argo*: The ship in which Jason sought the Golden fleece.

Bears vegetables, in a grumbling way,
Your labouring people think, beyond all question,
Beef, veal, and mutton, better for digestion.

68

And thus it was with this our hapless crew;
   For on the third day there came on a calm,
And though at first their strength it might renew,
   And lying on their weariness like balm,
Lulled them like turtles sleeping on the blue
   Of Ocean, when they woke they felt a qualm,
And fell all ravenously on their provision,
Instead of hoarding it with due precision.

69

The consequence was easily foreseen —
   They ate up all they had, and drank their wine,
In spite of all remonstrances, and then
   On what, in fact, next day were they to dine?
They hoped the wind would rise, these foolish men!
   And carry them to shore; these hopes were fine,
But as they had but one oar, and that brittle,
It would have been more wise to save their victual.

70

The fourth day came, but not a breath of air,
   And Ocean slumbered like an unweaned child:
The fifth day, and their boat lay floating there,
   The sea and sky were blue, and clear, and mild —
With their one oar (I wish they had had a pair)
   What could they do? and Hunger's rage grew wild:
So Juan's spaniel, spite of his entreating,
Was killed, and portioned out for present eating.

71

On the sixth day they fed upon his hide,
   And Juan, who had still refused, because
The creature was his father's dog that died,

Now feeling all the vulture in his jaws,
With some remorse received (though first denied)
    As a great favour one of the fore-paws,
Which he divided with Pedrillo, who
Devoured it, longing for the other too.

72

The seventh day, and no wind — the burning sun
    Blistered and scorched, and, stagnant on the sea,
They lay like carcasses; and hope was none,
    Save in the breeze that came not: savagely
They glared upon each other — all was done,
    Water, and wine, and food, — and you might see
The longings of the cannibal arise
(Although they spoke not) in their wolfish eyes.

73

At length one whispered his companion, who
    Whispered another, and thus it went round,
And then into a hoarser murmur grew,
    An ominous, and wild, and desperate sound;
And when his comrade's thought each sufferer knew,
    'T was but his own, suppressed till now, he found;
And out they spoke of lots for flesh and blood,
And who should die to be his fellow's food.

74

But ere they came to this, they that day shared
    Some leathern caps, and what remained of shoes;
And then they looked around them, and despaired,
    And none to be the sacrifice would choose;
At length the lots were torn up, and prepared,
    But of materials that must shock the Muse —
Having no paper, for the want of better,
They took by force from Juan Julia's letter.

75

The lots were made, and marked, and mixed, and handed,
    In silent horror, and their distribution

Lulled even the savage hunger which demanded,
 Like the Promethean vulture, this pollution;
None in particular had sought or planned it,
 'T was Nature gnawed them to this resolution,
By which none were permitted to be neuter —
And the lot fell on Juan's luckless tutor.

76

He but requested to be bled to death:
 The surgeon had his instruments, and bled
Pedrillo, and so gently ebbed his breath,
 You hardly could perceive when he was dead.
He died as born, a Catholic in faith,
 Like most in the belief in which they 're bred,
And first a little crucifix he kissed,
And then held out his jugular and wrist.

77

The surgeon, as there was no other fee,
 Had his first choice of morsels for his pains;
But being thirstiest at the moment, he
 Preferred a draught from the fast-flowing veins:
Part was divided, part thrown in the sea,
 And such things as the entrails and the brains
Regaled two sharks, who followed o'er the billow —
The sailors ate the rest of poor Pedrillo.

78

The sailors ate him, all save three or four,
 Who were not quite so fond of animal food;
To these was added Juan, who, before
 Refusing his own spaniel, hardly could
Feel now his appetite increased much more;
 'T was not to be expected that he should,
Even in extremity of their disaster,
Dine with them on his pastor and his master.

79

'T was better that he did not; for, in fact,
 The consequence was awful in the extreme;

For they, who were most ravenous in the act,
    Went raging mad — Lord! how they did blaspheme!
And foam, and roll, with strange convulsions racked,
    Drinking salt-water like a mountain-stream,
Tearing, and grinning, howling, screeching, swearing,
And, with hyæna-laughter, died despairing.

80

Their numbers were much thinned by this infliction,
    And all the rest were thin enough, Heaven knows;
And some of them had lost their recollection,
    Happier than they who still perceived their woes;
But other pondered on a new dissection,
    As if not warned sufficiently by those
Who had already perished, suffering madly,
For having used their appetites so sadly.

81

And next they thought upon the master's mate,
    As fattest; but he saved himself, because,
Besides being much averse from such a fate,
    There were some other reasons: the first was,
He had been rather indisposed of late;
    And — that which chiefly proved his saving clause —
Was a small present made to him at Cadiz,
By general subscription of the ladies.

82

Of poor Pedrillo something still remained,
    But was used sparingly, — some were afraid,
And others still their appetites constrained,
    Or but at times a little supper made;
All except Juan, who throughout abstained,
    Chewing a piece of bamboo, and some lead:
At length they caught two Boobies, and a Noddy,
And then they left off eating the dead body.

82:7. *Boobies . . . Noddy*: sea fowl, so called because they were so easy
to catch.

83

And if Pedrillo's fate should shocking be,
   Remember Ugolino condescends
To eat the head of his arch-enemy
   The moment after he politely ends
His tale: if foes be food in Hell, at sea
   'T is surely fair to dine upon our friends,
When Shipwreck's short allowance grows too scanty,
Without being much more terrible than Dante.

84

And the same night there fell a shower of rain,
   For which their mouths gaped, like the cracks of earth
When dried to summer dust; till taught by pain,
   Men really know not what good water 's worth;
If you had been in Turkey or in Spain,
   Or with a famished boat's-crew had your berth,
Or in the desert heard the camel's bell,
You 'd wish yourself where Truth is — in a well.

85

It poured down torrents, but they were no richer
   Until they found a ragged piece of sheet,
Which served them as a sort of spongy pitcher,
   And when they deemed its moisture was complete,
They wrung it out, and though a thirsty ditcher
   Might not have thought the scanty draught so sweet
As a full pot of porter, to their thinking
They ne'er till now had known the joys of drinking.

86

And their baked lips, with many a bloody crack,
   Sucked in the moisture, which like nectar streamed;
Their throats were ovens, their swollen tongues were black,
   As the rich man's in Hell, who vainly screamed
To beg the beggar, who could not rain back

83:2. *Ugolino*: See Dante's *Inferno*, XXXIII, 76–78.

A drop of dew, when every drop had seemed
To taste of Heaven — If this be true, indeed,
Some Christians have a comfortable creed.

87

There were two fathers in this ghastly crew,
 And with them their two sons, of whom the one
Was more robust and hardy to the view,
 But he died early; and when he was gone,
His nearest messmate told his sire, who threw
 One glance at him, and said, "Heaven's will be done!
I can do nothing," and he saw him thrown
Into the deep without a tear or groan.

88

The other father had a weaklier child,
 Of a soft cheek, and aspect delicate;
But the boy bore up long, and with a mild
 And patient spirit held aloof his fate;
Little he said, and now and then he smiled,
 As if to win a part from off the weight
He saw increasing on his father's heart,
With the deep deadly thought, that they must part.

89

And o'er him bent his sire, and never raised
 His eyes from off his face, but wiped the foam
From his pale lips, and ever on him gazed,
 And when the wished-for shower at length was come,
And the boy's eyes, which the dull film half glazed,
 Brightened, and for a moment seemed to roam,
He squeezed from out a rag some drops of rain
Into his dying child's mouth — but in vain.

90

The boy expired — the father held the clay,
 And looked upon it long, and when at last
Death left no doubt, and the dead burthen lay

Stiff on his heart, and pulse and hope were past,
He watched it wistfully, until away
   'T was borne by the rude wave wherein 't was cast;
Then he himself sunk down all dumb and shivering,
And gave no sign of life, save his limbs quivering.

91

Now overhead a rainbow, bursting through
   The scattering clouds, shone, spanning the dark sea,
Resting its bright base on the quivering blue;
   And all within its arch appeared to be
Clearer than that without, and its wide hue
   Waxed broad and waving, like a banner free,
Then changed like to a bow that 's bent, and then
Forsook the dim eyes of these shipwrecked men.

92

It changed, of course; a heavenly Chameleon,
   The airy child of vapour and the sun,
Brought forth in purple, cradled in vermilion,
   Baptized in molten gold, and swathed in dun,
Glittering like crescents o'er a Turk's pavilion,
   And blending every colour into one,
Just like a black eye in a recent scuffle
(For sometimes we must box without the muffle).

93

Our shipwrecked seamen thought it a good omen —
   It is as well to think so, now and then;
'T was an old custom of the Greek and Roman,
   And may become of great advantage when
Folks are discouraged; and most surely no men
   Had greater need to nerve themselves again
Than these, and so this rainbow looked like Hope —
Quite a celestial Kaleidoscope.

94

About this time a beautiful white bird,
   Webfooted, not unlike a dove in size

And plumage (probably it might have erred
   Upon its course), passed oft before their eyes,
And tried to perch, although it saw and heard
   The men within the boat, and in this guise
It came and went, and fluttered round them till
Night fell: — this seemed a better omen still.

95

But in this case I also must remark,
   'T was well this bird of promise did not perch,
Because the tackle of our shattered bark
   Was not so safe for roosting as a church;
And had it been the dove from Noah's ark,
   Returning there from her successful search,
Which in their way that moment chanced to fall
They would have eat her, olive-branch and all.

96

With twilight it again come on to blow,
   But now with violence; the stars shone out,
The boat made way; yet now they were so low,
   They knew not where or what they were about;
Some fancied they saw land, and some said "No!"
   The frequent fog-banks gave them cause to doubt —
Some swore that they heard breakers, others guns,
And all mistook about the latter once.

97

As morning broke, the light wind died away,
   When he who had the watch sung out and swore,
If 't was not land that rose with the Sun's ray,
   He wished that land he never might see more;
And the rest rubbed their eyes and saw a bay,
   Or thought they saw, and shaped their course for shore;
For shore it was, and gradually grew
Distinct, and high, and palpable to view.

98

And then of these some part burst into tears,
   And others, looking with a stupid stare,
Could not yet separate their hopes from fears,
   And seemed as if they had no further care;
While a few prayed — (the first time for some years) —
   And at the bottom of the boat three were
Asleep: they shook them by the hand and head,
And tried to awaken them, but found them dead.

99

The day before, fast sleeping on the water,
   They found a turtle of the hawk's-bill kind,
And by good fortune, gliding softly, caught her,
   Which yielded a day's life, and to their mind
Proved even still a more nutritious matter,
   Because it left encouragement behind:
They thought that in such perils, more than chance
Had sent them this for their deliverance.

100

The land appeared a high and rocky coast,
   And higher grew the mountains as they drew,
Set by a current, toward it: they were lost
   In various conjectures, for none knew
To what part of the earth they had been tost,
   So changeable had been the winds that blew;
Some thought it was Mount Ætna, some the highlands
Of Candia, Cyprus, Rhodes, or other islands.

101

Meantime the current, with a rising gale,
   Still set them onwards to the welcome shore,
Like Charon's bark of spectres, dull and pale:

100:8. *Candia*: Crete.
101:3. *Charon's Bark*: In Greek myth, Charon ferried the souls of the
dead over the Styx to Hades.

Their living freight was now reduced to four,
And three dead, whom their strength could not avail
    To heave into the deep with those before,
Though the two sharks still followed them, and dashed
The spray into their faces as they splashed.

102

Famine — despair — cold thirst and heat, had done
    Their work on them by turns, and thinned them to
Such things a mother had not known her son
    Amidst the skeletons of that gaunt crew;
By night chilled, by day scorched, thus one by one
    They perished, until withered to these few,
But chiefly by a species of self-slaughter,
In washing down Pedrillo with salt water.

103

As they drew nigh the land, which now was seen
    Unequal in its aspect here and there,
They felt the freshness of its growing green,
    That waved in forest-tops, and smoothed the air,
And fell upon their glazed eyes like a screen
    From glistening waves, and skies so hot and bare —
Lovely seemed any object that should sweep
Away the vast —salt — dread — eternal Deep.

104

The shore looked wild, without a trace of man,
    And girt by formidable waves; but they
Were mad for land, and thus their course they ran,
    Though right ahead the roaring breakers lay:
A reef between them also now began
    To show its boiling surf and bounding spray,
But finding no place for their landing better,
They ran the boat for shore, — and overset her.

105

But in his native stream, the Guadalquivir,
  Juan to lave his youthful limbs was wont;
And having learnt to swim in that sweet river,
  Had often turned the art to some account:
A better swimmer you could scarce see ever,
  He could, perhaps, have passed the Hellespont,
As once (a feat on which ourselves we prided)
Leander, Mr. Ekenhead, and I did.

106

So here, though faint, emaciated, and stark,
  He buoyed his boyish limbs, and strove to ply
With the quick wave, and gain, ere it was dark,
  The beach which lay before him, high and dry:
The greatest danger here was from a shark,
  That carried off his neighbour by the thigh;
As for the other two, they could not swim,
So nobody arrived on shore but him.

107

Nor yet had he arrived but for the oar,
  Which, providentially for him, was washed
Just as his feeble arms could strike no more,
  And the hard wave o'erwhelmed him as 't was dashed
Within his grasp; he clung to it, and sore
  The waters beat while he thereto was lashed;
At last, with swimming, wading, scrambling, he
Rolled on the beach, half-senseless, from the sea:

108

There, breathless, with his digging nails he clung
  Fast to the sand, lest the returning wave,
From whose reluctant roar his life he wrung,

105:8. *Mr. Ekenhead and I did*: See *Written after Swimming from Sestos to Abydos* and note, above.

Should suck him back to her insatiate grave:
And there he lay, full length, where he was flung,
  Before the entrance of a cliff-worn cave,
With just enough of life to feel its pain,
And deem that it was saved, perhaps, in vain.

109

With slow and staggering effort he arose,
  But sank again upon his bleeding knee
And quivering hand; and then he looked for those
  Who long had been his mates upon the sea;
But none of them appeared to share his woes,
  Save one, a corpse, from out the famished three,
Who died two days before, and now had found
An unknown barren beach for burial ground.

110

And as he gazed, his dizzy brain spun fast,
  And down he sunk; and as he sunk, the sand
Swam round and round, and all his senses passed:
  He fell upon his side, and his stretched hand
Drooped dripping on the oar (their jury-mast),
  And, like a withered lily, on the land
His slender frame and pallid aspect lay,
As fair a thing as e'er was formed of clay.

111

How long in his damp trance young Juan lay
  He knew not, for the earth was gone for him,
And Time had nothing more of night nor day
  For his congealing blood, and senses dim;
And how this heavy faintness passed away
  He knew not, till each painful pulse and limb,
And tingling vein, seemed throbbing back to life,
For Death, though vanquished, still retired with strife.

112

His eyes he opened, shut, again unclosed,
  For all was doubt and dizziness; he thought

He still was in the boat, and had but dozed,
    And felt again with his despair o'erwrought,
And wished it Death in which he had reposed,
    And then once more his feelings back were brought,
And slowly by his swimming eyes was seen
A lovely female face of seventeen.

113

'T was bending close o'er his, and the small mouth
    Seemed almost prying into his for breath;
And chafing him, the soft warm hand of youth
    Recalled his answering spirits back from Death:
And, bathing his chill temples, tried to soothe
    Each pulse to animation, till beneath
Its gentle touch and trembling care, a sigh
To these kind efforts made a low reply.

114

Then was the cordial poured, and mantle flung
    Around his scarce-clad limbs; and the fair arm
Raised higher the faint head which o'er it hung;
    And her transparent cheek, all pure and warm,
Pillowed his death-like forehead; then she wrung
    His dewy curls, long drenched by every storm;
And watched with eagerness each throb that drew
A sigh from his heaved bosom — and hers, too.

115

And lifting him with care into the cave,
    The gentle girl, and her attendant, — one
Young, yet her elder, and of brows less grave,
    And more robust of figure, — then begun
To kindle fire, and as the new flames gave
    Light to the rocks that roofed them, which the sun
Had never seen, the maid, or whatsoe'er
She was, appeared, distinct, and tall, and fair.

116

Her brow was overhung with coins of gold,
   That sparkled o'er the auburn of her hair —
Her clustering hair, whose longer locks were rolled
   In braids behind; and though her stature were
Even of the highest for a female mould,
   They nearly reached her heel; and in her air
There was a something which bespoke command,
As one who was a Lady in the land.

117

Her hair, I said, was auburn; but her eyes
   Were black as Death, their lashes the same hue,
Of downcast length, in whose silk shadow lies
   Deepest attraction, for when to the view
Forth from its raven fringe the full glance flies,
   Ne'er with such force the swiftest arrow flew;
'T is as the snake late coiled, who pours his length,
And hurls at once his venom and his strength.

118

Her brow was white and low, her cheek's pure dye
   Like twilight rosy still with the set sun;
Short upper lip — sweet lips! that make us sigh
   Ever to have seen such; for she was one
Fit for the model of a statuary
   (A race of mere impostors, when all's done —
I've seen much finer women, ripe and real,
Than all the nonsense of their stone ideal).

119

I 'll tell you why I say so, for 't is just
   One should not rail without a decent cause:
There was an Irish lady, to whose bust
   I ne'er saw justice done, and yet she was
A frequent model; and if e'er she must
   Yield to stern Time and Nature's wrinkling laws,
They will destroy a face which mortal thought
Ne'er compassed, nor less mortal chisel wrought.

120

And such was she, the lady of the cave:
    Her dress was very different from the Spanish,
Simpler, and yet of colours not so grave;
    For, as you know, the Spanish women banish
Bright hues when out of doors, and yet, while wave
    Around them (what I hope will never vanish)
The basquiña and the mantilla, they
Seem at the same time mystical and gay.

121

But with our damsel this was not the case:
    Her dress was many-coloured, finely spun;
Her locks curled negligently round her face,
    But through them gold and gems profusely shone:
Her girdle sparkled, and the richest lace
    Flowed in her veil, and many a precious stone
Flashed on her little hand; but, what was shocking,
Her small snow feet had slippers, but no stocking.

122

The other female's dress was not unlike,
    But of inferior materials: she
Had not so many ornaments to strike,
    Her hair had silver only, bound to be
Her dowry; and her veil, in form alike,
    Was coarser; and her air, though firm, less free;
Her hair was thicker, but less long; her eyes
As black, but quicker, and of smaller size.

123

And these two tended him, and cheered him both
    With food and raiment, and those soft attentions,
Which are — as I must own — of female growth,
    And have ten thousand delicate inventions:
They made a most superior mess of broth,

120:7. *basquina and the mantilla*: The first is a dark outer skirt worn
on going out of doors; the second, a capelike cloak.

A thing which poesy but seldom mentions,
But the best dish that e'er was cooked since Homer's
Achilles ordered dinner for new comers.

124

I'll tell you who they were, this female pair,
   Lest they should seem Princesses in disguise;
Besides, I hate all mystery, and that air
   Of clap-trap, which your recent poets prize;
And so, in short, the girls they really were
   They shall appear before your curious eyes,
Mistress and maid; the first was only daughter
Of an old man, who lived upon the water.

125

A fisherman he had been in his youth,
   And still a sort of fisherman was he;
But other speculations were, in sooth,
   Added to his connection with the sea,
Perhaps not so respectable, in truth:
   A little smuggling, and some piracy,
Left him, at last, the sole of many masters
Of an ill-gotten million of piastres.

126

A fisher, therefore, was he, — though of men,
   Like Peter the Apostle, and he fished
For wandering merchant-vessels, now and then,
   And sometimes caught as many as he wished;
The cargoes he confiscated, and gain
   He sought in the slave-market too, and dished
Full many a morsel for that Turkish trade,
By which, no doubt, a good deal may be made.

123:8. *Achilles order'd dinner*: When Ajax, Ulysses and Phoenix came
to Achilles' tent to persuade him to return to the battle against Troy,
he prepared a great feast for them (*Iliad*, IX).
125:8. *piastres*: Turkish coins.

127

He was a Greek, and on his isle had built
   (One of the wild and smaller Cyclades)
A very handsome house from out his guilt,
   And there he lived exceedingly at ease;
Heaven knows what cash he got, or blood he spilt,
   A sad old fellow was he, if you please;
But this I know, it was a spacious building,
Full of barbaric carving, paint, and gilding.

128

He had an only daughter, called Haidée,
   The greatest heiress of the Eastern Isles;
Besides, so very beautiful was she,
   Her dowry was as nothing to her smiles:
Still in her teens, and like a lovely tree
   She grew to womanhood, and between whiles
Rejected several suitors, just to learn
How to accept a better in his turn.

129

And walking out upon the beach, below
   The cliff, towards sunset, on that day she found,
Insensible, — not dead, but nearly so, —
   Don Juan, almost famished, and half drowned;
But being naked, she was shocked, you know,
   Yet deemed herself in common pity bound,
As far as in her lay, "to take him in,
A stranger" dying — with so white a skin.

130

But taking him into her father's house
   Was not exactly the best way to save,
But like conveying to the cat the mouse,
   Or people in a trance into their grave;

127:2. *Cyclades*: Greek islands in the Aegean Sea.
128:1. *Haidée*: Byron probably took the name (meaning "the caressed one") from a Greek folk song which he translated in Athens in 1811.

Because the good old man had so much "νους,"
   Unlike the honest Arab thieves so brave,
He would have hospitably cured the stranger,
And sold him instantly when out of danger.

131

And therefore, with her maid, she thought it best
   (A virgin always on her maid relies)
To place him in the cave for present rest:
   And when, at last, he opened his black eyes,
Their charity increased about their guest;
   And their compassion grew to such a size,
It opened half the turnpike-gates to Heaven —
(St. Paul says, 't is the toll which must be given).

132

They made a fire, — but such a fire as they
   Upon the moment could contrive with such
Materials as were cast up round the bay, —
   Some broken planks, and oars, that to the touch
Were nearly tinder, since, so long they lay,
   A mast was almost crumbled to a crutch;
But, by God's grace, here wrecks were in such plenty,
That there was fuel to have furnished twenty.

133

He had a bed of furs, and a pelisse,
   For Haidée stripped her sables off to make
His couch; and, that he might be more at ease,
   And warm, in case by chance he should awake,
They also gave a petticoat apiece,
   She and her maid, — and promised by daybreak
To pay him a fresh visit, with a dish
For breakfast, of eggs, coffee, bread, and fish.

130:5. "νους": Mind or intelligence.
131:8. *St. Paul says*: *Hebrews* 10:34.
133:1. *pelisse*: Long cloak made of or lined with furs.

134

And thus they left him to his lone repose:
    Juan slept like a top, or like the dead,
Who sleep at last, perhaps (God only knows),
    Just for the present: and in his lulled head
Not even a vision of his former woes
    Throbbed in accurséd dreams, which sometimes spread
Unwelcome visions of our former years,
Till the eye, cheated, opens thick with tears.

135

Young Juan slept all dreamless: — but the maid,
    Who smoothed his pillow, as she left the den
Looked back upon him, and a moment stayed
    And turned, believing that he called again.
He slumbered; yet she thought, at least she said
    (The heart will slip, even as the tongue and pen),
He had pronounced her name — but she forgot
That at this moment Juan knew it not.

136

And pensive to her father's house she went,
    Enjoining silence strict to Zoe, who
Better than her knew what, in fact, she meant,
    She being wiser by a year or two:
A year or two 's an age when rightly spent,
    And Zoe spent hers, as most women do,
In gaining all that useful sort of knowledge
Which is acquired in Nature's good old college.

137

The morn broke, and found Juan slumbering still
    Fast in his cave, and nothing clashed upon
His rest; the rushing of the neighbouring rill,
    And the young beams of the excluded Sun,
Troubled him not, and he might sleep his fill;
    And need he had of slumber yet, for none

Had suffered more — his hardships were comparative
To those related in my grand-dad's "Narrative."

138

Not so Haidée; she sadly tossed and tumbled,
    And started from her sleep, and, turning o'er,
Dreamed of a thousand wrecks, o'er which she stumbled,
    And handsome corpses strewed upon the shore;
And woke her maid so early that she grumbled,
    And called her father's old slaves up, who swore
In several oaths — Armenian, Turk, and Greek —
They knew not what to think of such a freak.

139

But up she got, and up she made them get,
    With some pretence about the Sun, that makes
Sweet skies just when he rises, or is set;
    And 't is, no doubt, a sight to see when breaks
Bright Phœbus, while the mountains still are wet
    With mist, and every bird with him awakes,
And night is flung off like a mourning suit
Worn for a husband, — or some other brute.

140

I say, the Sun is a most glorious sight,
    I 've seen him rise full oft, indeed of late
I have sat up on purpose all the night,
    Which hastens, as physicians say, one's fate;
And so all ye, who would be in the right
    In health and purse, begin your day to date
From daybreak, and when coffined at four-score,
Engrave upon the plate, you rose at four.

141

And Haidée met the morning face to face;
    Her own was freshest, though a feverish flush

137:8. *grand-dad's Narrative*: Byron's grandfather had been shipwrecked
on the coast of Patagonia in 1740, and suffered great hardships in getting
back to England. He published his *Narrative* in 1768.

Had dyed it with the headlong blood; whose race
   From heart to cheek is curbed into a blush,
Like to a torrent which a moutain's base,
   That overpowers some Alpine river's rush,
Checks to a lake, whose waves in circles spread;
Or the Red Sea — but the sea is not red.

142

And down the cliff the island virgin came,
   And near the cave her quick light footsteps drew,
While the Sun smiled on her with his first flame,
   And young Aurora kissed her lips with dew,
Taking her for a sister; just the same
   Mistake you would have made on seeing the two,
Although the mortal, quite as fresh and fair,
Had all the advantage, too, of not being air.

143

And when into the cavern Haidée stepped
   All timidly, yet rapidly, she saw
That like an infant Juan sweetly slept;
   And then she stopped, and stood as if in awe
(For sleep is awful), and on tiptoe crept
   And wrapped him closer, lest the air, too raw,
Should reach his blood, then o'er him still as Death
Bent, with hushed lips, that drank his scarce-drawn breath.

144

And thus like to an Angel o'er the dying
   Who die in righteousness, she leaned; and there
All tranquilly the shipwrecked boy was lying,
   As o'er him lay the calm and stirless air:
But Zoe the meantime some eggs was frying,
   Since, after all, no doubt the youthful pair
Must breakfast — and betimes, lest they should ask it,
She drew out her provision from the basket.

145

She knew that the best feelings must have victual,
　　And that a shipwrecked youth would hungry be;
Besides, being less in love, she yawned a little,
　　And felt her veins chilled by the neighbouring sea;
And so, she cooked their breakfast to a tittle;
　　I can't say that she gave them any tea,
But there were eggs, fruit, coffee, bread, fish, honey,
With Scio wine, — and all for love, not money.

146

And Zoe, when the eggs were ready, and
　　The coffee made, would fain have wakened Juan;
But Haidée stopped her with her quick small hand,
　　And without a word, a sign her finger drew on
Her lip, which Zoe needs must understand;
　　And, the first breakfast spoilt, prepared a new one,
Because her mistress would not let her break
That sleep which seemed as it would ne'er awake.

147

For still he lay, and on his thin worn cheek
　　A purple hectic played like dying day
On the snow-tops of distant hills; the streak
　　Of sufferance yet upon his forehead lay,
Where the blue veins looked shadowy, shrunk, and weak;
　　And his black curls were dewy with the spray,
Which weighed upon them yet, all damp and salt,
Mixed with the stony vapours of the vault.

148

And she bent o'er him, and he lay beneath,
　　Hushed as a babe upon its mother's breast,
Drooped as the willow when no winds can breathe,
　　Lulled like the depth of Ocean when at rest,
Fair as the crowning rose of the whole wreath,
　　Soft as the callow cygnet in its nest;
In short, he was a very pretty fellow,
Although his woes had turned him rather yellow.

149

He woke and gazed, and would have slept again,
    But the fair face which met his eye forbade
Those eyes to close, though weariness and pain
    Had further sleep a further pleasure made:
For Woman's face was never formed in vain
    For Juan, so that even when he prayed
He turned from grisly saints, and martyrs hairy,
To the sweet portraits of the Virgin Mary.

150

And thus upon his elbow he arose,
    And looked upon the lady, in whose cheek
The pale contended with the purple rose,
    As with an effort she began to speak;
Her eyes were eloquent, her words would pose,
    Although she told him, in good modern Greek,
With an Ionian accent, low and sweet,
That he was faint, and must not talk, but eat.

151

Now Juan could not understand a word,
    Being no Grecian; but he had an ear,
And her voice was the warble of a bird,
    So soft, so sweet, so delicately clear,
That finer, simpler music ne'er was heard;
    The sort of sound we echo with a tear,
Without knowing why — an overpowering tone,
Whence Melody descends as from a throne.

152

And Juan gazed as one who is awoke
    By a distant organ, doubting if he be
Not yet a dreamer, till the spell is broke
    By the watchman, or some such reality,
Or by one's early valet's curséd knock;
    At least it is a heavy sound to me,
Who like a morning slumber — for the night
Shows stars and women in a better light.

153

And Juan, too, was helped out from his dream,
  Or sleep, or whatsoe'er it was, by feeling
A most prodigious appetite; the steam
  Of Zoe's cookery no doubt was stealing
Upon his senses, and the kindling beam
  Of the new fire, which Zoe kept up, kneeling,
To stir her viands, made him quite awake
And long for food, but chiefly a beef-steak.

154

But beef is rare within these oxless isles;
  Goat's flesh there is, no doubt, and kid, and mutton,
And, when a holiday upon them smiles,
  A joint upon their barbarous spits they put on:
But this occurs but seldom, between whiles,
  For some of these are rocks with scarce a hut on;
Others are fair and fertile, among which
This, though not large, was one of the most rich.

155

I say that beef is rare, and can't help thinking
  That the old fable of the Minotaur —
From which our modern morals, rightly shrinking,
  Condemn the royal lady's taste who wore
A cow's shape for a mask — was only (sinking
  The allegory) a mere type, no more,
That Pasiphae promoted breeding cattle,
To make the Cretans bloodier in battle.

156

For we all know that English people are
  Fed upon beef — I won't say much of beer,
Because 't is liquor only, and being far

155:2. *Minotaur*: Pasiphae, wife of Minos, king of Crete, fell in love
with a white bull presented to her husband by Poseidon, the sea god, and
gave birth to the Minotaur, a monster with the head of a bull and body
of a man.

From this my subject, has no business here;
We know, too, they are very fond of war,
    A pleasure — like all pleasures — rather dear;
So were the Cretans — from which I infer,
That beef and battles both were owing to her.

157

But to resume. The languid Juan raised
    His head upon his elbow, and he saw
A sight on which he had not lately gazed,
    As all his latter meals had been quite raw,
Three or four things, for which the Lord he praised,
    And, feeling still the famished vulture gnaw,
He fell upon whate'er was offered, like
A priest, a shark, an alderman, or pike.

158

He ate, and he was well supplied; and she,
    Who watched him like a mother, would have fed
Him past all bounds, because she smiled to see
    Such appetite in one she had deemed dead:
But Zoe, being older than Haidée,
    Knew (by tradition, for she ne'er had read)
That famished people, must be slowly nurst,
And fed by spoonfuls, else they always burst.

159

And so she took the liberty to state,
    Rather by deeds than words, because the case
Was urgent, that the gentleman, whose fate
    Had made her mistress quit her bed to trace
The sea-shore at this hour, must leave his plate,
    Unless he wished to die upon the place —
She snatched it, and refused another morsel,
Saying, he had gorged enough to make a horse ill.

160

Next they — he being naked, save a tattered
    Pair of scarce trowsers — went to work,

And in the fire his recent rags they scattered,
    And dressed him, for the present, like a Turk,
Or Greek — that is, although it not much mattered,
    Omitting turban, slippers, pistol, dirk, —
They furnished him, entire, except some stitches,
With a clean shirt, and very spacious breeches.

161

And then fair Haidée tried her tongue at speaking,
    But not a word could Juan comprehend,
Although he listened so that the young Greek in
    Her earnestness would ne'er have made an end;
And, as he interrupted not, went eking
    Her speech out to her protégé and friend,
Till pausing at the last her breath to take,
She saw he did not understand Romaic.

162

And then she had recourse to nods, and signs,
    And smiles, and sparkles of the speaking eye,
And read (the only book she could) the lines
    Of his fair face, and found, by sympathy,
The answer eloquent, where the Soul shines
    And darts in one quick glance a long reply;
And thus in every look she saw expressed
A world of words, and things at which she guessed.

163

And now, by dint of fingers and of eyes,
    And words repeated after her, he took
A lesson in her tongue; but by surmise,
    No doubt, less of her language than her look:
As he who studies fervently the skies
    Turns oftener to the stars than to his book,
Thus Juan learned his *alpha beta* better
From Haidée's glance than any graven letter.

161:8. *Romaic*: Modern Greek vernacular.

164

'T is pleasing to be schooled in a strange tongue
 By female lips and eyes — that is, I mean,
When both the teacher and the taught are young,
 As was the case, at least, where I have been;
They smile so when one 's right, and when one 's wrong
 They smile still more, and then there intervene
Pressure of hands, perhaps even a chaste kiss; —
I learned the little that I know by this:

165

That is, some words of Spanish, Turk, and Greek,
 Italian not at all, having no teachers;
Much English I cannot pretend to speak,
 Learning that language chiefly from its preachers,
Barrow, South, Tillotson, whom every week
 I study, also Blair — the highest reachers
Of eloquence in piety and prose —
I hate your poets, so read none of those.

166

As for the ladies, I have nought to say,
 A wanderer from the British world of Fashion,
Where I, like other "dogs, have had my day,"
 Like other men, too, may have had my passion —
But that, like other things, has passed away,
 And all her fools whom I *could* lay the lash on:
Foes, friends, men, women, now are nought to me
But dreams of what has been, no more to be.

167

Return we to Don Juan. He begun
 To hear new words, and to repeat them; but

165:2. Byron had originally written "Italian rather more, having more teachers" which was closer to the truth. But the change suits the role of ironic narrator that he is cultivating.

165:5–6. *Barrow* (1630–1677); *South* (1633–1716); and *Tillotson* (1630–1694) were all theological writers. Hugh *Blair* (1718–1800) wrote *Lectures on Rhetoric*, an influential textbook.

Some feelings, universal as the Sun,
 Were such as could not in his breast be shut
More than within the bosom of a nun:
 He was in love, — as you would be, no doubt,
With a young benefactress, — so was she,
Just in the way we very often see.

168

And every day by daybreak — rather early
 For Juan, who was somewhat fond of rest —
She came into the cave, but it was merely
 To see her bird reposing in his nest;
And she would softly stir his locks so curly,
 Without disturbing her yet slumbering guest,
Breathing all gently o'er his cheek and mouth,
As o'er a bed of roses the sweet South.

169

And every morn his colour freshlier came,
 And every day helped on his convalescence;
'T was well, because health in the human frame
 Is pleasant, besides being true Love's essence,
For health and idleness to Passion's flame
 Are oil and gunpowder; and some good lessons
Are also learnt from Ceres and from Bacchus,
Without whom Venus will not long attack us.

170

While Venus fills the heart, (without heart, really,
 Love, though good always, is not quite so good,)
Ceres presents a plate of vermicelli, —
 For Love must be sustained like flesh and blood, —
While Bacchus pours out wine, or hands a jelly:
 Eggs, oysters, too, are amatory food;
But who is their purveyor from above
Heaven knows, — it may be Neptune, Pan, or Jove.

169:7–8. *Ceres . . . Bacchus . . . Venus*: i.e. Venus (Love) cannot continue without support from Ceres (food) and Bacchus (wine).

171

When Juan woke he found some good things ready,
   A bath, a breakfast, and the finest eyes
That ever made a youthful heart less steady,
   Besides her maid's, as pretty for their size;
But I have spoken of all this already —
   A repetition 's tiresome and unwise, —
Well — Juan, after bathing in the sea,
Came always back to coffee and Haidée.

172

Both were so young, and one so innocent,
   That bathing passed for nothing; Juan seemed
To her, as 't were, the kind of being sent,
   Of whom these two years she had nightly dreamed,
A something to be loved, a creature meant
   To be her happiness, and whom she deemed
To render happy; all who joy would win
Must share it, — Happiness was born a Twin.

173

It was such pleasure to behold him, such
   Enlargement of existence to partake
Nature with him, to thrill beneath his touch,
   To watch him slumbering, and to see him wake:
To live with him for ever were too much;
   But then the thought of parting made her quake;
He was her own, her ocean-treasure, cast
Like a rich wreck — her first love, and her last.

174

And thus a moon rolled on, and fair Haidée
   Paid daily visits to her boy, and took
Such plentiful precautions, that still he
   Remained unknown within his craggy nook;
At last her father's prows put out to sea,
   For certain merchantmen upon the look,

Not as of yore to carry off an Io,
But three Ragusan vessels, bound for Scio.

175

Then came her freedom, for she had no mother,
    So that, her father being at sea, she was
Free as a married woman, or such other
    Female, as where she likes may freely pass,
Without even the encumbrance of a brother,
    The freest she that ever gazed on glass:
I speak of Christian lands in this comparison,
Where wives, at least, are seldom kept in garrison.

176

Now she prolonged her visits and her talk
    (For they must talk), and he had learnt to say
So much as to propose to take a walk, —
    For little had he wandered since the day
On which, like a young flower snapped from the stalk,
    Drooping and dewy on the beach he lay, —
And thus they walked out in the afternoon,
And saw the sun set opposite the moon.

177

It was a wild and breaker-beaten coast,
    With cliffs above, and a broad sandy shore,
Guarded by shoals and rocks as by an host,
    With here and there a creek, whose aspect wore
A better welcome to the tempest-tost;
    And rarely ceased the haughty billow's roar,
Save on the dead long summer days, which make
The outstretched Ocean glitter like a lake.

   174:7. *Io*: According to Greek myth she was carried off by Phoenician traders.
   174:8. *Ragusan vessels, bound for Scio*: Ragusa is the Italian name for Dubrovnik on the Adriatic coast in Yugoslavia; Scio (Chios) is an Aegean island.

178

And the small ripple spilt upon the beach
   Scarcely o'erpassed the cream of your champagne,
When o'er the brim the sparkling bumpers reach,
   That spring-dew of the spirit! the heart's rain!
Few things surpass old wine; and they may preach
   Who please, — the more because they preach in vain, —
Let us have Wine and Woman, Mirth and Laughter,
Sermons and soda-water the day after.

179

Man, being reasonable, must get drunk;
   The best of Life is but intoxication:
Glory, the Grape, Love, Gold, in these are sunk
   The hopes of all men, and of every nation;
Without their sap, how branchless were the trunk
   Of Life's strange tree, so fruitful on occasion!
But to return, — Get very drunk, and when
You wake with headache — you shall see what then!

180

Ring for your valet — bid him quickly bring
   Some hock and soda-water, then you 'll know
A pleasure worthy Xerxes the great king;
   For not the blest sherbet, sublimed with snow,
Nor the first sparkle of the desert-spring,
   Nor Burgundy in all its sunset glow,
After long travel, Ennui, Love, or Slaughter,
Vie with that draught of hock and soda-water!

181

The coast — I think it was the coast that I
   Was just describing — Yes, it *was* the coast —
Lay at this period quiet as the sky,
   The sands untumbled, the blue waves untossed,
And all was stillness, save the sea-bird's cry,
   And dolphin's leap, and the little billow crossed

By some low rock or shelve, that made it fret
Against the boundary it scarcely wet.

182

And forth they wandered, her sire being gone,
    As I have said, upon an expedition;
And mother, brother, guardian, she had none,
    Save Zoe, who, although with due precision
She waited on her lady with the Sun,
    Thought daily service was her only mission,
Bringing warm water, wreathing her long tresses,
And asking now and then for cast-off dresses.

183

It was the cooling hour, just when the rounded
    Red sun sinks down behind the azure hill,
Which then seems as if the whole earth it bounded,
    Circling all Nature, hushed, and dim, and still,
With the far mountain-crescent half surrounded
    On one side, and the deep sea calm and chill
Upon the other, and the rosy sky
With one star sparkling through it like an eye.

184

And thus they wandered forth, and hand in hand,
    Over the shining pebbles and the shells,
Glided along the smooth and hardened sand,
    And in the worn and wild receptacles
Worked by the storms, yet worked as it were planned —
    In hollow halls, with sparry roofs and cells,
They turned to rest; and, each clasped by an arm,
Yielded to the deep Twilight's purple charm.

185

They looked up to the sky, whose floating glow
    Spread like a rosy Ocean, vast and bright;
They gazed upon the glittering sea below,

Whence the broad Moon rose circling into sight;
They heard the waves' splash, and the wind so low,
    And saw each other's dark eyes darting light
Into each other — and, beholding this,
Their lips drew near, and clung into a kiss;

186

A long, long kiss, a kiss of Youth, and Love,
    And Beauty, all concentrating like rays
Into one focus, kindled from above;
    Such kisses as belong to early days,
Where Heart, and Soul, and Sense, in concert move,
    And the blood 's lava, and the pulse a blaze,
Each kiss a heart-quake, — for a kiss's strength,
I think, it must be reckoned by its length.

187

By length I mean duration; theirs endured
    Heaven knows how long — no doubt they never reckoned;
And if they had, they could not have secured
    The sum of their sensations to a second:
They had not spoken, but they felt allured,
    As if their souls and lips each other beckoned,
Which, being joined, like swarming bees they clung —
Their hearts the flowers from whence the honey sprung.

188

They were alone, but not alone as they
    Who shut in chambers think it loneliness;
The silent Ocean, and the starlight bay,
    The twilight glow, which momently grew less,
The voiceless sands, and dropping caves, that lay
    Around them, made them to each other press,
As if there were no life beneath the sky
Save theirs, and that their life could never die.

189

They feared no eyes nor ears on that lone beach;
    They felt no terrors from the night; they were

All in all to each other: though their speech
   Was broken words, they *thought* a language there, —
And all the burning tongues the Passions teach
   Found in one sigh the best interpreter
Of Nature's oracle — first love, — that all
Which Eve has left her daughters since her fall.

190

Haidée spoke not of scruples, asked no vows,
   Nor offered any; she had never heard
Of plight and promises to be a spouse,
   Or perils by a loving maid incurred;
She was all which pure Ignorance allows,
   And flew to her young mate like a young bird;
And, never having dreamt of falsehood, she
Had not one word to say of constancy.

191

She loved, and was belovéd — she adored,
   And she was worshipped after Nature's fashion —
Their intense souls, into each other poured,
   If souls could die, had perished in that passion, —
But by degrees their senses were restored,
   Again to be o'ercome, again to dash on;
And, beating 'gainst *his* bosom, Haidée's heart
Felt as if never more to beat apart.

192

Alas! they were so young, so beautiful,
   So lonely, loving, helpless, and the hour
Was that in which the Heart is always full,
   And, having o'er itself no further power,
Prompts deeds Eternity can not annul,
   But pays off moments in an endless shower
Of hell-fire — all prepared for people giving
Pleasure or pain to one another living.

193

Alas! for Juan and Haidée! they were
    So loving and so lovely — till then never,
Excepting our first parents, such a pair
    Had run the risk of being damned for ever:
And Haidée, being devout as well as fair,
    Had, doubtless, heard about the Stygian river,
And Hell and Purgatory — but forgot
Just in the very crisis she should not.

194

They look upon each other, and their eyes
    Gleam in the moonlight; and her white arm clasps
Round Juan's head, and his around her lies
    Half buried in the tresses which it grasps;
She sits upon his knee, and drinks his sighs,
    He hers, until they end in broken gasps;
And thus they form a group that 's quite antique,
Half naked, loving, natural, and Greek.

195

And when those deep and burning moments passed,
    And Juan sunk to sleep within her arms,
She slept not, but all tenderly, though fast,
    Sustained his head upon her bosom's charms;
And now and then her eye to Heaven is cast,
    And then on the pale cheek her breast now warms,
Pillowed on her o'erflowing heart, which pants
With all it granted, and with all it grants.

196

An infant when it gazes on a light,
    A child the moment when it drains the breast,
A devotee when soars the Host in sight,
    An Arab with a stranger for a guest,

193:6. *Stygian river*: See above, note to 101:3.

A sailor when the prize has struck in fight,
    A miser filling his most hoarded chest,
Feel rapture; but not such true joy are reaping
As they who watch o'er what they love while sleeping.

197

For there it lies so tranquil, so beloved,
    All that it hath of Life with us is living;
So gentle, stirless, helpless, and unmoved,
    And all unconscious of the joy 't is giving;
All it hath felt, inflicted, passed, and proved,
    Hushed into depths beyond the watcher's diving:
There lies the thing we love with all its errors
And all its charms — like Death without its terrors.

198

The Lady watched her lover — and that hour
    Of Love's, and Night's, and Ocean's solitude,
O'erflowed her soul with their united power;
    Amidst the barren sand and rocks so rude
She and her wave-worn love had made their bower,
    Where nought upon their passion could intrude,
And all the stars that crowded the blue space
Saw nothing happier than her glowing face.

199

Alas! the love of Women! it is known
    To be a lovely and a fearful thing;
For all of theirs upon that die is thrown,
    And if 't is lost, Life hath no more to bring
To them but mockeries of the past alone,
    And their revenge is as the tiger's spring,
Deadly, and quick, and crushing; yet, as real
Torture is theirs — what they inflict they feel.

200

They are right; for Man, to man so oft unjust,
    Is always so to Women: one sole bond

Awaits them — treachery is all their trust;
   Taught to conceal, their bursting hearts despond
Over their idol, till some wealthier lust
   Buys them in marriage — and what rests beyond?
A thankless husband — next, a faithless lover —
Then dressing, nursing, praying — and all's over.

201

Some take a lover, some take drams or prayers,
   Some mind their household, others dissipation,
Some run away, and but exchange their cares,
   Losing the advantage of a virtuous station;
Few changes e'er can better their affairs,
   Theirs being an unnatural situation,
From the dull palace, to the dirty hovel:
Some play the devil, and then write a novel.

202

Haidée was Nature's bride, and knew not this;
   Haidée was Passion's child, born where the Sun
Showers triple light, and scorches even the kiss
   Of his gazelle-eyed daughters; she was one
Made but to love, to feel that she was his
   Who was her chosen: what was said or done
Elsewhere was nothing. She had nought to fear,
Hope, care, nor love, beyond, — her heart beat *here*.

203

And oh! that quickening of the heart, that beat!
   How much it costs us! yet each rising throb
Is in its cause as its effect so sweet,
   That Wisdom, ever on the watch to rob
Joy of its alchemy, and to repeat
   Fine truths; even Conscience, too, has a tough job

201:8. *write a novel*: Lady Caroline Lamb wrote a novel, *Glenarvon* (1816), in which she gave an account of her affair with Byron. See *Remember Thee!*

To make us understand each good old maxim,
So good — I wonder Castlereagh don't tax 'em.

204

And now 't was done — on the lone shore were plighted
   Their hearts; the stars, their nuptial torches, shed
Beauty upon the beautiful they lighted:
   Ocean their witness, and the cave their bed,
By their own feelings hallowed and united,
   Their priest was Solitude, and they were wed:
And they were happy — for to their young eyes
Each was an angel, and earth Paradise.

205

Oh, Love! of whom great Cæsar was the suitor,
   Titus the master, Antony the slave,
Horace, Catullus, scholars — Ovid tutor —
   Sappho the sage blue-stocking, in whose grave
All those may leap who rather would be neuter —
   (Leucadia's rock still overlooks the wave) —
Oh, Love! thou art the very God of evil,
For, after all, we cannot call thee Devil.

206

Thou mak'st the chaste connubial state precarious,
   And jestest with the brows of mightiest men:
Cæsar and Pompey, Mahomet, Belisarius;
   Have much employed the Muse of History's pen:

203:8. *Castlereagh*: See note to Dedication, 11:8.

205:2–3. *Titus* conquered his passion for the licentious Berenice and
sent her away from Rome when he became emperor; *Anthony* was enslaved by love for Cleopatra; *Horace* and *Catullus* wrote love lyrics; and
Ovid wrote the *Art of Love*. See above, I, 42.

205:4–6. *Sappho . . . Leucadia's rock*: According to legend, Sappho
leaped from a rock on the island of Leucadia because of unrequited love
for the youth Phaon.

206:3. The wives of all these men were rumored to have been unfaith-
ful. Belisarius (c. 505–565) was a famous general during the reign of
Justinian.

Their lives and fortunes were extremely various,
 Such worthies Time will never see again;
Yet to these four in three things the same luck holds,
They all were heroes, conquerors, and cuckolds.

207

Thou mak'st philosophers; there 's Epicurus
 And Aristippus, a material crew!
Who to immoral courses would allure us
 By theories quite practicable too;
If only from the Devil they would insure us,
 How pleasant were the maxim (not quite new),
"Eat, drink, and love, what can the rest avail us?"
So said the royal sage Sardanapalus.

208

But Juan! had he quite forgotten Julia?
 And should he have forgotten her so soon?
I can't but say it seems to me most truly a
 Perplexing question; but, no doubt, the moon
Does these things for us, and whenever newly a
 Strong palpitation rises, 't is her boon,
Else how the devil is it that fresh features
Have such a charm for us poor human creatures?

209

I hate inconstancy — I loathe, detest,
 Abhor, condemn, abjure the mortal made
Of such quicksilver clay that in his breast
 No permanent foundation can be laid;
Love, constant love, has been my constant guest,
 And yet last night, being at a masquerade,
I saw the prettiest creature, fresh from Milan,
Which gave me some sensations like a villain.

207:2. *Aristippus*: Greek hedonist philosopher (d. 356 B.C.).
207:8. *Sardanapalus*: Legendary king of Assyria (possibly ninth century B.C.) about whom Byron wrote a poetical drama (1821).

210

But soon Philosophy came to my aid,
   And whispered, "Think of every sacred tie!"
"I will, my dear Philosophy!" I said,
   "But then her teeth, and then, oh, Heaven! her eye!
I 'll just inquire if she be wife or maid,
   Or neither — out of curiosity."
"Stop!" cried Philosophy, with air so Grecian,
(Though she was masqued then as a fair Venetian;)

211

"Stop!" so I stopped. — But to return: that which
   Men call inconstancy is nothing more
Than admiration due where Nature's rich
   Profusion with young beauty covers o'er
Some favoured object; and as in the niche
   A lovely statue we almost adore,
This sort of adoration of the real
Is but a heightening of the *beau ideal*.

212

'T is the perception of the Beautiful,
   A fine extension of the faculties,
Platonic, universal, wonderful,
   Drawn from the stars, and filtered through the skies,
Without which Life would be extremely dull;
   In short, it is the use of our own eyes,
With one or two small senses added, just
To hint that flesh is formed of fiery dust.

213

Yet 't is a painful feeling, and unwilling,
   For surely if we always could perceive
In the same object graces quite as killing
   As when she rose upon us like an Eve,
'T would save us many a heartache, many a shilling,
   (For we must get them anyhow, or grieve),
Whereas if one sole lady pleased for ever,
How pleasant for the heart, as well as liver!

214

The Heart is like the sky, a part of Heaven,
  But changes night and day, too, like the sky;
Now o'er it clouds and thunder must be driven,
  And Darkness and Destruction as on high:
But when it hath been scorched, and pierced, and riven,
  Its storms expire in water-drops; the eye
Pours forth at last the Heart's blood turned to tears,
Which make the English climate of our years.

215

The liver is the lazaret of bile,
  But very rarely executes its function,
For the first passion stays there such a while,
  That all the rest creep in and form a junction,
Like knots of vipers on a dunghill's soil —
  Rage, fear, hate, jealousy, revenge, compunction —
So that all mischiefs spring up from this entrail,
Like Earthquakes from the hidden fire called "central."

216

In the mean time, without proceeding more
  In this anatomy, I 've finished now
Two hundred and odd stanzas as before,
  That being about the number I 'll allow
Each canto of the twelve, or twenty-four;
  And, laying down my pen, I make my bow,
Leaving Don Juan and Haidée to plead
For them and theirs with all who deign to read.

1819   *1819*

CANTO THE THIRD

1

HAIL, Muse! *et cetera*. — We left Juan sleeping,
  Pillowed upon a fair and happy breast,
And watched by eyes that never yet knew weeping,
  And loved by a young heart, too deeply blest

To feel the poison through her spirit creeping,
   Or know who rested there, a foe to rest,
Had soiled the current of her sinless years,
And turned her pure heart's purest blood to tears!

2

Oh, Love! what is it in this world of ours
   Which makes it fatal to be loved? Ah why
With cypress branches hast thou wreathed thy bowers,
   And made thy best interpreter a sigh?
As those who dote on odours pluck the flowers,
   And place them on their breast — but place to die —
Thus the frail beings we would fondly cherish
Are laid within our bosoms but to perish.

3

In her first passion Woman loves her lover,
   In all the others all she loves is Love,
Which grows a habit she can ne'er get over,
   And fits her loosely — like an easy glove,
As you may find, whene'er you like to prove her:
   One man alone at first her heart can move;
She then prefers him in the plural number,
Not finding that the additions much encumber.

4

I know not if the fault be men's or theirs;
   But one thing 's pretty sure; a woman planted
(Unless at once she plunge for life in prayers) —
   After a decent time must be gallanted;
Although, no doubt, her first of love affairs
   Is that to which her heart is wholly granted;
Yet there are some, they say, who have had *none*,
But those who have ne'er end with only *one*.

5

'T is melancholy, and a fearful sign
   Of human frailty, folly, also crime,

4:2. *planted*: Betrayed, abandoned.

That Love and Marriage rarely can combine,
    Although they both are born in the same clime;
Marriage from Love, like vinegar from wine —
    A sad, sour, sober beverage — by Time
Is sharpened from its high celestial flavour
Down to a very homely household savour.

6

There's something of antipathy, as 't were,
    Between their present and their future state;
A kind of flattery that 's hardly fair
    Is used until the truth arrives too late —
Yet what can people do, except despair?
    The same things change their names at such a rate;
For instance — Passion in a lover 's glorious,
But in a husband is pronounced uxorious.

7

Men grow ashamed of being so very fond;
    They sometimes also get a little tired
(But that, of course, is rare), and then despond:
    The same things cannot always be admired,
Yet 't is "so nominated in the bond,"
    That both are tied till one shall have expired.
Sad thought! to lose the spouse that was adorning
Our days, and put one's servants into mourning.

8

There 's doubtless something in domestic doings
    Which forms, in fact, true Love's antithesis;
Romances paint at full length people's wooings,
    But only give a bust of marriages;
For no one cares for matrimonial cooings,
    There 's nothing wrong in a connubial kiss:
Think you, if Laura had been Petrarch's wife,
He would have written sonnets all his life?

9

All tragedies are finished by a death,
    All comedies are ended by a marriage;

The future states of both are left to faith,
  For authors fear description might disparage
The worlds to come of both, or fall beneath,
  And then both worlds would punish their miscarriage;
So leaving each their priest and prayer-book ready,
They say no more of Death or of the Lady.

10

The only two that in my recollection,
  Have sung of Heaven and Hell, or marriage, are
Dante and Milton, and of both the affection
  Was hapless in their nuptials, for some bar
Of fault or temper ruined the connection
  (Such things, in fact, it don't ask much to mar);
But Dante's Beatrice and Milton's Eve
Were not drawn from their spouses, you conceive.

11

Some persons say that Dante meant Theology
  By Beatrice, and not a mistress — I,
Although my opinion may require apology,
  Deem this a commentator's phantasy,
Unless indeed it was from his own knowledge he
  Decided thus, and showed good reason why;
I think that Dante's more abstruse ecstatics
Meant to personify the Mathematics.

12

Haidée and Juan were not married, but
  The fault was theirs, not mine: it is not fair,
Chaste reader, then, in any way to put
  The blame on me, unless you wish they were;
Then if you 'd have them wedded, please to shut
  The book which treats of this erroneous pair,

9:8. *of Death or of the Lady*: A morbid ballad, "Death and the Lady," printed in 1736 in a volume called *A Guide to Heaven*, became very popular.

Before the consequences grow too awful;
'T is dangerous to read of loves unlawful.

13

Yet they were happy, — happy in the illicit
   Indulgence of their innocent desires;
But more imprudent grown with every visit,
   Haidée forgot the island was her Sire's;
When we have what we like 't is hard to miss it,
   At least in the beginning, ere one tires;
Thus she came often, not a moment losing,
Whilst her piratical papa was cruising.

14

Let not his mode of raising cash seem strange,
   Although he fleeced the flags of every nation,
For into a Prime Minister but change
   His title, and 't is nothing but taxation;
But he, more modest, took an humbler range
   Of Life, and in an honester vocation
Pursued o'er the high seas his watery journey,
And merely practised as a sea-attorney.

15

The good old gentleman had been detained
   By winds and waves, and some important captures;
And, in the hope of more, at sea remained,
   Although a squall or two had damped his raptures,
By swamping one of the prizes; he had chained
   His prisoners, dividing them like chapters
In numbered lots; they all had cuffs and collars,
And averaged each from ten to a hundred dollars.

16

Some he disposed of off Cape Matapan,
   Among his friends the Mainots; some he sold

16:1. *Cape Matapan*: At the southern point of the Greek peninsula.
16:2. *Mainots*: Greek pirates.

To his Tunis correspondents, save one man
    Tossed overboard unsaleable (being old):
The rest — save here and there some richer one,
    Reserved for future ransom — in the hold,
Were linked alike, as, for the common people, he
Had a large order from the Dey of Tripoli.

17

The merchandise was served in the same way,
    Pieced out for different marts in the Levant,
Except some certain portions of the prey,
    Like classic articles of female want,
French stuffs, lace, tweezers, toothpicks, teapot, tray,
    Guitars and castanets from Alicant,
All which selected from the spoil he gathers,
Robbed for his daughter by the best of fathers.

18

A monkey, a Dutch mastiff, a mackaw,
    Two parrots, with a Persian cat and kittens,
He chose from several animals he saw —
    A terrier, too, which once had been a Briton's,
Who dying on the coast of Ithaca,
    The peasants gave the poor dumb thing a pittance:
These to secure in this strong blowing weather,
He caged in one huge hamper altogether.

19

Then, having settled his marine affairs,
    Despatching single cruisers here and there,
His vessel having need of some repairs,
    He shaped his course to where his daughter fair
Continued still her hospitable cares;
    But that part of the coast being shoal and bare,
And rough with reefs which ran out many a mile,
His port lay on the other side o' the isle.

17:6. *Alicant*: A city and province in southeast Spain on the Mediterranean.

20

And there he went ashore without delay,
   Having no custom-house nor quarantine
To ask him awkward questions on the way,
   About the time and place where he had been:
He left his ship to be hove down next day,
   With orders to the people to careen;
So that all hands were busy beyond measure,
In getting out goods, ballast, guns, and treasure.

21

Arriving at the summit of a hill
   Which overlooked the white walls of his home,
He stopped. — What singular emotions fill
   Their bosoms who have been induced to roam!
With fluttering doubts if all be well or ill —
   With love for many, and with fears for some;
All feelings which o'erleap the years long lost,
And bring our hearts back to their starting-post.

22

The approach of home to husbands and to sires,
   After long travelling by land or water,
Most naturally some small doubt inspires —
   A female family 's a serious matter,
(None trusts the sex more, or so much admires —
   But they hate flattery, so I never flatter);
Wives in their husbands' absences grow subtler,
And daughters sometimes run off with the butler.

23

An honest gentleman at his return
   May not have the good fortune of Ulysses;
Not all lone matrons for their husbands mourn,
   Or show the same dislike to suitors' kisses;
The odds are that he finds a handsome urn

20:6. *to careen*: To tip a vessel on its side in order to clean its hull.

To his memory — and two or three young misses
Born to some friend, who holds his wife and riches —
And that *his* Argus — bites him by the breeches.

24

If single, probably his plighted Fair
   Has in his absence wedded some rich miser;
But all the better, for the happy pair
   May quarrel, and, the lady growing wiser,
He may resume his amatory care
   As *cavalier servente*, or despise her;
And that his sorrow may not be a dumb one,
Writes odes on the Inconstancy of Woman.

25

And oh! ye gentlemen who have already
   Some chaste *liaison* of the kind — I mean
An honest friendship with a married lady —
   The only thing of this sort ever seen
To last — of all connections the most steady,
   And the true Hymen, (the first 's but a screen) —
Yet, for all that, keep not too long away —
I 've known the absent wronged four times a day.

26

Lambro, our sea-solicitor, who had
   Much less experience of dry land than Ocean,
On seeing his own chimney-smoke, felt glad;
   But not knowing metaphysics, had no notion

23:8. *Argus*: In the Odyssey, Argus is the old dog who recognizes his master on his return home from his twenty years' wanderings and dies of joy. Byron wrote to Moore, January 19, 1815, about one of his dogs "that doted on me at ten years old, and very nearly ate me at twenty. When I thought he was going to enact Argus, he bit away the backside of my breeches . . . ."

26:1. *Lambro*: Byron may have taken the name and some characteristics from the Greek pirate, Lambro Katzones, about whom he heard stories when he was in Greece in 1809–1810. But much of the characterization is built upon Byron's memories of Ali Pasha, the Albanian tyrant whom he met in 1809.

Of the true reason of his not being sad,
   Or that of any other strong emotion;
He loved his child, and would have wept the loss of her,
But knew the cause no more than a philosopher.

27

He saw his white walls shining in the sun,
   His garden trees all shadowy and green;
He heard his rivulet's light bubbling run,
   The distant dog-bark; and perceived between
The umbrage of the wood, so cool and dun,
   The moving figures, and the sparkling sheen
Of arms (in the East all arm) — and various dyes
Of coloured garbs, as bright as butterflies.

28

And as the spot where they appear he nears,
   Surprised at these unwonted signs of idling,
He hears — alas! no music of the spheres,
   But an unhallowed, earthly sound of fiddling!
A melody which made him doubt his ears,
   The cause being past his guessing or unriddling;
A pipe, too, and a drum, and shortly after —
A most unoriental roar of laughter.

29

And still more nearly to the place advancing,
   Descending rather quickly the declivity,
Through the waved branches o'er the greensward glancing,
   'Midst other indications of festivity,
Seeing a troop of his domestics dancing
   Like Dervises, who turn as on a pivot, he
Perceived it was the Pyrrhic dance so martial,
To which the Levantines are very partial.

29:7. *Pyrrhic dance*: Greek war dance in quick time, with movements simulating combat.

30

And further on a troop of Grecian girls,
   The first and tallest her white kerchief waving,
Were strung together like a row of pearls,
   Linked hand in hand, and dancing; each too having
Down her white neck long floating auburn curls —
   (The least of which would set ten poets raving);
Their leader sang — and bounded to her song
With choral step and voice the virgin throng.

31

And here, assembled cross-legged round their trays,
   Small social parties just begun to dine;
Pilaus and meats of all sorts met the gaze,
   And flasks of Samian and of Chian wine,
And sherbet cooling in the porous vase;
   Above them their dessert grew on its vine; —
The orange and pomegranate nodding o'er,
Dropped in their laps, scarce plucked, their mellow store.

32

A band of children, round a snow-white ram,
   There wreathe his venerable horns with flowers;
While peaceful as if still an unweaned lamb,
   The patriarch of the flock all gently cowers
His sober head, majestically tame,
   Or eats from out the palm, or playful lowers
His brow, as if in act to butt, and then
Yielding to their small hands, draws back again.

33

Their classical profiles, and glittering dresses,
   Their large black eyes, and soft seraphic cheeks,
Crimson as cleft pomegranates, their long tresses,
   The gesture which enchants, the eye that speaks,

30:1–8. Probably the Greek folk dance, the Romaika.
31:4. *Samian and . . . Chian wine*: From Samos and Chios (Scio), Greek islands in the Aegean.

The innocence which happy childhood blesses,
    Made quite a picture of these little Greeks;
So that the philosophical beholder
Sighed for their sakes — that they should e'er grow older.

34

Afar, a dwarf buffoon stood telling tales
    To a sedate grey circle of old smokers,
Of secret treasures found in hidden vales,
    Of wonderful replies from Arab jokers,
Of charms to make good gold and cure bad ails,
    Of rocks bewitched that open to the knockers,
Of magic ladies who, by one sole act,
Transformed their lords to beasts (but that 's a fact).

35

Here was no lack of innocent diversion
    For the imagination or the senses,
Song, dance, wine, music, stories from the Persian,
    All pretty pastimes in which no offence is;
But Lambro saw all these things with aversion,
    Perceiving in his absence such expenses,
Dreading that climax of all human ills,
The inflammation of his weekly bills.

36

Ah! what is man? what perils still environ
    The happiest mortals ever after dinner!
A day of gold from out of age of iron
    Is all that Life allows the luckiest sinner;
Pleasure (whene'er she sings, at least) 's a Siren,
    That lures, to flay alive, the young beginner;
Lambro's reception at his people's banquet
Was such as fire accords to a wet blanket.

37

He — being a man who seldom used a word
    Too much, and wishing gladly to surprise

(In general he surprised men with the sword)
 His daughter — had not sent before to advise
Of his arrival, so that no one stirred;
 And long he paused to re-assure his eyes,
In fact much more astonished than delighted,
To find so much good company invited.

38

He did not know (alas! how men will lie)
 That a report (especially the Greeks)
Avouched his death (such people never die),
 And put his house in mourning several weeks, —
But now their eyes and also lips were dry;
 The bloom, too, had returned to Haidée's cheeks:
Her tears, too, being returned into their fount,
She now kept house upon her own account.

39

Hence all this rice, meat, dancing, wine, and fiddling,
 Which turned the isle into a place of pleasure;
The servants all were getting drunk or idling,
 A life which made them happy beyond measure.
Her father's hospitality seemed middling,
 Compared with what Haidée did with his treasure;
'T was wonderful how things went on improving,
While she had not one hour to spare from loving.

40

Perhaps you think, in stumbling on this feast,
 He flew into a passion, and in fact
There was no mighty reason to be pleased;
 Perhaps you prophesy some sudden act,
The whip, the rack, or dungeon at the least,
 To teach his people to be more exact,
And that, proceeding at a very high rate,
He showed the royal *penchants* of a pirate.

41

You 're wrong. — He was the mildest mannered man
 That ever scuttled ship or cut a throat;

With such true breeding of a gentleman,
   You never could divine his real thought;
No courtier could, and scarcely woman can
   Gird more deceit within a petticoat;
Pity he loved adventurous life's variety,
He was so great a loss to good society.

42

Advancing to the nearest dinner tray,
   Tapping the shoulder of the nighest guest,
With a peculiar smile, which, by the way,
   Boded no good, whatever it expressed,
He asked the meaning of this holiday;
   The vinous Greek to whom he had addressed
His question, much too merry to divine
The questioner, filled up a glass of wine,

43

And without turning his facetious head,
   Over his shoulder, with a Bacchant air,
Presented the o'erflowing cup, and said,
   "Talking 's dry work, I have no time to spare."
A second hiccuped, "Our old Master 's dead,
   You 'd better ask our Mistress who 's his heir."
"Our Mistress!" quoth a third: "Our Mistress! — pooh! —
You mean our Master — not the old, but new."

44

These rascals, being new comers, knew not whom
   They thus addressed — and Lambro's visage fell —
And o'er his eye a momentary gloom
   Passed, but he strove quite courteously to quell
The expression, and endeavouring to resume
   His smile, requested one of them to tell
The name and quality of his new patron,
Who seemed to have turned Haidée into a matron.

45

"I know not," quoth the fellow, "who or what
   He is, nor whence he came — and little care;

But this I know, that this roast capon 's fat,
    And that good wine ne'er washed down better fare;
And if you are not satisfied with that,
    Direct your questions to my neighbour there;
He 'll answer all for better or for worse,
For none likes more to hear himself converse."

46

I said that Lambro was a man of patience,
    And certainly he showed the best of breeding,
Which scarce even France, the Paragon of nations,
    E'er saw her most polite of sons exceeding;
He bore these sneers against his near relations,
    His own anxiety, his heart, too, bleeding,
The insults, too, of every servile glutton,
Who all the time was eating up his mutton.

47

Now in a person used to much command —
    To bid men come, and go, and come again —
To see his orders done, too, out of hand —
    Whether the word was death, or but the chain —
It may seem strange to find his manners bland;
    Yet such things are, which I cannot explain,
Though doubtless, he who can command himself
Is good to govern — almost as a Guelf.

48

Not that he was not sometimes rash or so,
    But never in his real and serious mood;
Then calm, concentrated, and still, and slow,
    He lay coiled like the Boa in the wood;
With him it never was a word and blow,
    His angry word once o'er, he shed no blood,

47:8. *Guelph*: The House of Hanover was descended from the German
royal family of Guelph. Byron is making a sly dig at the mad George III
and the frivolous Prince Regent. See also *Vision of Judgment*, st. 49:7.

But in his silence there was much to rue,
And his *one* blow left little work for *two*.

49

He asked no further questions, and proceeded
    On to the house, but by a private way,
So that the few who met him hardly heeded,
    So little they expected him that day;
If love paternal in his bosom pleaded
    For Haidée's sake, is more than I can say,
But certainly to one deemed dead returning,
This revel seemed a curious mode of mourning.

50

If all the dead could now return to life,
    (Which God forbid!) or some, or a great many,
For instance, if a husband or his wife
    (Nuptial examples are as good as any),
No doubt whate'er might be their former strife,
    The present weather would be much more rainy —
Tears shed into the grave of the connection
Would share most probably its resurrection.

51

He entered in the house no more his home,
    A thing to human feelings the most trying,
And harder for the heart to overcome,
    Perhaps, than even the mental pangs of dying;
To find our hearthstone turned into a tomb,
    And round its once warm precincts palely lying
The ashes of our hopes, is a deep grief,
Beyond a *single gentleman's* belief.

52

He entered in the house — his home no more,
    For without hearts there is no home; — and felt
The solitude of passing his own door
    Without a welcome: *there* he long had dwelt,

There his few peaceful days Time had swept o'er,
  There his worn bosom and keen eye would melt
Over the innocence of that sweet child,
His only shrine of feelings undefiled.

53

He was a man of a strange temperament,
  Of mild demeanour though of savage mood,
Moderate in all his habits, and content
  With temperance in pleasure, as in food,
Quick to perceive, and strong to bear, and meant
  For something better, if not wholly good;
His Country's wrongs and his despair to save her
Had stung him from a slave to an enslaver.

54

The love of power, and rapid gain of gold,
  The hardness by long habitude produced,
The dangerous life in which he had grown old,
  The mercy he had granted oft abused,
The sights he was accustomed to behold,
  The wild seas, and wild men with whom he cruised,
Had cost his enemies a long repentance,
And made him a good friend, but bad acquaintance.

55

But something of the spirit of old Greece
  Flashed o'er his soul a few heroic rays,
Such as lit onward to the Golden Fleece
  His predecessors in the Colchian days;
'T is true he had no ardent love for peace —
  Alas! his country showed no path to praise:
Hate to the world and war with every nation
He waged, in vengeance of her degradation.

55:4. *Colchian days*: The Argonauts sailed to Colchis on the Black Sea
in search of the Golden Fleece.

56

Still o'er his mind the influence of the clime
   Shed its Ionian elegance, which showed
Its power unconsciously full many a time, —
   A taste seen in the choice of his abode,
A love of music and of scenes sublime,
   A pleasure in the gentle stream that flowed
Past him in crystal, and a joy in flowers,
Bedewed his spirit in his calmer hours.

57

But whatsoe'er he had of love reposed
   On that belovéd daughter; she had been
The only thing which kept his heart unclosed
   Amidst the savage deeds he had done and seen,
A lonely pure affection unopposed:
   There wanted but the loss of this to wean
His feelings from all milk of human kindness,
And turn him like the Cyclops mad with blindness.

58

The cubless tigress in her jungle raging
   Is dreadful to the shepherd and the flock;
The Ocean when its yeasty war is waging
   Is awful to the vessel near the rock;
But violent things will sooner bear assuaging,
   Their fury being spent by its own shock,
Than the stern, single, deep, and wordless ire
Of a strong human heart, and in a Sire.

59

It is a hard although a common case
   To find our children running restive — they
In whom our brightest days we would retrace,

57:8. *Cyclops*: Ulysses blinded the one-eyed Polyphemus with a hot brand.

Our little selves re-formed in finer clay,
Just as old age is creeping on apace,
    And clouds come o'er the sunset of our day,
They kindly leave us, though not quite alone,
But in good company — the gout or stone.

60

Yet a fine family is a fine thing
    (Provided they don't come in after dinner);
'T is beautiful to see a matron bring
    Her children up (if nursing them don't thin her);
Like cherubs round an altar-piece they cling
    To the fire-side (a sight to touch a sinner).
A lady with her daughters or her nieces
Shine like a guinea and seven-shilling pieces.

61

Old Lambro passed unseen a private gate,
    And stood within his hall at eventide;
Meantime the lady and her lover sate
    At wassail in their beauty and their pride:
An ivory inlaid table spread with state
    Before them, and fair slaves on every side;
Gems, gold, and silver, formed the service mostly,
Mother of pearl and coral the less costly.

62

The dinner made about a hundred dishes;
    Lamb and pistachio nuts — in short, all meats
And saffron soups, and sweetbreads; and the fishes
    Were of the finest that e'er flounced in nets,
Dressed to a Sybarite's most pampered wishes;
    The beverage was various sherbets
Of raisin, orange, and pomegranate juice,
Squeezed through the rind, which makes it best for use.

61:5 ff. Byron wrote to Murray, August 23, 1821, that he had taken much of the description of the furniture from his own observation and from Richard Tully's *Narrative of a Ten Years' Residence at Tripoli* (1816).

63

These were ranged round, each in its crystal ewer,
　　And fruits, and date-bread loaves closed the repast,
And Mocha's berry, from Arabia pure,
　　In small fine China cups, came in at last;
Gold cups of filigree, made to secure
　　The hand from burning, underneath them placed;
Cloves, cinnamon, and saffron too were boiled
Up with the coffee, which (I think) they spoiled.

64

The hangings of the room were tapestry, made
　　Of velvet panels, each of different hue,
And thick with damask flowers of silk inlaid;
　　And round them ran a yellow border too;
The upper border, richly wrought, displayed,
　　Embroidered delicately o'er with blue,
Soft Persian sentences, in lilac letters,
From poet's or the moralists their betters.

65

These Oriental writings on the wall,
　　Quite common in those countries, are a kind
Of monitors adapted to recall,
　　Like skulls at Memphian banquets, to the mind,
The words which shook Belshazzar in his hall,
　　And took his kingdom from him: You will find,
Though sages may pour out their wisdom's treasure,
There is no sterner moralist than Pleasure.

66

A Beauty at the season's close grown hectic,
　　A Genius who has drunk himself to death,
A Rake turned methodistic, or Eclectic —

65:4. *Memphian banquets*: Royal feasts in Memphis, capital of ancient
Egypt.
65:5. *Belshazzar*: See, below, note to Canto 8, 134:2.
66:3. *Eclectic*: A reference to the *Eclectic Review* which took a high moral

(For that's the name they like to pray beneath) —
But most, an Alderman struck apoplectic,
   Are things that really take away the breath, —
And show that late hours, wine, and love are able
To do not much less damage than the table.

67

Haidée and Juan carpeted their feet
   On crimson satin, bordered with pale blue;
Their sofa occupied three parts complete
   Of the apartment — and appeared quite new;
The velvet cushions (for a throne more meet)
   Were scarlet, from whose glowing centre grew
A sun embossed in gold, whose rays of tissue,
Meridian-like, were seen all light to issue.

68

Crystal and marble, plate and porcelain,
   Had done their work of splendour; Indian mats
And Persian carpets, which the heart bled to stain,
   Over the floors were spread; gazelles and cats,
And dwarfs and blacks, and such like things, that gain
   Their bread as ministers and favourites (that's
To say, by degradation) mingled there
As plentiful as in a court, or fair.

69

There was no want of lofty mirrors, and
   The tables, most of ebony inlaid
With mother of pearl or ivory, stood at hand,
   Or were of tortoise-shell or rare woods made,
Fretted with gold or silver: — by command
   The greater part of these were ready spread
With viands and sherbets in ice — and wine —
Kept for all comers at all hours to dine.

tone toward Byron: "the Poet's pathos is but the sentimentalism of the
drunkard between his cups."

70

Of all the dresses I select Haidée's;
    She wore two jelicks — one was of pale yellow;
Of azure, pink, and white was her chemise —
    'Neath which her breast heaved like a little billow:
With buttons formed of pearls as large as peas,
    All gold and crimson shone her jelick's fellow,
And the striped white gauze baracan that bound her,
Like fleecy clouds about the moon, flowed round her.

71

One large gold bracelet clasped each lovely arm,
    Lockless — so pliable from the pure gold
That the hand stretched and shut it without harm,
    The limb which it adorned its only mould;
So beautiful — its very shape would charm,
    And clinging, as if loath to lose its hold,
The purest ore enclosed the whitest skin
That e'er by precious metal was held in.

72

Around, as Princess of her father's land,
    A like gold bar above her instep rolled
Announced her rank; twelve rings were on her hand;
    Her hair was starred with gems, her veil's fine fold
Below her breast was fastened with a band
    Of lavish pearls, whose worth could scarce be told;
Her orange silk full Turkish trousers furled
About the prettiest ankle in the world.

73

Her hair's long auburn waves down to her heel
    Flowed like an Alpine torrent which the sun
Dyes with his morning light, — and would conceal
    Her person if allowed at large to run,

70:2. *jelicks*: Sleeveless jackets or bodices.
70:7. *baracan*: A mantle or wrap.

And still they seemed resentfully to feel
   The silken fillet's curb, and sought to shun
Their bonds whene'er some Zephyr caught began
To offer his young pinion as her fan.

74

Round her she made an atmosphere of life,
   The very air seemed lighter from her eyes,
They were so soft and beautiful, and rife
   With all we can imagine of the skies,
And pure as Psyche ere she grew a wife
   Too pure even for the purest human ties;
Her overpowering presence made you feel
It would not be idolatry to kneel.

75

Her eyelashes, though dark as night, were tinged
   (It is the country's custom, but in vain),
For those large black eyes were so blackly fringed,
   The glossy rebels mocked the jetty stain,
And in their native beauty stood avenged:
   Her nails were touched with henna; but, again,
The power of Art was turned to nothing, for
They could not look more rosy than before.

76

The henna should be deeply dyed to make
   The skin relieved appear more fairly fair;
She had no need of this, day ne'er will break
   On mountain tops more heavenly white than her:
The eye might doubt if it were well awake,
   She was so like a vision; I might err,
But Shakespeare also says, 't is very silly
"To gild refinéd gold, or paint the lily."

77

Juan had on a shawl of black and gold,
   But a white baracan, and so transparent

76:8. ". . . *paint the lily*": *King John* IV. ii. 11.

The sparkling gems beneath you might behold,
   Like small stars through the milky way apparent;
His turban, furled in many a graceful fold,
   An emerald aigrette, with Haidée's hair in 't,
Surmounted, as its clasp, a glowing crescent,
Whose rays shone ever trembling, but incessant.

78

And now they were diverted by their suite,
   Dwarfs, dancing girls, black eunuchs, and a poet,
Which made their new establishment complete;
   The last was of great fame, and liked to show it;
His verses rarely wanted their due feet —
   And for his theme — he seldom sung below it,
He being paid to satirise or flatter,
As the Psalm says, "inditing a good matter."

79

He praised the present, and abused the past,
   Reversing the good custom of old days,
An Eastern anti-jacobin at last
   He turned, preferring pudding to *no* praise —
For some few years his lot had been o'ercast
   By his seeming independent in his lays,
But now he sung the Sultan and the Pacha —
With truth like Southey, and with verse like Crashaw.

80

He was a man who had seen many changes,
   And always changed as true as any needle;
His Polar Star being one which rather ranges,
   And not the fixed — he knew the way to wheedle:
So vile he 'scaped the doom which oft avenges;
   And being fluent (save indeed when fee'd ill),

78:2. *a poet*: Another satiric portrait of the opportunist poet, modeled on Southey. For "sad trimmer" (82:1) Byron had originally written "sad Southey." See notes to *Vision of Judgment* and *Dedication*, above.
78:8. *"inditing a good matter"*: Psalms 45:1.

He lied with such a fervour of intention —
There was no doubt he earned his laureate pension.

81

But *he* had genius — when a turncoat has it,
   The *Vates irritabilis* takes care
That without notice few full moons shall pass it;
   Even good men like to make the public stare: —
But to my subject — let me see — what was it? —
   Oh! — the third canto — and the pretty pair —
Their loves, and feasts, and house, and dress, and mode
Of living in their insular abode.

82

Their poet, a sad trimmer, but, no less,
   In company a very pleasant fellow,
Had been the favourite of full many a mess
   Of men, and made them speeches when half mellow;
And though his meaning they could rarely guess,
   Yet still they deigned to hiccup or to bellow
The glorious meed of popular applause,
Of which the first ne'er knows the second cause.

83

But now being lifted into high society,
   And having picked up several odds and ends
Of free thoughts in his travels for variety,
   He deemed, being in a lone isle, among friends,
That, without any danger of a riot, he
   Might for long lying make himself amends;
And, singing as he sung in his warm youth,
Agree to a short armistice with Truth.

84

He had travelled 'mongst the Arabs, Turks, and Franks,
   And knew the self-loves of the different nations;

81:2. *Vates irritabilis*: "Irritable seer or poet." Coleridge in *Biographia Literaria* had written on "the supposed irritability of men of genius."
84:1. *Franks*: The common Eastern term for Western Europeans.

And having lived with people of all ranks,
    Had something ready upon most occasions —
Which got him a few presents and some thanks.
    He varied with some skill his adulations;
To "do at Rome as Romans do," a piece
Of conduct was which *he* observed in Greece.

85

Thus, usually, when *he* was asked to sing,
    He gave the different nations something national;
'T was all the same to him — "God save the King,"
    Or "Ça ira," according to the fashion all:
His Muse made increment of anything,
    From the high lyric down to the low rational;
If Pindar sang horse-races, what should hinder
Himself from being as pliable as Pindar?

86

In France, for instance, he would write a chanson;
    In England a six canto quarto tale;
In Spain he 'd make a ballad or romance on
    The last war — much the same in Portugal;
In Germany, the Pegasus he 'd prance on
    Would be old Goethe's — (see what says De Staël);
In Italy he 'd ape the "Trecentisti";
In Greece, he 'd sing some sort of hymn like this t' ye:

1

The Isles of Greece, the Isles of Greece!
    Where burning Sappho loved and sung,
    Where grew the arts of War and Peace,

  85:4. *"Ça ira"*: "It will succeed," the popular song of the French Revolution.

  85:8. *Pindar*: Several of Pindar's Odes celebrate victors in chariot races.

  86:6. *De Staël*: Madame de Staël had said that Goethe alone could represent the literature of Germany.

  86:7. *"Trecentisti"*: The poets of the fourteenth century, including Dante and Petrarch.

Where Delos rose, and Phœbus sprung!
Eternal summer gilds them yet,
But all, except their Sun, is set.

2

The Scian and the Teian muse,
    The Hero's harp, the Lover's lute,
Have found the fame your shores refuse:
    Their place of birth alone is mute
To sounds which echo further west
Than your Sires' "Islands of the Blest."

3

The mountains look on Marathon —
    And Marathon looks on the sea;
And musing there an hour alone,
    I dreamed that Greece might still be free;
For standing on the Persians' grave,
I could not deem myself a slave.

4

A King sate on the rocky brow
    Which looks o'er sea-born Salamis;
And ships, by thousands, lay below,
    And men in nations; — all were his!
He counted them at break of day —
And, when the Sun set, where were they?

5

And where are they? and where art thou,
    My country? On thy voiceless shore

1:4. *Delos*: An island in the Cyclades which Poseidon raised from the
sea and where Phoebus Apollo was born, according to legend.
2:1. *Scian and the Teian muse*: Homer was supposed to have been born
on Scio (Chios), an Aegean island, and Anacreon in Teos, a city in Asia
Minor.
2:6. *"Islands of the Blest"*: The Greek poets supposed them to be the
Cape Verde Islands or the Canaries.
3:1. *Marathon*: The Greeks defeated the Persians at Marathon in 490
B.C. A mound marks the graves of the Greeks, not the Persians (1.5).
4:1–8. *king*: Xerxes, king of the Persians, watched the defeat of his
fleet by the Greeks in the battle off Salamis in 480 B.C.

The heroic lay is tuneless now —
 The heroic bosom beats no more!
And must thy Lyre, so long divine,
Degenerate into hands like mine?

6

'T is something, in the dearth of Fame,
 Though linked among a fettered race,
To feel at least a patriot's shame,
 Even as I sing, suffuse my face;
For what is left the poet here?
For Greeks a blush — for Greece a tear.

7

Must *we* but weep o'er days more blest?
 Must *we* but blush? — Our fathers bled.
Earth! render back from out thy breast
 A remnant of our Spartan dead!
Of the three hundred grant but three,
To make a new Thermopylæ!

8

What, silent still? and silent all?
 Ah! no; — the voices of the dead
Sound like a distant torrent's fall,
 And answer, "Let one living head,
But one arise, — we come, we come!"
'T is but the living who are dumb.

9

In vain — in vain: strike other chords;
 Fill high the cup with Samian wine!
Leave battles to the Turkish hordes,
 And shed the blood of Scio's vine!

 7:8. *Thermopylae*: Three hundred Spartans under Leonidas held off the
Persian army of Xerxes for three days in this narrow pass (480 B.C.).
 9:2. *Samian wine*: See above 3, 31:4.
 9:4. *Scio's vine*: Chian wine.

Hark! rising to the ignoble call —
How answers each bold Bacchanal!

10

You have the Pyrrhic dance as yet,
    Where is the Pyrrhic phalanx gone?
Of two such lessons, why forget
    The noblier and manlier one?
You have the letters Cadmus gave —
Think ye he meant them for a slave?

11

Fill high the bowl with Samian wine!
    We will not think of themes like these!
It made Anacreon's song divine:
    He served — but served Polycrates —
A Tyrant; but our masters then
Were still, at least, our countrymen.

12

The Tyrant of the Chersonese
    Was Freedom's best and bravest friend;
That tyrant was Miltiades!
    Oh! that the present hour would lend
Another despot of the kind!
Such chains as his were sure to bind.

13

Fill high the bowl with Samian wine!
    On Suli's rock, and Parga's shore,

10:1. *Pyrrhic dance*: See above 3, 29:7.
10:2. *Pyrrhic Phalanx*: A close formation devised by Pyrrhus, king of Epirus, in the third century B.C.
10:5. *Cadmus*: According to legend, he brought the Phoenician alphabet to Greece.
11:4. *Polycrates*: Anacreon, famous for his drinking songs, lived on the island of Samos, ruled by the tyrant Polycrates, after Teos, his birthplace, was captured by the Persians (510 B.C.).
12:1. *Tyrant of the Chersonese*: Miltiades, dictator of the Thracian Cheronesus (modern Gallipoli), led the Greeks in their victory at Marathon.
13:2. *Suli's rock and Parga's shore*: Suli is a cliff overlooking the Ionian

Exists the remnant of a line
    Such as the Doric mothers bore;
And there, perhaps, some seed is sown,
The Heracleidan blood might own.

14

Trust not for freedom to the Franks —
    They have a king who buys and sells;
In native swords, and native ranks,
    The only hope of courage dwells;
But Turkish force, and Latin fraud,
Would break your shield, however broad.

15

Fill high the bowl with Samian wine!
    Our virgins dance beneath the shade —
I see their glorious black eyes shine;
    But gazing on each glowing maid,
My own the burning tear-drop laves,
To think such breasts must suckle slaves.

16

Place me on Sunium's marbled steep,
    Where nothing, save the waves and I,
May hear our mutual murmurs sweep;
    There, swan-like, let me sing and die:
A land of slaves shall ne'er be mine —
Dash down yon cup of Samian wine!

Sea on the Greek-Albanian border; Parga is in Albania. Byron greatly admired the warlike spirit of the Suliotes and tried to mold several hundred of them into a disciplined fighting force in Missolonghi.

13:6. *Heracleidan*: Descended from Hercules. According to the legend, the Dorians invaded Peloponnesus after the Trojan War to restore the sons of Hercules to their rightful home.

14:1. *Franks*: Here probably the English who had commercial agreements with Turkey. The Greek war for Independence did not begin until 1821.

16:1. *Sunium*: Ancient name for a promontory (modern Cape Colonna) in southeastern Attica.

87

Thus sung, or would, or could, or should have sung,
    The modern Greek, in tolerable verse;
If not like Orpheus quite, when Greece was young,
    Yet in these times he might have done much worse:
His strain displayed some feeling — right or wrong;
    And feeling, in a poet, is the source
Of others' feeling; but they are such liars,
And take all colours — like the hands of dyers.

88

But words are things, and a small drop of ink,
    Falling like dew, upon a thought, produces
That which makes thousands, perhaps millions, think;
    'T is strange, the shortest letter which man uses
Instead of speech, may form a lasting link
    Of ages; to what straits old Time reduces
Frail man, when paper — even a rag like this,
Survives himself, his tomb, and all that 's his!

89

And when his bones are dust, his grave a blank,
    His station, generation, even his nation,
Become a thing, or nothing, save to rank
    In chronological commemoration,
Some dull MS. Oblivion long has sank,
    Or graven stone found in a barrack's station
In digging the foundation of a closet,
May turn his name up, as a rare deposit.

90

And Glory long has made the sages smile;
    'T is something, nothing, words, illusion, wind —
Depending more upon the historian's style
    Than on the name a person leaves behind:
Troy owns to Homer what whist owes to Hoyle:
    The present century was growing blind

90:5. *Hoyle*: Edmund Hoyle (1672–1769) was the author of a treatise on Whist (1742).

To the great Marlborough's skill in giving knocks,
Until his late Life by Archdeacon Coxe.

91

Milton 's the Prince of poets — so we say;
  A little heavy, but no less divine:
An independent being in his day —
  Learned, pious, temperate in love and wine;
But, his life falling into Johnson's way,
  We 're told this great High Priest of all the Nine
Was whipped at college — a harsh sire — odd spouse,
For the first Mrs. Milton left his house.

92

All these are, *certes,* entertaining facts,
  Like Shakespeare's stealing deer, Lord Bacon's bribes;
Like Titus' youth, and Cæsar's earliest acts;
  Like Burns (whom Doctor Currie well describes);
Like Cromwell's pranks; — but although Truth exacts
  These amiable descriptions from the scribes.
As most essential to their hero's story,
They do not much contribute to his glory.

93

All are not moralists, like Southey, when
  He prated to the world of "Pantisocracy";
Or Wordsworth unexcised, unhired, who then
  Seasoned his pedlar poems with Democracy;
Or Coleridge long before his flighty pen

90:8. *Coxe*: William Coxe (1747–1828), *Memoirs of John, Duke of Marlborough* (1818–1819).
  91:5. *Johnson's way*: See the essay on "Milton" in Samuel Johnson's *Lives of the Poets.*
  92:2–4. *Titus' youth . . . Cromwell's pranks*: The Emperor Titus, Caesar, and Robert Burns were all notorious for dissipation in youth. Burns' *Life and Works* was published in 1800 by Dr. James Currie (1757–1805). As a boy, Oliver Cromwell got in trouble through robbing orchards.
  93:2. *"Pantisocracy"*: See *Vision of Judgment,* 97:5.
  93:3. *Wordsworth unexcised*: See *Dedication,* 6:6 note.

Let to the Morning Post its aristocracy;
When he and Southey, following the same path,
Espoused two partners (milliners of Bath).

94

Such names at present cut a convict figure,
    The very Botany Bay in moral geography;
Their loyal treason, renegado rigour,
    Are good manure for their more bare biography;
Wordsworth's last quarto, by the way, is bigger
    Than any since the birthday of typography;
A drowsy, frowzy poem, called the "Excursion,"
Writ in a manner which is my aversion.

95

He there builds up a formidable dyke
    Between his own and others' intellect;
But Wordsworth's poem, and his followers, like
    Joanna Southcote's Shiloh and her sect,
Are things which in this century don't strike
    The public mind, — so few are the elect;
And the new births of both their stale Virginities
Have proved but Dropsies, taken for Divinities.

96

But let me to my story: I must own,
    If I have any fault, it is digression,
Leaving my people to proceed alone,
    While I soliloquise beyond expression;
But these are my addresses from the throne,

93:6. *Morning Post*: Coleridge contributed poems and articles to the Tory *Morning Post* in 1798–1802.

93:8. *milliners of Bath*: Coleridge and Southey married two of the Fricker sisters in 1795. They had not been milliners so far as is known. Byron says that he picked up the gossip from a friend.

94:2. *Botany Bay*: On the eastern coast of Australia where convicts and political prisoners were sent.

94:7. *"Excursion"*: Published in 1814. See Dedication, 4:1.

95:4. *Joanna Southcote's Shiloh*: See *Vision of Judgment*, 28:8.

Which put off business to the ensuing session: —
Forgetting each omission is a loss to
The world, not quite so great as Ariosto.

97

I know that what our neighbours call *"longueurs,"*
   (We 've not so good a *word,* but have the *thing,*
In that complete perfection which insures
   An epic from Bob Southey every spring —)
Form not the true temptation which allures
   The reader; but 't would not be hard to bring
Some fine examples of the *Epopée,*
To prove its grand ingredient is *Ennui.*

98

We learn from Horace, "Homer sometimes sleeps;"
   We feel without him, — Wordsworth sometimes wakes, —
To show with what complacency he creeps,
   With his dear *"Waggoners,"* around his lakes.
He wishes for "a boat" to sail the deeps —
   Of Ocean? — No, of air; and then he makes
Another outcry for "a little boat,"
And drivels seas to set it well afloat.

99

If he must fain sweep o'er the ethereal plain,
   And Pegasus runs restive in his "Waggon,"
Could he not beg the loan of Charles's Wain?
   Or pray Medea for a single dragon?

96:8. *Ariosto*: Italian poet (1474–1533) author of *Orlando Furioso,* for which Byron had high regard.

97:1. *"longueurs"*: Dullness, tedious writing.

97:7. *Epopée*: Epic.

98:1. *"Homer . . . sleeps"*: Horace, *Epistle ad Pisones* (Art of Poetry), l. 359.

98:4–7. *"Waggoners"*: Wordsworth's *Waggoner* and *Peter Bell*, in the first stanza of which he wishes for "a little boat," were published in 1819.

99:3. *Charles's Wain*: The Big Dipper.

99:4. *Medea . . . dragon*: In the final scene in Euripides' *Medea,* Medea fled in a chariot drawn by dragons.

Or if, too classic for his vulgar brain,
　　He feared his neck to venture such a nag on,
And he must needs mount nearer to the moon,
　　Could not the blockhead ask for a balloon?

100

"Pedlars," and "Boats," and "Waggons!" Oh, ye shades
　　Of Pope and Dryden, are we come to this?
That trash of such sort not alone evades
　　Contempt, but from the bathos' vast abyss
Floats scumlike uppermost, and these Jack Cades
　　Of sense and song above your graves may hiss —
The "little boatman" and his *Peter Bell*
Can sneer at him who drew "Achitophel"!

101

T' our tale. — The feast was over, the slaves gone,
　　The dwarfs and dancing girls had all retired;
The Arab lore and Poet's song were done,
　　And every sound of revelry expired;
The lady and her lover, left alone,
　　The rosy flood of Twilight's sky admired; —
Ave Maria! o'er the earth and sea,
That heavenliest hour of Heaven is worthiest thee!

102

Ave Maria! blessèd be the hour!
　　The time, the clime, the spot, where I so oft
Have felt that moment in its fullest power
　　Sink o'er the earth — so beautiful and soft —
While swung the deep bell in the distant tower,
　　Or the faint dying day-hymn stole aloft,
And not a breath crept through the rosy air,
And yet the forest leaves seemed stirred with prayer.

100:5. *Jack Cades*: Jack Cade led a rebellion of commoners against Henry VI in 1450; his name became synonymous with ignorant rebelliousness.

100:8. *"Achitophel"*: In his "Essay, Supplementary to the Preface" in *Poems*, 1815, Wordsworth made uncomplimentary remarks about Dryden.

103

Ave Maria! 't is the hour of prayer!
  Ave Maria! 't is the hour of Love!
Ave Maria! may our spirit dare
  Look up to thine and to thy Son's above!
Ave Maria! oh that face so fair!
  Those downcast eyes beneath the Almighty Dove —
What though 't is but a pictured image? — strike —
That painting is no idol, — 't is too like.

104

Some kinder casuists are pleased to say,
  In nameless print — that I have no devotion;
But set those persons down with me to pray,
  And you shall see who has the properest notion
Of getting into Heaven the shortest way;
  My altars are the mountains and the Ocean,
Earth — air — stars, — all that springs from the great Whole,
Who hath produced, and will receive the Soul.

105

Sweet Hour of Twilight! — in the solitude
  Of the pine forest, and the silent shore
Which bounds Ravenna's immemorial wood,
  Rooted where once the Adrian wave flowed o'er,
To where the last Cæsarean fortress stood,
  Evergreen forest! which Boccaccio's lore
And Dryden's lay made haunted ground to me,
How have I loved the twilight hour and thee!

105:2–5. *pine forest . . . Caesarian fortress*: Pine forests stood on ground which had been the Roman port, Caesarea, but the Adriatic had receded by the sixth century leaving the port landlocked. Honorius, the last Western Emperor, died here in A.D. 423.

105:6–7. *Boccaccio's lore . . . . Dryden's lay*: Dryden's *Theodore and Honoria,* a tale of a specter huntsman of Ravenna, alluded to in the last four lines of the next stanza, was adopted from Boccaccio's *Decameron,* Day 5, Novel 8. See Excerpts from a Diary, February 20, 1821, p. 677 below.

106

The shrill cicalas, people of the pine,
   Making their summer lives one ceaseless song,
Were the sole echoes, save my steed's and mine,
   And Vesper bell's that rose the boughs along;
The spectre huntsman of Onesti's line,
   His hell-dogs, and their chase, and the fair throng
Which learned from this example not to fly
From a true lover, — shadowed my mind's eye.

107

Oh, Hesperus! thou bringest all good things —
   Home to the weary, to the hungry cheer,
To the young bird the parent's brooding wings;
   The welcome stall to the o'erlaboured steer;
Whate'er of peace about our hearthstone clings,
   Whate'er our household gods protect of dear,
Are gathered round us by thy look of rest;
Thou bring'st the child, too, to the mother's breast.

108

Soft Hour! which wakes the wish and melts the heart
   Of those who sail the seas, on the first day
When they from their sweet friends are torn apart;
   Or fills with love the pilgrim on his way
As the far bell of Vesper makes him start,
   Seeming to weep the dying day's decay;
Is this a fancy which our reason scorns?
Ah! surely Nothing dies but Something mourns!

109

When Nero perished by the justest doom
   Which ever the Destroyer yet destroyed,
Amidst the roar of liberated Rome,
   Of nations freed, and the world overjoyed,
Some hands unseen strewed flowers upon his tomb:
   Perhaps the weakness of a heart not void
Of feeling for some kindness done, when Power
Had left the wretch an uncorrupted hour.

110

But I 'm digressing; what on earth has Nero,
  Or any such like sovereign buffoons,
To do with the transactions of my hero,
  More than such madmen's fellow man — the moon's?
Sure my invention must be down at zero,
  And I grown one of many "Wooden Spoons"
Of verse, (the name with which we Cantabs please
To dub the last of honours in degrees).

111

I feel this tediousness will never do —
  'T is being *too* epic, and I must cut down
(In copying) this long canto into two;
  They 'll never find it out, unless I own
The fact, excepting some experienced few;
  And then as an improvement 't will be shown:
I 'll prove that such the opinion of the critic is
From Aristotle *passim*. — See ΠΟΙΗΤΙΚΗΣ.

1819   *1821*

CANTO THE FOURTH

1

NOTHING so difficult as a beginning
  In poesy, unless perhaps the end;
For oftentimes when Pegasus seems winning
  The race, he sprains a wing, and down we tend,
Like Lucifer when hurled from Heaven for sinning;
  Our sin the same, and hard as his to mend,
Being Pride, which leads the mind to soar too far,
Till our own weakness shows us what we are.

110:6–7. *"Wooden Spoons"* . . . *Cantabs*: Wooden spoons were once given to the lowest on the honors list in mathematical tripos (final examination) at Cambridge. *Cantabs* is the abbreviation of Cantabridgians, students of Cambridge.

111:8. ΠΟΙΗΤΙΚΗΣ: In his *Poetics* Aristotle had said that "the increase in bulk tends to the advantage of the Epic in grandeur."

2

But Time, which brings all beings to their level,
    And sharp Adversity, will teach at last
Man, — and, as we would hope, — perhaps the Devil,
    That neither of their intellects are vast:
While Youth's hot wishes in our red veins revel,
    We know not this — the blood flows on too fast;
But as the torrent widens towards the Ocean,
We ponder deeply on each past emotion.

3

As boy, I thought myself a clever fellow,
    And wished that others held the same opinion;
They took it up when my days grew more mellow,
    And other minds acknowledged my dominion:
Now my sere Fancy "falls into the yellow
    Leaf," and Imagination droops her pinion,
And the sad truth which hovers o'er my desk
Turns what was once romantic to burlesque.

4

And if I laugh at any mortal thing,
    'T is that I may not weep; and if I weep,
'T is that our nature cannot always bring
    Itself to apathy, for we must steep
Our hearts first in the depths of Lethe's spring,
    Ere what we least wish to behold will sleep:
Thetis baptized her mortal son in Styx;
A mortal mother would on Lethe fix.

5

Some have accused me of a strange design
    Against the creed and morals of the land,
And trace it in this poem every line:
    I don't pretend that I quite understand

3:5–6. "falls into the yellow/ Leaf": *Macbeth* V. iii. 22–23.
4:7–8. *Styx* . . . . *Lethe*: Thetis dipped her son, Achilles, in the river
Styx (See 2, 101:3 note). Lethe is the river of oblivion.

My own meaning when I would be *very* fine;
   But the fact is that I have nothing planned,
Unless it were to be a moment merry —
A novel word in my vocabulary.

6

To the kind reader of our sober clime
   This way of writing will appear exotic;
Pulci was sire of the half-serious rhyme,
   Who sang when Chivalry was more quixotic,
And revelled in the fancies of the time,
   True Knights, chaste Dames, huge Giants, Kings despotic;
But all these, save the last, being obsolete,
I chose a modern subject as more meet.

7

How I have treated it, I do not know;
   Perhaps no better than *they* have treated me,
Who have imputed such designs as show
   Not what they saw, but what they wished to see:
But if it gives them pleasure, be it so;
   This is a liberal age, and thoughts are free:
Meantime Apollo plucks me by the ear,
And tells me to resume my story here.

8

Young Juan and his lady-love were left
   To their own hearts' most sweet society;
Even Time the pitiless in sorrow cleft
   With his rude scythe such gentle bosoms; he
Sighed to behold them of their hours bereft,
   Though foe to Love; and yet they could not be
Meant to grow old, but die in happy Spring,
Before one charm or hope had taken wing.

6:3. *Pulci*: Luigi Pulci (1432–1487) wrote *Morgante Maggiore*, a mock-heroic poem in *ottava rima*, of which Byron translated the first canto in 1819–1820. Pulci became an increasingly important influence on *Don Juan*. See headnote to *Beppo*.

9

Their faces were not made for wrinkles, their
    Pure blood to stagnate, their great hearts to fail;
The blank grey was not made to blast their hair,
    But like the climes that know nor snow nor hail,
They were all summer; lightning might assail
    And shiver them to ashes, but to trail
A long and snake-like life of dull decay
Was not for them — they had too little clay.

10

They were alone once more; for them to be
    Thus was another Eden; they were never
Weary, unless when separate: the tree
    Cut from its forest root of years — the river
Dammed from its fountain — the child from the knee
    And breast maternal weaned at once for ever, —
Would wither less than these two torn apart;
Alas! there is no instinct like the Heart —

11

The Heart — which may be broken: happy they!
    Thrice fortunate! who of that fragile mould,
The precious porcelain of human clay,
    Break with the first fall: they can ne'er behold
The long year linked with heavy day on day,
    And all which must be borne, and never told;
While Life's strange principle will often lie
Deepest in those who long the most to die.

12

"Whom the gods love die young," was said of yore,
    And many deaths do they escape by this:
The death of friends, and that which slays even more —
    The death of Friendship, Love, Youth, all that is,

12:1. "Whom the gods love die young": See Herodotus [*Cleobis and Biton*, 1. 31–32] — Byron's note. Also in Menander. See letter to Hodgson, below, p. 639.

Except mere breath; and since the silent shore
    Awaits at last even those who longest miss
The old Archer's shafts, perhaps the early grave
Which men weep over may be meant to save.

13

Haidée and Juan thought not of the dead —
    The Heavens, and Earth, and Air, seemed made for them:
They found no fault with Time, save that he fled;
    They saw not in themselves aught to condemn:
Each was the other's mirror, and but read
    Joy sparkling in their dark eyes like a gem,
And knew such brightness was but the reflection
Of their exchanging glances of affection.

14

The gentle pressure, and the thrilling touch,
    The least glance better understood than words,
Which still said all, and ne'er could say too much;
    A language, too, but like to that of birds,
Known but to them, at least appearing such
    As but to lovers a true sense affords;
Sweet playful phrases, which would seem absurd
To those who have ceased to hear such, or ne'er heard —

15

All these were theirs, for they were children still,
    And children still they should have ever been;
They were not made in the real world to fill
    A busy character in the dull scene,
But like two beings born from out a rill,
    A Nymph and her belovéd, all unseen
To pass their lives in fountains and on flowers,
And never know the weight of human hours.

16

Moons changing had rolled on, and changeless found
    Those their bright rise had lighted to such joys

As rarely they beheld throughout their round;
　　And these were not of the vain kind which cloys,
For theirs were buoyant spirits, never bound
　　By the mere senses; and that which destroys
Most love — possession — unto them appeared
A thing which each endearment more endeared.

17

Oh beautiful! and rare as beautiful!
　　But theirs was Love in which the Mind delights
To lose itself, when the old world grows dull,
　　And we are sick of its hack sounds and sights,
Intrigues, adventures of the common school,
　　Its petty passions, marriages, and flights,
Where Hymen's torch but brands one strumpet more,
Whose husband only knows her not a whore.

18

Hard words — harsh truth! a truth which many know.
　　Enough. — The faithful and the fairy pair,
Who never found a single hour too slow,
　　What was it made them thus exempt from care?
Young innate feelings all have felt below,
　　Which perish in the rest, but in them were
Inherent — what we mortals call romantic,
And always envy, though we deem it frantic.

19

This is in others a factitious state,
　　An opium dream of too much youth and reading,
But was in them their nature or their fate:
　　No novels e'er had set their young hearts bleeding,
For Haidée's knowledge was by no means great,
　　And Juan was a boy of saintly breeding;
So that there was no reason for their loves
More than for those of nightingales or doves.

20

They gazed upon the sunset; 't is an hour
　　Dear unto all, but dearest to *their* eyes,

For it had made them what they were: the power
 Of Love had first o'erwhelmed them from such skies,
When Happiness had been their only dower,
 And Twilight saw them linked in Passion's ties;
Charmed with each other, all things charmed that brought
The past still welcome as the present thought.

21

I know not why, but in that hour to-night,
 Even as they gazed, a sudden tremor came,
And swept, as 't were, across their hearts' delight,
 Like the wind o'er a harp-string, or a flame,
When one is shook in sound, and one in sight:
 And thus some boding flashed through either frame,
And called from Juan's breast a faint low sigh,
While one new tear arose in Haidée's eye.

22

That large black prophet eye seemed to dilate
 And follow far the disappearing sun,
As if their last day of a happy date
 With his broad, bright, and dropping orb were gone;
Juan gazed on her as to ask his fate —
 He felt a grief, but knowing cause for none,
His glance inquired of hers for some excuse
For feelings causeless, or at least abstruse.

23

She turned to him, and smiled, but in that sort
 Which makes not others smile; then turned aside:
Whatever feeling shook her, it seemed short,
 And mastered by her wisdom or her pride;
When Juan spoke, too — it might be in sport —
 Of this their mutual feeling, she replied —
"If it should be so, — but — it cannot be —
Or I at least shall not survive to see."

24

Juan would question further, but she pressed
 His lip to hers, and silenced him with this,

And then dismissed the omen from her breast,
  Defying augury with that fond kiss;
And no doubt of all methods 't is the best:
  Some people prefer wine — 't is not amiss;
I have tried both — so those who would a part take
May choose between the headache and the heartache.

25

One of the two, according to your choice,
  Woman or wine, you 'll have to undergo;
Both maladies are taxes on our joys:
  But which to choose, I really hardly know;
And if I had to give a casting voice,
  For both sides I could many reasons show,
And then decide, without great wrong to either,
It were much better to have both than neither.

26

Juan and Haidée gazed upon each other
  With swimming looks of speechless tenderness,
Which mixed all feelings — friend, child, lover, brother —
  All that the best can mingle and express
When two pure hearts are poured in one another,
  And love too much, and yet can not love less;
But almost sanctify the sweet excess
By the immortal wish and power to bless.

27

Mixed in each other's arms, and heart in heart,
  Why did they not then die? — they had lived too long
Should an hour come to bid them breathe apart;
  Years could but bring them cruel things or wrong;
The World was not for them — nor the World's art
  For beings passionate as Sappho's song;
Love was born *with* them, *in* them, so intense,
It was their very Spirit — not a sense.

28

They should have lived together deep in woods,
  Unseen as sings the nightingale; they were

Unfit to mix in these thick solitudes
    Called social, haunts of Hate, and Vice, and Care:
How lonely every freeborn creature broods!
    The sweetest song-birds nestle in a pair;
The eagle soars alone; the gull and crow
Flock o'er their carrion, just like men below.

29

Now pillowed cheek to cheek, in loving sleep,
    Haidée and Juan their siesta took,
A gentle slumber, but it was not deep,
    For ever and anon a something shook
Juan, and shuddering o'er his frame would creep;
    And Haidée's sweet lips murmured like a brook
A wordless music, and her face so fair
Stirred with her dream, as rose-leaves with the air.

30

Or as the stirring of a deep clear stream
    Within an Alpine hollow, when the wind
Walks o'er it, was she shaken by the dream,
    The mystical Usurper of the mind —
O'erpowering us to be whate'er may seem
    Good to the soul which we no more can bind;
Strange state of being! (for 't is still to be)
Senseless to feel, and with sealed eyes to see.

31

She dreamed of being alone on the sea-shore,
    Chained to a rock; she knew not how, but stir
She could not from the spot, and the loud roar
    Grew, and each wave rose roughly, threatening her;
And o'er her upper lip they seemed to pour,
    Until she sobbed for breath, and soon they were
Foaming o'er her lone head, so fierce and high —
Each broke to drown her, yet she could not die.

32

Anon — she was released, and then she strayed
    O'er the sharp shingles with her bleeding feet,

And stumbled almost every step she made:
   And something rolled before her in a sheet,
Which she must still pursue howe'er afraid:
   'T was white and indistinct, nor stopped to meet
Her glance nor grasp, for still she gazed and grasped,
And ran, but it escaped her as she clasped.

33

The dream changed: — in a cave she stood, — its walls
   Were hung with marble icicles; the work
Of ages on its water-fretted halls,
   Where waves might wash, and seals might breed and lurk;
Her hair was dripping, and the very balls
   Of her black eyes seemed turned to tears, and mirk
The sharp rocks looked below each drop they caught,
Which froze to marble as it fell, — she thought.

34

And wet, and cold, and lifeless at her feet,
   Pale as the foam that frothed on his dead brow,
Which she essayed in vain to clear, (how sweet
   Were once her cares, how idle seemed they now!)
Lay Juan, nor could aught renew the beat
   Of his quenched heart: and the sea dirges low
Rang in her sad ears like a Mermaid's song,
And that brief dream appeared a life too long.

35

And gazing on the dead, she thought his face
   Faded, or altered into something new —
Like to her Father's features, till each trace
   More like and like to Lambro's aspect grew —
With all his keen worn look and Grecian grace;
   And starting, she awoke, and what to view?
Oh! Powers of Heaven! what dark eye meets she there?
'T is — 't is her Father's — fixed upon the pair!

36

Then shrieking, she arose, and shrieking fell,
   With joy and sorrow, hope and fear, to see

Him whom she deemed a habitant where dwell
　　The ocean-buried, risen from death, to be
Perchance the death of one she loved too well:
　　Dear as her father had been to Haidée,
It was a moment of that awful kind —
I have seen such — but must not call to mind.

37

Up Juan sprang to Haidée's bitter shriek,
　　And caught her falling, and from off the wall
Snatched down his sabre, in hot haste to wreak
　　Vengeance on him who was the cause of all:
Then Lambro, who till now forebore to speak,
　　Smiled scornfully, and said, "Within my call,
A thousand scimitars await the word;
Put up, young man, put up your silly sword."

38

And Haidée clung around him; "Juan, 't is —
　　'T is Lambro — 't is my father! Kneel with me —
He will forgive us — yes — it must be — yes.
　　Oh! dearest father, in this agony
Of pleasure and of pain — even while I kiss
　　Thy garment's hem with transport, can it be
That doubt should mingle with my filial joy?
Deal with me as thou wilt, but spare this boy."

39

High and inscrutable the old man stood,
　　Calm in his voice, and calm within his eye —
Not always signs with him of calmest mood:
　　He looked upon her, but gave no reply;
Then turned to Juan, in whose cheek the blood
　　Oft came and went, as there resolved to die;
In arms, at least, he stood, in act to spring
On the first foe whom Lambro's call might bring.

40

"Young man, your sword;" so Lambro once more said:
　　Juan replied, "Not while this arm is free."

The old man's cheek grew pale, but not with dread,
　　And drawing from his belt a pistol he
Replied, "Your blood be then on your own head."
　　Then looked close at the flint, as if to see
'T was fresh — for he had lately used the lock —
And next proceeded quietly to cock.

41

It has a strange quick jar upon the ear,
　　That cocking of a pistol, when you know
A moment more will bring the sight to bear
　　Upon your person, twelve yards off, or so;
A gentlemanly distance, not too near,
　　If you have got a former friend for foe;
But after being fired at once or twice,
The ear becomes more Irish, and less nice.

42

Lambro presented, and one instant more
　　Had stopped this Canto, and Don Juan's breath,
When Haidée threw herself her boy before;
　　Stern as her sire: "On me," she cried, "let Death
Descend — the fault is mine; this fatal shore
　　He found — but sought not. I have pledged my faith;
I love him — I will die with him: I knew
Your nature's firmness — know your daughter's too."

43

A minute past, and she had been all tears,
　　And tenderness, and infancy; but now
She stood as one who championed human fears —
　　Pale, statue-like, and stern, she wooed the blow;
And tall beyond her sex, and their compeers,
　　She drew up to her height, as if to show
A fairer mark; and with a fixed eye scanned
Her Father's face — but never stopped his hand.

41:8. *more Irish and less nice*: I.e. more truculent, and less fastidious.

44

He gazed on her, and she on him; 't was strange
   How like they looked! the expression was the same;
Serenely savage, with a little change
   In the large dark eye's mutual-darted flame;
For she, too, was as one who could avenge,
   If cause should be — a Lioness, though tame.
Her Father's blood before her Father's face
Boiled up, and proved her truly of his race.

45

I said they were alike, their features and
   Their stature, differing but in sex and years;
Even to the delicacy of their hand
   There was resemblance, such as true blood wears;
And now to see them, thus divided, stand
   In fixed ferocity, when joyous tears
And sweet sensations should have welcomed both,
Shows what the passions are in their full growth.

46

The father paused a moment, then withdrew
   His weapon, and replaced it; but stood still,
And looking on her, as to look her through,
   "Not *I*," he said, "have sought this stranger's ill!
Not *I* have made this desolation: few
   Would bear such outrage, and forbear to kill;
But I must do my duty — how thou hast
Done thine, the present vouches for the past.

47

"Let him disarm; or, by my father's head,
   His own shall roll before you like a ball!"
He raised his whistle, as the word he said,
   And blew; another answered to the call,
And rushing in disorderly, though led,
   And armed from boot to turban, one and all,

Some twenty of his train came, rank on rank;
He gave the word, — "Arrest or slay the Frank."

48

Then, with a sudden movement, he withdrew
    His daughter; while compressed within his clasp,
'Twixt her and Juan interposed the crew;
    In vain she struggled in her father's grasp —
His arms were like a serpent's coil: then flew
    Upon their prey, as darts an angry asp,
The file of pirates — save the foremost, who
Had fallen, with his right shoulder half cut through.

49

The second had his cheek laid open; but
    The third, a wary, cool old sworder, took
The blows upon his cutlass, and then put
    His own well in; so well, ere you could look,
His man was floored, and helpless at his foot,
    With the blood running like a little brook
From two smart sabre gashes, deep and red —
One on the arm, the other on the head.

50

And then they bound him where he fell, and bore
    Juan from the apartment: with a sign
Old Lambro bade them take him to the shore,
    Where lay some ships which were to sail at nine.
They laid him in a boat, and plied the oar
    Until they reached some galliots, placed in line;
On board of one of these, and under hatches,
They stowed him, with strict orders to the watches.

51

The world is full of strange vicissitudes,
    And here was one exceedingly unpleasant:

50.6. *galliots*: Small swift galleys.

A gentleman so rich in the world's goods,
    Handsome and young, enjoying all the present,
Just at the very time when he least broods
    On such a thing, is suddenly to sea sent,
Wounded and chained, so that he cannot move,
And all because a lady fell in love.

52

Here I must leave him, for I grow pathetic,
    Moved by the Chinese nymph of tears, green tea!
Than whom Cassandra was not more prophetic;
    For if my pure libations exceed three,
I feel my heart become so sympathetic,
    That I must have recourse to black Bohea:
'T is pity wine should be so deleterious,
For tea and coffee leave us much more serious,

53

Unless when qualified with thee, Cogniac!
    Sweet Naïad of the Phlegethontic rill!
Ah! why the liver wilt thou thus attack,
    And make, like other nymphs, thy lovers ill?
I would take refuge in weak punch, but *rack*
    (In each sense of the word), whene'er I fill
My mild and midnight beakers to the brim,
Wakes me next morning with its synonym.

54

I leave Don Juan for the present, safe —
    Not sound, poor fellow, but severely wounded;
Yet could his corporal pangs amount to half
    Of those with which his Haidée's bosom bounded?
She was not one to weep, and rave, and chafe,
    And then give way, subdued because surrounded;

52:6. *Bohea*: A strong, inferior black tea.
53:1. *qualified*: Mixed with brandy.
53:2. *Phlegethontic rill*: River of fire in Hades.
53:5. *rack*: Means both rum punch and a hangover.

Her mother was a Moorish maid from Fez,
Where all is Eden, or a wilderness.

55

There the large olive rains its amber store
   In marble fonts; there grain, and flower, and fruit,
Gush from the earth until the land runs o'er;
   But there, too, many a poison-tree has root,
And Midnight listens to the lion's roar,
   And long, long deserts scorch the camel's foot,
Or heaving whelm the helpless caravan;
And as the soil is, so the heart of man.

56

Afric is all the Sun's, and as her earth
   Her human clay is kindled; full of power
For good or evil, burning from its birth,
   The Moorish blood partakes the planet's hour,
And like the soil beneath it will bring forth:
   Beauty and love were Haidée's mother's dower;
But her large dark eye showed deep Passion's force,
Though sleeping like a lion near a source.

57

Her daughter, tempered with a milder ray,
   Like summer clouds all silvery, smooth, and fair,
Till slowly charged with thunder they display
   Terror to earth, and tempest to the air,
Had held till now her soft and milky way;
   But overwrought with Passion and Despair,
The fire burst forth from her Numidian veins,
Even as the Simoom sweeps the blasted plains.

58

The last sight which she saw was Juan's gore,
   And he himself o'ermastered and cut down;
His blood was running on the very floor
   Where late he trod, her beautiful, her own;

Thus much she viewed an instant and no more, —
  Her struggles ceased with one convulsive groan;
On her Sire's arm, which until now scarce held
Her writhing, fell she like a cedar felled.

59

A vein had burst, and her sweet lips' pure dyes
  Were dabbled with the deep blood which ran o'er;
And her head drooped, as when the lily lies
  O'ercharged with rain: her summoned handmaids bore
Their lady to her couch with gushing eyes;
  Of herbs and cordials they produced their store,
But she defied all means they could employ,
Like one Life could not hold, nor Death destroy.

60

Days lay she in that state unchanged, though chill —
  With nothing livid, still her lips were red;
She had no pulse, but Death seemed absent still;
  No hideous sign proclaimed her surely dead;
Corruption came not in each mind to kill
  All hope; to look upon her sweet face bred
New thoughts of Life, for it seemed full of soul —
She had so much, Earth could not claim the whole.

61

The ruling passion, such as marble shows
  When exquisitely chiselled, still lay there,
But fixed as marble's unchanged aspect throws
  O'er the fair Venus, but for ever fair;
O'er the Laocoön's all eternal throes,
  And ever-dying Gladiator's air,
Their energy like life forms all their fame,
Yet looks not life, for they are still the same. —

  61:4. *fair Venus*: The Venus of Medici.
  61:5–6. *Laocoön's . . . Gladiator's*: For Byron's description of these
sculptures, see *CH* IV, stanzas 140 and 160.

62

She woke at length, but not as sleepers wake,
  Rather the dead, for Life seemed something new,
A strange sensation which she must partake
  Perforce, since whatsoever met her view
Struck not on memory, though a heavy ache
  Lay at her heart, whose earliest beat still true
Brought back the sense of pain without the cause,
For, for a while, the Furies made a pause.

63

She looked on many a face with vacant eye,
  On many a token without knowing what:
She saw them watch her without asking why,
  And recked not who around her pillow sat;
Not speechless, though she spoke not — not a sigh
  Relieved her thoughts — dull silence and quick chat
Were tried in vain by those who served; she gave
No sign, save breath, of having left the grave.

64

Her handmaids tended, but she heeded not;
  Her Father watched, she turned her eyes away;
She recognised no being, and no spot,
  However dear or cherished in their day;
They changed from room to room — but all forgot —
  Gentle, but without memory she lay;
At length those eyes, which they would fain be weaning
Back to old thoughts, waxed full of fearful meaning.

65

And then a slave bethought her of a harp;
  The harper came, and tuned his instrument;
At the first notes, irregular and sharp,
  On him her flashing eyes a moment bent,
Then to the wall she turned as if to warp
  Her thoughts from sorrow through her heart re-sent;
And he began a long low island-song
Of ancient days, ere Tyranny grew strong.

66

Anon her thin wan fingers beat the wall
  In time to his old tune: he changed the theme,
And sung of Love; the fierce name struck through all
  Her recollection; on her flashed the dream
Of what she was, and is, if ye could call
  To be so being; in a gushing stream
The tears rushed forth from her o'erclouded brain,
Like mountain mists at length dissolved in rain.

67

Short solace, vain relief! — Thought came too quick,
  And whirled her brain to madness; she arose
As one who ne'er had dwelt among the sick,
  And flew at all she met, as on her foes;
But no one ever heard her speak or shriek,
  Although her paroxysm drew towards its close; —
Hers was a frenzy which disdained to rave,
Even when they smote her, in the hope to save.

68

Yet she betrayed at times a gleam of sense;
  Nothing could make her meet her Father's face,
Though on all other things with looks intense
  She gazed, but none she ever could retrace;
Food she refused, and raiment; no pretence
  Availed for either; neither change of place,
Nor time, nor skill, nor remedy, could give her
Senses to sleep — the power seemed gone for ever.

69

Twelve days and nights she withered thus; at last,
  Without a groan, or sigh, or glance, to show
A parting pang, the spirit from her passed:
  And they who watched her nearest could not know
The very instant, till the change that cast
  Her sweet face into shadow, dull and slow,
Glazed o'er her eyes — the beautiful, the black —
Oh! to possess such lustre — and then lack!

70

She died, but not alone; she held, within,
    A second principle of Life, which might
Have dawned a fair and sinless child of sin; ˙
    But closed its little being without light,
And went down to the grave unborn, wherein
    Blossom and bough lie withered with one blight;
In vain the dews of Heaven descend above
The bleeding flower and blasted fruit of Love.

71

Thus lived — thus died she; never more on her
    Shall Sorrow light, or Shame. She was not made
Through years or moons the inner weight to bear,
    Which colder hearts endure till they are laid
By age in earth: her days and pleasures were
    Brief, but delightful — such as had not staid
Long with her destiny; but she sleeps well
By the sea-shore, whereon she loved to dwell.

72

That isle is now all desolate and bare,
    Its dwellings down, its tenants passed away;
None but her own and Father's grave is there,
    And nothing outward tells of human clay;
Ye could not know where lies a thing so fair,
    No stone is there to show, no tongue to say,
What was; no dirge, except the hollow sea's,
Mourns o'er the Beauty of the Cyclades.

73

But many a Greek maid in a loving song
    Sighs o'er her name; and many an islander
With her Sire's story makes the night less long;
    Valour was his, and Beauty dwelt with her:
Is she loved rashly, her life paid for wrong —
    A heavy price must all pay who thus err,

In some shape; let none think to fly the danger,
For soon or late Love is his own avenger.

• • • • • • •

1819   *1821*

[In Canto 5, Juan is sold as a slave to the Turkish Sultana,
Gulbeyaz. His experiences in the Harem are related in Cantos
5 and 6. In Canto 7 he escapes from the Harem and makes
his way into the lines of the Russian army which is about
to attack the Turkish city of Ismail, situated near the mouth
of the Danube in what is today Rumania. Juan joins the
Russian army and takes part in the attack.]

CANTO THE SEVENTH

1

O Love! O Glory! what are ye who fly
    Around us ever, rarely to alight?
There's not a meteor in the polar sky
    Of such transcendent and more fleeting flight.
Chill, and chained to cold earth, we lift on high
    Our eyes in search of either lovely light;
A thousand and a thousand colours they
Assume, then leave us on our freezing way.

2

And such as they are, such my present tale is,
    A nondescript and ever-varying rhyme,
A versified Aurora Borealis,
    Which flashes o'er a waste and icy clime.
When we know what all are, we must bewail us,
    But ne'ertheless I hope it is no crime
To laugh at *all* things — for I wish to know
What, after *all*, are *all* things — but a *show*?

3

They accuse me — *Me* — the present writer of
    The present poem — of — I know not what —

A tendency to under-rate and scoff
   At human power and virtue, and all that;
And this they say in language rather rough.
   Good God! I wonder what they would be at!
I say no more than hath been said in Danté's
Verse, and by Solomon and by Cervantes;

4

By Swift, by Machiavel, by Rochefoucault,
   By Fénélon, by Luther, and by Plato;
By Tillotson, and Wesley, and Rousseau,
   Who knew this life was not worth a potato.
'T is not their fault, nor mine, if this be so, —
   For my part, I pretend not to be Cato,
Nor even Diogenes. — We live and die,
But which is best, *you* know no more than I.

5

Socrates said, our only knowledge was
   "To know that nothing could be known;" a pleasant
Science enough, which levels to an ass
   Each man of wisdom, future, past, or present.
Newton (that proverb of the mind), alas!
   Declared, with all his grand discoveries recent,
That he himself felt only "like a youth
Picking up shells by the great ocean — Truth."

6

Ecclesiastes said, "that all is vanity" —
   Most modern preachers say the same, or show it

4:1. *Rochefoucault*: François de La Rochefoucauld (1613–1680), author of the famous *Maxims* (1665).

4:2. *Fénélon*: François de Fénélon (1651–1715), French theologian who fell in disfavor with church and court for his Quietism, a mystical faith involving renunciation of self.

4:3. *Tillotson*: John Tillotson (1630–1694), archbishop of Canterbury.

4:6. *Cato*: Probably Cato the Censor (234–149 B.C.) who rebuked the Romans for their luxurious living and cried, "Carthage must be destroyed."

4:7. *Diogenes*: The Cynic philosopher (c. 412 B.C.) who lived a life of great austerity.

By their examples of true Christianity:
 In short, all know, or very soon may know it;
And in this scene of all-confessed inanity,
 By Saint, by Sage, by Preacher, and by Poet,
Must I restrain me, through the fear of strife,
From holding up the nothingness of Life?

7

Dogs, or men! — for I flatter you in saying
 That ye are dogs — your betters far — ye may
Read, or read not, what I am now essaying
 To show ye what ye are in every way.
As little as the moon stops for the baying
 Of wolves, will the bright Muse withdraw one ray
From out her skies — then howl your idle wrath!
While she still silvers o'er your gloomy path.

8

"Fierce loves and faithless wars" — I am not sure
 If this be the right reading — 't is no matter;
The fact 's about the same, I am secure;
 I sing them both, and am about to batter
A town which did a famous siege endure,
 And was beleagured both by land and water
By Souvaroff, or Anglicè Suwarrow,
Who loved blood as an alderman loves marrow.

• • • • • • •

80

Oh, thou eternal Homer! I have now
 To paint a siege, wherein more men were slain,
With deadlier engines and a speedier blow,

8:7. *Souvaroff*: Alexander Suvarov (variously spelled) (1729–1800) was the Russian general who attacked Ismail on November 30, 1790. The names and details which follow Byron took from an account of the siege in the Marquis de Castelnau's *Histoire de la Nouvelle Russie* (1820).

Than in thy Greek gazette of that campaign;
And yet, like all men else, I must allow,
    To vie with thee would be about as vain
As for a brook to cope with Ocean's flood, —
But still we moderns equal you in blood:

81

If not in poetry, at least in fact;
    And fact is Truth, the grand desideratum!
Of which, howe'er the Muse describes each act,
    There should be ne'ertheless a slight substratum.
But now the town is going to be attacked;
    Great deeds are doing — how shall I relate 'em?
Souls of immortal Generals! Phœbus watches
To colour up his rays from your despatches.

82

Oh, ye great bulletins of Bonaparte!
    Oh, ye less grand long lists of killed and wounded!
Shade of Leonidas, who fought so hearty,
    When my poor Greece was once, as now, surrounded!
Oh, Cæsar's Commentaries! now impart, ye
    Shadows of Glory! (lest I be confounded),
A portion of your fading twilight hues —
So beautiful, so fleeting — to the Muse.

83

When I call "fading" martial immortality,
    I mean, that every age and every year,
And almost every day, in sad reality,
    Some sucking hero is compelled to rear,
Who, when we come to sum up the totality
    Of deeds to human happiness most dear,
Turns out to be a butcher in great business,
Afflicting young folks with a sort of dizziness.

82:3. *Leonidas*: The hero of Thermopylae.

84

Medals, rank, ribands, lace, embroidery, scarlet,
   Are things immortal to immortal man,
As purple to the Babylonian harlot:
   An uniform to boys is like a fan
To women; there is scarce a crimson varlet
   But deems himself the first in Glory's van.
But Glory's glory; and if you would find
What *that* is — ask the pig who sees the wind!

85

At least *he feels it,* and some say he *sees,*
   Because he runs before it like a pig;
Or, if that simple sentence should displease,
   Say, that he scuds before it like a brig,
A schooner, or — but it is time to ease
   This Canto, ere my Muse perceives fatigue,
The next shall ring a peal to shake all people,
Like a bob-major from a village steeple.

86

Hark! through the silence of the cold, dull night,
   The hum of armies gathering rank on rank!
Lo! dusky masses steal in dubious sight
   Along the leaguered wall and bristling bank
Of the armed river, while with straggling light
   The stars peep through the vapours dim and dank,
Which curl in various wreaths: — how soon the smoke
Of Hell shall pall them in a deeper cloak!

87

Here pause we for the present — as even then
   That awful pause, dividing Life from Death,
Struck for an instant on the hearts of men, —
   Thousands of whom were drawing their last breath!
A moment — and all will be Life again!
   The march! the charge! the shouts of either faith,

Hurrah! and Allah! and one moment more —
The death-cry drowning in the Battle's roar.

1822 *1823*

CANTO THE EIGHTH

• • • • • • •

6

The night was dark, and the thick mist allowed
   Nought to be seen save the artillery's flame,
Which arched the horizon like a fiery cloud,
   And in the Danube's waters shone the same —
A mirrored Hell! the volleying roar, and loud
   Long booming of each peal on peal, o'ercame
The ear far more than thunder; for Heaven's flashes
Spare, or smite rarely — Man's make millions ashes!

7

The column, ordered on the assault, scarce passed
   Beyond the Russian batteries a few toises,
When up the bristling Moslem rose at last,
   Answering the Christian thunders with like voices:
Then one vast fire, air, earth, and stream embraced,
   Which rocked as 't were beneath the mighty noises;
While the whole rampart blazed like Etna, when
The restless Titan hiccups in his den;

8

And one enormous shout of "Allah!" rose
   In the same moment, loud as even the roar
Of War's most mortal engines, to their foes
   Hurling defiance: city, stream, and shore
Resounded "Allah!" and the clouds which close
   With thickening canopy the conflict o'er,

7:8. *The restless Titan*: Enceladus, the hundred-armed giant, was buried
by Zeus under Mt. Aetna.

Vibrate to the Eternal name. Hark! through
All sounds it pierceth — "Allah! Allah Hu!"

9

The columns were in movement one and all,
  But of the portion which attacked by water,
Thicker than leaves the lives began to fall,
  Though led by Arseniew, that great son of slaughter,
As brave as ever faced both bomb and ball.
  "Carnage" (so Wordsworth tells you) "is God's daughter:"
If *he* speak truth, she is Christ's sister, and
Just now behaved as in the Holy Land.

10

The Prince de Ligne was wounded in the knee;
  Count Chapeau-Bras, too, had a ball between
His cap and head, which proves the head to be
  Aristocratic as was ever seen,
Because it then received no injury
  More than the cap; in fact, the ball could mean
No harm unto a right legitimate head;
"Ashes to ashes" — why not lead to lead?

11

Also the General Markow, Brigadier,
  Insisting on removal of *the Prince*
Amidst some groaning thousands dying near, —
  All common fellows, who might writhe and wince,
And shriek for water into a deaf ear, —

8:8. *"Allah Hu!"*: "Allah Hu is properly the war cry of the Mussulmans, and they dwell on the last syllable, which gives it a wild and peculiar effect" (Byron's note).

9:4. *Arseniew*: Arseniev, the Prince de Ligne (10:1) and Markov (11:1) were generals in the Russian army. Count Chapeau Bras (10:2) is Byron's caricature of the thick-skulled aristocratic officer. In Castelnau, he is the Duc de Richelieu.

9:6. *"Carnage . . . is God's daughter"*: In his Thanksgiving Ode (1816) on the defeat of Napoleon, Wordsworth wrote: "But *Thy* most dreaded instrument / In working out a pure intent, / Is man arrayed for mutual slaughter; / Yea, Carnage is thy daughter!"

The General Markow, who could thus evince
His sympathy for rank, by the same token,
To teach him greater, had his own leg broken.

12

Three hundred cannon threw up their emetic,
   And thirty thousand muskets flung their pills
Like hail, to make a bloody Diuretic.
   Mortality! thou hast thy monthly bills:
Thy plagues — thy famines — thy physicians — yet tick,
   Like the death-watch, within our ears the ills
Past, present, and to come; — but all may yield
To the true portrait of one battle-field;

13

There the still varying pangs, which multiply
   Until their very number makes men hard
By the infinities of agony,
   Which meet the gaze, whate'er it may regard —
The groan, the roll in dust, the all-*white* eye
   Turned back within its socket, — these reward
Your rank and file by thousands, while the rest
May win perhaps a riband at the breast!

14

Yet I love Glory; — Glory 's a great thing: —
   Think what it is to be in your old age
Maintained at the expense of your good King:
   A moderate pension shakes full many a sage,
And Heroes are but made for bards to sing,
   Which is still better — thus, in verse, to wage
Your wars eternally, besides enjoying
Half-pay for life, make Mankind worth destroying.

15

The troops, already disembarked, pushed on
   To take a battery on the right: the others,
Who landed lower down, their landing done,
   Had set to work as briskly as their brothers:

Being grenadiers, they mounted one by one,
   Cheerful as children climb the breasts of mothers,
O'er the intrenchment and the palisade,
Quite orderly, as if upon parade.

16

And this was admirable: for so hot
   The fire was, that were red Vesuvius loaded,
Besides its lava, with all sorts of shot
   And shells or hells, it could not more have goaded.
Of officers a third fell on the spot,
   A thing which Victory by no means boded
To gentlemen engaged in the assault:
Hounds, when the huntsmen tumbles, are at fault.

17

But here I leave the general concern
   To track our Hero on his path of Fame:
He must his laurels separately earn —
   For fifty thousand heroes, name by name,
Though all deserving equally to turn
   A couplet, or an elegy to claim,
Would form a lengthy lexicon of Glory,
And, what is worse still, a much longer story:

18

And therefore we must give the greater number
   To the Gazette — which doubtless fairly dealt
By the deceased, who lie in famous slumber
   In ditches, fields, or wheresoe'er they felt
Their clay for the last time their souls encumber; —
   Thrice happy he whose name has been well spelt
In the despatch: I knew a man whose loss
Was printed *Grove*, although his name was Grose.

• • • • • • •

18:8. *Grose*: "A fact: see the Waterloo Gazette" (Byron's note). Byron was at college with Grose.

82

The city's taken — only part by part —
  And Death is drunk with gore: there 's not a street
Where fights not to the last some desperate heart
  For those for whom it soon shall cease to beat.
Here War forgot his own destructive art
  In more destroying Nature; and the heat
Of Carnage, like the Nile's sun-sodden slime,
Engendered monstrous shapes of every crime.

83

A Russian officer, in martial tread
  Over a heap of bodies, felt his heel
Seized fast, as if 't were by the serpent's head
  Whose fangs Eve taught her human seed to feel;
In vain he kicked, and swore, and writhed, and bled,
  And howled for help as wolves do for a meal —
The teeth still kept their gratifying hold,
As do the subtle snakes described of old.

84

A dying Moslem, who had felt the foot
  Of a foe o'er him, snatched at it, and bit
The very tendon which is most acute —
  (That which some ancient Muse or modern wit
Named after thee, Achilles!) and quite through 't
  He made the teeth meet, nor relinquished it
Even with his life — for (but they lie) 't is said
To the live leg still clung the severed head.

85

However this may be, 't is pretty sure
  The Russian officer for life was lamed,
For the Turk's teeth stuck faster than a skewer,
  And left him 'midst the invalid and maimed:
The regimental surgeon could not cure
  His patient, and, perhaps, was to be blamed
More than the head of the inveterate foe,
Which was cut off, and scare even then let go.

86

But then the fact 's a fact — and 't is the part
    Of a true poet to escape from fiction
Whene'er he can; for there is little art
    In leaving verse more free from the restriction
Of Truth than prose, unless to suit the mart
    For what is sometimes called poetic diction,
And that outrageous appetite for lies
Which Satan angles with for souls, like flies.

87

The city 's taken, but not rendered! — No!
    There 's not a Moslem that hath yielded sword:
The blood may gush out, as the Danube's flow
    Rolls by the city wall; but deed nor word
Acknowledge aught of dread of Death or foe:
    In vain the yell of victory is roared
By the advancing Muscovite — the groan
Of the last foe is echoed by his own.

88

The bayonet pierces and the sabre cleaves,
    And human lives are lavished everywhere,
As the year closing whirls the scarlet leaves
    When the stripped forest bows to the bleak air,
And groans; and thus the peopled city grieves,
    Shorn of its best and loveliest, and left bare;
But still it falls in vast and awful splinters,
As oaks blown down with all their thousand winters.

89

It is an awful topic — but 't is not
    My cue for any time to be terrific:
For checkered as is seen our human lot
    With good, and bad, and worse, alike prolific
Of melancholy merriment, to quote
    Too much of one sort would be soporific; —
Without, or with, offence to friends or foes,
I sketch your world exactly as it goes.

90

And one good action in the midst of crimes
  Is "quite refreshing," in the affected phrase
Of these ambrosial, Pharisaic times,
  With all their pretty milk-and-water ways,
And may serve therefore to bedew these rhymes,
  A little scorched at present with the blaze
Of conquest and its consequences, which
Make Epic poesy so rare and rich.

91

Upon a taken bastion, where there lay
  Thousands of slaughtered men, a yet warm group
Of murdered women, who had found their way
  To this vain refuge, made the good heart droop
And shudder; — while, as beautiful as May,
  A female child of ten years tried to stoop
And hide her little palpitating breast
Amidst the bodies lulled in bloody rest.

92

Two villanous Cossacques pursued the child
  With flashing eyes and weapons: matched with *them,*
The rudest brute that roams Siberia's wild
  Has feelings pure and polished as a gem —
The bear is civilised, the wolf is mild;
  And whom for this at last must we condemn?
Their natures? or their sovereigns, who employ
All arts to teach their subjects to destroy?

93

Their sabres glittered o'er her little head,
  Whence her fair hair rose twining with affright,
Her hidden face was plunged amidst the dead:
  When Juan caught a glimpse of this sad sight,
I shall not say exactly what he *said,*
  Because it might not solace "ears polite";

93:6. *"ears polite"*: "Who never mentions Hell to ears polite." Pope,
Moral Essays, Epistle 4, 1. 150.

But what he *did,* was to lay on their backs,
The readiest way of reasoning with Cossacques.

94

One's hip he slashed, and split the other's shoulder,
   And drove them with their brutal yells to seek
If there might be chirugeons who could solder
   The wounds they richly merited, and shriek
Their baffled rage and pain; while waxing colder
   As he turned o'er each pale and gory cheek,
Don Juan raised his little captive from
The heap a moment more had made her tomb.

95

And she was chill as they, and on her face
   A slender streak of blood announced how near
Her fate had been to that of all her race;
   For the same blow which laid her mother here
Had scarred her brow, and left its crimson trace,
   As the last link with all she had held dear;
But else unhurt, she opened her large eyes,
And gazed on Juan with a wild surprise.

● ● ● ● ● ● ●

120

But the stone bastion still kept up its fire,
   Where the chief Pacha calmly held his post:
Some twenty times he made the Russ retire,
   And baffled the assaults of all their host;
At length he condescended to inquire
   If yet the city's rest were won or lost;
And being told the latter, sent a Bey
To answer Ribas' summons to give way.

121

In the meantime, cross-legged, with great sang-froid,
   Among the scorching ruins he sat smoking
Tobacco on a little carpet; — Troy

Saw nothing like the scene around; — yet looking
With martial Stoicism, nought seemed to annoy
    His stern philosophy; but gently stroking
His beard, he puffed his pipe's ambrosial gales,
As if he had three lives, as well as tails.

122

The town was taken — whether he might yield
    Himself or bastion, little mattered now:
His stubborn valour was no future shield.
    Ismail 's no more! The Crescent's silver bow
Sunk, and the crimson Cross glared o'er the field,
    But red with no *redeeming* gore: the glow
Of burning streets, like moonlight on the water,
Was imaged back in blood, the sea of slaughter.

123

All that the mind would shrink from of excesses —
    All that the body perpetrates of bad;
All that we read — hear — dream, of man's distresses —
    All that the Devil would do if run stark mad;
All that defies the worst which pen expresses, —
    All by which Hell is peopled, or as sad
As Hell — mere mortals, who their power abuse —
Was here (as heretofore and since) let loose.

124

If here and there some transient trait of pity
    Was shown, and some more noble heart broke through
Its bloody bond, and saved, perhaps, some pretty
    Child, or an agéd, helpless man or two —
What's this in one annihilated city,
    Where thousand loves, and ties, and duties grew?
Cockneys of London! Muscadins of Paris!
Just ponder what a pious pastime War is.

121:8. *three lives, as well as tails*: A Turkish Pasha's rank was indicated by the number of horses' tails borne before him. Three tails indicated the highest rank.

124:7. *Muscadins*: Dandies. During the French Revolution, a term of contempt.

125

Think how the joys of reading a Gazette
    Are purchased by all agonies and crimes:
Or if these do not move you, don't forget
    Such doom may be your own in after-times.
Meantime the Taxes, Castlereagh, and Debt,
    Are hints as good as sermons, or as rhymes.
Read your own hearts and Ireland's present story,
Then feed her famine fat with Wellesley's glory.

126

But still there is unto a patriot nation,
    Which loves so well its country and its King,
A subject of sublimest exultation —
    Bear it, ye Muses, on your brightest wing!
Howe'er the mighty locust, Desolation,
    Strip your green fields, and to your harvests cling,
Gaunt famine never shall approach the throne —
Though Ireland starve, great George weighs twenty stone.

127

But let me put an end unto my theme:
    There was an end of Ismail — hapless town!
Far flashed her burning towers o'er Danube's stream,
    And redly ran his blushing waters down.
The horrid war-whoop and the shriller scream
    Rose still; but fainter were the thunders grown:
Of forty thousand who had manned the wall,
Some hundreds breathed — the rest were silent all!

• • • • • • •

125:5. *Taxes, Castlereagh, and Debt*: For Castlereagh, see *Dedication*. The enormous national debt as a result of the Napoleonic wars led to a period of inflation.

125:8. *Wellesley's glory*: The Irish potato crop failed in 1822 and resulted in famine. Wellesley, the brother of the Duke of Wellington, organized a system of relief.

133

Suwarrow now was conqueror — a match
  For Timour or for Zinghis in his trade.
While mosques and streets, beneath his eyes, like thatch
  Blazed, and the cannon's roar was scarce allayed,
With bloody hands he wrote his first despatch;
  And here exactly follows what he said: —
"Glory to *God* and to the Empress!" (*Powers
Eternal! such names mingled!*) "Ismail 's ours."

134

Methinks these are the most tremendous words,
  Since "MENE, MENE, TEKEL," and "UPHARSIN,"
Which hands or pens have ever traced of swords.
  Heaven help me! I 'm but little of a parson:
What Daniel read was short-hand of the Lord's,
  Severe, sublime; the prophet wrote no farce on
The fate of nations; — but this Russ so witty
Could rhyme, like Nero, o'er a burning city.

135

He wrote this Polar melody, and set it,
  Duly accompanied by shrieks and groans,
Which few will sing, I trust, but none forget it —
  For I will teach, if possible, the stones
To rise against Earth's tyrants. Never let it
  Be said that we still truckle unto thrones; —
But ye — our children's children! think how we
Showed *what things were* before the World was free!

136

That hour is not for us, but 't is for you:
  And as, in the great joy of your Millennium,

  133:2. *Timour . . . . Zinghis*: Zinghis or Genghis Khan (1162–1227) was
the great Mongol Emperor; Timour (1336?–1405), his descendant, was the
hero-villain in Marlowe's play *Tamburlaine the Great*.
  133:7–8. *"Ismail's ours"*: "In the original Russian . . . a kind of
couplet; for he was a poet." (Byron's note.)
  134:2. *Upharsin*: The words written on the wall at Belshazzar's Feast,
prophesying his destruction. See *Daniel* 5:25–28.

You hardly will believe such things were true
    As now occur, I thought that I would pen you 'em;
But may their very memory perish too! —
    Yet if perchance remembered, still disdain you 'em
More than you scorn the savages of yore,
Who *painted* their *bare* limbs, but *not* with gore.

137

And when you hear historians talk of thrones,
    And those that sate upon them, let it be
As we now gaze upon the mammoth's bones,
    And wonder what old world such things could see,
Or hieroglyphics on Egyptian stones,
    The pleasant riddles of futurity —
Guessing at what shall happily be hid,
As the real purpose of a pyramid.

138

Reader! I have kept my word, — at least so far
    As the first Canto promised. You have now
Had sketches of Love — Tempest — Travel — War, —
    All very accurate, you must allow,
And *Epic,* if plain truth should prove no bar;
    For I have drawn much less with a long bow
Than my forerunners. Carelessly I sing,
But Phoebus lends me now and then a string,

139

With which I still can harp, and carp, and fiddle.
    What further hath befallen or may befall
The hero of this grand poetic riddle,
    I by and by may tell you, if at all:
But now I choose to break off in the middle,
    Worn out with battering Ismail's stubborn wall,
While Juan is sent off with the despatch,
For which all Petersburgh is on the watch.

137:5. *Egyptian stones*: The Rosetta stone was discovered in 1799.

140

This special honour was conferred, because
　　He had behaved with courage and humanity —
Which *last* men like, when they have time to pause
　　From their ferocities produced by vanity.
His little captive gained him some applause
　　For saving her amidst the wild insanity
Of carnage, — and I think he was more glad in her
Safety, than his new order of St. Vladimir.

141

The Moslem orphan went with her protector,
　　For she was homeless, houseless, helpless; all
Her friends, like the sad family of Hector,
　　Had perished in the field or by the wall:
Her very place of birth was but a spectre
　　Of what it had been; there the Muezzin's call
To prayer was heard no more! — and Juan wept,
And made a vow to shield her, which he kept.

1822　　　　　　　　　　　　　　　　　　　　　　*1823*

[In Canto 9 Juan becomes the newest favorite of Catherine
the Great. But he falls ill and Catherine in the hope that
a change of climate will restore his health sends him on a secret mission to England.]

CANTO THE TENTH

1

WHEN Newton saw an apple fall, he found
　　In that slight startle from his contemplation —
'T is *said* (for I 'll not answer above ground
　　For any sage's creed or calculation) —
A mode of proving that the Earth turned round
　　In a most natural whirl, called "gravitation";
And this is the sole mortal who could grapple,
Since Adam — with a fall — or with an apple.

2

Man fell with apples, and with apples rose,
    If this be true; for we must deem the mode
In which Sir Isaac Newton could disclose
    Through the then unpaved stars the turnpike road,
A thing to counterbalance human woes:
    For, ever since, immortal man hath glowed
With all kinds of mechanics, and full soon
Steam-engines will conduct him to the moon.

3

And wherefore this exordium? — Why, just now,
    In taking up this paltry sheet of paper,
My bosom underwent a glorious glow,
    And my internal spirit cut a caper:
And though so much inferior, as I know,
    To those who, by the dint of glass and vapour,
Discover stars, and sail in the wind's eye,
I wish to do as much by Poesy.

4

In the wind's eye I have sailed, and sail; but for
    The stars, I own my telescope is dim;
But at the least I have shunned the common shore,
    And leaving land far out of sight, would skim
The Ocean of Eternity: the roar
    Of breakers has not daunted my slight, trim,
But *still* sea-worthy skiff; and she may float
Where ships have foundered, as doth many a boat.

· · · · · · ·

66

I've no great cause to love that spot on earth,
    Which holds what *might have been* the noblest nation;

2:8. *Steam-engines . . . to the moon*: In a conversation with Medwin,
Byron said, "Who would not wish to have been born two or three centuries later? . . . I suppose we shall soon travel by air-vessels, make air
instead of sea-voyages, and at length find our way to the moon, in spite
of the want of atmosphere."

But though I owe it little but my birth,
   I feel a mixed regret and veneration
For its decaying fame and former worth.
   Seven years (the usual term of transportation)
Of absence lay one's old resentments level,
When a man's country 's going to the devil.

67

Alas! could she but fully, truly, know
   How her great name is now throughout abhorred;
How eager all the Earth is for the blow
   Which shall lay bare her bosom to the sword;
How all the nations deem her their worst foe
   That worse than *worst of foes,* the once adored
False friend, who held out Freedom to Mankind,
And now would chain them — to the very *mind;* —

68

Would she be proud, or boast herself the free,
   Who is but first of slaves? The nations are
In prison, — but the gaoler, what is he?
   No less a victim to the bolt and bar.
Is the poor privilege to turn the key
   Upon the captive, Freedom? He 's as far
From the enjoyment of the earth and air
Who watches o'er the chain, as they who wear.

69

Don Juan now saw Albion's earliest beauties,
   Thy cliffs, *dear* Dover! harbour, and hotel;
Thy custom-house, with all its delicate duties;
   Thy waiters running mucks at every bell;
Thy packets, all whose passengers are booties
   To those who upon land or water dwell;
And last, not least, to strangers uninstructed,
Thy long, long bills, whence nothing is deducted.

70

Juan, though careless, young, and *magnifique,*
   And rich in rubles, diamonds, cash, and credit,

Who did not limit much his bills per week,
    Yet stared at this a little, though he paid it, —
(His Maggior Duomo, a smart, subtle Greek,
    Before him summed the awful scroll and read it):
But, doubtless, as the air — though seldom sunny —
Is free, the respiration 's worth the money.

71

On with the horses! Off to Canterbury!
    Tramp, tramp o'er pebble, and splash, splash through
       puddle;
Hurrah! how swiftly speeds the post so merry!
    Not like slow Germany, wherein they muddle
Along the road, as if they went to bury
    Their fare; and also pause besides, to fuddle
With "schnapps" — sad dogs! whom "Hundsfot," or
    "Verflucter,"
Affect no more than lightning a conductor.

72

Now there is nothing gives a man such spirits,
    Leavening his blood as cayenne doth a curry,
As going at full speed — no matter where its
    Direction be, so 't is but in a hurry,
And merely for the sake of its own merits;
    For the less cause there is for all this flurry,
The greater is the pleasure in arriving
At the great *end* of travel — which is driving.

73

They saw at Canterbury the cathedral;
    Black Edward's helm, and Becket's bloody stone,
Were pointed out as usual by the bedral,

71:7. *"Hundsfot"*; *"Verflucter"*: German oaths.
73:2. *Black Edward*: Edward the Black Prince (1330–1376).
 Becket's bloody stone: Thomas à Becket, Archbishop of Canterbury,
was murdered in the Cathedral in 1170.
73:3. *bedral*: Usher.

In the same quaint, uninterested tone: —
There's glory again for you, gentle reader! All
    Ends in a rusty casque and dubious bone,
Half-solved into these sodas or magnesias,
Which form that bitter draught, the human species.

74

The effect on Juan was of course sublime:
    He breathed a thousand Cressys, as he saw
That casque, which never stooped except to Time.
    Even the bold Churchman's tomb excited awe,
Who died in the then great attempt to climb
    O'er Kings, who *now* at least *must talk* of Law
Before they butcher. Little Leila gazed,
And asked why such a structure had been raised:

75

And being told it was "God's House," she said
    He was well lodged, but only wondered how
He suffered Infidels in his homestead,
    The cruel Nazarenes, who had laid low
His holy temples in the lands which bred
    The True Believers; — and her infant brow
Was bent with grief that Mahomet should resign
A mosque so noble, flung like pearls to swine.

76

On! on! through meadows, managed like a garden,
    A paradise of hops and high production;
For, after years of travel by a bard in
    Countries of greater heat, but lesser suction,
A green field is a sight which makes him pardon
    The absence of that more sublime construction,
Which mixes up vines — olives — precipices —
Glaciers — volcanoes — oranges and ices.

74:2. *Cressy*: Crécy, a village in northern France at which the English
won a great victory in 1346. Edward played a hero's role.

77

And when I think upon a pot of beer —
  But I won't weep! — and so drive on, postilions!
As the smart boys spurred fast in their career,
  Juan admired these highways of free millions —
A country in all senses the most dear
  To foreigner or native, save some silly ones,
Who "kick against the pricks" just at this juncture,
And for their pains get only a fresh puncture.

78

What a delightful thing 's a turnpike road!
  So smooth, so level, such a mode of shaving
The Earth, as scarce the eagle in the broad
  Air can accomplish, with his wide wings waving.
Had such been cut in Phaeton's time, the god
  Had told his son to satisfy his craving
With the York mail; — but onward as we roll,
Surgit amari aliquid — the toll!

79

Alas! how deeply painful is all payment!
  Take lives — take wives — take aught except men's purses:
As Machiavel shows those in purple raiment,
  Such is the shortest way to general curses.
They hate a murderer much less than a claimant
  On that sweet ore which everybody nurses. —
Kill a man's family, and he may brook it,
But keep your hands out of his breeches' pocket:

80

So said the Florentine: ye monarchs, hearken
  To your instructor. Juan now was borne,
Just as the day began to wane and darken,
  O'er the high hill, which looks with pride or scorn

78:8. *Surgit amari aliquid*: Something bitter wells up.
79:3. *Machiavel*: In the *Prince*, ch. 17, Machiavelli warns Princes above all to "abstain from the property of others."

Toward the great city. — Ye who have a spark in
   Your veins of Cockney spirit, smile or mourn
According as you take things well or ill; —
Bold Britons, we are now on Shooter's Hill!

81

The Sun went down, the smoke rose up, as from
   A half-unquenched volcano, o'er a space
Which well beseemed the "Devil's drawing-room,"
   As some have qualified that wondrous place:
But Juan felt, though not approaching *Home,*
   As one who, though he were not of the race,
Revered the soil, of those true sons the mother,
Who butchered half the earth, and bullied t' other.

82

A mighty mass of brick, and smoke, and shipping,
   Dirty and dusky, but as wide as eye
Could reach, with here and there a sail just skipping
   In sight, then lost amidst the forestry
Of masts; a wilderness of steeples peeping
   On tiptoe through their sea-coal canopy;
A huge, dun Cupola, like a foolscap crown
On a fool's head — and there is London Town!

83

But Juan saw not this: each wreath of smoke
   Appeared to him but as the magic vapour
Of some alchymic furnace, from whence broke
   The wealth of worlds (a wealth of tax and paper):
The gloomy clouds, which o'er it as a yoke
   Are bowed, and put the Sun out like a taper,
Were nothing but the natural atmosphere,
Extremely wholesome, though but rarely clear.

● ● ● ● ● ● ●

1822   *1823*

80:8. *Shooter's Hill:* On the southeast approach to London.
81:8. . . . *bullied t'other:* India, America (Byron's note).

1

WHEN Bishop Berkeley said "there was no matter,"
  And proved it — 't was no matter what he said:
They say his system 't is in vain to batter,
  Too subtle for the airiest human head;
And yet who can believe it? I would shatter
  Gladly all matters down to stone or lead,
Or adamant, to find the World a spirit,
And wear my head, denying that I wear it.

2

What a sublime discovery 't was to make the
  Universe universal egotism,
That all 's ideal — *all ourselves!* — I 'll stake the
  World (be it what you will) that *that's* no schism.
Oh Doubt! — if thou be'st Doubt, for which some take thee.
  But which I doubt extremely — thou sole prism
Of the Truth's rays, spoil not my draught of spirit!
Heaven's brandy, though our brain can hardly bear it.

3

For ever and anon comes Indigestion
  (Not the most "dainty Ariel"), and perplexes
Our soarings with another sort of question:
  And that which after all my spirit vexes,
Is, that I find no spot where Man can rest eye on,
  Without confusion of the sorts and sexes,
Of Beings, Stars, and this unriddled wonder,
The World, which at the worst 's a *glorious* blunder —

4

If it be chance — or, if it be according
  To the old text, still better: — lest it should

1:1. *Bishop Berkeley*: Irish philosopher (1685–1753) who in *On the Principles of Human Knowledge* (1754) argued that "extension, figure, and motion are only ideas existing in the mind."

Turn out so, we 'll say nothing 'gainst the wording,
    As several people think such hazards rude.
They 're right; our days are too brief for affording
    Space to dispute what *no one* ever could
Decide, and *everybody one day* will
Know very clearly — or at least lie still.

5

And therefore will I leave off metaphysical
    Discussion, which is neither here nor there:
If I agree that what is, is; — then this I call
    Being quite perspicuous and extremely fair;
The truth is, I 've grown lately rather phthisical:
    I don't know what the reason is — the air
Perhaps; but as I suffer from the shocks
Of illness, I grow much more orthodox.

6

The first attack at once proved the Divinity
    (But *that* I never doubted, nor the Devil);
The next, the Virgin's mystical virginity;
    The third, the usual Origin of Evil;
The fourth at once established the whole Trinity
    On so uncontrovertible a level,
That I devoutly wished the three were four —
On purpose to believe so much the more.

7

To our theme. — The man who has stood on the Acropolis,
    And looked down over Attica; or he
Who has sailed where picturesque Constantinople is,
    Or seen Timbuctoo, or hath taken tea
In small-eyed China's crockery-ware metropolis,
    Or sat amidst the bricks of Nineveh,
May not think much of London's first appearance —
But ask him what he thinks of it a year hence!

8

Don Juan had got out on Shooter's Hill;
    Sunset the time, the place the same declivity

Which looks along that vale of Good and Ill
    Where London streets ferment in full activity,
While everything around was calm and still,
    Except the creak of wheels, which on their pivot he
Heard, — and that bee-like, bubbling, busy hum
Of cities, that boil over with their scum: —

9

I say, Don Juan, wrapped in contemplation,
    Walked on behind his carriage, o'er the summit,
And lost in wonder of so great a nation,
    Gave way to 't, since he could not overcome it.
"And here," he cried, "is Freedom's chosen station;
    Here peals the People's voice nor can entomb it
Racks — prisons — inquisitions; Resurrection
Awaits it, each new meeting or election.

10

"Here are chaste wives, pure lives; here people pay
    But what they please; and if that things be dear,
'T is only that they love to throw away
    Their cash, to show how much they have a-year.
Here laws are all inviolate — none lay
    Traps for the traveller — every highway 's clear —
Here" — he was interrupted by a knife,
With — "Damn your eyes! your money or your life!" —

11

These free-born sounds proceeded from four pads
    In ambush laid, who had perceived him loiter
Behind his carriage; and, like handy lads,
    Had seized the lucky hour to reconnoitre,
In which the heedless gentleman who gads
    Upon the road, unless he prove a fighter
May find himself within that isle of riches
Exposed to lose his life as well as breeches.

12

Juan, who did not understand a word
    Of English, save their shibboleth, "God damn!"

And even that he had so rarely heard,
 He sometimes thought 't was only their "Salām,"
Or "God be with you!" — and 't is not absurd
 To think so, — for half English as I am
(To my misfortune), never can I say
I heard them wish "God with you," save that way; —

13

Juan yet quickly understood their gesture,
 And being somewhat choleric and sudden,
Drew forth a pocket pistol from his vesture,
 And fired it into one assailant's pudding —
Who fell, as rolls an ox o'er in his pasture,
 And roared out, as he writhed his native mud in,
Unto his nearest follower or henchman,
"Oh Jack! I 'm floored by that ere bloody Frenchman!"

14

On which Jack and his train set off at speed,
 And Juan's suite, late scattered at a distance,
Came up, all marvelling at such a deed,
 And offering, as usual, late assistance.
Juan, who saw the moon's late minion bleed
 As if his veins would pour out his existence,
Stood calling out for bandages and lint,
And wished he had been less hasty with his flint.

15

"Perhaps," thought he, "it is the country's wont
 To welcome foreigners in this way: now
I recollect some innkeepers who don't
 Differ, except in robbing with a bow,
In lieu of a bare blade and brazen front —
 But what is to be done? I can't allow
The fellow to lie groaning on the road:
So take him up — I 'll help you with the load."

14:5. *the moon's late minion*: i.e. highwayman. See Falstaff's phrase "minions of the moon" in *I Henry IV* I. ii. 28.

16

But ere they could perform this pious duty,
    The dying man cried, "Hold! I 've got my gruel!
Oh! for a glass of *max*! We 've missed our booty;
    Let me die where I am!" And as the fuel
Of Life shrunk in his heart, and thick and sooty
    The drops fell from his death-wound, and he drew ill
His breath, — he from his swelling throat untied
A kerchief, crying, "Give Sal that!" — and died.

17

The cravat stained with bloody drops fell down
    Before Don Juan's feet: he could not tell
Exactly why it was before him thrown,
    Nor what the meaning of the man's farewell.
Poor Tom was once a kiddy upon town,
    A thorough varmint, and a *real* swell,
Full flash, all fancy, until fairly diddled,
His pockets first and then his body riddled.

18

Don Juan, having done the best he could
    In all the circumstances of the case,
As soon as "Crowner's quest" allowed, pursued
    His travels to the capital apace; —
Esteeming it a little hard he should
    In twelve hours' time, and very little space,
Have been obliged to slay a free-born native
In self-defence: this made him meditative.

19

He from the world had cut off a great man,
    Who in his time had made heroic bustle.

16:3. *max*: Gin.
17:5. *kiddy upon town*: A petty thief.
17:7. *Full flash*: "Flashy"; a Show-off.
18:3. *"Crowner's quest*: Inquest. See *Hamlet* V. i. 21.
19. The "flash" language or underworld slang in this stanza is trans-

Who in a row like Tom could lead the van,
  Booze in the ken, or at the spellken hustle?
Who queer a flat? Who (spite of Bowstreet's ban)
  On the high toby-spice so flash the muzzle?
Who on a lark with black-eyed Sal (his blowing),
So prime — so swell — so nutty — and so knowing?

20

But Tom 's no more — and so no more of Tom.
  Heroes must die; and by God's blessing 't is
Not long before the most of them go home.
  Hail! Thamis, hail! Upon thy verge it is
That Juan's chariot, rolling like a drum
  In thunder, holds the way it can't well miss,
Through Kennington and all the other "tons,"
Which make us wish ourselves in town at once; —

● ● ● ● ● ● ●

45

In the great world, — which, being interpreted,
  Meaneth the West or worst end of a city,
And about twice two thousand people bred
  By no means to be very wise or witty,
But to sit up while others lie in bed,
  And look down on the Universe with pity, —
Juan, as an inveterate patrician,
Was well received by persons of condition.

46

He was a bachelor, which is a matter
  Of import both to virgin and to bride,

---

lated in Thomas Moore's 1833 edition of Byron: *ken*, a house that harbors thieves; *spelken*, the play-house; *queer a flat*, confound a gull or silly fellow; *high toby-spice*, robbery on horseback; *a lark*, fun or sport; *blowing*, a pickpocket's trull [moll]; *so swell*, so gentlemanly; *so nutty*, pleased or gratified with, as of someone of the opposite sex.

45:2. *West or worst end*: The west end was the fashionable section of London.

The former's hymeneal hopes to flatter;
   And (should she not hold fast by Love or Pride)
'T is also of some moment to the latter:
   A rib 's a thorn in a wed gallant's side,
Requires decorum, and is apt to double
The horrid sin — and what 's still worse the trouble.

47

But Juan was a bachelor — of arts,
   And parts, — and hearts: he danced and sung, and had
An air as sentimental as Mozart's
   Softest of melodies; and could be sad
Or cheerful, without any "flaws or starts,"
   Just at the proper time: and though a lad,
Had seen the world — which is a curious sight,
And very much unlike what people write.

48

Fair virgins blushed upon him; wedded dames
   Bloomed also in less transitory hues;
For both commodities dwell by the Thames
   The painting and the painted; Youth, Ceruse,
Against his heart preferred their usual claims,
   Such as no gentleman can quite refuse:
Daughters admired his dress, and pious mothers
Inquired his income, and if he had brothers.

49

The milliners who furnish "drapery Misses"
   Throughout the season, upon speculation
Of payment ere the Honeymoon's last kisses
   Have waned into a crescent's coruscation,
Thought such an opportunity as this is,
   Of a rich foreigner's initiation,

48:4. *Ceruse*: A cosmetic, i.e. "the wedded dame" or older woman.
49:1. *"drapery Misses"*: Fashionable young women, furnished with a wardrobe on credit, to be paid for by the husband after marriage.

Not to be overlooked — and gave such credit,
That future bridegrooms swore, and sighed, and paid it.

50

The Blues, that tender tribe, who sigh o'er sonnets,
 And with the pages of the last Review
Line the interior of their heads or bonnets,
 Advanced in all their azure's highest hue:
They talked bad French or Spanish, and upon its
 Late authors asked him for a hint or two;
And which was softest, Russian or Castilian?
And whether in his travels he saw Ilion?

51

Juan, who was a little superficial,
 And not in literature a great Drawcansir,
Examined by this learnéd and especial
 Jury of matrons, scarce knew what to answer:
His duties warlike, loving or official,
 His steady application as a dancer,
Had kept him from the brink of Hippocrene,
Which now he found was blue instead of green.

52

However, he replied at hazard, with
 A modest confidence and calm assurance,
Which lent his learnéd lucubrations pith,
 And passed for arguments of good endurance.
That prodigy, Miss Araminta Smith
 (Who at sixteen translated "Hercules Furens"
Into as furious English), with her best look,
Set down his sayings in her common-place book.

 51:2. *Drawcansir*: The name of a swaggering braggart in the play, *The Rehearsal*, by George Villiers (1671).
 51:7. *Hippocrene*: The fountain on Mt. Helicon, sacred to the muses.
 52:6. *"Hercules Furens"*: *Furious Hercules*, a drama by Seneca.

53

Juan knew several languages — as well
   He might — and brought them up with skill, in time
To save his fame with each accomplished belle,
   Who still regretted that he did not rhyme.
There wanted but this requisite to swell
   His qualities (with them) into sublime:
Lady Fitz-Frisky, and Miss Mævia Mannish,
Both longed extremely to be sung in Spanish.

54

However, he did pretty well, and was
   Admitted as an aspirant to all
The coteries, and, as in Banquo's glass,
   At great assemblies or in parties small,
He saw ten thousand living authors pass,
   That being about their average numeral;
Also the eighty "greatest living poets,"
As every paltry magazine can show *it 's*.

55

In twice five years the "greatest living poet,"
   Like to the champion in the fisty ring,
Is called on to support his claim, or show it,
   Although 't is an imaginary thing.
Even I — albeit I 'm sure I did not know it,
   Nor sought of foolscap subjects to be king, —
Was reckoned, a considerable time,
The grand Napoleon of the realms of rhyme.

56

But Juan was my Moscow, and Faliero
   My Leipsic, and my Mont Saint Jean seems Cain:

54:3. *Banquo's glass*: Mirror in which Macbeth saw Banquo and his
descendants as kings of Scotland. *Macbeth* IV. i. 112f.
56:1–2. *Moscow . . . Leipsic . . . Mont Saint Jean*: Napoleon retreated
from Moscow in the autumn of 1812, was defeated at Leipzig in October

La Belle Alliance of dunces down at zero,
    Now that the Lion 's fallen, may rise again:
But I will fall at least as fell my Hero;
    Nor reign at all, or as a *monarch* reign;
Or to some lonely isle of gaolers go,
With turncoat Southey for my turnkey Lowe.

* * * * * * *

60

John Keats, who was killed off by one critique,
    Just as he really promised something great,
If not intelligible, without Greek
    Contrived to talk about the gods of late,
Much as they might have been supposed to speak.
    Poor fellow! His was an untoward fate;
'T is strange the mind, that very fiery particle,
Should let itself be snuffed out by an article.

61

The list grows long of live and dead pretenders
    To that which none will gain — or none will know
The conqueror at least; who, ere Time renders
    His last award, will have the long grass grow
Above his burnt-out brain, and sapless cinders.
    If I might augur, I should rate but low
Their chances; — they 're too numerous, like the thirty
Mock tyrants, when Rome's annals waxed but dirty.

1813. Mont Saint Jean was a farmhouse on the battlefield of Waterloo.
Byron's dramas, *Marino Faliero* and *Cain*, were severely attacked by critics.
    56:3. *La Belle Alliance*: Byron is alluding to the "beautiful alliance"
of England, Prussia, Russia and Austria. Actually *La Belle Alliance* was
the farmhouse at Waterloo where Wellington and Blucher met and con-
gratulated each other as victors.
    56:8. *Lowe*: Sir Hudson Lowe was Napoleon's governor at St. Helena.
    60:5. . . . *supposed to speak*: Keats' unfinished epic, *Hyperion*. For
Keats' death see below pp. 679 and 681.
    61:7–8. *thirty/Mock tyrants*: The thirty pretenders to the throne in the
reign of the Roman Emperor, Gallienus, in the third century A.D.

62

This is the literary *lower* empire,
  Where the prætorian bands take up the matter; —
A "dreadful trade," like his who "gathers samphire,"
  The insolent soldiery to soothe and flatter,
With the same feelings as you 'd coax a vampire.
  Now, were I once at home, and in good satire,
I 'd try conclusions with those Janizaries,
And show them *what* an intellectual war is.

63

I think I know a trick or two, would turn
  Their flanks; — but it is hardly worth my while,
With such small gear to give myself concern:
  Indeed I 've not the necessary bile;
My natural temper 's really aught but stern,
  And even my Muse's worst reproof 's a smile;
And then she drops a brief and modern curtsy,
And glides away, assured she never hurts ye.

64

My Juan, whom I left in deadly peril
  Amongst live poets and *blue* ladies, passed
With some small profit through that field so sterile,
  Being tired in time — and, neither least nor last,
Left it before he had been treated very ill;
  And henceforth found himself more gaily classed
Amongst the higher spirits of the day,
The Sun's true son, no vapour, but a ray.

65

His morns he passed in business — which dissected,
  Was, like all business, a laborious nothing
That leads to lassitude, the most infected

62:2. *praetorian bands*: Special guard of the Roman emperors, who in the decline of the Empire frequently controlled the selection of emperor.
62:3. *"gathers samphire"*: *King Lear* IV. vi. 15–16.
62:7. *Janizaries*: Private guard of the Turkish sultan.

And Centaur Nessus garb of mortal clothing,
   And on our sofas makes us lie dejected,
      And talk in tender horrors of our loathing
All kinds of toil, save for our country's good —
Which grows no better, though 't is time it should.

66

His afternoons he passed in visits, luncheons,
   Lounging and boxing; and the twilight hour
In riding round those vegetable puncheons
   Called "Parks," where there is neither fruit nor flower
Enough to gratify a bee's slight munchings;
   But after all it is the only "bower"
(In Moore's phrase) where the fashionable fair
Can form a slight acquaintance with fresh air.

67

Then dress, then dinner, then awakes the world!
   Then glare the lamps, then whirl the wheels, then roar
Through street and square fast flushing chariots hurled
   Like harnessed meteors; then along the floor
Chalk mimics painting; then festoons are twirled;
   Then roll the brazen thunders of the door,
Which opens to the thousand happy few
An earthly Paradise of *Or Molu*.

68

There stands the noble hostess, nor shall sink
   With the three-thousandth curtsy; there the waltz,
The only dance which teaches girls to think,
   Makes one in love even with its very faults.
Saloon, room, hall, o'erflow beyond their brink,

65:4. *Centaur Nessus garb*: Poisoned robe. Hercules was killed by wearing a robe poisoned in the blood of the Centaur Nessus.

67:4–5. *Chalk mimics painting*: Ballroom and dining room floors were often decorated with pictures in chalk.

67:8. *Or Molu*: Gilded bronze decorations fashionable during the Regency.

And long the latest of arrivals halts,
'Midst royal dukes and dames condemned to climb,
And gain an inch of staircase at a time.

69

Thrice happy he who, after a survey
  Of the good company, can win a corner,
A door that 's *in* or boudoir *out* of the way,
  Where he may fix himself like small "Jack Horner,"
And let the Babel round run as it may,
  And look on as a mourner, or a scorner,
Or an approver, or a mere spectator,
Yawning a little as the night grows later.

70

But this won't do, save by and by; and he
  Who, like Don Juan, takes an active share,
Must steer with care through all that glittering sea
  Of gems and plumes and pearls and silks, to where
He deems it is his proper place to be;
  Dissolving in the waltz to some soft air,
Or proudlier prancing with mercurial skill,
Where Science marshals forth her own quadrille.

71

Or, if he dance not, but hath higher views
  Upon an heiress or his neighbour's bride,
Let him take care that that which he pursues
  Is not at once too palpably descried:
Full many an eager gentleman oft rues
  His haste; Impatience is a blundering guide
Amongst a people famous for reflection,
Who like to play the fool with circumspection.

72

But, if you can contrive, get next at supper;
  Or, if forestalled, get opposite and ogle: —
Oh, ye ambrosial moments! always upper

In mind, a sort of sentimental bogle,
Which sits for ever upon Memory's crupper,
    The ghost of vanished pleasures once in vogue! Ill
Can tender souls relate the rise and fall
Of hopes and fears which shake a single ball.

73

But these precautionary hints can touch
    Only the common run, who must pursue,
And watch and ward; whose plans a word too much
    Or little overturns; and not the few
Or many (for the number 's sometimes such)
    Whom a good mien, especially if new,
Or fame — or name — for Wit, War, Sense, or Nonsense,
Permits whate'er they please, — or *did* not long since.

74

Our Hero — as a hero — young and handsome,
    Noble, rich, celebrated, and a stranger,
Like other slaves of course must pay his ransom,
    Before he can escape from so much danger
As will environ a conspicuous man. Some
    Talk about poetry, and "rack and manger,"
And ugliness, disease, as toil and trouble; —
I wish they knew the life of a young noble.

75

They are young, but know not Youth — it is anticipated;
    Handsome but wasted, rich without a sou;
Their vigour in a thousand arms is dissipated;
    Their cash comes *from,* their wealth goes *to* a Jew;
Both senates see their nightly votes participated
    Between the Tyrant's and the Tribunes' crew;
And having voted, dined, drunk, gamed and whored,
The family vault receives another Lord.

72:4. *bogle*: Goblin.
74:6. *"rack and manger"*: Waste and disorder.

76

"Where is the World?" cries Young, "at *eighty*" — "Where
  The World in which a man was born?" Alas!
Where is the world of *eight* years past? *'T was there* —
  I look for it — 't is gone, a globe of glass!
Cracked, shivered, vanished, scarcely gazed on, ere
  A silent change dissolves the glittering mass.
Statesmen, Chiefs, Orators, Queens, Patriots, Kings,
And Dandies — all are gone on the Wind's wings.

77

Where is Napoleon the Grand? God knows!
  Where little Castlereagh? The devil can tell!
Where Grattan, Curran, Sheridan — all those
  Who bound the Bar or Senate in their spell?
Where is the unhappy Queen, with all her woes?
  And where the Daughter, whom the Isles loved well?
Where are those martyred saints the Five per Cents?
And where — oh, where the devil are the Rents?

78

Where's Brummell? Dished. Where 's Long Pole Wellesley?
  Diddled.

76:1. *Young*: Edward Young, author of *Night Thoughts,* wrote a poem,
Resignation, on this theme when he was over eighty.
   77:1. *Napoleon*: He had died on May 5, 1821.
   77:2. *Castlereagh*: See notes to *Dedication,* 11:8. He committed suicide
in 1822.
   77:3. *Gratton, Curran, Sheridan*: Famous Parliamentary orators and
wits, who died respectively in 1820, 1817, and 1816. Sheridan was the
dramatist.
   77:5. *unhappy Queen*: Queen Caroline, wife of George IV, had died
in August 1821.
   77:6. *daughter*: Princess Charlotte had died in childbirth, November
1817.
   77:7. *Five per cents*: British bonds, very unstable at the time.
   77:8. *Rents*: Farm rents, which had fallen very low.
   78:1. *Brummell*: The famous "beau" (1778–1840) who had fallen into
debt and "retired" to France.
   Wellesley: William Pole Tylney Long Wellesley (1788–1857), nephew of
the Duke of Wellington, and notorious for riotous living, was on his way
to bankruptcy.

Where 's Whitbread? Romilly? Where 's George the Third
Where is his will? (That 's not so soon unriddled.)
    And where is "Fum" the Fourth, our "royal bird"?
Gone down, it seems, to Scotland to be fiddled
    Unto by Sawney's violin, we have heard:
"Caw me, caw thee" — for six months hath been hatching
This scene of royal itch and loyal scratching.

79

Where is Lord This? And where my Lady That?
    The Honourable Mistresses and Misses?
Some laid aside like an old Opera hat,
    Married, unmarried, and remarried: (this is
An evolution oft performed of late).
    Where are the Dublin shouts — and London hisses?
Where are the Grenvilles? Turned as usual. Where
My friends the Whigs? Exactly where they were.

80

Where are the Lady Carolines and Franceses?
    Divorced or doing thereanent. Ye annals
So brilliant, where the list of routs and dances is, —
    Thou Morning Post, sole record of the panels
Broken in carriages, and all the phantasies
    Of fashion, — say what streams now fill those channels?

78.2. *Whitbread . . . Romilly*: Whitbread, Whig Politician, had committed suicide in 1815, Romilly (see I, 15:4n.) in 1818.

78:3. *. . . his will*: George III had left two wills, the second one unsigned. There was a rumor that George IV, who in the confusion appropriated the inheritance to himself, had destroyed his father's will.

78:4. *"Fum" the Fourth*: The nickname for George IV after "Fum, the Chinese bird of Royalty," an ornament in the king's Pavilion at Brighton.

78:8. *. . . loyal scratching*: George IV visited Scotland in 1822 where he was obsequiously received. *"Caw me, Caw thee"*: "Scratch me, I'll scratch you" in the sense of flattery.

79:7. *Grenvilles*: William Wyndham, Baron Grenville (1759–1834), a social reformer in his youth, now advocated repressive legislation.

79:8. *Whigs*: They had long been out of power.

80:1. *Lady Caroline and Franceses*: Lady Caroline Lamb and Lady Frances Webster, two of the women in Byron's life between 1812 and 1814, were now both separated from their husbands.

Some die, some fly, some languish on the Continent,
Because the times have hardly left them *one* tenant.

81

Some who once set their caps at cautious dukes,
    Have taken up at length with younger brothers:
Some heiresses have bit at sharper's hooks:
    Some maids have been made wives, some merely mothers:
Others have lost their fresh and fairy looks:
    In short, the list of alterations bothers.
There 's little strange in this, but something strange is
The unusual quickness of these common changes.

82

Talk not of seventy years as age; in seven
    I have seen more changes, down from monarchs to
The humblest individuals under Heaven,
    Than might suffice a moderate century through.
I knew that nought was lasting, but now even
    Change grows too changeable, without being new:
Nought 's permanent among the human race,
Except the Whigs *not* getting into place.

83

I have seen Napoleon, who seemed quite a Jupiter,
    Shrink to a Saturn. I have seen a Duke
(No matter which) turn politician stupider,
    If that can well be, than his wooden look.
But it is time that I should hoist my "blue Peter,"
    And sail for a new theme: — I have seen — and shook
To see it — the King hissed, and then caressed;
But don't pretend to settle which was best.

83:2. *a Duke*: Probably the Duke of Wellington.
83:5. *"blue Peter"*: A blue flag with a white square in the center, hoisted as the signal for immediate departure.
83:7. *the king hissed and then caressed*: Perhaps a reference to George IV's unpopularity when he tried to divorce Caroline in 1820, followed by the adulation he received in visits to Ireland (1821) and Scotland (1822).

84

I have seen the Landholders without a rap —
  I have seen Joanna Southcote — I have seen
The House of Commons turned to a taxtrap —
  I have seen that said affair of the late Queen —
I have seen crowns worn instead of a fool's cap —
  I have seen a Congress doing all that 's mean —
I have seen some nations, like o'erloaded asses,
Kick off their burthens — meaning the high classes.

85

I have seen small poets, and great prosers, and
  Interminable — *not eternal* — speakers —
I have seen the funds at war with house and land —
  I have seen the country gentlemen turn squeakers —
I have seen the people ridden o'er like sand
  By slaves on horseback — I have seen malt liquors
Exchanged for "thin potations" by John Bull —
I have seen John half detect himself a fool. —

86

But "*carpe diem*," Juan, "*carpe, carpe!*"
  To-morrow sees another race as gay

84:1. *Landholders without a rap*: In the period of economic instability following the Napoleonic war there were severe agricultural depressions (the price of grain fell, rents were unpaid and taxes high).

84:2. *Joanna Southcote*: See *Vision of Judgment*, stanza 28, note.

84:3. *tax trap*: Perhaps a reference to the imposition of an income tax in 1799.

84:4. *late queen*: The trial of Queen Caroline for adultery with her chamberlain in 1820.

84:6. *Congress*: The Congress of Verona in 1822 in which the Allied Sovereigns made plans to prevent the spread of popular uprisings.

85:3. *funds at war*: Probably a reference to government efforts to pay off the national debt. See note on 16, 99:6–8.

85:4. *squeakers*: I.e. "squawkers" at having their taxes raised.

85:5. *people ridden o'er*: Byron may have in mind the efforts to suppress unrest in Italy; or perhaps the Manchester "Peterloo" massacre of 1819.

85:7. *"Thin potations"*: Brewers were thinning beer to avoid the malt tax. For the phrase, see *II Henry IV*. IV. iii. 133–136.

86:1. *"Carpe Diem"*: Seize the day. See Horace, *Odes* I, 8.

And transient, and devoured by the same harpy.
   "Life 's a poor player," — then "play out the play,
Ye villains!" and above all keep a sharp eye
   Much less on what you do than what you say:
Be hypocritical, be cautious, be
Not what you *seem*, but always what you *see*.

87

But how shall I relate in other cantos
   Of what befell our hero in the land,
Which 't is the common cry and lie to vaunt as
   A moral country? But I hold my hand —
For I disdain to write an Atalantis;
   But 't is as well at once to understand,
You are *not* a moral people, and you know it,
Without the aid of too sincere a poet.

88

What Juan saw and underwent shall be
   My topic, with of course the due restriction
Which is required by proper courtesy;
   And recollect the work is only fiction,
And that I sing of neither mine nor me,
   Though every scribe, in some slight turn of diction,
Will hint allusions never *meant*. Ne'er doubt
This — when I speak, I *don't hint*, but *speak out*.

89

Whether he married with the third or fourth
   Offspring of some sage husband-hunting countess,
Or whether with some virgin of more worth
   (I mean in Fortune's matrimonial bounties),
He took to regularly peopling Earth,

86:4–5. ". . . *ye villains*": See *Macbeth* V. v. 24. and I *Henry IV*. II. iv. 539.

87:5. *Atalantis*: *Secret Memoirs and Manners from the New Atalantis* (1709) by Mrs. Manley, full of gossip and scandal about important people of the time. Swift and Pope refer to it.

Of which your lawful, awful wedlock fount is, —
Or whether he was taken in for damages,
For being too excursive in his homages, —

90

Is yet within the unread events of Time.
  Thus far, go forth, thou Lay, which I will back
Against the same given quantity of rhyme,
  For being as much the subject of attack
As ever yet was any work sublime,
  By those who love to say that white is black.
So much the better! — I may stand alone,
But would not change my free thoughts for a throne.

1822   *1823*

CANTO THE TWELFTH

• • • • • • •

40

But now I 'm going to be immoral; now
  I mean to show things really as they are,
Not as they ought to be: for I avow,
  That till we see what 's what in fact, we 're far
From much improvement with that virtuous plough
  Which skims the surface, leaving scarce a scar
Upon the black loam long manured by Vice,
Only to keep its corn at the old price.

41

But first of little Leila we 'll dispose,
  For like a day-dawn she was young and pure —
Or like the old comparison of snows,
  (Which are more pure than pleasant, to be sure,
Like many people everybody knows), —
  Don Juan was delighted to secure
A goodly guardian for his infant charge,
Who might not profit much by being at large.

42

Besides, he had found out he was no tutor
   (I wish that others would find out the same),
And rather wished in such things to stand neuter,
   For silly wards will bring their guardians blame:
So when he saw each ancient dame a suitor
   To make his little wild Asiatic tame,
Consulting "the Society for Vice
Suppression," Lady Pinchbeck was his choice.

43

Olden she was — but had been very young;
   Virtuous she was — and had been, I believe;
Although the World has such an evil tongue
   That — but my chaster ear will not receive
An echo of a syllable that's wrong:
   In fact, there 's nothing makes me so much grieve,
As that abominable tittle-tattle,
Which is the cud eschewed by human cattle.

44

Moreover I 've remarked (and I was once
   A slight observer in a modest way),
And so may every one except a dunce,
   That ladies in their youth a little gay,
Besides their knowledge of the World, and sense
   Of the sad consequence of going astray,
Are wiser in their warnings 'gainst the woe
Which the mere passionless can never know.

● ● ● ● ● ●

54

But now I will begin my poem. 'Tis
   Perhaps a little strange, if not quite new,

42:7–8. "the Society for Vice/Suppression": Society for the Suppression of Vice (used mainly for repression of political liberals and the press) was instituted in 1802.
43:8. eschewed: Apparently a mistake for "chewed."

That from the first of Cantos up to this
   I 've not begun what we have to go through.
These first twelve books are merely flourishes,
   Preludios, trying just a string or two
Upon my lyre, or making the pegs sure;
And when so, you shall have the overture.

55

My Muses do not care a pinch of rosin
   About what 's called success, or not succeeding:
Such thoughts are quite below the strain they have chosen;
   'T is a "great moral lesson" they are reading.
I thought, at setting off, about two dozen
   Cantos would do; but at Apollo's pleading,
If that my Pegasus should not be foundered,
I think to canter gently through a hundred.

• • • • • • •

1822   *1823*

CANTO THE THIRTEENTH

• • • • • • •

12

I 'm "at my old lunes" — digression, and forget
   The lady Adeline Amundeville;
The fair most fatal Juan ever met,
   Although she was not evil nor meant ill;
But Destiny and Passion spread the net
   (Fate is a good excuse for our own will),
And caught them; — what do they *not* catch, methinks?
But I 'm not Œdipus, and Life 's a Sphinx.

13

I tell the tale as it is told, nor dare
   To venture a solution: *"Davus sum!"*

12:1. *"at my old Lunes"*: See *Merry Wives of Windsor* IV. ii. 16–17.
"Lunes" means lunacy.
13:2. *"Davus sum"*: In Terence's comedy *Andrea* I. 2. 23 the slave

And now I will proceed upon the pair.
　　Sweet Adeline, amidst the gay World's hum,
Was the Queen-Bee, the glass of all that 's fair;
　　Whose charms made all men speak, and women dumb.
The last 's a miracle, and such was reckoned,
And since that time there has not been a second.

14

Chaste was she, to Detraction's desperation,
　　And wedded unto one she had loved well —
A man known in the councils of the Nation,
　　Cool, and quite English, imperturbable,
Though apt to act with fire upon occasion,
　　Proud of himself and her: the World could tell
Nought against either, and both seemed secure —
She in her virtue, he in his hauteur.

15

It chanced some diplomatical relations,
　　Arising out of business, often brought
Himself and Juan in their mutual stations
　　Into close contact. Though reserved, nor caught
By specious seeming, Juan's youth, and patience,
　　And talent, on his haughty spirit wrought,
And formed a basis of esteem, which ends
In making men what Courtesy calls friends.

16

And thus Lord Henry, who was cautious as
　　Reserve and Pride could make him, and full slow
In judging men — when once his judgment was
　　Determined, right or wrong, on friend or foe,
Had all the pertinacity Pride has,
　　Which knows no ebb to its imperious flow,
And loves or hates, disdaining to be guided,
Because its own good pleasure hath decided.

Davus says, "I am Davus, not Oedipus," meaning that he could not solve
the riddle of the Sphinx.

• • • • • • •

28

At Henry's mansion then, in Blank-Blank Square,
　Was Juan a *recherché*, welcome guest,
As many other noble scions were;
　And some who had but Talent for their crest;
Or Wealth, which is a passport everywhere;
　Or even mere Fashion, which indeed 's the best
Recommendation; and to be well dressed
Will very often supersede the rest.

29

And since "there 's safety in a multitude
　Of counsellors," as Solomon has said,
Or some one for him, in some sage, grave mood; —
　Indeed we see the daily proof displayed
In Senates, at the Bar, in wordy feud,
　Where'er collective wisdom can parade,
Which is the only cause that we can guess
Of Britain's present wealth and happiness; —

30

But as "there 's safety" grafted in the number
　"Of counsellors," for men, — thus for the sex
A large acquaintance lets not Virtue slumber;
　Or should it shake, the choice will more perplex —
Variety itself will more encumber.
　'Midst many rocks we guard more against wrecks —
And thus with women: howsoe'er it shocks some's
Self-love, there 's safety in a crowd of coxcombs.

31

But Adeline had not the least occasion

28:1. *Blank-Blank Square*: In 25:1–2, Byron had written, "for we will break no squares [i.e. violate no privacy] by naming streets."
28:2. *recherché*: Sought after.
29:1–2. *". . . counsellors"*: See *Proverbs* 11:14, 24:6.

For such a shield, which leaves but little merit
To Virtue proper, or good education.
  Her chief resource was in her own high spirit,
Which judged Mankind at their due estimation;
  And for coquetry, she disdained to wear it —
Secure of admiration: its impression
Was faint — as of an every-day possession.

· · · · · · ·

34

There also was of course in Adeline
  That calm patrician polish in the address,
Which ne'er can pass the equinoctial line
  Of anything which Nature would express;
Just as a Mandarin finds nothing fine, —
  At least his manner suffers not to guess,
That anything he views can greatly please:
Perhaps we have borrowed this from the Chinese —

35

Perhaps from Horace: his *"Nil admirari"*
  Was what he called the "Art of Happiness" —
An art on which the artists greatly vary,
  And have not yet attained to much success.
However, 't is expedient to be wary:
  Indifference, certes, don't produce distress;
And rash Enthusiasm in good society
Were nothing but a moral inebriety.

36

But Adeline was not indifferent: for
  (*Now* for a common-place!) beneath the snow,
As a Volcano holds the lava more
  Within — *et cætera*. Shall I go on? — No!

35:1. *"Nil Admirari"*: Horace, *Epistles*, i, 6, 1–2. Earlier (Canto 5, 101)
Byron quotes Pope's translation: "Not to admire, is all the Art I know
/To make men happy, and to keep them so."

I hate to hunt down a tired metaphor,
   So let the often-used Volcano go.
Poor thing! How frequently, by me and others,
It hath been stirred up till its smoke quite smothers!

37

I 'll have another figure in a trice: —
   What say you to a bottle of champagne?
Frozen into a very vinous ice,
   Which leaves few drops of that immortal rain,
Yet in the very centre, past all price,
   About a liquid glassful will remain;
And this is stronger than the strongest grape
Could e'er express in its expanded shape:

38

'T is the whole spirit brought to a quint-essence;
   And thus the chilliest aspects may concentre
A hidden nectar under a cold presence.
   And such are many — though I only meant her
From whom I now deduce these moral lessons,
   On which the Muse has always sought to enter.
And your cold people are beyond all price,
When once you've broken their confounded ice.

39

But after all they are a North-West Passage
   Unto the glowing India of the soul;
And as the good ships sent upon that message
   Have not exactly ascertained the Pole
(Though Parry's efforts look a lucky presage),
   Thus gentlemen may run upon a shoal;
For if the Pole 's not open, but all frost
(A chance still), 't is a voyage or vessel lost.

39:5. *Parry's efforts*: Sir William Parry (1790–1855) led several expeditions in search of a northwest passage. See *Vision of Judgment*, stanza 27 and note.

40

And young beginners may as well commence
   With quiet cruising o'er the ocean, Woman;
While those who are not beginners should have sense
   Enough to make for port, ere Time shall summon
With his grey signal-flag; and the past tense,
   The dreary *Fuimus* of all things human,
Must be declined, while Life's thin thread 's spun out
Between the gaping heir and gnawing gout.

• • • • • • •

42

The English winter — ending in July,
   To recommence in August — now was done.
'T is the postilion's paradise: wheels fly;
   On roads, East, South, North, West, there is a run.
But for post-horses who finds sympathy?
   Man's pity 's for himself, or for his son,
Always premising that said son at college
Has not contracted much more debt than knowledge.

• • • • • • •

50

Lord Henry and the Lady Adeline
   Departed like the rest of their compeers,
The peerage, to a mansion very fine —
   The Gothic Babel of a thousand years.
None than themselves could boast a longer line,
   Where Time through heroes and through beauties steers;
And oaks as olden as their pedigree
Told of their Sires — a tomb in every tree.

51

A paragraph in every paper told
   Of their departure — such is modern fame:

40:6. *Fuimus*: "We have been."

'T is pity that it takes no further hold
  Than an advertisement, or much the same;
When, ere the ink be dry, the sound grows cold.
  The Morning Post was foremost to proclaim —
"Departure, for his country seat, to-day,
Lord H. Amundeville and Lady A.

52

"We understand the splendid host intends
  To entertain, this autumn, a select
And numerous party of his noble friends;
  'Midst whom we have heard, from sources quite correct,
The Duke of D— the shooting season spends,
  With many more by rank and fashion decked;
Also a foreigner of high condition,
The envoy of the secret Russian mission."

53

And thus we see — who doubts the Morning Post?
  (Whose articles are like the "Thirty-nine,"
Which those most swear to who believe them most) —
  Our gay Russ Spaniard was ordained to shine,
Decked by the rays reflected from his host,
  With those who, Pope says, "Greatly daring dine." —
'T is odd, but true, — last war the News abounded
More with these dinners than the killed or wounded; —

54

As thus: "On Thursday there was a grand dinner;
  Present, Lords A. B. C." Earls, dukes, by name
Announced with no less pomp than Victory's winner:
  Then underneath, and in the very same
Column: date, "Falmouth. There has lately been here
  The Slap-dash regiment, so well known to Fame,
Whose loss in the late action we regret:
The vacancies are filled up — see Gazette."

53:2. *The Thirty Nine*: The 39 statements to which those taking orders in the Church of England subscribe.
53:6. *"Greatly daring dine"*: *The Dunciad*, IV, 318.

55

To Norman Abbey whirled the noble pair, —
　An old, old Monastery once, and now
Still older mansion — of a rich and rare
　Mixed Gothic, such as artists all allow
Few specimens yet left us can compare
　Withal: it lies, perhaps, a little low,
Because the monks preferred a hill behind,
To shelter their devotion from the wind.

●　●　●　●　●　●　●

1823　　　　　　　　　　　　　　　　　　　　　*1823*

CANTO THE FOURTEENTH

1

If from great Nature's or our own abyss
　Of Thought we could but snatch a certainty,
Perhaps Mankind might find the path they miss —
　But then 't would spoil much good philosophy.
One system eats another up, and this
　Much as old Saturn ate his progeny;
For when his pious consort gave him stones
In lieu of sons, of these he made no bones.

2

But System doth reverse the Titan's breakfast,
　And eats her parents, albeit the digestion
Is difficult. Pray tell me, can you make fast,
　After due search, your faith to any question?
Look back o'er ages, ere unto the stake fast
　You bind yourself, and call some mode the best one.
Nothing more true than *not* to trust your senses;
And yet what are your other evidences?

55:1. *Norman Abbey*: Byron used Newstead Abbey as the model for
Norman Abbey.
1:8. *made no bones*: Rhea, Saturn's wife, hid Jupiter, Neptune, and
Pluto from him at their births and gave him stones instead.

3

For me, I know nought; nothing I deny,
    Admit — reject — contemn: and what know *you,*
Except perhaps that you were born to die?
    And both may after all turn out untrue.
An age may come, Font of Eternity,
    When nothing shall be either old or new.
Death, so called, is a thing which makes men weep,
And yet a third of Life is passed in sleep.

4

A sleep without dreams, after a rough day
    Of toil, is what we covet most; and yet
How clay shrinks back from more quiescent clay!
    The very Suicide that pays his debt
At once without instalments (an old way
    Of paying debts, which creditors regret),
Lets out impatiently his rushing breath,
Less from disgust of Life than dread of Death.

5

'T is round him — near him — here — there — everywhere —
    And there 's a courage which grows out of fear,
Perhaps of all most desperate, which will dare
    The worst to *know* it: — when the mountains rear
Their peaks beneath your human foot, and there
    You look down o'er the precipice, and drear
The gulf or rock yawns, — you can't gaze a minute,
Without an awful wish to plunge within it.

6

'T is true, you don't — but, pale and struck with terror,
    Retire: but look into your past impression!
And you will find, though shuddering at the mirror
    Of your own thoughts, in all their self-confession,
The lurking bias, be it truth or error,
    To the *unknown*; a secret prepossession,

To plunge with all your fears — but where? You know not,
And that 's the reason why you do — or do not.

7

But what 's this to the purpose? you will say.
   Gent. reader, nothing; a mere speculation,
For which my sole excuse is — 't is my way;
   Sometimes *with* and sometimes without occasion.
I write what 's uppermost, without delay;
   This narrative is not meant for narration,
But a mere airy and fantastic basis,
To build up common things with common places.

8

You know, or don't know, that great Bacon saith,
   "Fling up a straw, 't will show the way the wind blows;"
And such a straw, borne on by human breath,
   Is Poesy, according as the Mind glows;
A paper kite which flies 'twixt Life and Death,
   A shadow which the onward Soul behind throws:
And mine 's a bubble, not blown up for praise,
But just to play with, as an infant plays.

9

The World is all before me — or behind;
   For I have seen a portion of that same,
And quite enough for me to keep in mind: —
   Of passions, too, I have proved enough to blame,
To the great pleasure of our friends, Mankind,
   Who like to mix some slight alloy with fame;
For I was rather famous in my time,
Until I fairly knocked it up with rhyme.

10

I have brought this world about my ears, and eke
   The other; that 's to say, the Clergy — who

8:1. *Bacon saith*: In his *Natural History*, No. 820.

Upon my head have bid their thunders break
   In pious libels by no means a few.
And yet I can't help scribbling once a week,
   Tiring old readers, nor discovering new.
In Youth I wrote because my mind was full,
And *now* because I feel it growing dull.

11

But "why then publish?" — There are no rewards
   Of fame or profit when the World grows weary.
I ask in turn, — Why do you play at cards?
   Why drink? Why read? — To make some hour less dreary.
It occupies me to turn back regards
   On what I 've seen or pondered, sad or cheery;
And what I write I cast upon the stream,
To swim or sink — I have had at least my dream.

12

I think that were I *certain* of success,
   I hardly could compose another line:
So long I 've battled either more or less,
   That no defeat can drive me from the Nine.
This feeling 't is not easy to express,
   And yet 't is not affected, I opine.
In play, there are two pleasures for your choosing —
The one is winning, and the other losing.

13

Besides, my Muse by no means deals in fiction:
   She gathers a repertory of facts,
Of course with some reserve and slight restriction,
   But mostly sings of human things and acts —
And that 's one cause she meets with contradiction;
   For too much truth, at first sight, ne'er attracts;
And were her object only what 's called Glory,
With more ease, too, she 'd tell a different story.

14

Love — War — a tempest — surely there 's variety;
   Also a seasoning slight of lucubration;
A bird's-eye view, too, of that wild, Society;
   A slight glance thrown on men of every station.
If you have nought else, here 's at least satiety,
   Both in performance and in preparation;
And though these lines should only line portmanteaus,
Trade will be all the better for these Cantos.

15

The portion of this World which I at present
   Have taken up to fill the following sermon,
Is one of which there's no description recent:
   The reason why is easy to determine:
Although it seems both prominent and pleasant,
   There is a sameness in its gems and ermine,
A dull and family likeness through all ages,
Of no great promise for poetic pages.

16

With much to excite, there 's little to exalt;
   Nothing that speaks to all men and all times;
A sort of varnish over every fault;
   A kind of common-place, even in their crimes;
Factitious passions — Wit without much salt —
   A want of that true nature which sublimes
Whate'er it shows with Truth; a smooth monotony
Of character, in those at least who have got any.

17

Sometimes, indeed, like soldiers off parade
   They break their ranks and gladly leave the drill;
But then the roll-call draws them back afraid,
   And they must be or seem what they *were*: still
Doubtless it is a brilliant masquerade:
   But when of the first sight you have had your fill,

It palls — at least it did so upon me,
This paradise of Pleasure and *Ennui*.

18

When we have made our love, and gamed our gaming,
　Dressed, voted, shone, and, may be, something more —
With dandies dined — heard senators declaiming —
　Seen beauties brought to market by the score,
Sad rakes to sadder husbands chastely taming —
　There's little left but to be bored or bore:
Witness those *ci-devant jeunes hommes* who stem
The stream, nor leave the world which leaveth them.

19

'T is sad — indeed a general complaint —
　That no one has succeeded in describing
The *monde*, exactly as they ought to paint:
　Some say, that authors only snatch, by bribing
The porter, some slight scandals strange and quaint,
　To furnish matter for their moral gibing;
And that their books have but one style in common —
My Lady's prattle, filtered through her woman.

20

But this can't well be true, just now; for writers
　Are grown of the *beau monde* a part potential:
I 've seen them balance even the scale with fighters,
　Especially when young, for that 's essential.
Why do their sketches fail them as inditers
　Of what they deem themselves most consequential,
The *real* portrait of the highest tribe?
'T is that — in fact — there's little to describe.

●　●　●　●　●　●　●

18:7. *ci-devant jeunes hommes*: Once young men, i.e., aging dandies.

31

Juan — in this respect, at least, like saints —
  Was all things unto people of all sorts,
And lived contentedly, without complaints,
  In camps, in ships, in cottages, or courts —
Born with that happy soul which seldom faints,
  And mingling modestly in toils or sports.
He likewise could be most things to all women.
Without the coxcombry of certain *she* men.

• • • • • •

41

No marvel then he was a favourite;
  A full-grown Cupid, very much admired;
A little spoilt, but by no means so quite;
  At least he kept his vanity retired.
Such was his tact, he could alike delight
  The chaste, and those who are not so much inspired.
The Duchess of Fitz-Fulke, who loved *tracasserie,*
Began to treat him with some small *agacerie.*

42

She was a fine and somewhat full-blown blonde,
  Desirable, distinguished, celebrated
For several winters in the grand, *grand Monde*:
  I 'd rather not say what might be related
Of her exploits, for this were ticklish ground;
  Besides there might be falsehood in what 's stated:
Her late performance had been a dead set
At Lord Augustus Fitz-Plantagenet.

43

This noble personage began to look
  A little black upon this new flirtation;
But such small licences must lovers brook,

41:7–8. *tracasserie* . . . *agaceri*: Mischief-making . . . flirtatiousness.

Mere freedoms of the female corporation.
Woe to the man who ventures a rebuke!
'T will but precipitate a situation
Extremely disagreeable, but common
To calculators when they count on Woman.

44

The circle smiled, then whispered, and then sneered;
  The misses bridled, and the matrons frowned;
Some hoped things might not turn out as they feared;
  Some would not deem such women could be found;
Some ne'er believed one half of what they heard;
  Some looked perplexed, and others looked profound:
And several pitied with sincere regret
Poor Lord Augustus Fitz-Plantagenet.

45

But what is odd, none ever named the Duke,
  Who, one might think, was something in the affair:
True, he was absent, and, 't was rumoured, took
  But small concern about the when, or where,
Or what his consort did: if he could brook
  Her gaieties, none had a right to stare:
Theirs was that best of unions, past all doubt,
Which never meets, and therefore can't fall out.

46

But, oh! that I should ever pen so sad a line!
  Fired with an abstract love of Virtue, she,
My Dian of the Ephesians, Lady Adeline,
  Began to think the Duchess' conduct free;
Regretting much that she had chosen so bad a line,
  And waxing chiller in her courtesy,

46:3. *Dian of the Ephesians*: The temple of Artemis (Diana) at Ephesus, with its statue of the goddess, was considered by the Romans one of the seven wonders of the world. See note to *Childe Harold*, IV, 153: 2–4. See also *Acts* 19:27–28: "Whom all Asia and the world worshippeth . . . Great is Diana of the Ephesians."

Looked grave and pale to see her friend's fragility,
For which most friends reserve their sensibility.

•   •   •   •   •   •   •

51

The Lady Adeline's serene severity
 Was not confined to feeling for her friend,
Whose fame she rather doubted with posterity,
 Unless her habits should begin to mend:
But Juan also shared in her austerity,
 But mixed with pity, pure as e'er was penned:
His Inexperience moved her gentle ruth,
And (as her junior by six weeks) his Youth.

52

These forty days' advantage of her years —
 And hers were those which can face calculation,
Boldly referring to the list of Peers
 And noble births, nor dread the enumeration —
Gave her a right to have maternal fears
 For a young gentleman's fit education,
Though she was far from that leap year, whose leap,
In female dates, strikes Time all of a heap.

53

This may be fixed at somewhere before thirty —
 Say seven-and-twenty; for I never knew
The strictest in chronology and virtue
 Advance beyond, while they could pass for new.
O Time! why dost not pause? Thy scythe, so dirty
 With rust, should surely cease to hack and hew:
Reset it — shave more smoothly, also slower,
If but to keep thy credit as a mower.

54

But Adeline was far from that ripe age,
 Whose ripeness is but bitter at the best:

'T was rather her Experience made her sage,
  For she had seen the World and stood its test,
As I have said in — I forget what page;
  My Muse despises reference, as you have guessed
By this time: — but strike six from seven-and-twenty,
And you will find her sum of years in plenty.

• • • • • • •

60

With the kind view of saving an *éclat,*
  Both to the Duchess and Diplomatist,
The Lady Adeline, as soon 's she saw
  That Juan was unlikely to resist —
(For foreigners don't know that a *faux pas*
  In England ranks quite on a different list
From those of other lands unblest with juries,
Whose verdict for such sin a certain cure is; —)

61

The Lady Adeline resolved to take
  Such measures as she thought might best impede
The farther progress of this sad mistake.
  She thought with some simplicity indeed;
But Innocence is bold even at the stake,
  And simple in the World, and doth not need
Nor use those palisades by dames erected,
Whose virtue lies in never being detected.

62

It was not that she feared the very worst:
  His Grace was an enduring, married man,
And was not likely all at once to burst
  Into a scene, and swell the clients' clan
Of Doctors' Commons; but she dreaded first
  The magic of her Grace's talisman,

60:1. *éclat*: Explosion, scandal.

And next a quarrel (as he seemed to fret)
With Lord Augustus Fitz-Plantagenet.

63

Her Grace, too, passed for being an *intrigante,*
　And somewhat *méchante* in her amorous sphere;
One of those pretty, precious plagues, which haunt
　A lover with caprices soft and dear,
That like to *make* a quarrel, when they can't
　Find one, each day of the delightful year:
Bewitching, torturing, as they freeze or glow,
And — what is worst of all — won't let you go:

64

The sort of thing to turn a young man's head,
　Or make a Werter of him in the end.
No wonder then a purer soul should dread
　This sort of chaste *liaison* for a friend;
It were much better to be wed or dead,
　Than wear a heart a Woman loves to rend.
'T is best to pause, and think, ere you rush on,
If that a *bonne fortune* be really *bonne.*

65

And first, in the overflowing of her heart,
　Which really knew or thought it knew no guile,
She called her husband now and then apart,
　And bade him counsel Juan. With a smile
Lord Henry heard her plans of artless art
　To wean Don Juan from the Siren's wile;
And answered, like a statesman or a prophet,
In such guise that she could make nothing of it.

66

Firstly, he said, "he never interfered
　In anybody's business but the King's:"

64:2. *Werter*: In Goethe's *Sorrows of Young Werther,* the hero committed suicide because of unrequited love.

Next, that "he never judged from what appeared,
   Without strong reason, of those sort of things:"
Thirdly, that "Juan had more brain than beard,
   And was not to be held in leading strings;"
And fourthly, what need hardly be said twice,
"That good but rarely came from good advice."

67

And, therefore, doubtless to approve the truth
   Of the last axiom, he advised his spouse
To leave the parties to themselves, forsooth —
   At least as far as *bienséance* allows:
That time would temper Juan's faults of youth;
   That young men rarely made monastic vows;
That Opposition only more attaches —
But here a messenger brought in despatches:

68

And being of the council called "the Privy,"
   Lord Henry walked into his cabinet,
To furnish matter for some future Livy
   To tell how he reduced the Nation's debt;
And if their full contents I do not give ye,
   It is because I do not know them yet;
But I shall add them in a brief appendix,
To come between mine Epic and its index.

69

But ere he went, he added a slight hint,
   Another gentle common-place or two,
Such as are coined in Conversation's mint,
   And pass, for want of better, though not new:
Then broke his packet, to see what was in 't,
   And having casually glanced it through,
Retired: and, as he went out, calmly kissed her,
Less like a young wife than an agéd sister.

67:4. *bienséance*: Propriety.

70

He was a cold, good, honourable man,
  Proud of his birth, and proud of everything;
A goodly spirit for a state Divan,
  A figure fit to walk before a King;
Tall, stately, formed to lead the courtly van
  On birthdays, glorious with a star and string;
The very model of a chamberlain —
And such I mean to make him when I reign.

71

But there was something wanting on the whole —
  I don't know what, and therefore cannot tell —
Which pretty women — the sweet souls! — call *soul.*
  Certes it was not body; he was well
Proportioned, as a poplar or a pole,
  A handsome man, that human miracle;
And in each circumstance of Love or War
Had still preserved his perpendicular.

72

Still there was something wanting, as I 've said —
  That undefinable *"Je ne sçais quoi,"*
Which, for what I know, may of yore have led
  To Homer's Iliad, since it drew to Troy
The Greek Eve, Helen, from the Spartan's bed;
  Though on the whole, no doubt, the Dardan boy
Was much inferior to King Menelaüs: —
But thus it is some women will betray us.

● ● ● ● ● ●

85

Our gentle Adeline had one defect —
  Her heart was vacant, though a splendid mansion;

72:6. *the Dardan boy*: Paris, descended from Dardanus, mythical
founder of the Trojan race.

Her conduct had been perfectly correct,
 As she had seen nought claiming its expansion.
A wavering spirit may be easier wrecked,
 Because 't is frailer, doubtless, than a staunch one;
But when the latter works its own undoing,
Its inner crash is like an Earthquake's ruin.

86

She loved her Lord, or thought so; but *that* love
 Cost her an effort, which is a sad toil,
The stone of Sisyphus, if once we move
 Our feelings 'gainst the nature of the soil.
She had nothing to complain of, or reprove,
 No bickerings, no connubial turmoil:
Their union was a model to behold,
Serene and noble, — conjugal, but cold.

  ● ● ● ● ● ● ●

91

She knew not her own heart; then how should I?
 I think not she was *then* in love with Juan:
If so, she would have had the strength to fly
 The wild sensation, unto her a new one:
She merely felt a common sympathy
 (I will not say it was a false or true one)
In him, because she thought he was in danger, —
Her husband's friend — her own — young — and a stranger.

92

She was, or thought she was, his friend — and this
 Without the farce of Friendship, or romance
Of Platonism, which leads so oft amiss
 Ladies who have studied Friendship but in France

86:3. *Sisyphus*: Condemned in hell eternally to roll a large stone to the top of a hill from which it always rolled down again. See *Odyssey*, Bk. XI.

Or Germany, where people *purely* kiss.
    To thus much Adeline would not advance;
But of such friendship as Man's may to Man be
She was as capable as Woman can be.

93

No doubt the secret influence of the Sex
    Will there, as also in the ties of blood,
An innocent predominance annex,
    And tune the concord to a finer mood.
If free from Passion, which all Friendship checks,
    And your true feelings fully understood,
No friend like to a woman Earth discovers,
So that you have not been nor will be lovers.

•   •   •   •   •   •   •

97

Whether Don Juan and chaste Adeline
    Grew friends in this or any other sense
Will be discussed hereafter, I opine:
    At present I am glad of a pretence
To leave them hovering, as the effect is fine,
    And keeps the atrocious reader in *suspense*:
The surest way — for ladies and for books —
To bait their tender — or their tenter — hooks.

98

Whether they rode, or walked, or studied Spanish,
    To read Don Quixote in the original,
A pleasure before which all others vanish;
    Whether their talk was of the kind called "small,"
Or serious, are the topics I must banish
    To the next Canto; where perhaps I shall
Say something to the purpose, and display
Considerable talent in my way.

99

Above all, I beg all men to forbear
 Anticipating aught about the matter:
They 'll only make mistakes about the fair,
 And Juan, too, especially the latter.
And I shall take a much more serious air
 Than I have yet done, in this Epic Satire.
It is not clear that Adeline and Juan
Will fall; but if they do, 't will be their ruin.

100

But great things spring from little: — Would you think,
 That in our youth, as dangerous a passion
As e'er brought Man and Woman to the brink
 Of ruin, rose from such a slight occasion,
As few would ever dream could form the link
 Of such a sentimental situation?
You 'll never guess, I 'll bet you millions, milliards —
It all sprung from a harmless game at billiards.

101

'T is strange, — but true; for Truth is always strange —
 Stranger than fiction: if it could be told,
How much would novels gain by the exchange!
 How differently the World would men behold!
How oft would Vice and Virtue places change!
 The new world would be nothing to the old,
If some Columbus of the moral seas
Would show mankind their Souls' antipodes.

102

What "antres vast and deserts idle," then,
 Would be discovered in the human soul!
What icebergs in the hearts of mighty men,

100:8. *billiards*: Byron wrote to Lady Melbourne in 1813 the details
of his making love to Lady Frances Webster over a game of billiards. See
Marchand, *Byron*, I, 414. See also headnote to *When We Two Parted*.
102:1. . . . *"deserts idle"*: *Othello* I. 3. 140.

What self-love in the centre as their Pole!
What Anthropophagi are nine of ten
  Of those who hold the kingdoms in control!
Were things but only called by their right name,
Cæsar himself would be ashamed of Fame.

1823   *1823*

CANTO THE FIFTEENTH

• • • • • • •

17

Adeline, no deep judge of character,
  Was apt to add a colouring from her own:
'T is thus the Good will amiably err,
  And eke the Wise, as has been often shown.
Experience is the chief philosopher,
  But saddest when his science is well known:
And persecuted Sages teach the Schools
Their folly in forgetting there are fools.

18

Was it not so, great Locke? and greater Bacon?
  Great Socrates? and thou, Diviner still,
Whose lot it is by Man to be mistaken,
  And thy pure creed made sanction of all ill?
Redeeming Worlds to be by bigots shaken,
  How was thy toil rewarded? We might fill
Volumes with similar sad illustrations,
But leave them to the conscience of the nations.

19

I perch upon an humbler promontory,
  Amidst Life's infinite variety:

102:5. *Anthropophagi*: Man-eaters; cannibals.
18:2. *Diviner still*: Christ. In a note Byron wrote: "I never arraigned his creed, but the use or abuse made of it. Mr. Canning one day quoted

With no great care for what is nicknamed Glory,
  But speculating as I cast mine eye
On what may suit or may not suit my story,
  And never straining hard to versify,
I rattle on exactly as I 'd talk
With anybody in a ride or walk.

20

I don't know that there may be much ability
  Shown in this sort of desultory rhyme;
But there 's a conversational facility,
  Which may round off an hour upon a time.
Of this I 'm sure at least, there 's no servility
  In mine irregularity of chime,
Which rings what 's uppermost of new or hoary,
Just as I feel the *Improvvisatore*.

21

"*Omnia vult* belle *Matho dicere — dic aliquando*
  Et bene, *dic* neutrum, *dic aliquando* male."
The first is rather more than mortal can do;
  The second may be sadly done or gaily;
The third is still more difficult to stand to;
  The fourth we hear, and see, and say too, daily:
The whole together is what I could wish
To serve in this conundrum of a dish.

22

A modest hope — but Modesty 's my forte,
  And Pride my feeble: — let us ramble on.

Christianity to sanction negro slavery, and Mr. Wilberforce had little to
say in reply. And was Christ crucified, that black men might be scourged?
If so, he had better been born a Mulatto, to give both colours an equal
chance of freedom, or at least salvation."
  20:8. *Improvvisatore*: Byron admired the ability of Italian actors, like
Sgricci whom he knew well, to extemporize rhymes.
  21:1-2. "*omnia vult. . . .*": Martial, *Epigrams* x, 46. "You want all
you say to be smart, Matho. Say sometimes what also is good; say what
is middling; say sometimes what is bad."
  22:2. *feeble*: Archaic for "foible."

I meant to make this poem very short,
  But now I can't tell where it may not run.
No doubt, if I had wished to pay my court
  To critics, or to hail the *setting* sun
Of Tyranny of all kinds, my concision
Were more; — but I was born for opposition.

23

But then 't is mostly on the weaker side;
  So that I verily believe if they
Who now are basking in their full-blown pride
  Were shaken down, and "dogs had had their day,"
Though at the first I might perchance deride
  Their tumble, I should turn the other way,
And wax an ultra-royalist in Loyalty,
Because I hate even democratic Royalty.

24

I think I should have made a decent spouse,
  If I had never proved the soft condition;
I think I should have made monastic vows
  But for my own peculiar superstition:
'Gainst rhyme I never should have knocked my brows,
  Nor broken my own head, nor that of Priscian,
Nor worn the motley mantle of a poet,
If some one had not told me to forego it.

25

But *laissez aller* — Knights and Dames I sing,
  Such as the times may furnish. 'T is a flight
Which seems at first to need no lofty wing,
  Plumed by Longinus or the Stagyrite:

23:4. *"dogs had had their day"*: *Hamlet* V. i. 314.
24:6. *Priscian*: Roman grammarian.
24:8. *forego it*: Byron refers to Brougham's review of *Hours of Idleness* in the *Edinburgh Review,* in which he advised the young lord to "forthwith abandon poetry."
25:1. *laissez aller*: Let us proceed.
25:4. *Stagyrite*: Aristotle, who was a native of Stagira in Macedonia.

The difficulty lies in colouring
   (Keeping the due proportions still in sight)
With Nature manners which are artificial,
And rend'ring general that which is especial.

26

The difference is, that in the days of old
   Men made the Manners; Manners now make men —
Pinned like a flock, and fleeced too in their fold,
   At least nine, and a ninth beside of ten.
Now this at all events must render cold
   Your writers, who must either draw again
Days better drawn before, or else assume
The present, with their common-place costume.

27

We 'll do our best to make the best on 't: — March!
   March, my Muse! If you cannot fly, yet flutter;
And when you may not be sublime, be arch,
   Or starch, as are the edicts statesmen utter.
We surely may find something worth research:
   Columbus found a new world in a cutter,
Or brigantine, or pink, of no great tonnage,
While yet America was in her non-age.

28

When Adeline, in all her growing sense
   Of Juan's merits and his situation,
Felt on the whole an interest intense, —
   Partly perhaps because a fresh sensation,
Or that he had an air of innocence,
   Which is for Innocence a sad temptation,
As Women hate half measures, on the whole,
She 'gan to ponder how to save his soul.

29

She had a good opinion of Advice,
   Like all who give and eke receive it gratis,

For which small thanks are still the market price,
    Even where the article at highest rate is:
She thought upon the subject twice or thrice,
    And morally decided — the best state is
For Morals — Marriage; and, this question carried,
She seriously advised him to get married.

30

Juan replied, with all becoming deference,
    He had a predilection for that tie;
But that, at present, with immediate reference
    To his own circumstances, there might lie
Some difficulties, as in his own preference,
    Or that of her to whom he might apply:
That still he 'd wed with such or such a lady,
If that they were not married all already.

• • • • • • •

40

But Adeline determined Juan's wedding
    In her own mind, and that 's enough for Woman:
But then, with whom? There was the sage Miss Reading,
    Miss Raw, Miss Flaw, Miss Showman, and Miss Knowman,
And the two fair co-heiresses Giltbedding.
    She deemed his merits something more than common:
All these were unobjectionable matches,
And might go on, if well wound up, like watches.

41

There was Miss Millpond, smooth as summer's sea,
    That usual paragon, an only daughter,
Who seemed the cream of Equanimity,
    Till skimmed — and then there was some milk and water,
With a slight shade of blue, too, it might be,

41:1–8. *Miss Millpond*: An obvious dig at Lady Byron, who before her
marriage was Annabella Milbanke.

Beneath the surface; but what did it matter?
Love 's riotous, but Marriage should have quiet,
And being consumptive, live on a milk diet.

42

And then there was the Miss Audacia Shoestring,
  A dashing *demoiselle* of good estate,
Whose heart was fixed upon a star or blue string;
  But whether English Dukes grew rare of late,
Or that she had not harped upon the true string,
  By which such Sirens can attract our great,
She took up with some foreign younger brother,
A Russ or Turk — the one 's as good as t' other.

43

And then there was — but why should I go on,
  Unless the ladies should go off? — there was
Indeed a certain fair and fairy one,
  Of the best class, and better than her class, —
Aurora Raby, a young star who shone
  O'er Life, too sweet an image for such glass,
A lovely being, scarcely formed or moulded,
A rose with all its sweetest leaves yet folded;

44

Rich, noble, but an orphan — left an only
  Child to the care of guardians good and kind —
But still her aspect had an air so lonely;
  Blood is not water; and where shall we find
Feelings of Youth like those which overthrown lie
  By Death, when we are left, alas! behind,
To feel, in friendless palaces, a home
Is wanting, and our best ties in the tomb?

45

Early in years, and yet more infantine
  In figure, she had something of Sublime
In eyes which sadly shone, as Seraphs' shine.

42:2. *demoiselle*: Unmarried woman.

All Youth — but with an aspect beyond Time;
Radiant and grave — as pitying Man's decline;
    Mournful — but mournful of another's crime,
She looked as if she sat by Eden's door,
And grieved for those who could return no more.

46

She was a Catholic, too, sincere, austere,
    As far as her own gentle heart allowed,
And deemed that fallen worship far more dear
    Perhaps because 't was fallen: her Sires were proud
Of deeds and days when they had filled the ear
    Of nations, and had never bent or bowed
To novel power; and as she was the last,
She held their old faith and old feelings fast.

47

She gazed upon a World she scarcely knew,
    As seeking not to know it; silent, lone,
As grows a flower, thus quietly she grew,
    And kept her heart serene within its zone.
There was awe in the homage which she drew;
    Her Spirit seemed as seated on a throne
Apart from the surrounding world, and strong
In its own strength — most strange in one so young!

48

Now it so happened, in the catalogue
    Of Adeline, Aurora was omitted,
Although her birth and wealth had given her vogue,
    Beyond the charmers we have already cited;
Her beauty also seemed to form no clog
    Against her being mentioned as well fitted,
By many virtues, to be worth the trouble
Of single gentlemen who would be double.

49

And this omission, like that of the bust
    Of Brutus at the pageant of Tiberius,

49:2. *Tiberius*: The emperor Tiberius Caesar did not allow the bust

Made Juan wonder, as no doubt he must.
   This he expressed half smiling and half serious;
When Adeline replied with some disgust,
   And with an air, to say the least, imperious,
She marvelled "what he saw in such a baby
As that prim, silent, cold Aurora Raby?"

50

Juan rejoined — "She was a Catholic,
   And therefore fittest, as of his persuasion;
Since he was sure his mother would fall sick,
   And the Pope thunder excommunication,
If — " But here Adeline, who seemed to pique
   Herself extremely on the inoculation
Of others with her own opinions, stated —
As usual — the same reason which she late did.

51

And wherefore not? A reasonable reason,
   If good, is none the worse for repetition;
If bad, the best way 's certainly to tease on,
   And amplify: you lose much by concision,
Whereas insisting in or out of season
   Convinces all men, even a politician;
Or — what is just the same — it wearies out.
So the end 's gained, what signifies the route?

52

Why Adeline had this slight prejudice —
   For prejudice it was — against a creature
As pure, as Sanctity itself, from Vice, —
   With all the added charm of form and feature, —
For me appears a question far too nice,
   Since Adeline was liberal by nature;
But Nature 's Nature, and has more caprices
Than I have time, or will, to take to pieces.

of Brutus, assassin of Julius Caesar, to be carried in the funeral procession
of Brutus' sister.

53

Perhaps she did not like the quiet way
  With which Aurora on those baubles looked,
Which charm most people in their earlier day:
  For there are few things by Mankind less brooked,
And Womankind too, if we so may say,
  Than finding thus their genius stand rebuked,
Like "Antony's by Cæsar," by the few
Who look upon them as they ought to do.

54

It was not envy — Adeline had none;
  Her place was far beyond it, and her mind:
It was not scorn — which could not light on one
  Whose greatest *fault* was leaving few to find:
It was not jealousy, I think — but shun
  Following the *ignes fatui* of Mankind:
It was not — but 't is easier far, alas!
To say what it was *not* than what it was.

55

Little Aurora deemed she was the theme
  Of such discussion. She was there a guest;
A beauteous ripple of the brilliant stream
  Of Rank and Youth, though purer than the rest,
Which flowed on for a moment in the beam
  Time sheds a moment o'er each sparkling crest.
Had she known this, she would have calmly smiled —
She had so much, or little, of the child.

56

The dashing and proud air of Adeline
  Imposed not upon her; she saw her blaze
Much as she would have seen a glow-worm shine,
  Then turned unto the stars for loftier rays.
Juan was something she could not divine,

53:7. ". . . *by Caesar*": See *Macbeth* III. i. 55–57.

Being no Sibyl in the new world's ways;
Yet she was nothing dazzled by the meteor,
Because she did not pin her faith on feature.

57

His fame too, — for he had that kind of fame
   Which sometimes plays the deuce with Womankind,
A heterogeneous mass of glorious blame,
   Half virtues and whole vices being combined;
Faults which attract because they are not tame;
   Follies tricked out so brightly that they blind: —
These seals upon her wax made no impression,
Such was her coldness or her self-possession.

58

Juan knew nought of such a character —
   High, yet resembling not his lost Haidée;
Yet each was radiant in her proper sphere:
   The island girl, bred up by the lone sea,
More warm, as lovely, and not less sincere,
   Was Nature's all: Aurora could not be,
Nor would be thus: — the difference in them
Was such as lies between a flower and gem.

59

Having wound up with this sublime comparison,
   Methinks we may proceed upon our narrative,
And, as my friend Scott says, "I sound my warison;"
   Scott, the superlative of my comparative —
Scott, who can paint your Christian knight or Saracen,
   Serf — Lord — Man, with such skill as none would share it, if
There had not been one Shakespeare and Voltaire,
Of one or both of whom he seems the heir.

60

I say, in my slight way I may proceed
   To play upon the surface of Humanity.

59:3. *"I sound my warison"*: See *Lay of the Last Minstrel*, IV, 24:17–20.
Warison: war cry.

I write the World, nor care if the World read,
  At least for this I cannot spare its vanity.
My Muse hath bred, and still perhaps may breed
  More foes by this same scroll: when I began it, I
Thought that it might turn out so — *now* I *know* it,
But still I am, or was, a pretty poet.

61

The conference or congress (for it ended
  As Congresses of late do) of the Lady
Adeline and Don Juan rather blended
  Some acids with the sweets — for she was heady;
But, ere the matter could be marred or mended,
  The silvery bell rang, not for "dinner ready,"
But for that hour, called *half-hour*, given to dress,
Though ladies' robes seem scant enough for less.

62

Great things were now to be achieved at table,
  With massy plate for armour, knives and forks
For weapons; but what Muse since Homer's able
  (His feasts are not the worst part of his works)
To draw up in array a single day-bill
  Of modern dinners? where more mystery lurks,
In soups or sauces, or a sole *ragoût*,
Than witches, b—ches, or physicians, brew.

• • • • • • •

74

Amidst this tumult of fish, flesh, and fowl,
  And vegetables, all in masquerade,
The guests were placed according to their roll,
  But various as the various meats displayed:
Don Juan sat next an "à l'Espagnole" —
  No damsel, but a dish, as hath been said;

74:1. . . . *fowl:* Byron has just described the dinner in detail.

But so far like a lady, that 't was drest
Superbly, and contained a world of zest.

75

By some odd chance too, he was placed between
   Aurora and the Lady Adeline —
A situation difficult, I ween,
   For man therein, with eyes and heart, to dine.
Also the conference which we have seen
   Was not such as to encourage him to shine,
For Adeline, addressing few words to him,
With two transcendent eyes seemed to look through him.

76

I sometimes almost think that eyes have ears:
   This much is sure, that, out of earshot, things
Are somehow echoed to the pretty dears,
   Of which I can't tell whence their knowledge springs.
Like that same mystic music of the spheres,
   Which no one hears, so loudly though it rings,
'T is wonderful how oft the sex have heard
Long dialogues — which passed without a word!

77

Aurora sat with that indifference
   Which piques a *preux chevalier* — as it ought:
Of all offences that 's the worst offence,
   Which seems to hint you are not worth a thought.
Now Juan, though no coxcomb in pretence,
   Was not exactly pleased to be so caught,
Like a good ship entangled among ice —
And after so much excellent advice.

78

To his gay nothings, nothing was replied,
   Or something which was nothing, as Urbanity
Required. Aurora scarcely looked aside,

77:2. *preux chevalier*: Gallant knight.

Nor even smiled enough for any vanity.
The Devil was in the girl! Could it be pride?
    Or modesty, or absence, or inanity?
Heaven knows! But Adeline's malicious eyes
Sparkled with her successful prophecies,

79

And looked as much as if to say, "I said it;"
    A kind of triumph I 'll not recommend,
Because it sometimes, as I have seen or read it,
    Both in the case of lover and of friend,
Will pique a gentleman, for his own credit,
    To bring what was a jest to a serious end:
For all men prophesy what *is* or *was*,
And hate those who won't let them come to pass.

80

Juan was drawn thus into some attentions,
    Slight but select, and just enough to express,
To females of perspicuous comprehensions,
    That he would rather make them more than less.
Aurora at the last (so history mentions,
    Though probably much less a fact than guess)
So far relaxed her thoughts from their sweet prison,
As once or twice to smile, if not to listen.

81

From answering she began to question: this
    With her was rare; and Adeline, who as yet
Thought her predictions went not much amiss,
    Began to dread she 'd thaw to a coquette —
So very difficult, they say, it is
    To keep extremes from meeting, when once set
In motion; but she here too much refined —
Aurora's spirit was not of that kind.

82

But Juan had a sort of winning way,
    A proud humility, if such there be,

Which showed such deference to what females say,
    As if each charming word were a decree.
His tact, too, tempered him from grave to gay,
    And taught him when to be reserved or free:
He had the art of drawing people out,
Without their seeing what he was about.

83

Aurora, who in her indifference
    Confounded him in common with the crowd
Of flatterers, though she deemed he had more sense
    Than whispering foplings, or than witlings loud —
Commenced (from such slight things will great commence)
    To feel that flattery which attracts the proud
Rather by deference than compliment,
And wins even by a delicate dissent.

84

And then he had good looks; — that point was carried
    Nem. con. amongst the women, which I grieve
To say leads oft to *crim. con.* with the married —
    A case which to the juries we may leave,
Since with digressions we too long have tarried.
    Now though we know of old that looks deceive,
And always have done, — somehow these good looks
Make more impression than the best of books.

85

Aurora, who looked more on books than faces,
    Was very young, although so very sage,
Admiring more Minerva than the Graces,
    Especially upon a printed page.
But Virtue's self, with all her tightest laces,
    Has not the natural stays of strict old age;
And Socrates, that model of all duty,
Owned to a *penchant*, though discreet, for beauty.

84:2–3. *Nem. con . . . crim. con*: "Unanimously" . . . "criminal conversation." i.e., adultery.

86

And girls of sixteen are thus far Socratic,
    But innocently so, as Socrates;
And really, if the Sage sublime and Attic
    At seventy years had phantasies like these,
Which Plato in his dialogues dramatic
    Has shown, I know not why they should displease
In virgins — always in a modest way,
Observe, — for that with me 's a *sine quâ.*

87

Also observe, that, like the great Lord Coke
    (See Littleton), whene'er I have expressed
Opinions two, which at first sight may look
    Twin opposites, the second is the best.
Perhaps I have a third too, in a nook,
    Or none at all — which seems a sorry jest:
But if a writer should be quite consistent,
How could he possibly show things existent?

88

If people contradict themselves, can I
    Help contradicting them, and everybody,
Even my veracious self? — But that 's a lie:
    I never did so, never will — how should I?
He who doubts all things nothing can deny:
    Truth's fountains may be clear — her streams are muddy,
And cut through such canals of contradiction,
That she must often navigate o'er fiction.

89

Apologue, Fable, Poesy, and Parable,
    Are false, but may be rendered also true,
By those who sow them in a land that 's arable:
    'T is wonderful what Fable will not do!

87:2. *Littleton*: Lord Coke's commentary on Littleton's *Institutes of the Laws of England* (1628–1644).

'T is said it makes Reality more bearable:
   But what 's Reality? Who has its clue?
Philosophy? No; she too much rejects.
   Religion? *Yes;* but which of all her sects?

90

Some millions must be wrong, that 's pretty clear;
   Perhaps it may turn out that all were right.
God help us! Since we have need on our career
   To keep our holy beacons always bright,
'T is time that some new prophet should appear,
   Or *old* indulge man with a second sight.
Opinions wear out in some thousand years,
Without a small refreshment from the spheres.

91

But here again, why will I thus entangle
   Myself with Metaphysics? None can hate
So much as I do any kind of wrangle;
   And yet, such is my folly, or my fate,
I always knock my head against some angle
   About the present, past, or future state:
Yet I wish well to Trojan and to Tyrian,
For I was bred a moderate Presbyterian.

92

But though I am a temperate theologian,
   And also meek as a metaphysician,
Impartial between Tyrian and Trojan,
   As Eldon on a lunatic commission, —
In politics my duty is to show John
   Bull something of the lower world's condition.
It makes my blood boil like the springs of Hecla,
To see men let these scoundrel Sovereigns break law.

92:4. *Eldon*: John Scott, Earl of Eldon, was Lord Chancellor between 1801–1827. In 1822–1823 Eldon was sitting on a case involving the sanity of Lord Portsmouth.
92:7. *Hecla*: A volcano, rather than hot-spring, in Iceland.

93

But Politics, and Policy, and Piety,
    Are topics which I sometimes introduce,
Not only for the sake of their variety,
    But as subservient to a moral use;
Because my business is to *dress* society,
    And stuff with *sage* that very verdant goose.
And now, that we may furnish with some matter all
Tastes, we are going to try the Supernatural.

94

And now I will give up all argument;
    And positively, henceforth, no temptation
Shall "fool me to the top up of my bent"; —
    Yes, I 'll begin a thorough reformation.
Indeed, I never knew what people meant
    By deeming that my Muse's conversation
Was dangerous; — I think she is as harmless
As some who labour more and yet may charm less.

95

Grim reader! did you ever see a ghost?
    No; but you have heard — I understand — be dumb!
And don't regret the time you may have lost,
    For you have got that pleasure still to come:
And do not think I mean to sneer at most
    Of these things, or by ridicule benumb
That source of the Sublime and the Mysterious: —
For certain reasons my belief is serious.

96

Serious? You laugh; — you may: that will I not;
    My smiles must be sincere or not at all.
I say I do believe a haunted spot
    Exists — and where? That shall I not recall,
Because I 'd rather it should be forgot,

94:3. "... *bent*": *Hamlet* III. ii. 408.

"Shadows the soul of Richard" may appal.
In short, upon that subject I 've some qualms very
Like those of the philosopher of Malmsbury.

97

The night — (I sing by night — sometimes an owl,
    And now and then a nightingale) — is dim,
And the loud shriek of sage Minerva's fowl
    Rattles around me her discordant hymn:
Old portraits from old walls upon me scowl —
    I wish to Heaven they would not look so grim;
The dying embers dwindle in the grate —
I think too that I have sat up too late:

98

And therefore, though 't is by no means my way
    To rhyme at noon — when I have other things
To think of, if I ever think — I say
    I feel some chilly midnight shudderings,
And prudently postpone, until mid-day,
    Treating a topic which, alas! but brings
Shadows; — but you must be in my condition,
Before you learn to call this superstition.

99

Between two worlds Life hovers like a star,
    'Twixt Night and Morn, upon the horizon's verge.
How little do we know that which we are!
    How less what we may be! The eternal surge
Of Time and Tide rolls on and bears afar
    Our bubbles; as the old burst, new emerge,

96·6. "*. . . the soul of Richard*: *Richard III* V. iii. 217–220.

96:8. *philosopher of Malmsbury*: "Hobbes: who doubting of his own soul paid that compliment to the souls of other people as to decline their visits, of which he had some apprehension" (Byron's note), Thomas Hobbes was accused, probably falsely, of being afraid of ghosts. Byron picked up the story in Bayle's *Dictionary*.

Lashed from the foam of ages; while the graves
Of Empires heave but like some passing waves.

1823   *1824*

CANTO THE SIXTEENTH

1

The antique Persians taught three useful things,
    To draw the bow, to ride, and speak the truth.
This was the mode of Cyrus, best of kings —
    A mode adopted since by modern youth.
Bows have they, generally with two strings;
    Horses they ride without remorse or ruth;
At speaking truth perhaps they are less clever,
But draw the long bow better now than ever.

2

The cause of this effect, or this defect, —
    "For this effect defective comes by cause," —
Is what I have not leisure to inspect;
    But this I must say in my own applause,
Of all the Muses that I recollect,
    Whate'er may be her follies or her flaws
In some things, mine 's beyond all contradiction
The most sincere that ever dealt in fiction.

3

And as she treats all things, and ne'er retreats
    From anything, this Epic will contain
A wilderness of the most rare conceits,
    Which you might elsewhere hope to find in vain.
'T is true there be some bitters with the sweets,
    Yet mixed so slightly, that you can't complain,
But wonder they so few are, since my tale is
"*De rebus cunctis et quibusdam aliis.*"

2:2. "*. . . comes by cause*": *Hamlet* II, ii. 103.
3:8. "*. . . quibusdam aliis*": Concerning all things and some others.

4

But of all truths which she has told, the most
  True is that which she is about to tell.
I said it was a story of a ghost —
  What then? I only know it so befell.
Have you explored the limits of the coast,
  Where all the dwellers of the earth must dwell?
'T is time to strike such puny doubters dumb as
The sceptics who would not believe Columbus.

• • • • • • •

8

The dinner and the *soirée* too were done,
  The supper too discussed, the dames admired,
The banqueteers had dropped off one by one —
  The song was silent, and the dance expired.
The last thin petticoats were vanished, gone
  Like fleecy clouds into the sky retired,
And nothing brighter gleamed through the saloon
Than dying tapers — and the peeping moon.

9

The evaporation of a joyous day
  Is like the last glass of champagne, without
The foam which made its virgin bumper gay;
  Or like a system coupled with a doubt;
Or like a soda bottle when its spray
  Has sparkled and let half its spirit out;
Or like a billow left by storms behind,
Without the animation of the wind;

10

Or like an opiate, which brings troubled rest,
  Or none; or like — like nothing that I know

St. Thomas Aquinas is reported to have written two treatises, *De omnibus rebus* (On all things) and *De quibusdam aliis* (On some others).

Except itself; — such is the human breast;
　A thing, of which similitudes can show
No real likeness, — like the old Tyrian vest
　Dyed purple; none at present can tell how,
If from a shell-fish or from cochineal.
So perish every Tyrant's robe piece-meal!

11

But next to dressing for a rout or ball,
　Undressing is a woe; our *robe de chambre*
May sit like that of Nessus, and recall
　Thoughts quite as yellow, but less clear than amber.
Titus exclaimed, "I 've lost a day!" Of all
　The nights and days most people can remember,
(I have had of both, some not to be disdained,)
I wish they 'd state how many they have gained.

12

And Juan, on retiring for the night,
　Felt restless, and perplexed, and compromised:
He thought Aurora Raby's eyes more bright
　Than Adeline (such is advice) advised;
If he had known exactly his own plight,
　He probably would have philosophized:
A great resource to all, and ne'er denied
Till wanted; therefore Juan only sighed.

13

He sighed; — the next resource is the full moon,
　Where all sighs are deposited; and now
It happened luckily, the chaste orb shone
　As clear as such a climate will allow;

10:7. *cochineal*: An insect from which a scarlet dye was made.
11:3. *Nessus*: See canto 11, 65:4.
11:5. *"I've lost a day"*: Suetonius, in *Lives of the Twelve Caesars,* relates that the Roman Emperor Titus made it his duty to act on all petitions presented to him; once at supper, reflecting that he had done nothing for anyone that day, he made this remark.

And Juan's mind was in the proper tone
   To hail her with the apostrophe — "O thou!"
Of amatory egotism the *Tuism*,
Which further to explain would be a truism.

14

But Lover, Poet, or Astronomer —
   Shepherd, or swain — whoever may behold,
Feel some abstraction when they gaze on her;
   Great thoughts we catch from thence (besides a cold
Sometimes, unless my feelings rather err);
   Deep secrets to her rolling light are told;
The Ocean's tides and mortals' brains she sways,
And also hearts — if there be truth in lays.

15

Juan felt somewhat pensive, and disposed
   For contemplation rather than his pillow:
The Gothic chamber, where he was enclosed,
   Let in the rippling sound of the lake's billow,
With all the mystery by midnight caused:
   Below his window waved (of course) a willow;
And he stood gazing out on the cascade
That flashed and after darkened in the shade.

16

Upon his table or his toilet, — *which*
   Of these is not exactly ascertained, —
(I state this, for I am cautious to a pitch
   Of nicety, where a fact is to be gained,)
A lamp burned high, while he leant from a niche,
   Where many a Gothic ornament remained,
In chiselled stone and painted glass, and all
That Time has left our fathers of their Hall.

13:7. *Tuism*: The "thou" as opposed to the "I."
16:1. *toilet*: Dressing table or washstand.

17

Then, as the night was clear though cold, he threw
　　His chamber door wide open — and went forth
Into a gallery of a sombre hue,
　　Long, furnished with old pictures of great worth,
Of knights and dames heroic and chaste too,
　　As doubtless should be people of high birth;
But by dim lights the portraits of the dead
Have something ghastly, desolate, and dread.

18

The forms of the grim Knight and pictured Saint
　　Look living in the moon; and as you turn
Backward and forward to the echoes faint
　　Of your own footsteps — voices from the Urn
Appear to wake, and shadows wild and quaint
　　Start from the frames which fence their aspects stern,
As if to ask how you can dare to keep
A vigil there, where all but Death should sleep.

19

And the pale smile of Beauties in the grave,
　　The charms of other days, in starlight gleams,
Glimmer on high; their buried locks still wave
　　Along the canvas; their eyes glance like dreams
On ours, or spars within some dusky cave,
　　But Death is imaged in their shadowy beams.
A picture is the past; even ere its frame
Be gilt, who sate hath ceased to be the same.

20

As Juan mused on Mutability,
　　Or on his Mistress — terms synonymous —
No sound except the echo of his sigh
　　Or step ran sadly through that antique house;
When suddenly he heard, or thought so, nigh,
　　A supernatural agent — or a mouse,

Whose little nibbling rustle will embarrass
Most people as it plays along the arras.

21

It was no mouse — but lo! a monk, arrayed
  In cowl and beads, and dusky garb, appeared,
Now in the moonlight, and now lapsed in shade,
  With steps that trod as heavy, yet unheard;
His garments only a slight murmur made;
  He moved as shadowy as the Sisters weird,
But slowly; and as he passed Juan by,
Glanced, without pausing, on him a bright eye.

22

Juan was petrified; he had heard a hint
  Of such a Spirit in these halls of old,
But thought, like most men, that there was nothing in 't
  Beyond the rumour which such spots unfold,
Coined from surviving Superstition's mint,
  Which passes ghosts in currency like gold,
But rarely seen, like gold compared with paper.
And did he see this? or was it a vapour?

23

Once, twice, thrice passed, repassed — the thing of air,
  Or earth beneath, or Heaven, or t' other place;
And Juan gazed upon it with a stare,
  Yet could not speak or move; but, on its base
As stands a statue, stood: he felt his hair
  Twine like a knot of snakes around his face;
He taxed his tongue for words, which were not granted,
To ask the reverend person what he wanted.

24

The third time, after a still longer pause,
  The shadow passed away — but where? the hall
Was long, and thus far there was no great cause
  To think his vanishing unnatural:

Doors there were many, through which, by the laws
  Of physics, bodies whether short or tall
Might come or go; but Juan could not state
Through which the Spectre seemed to evaporate.

25

He stood — how long he knew not, but it seemed
  An age — expectant, powerless, with his eyes
Strained on the spot where first the figure gleamed;
  Then by degrees recalled his energies,
And would have passed the whole off as a dream,
  But could not wake; he was, he did surmise,
Waking already, and returned at length
Back to his chamber, shorn of half his strength.

26

All there was as he left it: still his taper
  Burned, and not *blue*, as modest tapers use,
Receiving sprites with sympathetic vapour;
  He rubbed his eyes, and they did not refuse
Their office: he took up an old newspaper;
  The paper was right easy to peruse;
He read an article the King attacking,
And a long eulogy of "Patent Blacking."

27

This savoured of this world; but his hand shook;
  He shut his door, and after having read
A paragraph, I think about Horne Tooke,
  Undressed, and rather slowly went to bed.
There, couched all snugly on his pillow's nook,
  With what he had seen his phantasy he fed;

26:2. *blue*: Candles were supposed to burn with a blue flame when the devil or ghosts were present.
26:8. *"Patent Blacking"*: Advertisements for shoe blacking were often written in doggeral rhymes (Pratt).
27:3. *Horne Tooke*: See *Vision of Judgment*, Stanza 84.

And though it was no opiate, slumber crept
Upon him by degrees, and so he slept.

28

He woke betimes; and, as may be supposed,
    Pondered upon his visitant or vision,
And whether it ought not to be disclosed,
    At risk of being quizzed for superstition.
The more he thought, the more his mind was posed:
    In the mean time, his valet, whose precision
Was great, because his master brooked no less,
Knocked to inform him it was time to dress.

29

He dressed; and like young people he was wont
    To take some trouble with his toilet, but
This morning rather spent less time upon 't;
    Aside his very mirror soon was put;
His curls fell negligently o'er his front,
    His clothes were not curbed to their usual cut,
His very neckcloth's Gordian knot was tied
Almost an hair's breadth too much on one side.

30

And when he walked down into the Saloon,
    He sate him pensive o'er a dish of tea,
Which he perhaps had not discovered soon,
    Had it not happened scalding hot to be,
Which made him have recourse unto his spoon;
    So much *distrait* he was, that all could see
That something was the matter — Adeline
The first — but *what* she could not well divine.

31

She looked, and saw him pale, and turned as pale
    Herself; then hastily looked down, and muttered
Something, but what 's not stated in my tale.
    Lord Henry said, his muffin was ill buttered;

The Duchess of Fitz-Fulke played with her veil,
    And looked at Juan hard, but nothing uttered.
Aurora Raby with her large dark eyes
Surveyed him with a kind of calm surprise.

32

But seeing him all cold and silent still,
    And everybody wondering more or less,
Fair Adeline inquired, "If he were ill?"
    He started, and said, "Yes — no — rather — yes."
The family physician had great skill,
    And being present, now began to express
His readiness to feel his pulse and tell
The cause, but Juan said, he was "quite well."

33

"Quite well; yes, — no." — These answers were mysterious,
    And yet his looks appeared to sanction both,
However they might savour of delirious;
    Something like illness of a sudden growth
Weighed on his spirit, though by no means serious:
    But for the rest, as he himself seemed loth
To state the case, it might be ta'en for granted
It was not the physician that he wanted.

34

Lord Henry, who had now discussed his chocolate,
    Also the muffin whereof he complained,
Said, Juan had not got his usual look elate,
    At which he marvelled, since it had not rained;
Then asked her Grace what news were of the Duke of late?
    Her Grace replied, *his* Grace was rather pained
With some slight, light, hereditary twinges
Of gout, which rusts aristocratic hinges.

35

Then Henry turned to Juan, and addressed
    A few words of condolence on his state:

"You look," quoth he, "as if you had had your rest
  Broke in upon by the Black Friar of late."
"What Friar?" said Juan; and he did his best
  To put the question with an air sedate,
Or careless; but the effort was not valid
To hinder him from growing still more pallid.

36

"Oh! have you never heard of the Black Friar?
  The Spirit of these walls?" — "In truth not I."
"Why Fame — but Fame you know 's sometimes a liar —
  Tells an odd story, of which by and by:
Whether with time the Spectre has grown shyer,
  Or that our Sires had a more gifted eye
For such sights, though the tale is half believed,
The Friar of late has not been oft perceived.

37

"The last time was —" —"I pray," said Adeline —
  (Who watched the changes of Don Juan's brow,
And from its context thought she could divine
  Connections stronger than he chose to avow
With this same legend) — "if you but design
  To jest, you 'll choose some other theme just now,
Because the present tale has oft been told,
And is not much improved by growing old."

38

"Jest!" quoth Milor; "why, Adeline, you know
  That we ourselves — 't was in the honey moon —
Saw —" — "Well, no matter, 't was so long ago;
  But, come, I 'll set your story to a tune."
Graceful as Dian when she draws her bow,
  She seized her harp, whose strings were kindled soon

35:4. *Black Friar*: Byron is drawing upon the legend of the Black Friar
whose ghost was supposed to haunt Newstead Abbey from the time of the
dissolution of the Monasteries. According to Moore's *Life*, Byron claimed
that he had seen the ghost.

As touched, and plaintively began to play
The air of " 'T was a Friar of Orders Gray."

● ● ● ● ● ● ●

87

Dully passed o'er the dinner of the day;
   And Juan took his place, he knew not where,
Confused, in the confusion, and *distrait*,
   And sitting as if nailed upon his chair:
Though knives and forks clanked round as in a fray,
   He seemed unconscious of all passing there,
Till some one, with a groan, expressed a wish
(Unheeded twice) to have a fin of fish.

88

On which, at the *third* asking of the banns,
   He started; and perceiving smiles around
Broadening to grins, he coloured more than once,
   And hastily — as nothing can confound
A wise man more than laughter from a dunce —
   Inflicted on the dish a deadly wound,
And with such hurry, that, ere he could curb it,
He had paid his neighbour's prayer with half a turbot.

89

This was no bad mistake, as it occurred,
   The supplicator being an amateur;
But others, who were left with scarce a third,
   Were angry — as they well might, to be sure,
They wondered how a young man so absurd
   Lord Henry at his table should endure;
And this, and his not knowing how much oats
Had fallen last market, cost his host three votes.

90

They little knew, or might have sympathized,
   That he the night before had seen a ghost,

A prologue which but slightly harmonized
  With the substantial company engrossed
By matter, and so much materialised,
  That one scarce knew at what to marvel most
Of two things — *how* (the question rather odd is)
Such bodies could have souls, or souls such bodies!

91

But what confused him more than smile or stare
  From all the 'squires and 'squiresses around,
Who wondered at the abstraction of his air,
  Especially as he had been renowned
For some vivacity among the fair,
  Even in the country circle's narrow bound —
(For little things upon my Lord's estate
Were good small talk for others still less great) —

92

Was, that he caught Aurora's eye on his,
  And something like a smile upon her cheek.
Now this he really rather took amiss;
  In those who rarely smile, their smile bespeaks
A strong external motive; and in this
  Smile of Aurora's there was nought to pique,
Or Hope, or Love — with any of the wiles
Which some pretend to trace in ladies' smiles.

93

'T was a mere quiet smile of contemplation,
  Indicative of some surprise and pity;
And Juan grew carnation with vexation,
  Which was not very wise, and still less witty,
Since he had gained at least her observation,
  A most important outwork of the city —
As Juan should have known, had not his senses
By last night's Ghost been driven from their defences.

94

But what was bad, she did not blush in turn,
    Nor seem embarrassed — quite the contrary;
Her aspect was as usual, still — *not* stern —
    And she withdrew, but cast not down, her eye,
Yet grew a little pale — with what? concern?
    I know not; but her colour ne'er was high —
Though sometimes faintly flushed — and always clear,
As deep seas in a sunny atmosphere.

95

But Adeline was occupied by fame
    This day; and watching, witching, condescending
To the consumers of fish, fowl, and game,
    And dignity with courtesy so blending,
As all must blend whose part it is to aim
    (Especially as the sixth year is ending)
At their lord's, son's, or similar connection's
Safe conduct through the rocks of re-elections.

96

Though this was most expedient on the whole
    And usual — Juan, when he cast a glance
On Adeline while playing her grand *rôle*,
    Which she went through as though it were a dance,
Betraying only now and then her soul
    By a look scarce perceptibly askance
(Of weariness or scorn), began to feel
Some doubt how much of Adeline was *real*;

97

So well she acted all and every part
    By turns — with that vivacious versatility,
Which many people take for want of heart.

95:6. *sixth year is ending*: Parliamentary elections are about to be held.
Lord Henry has invited the country squires and their wives to dinner.

They err — 't is merely what is called mobility,
A thing of temperament and not of art,
  Though seeming so, from its supposed facility;
And false — though true; for, surely, they 're sincerest
Who are strongly acted on by what is nearest.

98

This makes your actors, artists, and romancers,
  Heroes sometimes, though seldom — sages never:
But speakers, bards, diplomatists, and dancers,
  Little that 's great, but much of what is clever;
Most orators, but very few financiers,
  Though all Exchequer Chancellors endeavour,
Of late years, to dispense with Cocker's rigours,
And grow quite figurative with their figures.

99

The poets of Arithmetic are they
  Who, though they prove not two and two to be
Five, as they might do in a modest way,
  Have plainly made it out that four are three,
Judging by what they take, and what they pay:
  The Sinking Fund's unfathomable sea,
That most unliquidating liquid, leaves
The debt unsunk, yet sinks all it receives.

100

While Adeline dispensed her airs and graces,
  The fair Fitz-Fulke seemed very much at ease;

97:4. *mobility*: Byron's note: "I am not sure that mobility is English;
but it is expressive of a quality which rather belongs to other climates,
though it is sometimes seen to a great extent in our own. It may be de-
fined as an excessive susceptibility of immediate impressions — at the same
time without *losing* the past; and is, though sometimes apparently useful
to the possessor, a most painful and unhappy attribute."

98:7. *Cocker's rigours*: Cocker's *Arithmetic*, first published in 1677, was
still a standard work in Byron's day.

99:6–8. *The Sinking Fund's unfathomable sea*: The Sinking Fund, a
scheme devised by Walpole in 1717–1718 to reduce the national debt, instead cost the country an enormous sum before being abolished in 1823.

Though too well bred to quiz men to their faces,
　　Her laughing blue eyes with a glance could seize
The ridicules of people in all places —
　　That honey of your fashionable bees —
And store it up for mischievous enjoyment;
And this at present was her kind employment.

101

However, the day closed, as days must close;
　　The evening also waned — and coffee came.
Each carriage was announced, and ladies rose,
　　And curtsying off, as curtsies country dame,
Retired: with most unfashionable bows
　　Their docile Esquires also did the same,
Delighted with their dinner and their Host,
But with the Lady Adeline the most.

102

Some praised her beauty: others her great grace;
　　The warmth of her politeness, whose sincerity
Was obvious in each feature of her face,
　　Whose traits were radiant with the rays of verity.
Yes; *she* was truly worthy *her* high place!
　　No one could envy her reserved prosperity.
And then her dress — what beautiful simplicity
Draperied her form with curious felicity!

103

Meanwhile sweet Adeline deserved their praises,
　　By an impartial indemnification
For all her past exertion and soft phrases,
　　In a most edifying conversation,
Which turned upon their late guests' miens and faces,
　　Their families, even to the last relation;
Their hideous wives, their horrid selves and dresses,
And truculent distortion of their tresses.

104

True, *she* said little — 't was the rest that broke
    Forth into universal epigram;
But then 't was to the purpose what she spoke:
    Like Addison's "faint praise," so wont to damn,
Her own but served to set off every joke,
    As music chimes in with a melodrame.
How sweet the task to shield an absent friend!
I ask but this of mine, to —— *not* defend.

105

There were but two exceptions to this keen
    Skirmish of wits o'er the departed; one,
Aurora, with her pure and placid mien;
    And Juan, too, in general behind none
In gay remark on what he had heard or seen,
    Sate silent now, his usual spirits gone:
In vain he heard the others rail or rally,
He would not join them in a single sally.

106

'T is true he saw Aurora look as though
    She approved his silence; she perhaps mistook
Its motive for that charity we owe
    But seldom pay the absent, nor would look
Farther — it might or it might not be so.
    But Juan, sitting silent in his nook,
Observing little in his reverie,
Yet saw this much, which he was glad to see.

107

The Ghost at least had done him this much good,
    In making him as silent as a ghost,
If in the circumstances which ensued

104:4. *Addison's "faint praise"*: In *Prologue to the Satires*, ll. 201–202,
Pope writes of Addison:
        "Damn with faint praise, assent with civil leer,
        And without sneering, teach the rest to sneer."

He gained esteem where it was worth the most;
And, certainly, Aurora had renewed
  In him some feelings he had lately lost,
Or hardened; feelings which, perhaps ideal,
Are so divine, that I must deem them real: —

108

The love of higher things and better days;
  The unbounded hope, and heavenly ignorance
Of what is called the World, and the World's ways;
  The moments when we gather from a glance
More joy than from all future pride or praise,
  Which kindle manhood, but can ne'er entrance
The Heart in an existence of its own,
Of which another's bosom is the zone.

109

Who would not sigh Αἴ αἴ τὰν Κυθέρειαν
  That *hath* a memory, or that *had* a heart?
Alas! *her* star must fade like that of Dian:
  Ray fades on ray, as years on years depart.
Anacreon only had the soul to tie an
  Unwithering myrtle round the unblunted dart
Of Eros: but though thou hast played us many tricks
Still we respect thee, *"Alma Venus Genetrix!"*

110

And full of sentiments, sublime as billows
  Heaving between this World and Worlds beyond,
Don Juan, when the midnight hour of pillows
  Arrived, retired to his; but to despond
Rather than rest. Instead of poppies, willows

109:1. . . . . Κυθέρειαν: From Bion's *Elegy on Adonis*: "Woe, woe, for Cytherea." Cytherea was goddess of love.
109:6–7. *Anacreon*: The reference is to the *Odes* of Anacreon.
109:8. *"Alma Venus Genetrix"*: Bountiful life-giving (mother) Venus. From Lucretius, *De Rerum Natura*, I, 1, where the reference is to Venus as mother of Aeneas and his descendants (the Romans).

Waved o'er his couch; he meditated, fond
Of those sweet bitter thoughts which banish sleep,
And make the wordling sneer, the youngling weep.

111

The night was as before: he was undrest,
　　Saving his night-gown, which is an undress;
Completely *sans culotte*, and without vest;
　　In short, he hardly could be clothed with less:
But apprehensive of his spectral guest,
　　He sate with feelings awkward to express
(By those who have not had such visitations),
Expectant of the Ghost's fresh operations.

112

And not in vain he listened; — Hush! what 's that?
　　I see — I see — Ah, no! — 't is not — yet 't is —
Ye powers! it is the — the — the — Pooh! the cat!
　　The Devil may take that stealthy pace of his!
So like a spiritual pit-a-pat,
　　Or tiptoe of an amatory Miss,
Gliding the first time to a *rendezvous*,
And dreading the chaste echoes of her shoe.

113

Again — what is 't? The wind? No, no, — this time
　　It is the sable Friar as before,
With awful footsteps regular as rhyme,
　　Or (as rhymes may be in these days) much more.
Again through shadows of the night sublime,
　　When deep sleep fell on men, and the World wore
The starry darkness round her like a girdle
Spangled with gems — the Monk made his blood curdle.

114

A noise like to wet fingers drawn on glass,
　　Which sets the teeth on edge; and a slight clatter,

111:3. *sans culotte*: Without trousers.

Like showers which on the midnight gusts will pass,
   Sounding like very supernatural water,
Came over Juan's ear, which throbbed, alas!
   For Immaterialism 's a serious matter;
So that even those whose faith is the most great
In Souls immortal, shun them *tête-à-tête*.

115

Were his eyes open? — Yes! and his mouth too.
   Surprise has this effect — to make one dumb,
Yet leave the gate which Eloquence slips through
   As wide as if a long speech were to come.
Nigh and more nigh the awful echoes drew,
   Tremendous to a mortal tympanum:
His eyes were open, and (as was before
Stated) his mouth. What opened next? — the door.

116

It opened with a most infernal creak,
   Like that of Hell. "Lasciate ogni speranza,
Voi, ch' entrate!" The hinge seemed to speak,
   Dreadful as Dante's *rima*, or this stanza;
Or — but all words upon such themes are weak:
   A single shade 's sufficient to entrance a
Hero — for what is Substance to a Spirit?
Or how is 't *Matter* trembles to come near it?

117

The door flew wide, not swiftly, — but, as fly
   The sea-gulls, with a steady, sober flight —
And then swung back; nor close — but stood awry,
   Half letting in long shadows on the light,
Which still in Juan's candlesticks burned high,
   For he had two, both tolerably bright,
And in the doorway, darkening darkness, stood
The sable Friar in his solemn hood.

116:3. ". . . *Voi, ch'entrate*": "Abandon all hope, ye who enter here."
Dante, *Inferno*, III, 9.

118

Don Juan shook, as erst he had been shaken
   The night before; but being sick of shaking,
He first inclined to think he had been mistaken;
   And then to be ashamed of such mistaking;
His own internal ghost began to awaken
   Within him, and to quell his corporal quaking —
Hinting that Soul and Body on the whole
Were odds against a disembodied Soul.

119

And then his dread grew wrath, and his wrath fierce,
   And he arose, advanced — the Shade retreated;
But Juan, eager now the truth to pierce,
   Followed, his veins no longer cold, but heated,
Resolved to thrust the mystery *carte* and *tierce*,
   At whatsoever risk of being defeated:
The Ghost stopped, menaced, then retired, until
He reached the ancient wall, then stood stone still.

120

Juan put forth one arm — Eternal powers!
   It touched no soul, nor body, but the wall,
On which the moonbeams fell in silvery showers,
   Chequered with all the tracery of the Hall;
He shuddered, as no doubt the bravest cowers
   When he can't tell what 't is that doth appal.
How odd, a single hobgoblin's nonentity
Should cause more fear than a whole host's identity!

121

But still the Shade remained: the blue eyes glared,
   And rather variably for stony death;
Yet one thing rather good the grave had spared,
   The Ghost had a remarkably sweet breath:

119:5. *carte and tierce*: The fourth and third positions for thrusting in
fencing.

A straggling curl showed he had been fairhaired;
   A red lip, with two rows of pearls beneath,
Gleamed forth, as though the casement's ivy shroud
The Moon peeped, just escaped from a grey cloud.

122

And Juan, puzzled, but still curious, thrust
   His other arm forth — Wonder upon wonder!
It pressed upon a hard but glowing bust,
   Which beat as if there was a warm heart under.
He found, as people on most trials must,
   That he had made at first a silly blunder,
And that in his confusion he had caught
Only the wall, instead of what he sought.

123

The Ghost, if Ghost it were, seemed a sweet soul
   As ever lurked beneath a holy hood:
A dimpled chin, a neck of ivory, stole
   Forth into something much like flesh and blood;
Back fell the sable frock and dreary cowl,
   And they revealed — alas! that e'er they should!
In full, voluptuous, but *not o'er*grown bulk,
The phantom of her frolic Grace — Fitz-Fulke!

1823   *1824*

Selections *from* Letters, Diary, and Detached Thoughts

When Byron wrote exuberantly to his banker friend, Kinnaird, "As to 'Don Juan', confess, confess — you dog and be candid — that it is the sublime of that there sort of writing — it may be bawdy but is it not good English? It may be profligate but is it not life, is it not the thing?" (see below, p. 671), he could equally well have been characterizing his letters and journals. For the language of the prose, like that of *Don Juan*, is informal English used in all its range of idiom and flexibility of rhythm. Both the poem and prose possess the quality of immediacy that we associate with the spontaneous, uninhibited conversation of an articulate and witty man. As we read, we feel that we are *there*, listening to Byron, so graphically does he make his experiences and opinions live on the page. More often than not, as a matter of fact, he dashed off his letters in a great hurry at odd (sometimes very odd) moments of the day and night, frequently just after the experience that he was recording (see, for example, the letters on pp. 661, 672). At the same time the letters were conscious performances, written for the special audience represented by the person addressed. But though he could not resist showing off or shocking his reader, Byron was never simply playing a role or a game. His letters and journals shock mainly by their candour. Attacking cant, they are very free from cant. They are honest, sometimes aggressively honest in their self-revelation, and in the blunt expression of opinion. Always Byron speaks his mind according to the mood of the moment, even though he may contradict himself a letter later. In his 1813 diary he wrote "When I am tired — as I generally am — out comes this, and down goes everything. But I can't read it over; and God knows what contradiction it may contain. If I am sincere with myself (but I fear one lies more to one's self than to anyone else) every page should confute, refute, and utterly abjure its predecessor." Not even in *Don Juan* is the range and complexity of Byron's personality revealed as it is in the letters and journals. Since a selection can at best provide only a tantalizing sampling of their "infinite variety," it seemed most practical here to choose those that can be read in relation to or conjunction with the poetry. For a fully representative collection the student is referred to Quennell's *Byron: A Self-Portrait,* in which the whole sweep of Byron's life is covered.

TO FRANCIS HODGSON[1]

Newstead Abbey, Sept. 3, 1811.

MY DEAR HODGSON,

I will have nothing to do with your immortality; we are miserable enough in this life, without the absurdity of speculating upon another. If men are to live, why die at all? and if they die, why disturb the sweet and sound sleep that "knows no waking"? "Post Mortem nihil est, ipsaque Mors nihil . . . quæris quo jaceas post obitum loco? Quo *non* Nata jacent."[2]

As to revealed religion, Christ came to save men; but a good Pagan will go to heaven, and a bad Nazarene to hell; "Argal"[3] (I argue like the gravedigger) why are not all men Christians? or why are any? If mankind may be saved who never heard or dreamt, at Timbuctoo, Otaheite, Terra Incognita, etc., of Galilee and its Prophet, Christianity is of no avail: if they cannot be saved without, why are not all orthodox? It is a little hard to send a man preaching to Judæa, and leave the rest of the world — Negers and what not — *dark* as their complexions, without a ray of light for so many years to lead them on high; and who will believe that God will damn men for not knowing what they were never taught? I hope I am sincere; I was so at least on a bed of sickness in a far-distant

---

[1] Francis Hodgson (1781–1852) tutor at King's College, Cambridge, and intimate friend of Byron between 1807 and 1816, was disturbed by what he considered the irreligious views of *Childe Harold,* and wrote in protest. In 1812 Hodgson took orders and became a curate.

[2] *"Post . . . jacent"*: From Senaca's *Troades,* 397–402. "After death is nothing, and death itself is nothing . . . You ask, where shall you lie after death? Where the *un*born lie."

[3] *"Argal"*: Corruption of Latin *ergo* "therefore." See *Hamlet* V. 1. 21.

country, when I had neither friend, nor comforter, nor hope, to sustain me. I looked to death as a relief from pain, without a wish for an after-life, but a confidence that the God who punishes in this existence had left that last asylum for the weary.

Ὃν ὁ θεὸς ἀγαπάει ἀποθνήσκει νέος.[4]

I am no Platonist, I am nothing at all; but I would sooner be a Paulician,[5] Manichean,[6] Spinozist,[7] Gentile,[8] Pyrrhonian,[9] Zoroastrian,[10] than one of the seventy-two villainous sects who are tearing each other to pieces for the love of the Lord and hatred of each other. Talk of Galileeism? Show me the effects — are you better, wiser, kinder by your precepts? I will bring you ten Mussulmans shall shame you in all goodwill towards men, prayer to God, and duty to their neighbours. And is there a Talapoin, or a Bonze,[11] who is not superior to a fox-hunting curate? But I will say no more on this endless theme; let me live, well if possible, and die without pain. The rest is with God, who assuredly, had He *come* or *sent*, would have made Himself manifest to nations, and intelligible to all.

I shall rejoice to see you. My present intention is to accept Scrope Davies's[12] invitation; and then, if you accept mine, we shall meet *here* and *there*. Did you know poor Matthews?[13] I shall miss him much at Cambridge.

---

4 *"Ον . . . . véos*: "Whom the gods love die young" (Menander).

5 *Paulician*: Member of Christian heretical sect between the second and tenth century which rejected sacraments and dogma. It was probably dualistic like the Manicheans.

6 *Manichean*: See *Cain*, Preface, n. 8.

7 *Spinozist*: i.e. Pantheist.

8 *Gentile*: Pagan, heathen.

9 *Pyrrhonian*: Follower of Pyrrho (c. 360–270 B.C.) Greek skeptic philosopher, who taught that nothing can be known.

10 *Zoroastrian*: See *Manfred* II. iv. 17n.

11 *Talapoin, or a Bonze*: Buddhist monk.

12 *Scrope Davies* (1783–1852): Fellow at King's College, Cambridge, and a flamboyant gambler.

13 *Matthews*: Charles Matthews, one of Byron's closest friends at Cambridge, was drowned in August, 1811.

TO MISS MILBANKE,

September 6, 1813.

. . . . With all my presumed prejudice against your sex, or rather the perversion of manners and principle in many, which you admit in some circles, I think the worst woman that ever existed would have made a man of very passable reputation. They are all better than us, and their faults, such as they are, must originate with ourselves. Your sweeping sentence "on the circles where we have met" amuses me much when I recollect some of those who constituted that society. After all, bad as it is, it has its *agremens.* The great object of life is sensation — to feel that we exist, even though in pain. It is this "craving void" which drives us to gaming — to battle — to travel — to intemperate, but keenly felt pursuits of any description, whose principal attraction is the agitation inseparable from their accomplishment. I am but an awkward dissembler; as my friend you will bear with my faults. I shall have the less constraint in what I say to you — firstly because I may derive some benefit from your observations — and next because I am very sure you can never be perverted by any paradoxes of mine. . . .

TO MISS MILBANKE

Nov. 29, 1813.

. . . . I by no means rank poetry or poets high in the scale of intellect. This may look like affectation, but it is my real opinion. It is the lava of the imagination whose eruption prevents an earthquake. They say poets never or rarely go *mad.* Cowper and Collins are instances to the contrary (but Cowper was no poet). It is, however, to be remarked that they rarely do, but are generally so near it that I cannot help thinking rhyme is so far useful in anticipating and preventing the disorder. I prefer the talents of action — of war, or the senate, or even of science, — to all the speculations of those mere dreamers of another existence (I don't mean religiously but fancifully) and spectators of this apathy. Disgust and perhaps incapacity have rendered me now a mere spectator; but I have occasionally mixed in the active and tumultuous departments of existence, and in these alone my recollection rests with any satisfaction, though not the best parts of it. . . .

TO MISS MILBANKE

March 3, 1814.

. . . . I thank you very much for your suggestion on religion. But I must tell you, at the hazard of losing whatever good opinion your gentleness may have bestowed upon me, that it is a source from which I never did, and I believe never can, derive comfort. If I ever feel what is called devout, it is when I have met with some good of which I did not conceive myself deserving, and then I am apt to thank anything but mankind. On the other hand, when I am ill or unlucky, I philosophize as well as I can, and wish it were over one way or the other — without any glimpses at the future. Why I came here, I know not. Where I shall go to, it is useless to inquire. In the midst of myriads of the living and the dead worlds — stars — systems — infinity — why should I be anxious about an atom? . . .

TO MISS ANNE ISABELLA MILBANKE[1]

Septr. 18th 1814.

Your letter has given me a new existence — it was unexpected — I need not say welcome — but *that* is a poor word to express my present feelings — and yet equal to any other — for express them adequately I cannot. I have ever regarded you as one of the first of human beings — not merely from my own observation but that of others — as one whom it was as difficult *not* to love — as scarcely possible to deserve; — I know your worth — and revere your virtues as I love yourself and if every proof in my power of my full sense of what is due

---

[1] Byron is replying to her letter accepting his proposal of marriage.

to you will contribute to *your* happiness — I shall have secured my own. — It *is* in your power to render me happy — you have made me so already. — I wish to answer your letter immediately — but am at present scarcely collected enough to do it rationally — I was upon the point of leaving England without hope without fear — almost without feeling — but wished to make one effort to discover — not if I could pretend to your present affections — for to those I had given over all presumption — but whether time — and my most sincere endeavour to adopt any mode of conduct that might lead you to think well of me — might not eventually in securing your approbation awaken your regard. — These hopes are now dearer to me than ever; dear as they have ever been; — from the moment I became acquainted my attachment has been increasing and the very follies — give them a harsher name — with which I was beset and bewildered the conduct to which I had recourse for forgetfulness only made recollection more lively and bitter by the comparisons it forced on me in spite of Pride — and of Passions — which might have destroyed but never deceived me. —

I am going to London on some business which once over — I hope to be permitted to visit Seaham; your father I will answer immediately and in the mean time beg you will present my best thanks and respects to him and Lady Milbanke. Will you write to me? and permit me to assure you how faithfully I shall ever be

yr. most attached and obliged Sert.

TO THOMAS MOORE

Newstead Abbey, Sept. 20, 1814.

Here's to her who long
Hath waked the poet's sigh!
The girl who gave to song
What gold could never buy.

My dear Moore,

I am going to be married — that is, I am accepted, and one usually hopes the rest will follow. My mother of the Gracchi[1] (that *are* to be), *you* think too strait-laced for me, although the paragon of only children, and invested with 'golden opinions of all sorts of men,'[2] and full of 'most blest conditions'[3] as Desdemona herself. Miss Milbanke is the lady, and I have her father's invitation to proceed there in my elect capacity, — which however, I cannot do till I have settled some business in London, and got a blue coat.

She is said to be an heiress, but of that I really know nothing certainly, and shall not enquire. But I do know, that she has talents and excellent qualities; and you will not deny her judgment, after having refused six suitors and taken me.

Now, if you have any thing to say against this, pray do; my mind's made up, positively fixed, determined, and therefore I will listen to reason, because now it can do no harm. Things may occur to break it off, but I will hope not. In the mean time, I tell you (*a secret,* by the by, — at least, till I know she wishes it to be public) that I have proposed and am accepted. You need not be in a hurry to wish me joy, for one mayn't be married for months. I am going to town to-morrow: but expect to be here, on my way there, within a fortnight.

If this had not happened, I should have gone to Italy. In my way down, perhaps, you will meet me at Nottingham, and come over with me here. I need not say that nothing will give me greater pleasure. I must, of course, reform thoroughly; and, seriously, if I can contribute to her happiness, I shall secure my own. She is so good a person, that — that — in short, I wish I was a better.

Ever, etc.

[1] *Gracchi*: Twin brothers (163–121 B.C.) who championed the cause of the plebians against the Roman Senate.
[2] *"Golden opinion . . . . men"*: *Macbeth* I. vii. 33.
[3] *"most . . . . conditions"*: *Othello* II. i. 245–246.

TO LADY BYRON

Mivart's Hotel [Easter] Sunday April [14] 1816.

"More last words" — not many — & such as you will attend to — answer I do not expect — nor does it import — but you will hear me. — I have just parted from Augusta — almost the last being you had left me to part with — & the only unshattered tie of my existence — wherever I may go — & I am going far — you & I can never meet again in this world — nor in the next — Let this content or atone. — If any accident occurs to me — be kind to *her,* — if she is then nothing — to her children: —

Some time ago — I informed you that with the knowledge that any child of ours was already provided for by other & better means — I had made my will in favor of her & her children — as prior to my marriage: — this was not done in prejudice to you for we had not then differed — & even this is useless during your life by the settlements — I say therefore — be kind to her & hers — for never has she acted or spoken otherwise towards you — she has ever been your friend — this may seem valueless to one who has now so many: — be kind to her — however — & recollect that though it may be advantage to you to have lost your husband — it is sorrow to her to have the water now — or the earth hereafter — between her & her brother. —

She is gone — I need hardly add that of this request she knows nothing — your late compliances have not been so extensive — as to render this an encroachment: — I repeat it — (for deep resentments have but *half* recollections) that you once did promise me thus much — do not forget it — nor deem it cancelled — it was not a vow. ——

Mr. Wharton[1] has sent me a letter with one question & two pieces of intelligence — to the question I answer that the carriage is yours — & as it has only carried us to Halnaby[2]

---

[1] *Wharton:* Gerald Blesson Wharton, attorney to Lady Byron's father.
[2] *Halnaby:* Halnaby Hall where Byron and Lady Byron spent their honeymoon.

— & London — & you to Kirkby[3] — I hope it will take you many a more propitious journey. —

The receipts can remain — unless troublesome, if so — they can be sent to Augusta — & through her I would also hear of my little daughter — my address will be left for Mrs. Leigh. — The ring is of no lapidary value — but it contains the hair of a king & an ancestor — which I should wish to preserve to Miss Byron. —

To a subsequent letter of Mr. Wharton's I have to reply that it is the "law's delay" not mine, — & that when he & Mr. H[4] have adjusted the tenor of the bond[5] — I am ready to sign.

Yrs Ever
very truly
Byron

TO THE HON. AUGUSTA LEIGH

Ouchy, Sep^t 17, 1816

MY DEAREST AUGUSTA,

I am thus far on my way to the Bernese Alps and the Grindenwald, and the *Yung frau* (that is the "Wild woman" being interpreted — as it is so perverse a mountain that no other sex would suit it), which journey may occupy me about eight days or so, and then it is my intention to return to Geneva, preparatory to passing the Simplon[1] ——

Continue you to direct as usual to Geneva. I have lately written to you several letters (3 or 4 by post and two by hand) and I have received all yours very safely. I rejoice to have heard that you are well. You have been in London too lately, and H. tells me that at your levée he generally found Ld F. Bentinck — pray why is that fool so often a visitor? is he in love with you? I have recently broken through my resolution

---

3 *Kirkby*: Kirkby Mallory, where Lady Byron's parents lived, and where she had gone in January when she separated from Byron.

4 *Mr. H.*: Byron's lawyer, John Hanson.

5 *bond*: The legal bond of separation.

1 *Simplon*: The Simplon pass into Italy.

of not speaking to you of Lady B — but do not on that account name her to me. It is a relief — a partial relief to me to talk of her sometimes to you — but it would be none to hear of her. *Of* her you are to judge for yourself, but do not altogether forget that she has destroyed your brother. Whatever my faults might or may have been — *She* — was not the person marked out by providence to be their avenger. One day or another her conduct will recoil on her own head; *not* through *me,* for my feelings towards her are not those of Vengeance, but — mark — if she does not end miserably *tot ou tard.*[2] She may think — talk — or act as she will, and by any process of cold reasoning and a jargon of "duty and acting for the best" etc., etc., impose upon her own feelings and those of others for a time — but woe unto her — the wretchedness she has brought upon the man to whom she has been everything evil [except in one respect (effaced)] will flow back into its fountain. I may thank the strength of my constitution that has enabled me to bear all this, but those who bear the longest and the most do not suffer the least. I do not think a human being could endure more mental torture than that woman has directly and indirectly inflicted upon me — within the present year.

She has (for a time at least) separated me from my child — and from you — but I turn from the subject for the present.

To-morrow I repass Clarens and Vevey; if in the new and more extended tour I am making, anything that I think may please you occurs, I will detail it.

Scrope has by this time arrived with my little presents for you and yours and Ada. I still hope to be able to see you next Spring, perhaps you and one or two of the children could be spared some time next year for a little tour *here* or in France with me of a month or two. I think I could make it pleasing to you, and it should be no expense to L. or to yourself. Pray think of this hint. You have no idea how very beautiful great part of this country is — and *women* and *children* traverse it with ease and expedition. I would return from any distance

---

[2] *tot ou tard:* sooner or later. See *Childe Harold,* iv. 131 ff.

at any time to see you, and come to England for you; and when you consider the chances against our — but I won't relapse into the dismals and anticipate long absences ——

The great obstacle would be that you are so admirably yoked — and necessary as a housekeeper — and a letter writer — and a place-hunter to that very helpless gentleman your Cousin, that I suppose the usual self-love of an elderly person would interfere between you and any scheme of recreation or relaxation, for however short a period.

What a fool was I to marry — and *you* not very wise — my dear — we might have lived so single and so happy — as old maids and bachelors; I shall never find any one like you — nor you (vain as it may seem) like me. We are just formed to pass our lives together, and therefore — we — at least — I — am by a crowd of circumstances removed from the only being who could ever have loved me, or whom I can unmixedly feel attached to.

Had you been a Nun — and I a Monk — that we might have talked through a grate instead of across the sea — no matter — my voice and my heart are

ever thine — B.

A JOURNAL

Clarens, Septr 18th 1816

Yesterday September 17th 1816 — I set out (with H[obhouse]) on an excursion of some days to the Mountains. I shall keep a short journal of each day's progress for my Sister Augusta.

. . . . Arrived the second time (1st time was by water) at Clarens, beautiful Clarens! Went to Chillon through Scenery worthy of I know not whom; went over the Castle of Chillon again. On our return met an English party in a carriage; a lady in it fast asleep! — fast asleep in the most anti-narcotic spot in the world — excellent! I remember, at Chamouni, in the very eyes of Mont Blanc, hearing another woman, English also, exclaim to her party "did you ever see any thing more *rural?*" — as if it was Highgate, or Hampstead, or Brompton, or Hayes, — *"Rural!"* quotha! — Rocks, pines, torrents, Glaciers, Clouds, and Summits of eternal snow far above them — and *"Rural!"* I did not know the thus exclaiming fair one, but she was a very good kind of a woman.

After a slight and short dinner, we visited the Chateau de Clarens; an English woman has rented it recently (it was not let when I saw it first): the roses are gone with their Summer; the family out, but the servants desired us to walk over the interior of the mansion. Saw on the table of the saloon Blair's sermons and somebody else's (I forget who's) sermons, and a set of noisy children. Saw all worth seeing, and then descended to the "Bosquet de Julie",[1] etc., etc.; our Guide full of *Rousseau,* whom he is eternally confounding with *St. Preux,*[2] and mixing the man and the book. On the steps of a cottage in the village, I saw a young paysan*ne,* beautiful as Julie herself. Went again as far as Chillon to revisit the little torrent from the hill behind it. Sunset reflected in the lake. Have to get up at 5 tomorrow to cross the mountains on horseback — carriage to be sent round; lodged at my old Cottage — hospitable and comfortable; tired with a longish ride on the Colt, and the subsequent jolting of the Charaban, and my scramble in the hot sun. Shall go to bed, thinking of you, dearest Augusta.

Mem. The Corporal who showed the wonders of Chillon was as drunk as Blucher,[3] and (to my mind) as great a man. He was *deaf* also, and thinking every one else so, roared out the legends of the Castle so fearfully that H. got out of humour. However, we saw all things from the Gallows to the Dungeons (the *Potence* and the *Cachots*),[4] and returned to Clarens with more freedom than belonged to the 15th Century. . . .

Septr 22d

Left Thoun in a boat, which carried us the length of the lake in three hours. The lake small; but the banks fine: rocks

1 *Bosquet de Julie:* Julie's grove. See *Childe Harold,* III, 99–104.
2 *St. Preux:* The hero in Rousseau's *Julie* or *La Nouvelle Héloïse.*
3 *Blucher:* Prussian commander at Waterloo.
4 *Potense . . . Cachots:* Gallows . . . dungeons.

down to the water's edge. Landed at Neuhause; passed Inter-lachen; entered upon a range of scenes beyond all description or previous conception. Passed a rock; inscription — 2 brothers — one murdered the other; just the place for it. After a variety of windings came to an enormous rock. Girl with fruit — very pretty; blue eyes, good teeth, very fair: long but good features — reminded me rather of F*y* Bought some of her pears, and patted her upon the cheek; the expression of her face very mild, but good, and not at all coquettish. Arrived at the foot of the Mountain (the Yung frau, *i.e.* the Maiden); Glaciers; torrents; one of these torrents *nine hundred feet* in height of visible descent. Lodge at the Curate's. Set out to see the Valley; heard an Avalanche fall, like thunder; saw Glacier — enormous. Storm came on, thunder, lightning, hail; all in perfection, and beautiful. I was on horseback; Guide wanted to carry my cane; I was going to give it him, when I recollected that it was a Swordstick, and I thought the lightning might be attracted towards him; kept it myself; a good deal encumbered with it, and my cloak, as it was too heavy for a whip, and the horse was stupid, and stood still with every other peal. Got in, not very wet; the Cloak being staunch. H. wet through; H. took refuge in cottage; sent man, umbrella, and cloak (from the Curate's when I arrived) after him. Swiss Curate's house very good indeed, — much better than most English Vicarages. It is immediately opposite the torrent I spoke of. The torrent is in shape curving over the rock, like the *tail* of a white horse streaming in the wind, such as it might be conceived would be that of the "*pale* horse" on which *Death* is mounted in the Apocalypse.[1] It is neither mist nor water, but a something between both; it's immense height (nine hundred feet) gives it a wave, a curve, a spreading here, a condensation there, wonderful and indescribable. I think, upon the whole, that this day has been better than any of this present excursion.

Sept. 23ᵈ

Before ascending the mountain, went to the torrent (7 in the morning) again; the Sun upon it forming a *rainbow* of

[1] *Apocalypse*: See *Manfred* II. ii. 1–8.

the lower part of all colours, but principally purple and gold; the bow moving as you move; I never saw any thing like this; it is only in the Sunshine. Ascended the Wengen Mountain; at noon reached a valley on the summit; left the horses, took off my coat, and went to the summit, 7000 feet (English feet) above the level of the *sea,* and about 5000 above the valley we left in the morning. On one side, our view comprized the *Yung frau,* with all her glaciers; then the *Dent d'Argent,* shining like truth; then the *little Giant* (the Kleiner Eigher); and the great Giant (the Grosser Eigher), and last, not least, the Wetterhorn. The height of Jungfrau is 13,000 feet above the sea, 11,000 above the valley; she is the highest of this range. Heard the Avalanches falling every five minutes nearly — as if God was pelting the Devil down from Heaven with snow balls. From where we stood, on the *Wengen* Alp, we had all these in view on one side: on the other the clouds rose from the opposite valley, curling up perpendicular precipices like the foam of the Ocean of Hell, during a Springtide — it was white, and sulphury, and immeasurably deep in appearance.[1] The side we ascended was (of course) not of so precipitous a nature; but on arriving at the summit, we looked down the other side upon a boiling sea of cloud, dashing against the crags on which we stood (these crags on one side quite perpendicular). Staid a quarter of an hour; began to descend; quite clear from cloud on that side of the mountain. In passing the masses of snow, I made a snowball and pelted H. with it.

Got down to our horses again; eat something; remounted; heard the Avalanches still; came to a morass; H. dismounted; H. got over well: I tried to pass my horse over; the horse sunk up [to] the chin, and of course he and I were in the mud together; bemired all over, but not hurt; laughed, and rode on. Arrived at the Grindenwald; dined, mounted again, and rode to the higher Glacier — twilight, but distinct — very fine Glacier, like *a frozen hurricane.*[2] Starlight, beautiful, but

1 *appearance*: See *Manfred* I. ii. 74–79, 85–89.
2 *frozen hurricane*: See *Manfred* II. iii. 4–8.

a devil of a path! Never mind, got safe in; a little lightning; but the whole of the day as fine in point of weather as the day on which Paradise was made. Passed *whole woods of withered pines, all withered;* trunks stripped and barkless, branches lifeless; done by a single winter,[3] — their appearance reminded me of me and my family.

Septr 24th.

Set out at seven; up at five. Passed the black Glacier, the Mountain Wetterhorn on the right; crossed the Scheideck mountain; came to the *Rose* Glacier, said to be the largest and finest in Switzerland. *I* think the Bossons Glacier at Chamouni as fine; H. does not. Came to the Reichenback waterfall, two hundred feet high; halted to rest the horses. Arrived in the valley of Oberhasli; rain came on; drenched a little; only 4 hours' rain, however, in 8 days. Came to Lake of Brientz, then to town of Brientz; changed. H. hurt his head against door. In the evening, four Swiss Peasant Girls of Oberhasli came and sang the airs of their country; two of the voices beautiful — the tunes also: they sing too that *Tyrolese air* and song which you love, Augusta, because I love it — and I love, because you love it; they are still singing. Dearest, you do not know how I should have liked this, were you with me. The airs are so wild and original, and at the same time of great sweetness. The singing is over: but below stairs I hear the notes of a Fiddle, which bode no good to my night's rest. The *Lard* help us — I shall go down and see the dancing.

TO THOMAS MOORE

Venice, November 17, 1816

I wrote to you from Verona the other day in my progress hither, which letter I hope you will receive. Some three years ago, or it may be more, I recollect your telling me that you had received a letter from our friend Sam,[1] dated "On board

---

[3] *single winter:* See *Manfred* I. ii. 66–68.
[1] *friend Sam:* Samuel Rogers.

his gondola". *My* gondola is, at this present, waiting for me on the canal; but I prefer writing to you in the house, it being autumn — and rather an English autumn than otherwise. It is my intention to remain at Venice during the winter, probably, as it has always been (next to the East) the greenest island of my imagination. It has not disappointed me; though its evident decay would, perhaps, have that effect upon others. But I have been familiar with ruins too long to dislike desolation. Besides, I have fallen in love, which, next to falling into the canal, (which would be of no use, as I can swim,) is the best or the worst thing I could do. I have got some extremely good apartments in the house of a "Merchant of Venice", who is a good deal occupied with business, and has a wife in her twenty-second year. Marianna [Segati] (that is her name) is in her appearance altogether like an antelope. She has the large, black, oriental eyes, with that peculiar expression in them which is seen rarely among *Europeans* — even the Italians — and which many of the Turkish women give themselves by tinging the eyelid, — an art not known out of that country, I believe. This expression she has *naturally,* — and something more than this. In short, I cannot describe the effect of this kind of eye, — at least upon me. Her features are regular, and rather aquiline — mouth small — skin clear and soft, with a kind of hectic colour — forehead remarkably good: her hair is of the dark gloss, curl, and colour of Lady J[ersey]'s:[2] her figure is light and pretty, and she is a famous songstress — scientifically so; her natural voice (in conversation, I mean) is very sweet; and the naïveté of the Venetian dialect is always pleasing in the mouth of a woman.

November 23

You will perceive that my description, which was proceeding with the minuteness of a passport, has been interrupted for several days. In the mean time * * * *[3]

---

2 *Lady Jersey's:* "The reigning beauty and wit of the most select London society." It was at her party that Byron was snubbed just before he left England in 1816.

3 ***: The asterisks indicate passages omitted by Moore when he published the letters.

December 5

Since my former dates, I do not know that I have much to add on the subject, and, luckily, nothing to take away; for I am more pleased than ever with my Venetian, and begin to feel very serious on that point — so much so, that I shall be silent. * * * * *

By way of divertisement, I am studying daily, at an Armenian monastery, the Armenian language. I found that my mind wanted something craggy to break upon; and this — as the most difficult thing I could discover here for an amusement — I have chosen, to torture me into attention. It is a rich language, however, and would amply repay any one the trouble of learning it. I try, and shall go on; — but I answer for nothing, least of all for my intentions or my success.

TO THOMAS MOORE

Venice, January 28, 1817

. . . . I think of being in England in the spring. If there is a row, by the sceptre of King Ludd,[1] but I'll be there; and if there is none, and only a continuance of "this meek, piping time of peace", I will take a cottage a hundred yards to the south of your abode, and become your neighbour; and we will compose such canticles, and hold such dialogues, as shall be the terror of the *Times* (including the newspaper of that name), and the wonder, and honour, and praise, of the *Morning Chronicle* and posterity.

I rejoice to hear of your forthcoming[2] in February — though I tremble for the "magnificence", which you attribute to the new *Childe Harold*.[3] I am glad you like it; it is a fine indistinct piece of poetical desolation, and my favourite. I was half mad during the time of its composition, between metaphysics, mountains, lakes, love unextinguishable, thoughts

---

[1] *King Ludd*: Ned Ludd, leader of workmen who destroyed the cotton machinery for which they blamed unemployment and low wages. Byron's first parliamentary speech in 1811 had been on behalf of Nottingham Luddites.

[2] *forthcoming*: Probably Moore's oriental poem *Lallah Rookh*.

[3] *new Childe Harold*: Canto III.

unutterable, and the nightmare of my own delinquencies. I should, many a good day, have blown my brains out, but for the recollection that it would have given pleasure to my mother-in-law; and, even *then,* if I could have been certain to haunt her —— but I won't dwell upon these trifling family matters.

Venice is in the *estro*[4] of her carnival, and I have been up these last two nights at the ridotto[5] and the opera, and all that kind of thing. Now for an adventure. A few days ago a gondolier brought me a billet without a subscription, intimating a wish on the part of the writer to meet me either in gondola or at the island of San Lazaro, or at a third rendezvous, indicated in the note. "I know the country's disposition well" — in Venice "they do let Heaven see those tricks they dare not show",[6] etc., etc.; so, for all response, I said that neither of the three places suited me; but that I would either be at home at ten at night *alone,* or be at the ridotto at midnight, where the writer might meet me masked. At ten o'clock I was at home and alone (Marianna was gone with her husband to a conversazione), when the door of my apartment opened, and in walked a well-looking and (for an Italian) *bionda* girl of about nineteen, who informed me that she was married to the brother of my *amorosa,* and wished to have some conversation with me. I made a decent reply, and we had some talk in Italian and Romaic (her mother being a Greek of Corfu), when lo! in a very few minutes, in marches, to my very great astonishment, Marianna Segati, *in propriâ personâ,* and after making a most polite courtesy to her sister-in-law and to me, without a single word seizes her said sister-in-law by the hair, and bestows upon her some sixteen slaps, which would have made your ear ache only to hear their echo. I need not describe the screaming which ensued. The luckless visitor took flight. I seized Marianna, who, after several vain efforts to get away in pursuit of the enemy, fairly went into fits in my arms; and, in spite of reasoning,

4 *estro:* Fire, warmth.
5 *ridotto:* Masquerade.
6 "... *dare not show*": *Othello* III. iii. 201–203.

eau de Cologne, vinegar, half a pint of water, and God knows what other waters beside, continued so till past midnight.

After damning my servants for letting people in without apprizing me, I found that Marianna in the morning had seen her sister-in-law's gondolier on the stairs, and, suspecting that his apparition boded her no good, had either returned of her own accord, or been followed by her maids or some other spy of her people to the conversazione, from whence she returned to perpetrate this piece of pugilism. I had seen fits before, and also some small scenery of the same genus in and out of our island: but this was not all. After about an hour, in comes — who? why, Signor Segati, her lord and husband, and finds me with his wife fainting upon the sofa, and all the apparatus of confusion, dishevelled hair, hats, handkerchiefs, salts, smelling-bottles — and the lady as pale as ashes, without sense or motion. His first question was, "What is all this?" The lady could not reply — so I did. I told him the explanation was the easiest thing in the world; but in the mean time it would be as well to recover his wife — at least, her senses. This came about in due time of suspiration and respiration.

You need not be alarmed — jealousy is not the order of the day in Venice, and daggers are out of fashion; while duels, on love matters, are unknown — at least, with the husbands. But, for all this, it was an awkward affair; and though he must have known that I made love to Marianna, yet I believe he was not, till that evening, aware of the extent to which it had gone. It is very well known that almost all the married women have a lover; but it is usual to keep up the forms, as in other nations. I did not, therefore, know what the devil to say. I could not out with the truth, out of regard to her, and I did not choose to lie for my sake; — besides, the thing told itself. I thought the best way would be to let her explain it as she chose (a woman being never at a loss — the devil always sticks by them) — only determining to protect and carry her off, in case of any ferocity on the part of the Signor. I saw that he was quite calm. She went to bed, and next day — how they settled it, I know not, but settle it they did. Well — then

I had to explain to Marianna about this never-to-be-sufficiently-confounded sister-in-law; which I did by swearing innocence, eternal constancy, etc., etc. * * * But the sister-in-law, very much discomposed with being treated in such wise, has (not having her own shame before her eyes) told the affair to half Venice, and the servants (who were summoned by the fight and the fainting) to the other half. But, here, nobody minds such trifles, except to be amused by them. I don't know whether you will be so, but I have scrawled a long letter out of these follies.

> Believe me ever, etc.

TO THOMAS MOORE

Venice, February 28, 1817.

You will, perhaps, complain as much of the frequency of my letters now, as you were wont to do of their rarity. I think this is the fourth within as many moons. I feel anxious to hear from you, even more than usual, because your last indicated that you were unwell. At present, I am on the invalid regimen myself. The Carnival — that is, the latter part of it, and sitting up late o' nights, had knocked me up a little. But it is over — and it is now Lent, with all its abstinence and sacred music.

The mumming closed with a masked ball at the Fenice, where I went, as also to most of the ridottos, etc., etc.; and, though I did not dissipate much upon the whole, yet I find "the sword wearing out the scabbard", though I have but just turned the corner of twenty-nine.

> So we'll go no more a roving
> So late into the night,
> Though the heart be still as loving,
> And the moon be still as bright.
>
> For the sword outwears its sheath,
> And the soul wears out the breast,
> And the heart must pause to breathe,
> And Love itself have rest.

Though the night was made for loving,
  And the day returns too soon,
Yet we'll go no more a roving
  By the light of the moon.

• • • • • • •

If I live ten years longer, you will see, however, that it is
not over with me — I don't mean in literature, for that is
nothing; and it may seem odd enough to say, I do not think
it my vocation. But you will see that I shall do something or
other — the times and fortune permitting — that, "like the
cosmogony, or creation of the world, will puzzle the philosophers of all ages."[1] But I doubt whether my constitution will
hold out. I have, at intervals, ex*or*cised it most devilishly. . . .

TO JOHN MURRAY

Venice, April 9, 1817.

DEAR SIR,

Your letters of the 18th and 20th are arrived. In my own
I have given you the rise, progress, decline, and fall of my
recent malady. It is *gone* to the Devil: I won't pay him so bad
a compliment as to say it *came* from him; — *he* is too much
of a Gentleman. It was nothing but a slow fever, which
quickened its pace towards the end of its journey. I had been
bored with it some weeks — with nocturnal burnings and
morning perspirations; but I am quite well again, which I
attribute to having had neither medicine nor Doctor thereof.

In a few days I set off for Rome: such is my purpose. I shall
change it very often before Monday next, but do you continue
to direct and address to *Venice*, as heretofore. If I go, letters
will be forwarded: I say "*if*," because I never know what I
shall do till it is done; and as I mean most firmly to set out
for Rome, it is not unlikely I may find myself at St. Peters-
burg.

You tell me 'take care of myself'; — faith, and I will. I

---

[1] ". . . *philosophers of all ages*": Byron is quoting from Oliver Goldsmith's *The Vicar of Wakefield*, Chap. XIV.

won't be posthumous yet, if I can help it. Notwithstanding, only think what a "Life and Adventures," while I am in full scandal, would be worth, together with the *membra* of my writing-desk, the sixteen beginnings of poems never to be finished! Do you think I would not have shot myself last year had I not luckily recollected that Mrs. Clermont, and Lady Noel,[1] and all the old women in England would have been delighted; — besides the agreeable "Lunacy," of the "Crowner's Quest," and the regrets of two or three or half a dozen? Be assured that I *would live* for two reasons, or more; — there are one or two people whom I have to put out of the world, and as many into it, before I can "depart in peace"; if I do so before, I have not fulfilled my mission. Besides, when I turn thirty, I will turn devout; I feel a great vocation that way in Catholic churches, and when I hear the organ. . . .

TO JOHN MURRAY

Venice, May 30, 1817

DEAR SIR,

I returned from Rome two days ago, and have received your letter; but no sign nor tidings of the parcel sent through Sir —— Stuart, which you mention. After an interval of months, a packet of *Tales*, etc., found me at Rome; but this is all, and may be all that ever will find me. The post seems to be the only sane conveyance; and *that only for letters*. From Florence I sent you a poem on Tasso, and from Rome the new third act of *Manfred*, and by Dr. Polidori two pictures for my sister. I left Rome, and made a rapid journey home. You will continue to direct here as usual. Mr. Hobhouse is gone to Naples: I should have run down there too for a week, but for the quantity of English whom I heard of there. I prefer hating them at a distance; unless an earthquake, or a good real eruption of Vesuvius, were insured to reconcile me to their vicinity.

I know no other situation except Hell which I should feel

---

[1] *Mrs. Clermont and Lady Noel*: Lady Byron's governess and mother whom Byron blamed for malicious interference and malevolent influence on his wife.

inclined to participate with them — as a race, always excepting several individuals. There were few of them in Rome, and I believe none whom you know, except that old Blue-*bore* Sotheby,[1] who will give a fine account of Italy, in which he will be greatly assisted by his total ignorance of Italian, and yet this is the translator of Tasso.

The day before I left Rome I saw three robbers guillotined. The ceremony — including the *masqued* priests; the half-naked executioners; the bandaged criminals; the black Christ and his banner; the scaffold; the soldiery; the slow procession, and the quick rattle and heavy fall of the axe; the splash of the blood, and the ghastliness of the exposed heads — is altogether more impressive than the vulgar and ungentlemanly dirty "new drop", and dog-like agony of infliction upon the sufferers of the English sentence. Two of these men behaved calmly enough, but the first of the three died with great terror and reluctance, which was very horrible. He would not lie down; then his neck was too large for the aperture, and the priest was obliged to drown his exclamations by still louder exhortations. The head was off before the eye could trace the blow; but from an attempt to draw back the head, notwithstanding it was held forward by the hair, the first head was cut off close to the ears: the other two were taken off more cleanly. It is better than the oriental way, and (I should think) than the axe of our ancestors. The pain seems little; and yet the effect to the spectator, and the preparation to the criminal, are very striking and chilling. The first turned me quite hot and thirsty, and made me shake so that I could hardly hold the opera-glass (I was close, but determined to see, as one should see every thing, once, with attention); the second and third (which shows how dreadfully soon things grow indifferent), I am ashamed to say, had no effect on me as a horror, though I would have saved them if I could.

It is some time since I heard from you — the 12*th April* I believe.

Your ever truly,

B.

---

[1] *Sotheby*: See *Beppo*, stanza 72:7 n.

TO JOHN MURRAY

Venice, April 6, 1819.

DEAR SIR,

The Second Canto of *Don Juan* was sent, on Saturday last, by post, in 4 packets, two of 4, and two of three sheets each, containing in all two hundred and seventeen stanzas, octave measure. But I will permit no curtailments, except those mentioned about Castlereagh and the two *Bobs* in the Introduction.[1] You sha'n't make *Canticles* of my Cantos. The poem will please, if it is lively; if it is stupid, it will fail; but I will have none of your damned cutting and slashing. If you please, you may publish *anonymously;* it will perhaps be better; but I will battle my way against them all, like a Porcupine.

So you and Mr. Foscolo,[2] etc., want me to undertake what you call a "great Work"? an Epic poem, I suppose, or some such pyramid. I'll try no such thing; I hate tasks. And then "seven or eight years!" God send us all well this day three months, let alone years. If one's years can't be better employed than in sweating poesy, a man had better be a ditcher. And works, too! — is *Childe Harold* nothing? You have so many "*divine*" poems, is it nothing to have written a *Human* one? without any of your wornout machinery. Why, man, I could have spun the thoughts of the four cantos of that poem into twenty, had I wanted to book-make, and its passion into as many modern tragedies. Since you want *length*, you shall have enough of *Juan*, for I'll make 50 cantos.

And Foscolo, too! Why does *he* not do something more than the *Letters of Ortis*, and a tragedy, and pamphlets? He has good fifteen years more at his command than I have: what has he done all that time? — proved his Genius, doubtless, but not fixed its fame, nor done his utmost.

Besides, I mean to write my best work in *Italian*, and it

1 *Castlereagh and the two Bobs in the Introduction*: See Dedication to *Don Juan*, 11:8 n. and 3:8 n.
2 *Foscolo*: Ugo Foscolo (1778–1827) an Italian patriot and author who had settled in England. His most famous work, *Lettere de Jacapo Ortis,* was written in 1798.

will take me nine years more thoroughly to master the language; and then if my fancy exist, and I exist too, I will try What I *can* do *really*. As to the Estimation of the English which you talk of, let them calculate what it is worth, before they insult me with their insolent condescension.

I have not written for their pleasure. If they are pleased, it is that they chose to be so; I have never flattered their opinions, nor their pride; nor will I. Neither will I make "Ladies books" *al dilettar le femine e la plebe.*[3] I have written from the fullness of my mind, from passion, from impulse, from many motives, but not for their "sweet voices".

I know the precise worth of popular applause, for few Scribblers have had more of it; and if I chose to swerve into their paths, I could retain it, or resume it, or increase it. But I neither love ye, nor fear ye; and though I buy with ye and sell with ye, and talk with ye, I will neither eat with ye, drink with ye, nor pray with ye.[4] They made me, without my search, a species of popular Idol; they, without reason or judgement, beyond the caprice of their good pleasure, threw down the Image from its pedestal; it was not broken with the fall, and they would, it seems, again replace it — but they shall not.

You ask about my health: about the beginning of the year I was in a state of great exhaustion, attended by such debility of Stomach that nothing remained upon it; and I was obliged to reform my "way of life," which was conducting me from the "yellow leaf"[5] to the Ground, with all deliberate speed. I am better in health and morals, and very much yours ever,

B.

TO JOHN MURRAY

Venice, May 18, 1819

DEAR SIR,

. . . . I write to you in haste and at past two in the morning having besides had an accident. In going, about an hour and

---

[3] " . . . *a la plebe*": For the pleasure of women and the masses.

[4] *nor pray with ye*: A paraphrase of Shylock's speech in *Merchant of Venice* I. 3.

[5] *"yellow leaf"*: See *Don Juan* 3, 3:5–6.

a half ago, to a rendezvous with a Venetian girl (unmarried and the daughter of one of their nobles), I tumbled into the Grand Canal, and, not choosing to miss my appointment by the delays of changing, I have been perched in a balcony with my wet clothes on ever since, till this minute that on my return I have slipped into my dressing-gown. My foot slipped in getting into my Gondola to set out (owing to the cursed slippery steps of their palaces), and in I flounced like a Carp, and went dripping like a Triton to my Sea nymph and had to scramble up to a grated window: —

> Fenced with iron within and without
> Lest the lover get in or the Lady get out.

She is a very dear friend of mine, and I have undergone some trouble on her account, for last winter the truculent tyrant her flinty-hearted father, having been informed by an infernal German, Countess Vorsperg (their next neighbour), of our meetings, they sent a priest to me, and a Commissary of police, and they locked the Girl up, and gave her prayers and bread and water, and our connection was cut off for some time; but the father hath lately been laid up, and the brother is at Milan, and the mother falls asleep, and the Servants are naturally on the wrong side of the question, and there is no Moon at Midnight just now, so that we have lately been able to recommence; the fair one is eighteen; her name, Angelina; the family name, of course, I don't tell you.

She proposed to me to divorce my mathematical wife, and I told her that in England we can't divorce except for *female* infidelity. "And pray, (said she), how do you know what she may have been doing these last three years?" I answered that I could not tell, but that the state of Cuckoldom was not quite so flourishing in Great Britain as with us here. "But", she said, "can't you get rid of her?" "Not more than is done already (I answered): You would not have me *poison her*?" Would you believe it? She made me *no answer*. Is not that a true and odd national trait? It spoke more than a thousand words, and yet this is a little, pretty, sweet-tempered, quiet feminine being as ever you saw, but the Passions of a Sunny

Soil are paramount to all other considerations. An unmarried Girl naturally wishes to be married: if she can marry and love at the same time it is well, but at any rate she must love. I am not sure that my pretty paramour was herself fully aware of the inference to be drawn from her dead Silence, but even the unconsciousness of the latent idea was striking to an observer of the Passions; and I never strike out a thought of another's or of my own without trying to trace it to its Source.

I wrote to Mr. H. pretty fully about our matters. In a few days I leave Venice for Romagna. Excuse this scrawl, for I write in a state of shivering from having sat in my dripping drapery, and from some other little accessories which affect this husk of our immortal Kernel.

Tell Augusta that I wrote to her by yesterday's post, addressed to your care. Let me know if you come out this Summer that I may be in the way, and come to me; don't go to an Inn. I do not know that I can promise you any pleasure; "our way of life" is so different in these parts, but I insure to myself a great deal in seeing you, and in endeavouring (however vainly) to prove to you that I am, very truly

Yours ever,

B.

P.S. — I have read Parson Hodgson's *Friends*[1] in which he seems to display his knowledge of the subject by a Covert attack or two on some of his own. He probably wants another Living; at least I judge so by the prominence of his piety, although he was always pious — even when he was kept by a Washerwoman on the New Road. I have seen him cry over her picture, which he generally wore under his left Armpit. But he is a good man, and I have no doubt does his duty by his Parish. As to the poetry of his New-fangled Stanza, I wish they would write the octave or the Spenser; we have no other legitimate measure of that kind. He is right in defending *Pope*

---

1 *Hodgson's Friends: The Friends: a Poem.* In Four Books, published by Murray. In a note, Hodgson alludes to Byron's irreligiousness. See above, p. 638 (Letter to Hodgson, Sept. 3, 1811).

against the bastard Pelicans of the poetical winter day, who add insult to their Parricide by sucking the blood of the parent of English *real* poetry — poetry without fault, — and then spurning the bosoms which fed them.

TO JOHN MURRAY

Bologna, June 7, 1819

DEAR SIR,

Tell Mr. Hobhouse that I wrote to him a few days ago from Ferrara. It will therefore be idle in him or you to wait for any further answers or returns of proofs from Venice, as I have directed that no English letters be sent after me. The publication can be proceeded in without, and I am already sick of your remarks, to which I think not the least attention ought to be paid.

Tell Mr. Hobhouse that, since I wrote to him, I had availed myself of my Ferrara letters, and found the society much younger and better there than at Venice. I was very much pleased with the little the shortness of my stay permitted me to see of the Gonfaloniere Count Mosti, and his family and friends in general.

I have been picture-gazing this morning at the famous Domenichino and Guido,[1] both of which are superlative. I afterwards went to the beautiful Cimetery of Bologna, beyond the walls, and found, besides the superb Burial-ground, an original of a *Custode*, who reminded me of the grave-digger in Hamlet. He has a collection of Capuchins' skulls, labelled on the forehead, and taking down one of them, said, "This was Brother Desiderio Berro, who died at forty — one of my best friends. I begged his head of his brethren after his decease, and they gave it me. I put it in lime and then boiled it. Here it is, teeth and all, in excellent preservation. He was the merriest, cleverest fellow I ever knew. Wherever he went, he brought joy; and when any one was melancholy, the sight of him was enough to make him cheerful again. He walked so

---

[1] *Domenichino and Guido*: Domenico Zampieri (1581–1641) and Guido Reni (1575–1642), Italian painters, both born in Bologna.

actively, you might have taken him for a dancer — he joked — he laughed — oh! he was such a Frate as I never saw before, nor ever shall again!"

He told me that he had himself planted all the Cypresses in the Cimetery; that he had the greatest attachment to them and to his dead people; that since 1801 they had buried fifty three thousand persons. In showing some older monuments, there was that of a Roman girl of twenty, with a bust by Bernini.[2] She was a Princess Barberini, dead two centuries ago: he said that, on opening her grave, they had found her hair complete, and "as yellow as gold". Some of the epitaphs at Ferrara pleased me more than the more splendid monuments of Bologna; for instance: —

> "Martini Luigi
>   Implora pace."

> "Lucrezia Picini
>   Implora eterna quiete."

Can any thing be more full of pathos? Those few words say all that can be said or sought: the dead had had enough of life; all they wanted was rest, and this they *"implore"*. There is all the helplessness, and humble hope, and deathlike prayer, that can arise from the grave — *"implora pace"*. I hope, whoever may survive me, and shall see me put in the foreigners' burying-ground at the Lido, within the fortress by the Adriatic, will see those two words, and no more, put over me. I trust they won't think of "pickling, and bringing me home to Clod or Blunderbuss Hall".[3] I am sure my bones would not rest in an English grave, or my clay mix with the earth of that country. I believe the thought would drive me mad on my

---

2 *Bernini*: Giovanni Bernini (1598–1680), Italian sculptor.

3 *"Blunderbuss Hall"*: A paraphrase of Acre's words in Sheridan's *The Rivals*, V. 3: "I'll be your second with all my heart; and if you should get a *quietus*, you may command me, entirely. I'll get you *snug lying* in the *Abbey here*; or *pickle* you, and send you over to Blunderbuss Hall . . . with the greatest pleasure." The irony is that upon Byron's death in Greece his remains were shipped back to England in a cask containing 180 gallons of spirits.

deathbed, could I suppose that any of my friends would be base enough to convey my carcase back to your soil. I would not even feed your worms, if I could help it.

So, as Shakespeare says of Mowbray, the banished Duke of Norfolk, who died at Venice (see Richard II.), that he, after fighting

> "Against black pagans, Turks, and Saracens,
> And toil'd with works of war, retir'd himself
> To Italy; and there, at *Venice*, gave
> His body to that *pleasant* country's earth,
> And his pure soul unto his Captain Christ,
> Under whose colours he had fought so long."[4]

Before I left Venice, I had returned to you your late, and Mr. Hobhouse's, sheets of *Juan*. Don't wait for further answers from me, but address yours to Venice, as usual. I know nothing of my own movements; I may return there in a few days, or not for some time. All this depends on circumstances. I left Mr. Hoppner[5] very well, as well as his son and Mrs. Hoppner. My daughter Allegra was well too, and is growing pretty; her hair is growing darker, and her eyes are blue. Her temper and her ways, Mr. Hoppner says, are like mine, as well as her features: she will make, in that case, a manageable young lady.

I never hear any thing of Ada, the little Electra of my Mycenæ; the moral Clytemnestra[6] is not very communicative of her tidings, but there will come a day of reckoning, even if I should not live to see it.

I have at least seen Romilly[7] shivered who was one of the assassins. When that felon, or lunatic (take your choice he must be one and might be both), was doing his worst to uproot my whole family tree, branch, and blossoms; when, after taking my retainer, he went over to them; when he was bring-

---

4 "*. . . fought so long*": *Richard II* IV. i. 95–100.

5 *Hoppner*: Richard Hoppner, the British Consul in Venice.

6 *. . . Clytemnestra*: Lady Byron: Electra was Clytemnestra's daughter. See *Childe Harold*, IV, 132, n.

7 *Romilly*: See *Don Juan*, I, 15:4 n.

ing desolation on my hearth and destruction on my household
Gods, did he think that, in less than three years, a natural
event — a severe domestic — but an expected and common
domestic calamity, — would lay his carcase in a cross road,
or stamp his name in a verdict of Lunacy? Did he (who in
his drivelling sexagenary dotage had not the courage to survive his Nurse — for what else was a wife to him at his time
of life?) — reflect or consider what my feelings must have
been, when wife, and child, and sister, and name, and fame,
and country were to be my sacrifice on his legal altar — and
this at a moment when my health was declining, my fortune
embarrassed, and my mind had been shaken by many kinds
of disappointment, while I was yet young and might have
reformed what might be wrong in my conduct, and retrieved
what was perplexing in my affairs. But the wretch is in his
grave. I detested him living, and I will not affect to pity him
dead; I still loathe him — as much as we can hate dust — but
that is nothing.

What a long letter I have scribbled!

Yours truly,

B.

P.S. — Here, as in Greece, they strew flowers on the tombs.
I saw a quantity of rose-leaves, and entire roses, scattered over
the graves at Ferrara. It has the most pleasing effect you can
imagine.

TO JOHN MURRAY

Bologna, August 12, 1819

DEAR SIR,

I do not know how far I may be able to reply to your letter,
for I am not very well to-day. Last night I went to the repre-
sentation of Alfieri's *Mirra*,[1] the two last acts of which threw
me into convulsions. I do not mean by that word a lady's

---

[1] *Alfieri's Mirra*: a tragedy about a daughter's incestuous love for her
father. In the last act, she confesses to him and kills herself. For Alfieri,
see *Cain*, Preface, n. 12.

hysterics, but the agony of reluctant tears, and the choaking shudder, which I do not often undergo for fiction. This is but the second time for anything under reality; the first was on seeing Kean's Sir Giles Overreach.[2] The worst was, that the *"dama"*,[3] in whose box I was, went off in the same way, I really believe more from fright than any other sympathy — at least with the players: but she has been ill, and I have been ill, and we are all languid and pathetic this morning, with great expenditure of Sal Volatile. But, to return to your letter of the 23d of July.

You are right, Gifford is right, Crabbe is right, Hobhouse is right — you are all right, and I am all wrong;[4] but do, pray, let me have that pleasure. Cut me up root and branch; quarter me in the *Quarterly*; send round my *disjecti membra poetæ*, like those of the Levite's Concubine[5]; make me, if you will, a spectacle to men and angels; but don't ask me to alter, for I can't: — I am obstinate and lazy — and there's the truth.

But, nevertheless, I will answer your friend C[ohen],[6] who objects to the quick succession of fun and gravity, as if in that case the gravity did not (in intention, at least) heighten the fun. His metaphor is, that "we are never scorched and drenched at the same time". Blessings on his experience! Ask him these questions about "scorching and drenching". Did he never play at Cricket, or walk a mile in hot weather? Did he never spill a dish of tea over his testicles in handing the cup to his charmer, to the great shame of his nankeen breeches?[7] Did he never swim in the sea at Noonday with the Sun in his eyes and on his head, which all the foam of Ocean could not cool? Did he never draw his foot out of a tub of too hot water, damning his eyes and his valet's . . . . Was

---

[2] *Kean's Sir Giles Overreach*: Edmund Kean playing the principal character in Thomas Massinger's *New Way to Pay Old Debts* (1633).

[3] *"dama"*: The Countess Guiccioli.

[4] *I am all wrong*: Byron's publisher and friends were alarmed by what they considered the flippancy, the irreverence, and indecency of *Don Juan*, and were urging him to revise or omit portions of it.

[5] *Levite's Concubine*: See *Judges*, 19:29.

[6] *Cohen*: Afterwards Sir Francis Palgrave (1788–1861), editor of *The Golden Treasury*.

[7] *nankeen*: Cotton cloth.

he ever in a Turkish bath, that marble paradise of sherbet and Sodomy? Was he ever in a cauldron of boiling oil, like St. John? or in the sulphureous waves of hell? (where he ought to be for his "scorching and drenching at the same time"). Did he never tumble into a river or lake, fishing, and sit in his wet cloathes in the boat, or on the bank, afterwards "scorched and drenched," like a true sportsman? "Oh for breath to utter!" —[8] but make him my compliments; he is a clever fellow for all that — a very clever fellow.

You ask me for the plan of Donny Johnny: I *have* no plan — I *had* no plan; but I had or have materials; though if, like Tony Lumpkin,[9] I am "to be snubbed so when I am in spirits", the poem will be naught, and the poet turn serious again. If it don't take, I will leave it off where it is, with all due respect to the Public; but if continued, it must be in my own way. You might as well make Hamlet (or Diggory)[10] "act mad" in a strait waistcoat as trammel my buffoonery, if I am to be a buffoon: their gestures and my thoughts would only be pitiably absurd and ludicrously constrained. Why, Man, the Soul of such writing is its licence; at least the *liberty* of that *licence*, if one likes — *not* that one should abuse it: it is like trial by Jury and Peerage and the Habeas Corpus — a very fine thing, but chiefly in the *reversion*; because no one wishes to be tried for the mere pleasure of proving his possession of the privilege.

But a truce with these reflections. You are too earnest and eager about a work never intended to be serious. Do you suppose that I could have any intention but to giggle and make giggle? — a playful satire, with as little poetry as could be helped, was what I meant: and as to the indecency, do, pray, read in Boswell what *Johnson*, the sullen moralist, says of *Prior* and Paulo Purgante . . . .[11]

---

[8] *breath to utter*: *I Henry IV* II. iv. 217.

[9] *Tony Lumpkin*: In Goldsmith's *She Stoops to Conquer*, Act II.

[10] *Diggory*: "Diggery" is a stage struck servant in Isaac Jackman's farce *All the World's a Stage* (1777).

[11] *Paulo Purgante*: *Paulo Purgante and his Wife*, a poem by Matthew Prior. For Johnson's comment that "there is nothing in Prior that will excite to lewdness. If Lord Hailes thinks there is, he must be more com-

TO THE COUNTESS GUICCIOLI[1]

Bologna, August 25, 1819.

MY DEAR TERESA,

I have read this book in your garden; — my love, you were absent, or else I could not have read it. It is a favourite book of yours, and the writer was a friend of mine. You will not understand these English words, and *others* will not understand them — which is the reason I have not scrawled them in Italian. But you will recognize the handwriting of him who passionately loved you, and you will divine that, over a book which was yours, he could only think of love. In that word, beautiful in all languages, but most so in yours — *Amor mio* — is comprised my existence here and hereafter. I feel I exist here, and I fear that I shall exist hereafter, — to *what* purpose you will decide; my destiny rests with you, and you are a woman, eighteen years of age, and two out of a convent. I wish that you had stayed there, with all my heart, — or, at least, that I had never met you in your married state.

But all this is too late. I love you, and you love me, — at least, you *say so*, and *act* as if you *did* so, which last is a great consolation in all events. But *I* more than love you, and cannot cease to love you.

Think of me, sometimes, when the Alps and the ocean divide us, — but they never will, unless you *wish* it.

Byron

TO THE HON. DOUGLAS KINNAIRD[1]

Venice, Octr 26, 1819

MY DEAR DOUGLAS,

My late expenditure has arisen from living at a distance from Venice and being obliged to keep up two establishments,

bustible than other people," see entry for 22 September 1777 in Boswell's *Life*, ed. G. B. Hill, revised by L. F. Powell (1934), III, 192.

[1] Written in the Countess' copy of Madame de Stael's *Corinne*.
[1] Douglas Kinnaird (1788–1830) was Byron's banker and trusted friend.

from frequent journeys and buying some furniture and books as well as a horse or two — and not from any renewal of the *Epicurean* system as you suspect.

I have been faithful to my honest liaison with Countess Guiccioli and I can assure you that she has never cost me directly or indirectly a sixpence, indeed the circumstances of herself and family render this no merit. I never offered her but one present — a broach of brilliants and she sent it back to me with her *own hair* in it (I shall *not* say of *what part* but *that* is an Italian custom) and a note to say that she was not in the habit of receiving presents of that value, but hoped that I would not consider her sending it back as an affront, nor the value diminished by the enclosure. . . .

As to "Don Juan", confess, confess — you dog and be candid — that it is the sublime of *that there* sort of writing — it may be bawdy but is it not good English? It may be profligate but is it not *life,* is it not *the thing*? Could any man have written it who has not lived in the world? — and tooled in a post-chaise? — in a hackney coach? — in a gondola? — against a wall? — in a court carriage? — in a vis à vis?[2] — on a table? — and under it? I have written about a hundred stanzas of a third Canto, but it is damned modest — the outcry has frighted me. I had such projects for the Don but the Cant is so much stronger than the C——, nowadays, that the benefit of experience in a man who had well weighed the worth of both monosyllables must be lost to despairing posterity. After all what stuff this outcry is — Lalla Rookh and Little[3] are more dangerous than my burlesque poem can be. Moore has been here, we got tipsy together and were very amicable; he is gone to Rome. I put my life (in M.S.) into his hands (not for publication), you or anybody else may see it at his return. It only comes up to 1816. He is a noble fellow and looks quite fresh and poetical, nine years (the age of a poem's education) my senior. He looks younger. This comes from marriage and being settled in the country. I want to go to South America —

---

[2] *vis-à-vis*: A carriage with facing seats.

[3] *Little*: Moore's pseudonym in his early poems. Moore published *Lallah Rookh* in 1818.

I have written to Hobhouse all about it. I wrote to my wife, three months ago, under cover to Murray. Has she got the letter — or is the letter got into Blackwood's Magazine? . . .

TO JOHN MURRAY

Ravenna, Decr 9th 1820

DEAR MURRAY,

I intended to have written to you at some length by this post, but as the Military Commandant is now lying dead in my house, on Fletcher's bed, I have other things to think of.

He was shot at 8 o'clock this evening about two hundred paces from our door. I was putting on my great coat to pay a visit to the Countess G., when I heard a shot, and on going into the hall, found all my servants on the balcony exclaiming that "a Man was murdered". As it is the custom here to let people fight it through, they wanted to hinder me from going out; but I ran down into the Street: Tita, the bravest of them, followed me; and we made our way to the Commandant, who was lying on his back, with five wounds, of which three in the body — one in the heart. There were about him Diego, his Adjutant, crying like a Child; a priest howling; a surgeon who dared not touch him; two or three confused and frightened soldiers; one or two of the boldest of the mob; and the Street dark as pitch, with the people flying in all directions. As Diego could only cry and wring his hands, and the Priest could only pray, and nobody seemed able or willing to do anything except exclaim, shake and stare, I made my servant and one of the mob take up the body; sent off Diego crying to the Cardinal, the Soldiers for the Guard; and had the Commandant conveyed up Stairs to my own quarters. But he was quite gone. I made the surgeon examine him, and examined him myself. He had bled inwardly, and very little external blood was apparent. One of the slugs had gone quite through — all but the skin: I felt it myself. Two more shots in the body, one in a finger, and another in the arm. His face not at all disfigured: he seems asleep, but is growing livid. The assassin has not been taken; but the gun was found — a gun filed down to half the barrel.

He said nothing but *O Dio!* and *O Gesu* two or three times.

The house was filled at last with soldiers, officers, police, and military; but they are clearing away — all but the sentinels, and the body is to be removed tomorrow. It seems that, if I had not had him taken into my house, he might have lain in the Streets till morning; as here nobody meddles with such things, for fear of the consequences — either of public suspicion, or private revenge on the part of the slayers. They may do as they please: I shall never be deterred from a duty of humanity by all the assassins of Italy, and that is a wide word.

He was a brave officer, but an unpopular man. The whole town is in confusion.

You may judge better of things here by this detail, than by anything which I could add on the Subject: communicate this letter to Hobhouse and Douglas K^d, and believe me

Yours ever truly,

B.

P.S. — The poor Man's wife is not yet aware of his death: they are to break it to her in the morning.

The Lieutenant, who is watching the body, is smoking with the greatest *sangfroid*: a strange people.

EXTRACTS FROM A DIARY[1]

Jan 28, 1821

Memoranda.

What is Poetry? — The feeling of a Former world and Future.

Thought Second.

Why, at the very height of desire and human pleasure, — worldly, social, amorous, ambitious, or even avaricious, — does there mingle a certain sense of doubt and sorrow — a fear of what is to come — a doubt of what *is* — a retrospect to the

---

[1] Byron kept the Diary between January 4 and February 27, 1821.

past, leading to a prognostication of the future? (The best of Prophets of the future is the Past.) Why is this, or these? — I know not, except that on a pinnacle we are most susceptible of giddiness, and that we never fear falling except from a precipice — the higher, the more awful, and the more sublime; and, therefore, I am not sure that Fear is not a pleasurable sensation; at least, *Hope* is; and *what Hope* is there without a deep leaven of Fear? and what sensation is so delightful as Hope? and, if it were not for Hope, where would the Future be? — in hell. It is useless to say *where* the Present is, for most of us know; and as for the Past, *what* predominates in memory? — *Hope baffled.* Ergo, in all human affairs, it is Hope — Hope — Hope. I allow sixteen minutes, though I never counted them, to any given or supposed possession. From whatever place we commence, we know where it all must end. And yet, what good is there in knowing it? It does not make men better or wiser. During the greatest horrors of the greatest plagues, (Athens and Florence, for example — see Thucydides and Machiavelli,) men were more cruel and profligate than ever. It is all a mystery. I feel most things, but I know nothing, except

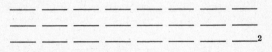

²

February 2, 1821

I have been considering what can be the reason why I always wake, at a certain hour in the morning, and always in very bad spirits — I may say, in actual despair and despondency, in all respects — even of that which pleased me over night. In about an hour or two, this goes off, and I compose either to sleep again, or, at least, to quiet. In England, five years ago, I had the same kind of hypochondria, but accompanied with so violent a thirst that I have drank as many as fifteen bottles of soda-water in one night, after going to bed,

---

² "Thus marked, with impatient stroke of the pen, by himself in the original." Moore.

and been still thirsty — calculating, however, some lost from the bursting out and effervescence and overflowing of the soda-water, in drawing the corks, or striking off the necks of the bottles from mere thirsty impatience. At present, I have *not* the thirst; but the depression of spirits is no less violent.

I read in Edgeworth's *Memoirs* of something similar (except that his thirst expended itself on *small beer*) in the case of Sir F. B. Delaval; — but then he was, at least, twenty years older. What is it? — liver? In England, Le Man (the apothecary) cured me of the thirst in three days, and it had lasted as many years. I suppose that it is all hypochondria.

What I feel most growing upon me are lazinesss, and a disrelish more powerful than indifference. If I rouse, it is into fury. I presume that I shall end (if not earlier by accident, or some such termination), like Swift — "dying at top". I confess I do not contemplate this with so much horror as he apparently did for some years before it happened. But Swift had hardly *begun life* at the very period (thirty-three) when I feel quite an *old sort* of feel.

Oh! there is an organ playing in the street — a waltz, too! I must leave off to listen. They are playing a waltz which I have heard ten thousand times at the balls in London, between 1812 and 1815. Music is a strange thing.

Feb. 18, 1821

. . . To-day I have had no communication with my Carbonari[1] cronies; but, in the mean time, my lower apartments are full of their bayonets, fusils, cartridges, and what not. I suppose that they consider me as a depôt, to be sacrificed, in

---

[1] *Carbonari*: (Charcoal burners) A secret revolutionary society in which the father and brother of Teresa Guiccioli were among the leaders, and Byron was an enthusiastic supporter. It was their hope to overthrow Austrian rule in northern Italy. In July 1820 the Carbonari in southern Italy had led a revolt which had forced a liberal constitution upon the King of Naples. But the Austrians (the Barbarians) sent an army to restore the absolute Monarchy, and in early March the Neopolitans were defeated and the revolution broken. At the same time, the leaders in Northern Italy were arrested. The Gambas were sent into exile in Tuscany. The diary entries record Byron's extravagant hopes and bitter disappointment at the climactic moment.

case of accidents. It is no great matter, supposing that Italy could be liberated, who or what is sacrificed. It is a grand object — the very *poetry* of politics. Only think — a free Italy!!! Why, there has been nothing like it since the days of Augustus. I reckon the times of Cæsar (Julius) free; because the commotions left every body a side to take, and the parties were pretty equal at the set out. But, afterwards, it was all prætorian and legionary business — and since! — we shall see, or, at least, some will see, what card will turn up. It is best to hope, even of the hopeless. The Dutch did more than these fellows have to do, in the Seventy Years' War.

February 19, 1821

Came home *solus* — very high wind — lightning — moonshine — solitary stragglers muffled in cloaks — women in masks — white houses — clouds hurrying over the sky, like spilt milk blown out of the pail — altogether very poetical. It is still blowing hard — the tiles flying, and the house rocking — rain splashing — lightning flashing — quite a fine Swiss Alpine evening, and the sea roaring in the distance.

Visited — conversazione.[1] All the women frightened by the squall: they won't go to the masquerade because it lightens — the pious reason!

Still blowing away. A. has sent me some news to-day. The war approaches nearer and nearer. Oh those scoundrel sovereigns! Let us but see them beaten — let the Neapolitans but have the pluck of the Dutch of old, or the Spaniards of now, or of the German Protestants, the Scotch Presbyterians, the Swiss under Tell, or the Greeks under Themistocles — *all* small and solitary nations (except the Spaniards and German Lutherans), and there is yet a resurrection for Italy, and a hope for the world.

February 20, 1821

The news of the day are, that the Neapolitans are full of energy. The public spirit *here* is certainly well kept up. The

[1] *conversazione*: Evening party.

Americani (a patriotic society here, an under branch of the *Carbonari*) give a dinner in *the Forest* in a few days, and have invited me, as one of the C[i]. It is to be in *the Forest* of Boccacio's and Dryden's "Huntsman's Ghost"[1]; and, even if I had not the same political feelings, (to say nothing of my old convivial turn, which every now and then revives,) I would go as a poet, or, at least, as a lover of poetry. I shall expect to see the spectre of "Ostasio degli Onesti" (Dryden has turned him into Guido Cavalcanti — an essentially different person, as may be found in Dante) come "thundering for his prey in the midst of the festival". At any rate, whether he does or no, I will get as tipsy and patriotic as possible.

Within these few days I have read, but not written.

February 24, 1821

Rode, etc., as usual. The secret intelligence arrived this morning from the frontier to the C[i]. is as bad as possible. The *plan* has missed — the Chiefs are betrayed, military, as well as civil — and the Neapolitans not only have *not* moved, but have declared to the P. government, and to the Barbarians, that they know nothing of the matter!!!

Thus the world goes; and thus the Italians are always lost for lack of union among themselves. What is to be done *here,* between the two fires, and cut off from the N[n]. frontier, is not decided. My opinion was, — better to rise than be taken in detail; but how it will be settled now, I cannot tell. Messengers are despatched to the delegates of the other cities to learn their resolutions.

I always had an idea that it would be *bungled*; but was willing to hope, and am so still. Whatever I can do by money, means, or person, I will venture freely for their freedom; and have so repeated to them (some of the Chiefs here) half an hour ago. I have two thousand five hundred scudi, better than five hundred pounds, in the house, which I offered to begin with.

---

[1] *Boccacio's and Dryden's "Huntsman's Ghost"*: See *Don Juan,* 3, 105: 6–7 n.

February 25, 1821

Came home — my head aches — plenty of news, but too tiresome to set down. I have neither read nor written, nor thought, but led a purely animal life all day. I mean to try to write a page or two before I go to bed. But, as Squire Sullen says, "My head aches consumedly: Scrub, bring me a dram!"[1] Drank some Imola wine, and some punch!

February 27, 1821

. . . Last night I suffered horribly — from an indigestion, I believe. I *never* sup — that is, never at home. But, last night, I was prevailed upon by the Countess Gamba's persuasion, and the strenuous example of her brother, to swallow, at supper, a quantity of boiled cockles, and to dilute them, *not* reluctantly, with some Imola wine. When I came home, apprehensive of the consequences, I swallowed three or four glasses of spirits, which men (the venders) call brandy, rum, or hollands, but which gods would entitle spirits of wine, coloured or sugared. All was pretty well till I got to bed, when I became somewhat swollen, and considerably vertiginous. I got out, and mixing some soda-powders, drank them off. This brought on temporary relief. I returned to bed; but grew sick and sorry once and again. Took more soda-water. At last I fell into a dreary sleep. Woke, and was ill all day, till I had galloped a few miles. Query — was it the cockles, or what I took to correct them, that caused the commotion? I think both. I remarked in my illness the complete inertion, inaction, and destruction of my chief mental faculties. I tried to rouse them, and yet could not — and this is the *Soul!!!* I should believe that it was married to the body, if they did not sympathise so much with each other. If the one rose, when the other fell, it would be a sign that they longed for the natural state of divorce. But as it is, they seem to draw together like post-horses.

Let us hope the best — it is the grand possession.

---

[1] *". . . Scrub, bring me a dram"*: In Farquhar's *Beaux Stratagem*, Act V, sc. 4.

TO PERCY BYSSHE SHELLEY

Ravenna, April 26, 1821

• • • • • • •

I am very sorry to hear what you say of Keats[1] — is it *actually* true? I did not think criticism had been so killing. Though I differ from you essentially in your estimate of his performances, I so much abhor all unnecessary pain, that I would rather he had been seated on the highest peak of Parnassus than have perished in such a manner. Poor fellow! though with such inordinate self-love he would probably have not been very happy. I read the review of *Endymion* in the *Quarterly*.[2] It was severe, — but surely not so severe as many reviews in that and other journals upon others.

I recollect the effect on me of the *Edinburgh* on my first poem; it was rage, and resistance, and redress — but not despondency nor despair. I grant that those are not amiable feelings; but, in this world of bustle and broil, and especially in the career of writing, a man should calculate upon his powers of *resistance* before he goes into the arena.

> "Expect not life from pain nor danger free,
> Nor deem the doom of man reversed for thee."[3]

You know my opinion of *that second-hand* school of poetry. You also know my high opinion of your own poetry, — because it is of *no* school. I read *Cenci*[4] — but, besides that I think the *subject* essentially *un*dramatic, I am not an admirer of our old dramatists *as models*. I deny that the English have hitherto had a drama at all. Your *Cenci*, however, was a work of power and

---

1 *Keats*: Keats died 23 February 1821 at Rome.

2 *Quarterly*: *The Quarterly Review*, XIX (1818), 204–208. Shelley believed that Keats' death had been brought on by the brutal review of his poems published in the *Quarterly*.

3 "*. . . reversed for thee*": See Samuel Johnson, *The Vanity of Human Wishes*, 153–154.

4 *Cenci*: Shelley's tragedy was published in the spring of 1820.

poetry. As to *my* drama,[5] pray revenge yourself upon it, by being as free as I have been with yours.

I have not yet got your *Prometheus*,[6] which I long to see. I have heard nothing of mine, and do not know that it is yet published. I have published a pamphlet on the Pope controversy,[7] which you will not like. Had I known that Keats was dead — or that he was alive and so sensitive — I should have omitted some remarks upon his poetry, to which I was provoked by his *attack* upon *Pope*,[8] and my disapprobation of *his own* style of writing.

You want me to undertake a great poem — I have not the inclination nor the power. As I grow older, the indifference — *not* to life, for we love it by instinct — but to the stimuli of life, increases. Besides, this late failure of the Italians[9] has latterly disappointed me for many reasons, — some public, some personal. My respects to Mrs. S.

Yours ever,

B.

P.S. — Could not you and I contrive to meet this summer? Could not you take a run here *alone?*

TO JOHN MURRAY

Ravenna, July 6, 1821.

• • • • • • •

P.S. — At the particular request of the Contessa G. I have promised not to continue *Don Juan.* You will therefore look upon these 3 cantos as the last of that poem. She had read the two first in the French translation, and never ceased beseeching me to write no more of it. The reason of this is not at first

---

5 *my drama*: *Marino Faliero,* just published.

6 *Prometheus Unbound*: Published in the summer of 1820.

7 *Pope controversy*: Byron's pamphlet *On the Rev. W. L. Bowles' Strictures on . . . Pope* was published in March, 1821.

8 *attack upon Pope*: In *Sleep and Poetry,* lines 193–206. Byron's remarks on Keats occurred in a second pamphlet, not published until 1835 (the remarks were deleted).

9 *late failure of the Italians*: The collapse of the Carbonari movement.

obvious to a superficial observer of FOREIGN manners; but it arises from the wish of all women to exalt the *sentiment* of the passions, and to keep up the illusion which is their empire. Now *Don Juan* strips off this illusion, and laughs at that and most other things. I never knew a woman who did *not* protect *Rousseau*, nor one who did not dislike de Grammont,[1] Gil Blas,[2] and all the *comedy* of the passions, when brought out naturally.

TO JOHN MURRAY

R[avenna] July 30th, 1821

• • • • • • •

Are you aware that Shelley has written an elegy on Keats, and accuses the *Quarterly* of killing him?

> "Who killed John Keats?"
> "I," says the Quarterly,
> So savage and Tartarly,
> " 'Twas one of my feats."

> "Who shot the arrow?"
> "The poet-priest Milman[1]
> (So ready to kill man),
> Or Southey or Barrow."[2]

You know very well that I did not approve of Keat's poetry, or principles of poetry, or of his abuse of Pope; but, as he is dead, omit *all* that is said *about him* in any *MSS.* of mine, or publication. His *Hyperion* is a fine monument, and will keep his name. I do not envy the man who wrote the article: your review people have no more right to kill than any other foot

---

1 *de Grammont*: Philibert, Comte de Gramont (1621–1707), French court-ier of Louis XVI, whose witty and cynical *Memoirs* were a revealing pic-ture of court life.

2 *Gil Blas*: A strongly realistic picaresque novel (1715–1735) by Alain René Le Sage (1668–1747). Translated by Smollet, it influenced his own *Roderick Random,* and in turn Byron's *Don Juan.*

1 *Milman*: See letter to Murray, November 3, 1821, below.

2 *Barrow*: J. Barrow, a "hatchet" reviewer for the *Quarterly.*

pads. However, he who would die of an article in a review would probably have died of something else equally trivial. . . .

FROM *DETACHED THOUGHTS*[1]

Oct. 1821

72

When I first went up to College, it was a new and a heavy hearted scene for me. Firstly, I so much disliked leaving Harrow, that, though it was time (I being seventeen), it broke my very rest for the last quarter with counting the days that remained. I always *hated* Harrow till the last year and half, but then I liked it. Secondly, I wished to go to Oxford and not to Cambridge. Thirdly, I was so completely alone in this new world, that it half broke my Spirits. My companions were not unsocial, but the contrary — lively, hospitable, of rank, and fortune, and gay far beyond my gaiety. I mingled with, and dined and supped, etc., with them; but, I know not how, it was one of the deadliest and heaviest feelings of my life to feel that I was no longer a boy. From that moment I began to grow old in my own esteem; and in my esteem age is not estimable. I took my gradations in the vices with great promptitude, but they were not to my taste; for my early passions, though violent in the extreme, were concentrated, and hated division or spreading abroad. I could have left or lost the world with or for that which I loved; but, though my temperament was naturally burning, I could not share in the common place libertinism of the place and time without disgust. And yet this very disgust, and my heart thrown back upon itself, threw me into excesses perhaps more fatal than those from which I shrunk, as fixing upon one (at a time) the passions, which, spread amongst many, would have hurt only myself.

73

People have wondered at the Melancholy which runs through my writings. Others have wondered at my personal gaiety; but

[1] Between Oct. 15, 1821 and May 18, 1822, Byron kept a notebook to which he gave this name.

I recollect once, after an hour, in which I had been sincerely and particularly gay, and rather brilliant, in company, my wife replying to me when I said (upon her remarking my high spirits) "and yet, Bell, I have been called and mis-called Melancholy — you must have seen how falsely, frequently". "No, B.," (she answered) "it is not so: at *heart* you are the most melancholy of mankind, and often when apparently gayest."

74

If I could explain at length the *real* causes which have contributed to increase this perhaps *natural* temperament of mine, this Melancholy which hath made me a bye-word, nobody would wonder; but this is impossible without doing much mischief. I do not know what other men's lives have been, but I cannot conceive any thing more strange than some of the earlier parts of mine. I have written my memoirs, but omitted *all* the really *consequential* and *important* parts, from deference to the dead, to the living, and to those who must be both.

75

I sometimes think that I should have written the *whole* as a *lesson*, but it might have proved a *lesson* to be *learnt* rather than *avoided*; for passion is a whirlpool, which is not to be viewed nearly without attraction from its Vortex.

76

I must not go on with these reflections, or I shall be letting out some secret or other to paralyze posterity.

● ● ● ● ● ● ●

95

If I had to live over again, I do not know what I would change in my life, unless it were *for not to have lived at all*. All history and experience, and the rest, teaches us that the good and evil are pretty equally balanced in this existence, and that what is most to be desired is an easy passage out of it.

What can it give us but *years*? and those have little of good but their ending.

96

Of the Immortality of the Soul, it appears to me that there can be little doubt, if we attend for a moment to the action of Mind. It is in perpetual activity. I used to doubt of it, but reflection has taught me better. It acts also so very independent of body: in dreams for instance incoherently and madly, I grant you; but still it is *Mind,* and much more *Mind* than when we are awake. Now, that *this* should not act *separately,* as well as jointly, who can pronounce? The Stoics, Epictetus and Marcus Aurelius, call the present state "a Soul which drags a Carcase": a heavy chain, to be sure; but all chains, being material, may be shaken off.

How far our future life will be individual, or, rather, how far it will at all resemble our *present* existence, is another question; but that the *Mind* is *eternal,* seems as probable as that the body is not so. Of course, I have ventured upon the question without recurring to Revelation, which, however, is at least as rational a solution of it as any other.

A *material* resurrection seems strange, and even absurd, except for purposes of punishment; and all punishment, which is to *revenge* rather than *correct,* must be *morally wrong.* And *when* the *World is at an end,* what moral or warning purpose *can* eternal tortures answer? Human passions have probably disfigured the divine doctrines here, but the whole thing is inscrutable. It is useless to tell me *not* to *reason,* but to *believe.* You might as well tell a man not to wake but *sleep.* And then to *bully* with torments! and all that! I cannot help thinking that the *menace* of Hell makes as many devils, as the severe penal codes of inhuman humanity make villains.

Man is born *passionate* of body, but with an innate though secret tendency to the love of Good in his Mainspring of Mind. But God help us all! It is at present a sad jar of atoms.

97

Matter is eternal, always changing, but reproduced, and, as far as we can comprehend Eternity, Eternal; and why not *Mind?* Why should not the Mind act with and upon the Universe? as portions of it act upon and with the congregated dust called Mankind? See, how one man acts upon himself and others, or upon multitudes? The same Agency, in a higher and purer degree, may act upon the Stars, etc., ad infinitum.

98

I have often been inclined to Materialism in philosophy but could never bear its introduction into *Christianity*, which appears to me essentially founded upon the *Soul*. For this reason, Priestley's Christian Materialism always struck me as deadly. Believe the resurrection of the body, if you will, but *not without* a *Soul*. The devil's in it, if, after having had a Soul (as surely the *Mind*, or whatever you call it, *is*) in this world, we must part with it in the next, even for an Immortal Materiality. I own my partiality for *Spirit*.

99

I am always most religious upon a sun-shiny day; as if there was some association between an internal approach to greater light and purity, and the kindler of this dark lanthorn of our eternal existence.

100

The Night is also a religious concern; and even more so, when I viewed the Moon and Stars through Herschell's telescope, and saw that they were worlds.

101

If, according to some speculations, you could prove the World many thousand years older than the Mosaic Chronology, or if you could knock up Adam and Eve and the Apple and Serpent, still what is to be put up in their stead? or how is the difficulty removed? Things must have had a beginning, and what matters it *when* or *how*?

I sometimes think that *Man* may be the relic of some higher material being, wrecked in a former world, and degenerated in the hardships and struggle through Chaos into Conformity — or something like it; as we see Laplanders, Esquimaux, etc., inferior in the present state, as the Elements become more inexorable. But even then this higher pre-Adamite supposititious Creation[2] must have had an Origin and a *Creator*; for a *Creator* is a more natural imagination than a fortuitous concourse of atoms. All things remount to a fountain, though they may flow to an Ocean.

102

What a strange thing is the propagation of life! A bubble of Seed which may be spilt in a whore's lap — or in the orgasm of a voluptuous dream — might (for aught we know) have formed a Caesar or a Buonaparte: there is nothing remarkable recorded of their Sires, that I know of.

TO JOHN MURRAY

Pisa, November 3, 1821.

DEAR MORAY,

The two passages[1] cannot be altered without making Lucifer talk like the Bishop of Lincoln — which would not be in the character of the former. The notion is from Cuvier[2] (that of the *old Worlds*), as I have explained in an additional note to the preface. The other passage is also in character: if *nonsense* — so much the better, because then it can do no harm, and the sillier Satan is made, the safer for every body. As to "alarms," etc., do you really think such things ever led any body astray? Are these people more impious than Milton's Satan? or the Prometheus of Æschylus? or even than the Sadducees of your envious parson, the *Fall of Jerusalem* fabricator?[3] Are not Adam, Eve, Adah, and Abel, as pious as the Catechism?

---

2 No. 101. *Higher pre-Adamite supposititious Creation*: See *Cain*, Preface, and II. ii. 44 ff.

1 *two passages*: The passages were from *Cain*, II. ii, in which Lucifer showed Cain the phantom of the superior beings who lived before Adam. See II. ii. 44 ff. and note.

2 *Cuvier*: See *Cain*, Preface, above p. 232.

3 *Fall of Jerusalem fabricator*: The Rev. H. H. Milman (1791–1868), Professor of Poetry, at Oxford had written an horrendous epic (1820) by this name. Byron believed that Milman was trying to get Murray to give up publishing *Don Juan*.

Gifford[4] is too wise a man to think that such things can have any *serious* effect: *who* was ever altered by a poem? I beg leave to observe, that there is no creed nor personal hypothesis of mine in all this: but I was obliged to make Cain and Lucifer talk consistently, and surely this has always been permitted to poesy. Cain is a proud man: if Lucifer promised him kingdoms, etc., it would *elate* him: the object of the Demon is to *depress* him still further in his own estimation than he was before, by showing him infinite things and his own abasement, till he falls into the frame of mind that leads to the Catastrophe, from mere *internal* irritation, *not* premeditation, or envy of *Abel* (which would have made him contemptible), but from the rage and fury against the inadequacy of his state to his conceptions, and which discharges itself rather against Life, and the Author of Life, than the mere living.

His subsequent remorse is the natural effect of looking on his sudden deed. Had the *deed* been *premeditated*, his repentance would have been tardier.

The three last MS. lines of Eve's curse[5] are replaced from *memory* on the proofs, but incorrectly (for I keep no copies). Either keep *these three*, or *replace* them with the *other three*, whichever are thought least bad by Mr. Gifford. There is no occasion for a *revise;* it is only losing time.

Either dedicate it to Walter Scott,[6] or, if you think he would like the dedication of *The Foscaris* better, put the dedication to *The Foscaris*. Ask him which.

Your first note was queer enough; but your two other letters, with Moore's and Gifford's opinions, set all right again. I told you before that I can never *recast* any thing. I am like the Tiger: if I miss the first spring, I go growling back to my Jungle again; but if I *do hit*, it is crushing. Now for Mr. Mawman,[7] I received him civilly as *your* friend, and he spoke of

4 *Gifford*: William Gifford, editor of the *Quarterly Review* and reader for Murray.

5 *Eve's curse*: See *Cain* III. 441–445 and note.

6 *Walter Scott*: *Cain* was dedicated to Scott.

7 *Mr. Mawman*: J. Mawman, publisher and friend of Murray who visited Byron at Ravenna. Byron gave him an inscribed copy of *Don Juan*, cantos 3–5, with the request that he show the copy to "the publisher" and

you in a friendly manner. As one of the squadron of Scribblers I could not but pay due reverence to a commissioned officer.

I gave him that book with the inscription to show to *you*, that you might correct the errors. With the rest I can have nothing to do; but he has served you very *right*. You have played the stepmother to *D[on] J[uan]* throughout, either ashamed or afraid, or negligent, to your own loss and nobody's credit. Who ever heard before of a *publisher's not* putting *his* name? The reasons for *my anonyme* I stated; they were family ones entirely. Some travelling Englishmen whom I met the other day at Bologna told me, that you affect to wish to be considered as *not* having anything to do with that work, which, by the way, is sad half and half dealing — for you will be a long time before you publish a better poem.

You seem hurt at the words *"the publisher." What!* you — who won't put your name on the title page — would have had me stick J. M. Esqre on the blank leaf. No, Murray! you are an excellent fellow, a little variable and somewhat of the opinion of every body you talk with (particularly the last person you see), but a good fellow for all that; yet nevertheless I can't tell you that I think you have acted very gallantly by that persecuted book — which has made its way entirely by *itself*, without the light of your countenance, or any kind of encouragement — critical — or bibliopolar. You disparaged the last three cantos to me, and kept them back above a year; but I have heard from England that (notwithstanding the errors of the press) they are well thought of; for instance, by American Irving, which last is a feather in my (fool's) cap.

You have received my letter (open) through Mr. Kinnaird, and so, pray, send me no more reviews of any kind. I will read no more of evil or good in that line. Walter Scott has not read a review of *himself* for *thirteen years*.

The bust[8] is not *my* property, but *Hobhouse's*. I addressed

---

point out the "gross printer's blunders." Murray had published the poem anonymously.

8 *bust*: Hobhouse had in 1817 commissioned a bust of Byron by the noted Danish sculptor, Bertal Thorwaldson.

it to you as an Admiralty man, great at the Custom house. Pray deduct the expenses of the same, and all others.

Yours ever,
Byron

TO THOMAS MOORE

Pisa, March 8, 1822.

You will have had enough of my letters by this time — yet one word in answer to your present missive. You are quite wrong in thinking that your *"advice"* had offended me; but I have already replied (if not answered) on that point.

With regard to Murray, as I really am the meekest and mildest of men since Moses (though the public and mine "excellent wife" cannot find it out), I had already pacified myself and subsided back to Albemarle Street, as my yesterday's *ye*pistle will have informed you. But I thought that I had explained my causes of bile — at least to you. Some instances of vacillation, occasional neglect, and troublesome sincerity, real or imagined, are sufficient to put your truly great author and man into a passion. But reflection, with some aid from hellebore, hath already cured me *pro tempore*, and, if it had not, a request from you and Hobhouse would have come upon me like two out of the *tribus Anticyris*,[1] — with which, however, Horace despairs of purging a poet. I really feel ashamed of having bored you so frequently and fully of late. But what could I do? You are a friend — an absent one, alas! — and as I trust no one more, I trouble you in proportion.

This war of "Church and State" has astonished me more than it disturbs; for I really thought *Cain* a speculative and hardy, but still a harmless, production. As I said before, I am really a great admirer of tangible religion; and am breeding

---

[1] *tribus Anticyris*: "three Anticyris" (Horace, *Ars Poetica*, 300). Three ancient Greek towns famous for Hellebore, an herb used in the treatment of madness. Horace writes of the bearded and long-haired poet, whose head even the three Anticyris could not cure.

one of my daughters a Catholic, that she may have her hands full. It is by far the most elegant worship, hardly excepting the Greek mythology. What with incense, pictures, statues, altars, shrines, relics, and the real presence, confession, absolution, — there is something sensible to grasp at. Besides, it leaves no possibility of doubt; for those who swallow their Deity, really and truly, in transubstantiation, can hardly find any thing else otherwise than easy of digestion.

I am afraid that this sounds flippant, but I don't mean it to be so; only my turn of mind is so given to taking things in the absurd point of view, that it breaks out in spite of me every now and then. Still, I do assure you that I am a very good Christian. Whether you will believe me in this, I do not know; but I trust you will take my word for being

Very truly and affectionately yours, etc.

TO THOMAS MOORE

Pisa, August 27, 1822

• • • • • • •

The other day, at Viareggio, I thought proper to swim off to my schooner (the Bolivar) in the offing, and thence to shore again — about three miles, or better, in all. As it was at midday, under a broiling sun, the consequence has been a feverish attack, and my whole skin's coming off, after going through the process of one large continuous blister, raised by the sun and sea together. I have suffered much pain; not being able to lie on my back, or even side; for my shoulders and arms were equally St. Bartholomewed. But it is over, — and I have got a new skin, and am as glossy as a snake in its new suit.

We have been burning[1] the bodies of Shelley and Williams on the sea-shore, to render them fit for removal and regular interment. You can have no idea what on extraordinary effect such a funeral pile has, on a desolate shore, with mountains in

---

[1] *We have been burning*: Shelley and Williams were drowned July 8, 1822. It was while Shelley's body was being burned that Byron swam out to his schooner.

the background and the sea before, and the singular appearance the salt and frankincense gave to the flame. All of Shelley was consumed, except his *heart*, which would not take the flame, and is now preserved in spirits of wine.

• • • • • • •

I have nearly (*quite three*) four new cantos of *Don Juan* ready. I obtained permission from the female Censor Morum of *my* morals to continue it, provided it were immaculate; so I have been as decent as need be. There is a deal of war — a siege, and all that, in the style, graphical and technical, of the shipwreck in Canto Second, which "took," as they say in the Row.

Yours, etc.

P.S. — That *** Galignani[2] has about ten lies in one paragraph. It was not a Bible that was found in Shelley's pocket, but John Keats's poems. However, it would not have been strange, for he was a great admirer of Scripture as a composition. *I* did not send my bust to the academy of New York; but I sat for my picture to young West,[3] an American artist, at the request of some members of that Academy to *him* that he would take my portrait, — for the Academy, I believe.

I had, and still have, thoughts of South America, but am fluctuating between it and Greece. I should have gone, long ago, to one of them, but for my liaison with the Countess G.; for love, in these days, is little compatible with glory. *She* would be delighted to go too; but I do not choose to expose her to a long voyage, and a residence in an unsettled country, where I shall probably take a part of some sort.

TO JOHN MURRAY

Genoa, 10bre 25º, 1822

I had sent you back the *Quarterly*, without perusal, having resolved to read no more reviews, good, bad, or indifferent;

---

2 *Galignani*: Galignani's *Messenger*, a newspaper published in English in Paris. The asterisks are Moore's.
3 *West*: William Edward West (1788–1857).

but "who can control his fate?"[1] Galignani, to whom my English studies are confined, has forwarded a copy of at least one half of it, in his indefatigable Catch-penny weekly compilation; and as, "like Honour, it came unlooked for",[2] I have looked through it. I must say that, upon the *whole*, that is, the whole of the *half* which I have read (for the other half is to be the Segment of Gal.'s next week's Circular), it is extremely handsome, and any thing but unkind or unfair. As I take the good in good part, I must not, nor will not, quarrel with the bad: what the Writer says of *Don Juan* is harsh, but it is inevitable. He must follow, or at least not directly oppose, the opinion of a prevailing, and yet not very firmly seated, party: a review may and will direct or "turn awry" the Currents of opinion, but it must not directly oppose them. *Don Juan* will be known by and bye, for what it is intended, — a *Satire* on *abuses* of the present states of Society, and not an eulogy of vice: it may be now and then voluptuous: I can't help that. Ariosto is worse; Smollett (see Lord Strutwell in vol. 2ᵈ of *R[oderick] R[andom]*) ten times worse; and Fielding no better. No Girl will ever be seduced by reading *D.J.*: — no, no; she will go to Little's poems[3] and Rousseau's romans for that, or even to the immaculate De Stael[4]: they will encourage her, and not the Don, who laughs at that, and — and — most other things. But never mind — Ça ira![5]

And now to a less agreeable topic, of which *pars magna es* — [6] you Murray of Albemarle Sᵗ and the other Murray of Bridge Street[7] — "Arcades Ambo" ("*Murrays both*") et *cant-*

---

1 ". . . *control his fate*": *Othello* V. 2. 265.
2 "*Like Honour, it came unlooked for*": *I Henry IV* V. 3. 64.
3 *Little's poems*: See Letter to Kinnaird above.
4 *De Stael*: See letter to Countess Guiccioli, above.
5 *Ça ira*: See *Don Juan*, 3, 85:4.
6 *pars magna es*: "You are the great part."
7 *Murray of Bridge Street*: Charles Murray, lawyer for the Constitutional Society which prosecuted John Hunt for libel against George III in publishing *The Vision of Judgment*. John Murray, Byron's publisher, was at fault because when, unwilling to publish the poem, he sent the manuscript to Hunt, he did not include the preface in which Byron had made clear that the poem was directed against Southey and not George III.

are pares"[8]: ye, I say, between you, are the Causes of the prosecution of John Hunt, Esq[re] on account of the *Vision*. You,
by sending him an incorrect copy, and the other, by his function. Egad, but H.'s Counsel will lay it on you with a trowel
for your tergiversifying as to the MSS., etc., whereby poor H.
(and, for anything I know, myself — I am willing enough) is
likely to be impounded.

Now, do you see what you and your friends do by your in-
judicious rudeness? — actually cement a sort of connection
which you strove to prevent, and which, had the H.'s *prospered*, would not in all probability have continued. As it is, I
will not quit them in their adversity, though it should cost me
character, fame, money, and the usual et cetera.

My original motives I already explained (in the letter which
you thought proper to show): they are the *true* ones, and I
abide by them, as I tell you, and I told L[h] H[t] [9] when he ques-
tioned me on the subject of that letter.[10] He was violently hurt,
and never will forgive me at bottom; but I can't help that.
I never meant to make a parade of it; but if he chose to question me, I could only answer the plain truth: and I confess
I did not see anything in the letter to hurt him, unless I said
he was "a *bore*", which I don't remember. Had their Journal
gone on well, and I could have aided to make it better for them,
I should then have left them, after my safe pilotage off a lee
shore, to make a prosperous voyage by themselves, As it is,
I can't, and would not, if I could, leave them amidst the
breakers.

As to any community of feeling, thought, or opinion, between L. H. and me, there is little or none: we meet rarely,
hardly ever; but I think him a good principled and able man,

8 *"Arcades Ambo . . . et cant-are pares"*: "Arcadians both and ready to
sing." Virgil's *Eclogues* 7.4. Byron is punning: both are purveyors of cant.
9 *L[h] H[t]*: Leigh Hunt.
10 *Subject of that letter*: In a letter to Murray October 9, 1822, Byron
said that he supported *The Liberal* because of the poverty of the Hunt
brothers, and not from an intrinsic interest in the Journal. He wrote:
"I have done all I can for Leigh Hunt since he came here; but it is almost
useless: his wife is ill, his six children not very tractable, and in the affairs
of this world he himself is a child."

and must do as I would be done by. I do not know what world he has lived in, but I have lived in three or four; and none of them like his Keats and Kangaroo *terra incognita*. Alas! poor Shelley! how he would have laughed had he lived, and how we used to laugh now and then, at various things, which are grave in the Suburbs!

You are all mistaken about Shelley. You do not know how mild, how tolerant, how good he was in Society; and as perfect a Gentleman as ever crossed a drawing-room, when he liked, and where he liked.

I have some thoughts of taking a run down to Naples (*solus*, or, at most, *cum solâ*) this Spring, and writing, when I have studied the Country, a fifth and sixth Canto of *Chᵉ Harolde*: but this is merely an idea for the present, and I have other excursions and voyages in my mind. The busts are finished: are you worthy of them?

Yours, etc., N.B.

TO [MARY SHELLEY]

[*December, 1822*]

• • • • • • •

I presume that you, at least, know enough of me to be sure that I could have no intention to insult Hunt's poverty. On the contrary, I honour him for it; for I know what it is, having been as much embarrassed as ever he was, without perceiving aught in it to diminish an honourable man's self-respect. If you mean to say that, had he been a wealthy man, I would have joined in this Journal, I answer in the negative. . . . I engaged in the Journal from good-will towards him, added to respect for his character, literary and personal; and no less for his political courage, as well as regret for his present circumstances: I did this in the hope that he might, with the same aid from literary friends of literary contributions (which is requisite for all journals of a mixed nature), render himself independent.

• • • • • • •

I have always treated him, in our personal intercourse, with such scrupulous delicacy, that I have forborne intruding advice which I thought might be disagreeable, lest he should impute it to what is called "taking advantage of a man's situation."

As to friendship, it is a propensity in which my genius is very limited. I do not know the *male* human being, except Lord Clare, the friend of my infancy, for whom I feel any thing that deserves the name. All my others are men-of-the-world friendships. I did not even feel it for Shelley, however much I admired and esteemed him; so that you see not even vanity could bribe me into it, for, of all men, Shelley thought highest of my talents, — and, perhaps, of my disposition.

I will do my duty by my intimates, upon the principle of doing as you would be done by. I have done so, I trust, in most instances. I may be pleased with their conservation — rejoice in their success — be glad to do them service, or to receive their counsel and assistance in return. But as for friends and friendship, I have (as I already said) named the only remaining male for whom I feel any thing of the kind, excepting, perhaps, Thomas Moore. I have had, and may have still, a thousand friends, as they are called, in *life*, who are like one's partners in the waltz of this world — not much remembered when the ball is over, though very pleasant for the time. Habit, business, and companionship in pleasure or in pain, are links of a similar kind, and the same faith in politics is another. . . .

TO THOMAS MOORE

Cephalonia, December 27, 1823.

I received a letter from you some time ago. I have been too much employed latterly to write as I could wish, and even now must write in haste.

I embark for Missolonghi to join Mavrocordato[1] in four-and-twenty hours. The state of parties (but it were a long story) has kept me here till *now*; but now that Mavrocordato (their Washington, or their Kosciusko) is employed again, I can act with a *safe conscience*. I carry money to pay the squadron, etc., and I have influence with the Suliotes, *supposed* sufficient to

---

1 *Mavrocordato*: Prince Alexander Mavrocordatos (1791–1865), the Greek leader whom Byron supported.

keep them in harmony with some of the dissentients; — for there are plenty of differences, but trifling.

It is imagined that we shall attempt either Patras or the castles on the Straits; and it seems, by most accounts, that the Greeks, at any rate the Suliotes, who are in affinity with me of "bread and salt," — expect that I should march with them, and — be it even so! If any thing in the way of fever, fatigue, famine, or otherwise, should cut short the middle age of a brother warbler, — like Garcilasso de la Vega, Kleist, Körner, Joukoffsky (a Russian nightingale — see Bowring's *Anthology*), or Thersander,[2] or, — or somebody else — but never mind — I pray you to remember me in your "smiles and wine."[3]

I have hopes that the cause will triumph; but whether it does or no, still "honour must be minded as strictly as milk diet." I trust to observe both.

Ever, etc.

TO THE HON. AUGUSTA LEIGH[1]

Missolonghi, [Monday] February 23, 1824.

My Dearest Augusta,

I received a few days ago yours and Lady B.'s report of Ada's health, with other letters from England for which I ought to be and am (I hope) sufficiently thankful, as they were of great comfort and I wanted some, having been recently unwell, but am now much better. So that you need not be alarmed.

You will have heard of our journeys and escapes, and so forth, perhaps with some exaggeration; but it is all very well now, and I have been for some time in Greece, which is in as good a state as could be expected considering circumstances.

---

[2] *Garcillasso de la Vega* (1503–1536); Ewald Christian *von Kleist* (1715–1759); Karl Theodor *Körner* (1791–1813); Vasil Andreevich *Zhukovsky* (1783–1852); and *Thersander* who accompanied Agamemnon to Troy. All except Zhukovsky were fatally wounded in battle.

[3] *"Smiles and wine"*: A phrase from Moore's poem *The Legacy*.

[1] This letter was found unfinished on Byron's desk after his death.

But I will not plague you with politics, wars, or *earthquakes*, though we had another very smart one three nights ago, which produced a scene ridiculous enough, as no damage was done except to those who stuck fast in the scuffle to get first out of the doors or windows, amongst whom some recent importations, fresh from England, who had been used to quieter elements, were rather squeezed in the press for precedence.

I have been obtaining the release of about nine and twenty Turkish prisoners — men, women, and children — and have sent them at my own expense home to their friends, but one, a pretty little girl of nine years of age named Hato[2] or Hatagèe, has expressed a strong wish to remain with me, or under my care, and I have nearly determined to adopt her. If I thought that Lady B. would let her come to England as a Companion to Ada — (they are about the same age), we could easily provide for her; if not, I can send her to Italy for education. She is very lively and quick, and with great black oriental eyes, and Asiatic features. All her brothers were killed in the Revolution; her mother wishes to return to her husband who is at Prevesa, but says that she would rather entrust the child to me in the present state of the Country. Her extreme youth and sex have hitherto saved her life, but there is no saying what might occur in the course of the *war* (and of *such* a war), and I shall probably commit her to the charge of some English lady in the islands for the present. The Child herself has the same wish, and seems to have a decided character for her age. You can mention this matter if you think it worth while. I merely wish her to be respectably educated and treated, and, if my years and all things be considered, I presume, it would be difficult to conceive me to have any other views.

With regard to Ada's health, I am glad to hear that it is so much better. But I think it right that Lady B. should be informed, and guard against it accordingly, that her description of much of her indisposition and tendencies very nearly resemble my *own* at a similar age, except that I was much

2 *Hato*: Compare with Don Juan's experience, Canto 8, 91 ff., as an example of the way in which art and life overlapped for Byron.

more impetuous. Her preference of *prose* (strange as it may seem) *was* and indeed *is* mine (for I hate *reading* verse, and always did), and I never invented anything but '*boats — ships*' and generally relating to the Ocean. I showed the report to Col. Stanhope, who was struck with the resemblance of *parts* of it to the *paternal* line even now. But it is also fit, though unpleasant, that I should mention that my recent attack, and a very severe one, had a strong appearance of *epilepsy*. *Why* — I know not, for it is late in life — its first appearance at thirty-six — and, as far as I *know*, it is not *hereditary*, and it is that it may not *become* so, that you should tell Lady B. to take some precautions in the case of Ada. My attack has not yet returned, and I am fighting it off with abstinence and exercise, and thus far with success; if merely casual, it is all very well.

Rinehart Editions